# Social Psychology in Court

**Michael J. Saks, Ph. D.**
Boston College

**Reid Hastie, Ph. D.**
Harvard University

**VNR** **VAN NOSTRAND REINHOLD COMPANY**
NEW YORK    CINCINNATI    ATLANTA    DALLAS    SAN FRANCISCO
LONDON    TORONTO    MELBOURNE

Van Nostrand Reinhold Company Regional Offices:
New York   Cincinnati   Atlanta   Dallas   San Francisco

Van Nostrand Reinhold Company International Offices:
London   Toronto   Melbourne

Library of Congress Catalog Card Number: 78-8664
ISBN: 0-442-23186-5

Manufactured in the United States of America

Published by Van Nostrand Reinhold Company
135 West 50th Street, New York, N.Y. 10020

Published simultaneously in Canada by Van Nostrand Reinhold Ltd.

15  14  13  12  11  10  9  8  7  6  5  4  3  2  1

**Library of Congress Cataloging in Publication Data**

Saks, Michael J.
    Social psychology in court.

    Includes bibliographical references and index.
    1. Sociological jurisprudence.  2. Social
psychology.  3. Psychology, Forensic.  4. Courts
—United States.  5. Social science research—
Law and legislation—United States.  I. Hastie,
Reid, joint author.  II. Title.
K380.S23          347'.73'5          78-8664
ISBN 0-442-23186-5

*To our legal friends,*
*whose interest in our field*
*has made us feel welcome in theirs.*

# Preface

One day one of the authors visited the office of an acquaintance who is widely respected nationally both as a practicing attorney and a professor of lawyering process. In a stack on his desk lay the following books:

*Judges*
*Attorney's Guide to Effective Discovery Techniques*
*How to Prepare and Negotiate Cases for Settlement*
*Proof, Persuasion and Cross-Examination: A Winning New Approach in the Courtroom*
*Contemporary Social Psychology*

The presence of a social psychology book in that little collection seems to us to be eminently sensible. Indeed, its absence might be even more noteworthy. Despite the proclivity of both persons in the legal system and social psychologists for ignoring each other, there is, we believe, a strikingly good fit between many of the behavioral questions with which lawyers, judges, and litigants must deal, and knowledge uncovered by social psychological research.

Courts could hardly be more like applied social psychology laboratories if they were intended to be. The tasks of participants in and around the courtroom read like the table of contents of a social psychology textbook: Lawyers bargain and negotiate outside of court, and in court try to change attitudes; jurors engage in social perception and social influence, and juries in group decision-making; judges integrate information to reach decisions; and evidence includes such matters as perception and recall by eyewitnesses, attributions induced through "character" testimony, and psychophysiological measures of stress (lie detection). These are but the more obvious examples.

Already we have hinted at the particular slice of the world of law and psychology that is this book's focus. We concentrate on litigation—what goes on in and about courtrooms. Thus, we trade away increased breadth (we do not cover—on the criminal side—citizen reports of crime, police, or prisons, or—on the civil side—dispute initiation, its alternative modes of resolution, remedies, or the like). We hope that the trade has obtained for the reader greater depth in the areas we do cover, and greater relevance to the psychology of both criminal and civil litigation.

The kinds of research on which this book is based fall essentially into three categories: studies made directly on the relevant legal processes or simulations of them (e.g., juries, polygraphy, eyewitnesses); more basic science research generalized to those legal processes (e.g., group decision making, psychophysiology, perception and memory); and less analytic, more descriptive work by sociologists, political scientists, and legal scholars, as well as psychologists.

We expect the book to illuminate the processes under study, as a good academic book should, but also to serve more action-oriented needs, such as improving the performance of present or future attorneys, judges, and litigants, and suggesting legal policy changes.

Accordingly, *Social Psychology in Court* should be appropriate for use in undergraduate courses in psychology and law, in certain courses in sociology or political science, and as a supplementary text in social psychology courses, where it would demonstrate the application of a great many social psychological concepts. The book could also be used in certain law courses, such as trial practice or lawyering process. Finally, it is intended for legal practitioners themselves to find much that is useful. In short, this is a book for both behavioral science people interested in areas of application of their knowledge, and legal people interested in better understanding their world and being more effective in it.

Two further notes are in order:

First, this book is written in nonsexist language, whereby the world is populated not by men and mankind but by people and humanity. This deliberate choice has been made in response to contemporary values, to the American Psychological Association's "Guidelines for Nonsexist Language in APA Journals" (*American Psy-*

*chologist*, 1977, *32*, 487–494), and to Meridith Miller's criticism of an early draft of the manuscript.

Second, Chapter 1, "Social Science Research and the Law," essentially offers an overview of social science research methods (any science research methods, actually) and of the legal process, for those readers who need it. Those who do not, will want to skip parts or all of Chapter 1.

M. J. S.
Chestnut Hill, Massachusetts
R. H.
Cambridge, Massachusetts

# Acknowledgments

The authors wish to thank a few people who helped us create this book. The usual disclaimers apply: whatever is good about this book they may be given credit for; whatever is wrong with it is the fault of the authors, who probably disregarded wise and knowledgeable counsel.

Steven Penrod, Robert Hallisey, David A. Rose, William Engels, and Meridith Miller provided answers to questions and/or comment and criticism of drafts of the manuscript. Assistance in preparation of the manuscript was provided by Mary Baker, Patty Mason, and Linda Berman. To these people, and others, go our thanks.

# Contents

# 1
# Social Science Research and the Law

Every law and every legal institution is based on assumptions about human nature and the manner in which human behavior is determined. We believe that scientific psychology can help us understand these institutions and improve them. This book is our attempt to test that belief. In it we examine one important legal institution, the trial court, from the point of view of the modern research psychologist. Our analysis is designed to show that principles of human behavior derived from laboratory and field research illuminate the behavior of the actors in the courtroom setting and even suggest ways to improve the trial process. We are putting psychology on trial, and you, the reader, are our judge.

## LAW AND PSYCHOLOGY

There is an interesting parallel between legal and scientific institutions. Both exist to make decisions about the real world. Both have elaborate "rules of evidence," which specify the facts that can be considered and the manner in which these facts can be presented. Both operate with traditional and rather conservative decision-making policies. And both have a means of recording past "cases" and applying them to current decisions. There are also a number of fascinating differences between the two systems. Legal systems are designed to guarantee "due process" as well as, perhaps even instead of, guaranteeing a "true" decision. Legal rules of evidence, designed to treat many unrelated cases, are consequently quite different from scientific standards of proof, which stress repeatability or reliability. The judge and "jury of amateurs" and adversarial attorneys who are the hallmark of the modern trial stand in stark contrast to the typical laboratory research team. The conventions of the jury trial, instructions about "presumption of innocence," "burden of proof," and the unanimous jury verdict requirement are quite unlike the statistical decision-making machinery that governs scientific proof.

We think that legal and scientific decision makers could profit from a bit more interaction. Participants in the legal justice system can improve their practice by learning about the psychology of personality and its application to jury selection, the psychology of memory and its application to eyewitness testimony, and the psychology of attitude change and its application to advocacy, to name a few areas where psychologists have conducted research that is directly relevant to courtroom practice. We also believe that knowledge of more abstract psychological theories, theories of memory, group dynamics, and personality, should be widespread among lawyers, judges, and court officials, and that a scientifically "enlightened" court will conduct its business more efficiently and fairly. Finally, we hope that this book will persuade participants in the legal justice system that the scientific experimental method is occasionally useful in evaluating legal practice.

A nice example of such experimentation is provided by recent legislation in our home state of Massachusetts. A bill was introduced into the state legislature that would change the manner in which jurors are called for jury duty and the requirements of their service. Debate in the legislature was heated, with opponents of the bill concerned about the costs of implementing the new procedures and the impracticality of calling new jurors to serve every day of the week (one of the innovations in the bill). The supporters of the bill attempted to convince the opposing legislators by citing examples of similar programs in other jurisdictions, but arguments about "what works in Houston or Detroit" were not persuasive. Finally, in order to break the deadlock, the supporters of the bill made an unexpected suggestion: Why not select one representative county in the state and during one year conduct a test, an experiment, with the new procedure? If the new jury selection plan is successful, if it is easy to implement and maintain, then we can adopt the plan statewide. If the new plan does not work, we can return to the old methods, and the state court system will continue to operate as before.  It is this attitude, "let us conduct an experiment," "let us attempt to answer policy questions by collecting empirical data relevant to practical questions," which we believe is the most valuable contribution that science has to offer our legal system.

It is important to emphasize that the law-psychology interface is not a one-way street.  Although we will concentrate on the contributions that social scientists can make in the courtroom, we must also acknowledge that science profits handsomely from the connection (Tapp, 1976).

First, an increasing number of psychologists, sociologists, and psychiatrists are participating in the justice system.  There is a long tradition of asking psychiatrists and psychologists to testify about the mental condition of a person accused of committing a crime (reviewed in Chapter 6 of this text).  Recently, psychologists have been called to assist the court in evaluating the reliability of eyewitness reports and lie detection techniques (reviewed in Chapter 7).  Social science experts have been making the news lately by assisting attorneys in jury selection (see Chapter 3) and in detecting and proving that economic or educational discrimination on the basis of sex, religion, or ethnicity has occurred.

Second, this text is a veritable catalog of social science research conducted in the courtroom or in simulated, mock-courtroom settings.  The extension, application, and revision of scientific theories is essential to their existence (Neisser, 1976).  The real-world, problem-oriented research setting nurtures theories.  It provides constant challenges and tests of a theory so that later versions of the formulation are better articulated, more general, and more useful.  It provides new support for the theory, most strongly when the theory conflicts with common sense and proves to be correct. And, last but not least, problem-oriented research attracts funding from government, institutional, and industry sources.

## RESEARCH METHODS

We will spend a considerable amount of time illustrating various empirical research methods, commenting on their strengths and weaknesses, and suggesting new applications for them.   Here we will introduce the major types of research methods that appear throughout the remainder of the book.

A first, fundamental distinction is between experimental and nonexperimental research.   Suppose we would like to study the effects of varying jury size on the performance of the jury.   In practice, two jury sizes are of interest: six-person juries and the traditional twelve-person juries.   We call jury size our *independent variable*, the variable that we hypothesize may be the *cause of* variations in jury performance.   In *experimental research* the experimenter creates two or more treatments or conditions conceptualized as levels of the independent variable.   In this example, an experiment to study the effects of varying jury size, the independent variable, which is manipulated or varied by the experimenter, is jury size, and the two levels of the variable or the experimental treatments are twelve-person juries and six-person juries.   Our *dependent variables* will be indices, measurements, or types of observation that we believe are good indicants of the jury's performance, the *effect* we want to study.   For a start we may want to look at each jury's verdict and the length of its deliberation time as measures of performance.   The question we want to answer with our research is: To what extent does jury performance (measured as verdict and length of time to reach the verdict) depend on jury size?

One approach to answering our question is to conduct an experiment in which we assign our independent variable, size of jury, to experimental units or subjects (our juries) and observe how these experimenter-created juries perform.   An ideal plan might be to descend on a local courthouse, sample jurors from the actual jury pool, present a real trial (a film of a real trial is probably the most practical option), and then send the jurors into a deliberation room at the courthouse with standard instructions.   The critical aspect of this procedure, which would make it an experiment in the scientific sense, is the *random* assignment of individual jurors to either six- or twelve-person juries.   For example, before composing each of our experimental juries, we might literally toss a coin to decide whether each jury studied would be in the twelve-person or the six-person treatment.   Whenever a head appeared, we would sample six jurors;

when a tail appeared, we would sample twelve. Use of the coin toss, a random event initiated by the experimenter, prevents *systematic* interference by any variables—other than our independent variable, jury size—with our results.   By rigorously following this random assignment procedure we can guard against any incidental biases influencing our answer to the original question: To what extent does jury performance *depend* on jury size? For if a coin toss determines the experimental treatment, what important causal variable (besides jury size) could possibly vary systematically with the assignment rule? Thus, if at the end of our experiment we have studied several juries of each size and there are differences between juries in the two groups, we can conclude with confidence that group size alone is responsible for the differences in performance.  On the other hand, if there were no differences in performance, we could conclude confidently that we had not allowed some biasing factor systematically to mask the effects of group size.

Consideration of an alternative to random assignment of juries to group size conditions shows how problems in interpreting the results of the study can arise when it is not a true, random-assignment, experiment.  Suppose we discover that in one state, Florida for example, six-person juries are the rule in criminal trials, while in another state, say Massachusetts, twelve-person juries are used in all such trials. This situation is similar to our original experimental design, in that we have six-person juries and twelve-person juries deciding quite similar cases.  Suppose that six-person juries convict more often than twelve-person juries.  Can we confidently conclude that our independent variable, jury size, is causing this difference? No, of course not.  Many other factors are varying systematically with jury size.  For example, if we restrict our consideration to the differences between Florida and Massachusetts juries, perhaps juries in Florida are composed of older citizens, or perhaps the Florida prosecutors bring different types of cases to trial from those brought by Massachusetts prosecutors; or perhaps the governor of Massachusetts has recently suggested that a "trigger happy" jury convicted Sacco and Vanzetti of murder . . . .  The point is that once other factors, really potential alternative causal variables, are allowed to *co-vary* with our dependent variable, we can no longer be sure that we are observing only the independent variable's effects. This is the main reason why we think that the experimental method is the strongest way to study causal relations.

To summarize our comments on the experimental method, we have introduced two important distinctions. First is the distinction between independent variables, which are "manipulated" or randomly assigned to experimental subjects, and dependent variables, which are observed or measured. In our example each jury was an experimental subject, and it was randomly composed of six or twelve persons. As each jury participated in our experiment, we recorded its verdict and its deliberation time as measures of performance. If there is a systematic difference in the verdicts returned by the two types of jury or in their deliberabion times, we conclude that the independent variable has *caused* the difference. Social scientists use modern statistical theory to help them summarize their data and to guide their decision that a true, reliable difference has been detected in their experiment. In this example, a statistical test could be performed to determine if an observed difference in proportion of guilty verdicts or in average deliberation times was "significant." This use of the word significant is a technical expression meaning reliable. A "significant" difference is a difference that we would expect to obtain again should the experiment be repeated.

Second, we have talked about a research method where the experimenter has "control" over the experimental subjects and independent variable treatments so that it is possible randomly to assign subjects to experimental conditions. The implication is that there are other methods which do not include the random-assignment device. We will discuss these nonexperimental *correlational methods* next.

Let us return to the example of studying the effects of jury size on jury performance. A correlational approach to our question might start with a search for data from many jurisdictions in hope that there are naturally occurring variations in the sizes of juries sitting in criminal courts and that data are available on conviction rates and possibly even deliberation times for some jurisdictions. In fact there is a good amount of variation in jury size across states and even from court to court within states. Since we are imagining in this example, we can imagine that it is possible to obtain data on conviction rates in several jurisdictions. We could summarize the results of our survey by drawing a graph in which the relation between jury size and conviction rate is represented as in Figure 1.1. Each point in the graph represents the data from one correlational unit, and we can see that there is a general pattern: smaller juries are likelier to convict than larger juries. The problem is that this approach does not rule out many alternative causal explanations for the size–conviction relation. Perhaps western states are likelier to have small juries than eastern states, and so our observed differences in conviction rates are caused by differences in "legal climate."

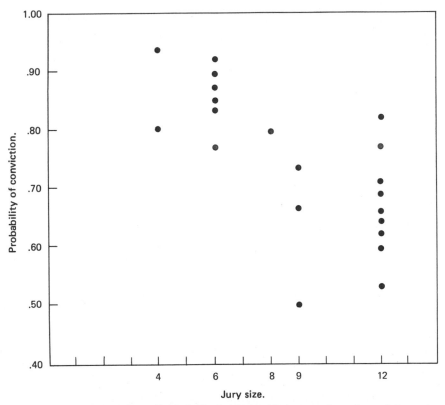

Figure 1.1. Graphs showing a (hypothetical) relationship between jury size and the probability of conviction in a jury trial in 21 jurisdictions. Each point represents the relation between jury size (horizontal axis) and conviction probability (vertical axis) in one jurisdiction. The relationship depicted here shows that large juries are less likely to convict than small juries.

Perhaps lower courts are likelier to have small juries than higher trial courts, and so our conviction rate differences are caused by characteristics of the cases. And, of course, we can go on generating plausible causal accounts for our dependent-variable difference.

The correlational approach is somewhat stronger than we have depicted it thus far. It is possible to eliminate some of our alternative causal accounts using the correlational method. For instance, if we have data on the types of cases that go to large and to small juries, we can directly examine the relation between case type and conviction rate. It is possible to go even further and evaluate the relative relationships between several potential causal variables and our dependent variables (Crano and Brewer, 1973). However, we will almost always find that our conclusions about "what causes what" are not as strong as when we are able to apply the true experimental method.

To repeat ourselves, there are two main reasons why the true experiment is a stronger method to study causal relations than the correlational method. First, the experimenter manipulates the independent variable and then measures the dependent variable. Thus, we can be sure that the causal event precedes its effect in time. This is an essential condition of cause–effect relationships. Second, the random assignment procedure of an experiment allows us to eliminate the multitude of competing causal variable accounts from consideration so that we can concentrate on the relationship between our independent and dependent variables.

Although we would always like to be able to construct experiments to study causal relations between events or variables, it is not always practical. Often there is no money to conduct an experiment, a policy decision must be made before an experiment can be conducted, or there is no possibility of executing an actual field experiment or a simulation experiment that is realistic enough to yield conclusions which will generalize to the problem of interest. The issue of the generality of a research result is extremely important when our goal is to apply research to solve practical problems.

Up to this point we have been concerned with the *internal validity* of experimental and correlational research methods. We have argued that experiments provide a tighter internal inferential logic to draw conclusions about causation than correlational methods. A different type of validity is involved when we ask ourselves, given the results of a particular study, experimental or correlational, to what other times, places, and settings can we generalize these conclusions? This second class of methodological issues is concerned with the *external validity* of research (Campbell and Stanley, 1963). Another example can help us see this distinction more clearly. Suppose we search the psychological literature for research relevant to our empirical question about the effects of jury size on performance. We find a well-designed true experiment in which college students were randomly assigned to six- or twelve-person mock juries. These juries listened to a short tape-recorded description of an assault and battery case while sitting in a classroom. After the tape recording the experimental juries deliberated to a unanimous verdict of guilty or innocent. The results of this study showed that six-person juries were likelier to convict than twelve-person juries. (A study similar to this one was conducted by Angelo Valenti and Leslie Downing at the University of Georgia in 1974.)   The question is, can we generalize from the results of this classroom experiment to draw conclusions about the behavior of actual juries?

Table 1.1 lists some of the dimensions of comparison that are relevant to our dilemma. The problem is that social scientists have not developed a rigorous approach to the problem of generality (Meehl, 1971).   We can certainly say that a comparison of the experimental situation and the situation to which we want to gen-

Table 1.1.  Summary comparison of a laboratory simulation experiment with the actual courtroom setting to which the research results may or may not generalize.

|  | *Experiment* | *Real World* |
|---|---|---|
| Subjects | Mostly upper middle class college students | Mostly lower class and lower middle class adults |
| Setting | College classroom | Courthouse |
| Materials | Tape-recorded assault and battery case summary (duration: 10 minutes) | Various actual legal trials (average duration: 3 days) |
| Task | Deliberate to a verdict (average duration: 20 minutes) | Deliberate to a verdict (average duration: 120 minutes) |

eralize along dimensions such as subjects, setting, materials, task, and so forth is relevant to our question. But, we do not have any rules to allow us to conclude definitely whether or not generalization is safe or even which of the dimensions is most important.

There are three solutions to this problem. First, we can trust our intuitions to tell us whether or not generalization is safe. We can strengthen our intuitive judgment somewhat if we exercise care to specify clearly the situation we wish to draw conclusions about or the research from which we want to generalize. Our example table above is a useful device to guide our intuitive judgments. Second, occasionally we will find several experiments and correlational studies that are relevant to our target situation. The reliability of the con- clusions across the related research settings is an indication of the likelihood that the results will generalize to a new, non-research setting. For example, if there were several experimental and corre- lational studies relevant to our jury-size question, we could compare studies to determine whether the results were consistent across the subjects, settings, and materials involved in the different studies. Third, an indirect approach to the generalizability problem may be available if there is a well-developed scientific theory for the phe- nomenon in the research from which we wish to generalize. In this case, where the research supports or is accounted for by a specific theory, the generality of that theory is an indirect indicant of the generalizability of the research. For example, if (a) our jury size experiment results agreed closely with the predictions of a general theory of group performance, and (b) this theory was useful in predicting group performance in a variety of circumstances (maybe even some naturally occurring, non-laboratory groups), then (c) we can have increased confidence in the generality of the results of the experiment.

Usually, but not always, experimental research will have higher internal validity than correlational research. That is, we believe experiments usually provide stronger answers to questions about causality. However, just the reverse seems to be true for external validity. Correlational studies are usually more closely related to natural problems than are experiments, for there are relatively few experiments conducted outside the laboratory, "in the field." How- ever, there is an increasing application of the experimental method to answering policy questions (Fairley and Mosteller, 1977), and we hope that this book will contribute to the creation of an "experimenting society" in this country (Campbell, 1969).

## THE UNITED STATES COURT SYSTEM

The court system in the United States is vast and vastly complex. For the purposes of this text, it is sufficient to keep in mind that we are concerned almost exclusively with trial courts and for the most part with criminal trial cases. Three distinctions should be useful to the reader. First of all, the United States Constitution provides for separate but parallel federal and state court systems. The diagram in Figure 1.2 indicates the parallel nature of the state and federal systems. Federal courts have jurisdiction over trials arising from violations of federal laws; state courts deal with state statute violations.

Second, the vertical dimension of Figure 1.2 represents a movement from lower trial courts to intermediate and higher appeals courts, to culminate in the highest appeals court in the country,

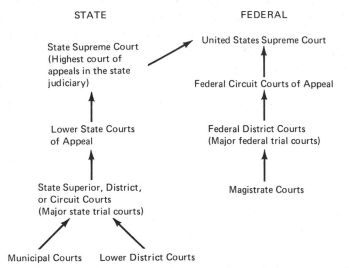

Figure 1.2. Parallel state and federal court systems. Arrows indicate routes of appeal. There is great variety in the organization of state court systems; so the left-hand column is only approximately correct for many jurisdictions.

the United States Supreme Court.  We will be concerned with the lower trial courts here; cases enter the justice system at this level.  In criminal cases most convictions are followed by appeals by the defendant, asking higher courts to review the trial court's action.  If the appeals court, usually a panel of from three to nine judges, feels that there were procedural irregularities or that the original trial verdict was improper, it can reverse the trial court's verdict.

A third distinction to keep in mind is between criminal and civil trial proceedings.  Criminal law is designed to regulate behavior by declaring some acts to be crimes and therefore unacceptable in the society.  In criminal cases the party initiating the trial is a state or federal prosecutor, usually a district attorney, who is acting on behalf of the public.  Criminal trial convictions, especially for serious "felony" crimes, carry jail sentences or severe fines as punishments.  Civil law is designed to settle disputes among individuals, organizations, and branches of the government.  Civil cases typically involve claims that one party has wrongfully injured another (torts) or claims that one party has broken a formal contract or agreement.  Most cases that reach federal and state trial courts involve civil matters.  This is one reason why the backlog of civil cases is enormous.  In Massachusetts, for example, major civil cases usually wait several years to come to trial.  The backlog of criminal cases is also large, but court systems are required to handle criminal matters expeditiously.   In Massachusetts the interval between arrest and trial rarely exceeds one year—although this too is a considerable delay.

Criminal and civil court proceedings have much in common; thus we have not hesitated to discuss psychological research on either type of case.  However, since most research has focused on criminal proceedings, most of our examples will be drawn from criminal trial settings.  There are numerous other special courts within both the federal and state systems—for example, state and city juvenile courts, military courts-martial, and many special administrative courts.  Those courts are outside the domain of this book.  More thorough introductions to the variety of court systems in America and abroad are available in elementary law texts (e.g., Prassel, 1975; Lieberman, 1966; Abraham, 1975).

## A TOUR OF THE CRIMINAL JUSTICE SYSTEM

Now that we have fixed our center of attention in the criminal trial courts, it is important to take a quick look at the entire criminal justice system. Only a small percentage of the cases that enter the system by attracting the attention of law enforcement officials lead to courtroom trials. Figure 1.3 outlines the operations of the criminal justice system.

First let us suppose that a criminal act has occurred. For example, two young men force their way into the cashier's booth of a supermarket, threaten the clerk with a pistol, and leave with the contents of the cash drawer in a paper bag. A crime such as this would almost certainly be reported to the police, who would appear at the market a few minutes after the robbers' departure. Note, however, that even if we restrict our attention to major crimes, fewer than half will be reported to the police.

The police go to work obtaining eyewitness accounts of the crime and descriptions of the robbers. Let us suppose that two clerks had unobstructed views of the robbers' faces; they would probably be taken to a police station and shown mugshot photographs of persons whom the police detectives think might have been involved in the robbery. Meanwhile, descriptions of the robbers and their getaway vehicle will have been broadcast to police in the area.

If the clerk-witnesses in our example identify any mugshot suspects as likely perpetrators of the crime, warrants for their arrest will be sought from a local lower court judge or magistrate. Alternatively, suspects matching the robbers' descriptions might be arrested on the street (without a "bench warrant") by patrolling police officers. Note once again that neither of these outcomes is likely to occur; even for major criminal offenses such as armed robbery, fewer than one-fourth of the reported incidents lead to arrests.

To continue our example, let us suppose that our witnesses select one mugshot photograph from the police file as very probably one of the robbers. The police obtain a bench warrant and accompanied by the two witnesses drive to the suspect's apartment, arrest him, and search the apartment. At this time the suspect is read his

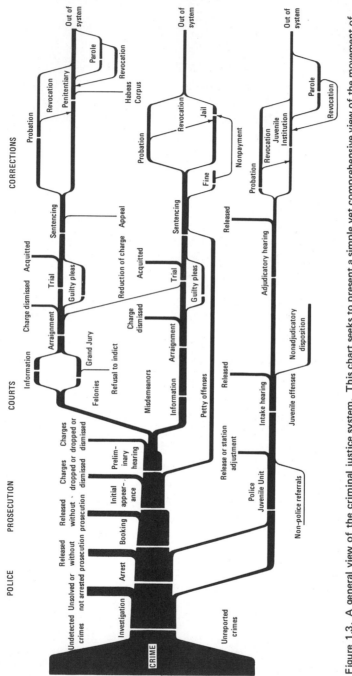

POLICE     PROSECUTION     COURTS     CORRECTIONS

Figure 1.3. A general view of the criminal justice system. This chart seeks to present a simple yet comprehensive view of the movement of cases through the criminal justice system. Procedures in individual jurisdictions may vary from the pattern shown here. The differing weights of line indicate the relative volumes of cases disposed of at various points in the system, but this is only suggestive, since no nation-wide data of this sort exist.

14

"Miranda Rights," which inform him that he is entitled to a lawyer and that he does not have to talk to the police. The suspect is taken to the police station, searched thoroughly, photographed, finger-printed, and placed in a jail cell. Additional statements are taken from the two clerks, identifying the suspect as one of the robbers.

The suspect is reminded of his right to be represented by an attorney and then interrogated for several hours, the police hoping to elicit a confession from the suspect using the strong eyewitness identifications to persuade him to cooperate. Let us suppose that the suspect does not confess and is returned to his cell until the next day. Here many cases leave the justice system because the police do not have sufficient evidence to support an indictment by a grand jury or judge-conducted preliminary hearing. No one has collected uniform statistics to show what proportion of arrests do not lead to preliminary hearings, but a large group of cases leaves the system at this point.

Next he is brought before a lower court judge and arraigned. A formal statement of the charge against the defendant is read; the judge determines that the charge is understood and that legal counsel has been secured (assigning an attorney, if necessary). The judge then asks a court probation officer for a report on the defendant's past criminal record and current living situation. The judge uses this information as well as recommendations from the prosecution and defense attorneys to set bail for the case.

Bail money is a monetary guarantee that the defendant, if released, will appear in court for trial. Many defendants are too poor to pay the bail money or to borrow it from a bail bondsman, and they remain in jail until their trial date. Today it is increasingly common to release defendants without bail payments, "on their own recognizance." Let us suppose our defendant is poor and that bail is set for $10,000. The defendant returns to a cell, where the court-appointed public defender interviews him to obtain information about the case and prepare for the events of the next few days.

The next day the preliminary hearing resumes, and the prosecution's eyewitnesses, the arresting officer, and a police detective present the evidence against the defendant. The defendant is called to testify but chooses to remain silent. The judge decides that there are sufficient grounds to conclude there is "probable cause" to hold the defendant, and the case is "bound over" to the local "grand jury."

The following day a grand jury of twenty-three citizens listens to the evidence presented at the preliminary hearing and, after deliberating, returns an indictment formally charging the defendant with armed robbery.   The day after the grand jury returns the indictment, the defendent is arraigned before the same judge who presided at the preliminary hearing.   The defendant is asked to enter a plea of guilty or not guilty to the formal charge of armed robbery.   The defendant pleads, "not guilty."   Bail is reviewed, and the defendant is returned to jail to await trial.

During the next five months, while the defendant is waiting for trial, the case is discussed with the attorney several times.   The attorney conducts an investigation of the crime and prepares witnesses.   These include the defendant and the defendant's cousin (in our example), who will testify they were together on the afternoon when the robbery occurred.   During the time between the preliminary hearing and the trial, about 80% of the defendants charged with major offenses plead guilty.   This usually occurs as a result of negotiations between the attorneys, and the process is called plea bargaining.   The prosecuting attorney may offer to alter the charges against the defendant, drop some charges, or recommend relatively low sentences to the trial judges (Rosett and Cressey, 1976).   It is clear that the prosecution and the defense are usually able to strike a bargain; the defendant changes the plea to "guilty," and the case does not go to trial.   This bargaining process is usually covert and certainly merits more attention than it has received to date.   In our view a promising innovation is to introduce the judge into the process and formalize it, as has occurred in some jurisdictions (e.g., Minnesota state courts).

To return to our example of armed robbery, we have now reached the beginning of the actual trial.   The first few hours of the trial are occupied with preliminaries, attorneys' motions to suppress evidence, and to permit special questions to be asked of jurors during jury selection, and so forth.   Then a number of potential jurors, usually about forty for a felony case, are brought into the courtroom.   A voir dire (old French for "to speak the truth") proceeding is held to select the actual trial jurors.   Both attorneys and the trial judge question each prospective juror about their acquaintance with the case, their ability to be impartial, and other related matters. Jurors who indicate they cannot be impartial or that they have a personal interest in the outcome of the trial (perhaps a prospective juror is employed in the supermarket that was robbed) are excused from service "for cause." Other jurors are excused by the attorneys "peremptorily" or "without cause" because one of the attorneys suspects bias but cannot demonstrate it. Peremptory challenges are limited in number by law to keep the selection process from becoming unwieldy. When a jury, usually of twelve plus two alternates, has been selected and sworn in, the trial begins.

The clerk of the court reads the indictment, and then the two attorneys make opening statements to the jury outlining the arguments they will present through their witnesses and evidential exhibits. Often the defense attorney withholds the opening statement until the prosecutor has presented the entire case against the defendant. The prosecutor is required to present the state's case first and to persuade the jury "beyond a reasonable doubt" that the defendant is guilty of all elements of the crime with which he is charged. This burden of proof is a manifestation of the "innocent until proven guilty" principle, which underlies American criminal law.

In our example, the district attorney opens by outlining the circumstances of the crime and introducing four witnesses—the two eyewitnesses, a police detective who interviewed the clerks and obtained the initial mugshot identifications, and a police officer who participated in the arrest. The prosecutor then calls each witness to the stand and elicits testimony from them supporting the prosecution's side of the case. It is established that the clerk was employed by the supermarket, and that $300 of the store's money was taken at gunpoint. The clerk is asked to describe the robbery and the robbers. Then the clerk describes the police identification procedures and finally identifies the defendant as one of the robbers.

After this direct examination is over, the defendant's lawyer is allowed to cross-examine the witness. The defense would doubtless concentrate on the identification evidence, attempting to weaken the witness's credibility. Was the market well-lighted, did the witness really see the robbers' faces, did the police bias the results of the mugshot examination, is the witness quite certain that the identification is correct, and so forth.  This back-and-forth, direct examination–cross-examination, pattern of questioning occurs with each prosecution witness.

After the final prosecution witness leaves the stand, the district attorney "rests" the state's case.  Then the defense lawyer makes an opening statement and calls the first defense witness, the defendant, to the witness stand.  The same pattern of direct examination followed by cross-examination occurs for defense witnesses, but, of course, the defense lawyer leads the direct examination.  Cross-examination of the defendant would include an effort to bring any prior criminal convictions to light.  This evidence, concerning the defendant's bad character, cannot be introduced into evidence simply to show that he is the sort of person who would perform criminal acts such as the crime with which he is charged.  However, American legal rules of evidence permit character evidence to enter the trial record for several other reasons.  In this case, for example, the prosecution might introduce evidence concerning a previous felony conviction, perhaps aggravated assault, to demonstrate that the defendant is not credible.  The jury would be instructed to separate issues of credibility (is the defendant's testimony truthful?) from culpability (is the defendant guilty of the crime with which he is charged?) and to use information about prior criminal convictions only in the first instance.

The defense attorney's second witness, the defendant's cousin, follows the defendant on the stand.  Direct examination aims to persuade the jury that they were together, in another part of town, at the time of the robbery in the supermarket.  The prosecutor's cross-examination is designed to undermine this testimony by emphasizing the witness's bias towards the defendant's acquital and inconsistencies in the alibi story.

After the last defense witness leaves the stand, the defense lawyer makes a summary statement of the defense case.  The unreliability of eyewitness identification evidence would be emphasized, as well as the strength of the defendant's alibi, and the importance of the presumption of innocence, with its requirement that the prosecution prove every element of the indictment "beyond a reasonable doubt."

Following the defense counsel, the prosecutor would summarize the state's case, stressing the certainty of the eyewitnesses and the weakness of the defendant's alibi defense.

During the body of the trial the judge plays a very modest role. The judge makes certain that the lawyer's conduct, particularly interrogation of witnesses, is proper and that the courtroom is orderly. After the lawyers finish, the judge assumes a prominent role, instructing the jury on the nature of the laws that it must apply during its deliberation on the case. The jury's responsibility is to decide what the facts of the case are as revealed in the complex, conflicting testimony heard during the trial. After deciding on the facts of the case, the jury is required to apply the relevant legal statutes, presented in the judge's instructions, to reach a proper verdict.

Most judges base their instructions to the jury on "pattern charges," which are available in judicial handbooks published in most states. Usually these standard charges are modified slightly from case to case at the attorneys' requests and the judge's discretion. For example, we have suggested that the trial judge in the supermarket robbery case might comment on the proper use of evidence about the defendant's prior criminal record. In addition to substantive instructions about the laws governing the particular case, the judge's charge instructs the jury about procedural matters. For example, the instructions describe the standard of proof, "beyond reasonable doubt" in criminal cases, and the verdict requirement, twelve out of twelve, or unanimous, in most jurisdictions. The judge must be extremely careful to instruct the jury properly both during the trial and in the final charge. Should the trial end with a conviction, most grounds for appealing the case to higher courts refer to alleged errors in the judge's instructions.

At the end of the judge's charge to the jury, the jury is taken to a deliberation room and required to deliberate to a verdict or until hopelessly deadlocked. If the jury reaches a verdict of not guilty, the trial is over and the defendant is freed. (Under the United States Constitution, the prosecution has no right to appeal an acquittal verdict.) If the verdict is guilty, the judge will typically ask for a week or more to review the defendant's record, supplemented by attorneys' recommendations, to set a sentence. In our example, let us suppose our defendant is convicted. The trial judge sets a date for sentencing two weeks later and, primarily because it is the defendant's second serious criminal conviction, imposes a sentence of ten years in prison.

The defendant goes to prison immediately to begin serving the sentence. Usually the time spent in jail awaiting trial is subtracted from the sentence. Most major criminal convictions are appealed, and it is likely that the defense attorney would continue to work on the case for several months pursuing any avenues of appeal which look promising. Cases that are successfully appealed, in which the defense lawyer is able to obtain a reversal of the trial court's verdict, are rare. Perhaps only 5% of criminal convictions are successful on appeal. However, the right to appeal is an extremely important aspect of the criminal justice system. One major source of judicial reform is the appeals court system, and the appeal process acts to maintain a fairly high standard of conduct in most trial courts.

The armed robbery case we have just outlined should serve to introduce to the reader the criminal justice system in this country. The example was designed to emphasize the small significance of courtroom activity within the larger system. Very, very few criminal acts lead to legal trials. However, it is important to realize that the courtroom is of critical importance in almost all parts of the system, in spite of its apparently narrowly confined influence. Police investigation procedures and lawyers' conduct are strongly determined by the anticipation that these behaviors may come under scrutiny of the court in the event that there is a trial. The conventions of courthouse plea bargaining are also powerfully affected by the possibility of a trial. It is difficult to conceive of any episode in the chain of events described here that is not influenced by the fact that the sequence may lead into the courtroom.

We will cite examples from both criminal and civil proceedings throughout this text. Although we have indicated the basic differences between the two types of adjudication, we have not developed a lengthly example of a civil case. We think that the two types of proceedings have much in common: a similar "cast of characters" and similar procedural rules. Of course, civil litigation usually involves two parties who disagree about responsibility for an accidental injury or a failure to fulfill a contract. The defendant in a civil suit is charged with responsibility for the accident or contract violation by another private party, the plaintiff. Issues of self-incrimination, bail, imprisonment, and so forth, do not arise.

We should warn the reader of one type of limitation on the examples we use in this text. Although we have selected or constructed each example to represent the general features of the legal institutions we review, there is so much diversity across jurisdictions in this country that no example can fit all relevant settings. The events we have described in our example robbery case are very close to those that would occur in our home state of Massachusetts. However, they are probably not exactly correct as a summary of the system in Pennsylvania or Texas state courts; and, of course, things are a bit different again in the federal courts.

We have not allowed the impossibility of finding perfectly general examples to deter us from constructing many example case situations or using examples from a variety of settings. The fine structure of legal institutions is just not important in a basic text that is designed to introduce general psychological principles and illustrate their application to courtroom phenomena.

We have organized this book into chapters on each of the major "actors" in the courtroom drama. There are chapters on the trial judge, the jury, the lawyers, the defendant, and the "evidence"; this last chapter is psychological in that it concentrates on the witness as the source of evidence. Each chapter includes a brief introduction to the actor's role in the trial as well as a thorough review of psychological research and theory relevant to that actor. The final chapter of the book is an overview of the courtroom, which concentrates on the relations between the actors within the small world of the courtroom, and the court within the larger world.

## SUMMARY

This introductory chapter started with a sketch of the connections between social science and legal justice institutions. We pointed out the advantages of the interchange for both parties: on one hand, increased understanding of legal institutions and their effects and, on the other, enrichment of scientific theory. We introduced social research methods, and made a fundamental distinction between experimental and correlational methods.   Next we discussed the two important types of research validity: (a) internal validity, concerned with the strength of a study's conclusions about causal relations between variables within the experimental or correlational design; (b) external validity, concerned with the generalizability of the results of a study to the sample of subjects, materials, and tasks in a new setting.  The final section of the chapter was an overview of the criminal and civil justice systems in this country.

# 2
# The Judge

## OVERVIEW OF THE JUDGE'S ROLE

In the public eye, the judge is the central actor in the courtroom. Of all the participants in the legal process, he or she is the most prominent symbolically, the most prestigious, and the most powerful during the trial itself. To begin this chapter we will review the judge's major activities in the criminal trial process.

Every person arrested must appear before a judge within a few hours of the arrest. During this initial presentment to the court the defendant is informed of legal rights, the criminal charges are explained, and the judge makes a preliminary decision about whether there is enough evidence to continue to hold the defendant in jail. At this preliminary hearing or shortly afterward the judge is required to set bail for the defendant, the bail being an amount of money that the defendant must pay to guarantee reappearance at subsequent court proceedings. Often the defendant is released without a monetary bail on his or her "own recognizance" or promise to return for further proceedings.

During the bail hearing or shortly before it, the judge presides over the arraignment, during which the accused is formally charged and enters a plea of guilty or not guilty. If the accused pleads guilty, the judge may interrogate him or her to ensure that the consequences of the plea are fully understood, and that it is entered without coercion by the police or others. Following a guilty plea, the judge usually decides on a sentence (often a fine, a short jail sentence, or probation) immediately.

If the defendant enters a not guilty plea, a trial date is set—usually several months after the date of the arraignment. During the interval between arraignment and trial most defendants, if they have not already done so, change their pleas to guilty. When this happens, the judge again assumes control of the proceedings, and the sentencing process begins. Most guilty pleas are entered after negotiations ("plea bargaining") take place between the prosecution and defense lawyers. The result of these negotiations is an agreement that the defendant will plead guilty to a lesser charge or that the prosecuting attorney will recommend reduced sentences to the judge during the pre-sentence hearing. Judges usually respect the terms of these bargains by following the prosecution's recommendations in sentencing. In some jurisdictions the judge actually participates in the bargaining process, acting as a mediator between the two attorneys.

If the case reaches trial, the judge (usually not the same judge who conducted the pretrial proceedings) presides over the case. If it is a jury trial he or she directs the impanelment of jurors, "umpires" the attorneys' presentations, and gives the jury final instructions on the law and evidence before they begin deliberation. In a few rare cases the judge exercises the court's power to intervene in the jury's decision either by directing them to return a particular verdict or even by reversing their judgment (this is called a judgment *non obstante verdicto*).

If the verdict is acquittal, the defendant leaves the criminal process. If the verdict is conviction, sentencing takes place. Usually the judge sentences the defendant a few days after the trial, allowing for a review of the facts of the case and a pre-sentence report prepared by the court's probation department.

On the surface we have presented an image of a powerful, autonomous trial judge. Of course, this picture is a simplification and even somewhat misleading. The judge's behavior is constrained by a great number of forces operating in the criminal justice system. First, there are conventions, rules, and laws that limit freedom. These factors specify the ordering and protocol for most of the events in the court's operation. For example, the law determines which hearings must be held, sets limits on bail levels for bailable offenses, controls the selection and instruction of juries, determines courtroom procedure, and limits or even prescribes sentences for various crimes. Second, relationships with other court officials, especially prosecutors and police, place limits on the judge's freedom. This is clear when we consider the paramount importance of the plea-bargaining process.

Finally, the sheer weight of the caseload in most courts will diminish the judge's role still further. To avoid even greater congestion in the criminal justice system, the judge is forced to hold brief hearings and constantly to press attorneys and juries for swift, decisive action within the law's formal procedural requirements.

Although these numerous unobtrusive constraints limit the judge's autonomy, he or she is still the most powerful actor in the legal system. A judge's personal predispositions determine which cases reach the courtroom, and influence prosecution and defense attorneys before the trial. The judge's discretion to set bail and determine sentences is still very broad. And the court* usually has recourse to exercise his or her prerogatives by reversing decisions made by others.

## JUDICIAL BACKGROUNDS

There is bewildering variety in the methods used to recruit trial judges. The variety chiefly reflects the workings of historical accidents and the great range of tasks that judges perform. Most state and municipal jurisdictions select judges through public elections; many depend on political officeholders such as governors, mayors, and legislators to appoint judges; and an increasing number of jurisdictions have panels composed of lawyers, citizens, and politicians to select judges on the basis of their professional records. Federal judgeships are filled by presidential appointment with a senate review. Each of these paths to the bench is tortuous and obscure, and each selection method serves some interests while neglecting others. The point for the present discussion is that this complexity is certain to produce a great diversity in the personal characteristics of judges.

There are numerous surveys of the characteristics of men and women serving on the bench (see Abraham, 1975, for a sampling), which provide a sense of the diversity in the profession. However, relatively little research has been devoted to the relationship between judicial background or personal differences and judicial performance.

Given the central role of the judge and the emphasis on rationality and impartiality in the legal system, social scientists have been interested in the manner in which individual differences influence the quality and direction of their decisions. Most of this research has

*"The court" is sometimes synonymous with "the judge."

focused on "sociological" rather than psychological variables. For example, Nagel (1962) conducted a large-scale study of the influence of background on state and federal supreme court judicial decisions. Nagel constructed an index of each judge's tendency to decide cases in favor of the defense or prosecution. He found that political party affiliation (Republican), bar association membership, high income, Protestant religious affiliation, low scores on a test of liberal political attitudes, and experience as a prosecuting attorney were all associated with a bias to favor the prosecution side of a case under appellate court review.

There have also been several efforts to characterize "personal styles" of judges and to relate style to family and educational background. An example of this approach is in the work of Smith and Blumberg (1967), who used a participant observation method to examine the differences among nine judges on the bench in a major criminal court. They developed a typology of six major judicial role patterns, which is perhaps best summarized by listing their labels: Intellectual-Scholar, Routineer-Hack, Political Adventurer-Careerist, Judicial Pensioner, the Hatchet-Man, the Tyrant-Showboat-Benevolent Despot. Smith and Blumberg discovered that the majority of the workload of the entire bench was handled by two justices, an Intellectual-Scholar and a Routineer-Hack. The authors noted that it was typical of large urban court systems to find one or two "workhorse" judges handling cases at a far higher rate than the other justices. However, they found it quite remarkable that the two "workhorses" in their study exhibited such great stylistic differences—the well-educated Intellectual-Scholar conducting an almost frenzied court, working weekends and evenings, and arousing antagonism from the rest of the bench; the more prosaic Routineer-Hack running a more traditional, but nonetheless efficient court.

To date there is no research on the effects of traditional personality variables on judicial decision making. To some extent this is due to judges' reluctance to open their profession to psychologists' scrutiny. Almost all of the research on individual differences has been accomplished by examining public records or by observing judges at work in the courtroom. However, it is also true that the current primitive state of the personality field provides a rather weak base for studying naturally occurring individual differences. Most personality constructs are as yet poorly developed, and reliable and valid assessment instruments are almost completely lacking (Mischel, 1968). The focus on social, attitudinal, and behavioral style differences is a conservative but sound beginning.

## ARRAIGNMENT AND BAIL

Judges are first involved in most criminal cases when they are called on to oversee arraignment and bail-setting hearings. In some cases a judge approves a warrant for the arrest of a suspect; but most arrests are made without a warrant, and in any case a warrant is issued routinely if the police do request one. The initial presentment of a defendant usually occurs within a day of arrest. During this proceeding the judge's duties are quite straightforward, although there is a wide range in the conscientiousness with which they are performed in the lower courts (President's Commission, 1967). Ordinarily the judge informs the defendant of the charges that led to the arrest, apprises him or her of legal rights, and arranges to have a defense attorney assigned to the case. Many minor cases are disposed of at this point; if the defendant pleads guilty, the judge imposes sentence at once. In most felony cases a brief hearing is held at this time to determine whether the prosecution has enough evidence to show probable cause to hold the defendant for trial.*  In these cases, following the probable cause hearing, the prosecutor's office prepares an "information" describing the charges against the defendant, and a formal arraignment is held. Many, probably most, defendants plead guilty at this point, and the sentencing process is started. For those defendants who plead innocent as charged, a trial date is set, usually months from the arraignment data, and the issue of bail is raised.

Bail, as we have said, is a monetary payment to ensure that the defendant will appear in court when required to do so. The legal object of the bail system is to ensure reappearance, but a number of factors that are not relevant to the risk of the defendant's fleeing probably enter into the judge's bail decision.

There are a multitude of problems with the bail system, most of

---

*In some jurisdictions a grand jury hearing replaces the probable cause hearing with a specially selected jury (usually of twenty-five persons) deciding if the prosecution case is strong enough to "indict" the defendant.

them deriving from the fact that while its object is to guarantee the defendant's appearance in court, the means to secure the appearance is monetary.  First of all, psychologists and other behavioral scientists have not developed prediction techniques powerful enough reliably to distinguish the high-risk defendants from the low-risk ones.  Second, the effects of the monetary bail system are critically dependent on the defendant's economic condition.  In fact, the bail payment is probably an effective sanction for only a small proportion of the defendants: many defendants cannot afford any bail costs no matter how low, and many are wealthy enough so that the bail payment is no guarantee of later appearance in court.  Third, it seems unjust to jail a person, who is presumed to be innocent until proven guilty, merely because he or she is unable to meet the costs of bail.

Research on defendants' behavior between arraignment and trial suggests that the likelihood a person will commit further crimes in the interval or flee is typically overestimated.  Efforts to reform bail laws (the 1966 federal bail reform law) and bail-setting practices such as the famous Manhattan Bail Project (Ares, Rankin, and Sturz, 1963) have promoted the use of "on own recognizance" releases, where the defendant is not required to post bail money but is released on his or her promise to return.  This method seems more consistent with the premise that a defendant is "innocent until proven guilty," and in practice an overwhelming number of recognizance-release defendants appear for trial.

In addition to the research by social scientists designed to predict the behavior of defendants awaiting trial, there are several studies of judges' bail-setting policies.  The research by Ebbe Ebbesen and Vladimir Konečni on bail-setting decisions is an excellent example of the application of social science methods to a natural domain.  We will spend some time on their research because it illustrates several theoretical, methodological, and substantive points.

Ebbesen and Konečni (1975) designed two studies to examine judges' decision making in the bail-hearing situation.  Typically the bail hearing in a minor case lasts a few minutes following arraignment. A lower court judge reviews a terse summary of the charges against the defendant, his or her economic status, ties to the local community, and prior criminal record.  Both attorneys present recommendations for bail and occasionally briefly emphasize details of the case in support of their recommendations.  Then in a matter of seconds the judge renders a decision based on the information in the probation officer's case file and the two recommendations.

The relative simplicity of the situation appealed to the two psychologists, and in their first experiment they enlisted the cooperation of eighteen lower court judges.  They asked each judge to review several model cases designed to mimic real case files and including written attorneys' recommendations, and then to set bail as though they were actually in court.  The simulation method allowed the experimenters to prepare case reports in which several variables were systematically manipulated.  Several levels of district attorney bail recommendations and defense recommendations were presented, along with information implying weak or strong local community ties and a previous criminal conviction record or no record.  Thirty-six files were created, so that every level of every variable occurred with every level of each other variable.  Other factors were presented at fixed levels in every case; for example, only robbery charges were included, the defendants always entered not guilty pleas, and they were always between the ages of twenty-one and twenty-five.  Finally, other details of the case, such as the exact nature of the stolen goods, were varied to increase the realism of the cases.

The advantages of the experimental plan are fairly obvious.  Any systematic variations in the judge's final bail levels can be unequivocally attributed to variations in the independent variables.  The relative effects of these experimenter-controlled variables can be assessed and clearly separated from the influences of the constant background variables (for example, type of crime).

Ebbesen and Konečni were not content with merely demonstrating that some variables influence bail levels while others do not. They hoped to "capture the judge's decision policy" by developing a simple mathematical equation that would predict actual final bail levels from information about each case.  In this situation they made the following theoretical assumptions about their judges:

1. The facts of each case can be viewed as forces acting on the judges' final bail decisions.

2. The strength of each fact's influence force on the final bail level can be characterized as acting in a specific *direction* with a particular *weight*.  For example, if we consider only the two attorneys'

recommendations, we can imagine that they will differ in *direction*, with the value of the district attorney's recommendation being "high" (he would urge the judge to set a high bail) and the defense recommendation being "low" (urging the judge to set a low bail or release the defendant on his own recognizance). The second, *weighting*, factor refers to the weight the judge gives to each recommendation. A prosecution-oriented judge might tend to weigh the district attorney's recommendations more heavily than those of the defense. Consequently we would expect his final decision to fall in the direction of the higher recommendation. The notion of weight in this sense is very close to the everyday usage of the term: the district attorney's recommendation has a greater weight in the judge's final decision.

3. Although it is fairly easy to think of the attorneys' recommendations as variables in an equation to predict final bail level—after all, the recommendations and the final bail are all stated in comparable dollar-value terms—it is not so easy to accept the authors' contention that factors such as prior record and local ties can also be represented quantitatively. Even psychologists who are eager to quantify or "scale" these apparently nonnumerical entities believe that the road to a successful mathematical formulation is steep and thorny. Suffice it to say for our present purposes that modern psychological measurement theory and scaling techniques provide a practical, although cumbersome, solution to the problem of quantifying variables such as local ties and prior record (see Dawes, 1972, and Anderson, 1974, for an introduction to these methods).

4. Next the authors proposed that the typical judge's bail decision could be described or modeled as a *weighted sum* of the values and weights of each of the types of information in the case. Since many background variables were fixed at constant levels in the experiment, the psychologists needed only to consider a simplified form of the model to account for the judges' decisions. The experimenters proposed a model of the following form:

$$[\text{WEIGHT}_1 \times \text{DISTRICT ATTORNEY'S RECOMMENDATION}]$$
$$+ [\text{WEIGHT}_2 \times \text{DEFENSE ATTORNEY'S RECOMMENDATION}]$$
$$+ [\text{WEIGHT}_3 \times \text{STRENGTH OF LOCAL TIES}]$$
$$+ [\text{WEIGHT}_4 \times \text{PRIOR CONVICTION RECORD}]$$

$$= \text{FINAL BAIL LEVEL}$$

Notice that although we have been quite precise about the conceptual meanings of the weights and scale values and the form of the model we have not committed ourselves to exact number values for these variables. The experimenter gives the model several advantages when he applies it to the data from an experiment. First, he tests only the general form of the model, assigning values to the four weights (WEIGHT$_1$ ... WEIGHT$_4$) and the scale values (DISTRICT ATTORNEY'S RECOMMENDATION ... PRIOR RECORD) to maximize the fit of the model to the data (and to satisfy a few constraints imposed by the measurement and scaling methods). Second, he is willing to assume that if the form of the model is successful in the simplified case, he can generalize it by merely adding new terms as new variables enter the judgment task (for instance, WEIGHT$_5$ × AMOUNT STOLEN).

(The model of the judge proposed by Ebbesen and Konecni is actually a special case of a very general mathematical model, called the linear multiple regression model by statisticians. This model is usually used to summarize the relationship between a single to-be-predicted dependent variable [the judge's bail decision in the Ebbesen and Konečni case] and a number of predictor independent variables [the information about attorney's recommendations, crime severity, strength of community ties, and so forth, in this case]. Details of the statistical model are available in many elementary texts on multivariate analysis.)

5. Finally, Ebbesen and Konečni assumed that the final bail judgment is not only a *weighted sum* but that it is a *weighted average* of the scale values of the case information. This final assumption is the most restrictive and the most controversial. The so-called averaging model has proved to be a valid representation in a number of decision-making situations similar to the bail-setting task (for instance, as a model of first-impression judgments in social acquaintance situations), but it has also failed as a psychological model (for instance, in predicting evaluations of economic and gambling problems).

The averaging constraint takes the form of an assumption that the sum of the weights in the model is equal to unity:

$$\text{WEIGHT}_1 + \text{WEIGHT}_2 + \text{WEIGHT}_3 + \text{WEIGHT}_4 = 1$$

The conception of a judge comprehending or "evaluating" and

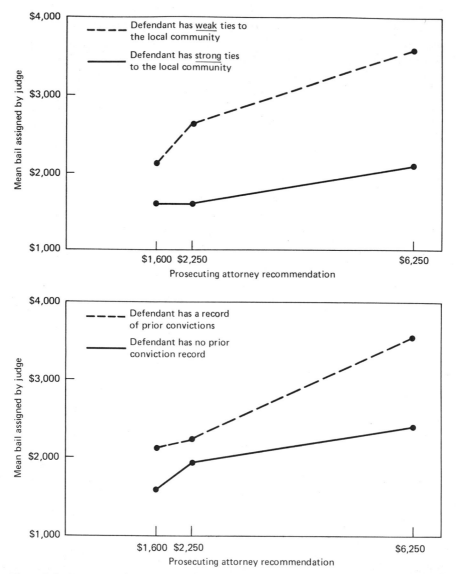

Figure 2.1. Summary of data from Ebbesen and Konečni's (1975) laboratory bail-setting experiment. The vertical axis represents the amount of the judge's bail decision, the dependent variable in the study. The horizontal axis represents the prosecuting attorney's recommendation, one of the independent variables. The fact that all four lines slope upward to the right indicates that these recommendations had an impact on the judgment; when the attorney recommended higher bail levels, the judge assigned higher bail requirements. The upper panel splits the data according to the "community ties" independent variable. The separation on the two lines indicates that this variable also had an effect

then weighting each fact relevant to a decision seems intuitively reasonable. Even the averaging rule, which implies that the weight given to each piece of information is dependent on the nature of the other facts in the case, is quite plausible. Resistance to the model usually arises because of its simplicity. Most experts, legal judges or otherwise, feel that their decisions are byzantine inferential masterpieces and that the prosaic averaging model is an insult to the richness of their intellectual creativity. There are several responses to this objection. First, experts almost always overestimate the complexity and sensitivity of their personal judgment strategies. Slovic and Lichtenstein (1971) reviewed several studies of expert decision making. They concluded that experts such as medical diagnosticians, stockbrokers, admission officers, and clinical psychologists have relatively poor insight into their decision policies. Generally these experts believed that they utilized many more sources of information and more complex judgment rules than they actually used. Interestingly, these experts appeared to become even less insightful as they gained professional experience: young judges were more accurate in assessing their personal decision policies than older ones. Second, the averaging model is not expected to reflect every detail of the judge's behavior. The model is a first approximation, which aims to capture the general features of the decision strategy while missing or ignoring the fine structure. After all, psychological research on expert judges is very new, less than ten years old, and the initial models must by necessity be overly simple.

Returning to Ebbesen and Konečni's experimental method, eighteen judges read the experimental materials for thirty-six arraignment-bail files and assigned a dollar-value bail to each case. The resulting judgments are displayed in Figure 2.1. The pattern of results shows that the district attorney's recommendation is important (all of the lines slope up to the right) and that both the local-ties variable and the prior-record variable have significant impacts on the final bail decision. The defense attorney's recommendation had no influence on the

---

on assigned bail levels: if the defendant had weak ties to the community, bail was set at a higher level than if his ties were strong. Finally, the lower panel shows that the existence of a record of prior criminal convictions affected bail levels: if the defendant had a record, bail was set higher than if his record was clean. Effects of the defense attorney's recommendation are not represented here because this independent variable had no reliable impact on the judge's bail decision.

judge—a fact which corresponds to the condition of an averaging model where this information receives no weight at all (WEIGHT$_2$ = 0).

Table 2.1 presents values for weights and scale values that might be derived to account for the present results (actually Ebbesen and Konečni proposed a slightly more elaborate model and analysis). We can use the weights and values in this table in conjunction with the averaging model to "predict" (actually *post*dict) the judges' decisions. For instance, the predicted bail for a defendant with strong local ties and a prior-conviction record, for whom the district attorney recommends a bail of $2250, and the defense recommends $1100 would be represented as follows:

$$[.50 \times \$2000] + [.00 \times \$1100] + [.30 \times \$0] + [.20 \times \$6000] = \$2200$$

This result is quite close to the actual figure obtained in the experiment ($1800).

Ebbesen and Konečni next attempted to apply their model to bail decisions occurring in actual arraignment hearings. They sent several observers to the courtrooms of the same judges who had participated in the pencil-and-paper laboratory study. These observers recorded information on the variables that had been manipulated in the laboratory along with the final bail set in hundreds of real bail hearings. The experimenters added a new variable, severity of the crime with which the defendant was charged, to the analysis.

Again they applied the averaging model. As before they found

Table 2.1. Example weights and scale values for the simple averaging model for the data from Ebbesen and Konečni, Experiment 1.

| | Weights | Subjective Scale Values | |
|---|---|---|---|
| District Attorney's Recommendation | .50 | recommendation: $1600 scale value: $1600 | recommendation: $2250 scale value: $2000 | recommendation: $6250 scale value: $4000 |
| Defense Attorney's Recommendation | .00 | recommendation: $0 scale value: $0 | recommendation: $550 scale value: $550 | recommendation: $1100 scale value: $1100 |
| Strength of Local Ties | .30 | Strong Local Ties scale value: $0 | Weak Local Ties scale value: $3000 | |
| Prior Conviction Record | .20 | No Prior Convictions scale value: $0 | Record of Prior Convictions scale value: $6000 | |

that the district attorney's recommendation had the greatest influence on the final bail value. They discovered that in the actual courtroom setting that strong or weak community ties and presence or absence of a prior criminal record did not have any simple effect on bail decisions. They also found that the defense attorneys' recommendations had little or no influence on the judges' decisions. They concluded that although the weights on the factors of the case had shifted from the laboratory setting to the courtroom, the averaging model was still valid.

Ebbesen and Konečni also found that the severity of the crime which the defendant was alleged to have committed was important, but the influence of this variable was indirect. Severity of the crime affected both attorneys' recommendations, and it is through these recommendations that the final decision was influenced. Note that one implication of these conclusions is that the judge does attend to the factors which predict the risk that the defendant will not reappear in court: local ties, attorneys' recommendations, and crime severity. Also it seems that the judge does ignore the existence of a prior record per se. Further, since the averaging model based on only these five factors does a good job of predicting the judge's decisions, it follows that the influence of irrelevant factors (such as press coverage, desire to punish the defendant immediately, favoritism for the district attorney) is relatively small.

One problem with the field study in contrast to the controlled laboratory experiment is that it is impossible completely to eliminate alternative accounts for the results based on the effects of "hidden" or "unmeasured" variables. For example, Anderson (1976) speculates that the Ebbesen and Konečni results reflect the effects of the defendants' race on bail decisions. Since Ebbesen and Konečni did not record defendants' race, and since race is plausibly related to some of the variables that were studied (e.g., prior record, crime severity), they cannot confidently eliminate interpretations of their results based on hypothetical race effects. (Of course this essential ambiguity is always present in nonexperimental field research. The conscientious researcher must be continually vigilant for plausible "hidden variable" explanations to turn them into testable hypotheses as best he can. Probably the best research strategy available is exemplified by Ebbesen and Konečni's approach: yoke the powerful, but unrepresentative, laboratory experiment to the inferentially weaker, but realistic, field study.)

Actually the hidden-variable problem is several subproblems. First, it could be that the researcher has completely missed the variable that is controlling the judge's decisions. The example outlined above illustrates this possibility. Anderson speculated that judges could be sensitive to the defendant's race, but Ebbesen and Konečni completely ignored the race variable in their analysis. If race were a crucial variable (and we don't know that it was), Ebbesen and Konečni's analysis would be flawed. Second, it could be that the researchers have defined a variable in one way (e.g., strength of community ties), but the judge is sensitive to a conceptually related but distinct variable (e.g., socioeconomic class). Here the problem is not that the researcher has failed to detect a relationship, but that he has "mislabeled" the relationship. Other researchers and theorists who do not carefully scrutinize the original data may then generate conclusions about residence patterns, geographical mobility, and so forth, while a correct analysis would have emphasized income, occupation, and the like. The solution to this problem is to consider a variety of empirically observable indices of a construct, such as "strength of community ties." The use of "multiple converging empirical operations" (i.e., many related measures of a construct) protects us from missing the correct conceptualization of measured variables.

Third, the researcher may have defined a dimension that is not treated as a single continuum by the judge. For example, although Ebbesen and Konečni defined severity of crime as a single dimension in their analysis, it is quite plausible that the judge distinguishes two (or more) categories of crime (violent *v.* nonviolent, or murder *v.* other crimes) and treats the two in very different ways as they appear in the arraignment docket. In fact, there was some evidence that the community-ties variable had one sort of effect for less severe crimes and exactly the opposite pattern of effects for more severe crimes in the Ebbesen and Konečni study.

To summarize, bail decisions in the laboratory setting reflected the prosecutor's recommendation, strength of local ties, and prior record. However, in actual bail hearings, the judge's final bail was directly related only to the prosecutor's recommendation. First, there are two ways to account for the correlation between the final bail and the prosecutor's recommendation: the judge depends heavily on the recommendation, or the judge and the prosecutor have highly similar decision policies (both depending on crime severity as the major cue to set bail).    In this case both the direct-dependence and use-of-similar-cues hypotheses are almost certainly valid.  Second, how can we account for the differences in policy, for the same judges, in the laboratory and the courtroom settings?  One rather unflattering possibility suggested by Ebbesen and Konečni is that the judges are on their best behavior in the laboratory, and they adopt an unnatural bail-setting policy carefully weighting prior record and community-ties information as they feel a proper judge should.  However, when they are back on the bench, unaware of the psychologists' scrutiny, they return to their irresponsible habits and listen only to the prosecutor.  This interpretation is probably incorrect.  A more likely account follows from an analysis of the flow of information in the disjointed, complex arraignment hearing.  The judge does his best to attend to all the sources of information relevant to his decisions.  Unfortunately, the irregular, muddled presentation of information and conflicting attention demands in the courtroom foil the judge's efforts to be open-minded, and leave him dependent on one or two imputs.  One implication of this interpretation is that the defense attorney, completely ignored in Ebbesen and Konečni's study, could exert more influence on the judge if he or she would clearly highlight the facts of a case that favor lower bail.  That is, we should not blame the overloaded judge but the defense attorney who fails to bring community ties and prior record to the court's attention when these variables are in favor of the accused.

We have invested so much time in reviewing the Ebbesen and Konečni paper because we feel that it foreshadows coming developments in psychological research on the trial judge.  The method is especially appealing because it allows comparisons between highly controlled laboratory settings and the actual courtroom.  The authors' arguments for the validity of the averaging model are very persuasive because of the convergence of results obtained in the two settings.  The theoretical section of their paper is also exemplary in that the model of the judge is plausible, precise, and empirically flexible.  It is interesting to see that the general form of the model, the averaging rule, is valid in both settings, but that details such as the weights vary with changes  in the setting.  One rather encouraging conclusion is that laboratory simulations are a useful method to explicate the judge's performance in the natural setting.

## PLEA BARGAINING

Most criminal cases (approximately 80%) end during the period following arrest before the trial begins, with a plea of guilty by the defendant.  Without this high rate of "plea copping" there would be no way for the present court systems to handle the volume of criminal cases that would reach the trial stage.  There are numerous sociological and participant observation studies of the plea bargaining process (Rosett and Cressey, 1976; Newman, 1956).  Most jurisdictions enjoin judges from participating in the negotiations for pleas, and the two attorneys deal with one another directly.  Recently there has been a shift in the procedure, and judges in some states (for example, parts of California and Minnesota) mediate discussions between the attorneys.  To date there is no research by psychologists on this problem.  It would seem that the Ebbesen and Konečni method for studying bail setting could be easily adapted for studying some aspects of the negotiated guilty plea.  Another approach is suggested by the simulation method employed by Thibaut and Walker (1975) in their experiments on conditions in pretrial settlement conferences in civil cases.

## THE JUDGE'S INSTRUCTIONS TO THE JURY

Once the trial begins, the judge takes a more prominent directive role. The judge usually conducts the voir dire proceedings during which the trial jury is selected if the defendant has not waived rights to a jury trial.  The judge reviews and decides on motions by the lawyers usually concerned with the admission of exhibits of evidence, deposition statements by witnesses who cannot be present at the trial, expert testimony, and so forth.  Finally, once the actual trial begins, the court assumes the role of "umpire," ruling on objections raised by the attorneys and occasionally directing attorneys and witnesses to improve the quality of the trial.

There has been no research on the variables that control the judge's behavior during the trial itself.  However, there are a number of experiments on the impact of the judge's instructions to the jury on the jury's behavior. Most of this research has focused on the effect of a judge's instruction to disregard a portion of the testimony on the jury's later use of the testimony.

Doob and Kirshenbaum (1973) conducted one of the neater experiments on this issue. In their simulation experiment, college-student subjects read a summary of a burglary case. For half of the subjects the case included information about the defendant's past record indicating that he had been convicted, five times, of breaking and entering charges. Subjects receiving this information were consistently more likely to judge the defendant guilty in the case. Of more interest to us is the fact that it made no difference whether or not the judge instructed the subject that the past-record evidence was only relevant to evaluating the witness's credibility and not relevant to deciding on his guilt or innocence. Clearly subjects ignored the judge's instructions; otherwise the instruction would have caused the subjects receiving it to judge the defendant as less likely to be guilty as charged than they did.

Sue, Smith, and Caldwell (1973), also using college-student subjects in a simulation of juror decision making, found that evidence ruled inadmissible had a significant effect on subjects' verdicts and assignments of punishment. The effects of inadmissible evidence were especially strong when the remaining, admissible, evidence was weak.

The disturbing implication of the Doob and Kirshenbaum and Sue, Smith, and Caldwell results, that jurors will typically ignore or misunderstand instructions from the bench, is echoed by a number of other empirical studies. Even more disquieting is contemplation of the fate of the judge's final instructions and charge to the jury at the end of the trial. Almost no research has been conducted on the extent to which jurors comprehend and apply the long difficult summary instructions. One section of the renowned "American Jury" study by Harry Kalven and Hans Zeisel of the University of Chicago bears on this issue indirectly (Kalven and Zeisel, 1966, 1967).

In this classic survey study, the two researchers mailed questionnaires to state and federal trial judges asking for information about recent case outcomes. The design of the survey emphasized comparisons between the juries' actual verdicts and the judges' (private) judgments. The general conclusion of the study was that in an overwhelming majority of cases judges' and juries' decisions were in agreement. The researchers went on to demonstrate that numerous characteristics of the trial—e.g., case difficulty, strength of evidence, length—affected both the jury and the judge similarly. For example, trial length was directly related to deliberation time, and judges' ratings of case difficulty predicted the likelihood that juries would request additional instructions from the judge during their deliberation. Judges' ratings of closeness of the case were related to the probability of disagreement between judge and jury on the verdict. Jury acquittal rates were related to judges' evaluations of the strength of the prosecution case, and so on. Taken together all of these correlations suggest that the jury and the judge are sensitive to the same characteristics of the case. Since the judge's instructions are the major communication between judge and jury, it seems plausible that jurors follow the case correctly and do a conscientious job of comprehending and applying rules of law outlined in the judge's final instructions. Unfortunately the logic behind this conclusion is not irresistible, and even in the Kalven and Zeisel survey there was a nonnegligible rate of judge–jury disagreements.

A few experiments have looked more directly at jurors' reactions to the judge's instructions, and the conclusions from this research are rather pessimistic. Several simulation experiments (DeSloovere, 1933; Forston, 1970; Henney, 1947; Hunter, 1935) assessed jurors' comprehension of the final instructions. All of these investigators concluded that the typical juror's grasp of the principles of law was weak at best and that legal definitions and rules were more often misapplied than used correctly.

There is currently considerable interest in developing more comprehensible "pattern instructions" and procedures that will deliver instructions to a jury in a maximally useful manner. Two promising suggestions are to present instructions before as well as after the trial evidence (Prettyman, 1960) and to allow jurors to take a written summary of the instructions into the deliberation room. In addition to these procedural improvements, researchers are studying ways in which psycholinguistic theory can be applied to render difficult instructions more understandable (Sales, Elwork, and Alfini, 1977).

Following the judge's final instructions, the case is in the jury's hands.    Upon the jury's request, the judge may be called on to decide whether to send evidence exhibits, sections of the trial transcript, or additional instructions to the deliberation room.  Should the jury return without reaching a verdict or "hang," the judge would exhort them to attempt once again to reach agreement.

When the jury returns with a verdict, the judge thanks them and dismisses them to return to the jury waiting room.  If the verdict is an acquittal, the legal process is finished and the defendant is released.  The prosecution side of the case has no rights to appeal the verdict.  If the verdict is for conviction, the judge begins a review of the guilty defendant's record to determine the disposition of the case.

## SENTENCING

Thus far in the legal process the judge's behavior has been strongly constrained by laws, court rules, and the roles of other participants in the legal system; however, the matter of sentencing is almost completely in the judge's hands.  In this country the judge reviews the facts of the case, a pre-sentence report prepared by a probation officer, and then simply determines the sentence.  It is something of an embarassment to observe the great range of sentences that different judges assign to apparently indistinguishable crimes.  Penologists, of course, have to live with these disparities, and they are particularly acerbic about sentencing practices.  James V. Bennett, former Director of the Federal Bureau of Prisons, has observed:

> In one of our institutions a middle-aged credit union treasurer is serving 117 days for embezzling $24,000 in order to cover his gambling debts.  On the other hand, another middle-aged embezzler with a fine past record and a fine family is serving 20 years, with 5 years probation to follow.  At the same institution is a war veteran, a 39-year-old attorney who has never been in trouble before, serving 11 years for illegally importing parrots into this country.  Another who is destined for the same institution is a middle-aged tax accountant who on tax fraud charges received 31 years and 31 days in consecutive sentences.  In stark contrast, at the same institution last year an unstable young man served out his 98-day sentence for armed bank robbery. [cited in Kaplan, 1973]

Federal and state laws provide limits that set upper and lower bounds on the penalties which can be imposed by the judge. But these boundaries usually allow wide lattitude for the judge's discretion to operate. For example, in Massachusetts a conviction for armed robbery can carry a sentence from five years to life in prison, and a conviction for manslaughter a sentence from two and one-half to twenty years in prison; and of course the judge may always grant a suspended sentence, allowing the defendant to return to society immediately. Furthermore, there is almost no appeals court review of sentences. Neither the prosecution nor the defense has a right to appeal the trial judge's sentence in most cases.

This lack of limitations and lack of review is accompanied by lack of control, leaving even the most conscientious judge at sea in an ocean of inconsistent standards and shifting guidelines. For example, at least four conflicting theories of sentencing policy are popular today:

(a) Case disposition should satisfy the victim's, friends of the victim's, and the public's need for *vengeance* on the criminal.

(b) Case disposition should demonstrate publicly the penalty a wrongdoer pays for his crime, to *deter* other potential offenders.

(c) Case disposition should aim to *protect* society from additional crimes by convicted criminals.

(d) Case disposition should aim to *rehabilitate* the criminal to prevent him or her from choosing to commit further crimes after leaving the correctional system.

Judges are left to their own devices to adopt or create sentencing policies. The result is that sentences in apparently identical crime circumstances vary widely. An early survey study by Gaudet (1938) found large disparities in the sentences assigned to similar offenders in lower courts in New Jersey. Gaudet found that judges tended to be consistent in assigning harsh or lenient sentences, but he was unable to isolate any relationships between sentencing policies and personal experience, local economic conditions, or imminence of reappointment.

The Gaudet result has been replicated in many other survey studies; however, we cannot conclude that this evidence for variation in sentences across similar *but different* cases proves that there is injustice in sentencing. It is possible that judges are attempting to sentence defendants justly and that the different circumstances of each case require considerable flexibility in sentencing. Unfortunately, a number of studies demonstrate that there is also great variation in the sentences imposed on the *same* defendants by different judges.

An experimental study in the Second Circuit of the federal court system (federal trial courts in New York, Connecticut, and Vermont) provides a clear demonstration that a defendant's sentence depends on the individual trial judge (Partridge and Eldridge, 1974). The study asked fifty federal judges to impose sentences on twenty different defendants charged with a range of offenses. Some example results are presented in Table 2.2. First, it is clear that there is enormous disagreement between judges. The authors of the

Table 2.2.  Second Circuit Sentencing Study. The numbers in the table indicate the federal judges' sentence assignments for seven cases. The range in sentences, the difference between the most and least severe figures for each case, is quite large, implying that disagreement between judges is high even when they review the same cases.

| Experimental Case | Most Severe Sentence | Median Sentence | Least Severe Sentence |
|---|---|---|---|
| Extortionate credit transactions; income tax violations | 20 yr prison $65,000 | 10 yr prison $50,000 | 3 yr prison |
| Bank robbery | 18 yr prison $5,000 | 10 yr prison | 5 yr prison |
| Sale of heroin | 10 yr prison 5 yr probation | 5 yr prison 3 yr probation | 1 yr prison 5 yr probation |
| Theft and possession of stolen goods | 7.5 yr prison | 3 yr prison | 4 yr probation |
| Operating an illegal gambling business | 1 yr prison $3,000 | 3 yr probation $10,000 | 1 yr probation $1,000 |
| Mail theft | 6 mos prison 18 mos probation | 3 yr probation | 1 yr probation |
| Perjury | 1 yr prison $1,000 | 2 yr probation $500 | $1,000 |

report concluded that, "for the most part, the pattern displayed is not one of substantial consensus with a few sentences falling outside the area of agreement.   Rather, it would appear that absence of consensus is the norm."   Second, the most troubling sentencing inequities occur when one person receives a prison sentence and another, charged with the same offense, does not.   Judges in the Second Circuit study disagreed on the issue of incarceration in sixteen out of the twenty cases studied.   Third, sentencing disparities were not related to the length of a judge's service.   There was no evidence that more experienced judges were closer to one another than less experienced judges.

There has been almost no research by psychologists on the problem of identifying and modeling individual differences in trial judges' sentencing behavior.   Ebbesen and Konečni (1976) have started to apply their techniques to the problem, but the trial judge is still the least well-understood actor in the courtroom.

Although the larger problem of modeling the trial judge's decision policy is still untouched, sociologists have pursued the problem of identifying the influences of "extralegal" factors (for instance, the defendant's race, sex, and socioeconomic status) on sentencing ever since the publication of a pioneering monograph by Sellin in 1928.   Sellin argued that although factors such as the defendant's race and economic status are legally irrelevant to the determination of sentence, the judge cannot escape their subtle influence.

Research on the problem has all followed a single methodological strategy.   One or more extralegal factors are isolated, and cases in which the defendant was convicted are classified on the basis of the factors.   Then the researcher employs statistical techniques to determine if the sentence imposed in each case is reliably correlated with the extralegal factor.   For example, Sellin hypothesized that when sentences are imposed, the most severe sentences will be assigned to blacks and other members of racial minorities.   The difficulty with this approach is that although a superficial survey of cases may appear to confirm the hypothesis, a thorough, convincing analysis must not only demonstrate that there is a relation between the extralegal factor and sentence severity, but further that the true source of the relationship is not another legally relevant factor (for instance, prior conviction record).   In Sellin's example, he needed to show that race and sentence are correlated, and in addition he needed to demonstrate that a correlation between race and prior record (black defendants were likelier than whites to have prior criminal convictions) did not exist, or did not account for the relation between race and sentence.  As it turns out, Sellin did not accomplish either objective.  He neither established the existence of a strong race–sentence correlation, nor did he attempt to rule out other legally relevant variables as competing explanations.  The statistical logic required to establish a variable as causal and to rule out explanations based on "co-varying" factors is extremely complex. In a recent review paper Hagan (1974) concludes that none of the thirty-odd studies to date has established the significance of extra-legal attributes in criminal sentencing.  Of course, this does not mean that extralegal considerations are negligible, but only that a clear case for their importance has yet to be advanced.

## THE APPELLATE COURT JUDGE

In addition to the research we have just reviewed on the psychology of the trial judge, there is a literature on appellate court judges.  The most prominent and most studied judges in the country are the nine justices of the Supreme Court of the United States, which is ex-clusively concerned with cases on appeal.  Unlike the trial judges we have discussed above, most appellate judges meet to make their decisions collegially.  Any successful analysis of these judges' be-havior must consider the dynamics of these small groups as well as the judges as individuals.  Social scientists and legal scholars have focused on four topics in collegial justice: first, the development of quantitative models to predict individual supreme court justices' decisions; second, comparisons between judges' behavior making decisions alone and (the same) judges' decisions as members of judicial tribunals; third, theoretical analyses of the relative accuracy of individual and group decisions; fourth, historical analyses of the patterns of clique formation and inter-judge influence in the Supreme Court.

Ulmer (1971) has written an excellent monograph introducing research on "courts as small groups."  We will not discuss appellate court decision making in this text because the procedures and functions of an appellate court are so different from those of the trial courtroom, which is the focus of our presentation.

## SUMMARY

This chapter on the psychology of the trial judge began with a review of the tasks performed by the judge in the courtroom. There followed a short section on the nature of individual differences between judges, emphasizing the diversity of personal characteristics to be found on the bench. Next the bail-setting process was explored in an extensive analysis of two studies by Ebbesen and Konecni. Experimental and correlational methods were compared, and a mathematical averaging model of the trial judge's decision-making policy was examined. A short review of research on the judge's communications with the trial jury, instructions during the trial, was presented. The general conclusion that the trial judge's instructions could be improved in comprehensibility and effectiveness was advanced. Finally, the chapter concluded with a summary of research on sentencing policies.

# 3
# Jury Behavior: Composition

Consider a jury that has finished hearing a trial and has just entered the jury room to begin its deliberations. The jurors are ordinary citizens untrained in the task they are performing. They have been drawn more or less at random from the eligible population, convened briefly for a particular trial, and given important powers of official decision making. Yet they will deliberate in complete secrecy, render their decision without explanation, and return to private life without accountability for that decision then or ever (Kalven and Zeisel, 1966).

If that jury is like most of the juries in the United States, it will deliberate for about one hour (for trials lasting up to two days, median deliberation time is under one hour; 74% of juries complete their deliberations in less than two hours); and if it is like approximately 95% of American juries, it will conclude its deliberations with a verdict (Kalven and Zeisel, 1966). What are the determinants of the outcome of that deliberation? What determines how the jury performs, whether the jury hangs or reaches a verdict, and whether that verdict will favor the prosecution or the defense, the plaintiff or the defendant?

The product of any group process depends upon four classes of variables: the composition of the group, its structure, the nature of the group process, and the task with which the group is confronted. By composition, we mean the characteristics of the people who constitute the group. Group structure refers to such variables as the group's size, spatial arrangements, social organization, or communication networks. Process refers to what the group does, in contrast to whom it is composed of or how they are organized. The group's task defines its purpose; it is the content of what the group was brought together to do. The specifics of each of these components lend precision to understanding, predicting, and changing what the jury will do. If we can fill in the details of this formula, we ought to be able to predict what verdict will be returned by a jury that entered the deliberation room and left us outside.

For many theorists of jury behavior, composition is not only the logical place to start but essentially gives the solution to the puzzle. An old textbook on lawyering process counsels:

> Many practitioners maintain that the selection of a jury is the most important step toward the winning of a case. This is not a compliment to the jury system, but if it expresses the truth, it is a condition which cannot be ignored by the practitioner. [Brumbaugh, 1917, p. 285]

Recently, lawyers and social scientists have collaborated to bring modern social and behavioral science techniques to bear on the selection of favorable juries. A book describing the new techniques introduces them by citing "a very obvious fact: the people who constitute the jury can have as much or more to do with the outcome of a trial as the evidence and arguments" (Kairys, Schulman, and Harring, 1975, p. 1).

This hypothesis, that the composition of the jury is the most important determinant of the trial's outcome, has been implicit in the practice of law for some time. What kinds of jurors are favorable and what kinds are unfavorable are contained in the folk wisdom of the law. Brumbaugh's (1917) chapter on "Estimating the Jury" details the major kinds of biases possessed by jurors: The Religious Bias, The Nationality Bias, The Political Bias, The Class Bias, the Bias of Education; along with advice on picking "The Best Jury."

> (A) juror should be a man carrying responsibilities, so that he has a due sense of obligation; he should be a family man, for this type of a man will weigh the effect of a verdict upon his own children and their future interests, in short, he has the welfare of society in his mind's eye. . . . (A) juror should have some regard in his practical life for religion. . . . This will tend to make him more conscientious in the fulfillment of his duty. . . . (He) should be a man of good habits. . . .

> Moreover, the men upon the jury should not only be respectable in every way, but be intelligent representative citizens who have a reputation for honor and fairness. . . . A set of twelve such men uniform in social rank and age make the best possible jury.

Simon (1967) cites some legal folklore on the impact of occupations upon juror behavior:

> As a rule, clergymen, school teachers, lawyers, and wives of lawyers do not make desirable jurors. They are too often sought out for advice and tend to be too opinionated.
>
> Retired businessmen are usually fair but disinclined to render wild verdicts. A reasonably well-educated laboring man is not to be despised. [pp. 103–104]

Other advice urges lawyers to avoid cabinetmakers because they want everything to fit together neatly, Germans or Scandinavians because those nationalities are too exacting, and so on (Mossman, 1973).

The theory underlying the core hypothesis, that the characteristics of jurors affect the decision they reach, can be stated fairly simply. A person's demographic background (socioeconomic class, race, religion, sex, age, education, and so forth) denotes a particular kind of socializing history for that person. If you are poor, young, black, and female, you will have been conditioned to view the world differently, to react to it differently, and to hold different attitudes compared with a person who is wealthy, old, white, and male. These perceptions, attitudes, and values, in turn, help determine the decision you make as a juror. In addition to demographic characteristics, personality type (whether personality arises through genetics, psychodynamic development, or conditioning history) is thought to predispose a juror to a particular decision. If you are highly dependent on order, for example, you might be conviction-prone. It is unclear whether the theory holds that personality type determines the substantive preference one has (e.g., always wanting to be punitive) or whether it influences the way one processes the evidence (giving more weight to the government's evidence than to the defense's). Thus, juror demographic characteristics, personality, and attitudes are thought to have substantial impact on their decisions.

We will shortly consider the evidence relating to this pervasive hypothesis, and the implications of its correctness or incorrectness for legal institutions as well as for practitioners.

First, however, we should briefly mention several issues closely related to jury composition, with which legal institutions have had and will have to grapple. First, there is the suggestion that jurors be routinely screened using psychological tests (e.g., Emerson, 1968; Mitchell and Byrne, 1973; also, cf. *People v. Craig*, 1968, which banned the use of intelligence tests in jury selection). The rationale is that if some people are more intelligent or more unbiased than others and those are the people who would do the ablest job as jurors, perhaps the law should establish the achievement of certain scores on certain psychological tests as a condition for serving on a jury.

A second issue is one which suggests that the courts are, in some cases, already following the first suggestion, and to the disadvantage of the defendant. In most jurisdictions where the death penalty is legal, "scrupled" jurors (persons who indicate that they would not find a defendant guilty if conviction would lead to execution) are not permitted serve on juries in capital cases. Such "death-qualified" juries are composed of a disproportionate number of conservative, authoritarian persons, since scrupled jurors, who tend to be liberal and nonauthoritarian, are excluded. And authoritarians, continues the argument, are more likely to convict. Thus, the act of death-qualifying a jury may stack the deck against the defendant; not only are the remaining jurors willing to convict, they are more likely to convict than a more representative jury would be (Jurow, 1971; *Witherspoon v. Illinois*, 1968). If all this is true, convictions by such juries may be unconstitutional, and certainly are unfair.

The jury's composition is influenced at two major stages of selection. From the eligible population a pool of prospective jurors, called the "venire," is selected to serve for a given period, usually about a month. From this pool, through voir dire (see Chapter 1), attorneys are able further to influence the composition of the jury by excluding persons they believe would be biased (that is, unfavorable to their side).

The first selection stage puts absolute limits on who can be a juror; anyone who does not get into the venire will not serve. Although venires are supposed to be representative of the community, the selection procedures will determine how closely the venire approximates the community. Many of the methods used to select the venire cause it to be unrepresentative. Even the widely accepted method of using voter registration lists will lead to an underrepresentation of young persons, ethnic minorities, or people who move frequently—all of whom are eligible to serve on juries, but are relatively unlikely to be registered to vote. Some jurisdictions use a "key man" system, where selected persons are asked to compile special jury lists of people they know. Other jurisdictions, as a matter of policy, may call jurors in an unrepresentative fashion, such as by choosing two males for every female, or no females at all (the practice, until recently, in Louisiana).

The U.S. Supreme Court has been ruling for nearly 100 years that jury pools must be representative of a cross section of the community from which they are drawn (Kairys, 1972); "cognizable classes" may not be discriminated against. Still, they are widely found to be unrepresentative (Mills, 1962; Vanderzell, 1966; Holbrook, 1956). For example, Figure 3.1 is a map of Philadelphia indicating the representation of each ward in the county's juries in 1970. The overrepresented wards tend to be in white, middle and upper socioeconomic areas; the underrepresented wards tend to be in black and lower socioeconomic areas.

In deciding whether a jury pool deviates significantly from a cross section of the community, justices have used an intuitive "feel" for a "significant" discrepancy, even though statistical techniques in common use permit the calculation of the exact probability that an observed difference between a community and its juries is due only to chance in sampling (Finkelstein, 1966). For a simple example, if females constitute 60% of a community and males 40%, and out of 200 jurors, 105 were female and 95 were male, what is the probability that this discrepancy was a chance result?

The answer can be found by using any of several statistical tests, but let us use the "z test for instances," an old (around since 1733) and simple one:

$$z = \frac{|nP_x - x| - c}{\sqrt{nP_xP_y}}$$

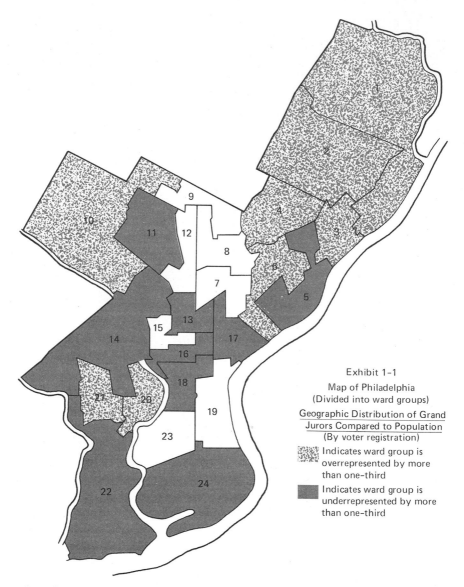

Exhibit 1-1

Map of Philadelphia
(Divided into ward groups)

Geographic Distribution of Grand
Jurors Compared to Population
(By voter registration)

Indicates ward group is
overrepresented by more
than one-third

Indicates ward group is
underrepresented by more
than one-third

Figure 3.1. Juries should be representative of the population from which they are drawn. In this map of Philadelphia, the city's wards are marked to show their citizens' representation on grand juries. Some are substantially overrepresented; others are under-represented. Anyone familiar with the city, like one of the authors (who grew up there), immediately recognizes that it is the relatively well-to-do areas in the northeast and northwest that are overrepresented and the relatively poor and/or minority-populated wards that are under-represented. (From Kairys et al., 1975.)

where,

$x$ = the number of persons in the smaller sample
$P_x$ = the proportion of persons in the smaller class
$P_y = 1 - P_x$
$n$ = the size of the sample
$c = 0.5$, a constant

If we insert into the equation the size of the sample (200 jurors), the proportion of persons in the smaller class (.40 of the community are males), the number of persons in the smaller sample (95 males), the constant (0.5), and the proportion of persons in the larger class (.60 of the community are females),

$$z = \frac{|(200 \cdot .40) - 95| - 0.5}{\sqrt{200 \cdot .40 \cdot .60}}$$

Solving for $z$,

$$z = 2.093$$

Looking up $z$ in a $z$-table of normal probabilities (found in any elementary statistics textbook), we discover that a $z$ of 2.093 is associated with a probability of less than .05, or 5%. Thus, we can say that the observed distribution of jurors, drawn from a community such as we have described, is likely to occur by chance fewer than 5 times in 100. This is below social scientists' conventional level of significance (which is .05), and we would reject as too improbable the hypothesis that the distribution of jurors was a chance occurrence.

Although Supreme Court justices have relied on subjective probability estimates and have not made their mathematics explicit, Ulmer (1962) studied the decision making of Supreme Court justices in racial exclusion cases decided between 1935 and 1960 and discovered that the Court found jury pools to be unrepresentative when the sample of jurors is greater than sixty and when the racial heterogeneity of the jury pool differed from that of the eligible population to an extent expected by chance less than 5% of the time. Otherwise the jury pools were declared acceptable. Interestingly enough, the conventional probability level used by scientists for rejecting the hypothesis that an observation occurred by chance is just that— $p < .05$.

When venire selection is thought to produce unrepresentative jury pools, surveys by social scientists have been used by lawyers to marshal evidence for declaring that jury system unconstitutional and obtaining jurors more representative of the community (Kairys et al., 1975).  At this first stage of jury selection, one tries to ensure that the venire is representative.

It is at the second stage of jury selection, voir dire, that attorneys can apply hypotheses about people's characteristics to try to produce a favorable jury.  During voir dire, prospective jurors are examined. This examination consists of questions being put to the jurors, sometimes by the judge, sometimes by the attorneys.  In addition, the examination provides an opportunity for observation of the physical appearance and demeanor of the prospective jurors.  Finally, certain other information gathered by the court about the jurors is available, such as name, residence, and occupation.  The purpose of voir dire is to eliminate jurors whose biases may interfere with a fair consideration of the evidence.  In addition to generalized biases, jurors may have been exposed to a particular source of biasing information, such as prejudicial pretrial news coverage.  Voir dire is the opportunity to identify and remove persons who have been exposed to such information (Padawer-Singer, Singer, and Singer, 1974).

Using any of the information available to them, the respective attorneys may challenge the seating of any person on the jury panel. Challenges may be for cause, where the lawyer asks the judge to exclude a particular person from the jury, offering reasons, and, if the judge agrees, the person is "excused."  Or an attorney may use one of a limited number of peremptory challenges to exclude a juror without having to offer reasons and without requiring the judge's consent.  The defense usually has more peremptory challenges available than the prosecution.  In this way, by excluding certain persons from the jury, attorneys are able to influence the jury's composition. Although the purpose of voir dire is to eliminate jurors whose biases may interfere with making a decision based only upon the evidence presented at the trial, for centuries attorneys have understandably sought to select juries favorable to their side.  Presumably, if both sides do this, and do it well, the result will be a jury composed of people leaning to neither side, that is, neutral jurors, the very ones who will be best able to let the evidence determine their decision and to have attitudes and personality play a minimal role. The question of immediate concern, however, is how can we tell which jurors are favorable to which side?

For centuries, the hypotheses lawyers used were based upon the kinds of folklore discussed earlier, hunches, unsystematic past experience, intuition, stabs in the dark. Scientific jury selection has moved this process from the level of hunches and folklore to a more sophisticated plane, enabling selection decisions to be made with the benefit of knowledge acquired through the use of systematic empirical techniques (Schulman, Shaver, Colman, Emrich, and Christie, 1973; Kairys et al., 1975; Saks, 1976).

Scientific jury selection was first used in the winter of 1971–1972, in the trial of the Harrisburg Seven, and has been further developed and used in numerous trials since then (Kairys et al., 1975; Saks, 1976). Actually, the techniques are far from new; it is the application of the techniques to the problem of jury selection that is new. The necessary mathematical techniques were developed before the twentieth century, the attitude-scaling techniques by the late 1920s, development of standardized attitude and personality scales, and studies of the relationships among them and demographic characteristics, were underway by 1950, and when computer technology came into common use by social scientists around 1960, the capability for selecting juries scientifically might have been described more as easy than as feasible. Surprisingly, the collaboration of lawyers and social scientists in the scientific selection of juries did not take place until the case of the Harrisburg Seven. Let us consider how it is done and what its advantages may be by examining that trial.

Philip Berrigan and his co-defendants were indicted by the federal government and charged with raiding a number of draft boards, conspiring to raid draft boards and destroy records, conspiring to kidnap Henry Kissinger, and conspiring to blow up heating tunnels in Washington, D.C. This was another in the government's continuing series of conspiracy trials against antiwar groups. Although the trial site could have been any of a number of large eastern cities, it was convened in Harrisburg, Pennsylvania, an area with a particularly conservative and pro-government population. A group of social scientists joined with the team of defense attorneys, headed by former U.S. Attorney General Ramsey Clark, to select from the highly conservative population a jury that would be more favorable to the defendants. The trial ended in a hung jury, split 10–2 in favor of the defense, and the Government dropped the charges.

Scientific jury selection proceeds as follows. Taking into consideration the issues on which the case is likely to hinge, the social scientists design questionnaires that include:

—Scales previously developed and validated to measure attitudes related to the crucial issues of the case, such as a Trust-in-Government measure;

—New attitude and information items written for the particular case at hand, such as knowledge of the defendants and their case;

—Measures of background characteristics, including: personality measures, such as a scale measuring authoritarianism; demographic characteristics, such as sex, occupation, race, education, socioeconomic status; media contact and preferences; spare-time activities; and organizational memberships.

Interviewers use these questionnaries to collect data from a sample of the population from which the juror pool will be drawn. They do not approach any of the prospective jurors themselves. By correlating the background characteristics with the attitude measures, it is possible to uncover the important variables that predict the population's attitudes. It might be found, for example, that females are more favorable to the defense than males, young people more than older people, egalitarians more than authoritarians, readers of *The New York Times* more than readers of the *New York Daily Times*, Elks more than Masons, and that level of education, introversion, age, political affiliation, and two dozen other things are not at all related to the critical attitudes.

The reason for surveying the local jurisdiction rather than examining national trends is that each community may have its own unusual circumstances which make, say, women more amenable to the defense's case in Harrisburg, but men more defense-prone in Gainesville. It is better to know what is happening in the particular community where the case is being tried than to rely on general trends, which may not hold in that locality. Moreover, key attitudes change not only with geography but with the passage of time or the rise of a new case to activate new issues.

One benefit of obtaining demographic correlates of attitudes related to the trial is that, during voir dire, jurors sometimes lie. They may say they are not biased against protesting priests when they actually are and want to be on the jury to punish the defendant. But background characteristics cannot be falsified. If the juror is a 54-year-old male registered Republican who is the proprietor of a sporting goods store, computer print-outs will tell what he is likely to believe, even if he will not. On the other hand, the data tell only about the probabilities for the population, not how any particular 54-year-old male Republican entrepreneur will vote. Like a baseball manager deciding on which pinch hitter to use, the social scientist cannot know if on a particular occasion player A will outhit player B. But he can know that against pitcher X left-handed hitters have, on the average, done better than right-handed hitters, and play the percentages accordingly. In the long run he will come out ahead.

The critical attitude measures can be reduced to a smaller set of indices by a technique (known as factor analysis) that tries to find the major factors underlying the variables. Those demographic and personality variables which predict the attitudes that are assumed to predict the jurors' verdicts may be formed into a prediction equation or into juror profiles, which allow one to arrange jurors according to their favorability (to the side doing the selecting). The prediction equation is derived from the survey data, always by computer these days, and shows which predictor variables (age, race, socioeconomic status [SES], or whatever) have the power to predict the criterion variable (the attitude index). Such an equation might look like the following:

$$\hat{Y} = (.6771)(\text{SES}) + (.3934)(\text{Sex}) + (.0561)(\text{Age}) + .1027$$

The equation shows which variables have predictive power for this population (in this hypothetical example they are SES, sex, and age), and how much weight (called regression coefficients) they receive (e.g., .6771 for SES). To predict a juror's attitude on the relevant dimension, you would multiply the juror's SES score by .6671, Sex score by .3934, Age by .0561, and add these together along with .1027 (the intercept constant). This gives the final sum, $\hat{Y}$, which is the predicted attitude for that juror. (The reader may recognize this as a minor elaboration of analytic geometry from high school, applied here to social rather than physical dimensions.) We know the distribution of attitudes, $Y$, in the population. The equation enables us to decide whether a given juror should be challenged off the jury by seeing where his or her score falls in that distribution. Using the equation and a pocket calculator (if not a remote computer terminal), we can compile the predicted attitude index for each juror under consideration. Or, alternatively, the data can be used to construct, in advance, profiles of what relatively positive and negative jurors look like.

Another way to use the survey data is by generating profiles through a computer program called the Automatic Interaction Detector. Such a profile might look like Figure 3.2. Although the illustration is simplified, with only three predictor variables, each having only two levels, the number of combinations of characteristics can be seen to grow large already. Generalizations according to a single variable ("middle income jurors are more favorable to the prosecution than low income jurors") are imprecise and often misleading. For example, we can see that while a middle SES female who is old is extremely prosecution-prone, a middle SES female who is young is quite the opposite. Any kinds of jurors (poor, young, male; middle

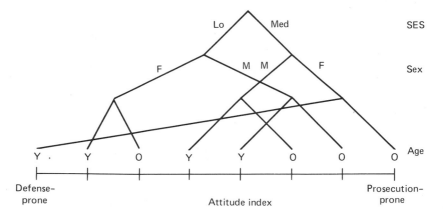

Figure 3.2. Example of data that might result from a demographic analysis of jurors and their attitudes using AID (Automatic Interaction Detector). "Interactions" refer to the fact that the joint impact of two or more variables may be different than the simple impact of one at a time. For example, while medium socioeconomic status is shown here to be generally prosecution-prone, a medium SES young male is considerably more defense-prone than a low SES older male. In this figure the eight combinations of SES × Sex × Age (2 × 2 × 2 = 8) are traced down to their various positions on a scale of prosecution- or defense-prone attitudes. Recognition of interactions improves predictive accuracy.

class, young, female; and so forth) could be traced through the branches of such a profile and their expected position on the attitude index found.  While prediction equations and profiles of favorable jurors will vary from community to community, the same socializing processes are assumed to lead to those differing results.  The survey and resulting equations nevertheless quantify and describe the existing relationships in the population under study.  This underscores the value of an empirical study of the population from which the jury is being drawn, rather than reliance upon superstitions or experience that may have worked somewhere else, but not in the jurisdiction where the case must be tried.

Not only individual characteristics but what is known about group dynamics is taken into account.  Which jurors are likely to take leadership roles in the group?  Which subgroups will form?  Who will be marginal participants?  Is the presence of a person of the defendant's ethnic group needed (regardless of that individual's attitudes) in order to suppress the expression of prejudice by the other jurors? Thus, the group is treated as more than a collection of individuals.

The social scientists in the Harrisburg case warned against placing too much faith in such technology as attitude scales and prediction equations.  In the courtroom, they also observed the prospective jurors and tried to discern which way each one leaned.  They relied on nonverbal behavior, what jurors said and how they said it, and appearance and "vibrations."  The attorneys, of course, did the same thing in their own way, as they would have even without the social scientists.  So did the defendants.  The results of these intuitive judgments were compared to the statistical findings; and when both agreed, the defense team could be confident that a favorable juror had been identified.  When the human and computerized indicators did not concur, the juror in question could be skipped over or investigated further.

While such caution agrees with the common sense of most of us, the caution is probably in the wrong direction. Intuitive, instinctive judgments, when put to the test, have proved notoriously unreliable (e.g., Mischel, 1968, 1971; Livermore, Malmquist, and Meehl, 1968). When the same information is available to both a human decision maker and a mathematical model, almost without exception the mathematical model makes more reliable and accurate predictions.

In sixty studies comparing clinical and statistical prediction, the humans beat the computer only once (Meehl, 1954; Gough, 1962). These findings were as much of a shock (and offense to the human ego) to the people who discovered them as to you who read about them. The original intention was to aid human decision makers by providing a floor of statistical accuracy below which they could not fall. But the floor turned out to be a ceiling (Dawes and Corrigan, 1974). We are indeed fallible creatures. In the Harrisburg trial, the selection of one of the two jurors who held out for conviction had been vetoed by the computer. That advice, however, was overruled by Ramsey Clark, who felt certain the juror was a good choice.

Fortunately, we need not choose between trusting the humans and trusting the technology. Both are available for use. If only jurors who are approved by both methods are selected, then many questionable jurors, who would have been picked by one or the other and turned out to be wrong, would be safely excluded. The wisdom of using both and looking for agreement is obvious.

Another part of the jury-selection art, which is really quite old, is investigation of members of the venire. Information about their backgrounds, habits, likes and dislikes, offers clues to their attitudes toward the case in progress. The new twist added by social scientists is the development of systematic "community networks," where people who "know people who know people who know people" serve as informants, providing information about prospective jurors. So long as the jurors and their families are not approached, such investigations are widely regarded as legal (e.g., Cullinan, 1956; *ABA Standards Relating to the Defense Function*, Standard 7.2; *Dow v. Carnegie*, 1954) and have been practiced, especially by the government, for many, many years. Indeed, historically, jurors were always well known to counsel.

In addition to psychological, paralinguistic, and kinesic observation, other techniques have, in one case or another, crept into the selection process. These include handwriting analysis and even astrological prediction. The value of any of these supplementary methods is questionable. Their validity has not been established through systematic empirical studies. No empirical studies known to us support the hypothesis that handwriting or astrological signs are predictive of juror attitudes or decision behavior. Even attempts to measure attitudes through unobtrusive nonverbal techniques seem to indicate that people can and do conceal their attitudes nonverbally as readily as they do verbally; only when people are asked to let their nonverbal movements reveal their feelings do consistent kinesic patterns emerge (Love, 1972). Most of these supplementary techniques are therefore not usually included in the arsenal of "scientific jury selection" techniques.

Regardless of the status of any of the supplementary techniques, there are some empirically verified techniques being used, notably demographic analysis. These do enable the prediction to some degree of peoples' attitudes toward specific trial-related issues, as well as attitudes toward aspects of the criminal justice system. In addition to studies conducted for the purpose of jury selection in particular trials, many studies show a relation between demographic characteristics and attitudes. Zeisel (1968) found that attitudes toward the death penalty were related to race and that among whites a large difference existed between males and females. For males, age and education were predictive. Overall, religion and age showed small effects. Rokeach and Vidmar (1973) reviewed research relating juror characteristics to attitudes relevant to the prosecution of a Black Panther for murder. Crosson (1967) and Jurow (1971) found that death-qualified jurors were more politically conservative than scrupled jurors. Indeed, it seems unlikely that any survey of a community's opinion on any important issue would not show some differences between demographic groups.

This still leaves a major gap unbridged, however. Being satisfied with predicting jurors' attitudes means that one is assuming that attitudes determine or at least predict actual behavior. The assumption of attitude–behavior consistency is, however, a questionable one (Wicker, 1969). Thus, we have yet to consider the final link: Do the attitudes predicted by the demographic and personality measures in turn predict juror decision making? That is, however well these techniques predict the attitudes of jurors, the next step is crucial—how well do the attitudes predict their behavior as jurors? In short, how well does scientific jury selection work?

We should keep in mind that assessing the practical benefits of scientific jury selection requires a comparison not between a scientifically selected jury and a randomly selected jury, but between a scientifically selected jury and a jury selected in the usual way by attorneys. Attorneys may do far better than chance (Diamond and Zeisel, 1974), so the added benefits of scientific jury selection may be modest.

The evidence for its effectiveness that has most excited or frightened people about scientific jury selection is the fact that virtually no one who has used scientific jury selection has lost a case. This seemingly impressive evidence is really no evidence at all. One cannot know the meaning of such an outcome without comparing it to a control group. For example, suppose each time juries selected scientifically heard a trial, a second jury selected the traditional way also heard the case. We could then compare the verdicts rendered by the scientifically selected juries with those rendered by the traditional juries. In this way, we could isolate the variable of interest—jury composition. If the scientifically selected juries convicted at the same rate as the conventional juries, we could infer that the selection had no impact on the jury's decision making. Only if the juries selected scientifically by the defense convicted less than their yoked counterparts, would we be able to be sure the technique was more effective than what lawyers did anyway. Such studies have not been made, so our knowledge on this question is less than certain. But other lines of evidence exist.

We know, for example, that cases in which scientific jury selection has been used have been almost uniformly "political" trials where most of the counts in the indictments were for conspiracy. In comparable trials, whether the defense used scientific jury selection or not, the jury usually did not convict. (Bermant, 1975). The prosecutors may, in "politically motivated" cases, fail to present a strong case or have none to begin with. Moreover, conspiracy charges are nearly always difficult to win convictions on. So it may be that the low conviction rate associated with scientific jury selection is due to the kind of case and evidence confronting the jury, rather than the composition of the jury.

None of this is to say that scientific jury selection did not have an important effect on verdicts in the cases where it has been used. It says only that we cannot know what the impact was because the necessary comparisons could not be made. The social scientists at Harrisburg understood all of this and, true to their training, they endeavored to measure the effectiveness of their selections. While the actual jury was deliberating, they reinterviewed a subsample of people from their original survey of the community. Fifty-four percent revealed a high presumption of the defendants' guilt. In contrast, only 17% (two of twelve) of the actual jurors voted to convict. But the surveyed citizens differed from the selected jurors in a very important way. The surveyed citizens had not heard the evidence—or the lack of it.

Most of the relevant evidence on the question of how well these techniques predict juror decision making comes from somewhat more basic research. In most of these studies, most variables do not emerge as having predictive power. Those that do emerge often vary from study to study. Simon (1967), studying jurors in Chicago, St. Louis, and Minneapolis, found that out of education, occupation, sex, income, religion, ethnicity, age, and several sets of attitude measures, only education and ethnicity correlated with verdicts. Out of twenty-seven predictors, Saks (1976) found only several attitude and value items and political-party preference to correlate with verdicts among jurors in Ohio. Buckhout (1973), studying jurors in California, found no correlation for age, income, education, and such personality measures as need for social approval, dogmatism, or Machiavellianism; the only significant predictor was jurors' affective rating of the prosecutor. While Crosson (1966) was finding that the Conservatism–Liberalism Scale was able to discriminate between scrupled and nonscrupled jurors, he was also finding that Rokeach's Dogmatism Scale, the Opinionation Scale, the Conservatism–Liberalism Scale, Watson-Glaser's Critical Thinking Scale, and Seigel's Manifest Hostility Scale were not. When variables do significantly predict juror behavior, they sometimes go in one direction (e.g., females acquit more than males) and sometimes in the opposite direction (e.g., males acquit more than females). Even within the same study, differences may emerge for one dependent variable (e.g., recommended sentence) but not for another (e.g., verdict). But usually, most variables do not emerge at all as having predictive power. Sex differences, for example, were found to predict verdicts significantly in some studies (e.g., Efran, 1974; Seely and Cornish, 1973 a,b) but not in others (e.g., Griffitt and Jackson, 1973; Seely and Cornish, 1973; Simon, 1967). As to predicting the sentence a juror recommends (a measure of punitiveness), Griffitt and Jackson did find sex to make a difference, but numerous other studies found no sex effect (e.g., Jones and Aronson, 1973; Landy and Aronson, 1969; Richey and Fichter, 1969).

These inconsistencies—perhaps it is more reasonable to call them variations—are not unexpected. Recall our discussion earlier that in different communities different socializing histories would occur. People of British ancestry are conviction-prone in some communities (Broeder, 1958) and acquittal-prone in others (Simon, 1967), presumably because of social, political, and economic arrangements of their home community. Indeed, to expect to find consistency for all males or females or all members of a particular ethnic group regardless of the particular social context of time and place would be even more peculiar. After all, attitudes are not transmitted genetically. And while the more immediate socializing influences of a person's life may reflect common historical conditioning trends, they will more strongly reflect the exigencies of the particular community or family situation. The social conditioning *process* is what is consistent, not the content of the socialization.

Nevertheless, these inconsistencies create practical problems for jury selection. Generalizations from one setting to another cannot be made easily. New jurisdictions, new defendants, or new trial issues are likely to require new studies if the jury selection is to be successful.

Some consistencies have arisen and are worth mentioning. Seely and Cornish (1973) found that, in general, jurors under thirty were more lenient than older jurors. Another consistent finding is that jurors are more lenient with defendants for whom they feel positive affect (Griffitt and Jackson, 1973; Mitchell and Byrne, 1973; Efran, 1974; Izzett and Leginski, 1974; Landy and Aronson, 1969). Note, however, that this is not a phenomenon related to the characteristics of the jurors such that one can employ a rule of thumb which says "Select jurors of type X." It is a phenomenon of the *relationship* between juror and defendant. The practical implication for an attorney is either to select jurors who are matched with the particular defendant, such as jurors who are similar in attitudes or demographic characteristics, or to make the defendant appear likable. Clarence Darrow had some extreme thoughts on this in 1933:

> Jurymen seldom convict a person they like or acquit one they
> dislike.  The main work of the trial lawyer is to make a jury like
> his client, or at least to feel sympathy for him; facts regarding the
> crime are relatively unimportant.  [Sutherland, 1966, p. 442]

Also, authoritarianism has often been found to correlate with antidefendant attitudes and greater punitiveness by jurors (Vidmar and
Crinkla, 1973; Jurow, 1971; Boehm, 1968; Crossen, 1966).  Authoritarianism is a constellation of politically and economically conservative attitudes (Adorno, Frenkel-Brunswick, Levinson, and Sanford,
1950).  It is usually measured with the California F-scale, on which
high scores represent high authoritarianism.  While high authoritarianism is predictive of high punitiveness, these same studies provide
very little support for the hypothesis that authoritarianism predicts
verdicts.  And it is the verdict that is the critical dependent variable
jury selectors are trying to predict.

Even when the studies are made and the findings are found, the
predictive power is relatively weak.  Recall that the methods increase
the probability of selecting a favorable juror; they do not create a
certainty.  Thus, if it is found that 60% of males are conviction-prone,
while only 55% of females are similarly disposed, that knowledge enables the defense to select jurors from the category in which fewer
conviction-prone jurors exist.  But that only increases the probability
of a favorable selection; it does not ensure it.

One may well select one of the 55% antidefendant females while
passing up one of the 40% prodefendant males.  Of course, more
than one variable is used in combination so that a multiple predictor
allows even better predictive strength.  But still, we are dealing in
probabilities that are by no means powerful.

In a study of 480 adult jurors in Columbus, Ohio, who were shown
the same videotape of a trial, deliberated in juries, and rendered verdicts, out of the twenty-seven predictor variables used, the single best
was whether jurors believed that crime was primarily the product of
"bad people" or "bad social conditions."  Those holding the latter
belief were more likely to regard the defendant as guilty.  (That's
right, guilty.)  This best predictor could account for only 9% of the
variance in jurors' judgments.  (The net quantity of variation in judgments in the sample studied is the "variance."  The greater the pro-

portion of that variance one can account for, the more powerful are the predictors and the more accurate the predictions. The ideal, of course, would be all 100% of it.) Using multiple prediction, the four best predictors (belief that crime is caused by bad people versus social conditions, personal valuation of obedience, personal valuation of leadership, and political party) in combination accounted for less than 13% of the variance in decisions. None of the remaining variables could add as much as 1% to the predictive accuracy (Saks, 1976). Similar weak relationships between the personal characteristics of jurors and the decisions they make are by far the rule, not the exception. And most variables show no relation. (See reviews in Saks, 1976; Davis, Bray, and Holt, 1977). Simon's (1967) conclusion for her own research could well be the summary to the bulk of the research: "The sharp lack of findings reported . . . rival in interest any data we have."

Despite a good deal of excitement about scientific jury selection (e.g. Kairys et al., 1975; Etzioni, 1974; Schulman et al., 1973; Shapley, 1974), and despite the apparently widely held assumption that the kind of person making a decision affects the decision made, the evidence consistently indicates that a jury's composition is a relatively minor determinant of the verdict. In the face of such enthusiastic countervailing belief, this conclusion may seem surprising. However, it should not. Small-group researchers have long recognized that individual difference variables account for little of the variation in group performance (McGrath and Altman, 1966). Juries are merely a special case of small-group decision making and are not exempt from the principles that apply to small groups generally. Nor should small-group researchers be surprised by the lack of impact of personality and attitude variables. The relative unimportance of personality (e.g., Mischel, 1968, 1969, 1971; Krasner and Ullman, 1973; Vernon, 1964) and attitudes (e.g., Wicker, 1969; Bem, 1970) as determinants of behavior has become increasingly evident in the study of human behavior generally. What, then, does determine the verdict a jury will render if it is not the characteristics of the group members? Put more precisely, since individual differences explain little of the variation in juror decisions, what accounts for a larger proportion of the variance? The answer is implied by studies that have measured or manipulated differences in trial evidence along with variations in the decision makers. Let us consider several of those studies.

Simon (1967) studied jurors in Chicago, St. Louis, and Minneapolis. Only education and ethnicity were able to predict jurors' votes (in two simulated cases where defendants were pleading "not guilty by reason of insanity" [NGI]. In one case, a housebreaking case, 66% of randomly selected jurors would have voted NGI, but persons with less than college education voted NGI at a rate of 72%—a difference of 6 percentage points. Blacks voted NGI at a rate of 85%—a difference of 19 percentage points compared to the general juror population. (Note that these reductions in uncertainty about juror tendencies cannot simply be added together, so that both pieces of knowledge improve your accuracy by 25%, because there will be much overlap. Many blacks will also have less than college education, so that the first cut will already filter out many jurors who are undesirable on the remaining criteria.) In Simon's other case, an incest case, a random selection of jurors would consist of people of whom 33% voted NGI. One's knowledge of education effects would improve selection of NGI jurors by 2 percentage points, and ethnicity would again improve it by 19 points. That is not insubstantial improvement. But the most powerful difference of all was the effect of the type of case: the housebreaking case produced 66% NGI voters compared to only 33% for the incest case—a difference of 33 percentage points. None of the demographic or attitudinal predictors approached that amount.

In another study (Saks, Werner, and Ostrom, 1975), a sample of former jurors from Columbus, Ohio, were asked to indicate their certainty of a defendant's guilt or innocence in a series of brief hypothetical cases, each consisting of a set of evidentiary statements. They were given cases in which the crime alleged differed, where the amount of evidence against the defendant differed, and in which the strength of the evidence varied; it was either moderately (prescaled to reflect a .44 probability of guilt) or highly (.77) incriminating. Jurors were also tested with a scale of defendant-related attitudes in order to classify them as favorable or unfavorable to the defense. The attitude scale did predict how the jurors would respond. Jurors designated "antidefendant" gave an average rating of guilt of 58 while "prodefendant" jurors gave ratings that averaged −20. (A score of zero would indicate a juror thought it was equally likely that the defendant was guilty as not guilty; positive scores are in the guilty direction; negative scores in the not guilty direction.)    That is a spread of 78 points. But the point spread between average certainty of guilt in response to one item of evidence compared to six items of evidence was 143 points. And presenting moderately incriminating evidence compared to highly incriminating evidence produced a spread of 172 points. In terms of the proportion of variance accounted for by each of the independent variables, the amount of evidence was more than three times as powerful, and the strength of evidence was more than seven times as powerful as attitudes were in determining the jurors' verdicts. Juror characteristics made a difference, but not nearly so much of a difference as characteristics of the trial evidence.

A study frequently cited by social scientists interested in jury selection is one by Boehm (1968), which reported a test of an instrument called the LAQ (Legal Attitudes Questionnaire) to predict how jurors would vote. The LAQ is essentially a courtroom measure of authoritarianism. Boehm used two forms of trial evidence, one which favored the defense and one which favored the prosecution. She examined the verdicts of jurors who "erred," that is, who voted guilty when the evidence favored the defense or voted leniently when the evidence favored the prosecution, and found that four-fifths of those designated by the LAQ as antiauthoritarian erred leniently, while only one-third of the authoritarians did so. However, only 38% of all the jurors erred. And only 28% erred in the direction predicted for them by the LAQ. (Some antiauthoritarians voted guilty in the face of pro-defense evidence and some authoritarians voted leniently on pro-prosecution evidence.) Most important is that fully 62% of the jurors voted exactly in line with the evidence.

The studies are unanimous in showing that evidence is a substantially more potent determinant of jurors' verdicts than the individual characteristics of jurors. Indeed, the power of evidence is so well recognized by jury researchers that when studying processes other than evidence, they must calibrate the evidence to be moderate so that it leaves some variance to be influenced by the variables under study. Manipulating the evidence powerfully influences the verdict the group renders. This finding also is consistent with findings from elsewhere in psychological research. However important personality and attitudes may be in determining overt behavior, they generally are not as important as stimulus features of the situation (e.g., Bandura, 1969; Staats, 1975; Mischel, 1968, 1969, 1971; Wicker, 1969).

What this implies about human behavior, on juries or off, is that while we are unique individuals, our differences are vastly overshadowed by our similarities. Moreover, the range of situations we are likely to encounter is far more varied than the range of human beings who will encounter them.

Additional research indicates that while situational variables are more determinative of behavior than individual difference variables, the statistical interaction between the two is the most powerful influence of all (Alker, 1972). This says that predictions of behavior are less accurate when individuals' characteristics alone are considered or when situational characteristics alone are considered, and more accurate when a properly understood *combination* of the two (the "interaction") is considered. The best predictor, then, would be a careful matching of jurors to the stimuli with which they will be presented. What little data we have on this point indicates that this does not hold for the kind of decision making jurors do. The variance due to the interaction between the person and the evidence is the smallest source of variance (Saks, 1976), individual differences are more important, and features of the evidence are most important.

An important possible limitation to these conclusions is that the relative contribution of evidence versus juror characteristics to the variance in verdicts depends partly upon the relative range of the two variables. If juror characteristics varied considerably, but evidence did not, that would make the proportion of variance due to juror characteristics increase. If evidence varied markedly but juror differences did not, then the proportion of variance due to evidence would increase. Ideally, we would like the same range of variation in our studies that exists in the real world of jury trials. In the studies cited, some used college student "jurors," a group more homogeneous than actual jurors. Those studies done on real jurors deciding real trials did not measure differences in evidence, so relative effects of the two could not be computed. It may be, then, that the consistent finding in these studies that evidence is more influential than juror characteristics is an accident of the range of evidence and jurors used. While this is a logical possibility, it seems unlikely. The one study that did measure the incriminatory strength of the evidence (Saks, Werner, and Ostrom, 1976) did not select extremely divergent levels of evidence—instead it used moderate (.44) and fairly high (.77) levels.

Similarly, Boehm (1968) did not use two forms of evidence that were extremely divergent. And the jurors in many of the studies did represent the available range of jurors in the venire, since they were not selected out to represent a narrow range. Thus, if the researchers wanted to alter the proportions of variance accounted for in their studies by these variables, they would have a difficult time doing so by altering the range of jurors (since the available range was already present), but they could quite easily alter the cases, making the weak ones weaker and the strong ones stronger.

The importance of juror characteristics would be at a maximum if the evidence were not strong in either direction. In actual trials, how often is the evidence ambiguous? An estimate is provided by Lempert (1975), who, inferring from Kalven and Zeisel's (1966) national jury data, concludes that at least 70% of cases are clear and unambiguous.

It follows, then, that if the cited studies fail to reflect the true state of affairs in jury trials, they do so by *underestimating* the impact of evidence relative to juror characteristics.

From the viewpoint of the jury system, these findings mean that jurors are much more responsive to the evidence placed before them than to their own personalities and attitudes. Our educated speculation is that this may well be due to the special social situation created by the court. Through learning outside of court and by the court's atmosphere, the judge's charges, and the rules of the game, jurors adopt a role of "fairness" and "objectivity" which may be as extreme as they ever have had or will have in their lives. That jurors are selected who do not have ongoing relationships with the parties or interests at stake in the case further enhances the success of the "objective factfinders'" role. Common-sense assumptions that the personal politics and prejudice which characterize much of human life invade the jury box ignore the special situational characteristics of the court and the human relationships constructed there.

This means that to a great degree, in most cases, the jury system is functioning as intended. It means that suggestions that courts narrow the range of jurors through psychological screening would have rather little impact on the quality of adjudication, though it would arouse serious controversy and, we think, diminish the quality of justice received by persons serving as jurors. And it means that suggestions to increase the range of jurors through eliminating many exemptions that now cause juries to be unrepresentative of the population would expand the control exerted through jury selection by attorneys and social scientists (cf., Etzioni, 1974; Saks, 1976, note 56).

From the viewpoint of attorneys and social scientists, working to serve a particular side of a particular case, these findings mean that while jury selection will have some impact on the outcome of the case, it is not as effective as directing their efforts at building and structuring the evidence to be presented to the jury. Interestingly, social psychologists have studied the process of persuasion and attribution of responsibility far more intensively than they have the role of individual differences in decision making. It is only in cases where the evidence is ambiguous that scientific jury selection would have its greatest utility.

## SUMMARY

The jury, like most other human groups, functions according to its composition, its structure, the nature of the group process, and the task confronting the group. The composition of the jury has long been of concern to the law. Work by social scientists has been useful in considering the constitutionality of jury pools, and assisting lawyers in selecting juries at trials. Folklore about, and modern techniques of scientific jury selection have important similarities and contrasts. Research findings suggest that jury composition has little influence on the outcome of a trial relative to other variables under the lawyer's control.

# 4
# Jury Behavior: Structure, Process, Outcome

In the previous chapter we examined the question of jury composition. The present chapter turns to several features of the jury's structure, the group decision-making process, and the outcome of the deliberation: the jury's verdict.

## STRUCTURE

By structure we mean the physical and social organization of the jury. Physical organization is perhaps the most readily apprehended. It refers to the number of jurors and their spatial arrangements—distance, geometric pattern, orientation. Social structure refers to such matters as role relationships (leaders, followers), faction memberships and subgroup formation, communication networks (who is accessible to whom, by what pattern), and ways in which the decision preferences of individuals are to be combined into a group decision, what we call a social decision rule (majority, unanimity, and so forth). Each of these structural variables is present when a group is engaged in decision making, and each may affect the process and product of the group deliberation. Our discussion of jury structure will address three issues: the geometry of the jury, the size of the jury, and the decision rule (unanimity versus quorum). The latter two have been both researched and litigated in recent years.

No doubt little thought is given to the shape of a jury table. Certainly, it must fit into the room where it will be used and into the judiciary's budget. But it is unlikely that the designers of courthouses and jury tables ask themselves questions about the impact of table geometry on the task that will have to be performed at the table.   Environmental psychologists and behavioral designers have found that questions of human functioning are the last to be asked by conventional architects and planners (see, e.g., Proshansky, Ittelson, and Rivlin, 1970, Part Five).

Research in "group geography" (Bass and Klubeck, 1952; Steinzor, 1950; Sommer, 1961) laid the groundwork for Strodtbeck and Hook's (1961) work on "The social dimensions of a twelve-man jury table." Figure 4.1 shows the arrangement of a jury table and the positions jurors may take around it.   Strodtbeck and Hook learned something about the impact of the table on the jury's behavior. The location of a juror affects the likelihood of the juror's being selected foreman. If the jury's choices of foreman were evenly distributed, each position should have held a foreman an average of 5.75 times in their study of sixty-nine juries.   The end position, however, was selected nearly three times more than it would have under an even distribution, as

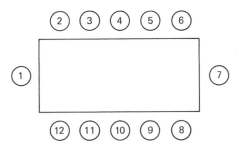

Figure 4.1. Jury geometry: positions, foreperson choices, communicative acts, and sociometric votes.  If people sitting around a jury table behaved and were treated equally, each would have the same likelihood of being selected foreperson, receive the same number of sociometric (group preference) votes, and make the same number of communicative acts. We can see in the data, however, that seat position about the table is systematically related to these variables.  End seats average much more than their expected share; other positions average at or less than that expected under an equality hypothesis. (Adapted from Strodtbeck and Hook, 1961.)

|  | Seat | Foreperson choices | Communicative acts | Sociometric votes |
|---|---|---|---|---|
| End | 1, 7 | 16.0 | 10.0 | 300 |
| Corner | 2, 6, 8, 12 | 5.5 | 7.5 | 241 |
| Flank | 3, 5, 9, 11 | 2.5 | 7.8 | 248 |
| Middle | 4, 10 | 2.5 | 8.4 | 274 |
| Expected value: |  | 5.75 | 8.3 |  |

we can see in the data in Figure 4.1. The amount of communication initiated from each of the positions is also different from that expected by an even distribution of communication, with the end and middle positions communicating more than their "share." And the gradient for communication is paralleled by the gradient for sociometric choices received by each position. The correlation within juries between communication and sociometric choice is +.69.

Strodtbeck and Hook carried the analysis a good deal further. Sheer physical distance between jurors accounted for only about 34% of the variance in sociometric choices. As an alternative, *social* distance, measured as an inverse function of the square root of each position's sociometric preferences received, was mathematically accounted for by three dimensions. The dimensions were the length and width of the table and the visual accessibility of the positions about the table. What this showed was that the tendency to be valued by other jurors and, presumably, the tendency to participate in the discussion, was a function of the person's location. End positions were the most centrally located in terms of social distance, middle positions next, and then the remaining positions at greater social distances. This finding makes sense in light of other research, which has found that in a group discussion, when one person stops talking, the person most likely to pick up the conversation is the person directly facing the previous speaker, with likelihoods decreasing in both directions away from the person opposite. The least likely next speakers are the two people sitting on either side of the previous speaker. It has been suggested that the reason for this is that the rules governing norms of conversation involve nonverbal signals by one person that he is finished and the verbal ball is passed to another person, who signals that he is picking it up next. This requires visual accessibility, and about a rectangular table the jurors most accessible are those at either end. The next most visible position belongs to those at the middle. The more visible a person is, the better that person will get to be known by the other jurors, both through repeated observation and by increased participation. The more active a participant one is in a group, the more influential he will be (Bavelas, Hastorf, Gross, and Kite, 1965). The only serious aberration in the findings is that the second most likely position to be selected foreman is the corner. That is explained by the fact that the ends are apparently widely held to be the "proper" location for a leader, and if not that position, then the position closest to it. Indeed, "corner" jurors about to become or having been selected foreman often move around the table to partially occupy the end position.

To these findings we must add the fact that persons of the proprietor and manager occupational classes take the end position about 15% more frequently than would be expected by chance. The social relations that have been reinforced in the outside world enter the jury room with the jurors. Proprietors and managers are more accustomed to taking the "in charge" position, are more comfortable with it, and the other jurors shy away from it. Added to the tendency of such persons already to be more verbal is the geometric advantage associated with the table position they have adopted. The shape of the table compounds the advantage some jurors arrived with.

*Recommendation.* The implication for designers of courthouses is simple. If the leveling out of participation in deliberation among jurors is a desirable goal, the introduction of round tables will contribute to that goal. It will not make the more verbal jurors talk as much as the less verbal; it will not make all jurors participate equally. One of the most ubiquitous findings of small group research is that group members participate unevenly, with a very few persons accounting for most of the discussion (Stephan and Mishler, 1952). But a round table would not exacerbate this tendency the way a rectangular table obviously does.

Another structural variable that affects the amount of communication is the size of the group. As groups grow larger, the disparity in participation increases. Those who talk a lot account for an even greater proportion of the discussion, and those who talk little account for a rapidly shrinking proportion. Another highly reliable finding in group research is that smaller groups produce greater member satisfaction than larger groups, and one of the reasons is the greater participation facilitated by the smaller group (Thomas and Fink, 1963). This and a number of other issues arose in 1970 when the U.S. Supreme Court was called upon to decide on the constitutionality of juries smaller than twelve (*Williams v. Florida*, 1970). Defendant Williams had been convicted by a jury of six after asking for trial by a jury of twelve. He was appealing the conviction to the Supreme Court on the ground that he had been unconstitutionally de-

prived of his right to a jury numbering twelve. After examining the
law and the history on this matter, the Court concluded that no clear
guidance came from those quarters, and they would have to turn to a
"functional analysis" of the jury's purpose. That is, if reduction in
the size of the jury adversely affected its functioning, then such a reduction would be unconstitutional. Mixed through the Court's ruling, five questions are discussed:

1. Are there differences in the amount or quality of group
   deliberation?
2. Are there differences in the accuracy or reliability of the jury?
3. Are there differences in the conviction–acquittal ratios or the
   proportion of hung juries?
4. Are there differences in the minority's ability to resist majority
   pressure to conform?
5. Are there differences in the likelihood of obtaining on the jury
   a representative cross section of the community?

Here is the Court's answer to these questions:

> The performance of [its role] is not a function of the particular
> number of the body that makes up the jury. To be sure, the
> number should probably be large enough to promote group de-
> liberation, free from outside attempts at intimidation, and to
> provide a fair possibility for obtaining a representative cross-
> section of the community. But we find little reason to think that
> these goals are in any meaningful sense less likely to be achieved
> when the jury numbers six, than when it numbers twelve—
> particularly if the requirement of unanimity is retained. And,
> certainly the reliability of the jury as a factfinder hardly seems
> likely to be a function of its size. [pp. 100–101]

Considering that these are empirical questions the court posed for itself, we may ask where the answers came from. One source would
appear to be "experiments."

> What few experiments have occurred—usually in the civil area—
> indicate that there is no discernible difference between the re-
> sults reached by the two different-sized juries. [p. 102]

An examination of the six "experiments" the court cites, however, indicates that they are "scant evidence by any standards" (Zeisel, 1971). Some were bald assertions based upon no observation at all; others were based on uncontrolled, haphazard observation by court clerks and attorneys interviewed about the matter after the fact; and one was simply irrelevant, discussing the economic advantages that might be expected from reduction in jury size, rather than the functioning of the jury. These "experiments" simply were not experiments.

On the question of size and cross-sectional community representation, the Court made no attempt to appeal to empirical data:

> (W)hile in theory the number of viewpoints represented on a randomly selected jury ought to increase as the size of the jury increases, in practice the difference between the 12-man and the six-man jury in terms of the cross-section of the community represented seems likely to be negligible. [*Williams*, p. 102]

These intuitive mathematics are a poor substitute for evidence or for explicit mathematics, as we will see shortly.

The best attempt to apply empirical evidence to the answering of the five empirical questions was in addressing the matter of differences in the minority's ability to resist majority pressure to conform. The Court concluded:

> Studies of the operative factors contributing to small group deliberation and decisionmaking suggest that jurors in the minority on the first ballot are likely to be influenced by the proportional size of the majority aligned against them. See H. Kalven and H. Zeisel, The American Jury 462–463, 488–489 (1966); C. Hawkins, Interaction and Coalition Realignments in Consensus-Seeking Groups: A Study of Experimental Jury Deliberations 13, 146, 156, Aug. 17, 1960 (unpublished thesis on file at Library of Congress); cf. Asch, Effects of Group Pressure Upon the Modification and Distortion of Judgments, In Readings in Social Psychology 2 (G. Swanson, T. Newcomb & E. Hartley et al., eds., 1952). See generally, Note, On Instructing Deadlocked Juries, 78, Yale L. J. 100, 108, and n. 30 (and authorities cited), 110–111 (1968). Thus, if a defendant needs initially to persuade four jurors that the State has not met its burden of proof in order to escape ulti-

mate conviction by a 12-man jury, he arguably escapes by initially persuading half that number in a six-man jury; random reduction, within limits, of the absolute number of the jury would
not affect the outcome. [*Williams*, n. 49, p. 101]

The principle of social influence being set forth by the Court is
that it is the proportional size of the majority that determines its social and psychological power over the minority. Thus, a jury split
5–1 (83%–17%) will exert pressure on its minority equivalent to that
of a jury split 10–2 (83%–17%). The statement is clear, obviously
relevant, and the Court cites a number of prominent psychological
and sociological studies to support its finding. The problem is that
each of the studies cited arrived at the opposite conclusion. Those
researchers can speak for themselves:

> Nevertheless for one or two jurors to hold out to the end, it
> would appear necessary that they had companionship at the be-
> ginning of the deliberations. The juror psychology recalls a fa-
> mous series of experiments by the psychologist Asch and others
> which showed that in an ambiguous situation a member of a
> group will doubt and finally disbelieve his own correct observa-
> tion if all other members of the group claim that he must have
> been mistaken. To maintain his original position, not only be-
> fore others but before himself, it is necessary for him to have at
> least one ally. [Kalven and Zeisel, 1966, p. 463]

> The results clearly demonstrate that a disturbance of the una-
> nimity of the majority markedly increased the independence of
> the critical subjects . . . . Indeed, we have been able to show that
> a unanimous majority of 3 is, under the given conditions, far
> more effective than a majority of 8 containing 1 dissenter. [Asch,
> 1952, p. 398–399]

> Consistent disapproval by the majority can shake a small mi-
> nority's faith even in judgments it believes to be right. Such pres-
> sures are most effective against a single dissenter and fall off rap-
> idly in efficacy as the size of the dissenting coalition increases. A
> single ally gives most dissenters the courage to voice their true
> convictions. [*Yale L. J.*, 1968, p. 111]

In contrast to the Supreme Court's reading of those studies, the clear finding is that the absolute, not the proportional, size of the factions is critical. The presence or absence of an ally is a most powerful determinant of a person's ability to resist majority pressure. Each additional ally adds decreasing increments of social support, such that eventually the relationship of size to resistance becomes asymptotic, the addition of further allies adding no more to the minority's ability to resist. In any event, the difference between one ally (10–2) for a person in the minority and no allies (5–1) is an enormous difference even though the proportional sizes are the same.

Many social and behavioral scientists and legal scholars who read the *Williams* opinion realized that the Court's holding rested on a weak foundation—"experiments" that were nothing of the sort, mathematical intuition that did not square with explicit mathematics, and real empirical studies that said quite the opposite of what the Court said they said. The opinion in *Williams v. Florida* came in for a good deal of criticism (Zeisel, 1971; Walbert, 1971; Saks, 1974, 1977), if not for the ultimate validity of its conclusions, then for the embarrassing collection of "evidence" on which the decision was based. The attorneys who submitted briefs on the case have generally escaped criticism, but they did so because they made no attempt at all to argue empirical questions from empirical evidence. One might want to say that their lapse was even greater; at least the Court tried to answer empirical questions with empirical answers.

Some social and behavioral scientists also realized that barely any research existed which specifically asked about the effects of group size on decision making in the context of juries. Four of these studies were conducted following *Williams v. Florida*; each found no effect of size, and were cited by the Supreme Court in a subsequent decision, *Colgrove v. Battin* (1973), as "convincing empirical evidence of the correctness of the *Williams* conclusion." The Court advanced to the use of real empirical studies and read their conclusions accurately. But the Court failed to read the studies critically. Empirical studies should neither be dismissed out of hand as meaningless nor accepted uncritically as necessarily true because they are empirical. All empirical studies are not created equal. Serious attention has to be paid to the methodology of a study, for its findings can be no better than the methods used to find them. The studies cited in *Colgrove* provide a good lesson on this point. (Saks, 1974, 1977; Zeisel and Diamond, 1974).

Two of the studies were conducted in jurisdictions where attorneys had a choice between six- and twelve-member juries (Bermant and Coppock, 1973; Institute of Judicial Administration, 1972). On comparing the verdicts rendered by the different-sized juries, the studies found no differences. But such an uncontrolled comparison misses the possibility that in choosing a jury size, attorneys were not selecting randomly, but were systematically choosing larger juries for some kinds of cases and smaller juries for others, thereby confounding the effects of jury size with the effects of the class of case. Careful reviews of the studies suggest that this may well have happened. Attorneys apparently chose larger juries for cases which were more complex or had larger amounts of money at stake. Thus, complex, costly cases tried to large juries were being compared to simpler, less costly cases tried to smaller juries, and the possible effects of jury size were masked by the case-type confound.

A third study compared juries' verdicts before and after a statutory change reducing the size of juries from twelve to six (Mills, 1973). Now, attorneys could not introduce selection confounds into the comparison between large and small juries. But history confounds— other changes occurring simultaneously with the reduction in jury size—may have been operating. For example, increases in the amount of damages awarded by the smaller juries may have been due not to the fact that smaller juries award higher amounts, but due to inflation. The researchers adjusted their data for the possible effects of inflation. They did not adjust for changes the legislature made at the same time it reduced the size of juries, such as the establishment of a mediation board to try to settle the cases. These confounding events may have had the effect of draining off one kind of case so that those tried to the six-person juries were systematically different from the mix of cases tried previously to twelve-person juries. Again, the same problem arises as in the previous studies.

One way to avoid these confounds is the conduct of a controlled simulation. The one that was cited by the Supreme Court (Kessler, 1973) found no differences between different-sized juries. Unfortunately, the study was not capable of finding any differences. For example, it used a videotaped trial so extreme that not one jury, regardless of size, reached a verdict favoring the plaintiff, and an unusually small sample size, which means it had very low statistical power to detect a difference even if one existed.

Thus, while these studies conclude that jury size has no effect, their methodology leaves their conclusions in great doubt. Can research on small groups, and sound statistical principles offer any answers?

Concerning quantity and quality of deliberation as a function of group size, smaller groups allow for greater participation per member and less disparity between the least and most talkative members. Because they spend more time deliberating, larger groups do more communicating collectively (Davis, 1969; Saks, 1977). Larger groups bring more and a wider range of human resources to the task. But increases in size produce increases in performance only up to the point where the process losses associated with group activity take away more from the deliberation than the added value of more members (Steiner, 1972). The phenomenon whereby smaller groups tend to inhibit the expression of disagreement among members (Bales and Borgatta, 1955; Slater, 1958) was found also in simulated juries: jurors' sociometric ratings of each others' "contributions" and "reasonableness" were higher in smaller juries (Saks, 1977). While the increased pleasantness and minimized disagreeableness may be desirable in many group contexts, juries may be one of the places where disagreement and contentiousness are precisely what we want stimulated. The hotter the deliberative fire, the more severely the evidence is tested.

Concerning the questions of accuracy and reliability and conviction–acquittal–hung ratios, we first need to operationalize the concepts of accuracy and reliability. They are so easy to say, but how do we measure them? Who knows the *correct* decision in a jury trial? If this were known, there would be no need for a trial. What we can do, however, is to define an accurate verdict as one that is consistent with what the population of jurors would have decided if the trial were held before the entire community, and the best estimate of what the community would have done comes from inferring from what the total sample in a study did. Reliability may be defined as it is in psychometrics: reproducibility of outcomes. A jury type that reaches the same verdict consistently (whether that verdict is accurate or not) is more reliable than one that reaches the verdict less consistently. Generally, larger groups will be more reliable and accurate than smaller groups. Twelve jurors are more accurate than six jurors for the same reason that twelve thermometers are more accurate than six thermometers: they cancel out random errors (Johnson, 1955). This holds for reliability as well; larger juries will produce more predictable verdicts than small juries in the same way that larger samples produce less variability in whatever it is they are measuring. This has the interesting implication for civil cases that while the average damage award rendered by a small jury will equal that of a large jury, the fluctuations about that mean will be greater for the smaller juries (Zeisel, 1971). In statistical vernacular, the means will be the same but the standard deviation will be larger for the smaller samples (juries). The reasons for expecting more accuracy and reliability among large juries are social as well as statistical. More resources, more contentiousness, more social support for the minority in larger juries should all add up to the necessity of stronger evidence to convince the whole group that the threshold of reasonable doubt has been exceeded. The data provided by verdicts in the study by Saks (1977) are consistent with these expectations, while failing to be statistically significant.

The question of minority resistance to majority pressure was discussed earlier, so we know that one would expect larger groups to provide more allies for the minorities and the allies will afford greater social support with which to resist the majority.

The cross-section issue was introduced earlier. Recall that the Court felt that although a community was likely to be less well represented on a jury of six than on a jury of twelve, "in practice the difference . . . seems likely to be negligible." Sampling theory enables us to restate the court's intuitive mathematics with some precision, and to replace their adjectives with numbers. Essentially we are confronting a sampling problem. Suppose we have a community that is stratified so that there are 90% of one kind of citizen and 10% of some other kind, say whites and blacks. And suppose we want to sample from that community population. If we draw samples of size twelve, the binomial expansion tells us that 72% of those samples will contain one or more members of the 10% minority. If, instead, we drew samples of size six, only 47% of the samples will contain one or more members of the minority group. This difference, 25 percentage points, in the ability of the different-sized juries to represent the community is what the Court termed a negligible difference. While the figures we have computed here come only from sampling theory, empirical data on the question have come quite close to the prediction (Saks, 1977).

In *Apodaca et al. v. Oregon* (1972) and *Johnson v. Louisiana* (1972), the Supreme Court encountered a similar set of questions about another aspect of jury structure, which were empirical in nature and for which law and constitutional history afforded no guide. Again the Court turned to a functional analysis of jury behavior—this time to decide whether a group decision rule (unanimous as compared to nonunanimous agreement required for a verdict) would have any effect upon jury behavior. And again, in 5–4 decisions, the Court decided that such structural changes would not influence jury behavior. Hardly any empirical research existed on this question. The issue invites mathematical modeling of the possible effects, and such models are fairly plentiful, starting with the work of nineteenth century mathematicians who studied the French judicial system and added to by contemporary work (e.g., Smoke and Zajonc, 1962; Walbert, 1971; Gelfand and Solomon, 1973, 1974; Davis, 1973; Saks and Ostrom, 1975). The Court, however, was unaware of the work that preceded its decision, as were the attorneys filing briefs in the case; again the null decision was made, again on intuitive grounds. The mathematical models deal with the effect of such group structure variables on verdicts. The Court's speculations included verdicts as well as some group process questions that sound like the kinds of questions small group researchers ask. The Court wondered whether, under a nonunanimous decision rule, juries would give due consideration to the views of the minority, particularly if minority views within a jury were held by a member of an ethnic minority, or would a relaxed decision rule lead to premature termination? Would groups under unanimity rules reach agreement only through compromises? And if quorum rules as small as 9-of-12 would not generate group processes or products different from unanimous rules, how much smaller could that quorum be allowed to shrink before some degradation of the group function occurred? On virtually all of these points, the Court concluded that jury behavior would not be altered by al-terations in the decision rule. The Court did expect, however, fewer hung juries to result. This was interpreted as an insubstantial (based on Kalven and Zeisel's [1966] data) change, and one that would af-fect convictions and acquittals equally.

Existing data and mathematical models would have provided some basis for formulating expectations regarding the effects of decision rules (Saks and Ostrom, 1975; Saks, 1977; Friedman, 1972; Davis et al., 1975). Some of these effects, based on some fundamental principles of probability, are shown in Table 4.1. Quorum juries are more likely to produce verdicts as opposed to hanging; this is accom-plished by reaching decisions on the basis of weaker evidence; and this means that more errors of both types will occur: convictions when the correct decision is acquittal; acquittals when the correct de-

**Table 4.1   Verdicts as a function of social decision rule and probability of an individual vote for conviction.**

| | Probability of an individual vote for conviction | | | | | | | | | | |
|---|---|---|---|---|---|---|---|---|---|---|---|
| | 0.0 | .1 | .2 | .3 | .4 | .5 | .6 | .7 | .8 | .9 | 1.0 |
| Probability of conviction | | | | | | | | | | | |
| Unanimous-12 | .00 | .00 | .00 | .00 | .00 | .00 | .00 | .01 | .07 | .28 | 1.00 |
| Quorum-12 | .00 | .00 | .00 | .01 | .06 | .19 | .44 | .72 | .93 | 1.00 | 1.00 |
| Probability of acquittal | | | | | | | | | | | |
| Unanimous-12 | 1.00 | .28 | .07 | .01 | .00 | .00 | .00 | .00 | .00 | .00 | .00 |
| Quorum-12 | 1.00 | 1.00 | .93 | .72 | .44 | .19 | .06 | .01 | .00 | .00 | .00 |
| Convictions as a proportion of verdicts | | | | | | | | | | | |
| Unanimous-12 | .00 | .00 | .00 | .00 | .00 | .00 | 1.00 | 1.00 | 1.00 | 1.00 | 1.00 |
| Quorum-12 | .00 | .00 | .00 | .01 | .12 | .50 | .88 | .99 | 1.00 | 1.00 | 1.00 |

The probability of a conviction by a whole jury increases with the probability that any given juror will vote to convict. However, with quorum juries that probability begins to increase at relatively low likelihoods of guilty votes by individual jurors, while unanimous juries require higher individual certainties before the likelihood of a group conviction starts to climb. Similarly, the probability of acquittal when individual jurors are not so sure the defendant is innocent are greater for quorum than for unanimous juries. The third pair of lines in the table show that while unanimous juries are less likely to deliver verdicts, those they do deliver are less likely to be a distorted reflection of the group: unanimous juries are more likely to convict only when the jurors lean toward conviction, and then to do so more surely, than is the quorum jury.

cision is conviction.  Increased efficiency is purchased at some cost in accuracy.  In practice, then, a relaxation in the decision rule should be expected to produce a *reduction* in the rate of convictions, since most trials currently result in convictions.  The decrease, however, is a result of increased error.

Kalven and Zeisel (1966) found that in jurisdictions requiring unanimous verdicts, 5.6% of juries hung compared to only 3.1% in jurisdictions that had quorum rules.  These were the findings the Court regarded as a difference that did not make much of a difference.  But other data of Kalven and Zeisel (1967) speak to the question of how juries respond to minority views that are not needed to reach consensus.  Jurisdictions requiring unanimous verdicts had only 5.6% of their juries fail to reach unanimity.  In jurisdictions where unanimity was not required, 25% of juries did not reach it.  One interpretation of these data is that once the requisite majority is reached, jurors do not bother to deliberate further with those whose agreement is not needed.  An alternative interpretation, of course, is that equally much deliberation occurs, but early "holdouts" can symbolically save some face by continuing to vote in the minority.  Data on deliberation times, for example, would allow a choice between these competing explanations.  Schachter's (1951) earlier research on how groups treat deviants indicates that those expressing minority views are at first given an increasingly inordinate amount of attention; but as communication continues without bringing about change in the deviants' views, communication to them drops off sharply, and they are perceived as no longer within the psychological boundaries of the group.

Quorum juries were found to generate more discussion per unit time, while unanimous juries took longer to reach the requisite consensus and deliberated longer.  Jurors in quorum-rule groups deliberated more inequitably (active talkers talked more, low participators talked less) than in unanimous-rule juries.  In a  close analysis of what happens after the requisite consensus is reached, it was found that when quorum juries reached minimum consensus, they did not spend more time talking with the minority, or at least no more time than unanimous juries did.  And in the unanimous juries there was no minority to talk to.  In that period in quorum juries, only 18% revoted and of those revotes, not one produced a vote change in the direction of the minority.  Considering how relieved juries often appear to be when consensus is finally reached, and how much pressure members of the quorum must feel to keep the consensus intact, it may be that the achievement of the minimum requisite consensus is as psychologically binding for quorum-rule juries as the unanimous consensus is for unanimous-rule juries.  In some cases, jurors even asked why time was being spent debating with the minority jurors when their votes were superfluous (Saks, 1977).

The question of a lower limit on jury size has recently reached the Supreme Court and has been decided (*Ballew v. Georgia*, 1978).  The decision is noteworthy in several respects.  The Court took serious note of the social science research, including critiques of its earlier decisions (much of which has been cited in this chapter), and has put the brakes on declining jury sizes, setting the constitutional minimum at six.  In addition, the Court's Opinion in this case represents the most extensive use of social science research by the Supreme Court to date.  No doubt future line-drawing awaits the Court when decision rules ranging down through simple majority are enacted by legislatures and tested in appeals courts.

Without some method for comparing the variety of jury structures likely to arise, the Courts may find themselves as perplexed as the Supreme Court was in *Johnson v. Louisiana.*  Johnson had been convicted by a 9–3 verdict in a three-tiered jury system that used 5-of-5 juries for more serious crimes, and twelve-member unanimous juries for capital crimes.  Johnson argued that the gradient of the tiers was not rational, that a more stringent standard (5-of-5) was used for serious potential deprivations of liberty, and that he should have been afforded at least as much protection as defendants in less serious cases were receiving.  The Court, faced with this question of whether a 9-of-12 structure was more or less likely to convict than a 5-of-5 jury, responded thusly:

> If appelant's position is that it is easier to convince nine of 12 jurors than to convince all of five, he is simply challenging the judgment of the Louisiana Legislature. [p. 4527]

The attorneys had not provided, and the Court apparently was not aware of, any probability models for such comparisons, and the matter was left to the vague realm of "legislative judgment."  An elementary probability model makes some distinct predictions. At all levels of individual jurors' guilt judgments (from completely certain of innocence to completely certain of guilt), the 9-or-more-of-12 structure is more likely to result in a verdict than the 5-of-5 structure (Saks and Ostrom, 1975). If the model is correct, Louisiana's inversion of the more (5-of-5) and less (9-of-12) stringent jury structures has the following implication. If the twelve jurors may be thought of as having fixed individual decisions regardless of what size or shape jury they are in, and if they are reconstituted into the $\left[ \binom{12}{5} = \dfrac{12!}{5!7!} = \right]$ 792 different combinations of five-member juries that could be made out of those twelve people, then only $\left[ \binom{9}{5} = \dfrac{9!}{5!4!} = \right]$ 126 or 16% of those juries would have been composed exclusively of jurors voting to convict. In short, if those same twelve jurors had been formed into a 5-of-5 jury, the probability is .84 that that jury would not have had enough votes to convict Johnson.

*Recommendations.* As long as we remain limited to comparing large juries to small, unanimous-rule juries to nonunanimous, or some combination of these, and try to find "the" best jury, given certain objectives of the jury function, any jury decided upon would represent a sacrifice of certain desirable performance features so that other features might be retained. For example, we might choose large juries for their superior ability to represent the community, and lose the small jury's superior ability to even out juror participation. A best-of-all-worlds solution might be possible by developing a novel jury structure that captures the best features of each jury type and makes those features available in a single jury structure. An example of such a synergistic jury might be the following "twin jury": A jury of size twelve (to provide better community representation), directed to self-select into twin juries of six persons each (making more likely social support for minorities in a single group and increased involvement per juror, and doubling the amount of total deliberation while reducing the court time required for the deliberation), where each jury is required to reach an independent 5-of-6 quorum (more communication per jury per unit time, better recall of arguments, and very few, if any, hung juries), and where the twin juries must agree on guilt independently in order for the verdict to be guilty—otherwise the verdict becomes not guilty (eliminating hung juries without introducing increased error into the decision process; requiring more certainty and consistency in perception of the evidence). Such group structures might provide greater efficiency while at the same time providing greater accuracy (with a built-in test of reliability of a verdict) with no change in cost to the courts.

## PROCESS

A model of jury decision making ought to explain how individual jurors reach their pre-deliberation voting stances, and how those individual preferences are combined into a group decision. One kind of theory that has been used to explain the first phase of this decision process is information integration theory (Anderson, 1974). Each juror begins with an initial, pretrial judgment that carries a particular weight. The trial, including both evidentiary and decision-irrelevant (legally speaking) information, is combined with the initial judgment through a weighted averaging process of all the elements. Some evidence is given more weight than other evidence; for example, perhaps one witness seems more credible than another—but it is all combined in this manner to yield a final judgment. The deliberation produces, through social influence and communication, some change in these individual preferences, adding more information, altering the weights assigned to old information. But mainly, the deliberation combines individual judgments. Let us develop some aspects of these pictures more fully.

The initial, pre-deliberation judgment has been a matter of more concern than the information that is processed during the trial, although one of the first empirical studies of jury decision making demonstrated the fluctuation in juror attitudes across the various stages of the trial (Weld and Danzig, 1940). The initial-judgment issue has been of interest because it has to do with juror bias, pretrial press-coverage effects, or other interferences with the presumption of innocence with which jurors are supposed to enter the trial. People involved in jury selection in celebrated trials have made much of the fact that in most surveys of the population from which jurors in those trials would be drawn, about 60% indicate a presumption of guilt for the defendant. This has been taken to indicate a departure from the defendant's right to be presumed innocent (Kairys, Schulman, and Harring, 1975). But it is not clear what this 60% figure means. That is, what *should* jurors' pretrial views be? In an attempt to find out, Saks, Werner, and Ostrom (1975) first asked subjects to respond to this hypothetical question: Imagine you are serving on a jury and the trial is about to begin. You have not yet seen the defendant, heard any of the evidence, or even the charges against the defendant. What do you think your decision will be in this trial when it is over? Most subjects indicated an exact .50 probability that they would vote guilty. It may be then that the 60% should be compared to the 50% who estimate they would vote guilty when they have no knowledge of a case. The degree of bias indicated by 60% may be rather small instead of rather large.

Thinking that jurors may not be able to tap their own pre-information judgment, and still wanting to know what the initial judgment was, the researchers tried a more inferential technique. Jurors were given varying amounts of information of varying levels of incriminatory strength, on several different crimes. They were asked, on the basis of the information given, to indicate the likelihood that the defendant was guilty. Now, knowing the judgments produced by a variety of evidentiary sets, it was possible to insert these values into a form of Anderson's information integration model, and solve for what was the only unknown: initial judgment. Whereas the model is usually used to predict the outcome assuming initial judgment and knowing information input, this study knew the input and the outcome, and used those to work backward to what the initial judgment must have been to produce the final judgments that occurred under the model. Figure 4.2 illustrates the data that resulted from the process. All data points were known except the 0-information point, and that could be solved for, under the model of human information integration used. The major finding was that the initial judgment was extremely close to zero certainty of defendant guilt. In fact, jurors identified by independent measures as antidefendant had slightly *lower* (albeit non–significantly lower) pretrial judgments. This suggests, first of all, that jurors do adopt a presumption of innocence that is nearly literal, even though if asked they think they are starting from around 50–50. (Compare this to Bem's [1966, 1967] suggestion that people do not have direct access to some of their own cognitive processes and must infer their attitudes from observing their own behavior; our jurors had not yet behaved, had nothing to infer

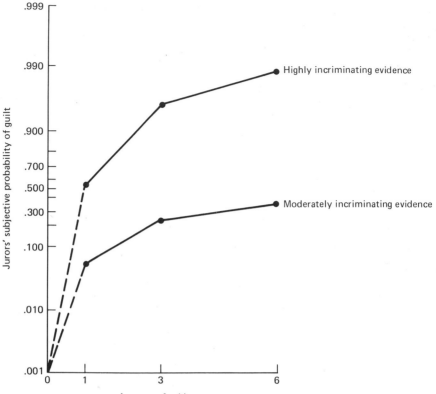

Figure 4.2. Locating jurors' pre-information judgments. Information integration theory provides equations that describe human information processing. It predicts people's final judgments on the basis of initial opinions combined with information (of known value) that has been given to them. These equations have been turned around to ask: if we know a person's final judgment and the information given to them, can we postdict their initial opinions? That would tell us what their "presumptions" were. This graph depicts that process of working backward and shows that the presumptions come very close to zero probability of guilt. (From Saks, Werner, and Ostrom, 1975.)

from, and hence offered a "rational" estimate of their pretrial judgments). It also suggests that juror bias may reside not in the substance of jurors' attitudes, in Andersonian terms the "scale value" of the judgment, but it may operate through the weights given to the initial judgment and subsequent information. Relatively antidefendant jurors more closely approximated the presumption of innocence, but arrived at greater judgments of guilt on the same evidence, so they must have given less weight to their prior judgment and/or more weight to the incriminating evidence than did the relatively more prodefendant jurors.

Whatever the initial judgment and however it was modified by the addition of information during the trial, jurors conclude the trial with some estimate of the probability that the defendant committed the crime charged. That degree of certainty is compared to the thresholds for voting guilty defined by the court and perceived by the juror.

Research evidence exists suggesting that different instructions from the bench regarding the standard of guilt to be applied do influence a juror's likelihood of voting guilty. The major standards are "preponderance of the evidence," used in civil trials and meaning that the juror should decide in the direction of the majority of the weight of the evidence; and "proof beyond a reasonable doubt," a more stringent standard used in criminal trials. If preponderance of the evidence means over 50% sure, beyond a reasonable doubt means something in the high nineties percent range. Thus, if a juror is 91% sure the defendant committed the crime, but has a threshold for converting that perception into a guilty vote that stands at 99%, the juror's probability of voting guilty will be low. Whatever the exact magnitudes are, the juror certainty of the defendant's guilt is compared to the threshold that must be exceeded in order to register a vote for conviction. This is the first decision rule a juror must apply. Each juror, then, enters the arena of deliberation with some probability of voting to acquit or convict. Before discussing the role of this "initial preference distribution," and it is indeed very important, let us examine briefly some of the processes that occur in the group deliberation.

An early step in the group process is to select a foreman. Some studies have shown females to be underrepresented and males overrepresented as foremen by a factor of five (Strodtbeck, James, and Hawkins, 1957). As we have already discussed, the physical location of a person at a rectangular table influences the probability of selection. The person who first speaks in the group is more likely than the others to be chosen foreman (Gordon, 1968; Strodtbeck, et al., 1957), often through a dialogue that begins, "Well, who should we pick as foreman?" and instantly ends, "Why don't you be foreman?" Finally, it has been found that the higher on the socioeconomic scale one's occupation is, the more likely one is to be selected foreman (Strodtbeck, et al., 1957). That behavior patterns in the outside world enter the deliberation room with the jurors is fairly obvious.

Combining these findings, we can see that the person most likely to be chosen foreman is a high-socioeconomic-status male who sits at the end of the table and initiates the discussion.

The distribution of participation by jurors, not surprisingly, reflects the same differences as foreman selection: males more than females, high SES more than low SES, ends and middles over the other positions. Also, higher levels of education are associated with greater participation. As the status of women has changed in the world, so it has changed in the jury. More recent studies show women's under-participation in deliberation being reduced, although one cannot be sure this is not a function, say, of different populations sampled, rather than an overall increase in female participation. Foremen communicate more than other jurors, but much of that is procedural communication rather than advocacy. The foreman tends to adopt a moderator rather than an advocate role.

The amount of participation varies also with the size faction a person is a member of, ranging from as much as 23% of the total discussion by a person in a one-person faction to a low of about 7% per person when the faction numbers seven through eleven. This indicates some tendency toward equilibrium, whereby within faction rates tend to adjust so that the average participation per faction member drops as the size of the faction increases. The process is not quite that straightforward and still awaits clearer conceptualization (Hawkins, 1962; Zeisel, 1963). A major concern in this area is how much communication a minority faction gets to engage in and how this participation rate is affected by such things as structural changes.

The absolute amount of participation by minorities (as well as anyone else) in six-person juries is greater than in twelve-person juries. Minorities do the same or better, however, in larger juries in terms of the proportional share of the communication they account for. As an individual, a minority person gets to talk more in a small jury; as a faction, minorities do (the same or) better when they are in large juries (Diamond, 1974; Saks, 1977).

What do juries do with their communication? In many respects a jury has a much less complicated task than other problem-solving or decision-making groups. They need not explore a problem and define the question facing that group; that is done for them by the court. They do have to reach consensus on the answer to the meta-question they are confronting (Is the defendant guilty or not guilty? Is the defendant in a civil action liable or not liable?). But unlike most problem-solving groups they need not worry about implementing their decisions; they need only report their finding to the court, and the institution will take over its implementation.

Juries, then, have only the core decision-making function—and that seems to be divided into two phases. The first is orientation, the exploration of the issues in the case, of the major items of evidence and inferences about those pieces of evidence. Very much as attorneys try to construct a "theory" to hold the facts, the jury tests competing theories to see which holds the evidence most plausibly. At first this is a general and softly focused exploration. After the first vote is taken, however, the focus becomes much sharper. Only points of disagreement are attended to, and the debate sharpens, with advocates of competing views confronting each other rather directly on the points of disagreement. Hawkins (1962) has called these phases two different strategies of handling the jury's task, the first characterized by a late first vote, the latter by an early first vote. An alternative interpretation is that both strategies are present in most juries, but the transistion from one to the other occurs at the taking of the first vote. If the first vote comes early enough, phase one will be obviated. Evidence for this is that the correlation between time to first vote and total length of deliberation is .48 (from data gathered for Saks, 1977). The importance of the first vote is not at all magical. It simply identifies the factions, or at least how big they are. The jury's task at that point is more simply defined as determining why each side has the views it has, and that focuses the debate on those points of disagreement. The task is as much to break down the minority as it is to examine the substantive issues of the case. The earlier the first vote occurs, the briefer and more pointed the deliberation will be. One might call that the point at which the jury gets down to serious business. Armed with this information, a foreman would be able to influence the tone of the jury's work by the timing of the first vote.

As we discussed earlier, the discussion is lopsided, with a core of jurors dominating the deliberation.  These high participators form the central work group of the jury; they are task- and decision-oriented more than the lesser participators.

Of interest to lawyers has been how specific matters are handled, such as reaching a consensus on the damages to be awarded in a civil trial or the matter of attorneys' contingent fees.  In deciding on the amount of an award, jurors are not supposed to take into account the fact that a portion of the plaintiff's award, usually one-third, goes to the attorney.  Kalven (1958) reported that the contingent fee is, and isn't, taken into account, finding that when it was brought up, it arose as a negotiation tactic.  The jurors favoring a higher award would point out to the jurors who favored a lower award that the difference they were arguing over would be contained in the attorney's fee.  That would tend to resolve the disagreement. The high-damage jurors could feel that they had prevailed because the higher award was being agreed upon; the low-damage jurors could feel they prevailed because the plaintiff was, after all, getting the lesser amount they had been advocating.  Kalven also reported that although jurors do not simply add up their different preferences for an award, divide by the number of jurors, and recommend that average as the award (the "quotient verdict"), they might as well do that because a simple arithmetic average is a good predictor of the award finally agreed upon.

Of interest to psychologists have been such group processes as decision shifts.  One consistent finding about group decision making is that the process of discussion causes judgmental shifts for the participants (Myers and Lamm, 1976).  In the classic paradigm in this research genre, the average risk-taking judgments of individuals reflect more conservatism before group discussion than either the group judgment or the average of individual judgments following group discussion.  Thus occurs a "risky shift," although it is better called a risk shift (because for some choice dilemmas the shift is consistently away from risk) or a decision shift (because shifts occur in nonrisk decisions such as jury verdicts).  Perhaps the most general and most accurate label for this process is Myers and Lamm's *group polarization phenomenon*.  In the case of jury decisions, how are the judgments of individual jurors transformed by group interaction?  Is there a tendency to shift toward conviction, or toward acquittal?

The findings of group polarization research and recent integrations of the research (Myers and Lamm, 1976) indicate that group interaction magnifies already existing tendencies in the individual preferences of group members.    Whether one is studying risk taking, ethical decision making, attitudes, negotiation and conflict, or jury decision making, if the members initially lean in one direction, the group interaction process draws them further in that same direction. This is shown most clearly in Figure 4.3, from Myers and Kaplan (1976).  Where the evidence made defendants appear innocent, group discussion made even more extreme the average judgment of innocence; where the evidence made the defendant appear guilty, group discussion caused judgmental shifts even further toward the guilty pole.  This phenomenon may be partly due to non–social-psychological, merely statistical, effects of decision schemes, where any majority process for combining individual decisions into one group

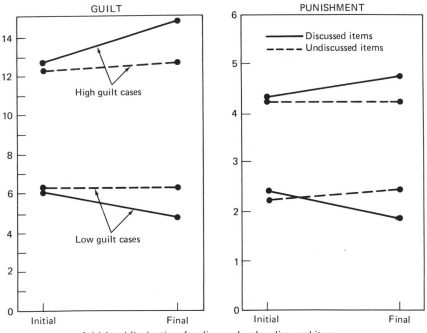

Initial and final ratings for discussed and undiscussed items

Figure 4.3. Group polarization phenomenon.  Both for ratings of guilt and recommended punishments, we can see that group discussion resulted in polarization of judgments—initially high judgments became even higher after discussion; initially low judgments became even lower after discussion.  Judgments on matters that were not included in discussion did not polarize. (From Myers and Kaplan, 1976.)

decision will lead to exaggeration of individual preference distributions (Davis, Kerr, Atkin, Holt, and Meek, 1975). But there are also social process effects involved, and research and conceptual work continue to examine such explanatory hypotheses as social comparison processes (where group members compare themselves to each other and modify their self presentations to elicit favorable reactions from other group members) and informational influence processes (where cognitive learning takes place in the direction of the dominant pole because that is where most of the argumentation and discussion centers) (Myers and Lamm, 1976).

The group polarization effect leads to a most important summary of group process effects upon the final decision rendered by the jury. It suggests that whatever the individual preferences are that enter the deliberation, the final outcome will be an exaggerated version of that distribution of individual judgments. That is, individual judgments are largely determinative of the group judgment. Other lines of evidence point strongly to this same conclusion. A variety of mathematical models have evolved to try to account for jury *group* decision processes (Davis, 1973; Gelfand and Solomon, 1973, 1974; see Davis, Bray, and Holt, 1977 for a survey of these theories of jury decision making). These models can predict verdicts, given initial preference distributions, with a fairly high degree of accuracy. When mathematical models do an effective job of predicting, their propositions come to be regarded as a theory or explanation of the processes. The theory one would have to draw from the success of these models is that the process of group decision making is one in which the majority preferences are highly predictive of the group decision. Further, Davis et al. (1975) point out that regardless of the court-imposed social decision rule (such as unanimity), an informal, normative, social decision rule (such as "if more than two-thirds of us favor a particular verdict, then we as a group will favor that verdict; otherwise we will hang") may be what is really the determining combinatorial rule.

When the various group processes are considered together, a consistent trend emerges. The jurors combine into factions and the majority communicates more. Explicit social decision rules, a structural feature, guide a combinatorial process that magnifies majority preferences. The group polarization phenomenon, be it through normative (social comparison) or informational influence, polarizes the existing group preference. The minority is subjected to pressures to conform, and can escape such aversive social stimuli by adopting the majority view. Implicit decision schemes show group deference to the majority. All of the processes begin with the initial distribution of preferences and convert that into a final verdict that is predictable from the preference distribution prior to the deliberation. Knowledge of individual differences in dominance, persuasibility, or whatever, and refinements in understanding the specific group processes will allow fine-tuning of the prediction of jury outcomes, but

> to a substantial degree the jury verdict is determined by the posture of the vote at the start of the deliberation process and not by the impact of this process as rational persuasion. [T]he deliberation process, though rich in human interest and color appears not to be at the heart of jury decision-making. [Kalven and Zeisel, 1966, p. 496]

Kalven and Zeisel found that only about 5% of juries hung. In order for a jury to hang a substantial split in opinion was required at the outset of deliberation. An initial minority of one, two, or three of twelve barely ever produces a hung jury. An initial minority of at least four is usually required to hang. In fewer than half of the instances of hung juries did the judge regard the deadlock as an unreasonable outcome, based on the trial evidence. Kalven and Zeisel have provided what is perhaps the most graphic summary of the process by which individual jurors' judgments are combined into a group decision:

> The deliberation process might well be likened to what the developer does for an exposed film: it brings out the picture, but the outcome is pre-determined. . . . [The developing process is] an interesting combination of rational persuasion, sheer social pressure, and the psychological mechanism by which individual perceptions undergo change when exposed to group discussion. [p. 489]

*Conclusions.* The hanging juror, the Henry Fonda minority of one who eventually turns the others among "twelve angry men" around from their initial preferences, and the juror who, for whatever out-side or intrapsychic reasons, is, as Lempert (1975) puts it, "beyond all reason," are statistical rarities.  Given that the outcome of the jury's decision is so heavily determined by the individual choices with which the deliberation begins, and given that those individual judgments are so heavily determined by the form and content of the information to which jurors are exposed during the trial, the practical lesson for attorneys seeking to win cases is that the presentation they design for the trial is the most important determinant of the outcome of that case.  Phenomena related to the presentation of information at the trial are discussed in the chapters on evidence and lawyering.

## OUTCOME

We have already discussed what is most important about outcomes of jury trials—the composition, structures, and processes that determine whether a verdict will be reached and what that verdict will be; and we have found that information presented at the trial is the major determinant of the trial's outcome.  This point about outcomes might best be made by turning our attention away, for a moment, from those components of jury decision making and looking only at its outcomes.  And compare those to outcomes reached by an altogether different decision-making device—the judge.  The judge's personal characteristics differ more from the jurors' than the jurors' do among each other.  And the judge decides as an individual, rendering group structure and process variables radically different from any variations among juries.  And yet the judge and the jury usually reach the same decision.  Kalven and Zeisel (1966) asked some 600 judges in some 8,000 cases to fill out a questionnaire about the case while the jury was out deliberating.  The data produced permit a comparison of judge and jury verdicts on the same case.  In criminal cases, judge and jury agreed on the verdict 80% of the time.  In civil cases they agreed 79% of the time.

While Kalven and Zeisel devote their book to explaining the sources of disagreement in the 20% of cases where there is judge-jury disagreement, we would prefer to point out the apparent cause of the massive *agreement* between judge and jury.  Both are responding to the same trial presentation and that presentation is the pre-potent determinant of trial outcome.    In spite of the differences between people, which are unusually large between judges and jurors, their similarities in responding to environmental stimuli exceed their differences.

## SUMMARY

Jury structure is illustrated by research on the geometry of the jury, the size of the jury, and the assigned decision rule of the jury. It is found, for example, that certain locations about the table give one more power than other locations. Variations in group size and social decision rule influence such things as the community representation on the jury, the process of deliberation, and other factors.    To exploit the most desirable group process effects within a single jury structure, a "synergistic" jury is recommended.  Jury process includes both how the individual juror reaches a judgment and how the individual judgments are combined to form a group decision.  Information integration theory is used to account for the individual process and to identify the pretrial presumptions of jurors. Jury process research has attended to participation in the delibera-tion, social influence, who is selected foreperson and how, compro-mises, and the group polarization of judgments.  The outcome of a trial is largely predictable from the stances of individual jurors at the outset of deliberation, and those stances are largely deter-mined by the evidence and arguments presented at trial.

# 5
# The Lawyer

*When I was a young man practicing at the bar, I lost a great many cases I should have won. As I got along, I won a great many cases I ought to have lost; so on the whole, justice was done.*

—Lord Justice Matthews

Trial lawyers are, to a remarkable degree, professional applied social psychologists. Much of their work directly parallels the traditional major research interests of social psychology, and they are daily in a position to manipulate key variables of social influence: they control information, manage impressions, influence attributions, make or withhold settlement offers, and so on.

In court, lawyers attempt to modify the beliefs and attitudes of judges and juries. Out of court, lawyers are bargainers and negotiators: approximately 90% of all litigation (both criminal and civil) is settled at some point prior to adjudication by a court. While interviewing a client or a witness, a lawyer is much like a research interviewer, attempting to establish rapport, to structure the interaction, to elicit needed information from the client. While giving advice and counsel, the lawyer may perform some of the functions of a counseling psychologist, or of a Machiavellian manipulator (e.g., Blumberg, 1967; Rosenthal, 1974). And much of the development and behavior of the lawyer is, like other organizational and institutional roles, susceptible to social psychological analysis: selection, education, and socialization of lawyers, cognitive re-structuring (what lawyers call "learning to think like a lawyer"), role-taking, and organizational and structural devices for shaping and maintaining the behavior of the profession.

While their interests in behavioral phenomena strongly parallel each other, the methods of the lawyer and social psychologist differ markedly. The lawyer relies upon intuition, personal and shared experience with other attorneys, and tradition to discover effective strategies for changing attitudes, securing favorable settlements, and so on. The social psychologist is suspicious of the opportunity for biased (i.e., unrepresentative) observations and lack of strong inference (cf., Platt, 1964; Campbell and Stanley, 1963) in such a naturalistic approach, and has typically resorted to carefully controlled experiments, field studies, or surveys to explore these same phenomena.

Another difference between the two enterprises is that while lawyers are interested in the empirical phenomena (i.e., what strategies work), most social psychologists regard these functional relationships between variables to be of far less interest than the creation and testing of theory to explain the phenomena. (A noteworthy exception is Zimbardo and Ebbesen, 1969.) Our approach is to draw from the social psychologist's store of findings, but to do so through the lawyer's highly applied perspective.

## PERSUASION AND THE MANAGEMENT OF SOCIAL PERCEPTION

### Attitude Change

During a trial, the lawyer's primary goal is to induce favorable attitudes among the factfinders in a case, the judge or jury. Attitude change may be regarded as the end product of a communication process, and variables affecting attitude change may accordingly be grouped into several classes. These classes of variables are features of the *source* of the communication, aspects of the *message* itself, and of the *channel* over which the message passes, and the characteristics of the *audience* to whom the message is transmitted. This communication model of attitude change is best suited to an audience that passively receives the message; and the attorney's audience during a trial is essentially passive. Juries and, during bench trials, judges, are perhaps the most attentive yet passive audience one is ever likely to address.

We have presented the better established phenomena of attitude change in Table 5.1, arranged according to the components of the

### Table 5.1.  Attitude change phenomena relevant to persuasion in the courtroom.

#### SOURCE

Attitude change in the advocated direction is increased if the source is high in:

*Credibility*, that is, perceived as possessing *expertise* and *objectivity* (not intending to persuade but disinterestedly to convey information).
*Attractiveness*, on the dimension of:
   *familiarity*
   *similarity*—both demographic and attitudinal/ideological (the latter may be induced by the Source initially expressing some views shared by the Receivers)
   *likability*—including personal style, physical appearance, etc.; and, if appearing highly competent, can be enhanced by a pratfall.
*Power, prestige, status.*

Attitude change is mediated by *attention* to the message (enhanced by attractiveness, status, expertise), *comprehension* of the message (arguments are better absorbed when the Source is ambiguously valenced; otherwise the conclusion is better absorbed), and *yielding* to the message (enhanced by credibility and high power).

#### CHANNEL

Attitude change in the advocated direction is enhanced by:

*Face-to-face verbal communications* over written, taped, or filmed communications.
*Direct contact with the attitude object* or objects related to the attitude issue. When people (like defendants) are the attitude objects, brief contact polarizes attitudes (initially positive become more positive; negative become more negative); long continuing contact at equal status levels leads to positive attitudes.
*Moderate levels of distraction* or interference; too much distortion precludes message reception.
*Nonverbal modes* to make evidence presentation more salient, more real, less monotonous.  Sensory modes (hearing, seeing, smelling, etc.) should be coordinated.

#### MESSAGE

Factors that increase message effectiveness are:

*Extremity*—attitude change increases with increasing extremity of the message advocated, up to very high levels of discrepancy from the Receiver's initial position.  If the Source's credibility is low or the Receiver is highly ego-involved in the attitude, a boomerang effect can occur.

**Table 5.1.** (*Continued*)

---

*Drawing explicit conclusions*, which is more effective than leaving them implicit and allowing the Receiver to draw them, unless the Receiver is especially intelligent or the explicitness is so strong that it arouses reactance in the Receiver.

*Emotional versus rational appeals*—appeals to emotion are equally effective or more effective than rational appeals. Messages including logical, factual, or substantive material, especially when it is subtle or complex, produce less change but change that decays more slowly. *Fear appeals* are generally more effective as the intensity of fear arousal increases, and are most effective when specific, doable actions can be prescribed as responses to the attitude, but can fall off in effectiveness at very high levels.

*Reinforcement*, which is effective in modifying attitudes in several ways:

*message-irrelevant*—when received under pleasant, reinforcing circumstances, attitude change communications produce more change.

*contingent*—when reinforcing events are contingent upon adoption of the advocated position.

*intrinsic*—when the message itself is a reinforcer, as when it answers questions the factfinder may have, or provides arguments to support an opinion the factfinder holds.

*Source derogation*—what a Receiver thinks of a Message affects evaluations of the Source, which in turn influences the persuasive impact of future communication from that Source.

*One-sidedness or two-sidedness*—if an advocate presents first, if the audience knows about the other side or knows there will be another side, has initial unfavorable attitudes, or is unusually intelligent, two-sided arguments are more effective; otherwise one-sided arguments are.

*Order effects*

*internal ordering*—when conclusions are presented first (anticlimactic ordering), the audience is alerted to the advocate's bias, but the attention-focusing power and comprehensibility of the message is enhanced; also, information presented early in a communication is learned best, middle is worst. Yielding is greatest to information that comes at the end of a message. Some information (nonsalient, controversial, interesting, or familiar) is primacy-bound; other is recency-bound.

*gross ordering*—the party presenting first has an advantage when a period of time will pass between the presentations and the time for a decision. The party presenting second has an advantage when a period of time will pass between the two presentations. When the two-sided nature of the attitude issue is salient, recency prevails.

*Memory for a message*, which is enhanced if the message is meaningful, familiar, a congruent, coherent whole, vivid, repeated (although the asymptote is reached quickly), and associated with known information.

*Attributions of responsibility*, which are facilitated by qualitative information, lexical choice, behavior (or reports of it) engulfing the perceptual field, non-

**Table 5.1.** *(Continued)*

common effects (the behavior could not produce multiple possible outcomes), high status of the behaver, serious harmful consequences of the behavior, placing the perceiver in an observer (rather than an actor) frame of reference. External attributions are facilitated by the counterparts to these.

**RECEIVER/DESTINATION**

The Receiver's characteristics, state, and circumstances that influence attitude change are:

*Involvement* with the consequences of one's response, which increases the probability of attitude change.

*Immunization*, or resistance to persuasion, which is facilitated by forewarning (of the intent to persuade), arousal of motivation (hostility, fear, etc.) to resist, critical ability, anchoring (initial attitude to relatively unambiguous positions), and inoculation (prior presentation of a weak form of the arguments accompanied by counterarguments to them).

(See also Chapter 3, on jury composition.)

communication model described above. (See Zimbardo and Ebbesen, 1969; Kiesler, Collins, and Miller, 1969; Oskamp, 1977.) Perusal of the table will inform the reader of what attitude change techniques "work." Many of these may strike you as convergent with common sense. The research findings do, indeed, often confirm the obvious, but sometimes they do a good bit more. Sometimes the research shows which of several competing common senses is correct, as in whether to draw conclusions explicitly or to leave them implicit, an instance in which intuition could lead one to either conclusion. Sometimes the research demonstrates the limits of the obvious, as when the superior persuasiveness of highly credible sources fades over time. And sometimes the research adds complexity to common sense, as in the finding of a curvilinear relationship between the extremity of an advocated position and the degree of change in the audience's attitude, leading ultimately to a "boomerang" effect. Let us focus on several of these phenomena of persuasion and discuss them in more concrete relation to lawyering and court procedure.

The famous advocate Clarence Darrow (1857–1938) is reputed to have employed the tactic of distraction to prevent the jury from hearing his opponent's closing arguments.  Darrow would insert a wire inside his cigar so that when he smoked it the ash would grow long without falling.  He would smoke it during his opponent's closing, and as the ash grew increasingly long, the jury (it is said) would become increasingly fascinated and not be able to attend to the opponent's arguments.  Research on the effects of distraction on attitude change shows that extreme enough levels of distraction will indeed prevent the audience from attending to a message.  Low to moderate levels of distraction, however, are sufficient only to distract the audience from silently counterarguing against the message they are listening to, while still allowing the message itself to be received.  (Counterarguing is a major way people resist persuasive influences.)  Thus, nonextreme distractors have been found to increase the persuasive impact of the message because they merely interfere with counterarguing (Zimbardo and Ebbesen, 1969).  An ash growing on a cigar is probably easy enough for a juror to monitor while still hearing the closing arguments.  But it would demand enough attention to interfere with counterarguing.  Thus, Darrow's tactic, while having intuitive appeal and being terribly clever, probably *increased* his opponent's effectiveness.

Lawyers can provide their audiences (judges and juries) with counterarguments against their adversaries' position and thereby increase resistance to subsequent persuasion by the opposition.  This is the technique known as "inoculation" (McGuire, 1964).  By giving the audience a weakened form of the opponent's argument and arguing against that view, the audience will have counterarguments to use against the opposition when it tries to persuade.  Many lawyers do use this technique during opening arguments.  They present their client's position as well as the adversary's position, and suggest arguments to vitiate the opponent's position.  Inoculation would be especially useful to the party that opens the trial, but obviously could be used by each in anticipating the other's case.

It has long been speculated that the order of presentation of arguments could inject some advantage to one side or the other.  This might apply to the gross ordering of presentations (the order in which advocates speak) or the internal ordering (whether any one advocate would increase his or her advantage by presenting the strong material early or late in the presentation). When information presented early is more persuasive, that is termed a primacy effect; when later information is found more effective, that is a recency effect. Early studies showed a primacy effect (Lund, 1925), suggesting that people are highly influenced by the information that establishes their first impression of an issue. Later studies found numerous exceptions to the first-enunciated "law of primacy." This easily posed question has had no simple answer. Sometimes primacy is found to operate; sometimes recency.

Obviously, interactions with other variables are critical in determining when one pattern will prevail and when the other. Some studies have indicated that the effects of primacy and recency are mediated by the kind of information transmitted. Some information activates primacy and thus is primacy-bound, such as that which is nonsalient, controversial, interesting, or highly familiar. Accordingly, information which is salient, noncontroversial, uninteresting, and familiar is recency-bound (Rosnow and Robinson, 1967; Rosnow and Goldstein, 1967; Kiesler, et al., 1969). Another mediating variable is time. The more time that passes, the more likely a communication is to have been forgotten, with the greatest memory decays occurring immediately, then tapering off. Generally, primacy will tend to prevail unless the first message is allowed to be forgotten before the second is heard. Then a recency effect will prevail. This is essentially what was found by Miller and Campbell (1959), who simulated the closing of a trial by presenting jurors with transcripts of lawyers' summations—first the plaintiff, then the defense: and then asked for a verdict. Four different conditions were run, in which they inserted: (a) a lengthy recess, after the second summation but before the decision; (b) the same, between the first summation and the second; (c) two recesses, between the first and second summations and the decision; and (d) no recesses at all. The first condition, in which the messages had a period of time in which to be forgotten, produced a primacy effect. In the second condition, where the first message was given time to be forgotten before presenting the second message, recency prevailed. And in the remaining two conditions, there was no differential effectiveness of the summations.

Thibaut and Walker (1975, Ch. 7) found dramatic recency effects in legal decision-making simulations. They attribute these to the nature of the issues typically in dispute in such arenas: whether particular behavior occurred or did not, rather than enduring qualities of a person or an issue.    Second, and more important, they conclude that the adversarial context of the trial causes decision makers to suspend early judgments, knowing that countervailing information from the other party will soon be presented.    Thibaut and Walker's findings showed the recency effect to hold for both gross and internal (climactic more effective than anticlimactic) orderings, except for the first presentation by innocence advocates, which had no recency effect.    Their data showed that the sequence of a typical adversary trial succeeded best in balancing out these decision-irrelevant effects of order.    The defense has the advantage of presenting second; the prosecution or plaintiff has the advantage of recency effects in both its opening and closing arguments.

The primacy–recency findings have less to offer attorneys planning trial strategies than they do to courts and legislatures designing trial procedures.    In most instances, the order of presentation is fixed by law.    And in criminal trials in most states the prosecution both opens and closes final arguments, the latter being a rebuttal, with the defense sandwiched in between.    The striking balance found by Thibaut and Walker (1975) is lost in favor of the prosecution, which has an extra recency opportunity, and which in closing arguments has the advantage of inoculation and primacy as well. Whether circumstances lend themselves to primacy or to recency effects does not matter; the prosecution has the advantage in either case (Lana, 1972).

Another classic variable in attitude change research is whether conclusions are drawn explicitly by the communicator or merely implied by the evidence and arguments.    Experiments have been conducted in which the same communicator source presenting the same arguments either draws conclusions explicitly or does not (Hovland and Mandell, 1952; Fine, 1957; Weiss and Steenbock, 1965).    The findings are rather clear: more attitude change in the direction advocated the source occurs when intended conclusions are made explicit. er who tries to allow the evidence and arguments to speak es runs a risk of allowing the factfinders to arrive at the lusion.    In our experience few lawyers do not make the and state the conclusion they wish their audience to nsidering all of the testimony I think and hope you will agree with me that there is but one verdict you can render in this case—that my client is not guilty." As with most of the processes we are discussing, there exist limits to the phenomenon, and it is possible to go too far: "After considering all of the testimony, I am absolutely certain that you cannot possibly reach any verdict in this case except one—that my client is not guilty." Conclusions stated *too* explicitly, such that they tend to restrict the decisional freedom of the factfinder, will arouse "reactance" (Brehm, 1966). To reduce reactance, a decision maker acts to restore that decisional freedom; in this context that would mean reacting against the conclusion stated by the source. Thus, maximum effectiveness with respect to this variable would be obtained by stating a conclusion explicitly, but not so much so that reactance is aroused.

When social psychologists study the persuasive impact of transmitting messages through different channels, they often mean live presentations versus written versus audio versus televised or filmed. Such research lends itself to identifying differential effectiveness of various media, whether, for example, a candidate's campaign funds are most cost-effectively invested in newspaper ads, billboards, radio or television spots, door-to-door canvassing, or some optimal mix of media. Until very recently, trial work has been far more restricted in the matter of communication channels. Some states have been experimenting with the use of edited videotapes as the trial that is presented to the jury. Research findings suggest that some differences in juror responses may be a function of the mode of presentation— between live trials and different types of videotaped trials (*Brigham Young University Law Review*, 1975). Other channel-shifting judicial experiments are being considered, such as hearing motions and trying cases by conference-telephone hook-ups to increase the efficiency and convenience of bringing people together for proceedings. Researchers will be concerned with evaluating the impact of such electronic trials on the nature of the communication and the effects, if any, on the product of the decision making.

Except for lobbying for or against these reforms, such a
board changes do not permit the adoption by attorneys
tial channel-use strategies—both sides will be trying th
both by videotape. One might say that both sides wi
the same court. Of more practical interest to the

what manipulations of the communication channel are available to increase the persuasive impact of his or her message.  Traditional courtroom options are limited to verbal testimony, exhibits of physical evidence, maps, photographs or diagrams, or, occasionally, site visits to the scene of the crime.  Typically, trials are overwhelmingly verbal affairs.  The judge speaks; the lawyers speak and ask questions; witnesses answer questions; and jurors listen.  The pictures of reality drawn for jurors are painted primarily with words.  Textbooks on trial practice (e.g., Keeton, 1973) generally encourage the use of audio-visual-olfactory aids: have witnesses draw on blackboards, play tapes, enter alcohol-reeking whisky bottles into evidence as exhibits, and so on.  These practical concerns (once again) point to a gap in the theory-guided research of social psychologists.  Very little research attention has been paid to the differential effectiveness of alternative communication modalities, though it is anticipated that future research will look into these ear-eye-nose-etc. issues (McGuire, 1969), as psychologists study the relative information-encoding capacity of different sensory modalities.

Some rules of thumb can, for now, be borrowed from basic research on perception and learning (Gibson, 1966; Neisser, 1976).  Attention, perception, and recall are facilitated by repetition.  But information can become lost in the midst of similar material that brings about habituation.  Thus, changes in energy level, movement, or use of a different sensory modality can help a stimulus stand out and be noticed.  Because trials are usually so verbal and monotonous, any use of nonverbal information (visual, olfactory, and so forth) will probably be salient and better attended to than had it been presented verbally.  Humans rely heavily on visual, in contrast to verbal, information to make their way through life, and may therefore place more credibility in what they can see for themselves.  Indeed, they likely place more credibility in anything they can sense for themselves than in what they are told verbally by lawyers and witnesses through such an easily manipulated and distortable medium as verbal report.  We have all experienced the palpable reality of being at a famous place or casting our eyes upon a historic artifact.  Interestingly, however, written information, though better remembered, is less persuasive than spoken information.  McGuire (1969) suggests that this paradoxical finding indicates much greater yielding to heard than to read communication.  Because people are accustomed to perceiving and learning through multiple modalities and coordinating the information, it would probably make sense for attorneys to use multiple, coordinated sensory modalities for presenting trial information.

In numerous trials the importance—perhaps overimportance—of physical exhibits has been evident.  In personal injury or medical malpractice cases, for example, photographs of the victim's injuries or the victim's injuries themselves are obviously appropriate and invariably exploited nonverbal evidence.  If the injuries are too gruesome or overused, however, their effect can be counterproductive.  As with most other stimulus–response relations, an optimal level of stimulation exists.  Too much perceived harm to a victim has led to the paradoxical finding that *less* blame is attributed to the harm-doer (Lerner, 1970).  In *U.S. v. Rosenberg* a torn Jello box was entered as evidence that a conspiracy had occurred, by showing how the two halves of the torn box were, allegedly, to be matched up.  The "reality" of the Jello box may be illusory, since anyone can tear a Jello box in half and bring it to court.  Nevertheless, both sides of the case agree it was an effective, if dubious, use of a communication mode.  A Boston obstetrician, convicted of manslaughter of a fetus in an otherwise legal abortion (*Commonwealth of Massachusetts v. Kenneth Edelin*, 1975), appealed the conviction on, among other grounds, the argument that the prosecution's use of color photographs of the abortus had been so effective as to prejudice the jury against the defendant.

## Attribution

The prosecutor or plaintiff's lawyer attempts to construct a picture in which the harm or wrongdoing in dispute is perceived as the responsibility of the defendant.  The defendant's lawyer, of course, attempts to draw a different picture, where most of the elements are the same but where the assignment of responsibility (or liability) does not fall upon the defendant.  Social psychologists call this process of perceiving causality in social events "attribution," and, in the specific circumstances we are discussing, "attribution of responsibility."  The competing images of reality propounded by the adverse parties in a trial seek to induce the factfinder to perceive the causal linkages differently.

One of the most easily comprehended ways of influencing the perception of a set of facts is in the coloring provided by the language chosen to construct the picture.  A dramatic example of the process is provided by the *Edelin* case.  The major issue in dispute was how the events were to be defined and labeled.  The defense wished the jury to perceive that a legal termination of a pregnancy had occurred, in which a fetus had been aborted.  The prosecution wanted the jury to perceive that following a legal termination of pregnancy, a baby boy had been smothered.  The trial made it clear that these choices of language were regarded as critically important.  The defense made a pretrial motion seeking to have certain words banned from the courtroom: suffocate, smother, murder, baby, baby boy.  In their place would go such words as fetus, abortus, subject, products of conception.  The importance of semantic issues was clear throughout this trial, in which a great deal of meta-talk—talk about talk—occurred. Consider this part of the defense opening statement:

> your effort . . . at all times [should be] to determine not what is said to have happened in terms of the words you hear, but what happened. [*Commonwealth of Mass. v. Edelin*, 1975, 5, 32]

While most social psychological research on persuasion focuses on the source, channel, and structure of the message, it should be clear that in the war of words that trials are, semantic content is also critically important.  The *Edelin* trial merely made explicit what is always implicit.  A sociolinguistic study by Danet (1975) makes clear that throughout the trial, lexical choices were correlated with the side making the statement, and were part of the tools that party was using to construct its preferred model of reality.  For example, during the direct examination of Edelin, his attorney chose prosecution-favorable terms 15% of the time; during cross-examination, the prosecution used such terms 49% of the time.  Assigning weighted values to lexical choices, Danet found that the prosecution won the war of words, managing to use more prosecution-loaded terms more often than the defense was able to use the defense-loaded terms, and the prosecution was even able to get the defendant to use them when he was under stress and speaking specifically about his own case (Danet, 1975).  The prosecution also won the trial.

Attributions of responsibility are associated not only with the choice of a trial lexicon; less obvious manipulations are fairly well understood by attribution researchers (Jones and Davis, 1965; Shaver, 1975). A *dispositional*, or *internal*, attribution is one in which the perceiver infers the "cause" of the actor's behavior to be the actor's own motives, intentions, and dispositions. A *situational*, or *external*, attribution is one in which the source of the act is perceived to be external to the actor, a result of situational pressures. The plaintiff or prosecution, obviously, seeks to produce a construction in which the factfinder will make a dispositional attribution; the defense seeks to paint a picture that will lead to a situational attribution. This distinction clearly is critical to issues of liability (Was the defendant negligent, responsible, accountable for the injury which befell the plaintiff?) and in the high-frequency "affirmative defense" in criminal cases ("Yes, I did it but I should not be held criminally liable because of mitigating circumstances").

The search by all humans for causality in everyday social events is termed "naive psychology" because these are nonrigorous causal searchings; yet they are nevertheless primitive forms of a scientific study of the causes of behavior. Attribution researchers try to determine the principles that govern people's "naive" perceptions of causality.

Researchers have found the direction of these attributions to be influenced by a number of variables. Heider (1958) has suggested that "behavior engulfs the field." That is, one's social perceptual field is dominated by behavior and the behaver who emitted it; we overlook situational determinants. Even when situational constraints on the behaver are made salient, perceivers still tend to make dispositional (or internal) attributions (e.g. Jones and Harris, 1967). Indeed, this quirk of naive causal attribution has been established as a truism by law; judges commonly instruct jurors that "people are assumed to intend the natural consequences of their actions." The defense lawyer's job is in large part to construct a picture that overrides this powerful and institutionally sanctioned tendency. Certainly the defense can attempt to bring forward information that makes situational constraints salient ("My client was forced by her captors to participate in the bank robbery; she did not do it on her own volition"). But more can be done.

Perceivers try to arrive at confident, *correspondent* inferences (i.e., hypothetical motives that fit both the behavior and its intentions).

Providing alternative plausible causes that are equally correspondent reduces the factfinder's ability to make a confident, culpable inference (Jones and Davis, 1965) ("My client was not running from the scene of the crime; he was going to call for help"). Even without the judge's urging, perceivers examine the effects of behavior to infer the intentions that may have motivated the behavior. And this process relies upon a *discounting principle* (Kelley, 1967, 1971): If a perceiver can discount alternative intended effects, one culpable inference can be confidently arrived at. But if several or many (reasonably intended) effects can be entertained, confident choices cannot be made among them ("Of course my client's actions resulted in the loss of the ship, but his actions were necessary to save the lives of the people on board"). These *common effects* of a single action make it impossible for perceivers to know which effect was intended. The importance of the discounting principle in drawing causal attributions is illustrated both in lay and in legal perceivers by the fact that statements against one's own interest are regarded as more informative and reliable. A statement consistent with one's own interests leaves a perceiver unsure of whether the statement is true or merely self-serving. When it is against interest, the self-serving alternative can be discounted, allowing a more certain inference to be made from the content of the statement.

Another example is the social status of the actor. Higher-status persons are perceived as more able to intend their actions; lower-status persons are more readily perceived as controlled by situational pressure (Thibaut and Riecken, 1955). In appropriate circumstances, an attorney might reduce the likelihood of an attribution of responsibility by reducing the perceived status of the defendant.

Walster (1966) conducted a study in which subjects were informed about a situation in which a person parked a car on a hill. Keeping that act constant, she varied the consequences of the car's accidentally rolling down the hill and causing either very minor or severe damage. The more serious the damage, the more the driver was perceived as responsible for its occurrence, even though the act itself did not vary. This process has been termed *defensive attribution:* serious harm, it has been theorized, cannot be perceived as a random event, because then it could unpredictably befall even the perceiver. Thus, the more serious the effect, the greater the need to attribute causality somewhere; and if that somewhere is a dispositional attribution to the actor, it is going to produce a stronger, more confident attribution of his responsibility for it.

The final attribution phenomenon we will mention is the actor–observer dichotomy (Jones and Nisbett, 1971). Actors tend to perceive their behavior as responses to the requirements of the situation; observers tend to perceive behavior as resulting from stable, dispositional characteristics of the behaver. Again, defendants, as the objects of factfinders' observations, are at a disadvantage. One solution for defense attorneys might be to present their client's side in a way that invites the jury to covertly role play (Jacobs and Sachs, 1971) the defendant's viewpoint, thereby making them vicarious actors and increasing the likelihood that they would make situational attributions (". . . and imagine that you are then suddenly confronted by a . . .").

## Language Style and the Verbal Control of Witnesses

Much of a lawyer's case is delivered from the mouths of witnesses. The lawyer, however, is in a position to exercise considerable influence over what comes out. The lawyer chooses the witnesses and the order in which to present them; the lawyer chooses the questions to ask and the pattern and rhythm of the answering. Lind and O'Barr (1977) have demonstrated the impact of speech style on the way a speaker is perceived, which in turn has impact on the persuasiveness of the message. The "powerless" style is characterized by the use of intensifiers ("so," "very," "too"), empty adjectives ("charming," "cute") hypercorrect grammar, polite forms, gestures, hedges, and rising intonations and a wider range of intonational patterns. The "powerful" style is the counterpart to the powerless. In their research, witnesses using the powerful style were perceived as more competent, attractive, trustworthy, dynamic, and convincing. While their study was on witness speech patterns, it seems safe to generalize it to the speech of the lawyers themselves.

Lawyers are generally advised (e.g., Keeton, 1973; Morrill, 1971) to allow longer, narrative responses from their own witnesses and briefer more fragmented responses from adverse witnesses, on the assumption that narrative answers are more persuasive to the factfinder.

Lind and O'Barr (1977) have shown how the training and expectations of the perceiver, the sex of the witness, and attributions about the lawyer's judgment of what the witness is saying, combine to place limits on the generality of that well-worn wisdom. Like many social psychological phenomena, it makes a poor main-effect generalization; it holds under certain conditions, not under others.

An interesting recent set of studies by Loftus and her associates shows how the lawyer can subtly control the facts witnesses report they have observed (Loftus and Palmer, 1974). For example, when asking a witness to estimate the speed an automobile was traveling when it smashed/collided/bumped/hit/contacted another car, the estimates of witnesses were systematically correlated with the word used to ask the question: 40.8 mph (smashed)/39.3 (collided)/38.1 (bumped)/34.0 (hit)/31.8 (contacted). Many lawyers who are sensitive to the importance of lexical choice as discussed earlier may already use such tactics. Loftus's studies, however, provide an unambiguous demonstration of its effectiveness. Another illustration from Loftus's research is the way facts not actually observed by a witness can be inserted as incidental features of early questions; they become incorporated into the witness's memory for the events under examination, and elicited in later questions as though they had been observed at the time of the event. Constructions of fact can be incorporated into the very question which purports to inquire about the fact ("Did you see the smashed headlight?" says that a smashed headlight existed; did you see it?). Questions posed that way elicit a higher proportion of agreeing responses by witnesses.

Suppose a lawyer wishes to establish a dispositional attribution for a person, and wishes that person to testify to the attribution himself. For example, say an attorney desires that a witness describe himself as "a nervous person" because that characterization is needed to make a later point. Through a leading question the attorney may ask: "You're a nervous person aren't you?" The witness will reply yes or no. If yes, the attorney has succeeded. If no, the attorney can then ask about a selected series of discrete behaviors that he knows will receive affirmative answers ("You're a bit shakey right now, aren't you?" "You smoke cigarettes, don't you?" "You dropped the scalpel, didn't you?"). Then the witness is asked, "Well, wouldn't you say these sound like the behavior of a nervous person?" The witness will then, or the next time around, acquiesce in the inference implied by those behaviors, and state the self-ascription the attorney is working for.  In short, a skillful attorney can elicit a great many responses from a witness, independent of what the witness would prefer to say.

## Audience

The audience to whom communication in a trial is generally directed is a judge or jury.  Separate chapters have been devoted to these participants.  At this point, we will mention only that the evidence is rather strong that the other classes of variables in the communication model, which we have been discussing, are more powerful determinants (than individual differences) of the verdict reached (Saks, 1976).  In the sizable majority of cases tried in U.S. courts or psychological laboratories, it matters less who is hearing the case than it does what is being heard; most cases are clear (Lempert, 1975).  Nevertheless, audience variables do exert some influence, and the wise practitioner does not neglect any difference that makes a difference.

## Summing Up

The research findings are atomistic; one who would apply them to a practical persuasion situation has to practice the art of weaving them together into an effective and coherent whole.  Biochemists study only one or a few processes in a given area of research; physicians must integrate the findings in the overall treatment of a whole patient.  A lawyer trying a case has to make decisions about the panoply of phenomena relating to persuasion and social perception—choice of language, choice of style, modalities of communication, whether and how to inoculate, whether to draw conclusions explicitly or implicitly, whether and how to increase credibility of favorable witnesses and reduce it in unfavorable witnesses, in what order to present information within arguments, the order of witnesses, how extreme a picture to paint without producing a boomerang effect, and on and on.  The number of variables to be considered is enormous.  The research findings are informative about individual variables and processes, but not very helpful about integrated packages of strategies.

Whatever the lawyer's total case presentation becomes, it is tried, obviously, in embrace with an adversary's case.  The two attorneys, or teams of attorneys, place antagonistic demands on the factfinder's beliefs and attitudes.  One of the earliest studies of the effects of adversary persuasion on juries, that of Weld and Danzig (1938), shows the back-and-forth pulls of plaintiff and defense counsel on the jury through the numerous stages of a mock civil trial.  The adversary's realistic goal is not to overwhelm, but to come out ahead in an obviously seesaw battle.  In Figure 5.1, the responses of the jury to the alternating antagonistic pulls are clear.

While social psychological research does not shed light on how an attorney can most effectively practice the art of organizing and making critical choices in presenting a coherent case, it does implicitly provide a method for comparing alternative trial strategies.  Suppose, for example, in a given case, an attorney has two or three different overall strategies that could be used, but is uncertain about which strategy would be most successful.  Time and resources allowing, the attorney could adopt the behavioral scientist's favorite tactic and test them.   A dress rehearsal of each of the alternative strategies could be presented to separate samples of twenty or thirty persons drawn from the population.  By asking the right questions of the "jurors," insight into the relative efficacy of the alternative available strategies could be obtained.  If lawyers videotaped their dress rehearsal, many advantages in case preparation could accrue from this method.  The tapes could be presented in a more methodologically sophisticated, counterbalanced order.  The attorneys could observe their own performances.  Specific portions of the tape could be altered and retested.

With or without videotape, the method of pretesting occasional cases on "jurors" would be most advantageous.  Lawyers rarely get detailed feedback from the ultimate decision makers; the feedback is usually limited to a verdict, and with only that the lawyer cannot identify with any precision what was done right and what was done wrong.  While the ultimate contingency in a trial is the jury's verdict, the lawyer is usually shaped instead by colleagues and professors, who necessarily do not know as much about what convinces juries as do juries.  Some lawyers sometimes use non-lawyer spouses or friends as sounding boards, which helps, and sometimes they question jurors after the verdict is delivered.  Using mock juries drawn from the same population as actual juries frees trial lawyers to be shaped by the people whose responses actually count.  This would also free the

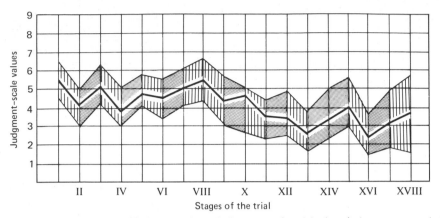

Figure 5.1. The course of judgments through the stages of a trial. Jury judgments are scaled from 1 (certain that the defendant is not liable for damages) through 9 (certain the defendant is liable). The solid center line represents the median judgment at each stage; the width of the figure shows quartile deviations above and below the median. The barred portion shows the effect of evidence for the defendant; the gray portion, that for the plaintiff. These data from a very early study show the seesaw effects of the adversarial process. Alternating presentations by plaintiff and defense push the jury's judgments back and forth. Note how the defense's cross-examination of the plaintiff's second witness hurt the defense. The zig-zag pattern is not balanced, but has an overall trend in it; by the end of the trial the defense has gained ground. (Weld and Danzig, 1938)

**Key to Figure 5.1**

Stages:
     I. Plaintiff opening statement
    II. Defense opening statement
   III. Direct examination of the plaintiff
   IV. Cross-examination of the plaintiff by the defense
    V. Direct examination of the plaintiff first witness
   VI. Cross-examination of plaintiff first witness
  VII. Direct examination of plaintiff second witness
 VIII. Cross-examination of plaintiff second witness
   IX. Direct examination of defense first witness
    X. Cross-examination of defense first witness
   XI. Direct examination of defense second witness
  XII. Cross-examination of defense second witness
 XIII. Direct examination of defense third witness
 XIV. Cross-examination of defense third witness
  XV. Rebuttal testimony for plaintiff
 XVI. Defense summation
XVII. Plaintiff summation
XVIII. Judge's charge

lawyers to experiment with inventive, novel strategies in a forum less risky than an actual trial.  If a strategy worked they could employ it at trial; if not, it could be discarded without serious cost.

We have suggested that more and less effective advocacy methods exist and can be identified; and, indeed, many lawyers do try to perfect their advocacy skills.  With the advice of trial tactics textbooks, law school mock trials, behavioral research findings, and the advice of colleagues, they attempt to identify the right speech style and the right amount of eye contact, to adeptly control witnesses, and so on, and try to become increasingly competent, polished, and skilled, until they perform with unerring aplomb.  But there is a little-appreciated danger in being too good.  Aronson, Willerman, and Floyd (1966) found that persons appearing to be of superior competence are liked even more after a minor blunder or pratfall.  Thus, a minor flaw makes a person better liked; and because people who are liked by their audiences are more influential sources of attitude-altering communications (Efran, 1974; Landy and Aronson, 1969; Osgood and Tannenbaum, 1955), a less perfect lawyer will be a more persuasive one.  The danger of being too good and the cure for it, however, exist only for the highly competent. Persons of average competence decline in attractiveness after a pratfall.  Before staging a stumble or spilling coffee all over themselves, attorneys should first be certain that they are perceived by jurors as highly, perhaps excessively, competent.

## BARGAINING AND NEGOTIATION

As we indicated earlier, the bulk of disputes resolved by the law and lawyers are not resolved through adjudication.  In their classic studies of civil suits, Franklin, Channin, and Mark (1961) found that fewer than 2% of the suits filed were ultimately settled by a court verdict; and of criminal convictions, Newman (1956) found that fewer than 7% resulted from trial court verdicts.  Subsequent patterns seem not to have changed.  The President's Commission on Law Enforcement and Administration of Justice (1967), examining criminal cases in a number of states and federal courts, found an average of only 13% of the convictions resulting from trials.  Only 8.4% of the cases filed in federal district courts in 1973 reached trial; the rest were settled out of court. Clearly, the majority of a lawyer's "trial" work is not persuasion in the courtroom but bargaining in the conference room. Knowledgeable litigants do not expect or hope or even want to go to trial; lawyers are sometimes even chosen for their reputations as effective negotiators.

It is, therefore, a stunning paradox, a failure of rationality, that when the public imagines a lawsuit it thinks of a trial; that the books written on effective lawyering, trial practice courses taught in law schools, and research done on lawyering processes are disproportionately concerned with trials to the neglect of bargaining. And yet this is not entirely illogical. As shall soon become clear, the trial remains the ultimate threat in negotiation: settle or we will see you in court. Thus, attorneys who are unwilling or unable or afraid to go to trial, will be unable to bargain successfully.

Why is bargaining used as extensively as it is? Because, generally, out-of-court settlement is advantageous to all concerned. It resolves issues faster than waiting for trial; gets defendants out of jail sooner and with lighter sentences (a benefit if they are actually guilty); gives prosecutors astronomical conviction rates; ensures plaintiffs they will recover some damages; ensures civil defendants they will not have to pay as much in damages as they would if they lost a court verdict; saves lawyers (and clients) the effort, time, and expense required for the preparation of an actual trial; allows lawyers and clients to retain control over case outcomes (which they give up once the decision is placed in the hands of a judge or jury); and reduces the court's caseload and ensures that the court spends its time only on the hardest cases (Pollack, 1975; Naythons, 1973; Ross, 1970; Cole, 1975). Judges encourage litigants to settle; lawyers find it more profitable to settle. Never mind for the moment that it may vitiate complete justice; bargaining provides a reward for nearly everyone, and if it stopped, the courts as presently constituted would be crushed by the nearly tenfold increase in the weight of the docket.

The distinction between "bargaining" and "negotiation" is often unclear, and for our purposes is unimportant. Stevens (1963), however, proposed the distinction that all exchange transactions involve the striking of a bargain, that is, the exchange of information about the terms of the transaction. Negotiation occurs when information is exchanged over and above that pertaining to the terms of the transaction and whether the terms are accepted or rejected.

The structure of bargaining situations is worthy of consideration. Whereas a trial is essentially a pure competition, zero-sum, all-or-none game, bargaining is a mixed-motive game—advocates are engaged in a transaction that simultaneously calls for competition and cooperation. Whereas in a trial disputants' outcomes are perfectly negatively correlated, in a bargaining situation they are not simply competing over conflicting interests, they must cooperate to achieve a mutually rewarding outcome. Kelley and Thibaut (1969) treat bargaining as a joint problem-solving venture, a conjunctive task whose solution requires joint agreement. The parties must both trust each other enough to exchange information vital to reaching agreement, and distrust each other enough so that they withhold information that the other side could use to dominate the bargain.

Unlike other social exchanges, the lawyers are unlikely to leave the bargaining field. Their role is to remain in the adversary relationship; alternative transactions are limited essentially to moving to a courtroom, a generally unattractive alternative (a low comparison level for alternatives exists, to use Thibaut and Kelley's [1959] terminology). The heavy use of bargaining tends to expose the myth that lawyers are essentially adversarial in their relations or work to maintain conflict. Lawyers benefit by being cooperative, by recognizing a mutual problem to be solved. Lawyers are sometimes (perhaps often) in a more adversarial relationship with their clients (trying to persuade them to accept a settlement offer) than with their institutional "adversaries." Indeed, a more realistic concern about the quality of justice is the lack of adversarial conflict (that is, due process) among lawyers and its replacement by routinized settlement-making (Blumberg, 1967; Cole, 1975; Downie, 1971).

The cooperativeness component of negotiations among attorneys is most evident in bargaining between prosecution and defense lawyers. They bargain not only for guilty pleas, but for bail, changes in charges, and sentencing, all subject to the approval (cooperation) of the judge. Negotiated pleas are so institutionalized and the respective "adversaries" so dependent upon each other to reach their respective goals, that they will share critical information about the case that likely would lead to defeat in court, because it is helpful to settlement. Each side knows the information may not be used against the other in court; to violate this tacit agreement would mean a breakdown of future accomodations. The defense needs future cooperation not only in reaching future settlements, but in obtaining police information on cases, access to the defendant in jail, and favors in bail setting. The prosecutor needs the defense lawyer's trust to dispose of future cases smoothly. Both profit from cooperation; thus more information is exchanged more freely between them (Blumberg, 1967; Alschuler, 1975) than otherwise would be.

The structure of the outcomes being bargained for in civil cases is illustrated in Figure 5.2. The assumption underlying a negotiation, and its necessary condition, is that a range of values exists that both parties prefer over no settlement. This range of values is called the *settlement range* or *contract zone*. In Figure 5.2, Defendant $A$ is willing to offer a settlement as high, if necessary, as $A$'s resistance point, $P_A$. Plaintiff $B$ is willing to accept an amount as low as, but no lower than, $B$'s resistance point, $P_B$. $A$ will be pleased to pay anything less than $P_A$ (the less, the better); $B$ would be happy to receive anything above $P_B$ (the more, the better). The resistance points mark the critical limits for the disputants, and only the range between them is set-

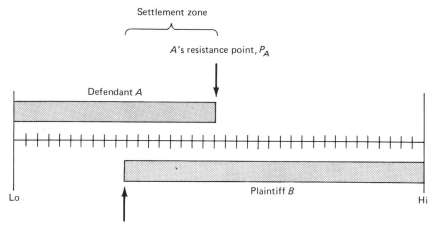

Figure 5.2. Structure of bargaining between plaintiff and defense. The range of possible settlements runs from very low (zero) to very high amounts. Each party to the negotiation has a "resistance point," the highest (for the defense) or lowest (plaintiff) each is willing to go. Each side would like to know and tries to discover what the other side's resistance point is, but can never be certain of it (compare with the dialogue in Table 5.2). If a settlement is to be reached, it must fall between the two resistance points, in the area known as the settlement zone.

tlement territory. If their individual ranges do not overlap, there will be no settlement. Among the most vital information either party can obtain is the other party's resistance point; it is carefully hidden information. On the contrary, $A$ wants $B$ to think $P_A$ is less than it is ("This is as high as I can go; I cannot offer more"), and $B$ wants $A$ to think $P_B$ is more than it is ("No way can I accept so low an offer; you'll simply have to do better").

This structure is, of course, an oversimplification. It portrays only one dimension (money) when in reality negotiations and the parties engaged in them may be responding to complex multiple dimensions. Not only may several material dimensions (money, benefits, control of land) be differently affected by alternative offers, but symbolic payoffs (prestige, honor, saving face) may also be involved (e.g., Gallo, Funk, and Levine, 1969; Brown, 1968, 1971). Nevertheless, the unidimensional dollar dimension is not a bad oversimplification. Considerable evidence exists showing that a variety of other variables are washed out by strong material stakes. Individual differences among bargainers fade when payoff matrices are strong enough, interactions last longer, and situations become more complex (Terhune, 1968, 1970; Uejio and Wrightsman, 1967; Wrightsman, Davis, et al., 1967; Rapoport and Chammah, 1965). (Also see Wrightsman, O'Connor, and Baker, 1972.)

Even some of the more disturbing laboratory findings, such as the reduced ability to reach mutually rewarding agreements with increasing ability to threaten and punish an opponent (Deutsch and Krauss, 1960) can disappear when real material payoffs are at stake (Gallo, 1968). Moreover, lawyers are professional bargainers. The "rational person model" of bargaining and negotiation probably applies as well to them as to anyone.

In criminal plea bargaining the defense has a guilty plea to offer in exchange for the prosecution's concession to (a) reduce the charges, (b) reduce the sentence associated with the guilty plea, (c) combine several similar charges into one concurrent charge, or (d) drop some of the charges (Newman, 1956). To try to win a settlement favorable to their own side, the prosecution will initially list many charges, some of them more serious than the prosecution can really hope to win if the case goes to trial. The defense may try to sound serious about going to trial (Alschuler, 1968; Cole, 1970). These stances provide bargaining chips to both sides while simultaneously applying pressure that will motivate settlement. In deciding what to settle for, prosecutors consider such factors as the strength of their case, their caseload, the harshness of the law, and the judge's likely sentence (Alschuler, 1968). These factors are not lost on defense attorneys in estimating what bargain can be struck with the prosecution.

The study of bargaining and negotiation by social psychologists (see generally, Rubin and Brown, 1976) has most often taken the form of experiments with the "Prisoner's Dilemma Game" in laboratory settings. In terms of external validity, that is, generalizability, these are perhaps the most suspect studies in social psychology (Apfelbaum, 1974; Gallo, 1966, 1968; Kelley, 1965). The laboratory bargaining games differ markedly from the situation in which lawyers bargain, and in critical ways. The former impose limits on the bargainers' response options and other variables that rarely constrain lawyers. In real negotiations lawyers can gather more resources with which to do bargaining battle, seek more information with which to apply leverage, imply future contingencies on other cases, stall, threaten to raise the amount of claims, bring reputations and power into the bargaining session with them, almost always have future interaction as a likely possibility, and so on. In Prisoner's Dilemma Games, experimental subjects have no real symbolic or material outcomes at stake. The major contingencies for which people enter bargaining sessions are absent. We will therefore place relatively little reliance on this research. And yet, some of the major PDG findings about bargaining strategies are surprisingly convergent with the findings of nonlaboratory researchers and professional negotiators (Gulliver, 1973; Schelling, 1960; Ross, 1970).

Generally, and it seems to be a reliable generalization, successful bargaining strategy involves making extreme initial offers, well above (or below) one's resistance point (Chertkoff and Conley, 1967); making concessions few, small (Komorita and Brenner, 1968), reciprocal, and each one rationalized, explained, justified on some basis other than the mere pursuit of agreement. Bear in mind that making and responding to offers and counter-offers is not all that is happening. A certain amount of outcome control (settlements, threat to go to trial) is bolstered by enormous amounts of information control. Each offer and counter-offer is also a message by which senders try to suggest that they are close to their resistance point and/or will not or need not go further, and through which receivers try to discern what the other side's position *really* is.  Attributions of the other side's position and intentions are inferred from available, limited, distorted information (Kelley and Thibaut, 1969).  Everything is a message and a clue; each side continually gives and conceals information.  For example, no one really wishes to make the opening suggestion of a settlement.  That may be interpreted as eagerness to settle because of a weak position.  Opening offers are not usually intended to be accepted; they are communications about where bargaining may begin (Ross, 1970).  Each concession must be made to look like what it is not, its real purpose concealed by its maker and read by its receiver (Schelling, 1960).  The norm of reciprocity, the making of reciprocal concessions (Gouldner, 1960; Ross, 1970), will not operate if one side tries unilateral concessions expecting the other side to come around (Solomon, 1960).  Two or more consecutive concessions by one party would be interpreted as indicating a weak position.  The negotiation could then easily be dominated by the recipient of the concession or break down and result in a trial.

Attributions are inferred not only from actions, from statements about what evidence the other side has, from its definition of the facts of the case and the likely outcome of a trial, but also from cues such as inconsistent behavior (statements that this is your last offer when it turns out not to be, threats that are not carried out), what it is that vacillation precedes or the opponent shows conflict about (is it to break off versus pursue the negotiation [in which case they may be very near their resistance point], or is it to make demands versus make concessions [in which case there probably is more room to bargain]?)  (Kelley and Thibaut, 1969; Shure, Meeker, and Hansford, 1965).

Experienced lawyers sometimes are able to extract valuable information from opponents without the opponents' notice.  Consider the dialogue in Table 5.2.  An experienced lawyer and an inexperienced lawyer were in the early stages of a negotiation.  After their colloquy, each reviewed the dialogue and explained to researchers what he was trying to accomplish with each remark and how he interpreted the other's responses.  Note how a question the young lawyer took for small talk told the older lawyer that he was dealing with an opponent who had not recently been in court nor was planning to be.

Meta-norms of how to engage each other always operate (Homans,

**Table 5.2.   Portions of a negotiation between older, experienced Attorney A and younger, inexperienced Attorney B.  Each lawyer's remarks (the center two columns) in the negotiation are accompanied by that lawyer's later comments, explaining how the opposing attorney's remark was interpreted and why the remark was made (the outermost columns).**

Courtesy of Gary Bellow and Jeanne Kettleson.

| Lawyer A's Comments | Lawyer A | Lawyer B | Lawyer B's Comments |
|---|---|---|---|
| I thought it best to begin with a strong line—a close to maximum demand and a non adversarial, frank, we're just professionals posture. | Look–let me be direct with you– unless you're willing to pay something close to the 5,000, we're asking, there's no sense in us talking. | | |
| | | And what about our counterclaim? | I didn't know whether to believe him or not—he's a very experienced lawyer. I thought I'd get a fix on exactly what he had in mind. |
| That seems a settlement-oriented response and I decided to continue taking a strong tack. | You'd have to dismiss it. I don't blame you for filing it, but if we ever gave in on something like that, we'd be mired in suits. | | |
| | | Well—I am authorized to settle both claims. We don't want to go to trial if we can avoid it any more than you do. | This seemed very plausible, given the weaknesses I knew about our claim. I decided not to put his back against the wall on what might be a matter of company policy. |
| I was glad to hear that settlement was possible, but I couldn't tell how far they'd go rather than try the case. | I don't know. It might be interesting. Do you know who's sitting next month? | | |

**Table 5.2.**  (*Continued*)

| Lawyer A's Comments | Lawyer A | Lawyer B | Lawyer B's Comments |
|---|---|---|---|
| I decided to probe his trial preparation and experience. | | | |
| | | No–I don't. | I don't know why he asked me that. Maybe just lawyer talk. |
| Might be a long way to preparing for trial. Although I usually like to make the first offer, he seemed sufficiently inexperienced to place this initiative on him. | Well, what have you got in mind? | | |
| | | I'm not sure. It depends on you, of course. What's your bottom line? | I wasn't sure what to ask for–5,000, 4,000. I preferred to react to his suggestion and work from there. |
| It's my policy to make small concessions always based in an apparent reason for going to that point. A drop of 1,000 from a claim could be a sensible trade-off for litigation costs and collection problems. | We'd take 4,000–if it's paid immediately on signing the agreement. | | |
| | | And dismissal of our counterclaims? | |
| It was clear that he was interested in offers by us that involved payment. My hunch was he was authorized to settle the case without any payment by us. | And dismissal of your counterclaims. | | |

**Table 5.2.** (*Continued*)

| Lawyer A's Comments | Lawyer A | Lawyer B | Lawyer B's Comments |
|---|---|---|---|
| | | That's way too much. We're entitled to some payment of our claim. | I think this was a mistake. It made me seem much too interested. I guess I was bothered by the lack of clarity about whether the offers included all charges or just their claim against us. I also probably didn't come back hard enough on the way I phrased my next comment. "Some" payment seems too much like a token to me. |
| I wasn't sure whether he would insist on a few hundred dollars or had real doubts about his case. I decided to reassert my original offer. | I just can't do that. I'd never be able to explain it to my client. Can you make the payment or not? | | |
| | | I'm afraid not—we would settle for dismissal of both claims, though. | This would certainly satisfy my client and seemed a lot to get, given how firm he appeared. |
| That was too big a concession to be a final offer. I decided to stay firm. | Not a chance. We're out $5,000. I can't go back to my client with a piece of paper on a $5,000 loss. | | |
| | | I have the same problem. Be reasonable. What will you accept? | When he didn't budge, I figured we really weren't in the same ball park and that he really had meant what he said at the beginning. |

**Table 5.2.** *(Continued)*

| Lawyer A's Comments | Lawyer A | Lawyer B | Lawyer B's Comments |
|---|---|---|---|
| It seemed time to come down again—not very far—and in the context of a projected image of an unwilling client. | I probably could get down another 1,000—but that's it—and I'm really not sure about that. | | |
| | | I'm afraid we really can't get an agreement then. I can't go above $2,000. | It was either offer the most we would pay or risk not settling. This was just carrying out my client's wishes, given what I had to work with. I was glad I did because my adversary may be able to convince his client to come down. |
| I figured that was the limit of his authority, but I didn't want to jump too fast. I planned to return from the phone call, jockey a little more and then not too enthusiastically accept it. It always makes sense to make him feel he did about as well as he could. | That's really low. But I'll try. Let me make a call and maybe we can work it out. | | |
| | | Fine. | |

1961; Donnell, 1970), and their violations often result in breakdown of negotiations. Such meta-norms are illustrated by Ikle's (1964) description of a code of bargaining conduct for international negotiators: the status of participants should not be disputed, concessions should be reciprocated, and lies, emotionalism, rudeness, and bargaining in bad faith are to be avoided. For lawyers we might add that participants must share a specialized body of knowledge, not act in self-interest in making professional decisions, and deal impersonally with their clients (Donnell, 1970). Norms relating to the substance of the agreement that "ought" to be reached are more likely raised when both sides have power and are tempted to use it, or by the weaker side in the negotiation.

Attorneys not only have a probability of future interaction, but have past relationships with each other that influence the negotiation (Apfelbaum, 1974), and a past that has constructed a reputation as to bargaining style and effectiveness (Gulliver, 1973). The reputation tells opponents what behavior and outcome they might expect. Some lawyers are regarded as "soft touches" (relatively easy to manipulate because they do not know the value of their cases), others as "tough settlers" (knowledgeable about their own and adversaries' cases and having the skill to win). Some start with astronomical demands that they quickly reduce because they are anxious to avoid trial. Others are "one-figure" bargainers, who simply state the sum they wish to obtain and adhere strictly to it. The "ultimatum" bargainer threatens that a failure immediately to agree to a settlement will result in an increase in demands, say, an additional $1,000 per week until a settlement is agreed to or the trial begins. Obviously, these varying strategies may have differential effectiveness, as discussed above, and reputations regarding lawyers' characteristic choices of strategy affect the way adversary negotiators will behave. To add weight to future negotiations, to build a reputation for credibility when making (implied or stated) threats, lawyers may occasionally have to do what is "just never done" to show they must be taken seriously.

Williams et al. (1976) attempted to identify the characteristics of "effective, average, and ineffective" bargainers through a questionnaire asking attorneys to rate colleagues with whom they had negotiated. It is unclear, however, what the definition of effective is. Does it mean a colleague whom you felt good after negotiating with (because you did well), or one you disliked (because that opponent was uncooperative and beat you severely)? Also, were these the "characteristics" of the negotiators or the attributions of the perceiver based on behavior that may have been compelled by situational variables not under the lawyer's control, such as the structure of the payoff matrix or the location of resistance points (cf. Kelley, 1966), or might the behavior be emanating from a strategy of deception that ultimately was effective because the other side still has not seen through it?

Ross (1970) notes a variety of other variables affecting negotiations—number of parties involved, balance of power between bargaining parties, number and clarity of issues, continuity of negotiations, available alternatives in the event of negotiation failure. A negotiation whose failure to reach settlement will result in a new negotiating session will not be taken as seriously as one whose failure will result in a trial. Obviously, a lawyer who is afraid to go to trial (owing either to personal lack of skill or weakness in the case) will be in a weak bargaining position because settlement is the only realistic alternative.

Much of what we said about persuasion and social perception applies in bargaining also, but here the "audience" is one's opponent. Again, a lawyer tries to appear credible, expert, and trustworthy; tries to paint a linguistic reality that will bring about a favorable settlement (on language choice in negotiating, see also Gallo, 1966, 1968; Gallo and Sheposh, 1971), and produce appropriate attributions as we have discussed above.

In brief, bargaining and negotiation depend upon the construction of socially defined realities, actual costs and rewards, norms, and strategies associated with the timing, amount, and justification of offers and counter-offers. With all of this involved in a negotiation, one can imagine the chagrin of a lawyer who finds that an opponent has been bargaining in bad faith; for example, the settlement was less the goal of the negotiation than was delay. Indeed, sometimes a case is such that both lawyer and client know they have a losing case and simply wish to delay the resolution as long as possible. A "victory" in such a context is maximization of the time required to lose.

Judges not only "encourage" settlements, but may subtly threaten altered outcomes if a bargain is not reached, such as the threat of a more severe sentence if plea bargaining is not successfully and expeditiously concluded (Dean, 1974; Thomas, 1973–1974). Of course, such judicial action is of questionable legality, and judges usually try to involve themselves only subtly and at a distance from the negotiations. In some jurisdictions, however, judges are formally involved in conferences designed to reach bargains (McIntyre and Lippman, 1970).

Though the generally competitive nature of trial and negotiation work has often been noted, as have the social psychological effects of competition, such as reduced information sharing, negative affect, and decreased cohesiveness (Crombag, 1966; Deutsch, 1949; Grossack, 1954; Raven and Eachus, 1963), often overlooked are the highly positive effects of intergroup competition coupled with intragroup cooperation. This is the "team-competitive" (Smead, 1972) situation common in legal practice, where a firm (team) works against another on a given case. Such a reward structure promotes strong within-group cohesiveness, high information-sharing, high morale, and positive affect. It also heightens the salience of boundary definition—we (our firm) versus them (Dunn and Goldman, 1966). This effect is much like the concept of superordinate goals (Sherif, Harvey, White, Hood, and Sherif, 1961); people who would be competitive with each other on smaller goals become highly cohesive and cooperative when their joint efforts are required for the achievement of greater goals.

We have discussed the whys and hows of bargaining as though it were a fact of life to be accepted and negotiated successfully. We should not fail to recognize that within a society's system of justice there are costs and benefits which ought to be noted. While keeping the courts from collapsing under the weight of the potential caseload (cf. Heumann, 1975), expediting the disposition of cases, and individualizing the law, bargaining may dilute justice. Especially in criminal plea bargaining, the innocent may be penalized. Because they fear the outcome of a trial, they sometimes plead guilty to crimes they did not commit; those who do insist on a trial may spend more time in jail awaiting trial and receiving harsh treatment from the prosecution and the court for their lack of cooperation. And bargaining has become so routinized that the defendant may receive less than zealous representation by his lawyer (Blumberg, 1967; Cole, 1975). Though bargaining seems less objectionable in resolving civil disputes, even there it may pose a threat to justice. Friedman and Macaulay (1977) have summed up these costs and benefits of bargaining as well as any:

> Bargaining was the dominant theme in our picture. The studies showed logrolling, settlements to avoid litigation, plea bargaining and even tacit bargains on the borders of bribery. Paradoxically, bargaining seems to offer both the benefits of tailoring

results to individual situations and of mass processing, it is faster to bargain, than to try and appeal a case.  Since in a bargain all those who participate are likely to get something, one avoids the risk of losing everything–a risk inherent in the zero-sum nature of most legal procedures.  Insofar as people must negotiate rather than impose their will on others, they must tolerate at least some diversity of conduct.  Those acting to benefit others have the satisfaction of knowing that they have or will be compensated.  However, there are good bargains and bad ones.  Any system resting on negotiation runs into all of the problems of inequalities of bargaining power and skill.  And some will find it distasteful to consider that the product the legal system is supposed to produce—justice—is transformed into a product to be bought and sold.  Those whose rights have been abridged are entitled to full vindication rather than the half loaf they get because of the unpredictability of the outcome of litigation, the expenses of the process and a discount for prompt payment. . . . On the other hand, perhaps one who has committed a serious crime should serve a substantial sentence in prison rather than benefit from a plea bargain in reward for testifying against his partners in crime. On a broader level, a system in which negotiation is the predominant style is one in which carrying out rational plans through law will be difficult if not impossible. [p. 190]

## SELECTION, EDUCATION, SOCIALIZATION, ROLE -TAKING, AND THE SHAPING, MAINTENANCE, AND MODIFICATION OF LAWYERS' BEHAVIOR

We began this chapter by alluding to some of the tasks lawyers perform and the skills required to perform those tasks.  We will close by asking how a society, a profession, or even an individual consumer of legal services can assure that these tasks are performed well rather than incompetently or dishonestly.  Indeed, how can one even distinguish good quality from poor quality lawyering, know a "good" lawyer from a "bad" lawyer?  In 1970 there were 350,000 lawyers in the U.S., with law schools turning out 33,000 more each year (Friedman, 1977).  Consider the diversity of lawyers and their tasks.  They may be government lawyers (e.g., regulatory agency lawyers, prosecutors), corporate counsel, public defenders or "legal services" attorneys, or lawyers in private practice. They may work in large firms, in which case they usually come from upper middle class families, attended the better universities, and handle the cases of wealthy clients; or they may work in small firms or solo practices, in which case they usually come from poorer, working class, ethnic backgrounds, attended nonnational, proprietary, or night law schools, and have clients who are not wealthy. The relative openness of the legal profession historically has made it a favorite arena of advancement for the children of immigrants, but how far they may climb is limited (Carlin, 1962; Ladinsky, 1963).

Not only do they try cases and negotiate settlements, but even more so lawyers draw up legal documents (e.g., wills, contracts), give advice and counsel about alternative courses of action and offer predictions about the likely outcomes of various courses, arrange the sale and purchase of property (the single most frequent legal problem of adult Americans being the purchase of real property [Special Committee to Survey Legal Needs, 1976]), handle matters before government agencies, arrange trusts, advise on tax matters, provide business advice, protect clients from abuse by business people, or try to undo damage once it is done. Prosecuting attorneys have to screen cases and, on the basis of evidential (do we have a case?), pragmatic (are the best interests of society going to be served?), and organizational (can the prosecutor's office, courts, etc., afford to handle the case?) considerations (Miller, 1969), decide whether to go ahead with the prosecution. Few of the nation's lawyers are prepared to practice before the courts, and the decline continues. "Although a lawyer must be prepared to look like a gladiator, most of the time he assumes the role of advisor and negotiator" (Jacob, 1972, p. 67).

How can we tell when a lawyer who is doing any of these things is doing them well—that an attorney who is supplying advice is supplying good advice, or interviewing a client effectively, or adopting good strategies and tactics in negotiating or trying a case? This has been a remarkably neglected topic until very recently. The profession (indeed, any profession) has an interest in making sure that it is neglected: that definitions of quality are kept vague, that judgments about competence are made rarely and then only by fellow members of the profession, that the mystical realm of professional judgment be the first and final arbiter of the quality of services (Rosenthal, 1974; Lieberman, 1970).   Notwithstanding some consumer-oriented evaluations (Nader and Green, 1976) and some fairly helpful advice (Denenberg, 1974), the answer is that no one (including the profession) has any sound ideas on the subject.   Work in the area is just beginning (Brickman and Lempert, 1976), in response to several changes in the legal services delivery system and its environment that have brought both pressures and potential for change.

These pressures come from at least three directions.  While lawyers have long been considered to have questionable ethics, evidenced by sociological findings of widespread ethical violations (e.g., Carlin, 1966; Handler, 1967) and by public opinion (e.g., Missouri Bar–Prentice-Hall, 1963), criticisms about ethics, and competence as well, have now surfaced from within the profession (e.g., Burger, 1974; Kaufman, 1975a, 1975b; Project '76, *Juris Doctor*, 1976).  Moreover, the frequency of professional malpractice actions against attorneys has been increasing (Luvera, 1975).  A second source of pressure comes from the growing consumer movement, which began with Corvairs and has spread to all areas of American life including lawyering (Nader and Green, 1976; Nader, 1976).  And third, two concurrent revolutions in the legal services delivery system: federally funded legal services for the poor, accompanied by the requirement for an empirical evaluation of the services as a matter of public law (The Legal Services Corporation Act, 1974); and legal services plans (sponsored by trade and credit unions, bar associations, and consumers groups) to bring legal services to the middle class.

Arrival at the threshold of a delivery system that would dramatically increase the public's access to lawyers has brought consumers, providers, and sponsors face to face with the problem of quality of services.   Increased access and utilization may exacerbate existing problems of competence and integrity; and the advent of third-party payment for services may repeat unfortunate experiences in the delivery of health care: costs up, quality down.  One reaction by the legal services community has been to plan research, innovation, and evaluation to improve the delivery system in all regards (see Brickman and Lempert, 1976), and particularly to grapple with the problem of quality: what is it, how do we measure it, how do we assure it (Carlson, 1976; Rosenthal, 1976; Saks and Benedict, 1976)?

Research in this area is at a very young stage—few of the projects in this new wave have been completed; therefore little has been learned as yet. But some broad outlines may be sketched.

Saks and Benedict (1976), drawing from analogous work on health care systems, point out that attention can be directed to the *outcome* of a legal transaction (e.g., verdict, settlement), the *processes* (behaviorally, what the service providers do), or the *structure* within which that transaction occurs (e.g., organizational environment, background characteristics of the service providers). Quality, from this viewpoint, means knowing what structures facilitate the processes known to effect the desired outcomes, and executing those processes within those structures. Assessment of quality within this framework ideally would mean explicit evaluation of these components; but since these things are not yet known, implicit assessment by peer (or consumer) review panels is the technique most feasible at this stage. Rosenthal (1976) points out that existing methods of evaluating the competence of lawyers are of this or lesser sorts. He identifies methods that rely upon evaluations of such structural variables as (a) quality of training received or performance on certification examinations or (b) the lawyer's status or reputation. Another method focuses on outcome variables such as (c) results of advocacy. And yet other methods examine process variables for (d) remaining above minimal standards of competent, nonnegligent conduct or, as Rosenthal (and Saks and Benedict) favor at this stage of the art, (e) the development of systematic and detailed evaluations of the way lawyers perform those functions that are central to effectively providing the services they offer.

Research by the Educational Testing Service has so far established that Law School Admissions Test (LSAT) scores predict performance in law school and on bar examinations with predictive validity coefficients of about .50 (Carlson and Wertz, 1976), and they are working toward developing measures of performance in law practice. While ETS's major interest is in seeing how well existing tests predict that performance and in developing better tests (perhaps non–paper-and-pencil tests), their performance measures will contribute to the evaluations Rosenthal has recommended.

Thus far we have addressed measurement and evaluation of the quality of legal services. What actions might be taken to improve quality?   Let us first briefly consider current practices, which may reveal some of the profession's assumptions about the determinants of ethical and competent behavior.  To become an attorney (see generally, Warkov and Zelan, 1965; Thorne, 1973) one must cross the hurdles of college, the LSAT, other admissions criteria, law school, and bar examinations, and then be admitted to the bar and to practice (beyond passing the bar examination, there are some vague criteria such as being of "good moral character").  Once in practice, lawyers are expected to adhere to codes of ethics and professional conduct and are subject to the sanctions of bar ethics and grievance committees and ultimately to civil suits for "professional negligence" as punishment for seriously unethical or incompetent conduct. (Any other controls over lawyers' behavior, as by colleagues in their firm or by clients in the office or the marketplace, are informal).  That such a system has been less than satisfactory—indeed, has prompted vociferous criticism of lawyers' performance from within and without the profession—should not be surprising to organizational social psychologists.

The structures and processes used to control the legal profession rely primarily on dispositional characteristics of attorneys-in-the-making.   Persons with particular characteristics (academic ability, knowledge, "good moral character," and so on) are filtered into the profession.   In law school they are socialized into the language and values of the profession, including a post-Watergate course in ethics; or at least the socialization process is begun.   The implicit theory here is that good and able people will behave well as professionals, so such people must be selected; and that particular behavior can be programmed by planting particular cognitions and cognitive styles ("learning to think like a lawyer"), so professional legal education is the answer.  Young lawyers are then expected to go into practice and behave competently.   The failure of input control to affect the quality of services has already been recognized in medicine (Derbyshire, 1969).  While specific skills and abilities do tend to remain consistent and predictable over time, it has been appreciated by social psychologists for a considerable period of time that complex social behaviors do not (Mischel, 1969), nor do attitudes have much effect on behavior (Deutsher, 1973), particularly if the attitudes are acquired in one setting (law school) and the behavior implied by the attitudes is called forth in a different setting (practice). Indeed, the classic study of complex social behavior and its nonpredictability from traits or other dispositional characteristics was concerned with "honesty" (Hartshorne and May, 1928). "Good moral *character*," even if it could be operationalized and measured, would not predict ethical behavior.

The legal profession has been suffering from the tendency to make dispositional attributions—honest behavior is perceived as emanating from a parallel internal trait—"good moral character," and certain classes of people who have such traits are sought. When the search fails, the seekers persist in the dispositional fallacy, and in discouragement conclude that  although they "know that some men are honest and some are dishonest," the behavior must flow from "private, personal standards" (Maru, 1972, p. 32).

Such behavior is more powerfully influenced by situational variables: more or less immediate contingencies, expectations of an interaction, social comparison with peers, and so on; and by person-by-situation interactions (Bem and Allen, 1974; Mischel, 1973). Scant attention is paid to these variables or to any situational or organizational variables, and yet it is these variables that the bulk of social psychological research indicates could be most effective in shaping and maintaining behavior (Saks and Benedict, 1976). It is not so surprising, after all, that the values learned years ago in law school have little influence under the weight of heavy caseloads that lead to neglect; pressures from clients to win at any price, of economics to earn a living, and from other lawyers to be "cooperative"; an occupational environment wherein the shedding of ethics that allows for success is widely tolerated if not encouraged, and where whistle-blowers invite assaults on their own professional survival. It is not accidental that professional fraternities such as law and medicine are infamous for their protection of unethical or incompetent colleagues. Even then, the only real situational sanctions that exist for lawyers are grievance committees and malpractice litigation—both being sanctions that require extremely high thresholds for activation. Conduct must be egregious before these machineries are set into motion. Disbarments have never exceeded 34 per 100,000 lawyers (Carlin, 1962; Smith, 1961; Kidney, 1977). Yet Supreme Court Chief Justice Burger suggests that as many as half of the trial bar are incompetent. ("Inept Lawyers," 1977.)

## SUMMARY

Lawyers are the professionals who come closest to being professional applied social psychologists. Their trial work involves attitude change, which is conceptualized as a source sending a message through a channel to a recipient. Research has been conducted on each of these components. A special task of trial attorneys is to effect the attribution of responsibility—having the factfinder make dispositional or situational attributions; this may be done through the careful use of language, noncommon effects, defensive attribution, and actor–observer effects, among other methods. Lawyers also use social control of witnesses, from whom much of the case is drawn. Another major area of lawyering as applied social psychology is in bargaining and negotiation for pleas and settlements in civil cases. Finally, we consider lawyer selection, education, and socialization, and the maintenance and modification of the behavior of lawyers in the context of the controversial quality of American lawyering.

# 6
# The Defendant

In this chapter on the defendant we will discuss two topics of considerable legal and psychological significance: first, the problem of determining the state of mind of the perpetrator of a crime, illustrated in a review of the history of the insanity defense in American courts; second, the influence of the defendant's appearance, demeanor, and prior criminal record on the trial jury and judge.

## THE MENTAL STATE OF THE DEFENDANT

### Introduction

A crime is usually defined in the law by specifying a set of "elements" or conditions that must be true for the defendant to be found guilty and subject to punishment. These elements typically include specific *acts*, which are performed in certain *"attendant circumstances,"* while in a certain *state of mind*. For example, the elements of the crime of burglary might be (a) breaking and entering (the act), (b) into a dwelling house by night (the attendant circumstances), (c) with intent to commit a felony therein (the state of mind). The definitions of some crimes, for example murder, also include a specified *result* (the unlawful death of a human being), which must also be true. In order for a defendant to be convicted of a crime, all of the elements of the crime must be established by credible evidence beyond a reasonable doubt in the minds of the jurors or a judge.

The intentions or states of mind of persons involved are relevant to many crimes, civil wrongs committed against persons or their property, and the interpretation of contracts and wills. In this chapter we will concentrate on the question of whether the defendant behaved with an evil intention, *mens rea*, when performing a legally sanctioned act, *actus rea.* It is important to note that this is only one example from the large range of cases in which the law is concerned with the negligent, reckless, intentional, willful, knowing, fraudulent, malicious, or premeditated commission of an evil act. Furthermore, the legal system is concerned with the mental state of a criminal both in determining culpability or guilt and in meting out an appropriate disposition of the case. Should the convicted criminal be imprisoned, be detained in an institution for the mentally ill, or be freed, and what conditions should be attached to the treatment? We will not deal with these issues in this chapter.

In criminal law the courts have developed a series of working definitions to handle the concept of intent applied to various crimes. For example, if we consider the homicidal crimes (murder in the first degree, murder in the second degree, manslaughter), the same act, killing another person, is involved in very different crimes with very different penalties, depending on the mental state of the actor. To establish the crime of first degree murder in some circumstances the defendant must be proved to have performed the murderous act *and* to have performed it with deliberately *premeditated malice* aforethought.

The law goes further and provides a more detailed characterization of the mental-state elements, premeditation and malice. The following selection is taken from a judge's oral instructions to a jury in a murder case. It illustrates the manner in which the mental state elements are defined in a typical murder trial.

Murder is the unlawful killing of a human being with malice aforethought.

Such malice may be express or implied. It is express when there is manifested a deliberate intention unlawfully to take away the life of a fellow creature. It is implied when no considerable provocation appears, or when the circumstances attending the killing show an abandoned and malignant heart.

The law prohibits acts highly dangerous to human life that cause serious injury or death unless legal cause or excuse is shown. Malice aforethought, either express or implied, is manifested by the doing of such an act by a person who is able to comprehend this prohibition and his obligation to conform his conduct to it. . . . Malice does not require a preexisting hatred or enmity toward the person injured.

All murder perpetrated by any kind of wilful, deliberate, and premeditated killing is murder of the first degree. . . .

Murder of the second degree must be distinguished not only from murder of the first degree, but also from manslaughter. Manslaughter shortly will be defined for you, and you will note that an essential feature of that offense, which distinguishes it from murder, is that the killing be done without malice.

If the unlawful killing of a human being is done with malice aforethought, but without deliberation and premeditation, that is, without the wilful, deliberate, and premeditated intent to take life that is an essential element of first degree murder, then the offense is murder in the second degree. . . .

Thus, if you find that the defendant killed the deceased while conscious and with malice, you will return a verdict of murder. If you find that this murder was committed wilfully, deliberately, and with premeditation, you will find the murder to be of the first degree.  If you find, however, that the defendant's mental capacity was so diminished that he did not, or you have a reasonable doubt whether he did, premeditate, deliberate, or form an intent to kill, you will find the murder to be of the second degree.

Premeditation, deliberation, an intent to kill, and malice must be present for the killing to be first degree murder.

Malice is an essential element of either degree of murder. Therefore, if you find that the defendant did not harbor malice, or have a reasonable doubt whether he harbored malice, you cannot find him guilty of a higher offense than manslaughter.

Manslaughter is the unlawful killing of a human being without malice.  Two kinds of manslaughter, the definitions of which are pertinent here, are:

1. Voluntary manslaughter, an intentional killing in which the law, recognizing human frailty, permits the defendant to establish the lack of malice either by

a. Showing provocation such as to rouse the reasonable man to heat of passion or sudden quarrel.  When such provocation is shown, the law will presume that the defendant who acts in the heat of passion or on sudden quarrel, acts without malice.

  b. Showing that due to diminished capacity caused by mental illness, mental defect, or intoxication, the defendant did not attain the mental state constituting malice.

  2. Involuntary manslaughter is a killing in the commission of an unlawful act not amounting to a felony, or in the commission of a lawful act which might produce death in an unlawful manner, or without due caution and circumspection.

For our purposes there are two important aspects of the legal approach to the definition of mental state. First, there is an implicit assumption underlying our definitions of common law felonies that the guilty individual must freely choose to perform the evil act. Second, there is a practical assumption that jurors or judges can make sharp distinctions between cases which fall into the mens rea categories (malicious, premeditated, . . .) and those which do not.

Probably the most controversy about determining the criminal's state of mind surrounds the legal issue of the insanity defense. The issue of criminal responsibility is most dramatic in cases in which the accused presents a defense for an unlawful act based on an alleged mental condition that renders the accused unable fully to control his or her actions. The clearest cases of this defense arise when the defendant enters a plea of not guilty by reason of insanity. In the western legal tradition it has been conventional to exempt a person from criminal responsibility, regardless of the acts he or she performs, if that person is insane. The rationale for the insanity defense against criminal responsibility is that a person who is insane, mentally ill, driven by an irresistible impulse, or unable to distinguish right from wrong lacks the capacity for free choice. If a person does not behave by his or her free will, then that person does not exhibit the mens rea condition essential to the assignment of criminal responsibility. Since the attribution of guilt requires that both the evil act, actus rea, and evil mind, mens rea, conditions be established, the wrongdoer cannot be judged guilty in the case where he or she is insane.

  Again, the two implicit assumptions, free will and the existence of a method to assess its presence (a practical sanity test), underlie the legal conventions. These assumptions have a foundation in the view of the individual as a free agent, capable of choosing to act for good or for evil, which is central to the western Judeo-Christian religious tradition.   One major problem with these legal conventions is that modern scientific psychology rejects both basic assumptions.

The two major traditions in modern psychology, deriving from the work of Freud on the psychodynamics of personality and from learning theorists such as Pavlov and Skinner, are both "deterministic." The modern academic psychologist supposes that a scientific analysis of behavior is possible only because behavior is powerfully determined by an individual's genetic makeup, personal developmental history, and present environment.   Students of Freud place a heavy emphasis on developmental events, while learning theorists stress the immediate environment; but both agree that the notion of "free will" is a myth.

Furthermore, there is massive disagreement among psychologists over the proper assessment of mental states, and even the possibility of such assessment.   Probably the only focus of agreement is that all current assessment methods are unreliable and of little or no utility in the prediction and control of behavior (Mischel, 1968; Bandura, 1969; Meehl, 1954).   Thus we have a situation today where legal conventions conflict with scientific suppositions, and where there is confusion and disarray in the scientific community about useful directions to take to improve legal practice.   For the moment let us put aside these practical problems and examine the history of legal standards of insanity in America.   We shall return to the disagreements between and within the legal, psychological, and psychiatric professions when we discuss the role of the psychiatric expert and proposed reforms of the insanity defense.

## American Standards of Legal Insanity

The first legal test for insanity to be widely adopted in this country was the so-called McNaghten test.   This rule was based on the holding of a British court in the murder trial of Daniel McNaghten who was accused of killing the prime minister's secretary in an attempt to kill the prime minister himself.   Evidence was presented that McNaghten believed he was being persecuted by the Tories and that he intended to kill the man who was attempting to kill him.   In his defense he pleaded not guilty and argued that he was subject to morbid delusions. He was acquitted, and the case was the subject of a debate in the House of Lords by fifteen criminal judges. The product of the debate was a set of critical questions to be answered to determine whether a defendant is not guilty by reason of insanity. These rules state that a defendant cannot be found responsible for a crime if it is shown that he was suffering such "a defect of reason, from a disease of the mind, as not to know the nature and the quality of the act he was doing, or if he did know it, that he did not know he was doing what was wrong?"

McNaghten's defense and the House of Lord's debate involved an extensive review of psychiatric theory and practice in Europe in 1843. The results of this review are surprisingly (and perhaps embarrassingly) contemporary. The barristers and judges discovered a great variety of diverging medical opinion on the issue. Probably the clearest source of the McNaghten Rules is the so-called wild beast test articulated by British courts in 1724. This prescription held that a defendant would not be criminally responsible "if he could not distinguish good from evil more than a wild beast."

The McNaghten Rules were accepted in virtually every American jurisdiction. Given the obvious practical problem of applying them decisively and the opposition to their use from many schools of medical and psychological thought, alternative formulations were certain to emerge. One source of dissatisfaction with the McNaghten Rules is the implicit hypothesis that sane behavior is based on intellectual, rational activity. Insanity is a "defect of reason." In 1954, motivated by the McNaghten Rules' undervaluation of emotional and unconscious determinants of behavior, David Bazelon, Circuit Judge in the United States Court of Appeals for the District of Columbia, drafted the so-called Durham Rule. The case involved the appeal by Monte Durham of his conviction on a charge of housebreaking. Durham's defense was that he was of unsound mind while committing the act. He appealed the conviction, claiming that the lower trial court had misapplied the existing (McNaghten) rules for the insanity defense.

Judge Bazelon hoped to remedy what he saw as pervasive defects in the McNaghten Rules by drafting a new standard to govern the insanity plea. The Durham Rule abandoned the right-and-wrong test, asserting instead that "an accused is not criminally responsible if his unlawful act was the product of a mental disease or mental defect." Bazelon (1974) drafted the rule in this form with the hope that it would solve some of the practical problems of eliciting psychiatric testimony which would be maximally useful to the trial jury and judge.  In a review of the rule written twenty years after its introduction, Bazelon summarized his motives: "Durham was not based on my notions that psychiatrists know everything there is to know about behavior.  Its purpose was to bring into the courtroom the knowledge they do have and to restore to the jury its traditional function of applying our inherited ideas of moral responsibility to those accused of crime."

Although the initial response of the psychiatric profession to the Durham Rule was enthusiastic, later opinion was almost uniformly critical.  A symposium published in 1959 in *The American Journal of Psychiatry* summarized the profession's criticisms (American Psychiatric Association, 1959).  Objections to the Durham Rule took almost the same form as those to the earlier McNaghten Rule.  The assumption that the defendant's actions can be said to be the *product* of his or her mental condition was seen to be as invalid as the notion that insanity is a *defect* of reason in the McNaghten Rules.  Bazelon himself seems to feel that the Durham Rule failed because the psychiatric profession was unwilling or unable to assume the heavier responsibilities assigned to it by the rule.

By 1961, the American Law Institute drafted a Model Penal Code that included a section governing the insanity defense.  In 1972, Judge Bazelon himself replaced the Durham Rule with a version of the Model Penal Code Rule in another murder case appeal, *U.S. v. Brawner*.  The American Law Institute and Brawner Rules are quite similar, stating that "a person is not responsible for criminal conduct if at the time of such conduct as a result of mental disease or defect he lacks substantial capacity either to appreciate the wrongfulness (criminality) of his conduct or to conform his conduct to the requirements of the law."  Of course, the Model Penal Code Rule does not settle the matter.  The quality of relations between the legal and psychiatric professions was hardly improved, and in the view of many critics the latest rules do not vary from the McNaghten Rule in any important respect (cf. Clyne, 1973; Monahan, 1973).

## Expert Psychiatric Testimony

Whatever we may think about the quality of the standards governing the insanity defense, they are a historical reality, and the use of expert testimony is a central part of their application. Loosely speaking, an expert in the legal sense is someone who has "special knowledge, skill, experience, training, or education" that is beyond the realm of ordinary experience. In the case of testimony concerning criminal responsibility, it is now routine to allow psychiatrists and clinical psychologists (cf. *Jenkins v. U.S.*, 1962) to testify. Court-appointed psychiatrists typically exhibit a bias towards the prosecution case, while defense psychiatrists favor the defendant's claim of reduced responsibility (Gardner, 1976).

As expert witnesses, psychiatrists have a special role. As experts they are the only witnesses who are permitted to present conclusions ("The defendant was insane") as well as facts ("The defendant has a measured intelligence quotient of 84") to the court. Because the experts' conclusions will almost surely, and predictably, favor one side in the trial, cross-examination is often vigorous and vicious. Furthermore, the most effective response to an expert's conclusion is to produce a second credible expert who reaches exactly the opposite conclusion. The ensuing "battle of experts"—for example, in the recent trial of Patricia Hearst for armed robbery—is quite a spectacle.

There are several reasons why psychiatric testimony can be expected to appear strained or inappropriate in court. First, the task of validly assessing a person's mental state while he or she performed an act months or years ago is simply beyond any extant medical or psychological science. Second, the questions the courts would like to answer derive from the legal conception of the individual, which, as we have indicated, is in fundamental disagreement with almost all modern psychiatric and psychological conceptions of the individual's nature. Legal criteria such as the McNaghten right-and-wrong test or the Durham mental product test are so alien to modern psychological theory that the experts are not qualified to apply them. Indeed, we have argued that the notions of free will and practical assessment will seem fundamentally and even dangerously incorrect to many psychologists. Third, because there are no simple, universally acknowledged definitions of concepts such as insanity or mental illness within the fields of clinical psychology and psychiatry, disagreement between experts with different theoretical attitudes will be easily available and quite sharp.  The prediction that a psychoanalyst and a behaviorist are going to disagree about the use of legal terms which are foreign to to both experts' professional experience is hardly a masterpiece of insight.  Fourth, psychiatrists and clinical psychologists are quite accustomed to presenting conclusions about particular cases, but they generally find it difficult to specify the premises, facts, and chain of inferences that led them to these conclusions.  Because there is usually disagreement between experts, direct examination and cross-examination aim to elucidate the facts and reasoning underlying the conclusions reached by each side's experts.  Experts are often unable to respond clearly to such interrogation.  In fact, there is reason to believe that the process of clinical judgment may not be completely conscious in the clinician (Nisbett and Wilson, 1977; Slovic and Lichtenstein, 1971).  Fifth, the recent legal criteria, Durham Rule and Model Penal Code Rule place an impossible practical burden on the expert.  Bazelon (1974) cites a conversation with a prominent psychiatrist in which the expert pointed out that a minimally adequate response to the Durham Rule, given today's limits on psychiatric science, would require 50 to 100 hours of interviewing and research for a single case.  The costs of such a task are quite beyond the means of any court system and almost all defendants.

Thus, we see that the current forms of the insanity plea in this country are in shabby condition.  Legal and medical opinion are out of step.  Intellectually adequate standards are probably impossible, given the state of psychological science.  And all current practical methods seem to be wrecked on the shoals of economic reality.  Still, there is strong sentiment in both the legal and medical professions to retain the insanity defense (cf. Monahan, 1973).

## Proposals to Reform the Insanity Defense

Currently in the United States the McNaghten test is still the most common insanity defense rule. Often the McNaghten Rule is used in conjunction with the "irresistible impulse test," which states that a defendant will be classed as insane if ". . . the governing power of his mind has been otherwise than voluntarily so completely destroyed that his actions are not subject to it, but are beyond his control." The Durham Rule, which was originally adopted in the District of Columbia and then rejected in the Brawner decision, is currently applied in very few jurisdictions (Maine and the Virgin Islands). The American Law Institute Model Penal Code standard, which closely resembles the Brawner Rule, is currently used in seven states and most federal circuit courts.

We have pointed out that although the insanity defense is a rare phenomenon in the courtroom, the philosophical, scientific, and political issues which arise in its consideration are crucial to the theory of justice manifested in our laws.  If the mens rea doctrine underlying the insanity defense were discarded, almost all of our criminal statutes would have to be rewritten.  This is because the notion of state of mind or intentionality is an integral part of the definitions of most criminal offenses.  For this reason it is extremely unlikely that the insanity defense will be abolished or even radically changed in the near future.

Scholars who support the mens rea doctrine have emphasized the historical tradition in which the doctrine is embedded, and have also made arguments for the principle's practical importance.  These arguments stress the usefulness of a system of laws based on the notion that an individual is free to choose to act in an evil or virtuous manner, and the responsibility for these freely chosen acts descends on the actor.  Further, the argument goes, the existence of institutions such as the insanity defense accentuates the distinction between the acts for which we are responsible and the small class of unintentioned, nonwillful behaviors.  Thus, the insanity defense reminds us that we are almost wholly responsible for our conduct.

Nonetheless, there is a large, varied literature advocating the abolition of the insanity defense.  Almost every conceivably relevant premise has been used as a foundation for abolitionist arguments. Rejection of the insanity defense comes from all sectors of the political spectrum.  It is attacked on one side because it excuses too many, and on the other because it excuses too few.  One abolitionist claims that it is unfair because it is available only to the rich.  Another claims it is applied only to the poor and minorities as a stigmatizing weapon of oppression.  Former President Nixon is concerned that the insanity defense allows dangerous criminals to go free, while others argue that the blameless mentally ill are confined longer than criminals. Whatever their reasons, a growing list of noteworthy persons are calling for the abolition of the insanity defense (Stone, 1975).

One point of view, the behavioral position, owes the most to academic psychology. This position is often attributed to Lady Barbara Wooten, a British legal expert, but it seems that the position is close (but not identical) to the views of clinical psychologists such as Karl Menninger or academic researchers such as B. F. Skinner. Herbert Packer (1968) has summarized this position neatly:

> First, free will is an illusion, because human conduct is determined by forces that lie beyond the power of the individual to modify.
>
> Second, moral responsibility, accordingly, is an illusion because blame cannot be ascribed for behavior that is ineluctably conditioned.
>
> Third, human conduct, being causally determined, can and should be scientifically studied and controlled.
>
> Fourth, the function of the criminal law should be purely and simply to bring into play processes for modifying the personality, and hence the behavior, of people who commit antisocial acts, so that they will not commit them in the future; or, if all else fails to restrain them from committing offenses by the use of external compulsion (e.g., confinement).
>
> [Fifth,] we have . . . real knowledge about how to rehabilitate people.
>
> [Sixth,] we know how to predict those who exhibit traits that are dangerous.

Proponents of the behavioral position have advocated a dramatic change in the nature of the decisions a court or jury would be required to make in criminal trials where the insanity defense is currently relevant. First, the trial court would decide whether the defendant had performed the criminal behavior of which he or she had been accused. Only after conviction would information about mens rea or intentionality be considered to decide on the disposition of the case: should the defendant be freed on probation, imprisoned, hospitalized, or placed in some other treatment facility. Figure 6.1 presents two decision charts that illustrate the difference between the traditional and the behavioral systems.

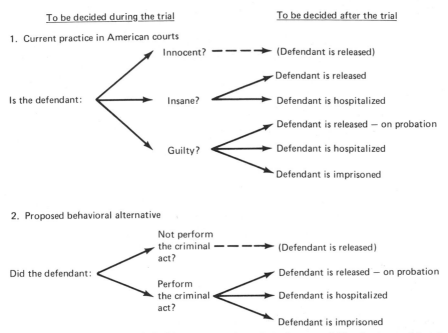

To be decided during the trial                    To be decided after the trial

1. Current practice in American courts

Is the defendant:

Innocent? — — — → (Defendant is released)

Insane?     Defendant is released
            Defendant is hospitalized

Guilty?     Defendant is released — on probation
            Defendant is hospitalized
            Defendant is imprisoned

2. Proposed behavioral alternative

Did the defendant:

Not perform the criminal — — — → (Defendant is released)
act?

Perform the criminal act?    Defendant is released — on probation
                             Defendant is hospitalized
                             Defendant is imprisoned

Figure 6.1. The ordering of decisions concerning criminal responsibility in the traditional American criminal justice system and in a proposed behavioral alternative.

We have already alluded to the massive statute reform that would have to occur to purge all crime definitions of intentionality requirements. Imagine how difficult it would be to redefine all of our current criminal acts in strict behavioral terms. There are additional problems with the proposed behavioral system. They derive from the last two assumptions in Packer's summary of the position. We have argued repeatedly that modern psychiatry and psychology are not up to the task of predicting behavior (for example, dangerousness [Dershowitz, 1971; Monahan, 1973]) or controlling behavior (for example, producing successful rehabilitation) to the extent assumed possible in the behavioral position.

For the present the behavioral position seems impractical and unjust. Perhaps the best solution is to leave decisions about insanity and mens rea conditions in the hands of the trial jury and judge. Their responsiveness to the particular conditions in each case and common-sense notions of responsibility seem to be as valid as any other available standard of judgment.

### The Insanity Defense in the Courtroom

We have spent some time on the insanity defense because it has received so much attention from legal authorities. During the 1950s and 1960s a large number of insanity defense cases moved through trial and appellate court systems and received extensive public media coverage. The validity of the convention of mens rea, which is central to American ideas of criminal responsibility, is the focus of attention in the controversies raised by each new insanity test. Thus, an enormous amount of legal and medical scholarship has been devoted to the topic.

It is interesting to assess the practical significance of the insanity defense in this context. Strictly speaking, the insanity defense is of little or no importance in current criminal litigation. Rita Simon (1967) guessed that fewer than 2% of criminal jury trials involved the issue. This figure is almost surely an overestimate today. Many states have abolished the capital punishment sentences that were the chief motivation for an insanity defense.

Although the insanity defense is relatively rare, there have been several well-executed studies of the jury's reaction to insanity pleas. These experiments diminish the apparent practical significance of variations in the insanity tests even further. We will review two experiments which demonstrate that jurors have great difficulty comprehending and applying the McNaghten and Durham tests, and, further, that not guilty verdict rates are affected only slightly by the choice of test.

Simon, working with the University of Chicago research group, published the results of a mock jury study that compared the effects of the McNaghten and Durham rules on jury decision making. Simon's experiment is one of the few to use actual jurors, sampled from courts in Chicago, St. Louis, and Minneapolis, realistic case materials (two 90-minute tape recordings), and realistically long deliberations. She found that mock jurors given the Durham Rule were slightly more likely to acquit on grounds of insanity than jurors given the McNaghten Rule. Further, jurors given no special insanity test instruction behaved similarly to the Durham Rule jurors. Thus, she concluded that the Durham Rule was close to the American juror's sense of equity in these matters. One concern voiced by critics of the Durham Rule was that it would deprive the jury of its basic responsibility to evaluate the defendant's mental state.   There was no evidence to support this contention; juries deliberated, if anything, longer and more vigorously under the Durham Rule than the McNaghten Rule or no rule.   Simon concluded that jurors were able to comprehend the special insanity instructions, but that they carefully and correctly separated the experts' task of advising from the jury's task of assigning criminal responsibility.

Simon interpreted her results to suggest that jurors recognized the psychiatrist as a qualified expert, but did not feel compelled to accept the professional's point of view.   In the jurors' eyes the psychiatrist was an expert advocating his or her profession's view of criminality.   For many of the jurors this point of view appeared extreme and even unreasonable, and in the final assessment most jurors rejected the psychiatrist's opinion.   The strong evidence for this interpretation comes from one statistic in the research: fewer than 15% of all juries that heard the experimental cases found the defendant not guilty by reason of insanity.

Recently Arens (1974) and his colleagues (Arens, Granfield, and Susman, 1965) have conducted research that argues against the conclusion that jurors understood the special insanity instructions.   They found that college student mock jurors, a social group which is relatively facile with verbal concepts, "manifested startlingly low comprehension of charge materials" presented on the insanity test.   Taken together, the Simon and Arens, Granfield, and Susman experiments suggest that the excitement over the proper standard for criminal insanity is of little practical importance in the courtroom.   However, the vast amount of scholarly attention is justified by the pervasive significance of the mens rea doctrine in western legal thought.   Alterations in our concept of the criminal mind have large, important effects on legislation and on post-conviction disposition of criminal offenders.

## THE DEFENDANT'S APPEARANCE AND CHARACTER

The defendant's appearance and conduct during the trial as well as information about his or her reputation in the community and prior criminal record, should they enter into the trial record, will influence the outcome of the case.   Lawyers are acutely aware of these factors, and they attempt to manipulate them to their advantage during the course of a trial. For example, in many criminal trials the defense lawyer is torn between the advantages of allowing the defendant to take the witness stand and tell his or her own story, and the disadvantages of exposing the jury to the accused's unattractive demeanor or prior record of unlawful activities. The well-publicized trial of Patricia Hearst is an example of a case where a defendant's appearance as a witness had mixed results for the defense. Her demeanor and initial direct testimony favored her side of the case. However, the prosecuting attorney was able to do considerable damage to her credibility during his cross-examination by focusing on events following the bank robbery for which she was on trial.

## The Defendant's Appearance and Personality

Aside from the research on extralegal factors in judge sentencing, reviewed in our chapter on the trial judge, almost all of the research on the defendant's appearance and demeanor has taken place in relatively unrealistic laboratory settings. We have argued that this does not nullify the research, and we are fairly comfortable about generalizing from the laboratory to the courtroom.

The experimental method used in this research provides a very elegant technique for isolating the defendant's appearance and character factors for study. It is relatively easy to prepare two "stimulus defendants" who vary noticeably in only a single respect—for example, occupation. Then one group of mock jurors can be exposed to one type of defendant (upper middle class, insurance adjustor), while a second group sees the other defendant (lower class, janitor). The results of this manipulation, holding everything constant except occupation, allow us confidently to assign responsibility for any obtained differences to occupation.

The major problems with laboratory research on defendant self-presentation effects stem from the fact that research on the topic has only just begun. Many of the experiments vary several factors together so that it is impossible to determine exactly which factors within the manipulated set are important. Also it is clear that the relative importance of the defendant's personal characteristics shifts from charge to charge. Since only a small sample of characteristics and crimes has been studied, it is imprudent to draw any general conclusions at present.

## Social Attractiveness

It is no surprise that attractive, socially successful people have an advantage in our courts of law as well as on our streets. However, most of us find this fact disquieting. After all, justice should be impartial, particularly with respect to the accused person's social status and appearance. Laboratory and field research serves to increase our discomfort, as the typical finding is that these "illegitimate" factors do weigh against the underdog in judgments of credibility, culpability, and punishment.

In a trend-setting experiment, Landy and Aronson (1969) studied the effects of varying a defendant's social characteristics on judgments of punishment in a negligent homicide traffic accident case. One group of subjects heard the defendant described as a relatively attractive person:

> Sander is a sixty-four-year-old insurance adjustor who has been employed by the same insurance firm for 42 years. Sander was friendly with everyone and was known as a good worker. Sander is a widower, his wife having died of cancer the previous year, and he is, consequently, spending Christmas Eve with his son and daughter-in-law. When the incident occurred, Sander's leg banged the steering column, reaggravating a gun wound which had been the source of a slight limp and much pain. Sander's traffic record shows he has received three tickets in the past five years, two of which were moving violations.

A second group heard the defendant described in less attractive terms:

> Sander is a thirty-three-year-old janitor. In the building where Sander has been working as a janitor for the past two months, he was not known by many of the firm employees, but was nevertheless invited to join the party. Sander is a two-time divorcee (sic), with three children by his first wife, who has since remarried. He was going to spend Christmas Eve with his girlfriend in her apartment. The effect of the incident on Sander was negligible; he was slightly shaken up by the impact, but suffered no major in-

juries.  Sander has two misdemeanors on his criminal record in the past five years—breaking and entering and a drug violation. His traffic record shows three tickets in the same space of time.

College-student mock jurors sentenced the unattractive defendant more harshly than the attractive defendant (twelve years versus nine years).  The Landy and Aronson result seems to confirm our worst fears; or does it?  The problem with the result is that because the experimenters loaded their descriptions with so many factors, truly a kitchen-sink manipulation of attractiveness, we are not sure just which differences affected the subjects. Perhaps, if age and prior record influence sentencing, we are not so uncomfortable.  In the chapter on the trial judge we note that factors such as these are normally, and reasonably, influential in actual sentencing decisions.  However, if we discovered that the defendant's occupation or marital status was an important determinant of sentencing, we might be quite disturbed.

Several follow-up studies have been conducted to separate out the effects of the factors manipulated together in the original Landy and Aronson experiments.  Reynolds and Sanders (1973) distinguished between the effects of age, injury, and "attractiveness," and found that attractiveness was important on its own.  Sigall and Landy (1972) separated injury and attractiveness, and again found attractiveness was important.  Defendants described as "loving and warm" received prison sentences three years shorter than defendants described as "cold and unapproachable."  Kaplan and Kemmerick (1974) obtained similar results varying trait adjective descriptions. Merely changing two trait labels in a traffic accident case affected liking for the defendant, guilt judgments, and sentencing.

Nemeth and Sosis (1973) used the Landy and Aronson materials in an experiment that also varied the race of the defendant.  They studied two college student subject populations: predominantly upper middle class University of Chicago students and lower middle class students at a midwestern junior college.  They found that the original Landy and Aronson attractiveness effect held up only in the junior college sample.  Furthermore, race affected the junior college subjects' sentences: they assigned the harshest sentences to white defendants.  These results remind us to exercise caution in generalizing from this loose network of laboratory findings to the real courtroom. Again, the problem is not that the laboratory research is misleading or inconclusive.  It is just that we must have results spanning several types of defendant characteristics, with a variety of criminal charges, and sampling a wide range of subjects.

As with "social attractiveness," it is no surprise that physically handsome people have an advantage in the legal world as well as elsewhere.  However, this inequity is particularly rankling to western conceptions of justice.  Berscheid, Walster, and their colleagues have conducted extensive research to document our predisposition to believe that "beautiful is good" (Berscheid and Walster, 1974; Dion, 1972).  Efran (1974) has demonstrated this phenomenon in a university examination cheating situation; college students judged unattractive cheaters guilty more often than attractive cheaters, and assigned harsher penalties to the less attractive accused.  There is also a growing laboratory literature on sex effects on judgment, which can be viewed as a type of attractiveness effect.  At the moment there do not seem to be consistent effects of sex of the mock juror and sex of the accused on guilt or punishment judgments.  One important determinant of such effects will doubtless be the nature of the crime involved in the case.

Sigall and Ostrove (1975) conducted an interesting experiment which supports the notion that the effects of defendant's sex and attractiveness will be conditional on the type of crime involved.  They argued that results like Dion's and Efran's could be explained by arguing that subjects believe that attractive people are more skillful in the social world than unattractive people.  Thus, attractive people would be induced to "break" social or legal rules less often than unattractive people.  Therefore, guilt and punishment judgments would (and should) reflect this differential likelihood of transgression. Sigall and Ostrove went on to suppose that if the criminal act was furthered by the perpetrator's attractiveness, then attractive defendants would be judged more harshly than unattractive ones.  The results of a laboratory experiment conducted by these two psychologists support this line of reasoning.  In a swindle case, where an attractive criminal could be expected to be more successful than an unattractive criminal, the attractive defendant's sentences were harsher than the unattractive defendant's.  The reverse was true when burglary, a crime in which success would not be related to attractiveness, was the charge.

One aspect of the defendant's appearance that has been reviewed by the judiciary is manner of dress. In many jurisdictions defendants who have been awaiting trial in jail appear in the courtroom clothed in their prison uniforms (Lown, 1977). Since these are defendants who were unable to raise the money to pay bail fees, they are usually from lower economic classes and charged with serious offenses. Defense lawyers have claimed that this treatment, failure to allow the defendants to dress in their usual street clothes, prejudices the jurors against them (cf. *Estelle v. Williams*, 1976).

Some social psychologists (Lerner, Miller, and Holmes, 1976) have advanced a rather ingenious hypothesis, and supported it with research, to explain such a bias on the part of the jurors. These researchers argued that the jurors, indeed all of us well-socialized westerners, are inclined to view our society as part of a "Just World." When misfortunes befall someone, we preserve our belief that our world is just by assuming the person deserves that fate. In the case of an accused criminal, we are biased to suppose that if that individual has been confined to jail awaiting trial, then he or she deserves this misfortune, that is, is guilty as charged. Generally our court system recognizes the possibility of such a source of bias against the defendant, and most rulings have supported the defendant's right to avoid prison clothing in the courtroom.

More delicate problems appear when we go beyond clothing to consider the prejudicial effects of other aspects of appearance, such as grooming and clothing style. Most courts have refused to extend the defendant's rights further than ruling that he or she must not be forced to wear a prison uniform. One rather fiendish argument is that if the defendant was unshaven, filthy, or unkempt when arrested, then that was how he or she must have chosen to appear to the world (Lown, 1977).

A dramatic example of changes in demeanor and appearance from arrest to trial is provided by the Patricia Hearst trial:

> Patricia Campbell Hearst looked small and pale as she sat on the witness stand today and told for the first time her story of the last two years. Sometimes her voice was barely audible; sometimes it was strong.
>
> But as she sat there, her knees were always together, her head was always up and she looked throughout well-bred and demure. In her rust-colored pants suit, she was again today the young

woman of wealth and good clothes and good manners that she has been in court every day for the last few weeks.

She has looked, all in all, in her silks and gabardines very different from the way she did the day she came in without planning at all. That was the day in September when she was arrested and came back before the eyes of the world looking like an unkempt gum-chewing teen-ager.

She wore baggy corduroys then, rubber sandals and a lavender T-shirt, the kind of clothes she tended to prefer when she was still a college student planning to get married.

But a lot has happened to Miss Hearst since her arrest and the time F. Lee Bailey was retained as her lawyer. Now, for example, she has white frosted nail polish.

She also has a brown jacket, a green jacket, a beige jacket and a blue jacket. She has blouses with ruffles and blouses with bows, trousers of various colors and a dress, all bought, some people say, by her mother and Mr. Bailey.

The clothes are large on her tiny frame, perhaps even a whole size too large and why she dressed–or is dressed–in a way that makes her look attractive but dowdy is unclear. [*The New York Times*, February 10, 1976]

Most of us are unhappy to discover that social and physical attractiveness enter into guilt and punishment judgments. However, there is some reassurance to be found in laboratory research which shows that the relative importance of these "illegitimate" factors may be considerably smaller in actual courtroom settings. One suggestion along these lines is provided by Izzett and Leginski (1974). They replicated Landy and Aronson's attractiveness findings for mock juries' pre-deliberation ratings, but found that the attractiveness effects were removed by the process of jury deliberation.

A third insidious class of variables which derive from the defendant's character involve personal and attitudinal similarity to the jurors and the judge who sit on the case. To some extent the jury selection process guards against the prominence of these effects. Presumably only a few jurors will be very similar or very dissimilar to the defendant and so biased for or against his or her case. However, the jury selection process does not eliminate all sources of similarity; indeed, race and social class of jury panels are often homogenized during their selection.  In any case, a clear scientific analysis will surely have to include an account of juror–defendant similarity effects. Furthermore, it is difficult to believe that the same analysis does not generalize even to the trial judge.  Certainly in some well-published draft resistance and antiwar demonstrator trials "political dissimilarity" between the judge and defendants had an obvious effect on the judge's behavior.

Byrne and his colleagues (Byrne, 1969; Byrne and Clore, 1970) have focused their research on the effect of degree of attitude similarity on attraction between individuals.  Griffitt and Jackson (1973) used the Landy and Aronson case materials but replaced the original attractiveness manipulation with the following summary of the defendant's attitudes and interests:

> He is described by a psychologist as a person with a firm belief in God, a strong allegiance to the American way of life, and as a person who feels that men cope with stress and financial matters better than women do.  Further, a social worker characterizes him as a person who enjoys sports, dancing, and involvement in current social problems such as promoting the cause of public school racial integration.  It was ascertained that he has no previous criminal record with the exception of one minor traffic violation.

They found that amount of agreement on these attitude issues was a potent determinant of both guilt and sentencing judgments.  Mitchell and Byrne (1973) conducted a similar experiment and included a personality test measuring their subjects' authoritarianism.  They found that authoritarian subjects were much less likely to find a similar defendant guilty than were nonauthoritarian subjects. In addition, authoritarian subjects assigned very harsh sentences to dissimilar defendants.  Unfortunately, there is no conclusive research on the effects of group discussion or deliberation on these sorts of attitude similarity effects.

## The Defendant's Reputation and Prior Criminal Record

"Evidence of good character is relevant in the determination of the probabilities of guilt; the purpose of the evidence as to the character of the accused is to show his disposition, and to base thereon a probable presumption that he would not be likely to commit, and there-fore, did not commit, the crime with which he is charged." This con-clusion from a decision by the Supreme Court of California (in Falknor and Steffen, 1954) is typical of legal rulings on the admissi-bility of evidence about a defendant's personality or moral character. The rules of evidence that govern the use of such testimony are elab-orate; we will summarize them briefly here (cf. Wigmore, 1935). In general the accused may offer testimony as to his or her good charac-ter with respect to traits germane to the unlawful acts with which the accused is charged. If charged with assault, the accused may offer testimony as to peaceableness; charged with embezzlement, testi-mony as to honesty; and so forth. Only after the defense has opened the issue of character, may the prosecution produce witnesses to re-fute the defense claims. Usually to circumvent the labyrinth of hear-say rules, the character evidence is presented in the form of a descrip-tion of the defendant's reputation in the community: "the shadow he casts on the community." Generally, testimony about specific conduct aside from that directly relevant to the crime with which the defendant is charged is excluded.

Similar rules apply to the introduction of evidence to impeach a witness's testimony. Again, there is considerable variation in the sorts of evidence that are admissible in different jurisdictions. For example, the California Code of Civil Procedure, which also applies to criminal trials, reads as follows:

> A witness may be impeached by the party against whom he was called . . . by evidence that his general reputation for truth, honesty, or integrity is bad, but not by evidence of particular wrongful acts, except that it may be shown by the examina-tion of the witness, or the record of the judgment, that he had been convicted of a felony. . . .

Notice again that there is an emphasis on the witness's "general repu-tation." In addition, evidence of prior criminal record may be brought in as an aid to evaluate *credibility*, but not *culpability*.

The implicit theory of personality underlying the use of character evidence in the courtroom has a great deal in common with tradi-tional personality theory in psychology. The theories both assume that a person's behavior reflects certain, relatively simple, personality traits. These traits are hypothesized to be a major determinant of behavior, and they are stably fixed for each individual during childhood and early adolescence. Therefore, if we can accurately assess these traits for an individual, we should be able to account for behavior in a variety of situations. Evidence from clinical interviews, paper-and-pencil personality tests, or the impression the individual makes on other members of his or her social world should allow us to make these personality assessments and help us to predict future behavior or reach a "verdict" about past behavior.

This common-sense theory of personality is almost irresistible to most of us. In fact a special field within social psychology has the problem of characterizing the "implicit personality theories" that each of us develops to make sense of our individual social worlds.

To those of us socialized in American and European cultures the tendency to "pigeon-hole" other people into relatively simple personality-trait categories is almost automatic (Hastorf, Schneider, and Polefka, 1970). For the most part it seems that this simplification is a benign habit because it enables us to impose some order on an extremely complex, potentially confusing social world (Kelley, 1973, Shaver, 1975). Of course, this orderliness is a simplification, and when specific detailed information is required to perform memory (D'Andrade, 1974) or judgment tasks (Slovic and Lichtenstein, 1971; Ross, 1977), trait attribution habits undoubtedly degrade our perceptions.

There are two especially troublesome features of our use of implicit personality theories to understand and predict behavior. First, the categorization processes are often so easy and so automatic that we are unaware of their significance (Nisbett and Wilson, 1977). Second, it seems that both common-sense and scientific personality theories are rather poor aids in predicting behavior. Mischel (1968) has been one of the most outspoken critics of traditional personality assessment. But even the most ardent personality theorists admit that their instruments are rudimentary.

For the moment in psychology there seems to be a shift of interest from the individual actor's personality to the causal force of his environment. The development of "situational" assessment techniques or "interactional" personality theories (Mischel, 1973, Alker, 1972; Bowers, 1973) seems to be the theme of the seventies.

Once again legal practice and scientific psychology are in conflict.

Legal statutes propose that testimony about the defendant's general predispositions or traits is the only admissible character evidence; psychological research implies that this testimony is unreliable and undermines judgment.

## SUMMARY

The chapter on the defendant was divided into two sections. The first section was concerned with the legal dependence on the "mental state" of the criminal in defining most criminal acts. The "insanity defense" was reviewed from historical, scientific, and practical perspectives. Finally, research on juries' reactions to variations in the insanity standard presented in the trial judge's instructions was summarized. The second part of the chapter reviewed research, mostly conducted in relatively artificial laboratory settings, on the impact of the defendant's appearance, demeanor, and attitudes on the jury. The chapter concluded with a comment on the use of character evidence to evaluate a witness's credibility. Our view is that such evidence is of little value in evaluating credibility.

# 7
# Evidence

Trial evidence comes into the courtroom in many forms. Written depositions, wills, and contracts, mechanical devices or models, physical objects, reports of chemical analyses, fingerprints, photographs, maps, and, of course, the spoken testimony of witnesses. Because the lay jury in Anglo-American courtrooms is unaccustomed to evaluating the merits of a disagreement on the basis of facts in the form of testimony, documents, and exhibits, an elaborate set of "Rules of Evidence" has developed to govern the admission and presentation of evidence (Wigmore, 1935). One of the foremost authorities on evidence, John Henry Wigmore has argued that these rules are consistent with scientific principles and facts. He even argues that the rules governing the admissibility of testimonial evidence are psychologically sound. (Interestingly, Wigmore also opposed the admissibility of expert testimony by psychologists.)

In this chapter we will concentrate on four areas in which scientific psychology bears on the presentation of evidence. First, we review some of the principles of persuasion and attitude change that apply to witness credibility. We spent some time on these same issues in our chapter on lawyering; thus this review will be brief, focusing on testimonial evidence. Second, we present a fairly thorough review of the psychology of eyewitness reliability. This section is a straightforward application of the vast and lively field of learning and memory. Third, we discuss modern techniques of lie detection from the psychologist's point of view. Fourth, we briefly summarize the research that has been conducted on the effects of sensational pretrial publicity on jury deliberation. In addition, we discuss the effects of a judge's instruction to exclude statements or exhibits that have been improperly presented to the jury. This last topic actually involves *extra*evidentiary influences. Related material is presented in

164

our chapters on the defendant (influence of the defendant's character) and the judge (extraevidentiary factors on sentencing).

## EVIDENCE AND BELIEF

We discussed the psychology of attitude change extensively in Chapter 5. However, there is one special topic, the psychology of the source of a persuasive message, that we need to develop in more detail in this chapter where we are concerned with the impact of the witness. Kelman (1961) has pointed out that the persuasiveness of a message depends on three aspects of its source: the source's credibility, the source's attractiveness, and the source's power over the listener. In the courtroom the witness's credibility is of primary concern.

McGuire (1968) has argued that credibility can be analyzed into two underlying components—expertise and objectivity. A related analysis by the renowned legal scholar Wigmore (1935) has listed five grounds on which a witness may be impeached or discredited:

1. The witness exhibits a defect in the capacity to observe, remember, or recount the events being reported. We discuss the psychology of eyewitness perception and memory in the next section of this chapter.

2. The witness is motivated to have a bias or interest in the outcome of the case. We used the example of bias imputed to a witness because of a close relationship to the defendant in our example case in Chapter 1. Human nature being as it is, there is virtually an infinite variety of ways in which testimony can be biased. Some common sources of bias in legal matters are friendship or kinship with parties in the case, hostility toward a defendant, plaintiff, or prosecutor, monetary interest in one side of a case (expert witnesses paid by one side to testify), or other self-interest (the government witness who testifies to avoid prosecution). Research by Carl Hovland and his associates at Yale University has confirmed the importance of perceived source objectivity or bias in determining the impact of a persuasive message (Hovland, Janis, and Kelley, 1953; Hovland and Weiss, 1951). Furthermore, it seems that it is important for a witness to admit the existence of a potentially biasing factor. In fact, under some circumstances, warning the audience (judge and jury) of persuasive intent may even enhance persuasive impact.

3. The character of a witness may be regarded as relevant to his or her credibility. We commented on this issue in our chapter on the defendant and argued that character appears to be an insubstantial basis on which to judge credibility. We are in hearty agreement with an appellate court opinion that reversed a trial court's decision to allow a twelve-year-old pandering charge to be introduced as circumstantial evidence to evaluate a witness's credibility:

> The logical connection between pandering and not testifying truthfully in auto accident litigation twelve years later completely escapes us. It would be surprising if any statistical correlation at all could be found between panders of twelve years ago and witness stand liars today. Indeed it is difficult to see why someone who was convicted of pandering twelve days ago necessarily would be more likely to lie on the witness stand than any other randomly chosen citizen. If there is any connection at all, its probative value is so slight as to be clearly outweighed by the prejudice created. [cited in Schum, 1977]

Furthermore, cross-examination of a witness which takes the form of character assassination is rarely an effective trial tactic (Keeton, 1973). For example, F. Lee Bailey's vicious cross-examination of prosecution psychiatrists during the Patricia Hearst trial, which went so far as to introduce personal notes from medical school records, was almost certainly useless.

4. One effective technique to impeach a witness's credibility is to show that the witness has made previous statements which conflict with current testimony. There has been almost no research relevant to the issue of self-consistency and persuasibility.

5. It is clear that when evidence from one side of a case conflicts with or contradicts another witness's testimony, the credibility of one or both witnesses is undermined. Again, there is little psychological research on this topic. We should cite the path-breaking research and theoretical analyses of Schum (1975, 1977), which apply probability theory to the courtroom situation. He has developed "cascaded inference models" from mathematical decision theory and applied them to judicial proceedings. "Cascaded inference" (Wigmore called it "concatenated inference") refers to the situation where evidence is related probabilistically to a verdict, *and* the veracity of the

evidence itself is uncertain.  Obviously, these conditional uncertainties are common in the courtroom, and it is possible that modern decision theory can simplify some judicial problems.  (See Finkelstein and Fairley, 1970, for another example, and Tribe, 1971, for a dissenting opinion.)

## EYEWITNESS RELIABILITY

Scientific and legal institutions share the goal of discovering the truth about real events.  Scientific and legal experts work together to uncover the truth under some circumstances.  Examples are provided by the ballistic, fingerprint, and chemical analyses that are commonly introduced as evidence in legal trials.  Another source of scientific expertise is the medical witness, who presents the conclusions of his diagnostic or autopsy analysis as testimony.  Occasionally psychologists are called on to evaluate the credibility of witnesses in a trial.  Psychologists have served as expert witnesses since at least the turn of the century; however, today their testimony is rarely sought and even more rarely admitted as evidence.  This is unfortunate, for we believe that a summary of relevant laboratory and field research would be a useful aid to the trial judge and jury in cases where eyewitness reliability is an issue.

The gap between the psychologist's understanding of human memory and the layman's is surprisingly large, given the role memory plays in individual experience and in human affairs.  There are several senses in which the scientific approach can be superior to common sense.  First, common sense may simply be incorrect.  For example, most lawyers, judges, or jurors would guess that an observer can best detect lies in a verbal conversation if he is able to view the faces and bodies of the conversationalists.  This is simply wrong.  Lie detection is most acute if the observer has verbal but not visual access to the liar (as we note in the section of this chapter on lie detection).  Second, common sense may be correct but imprecise.  Everyone would agree that estimates of time durations and vehicle speeds are inaccurate.  However, the critical question is what are the direction and magnitude of error in these judgments?  Third, the common-sense analysis may be partially correct but incomplete compared to the scientific analysis.  The non-scientist may correctly note the effects of lighting, interposed objects, color, shape, and movement on subjective judgments but then fail to consider all of the relevant factors together in estimating bias in a particular setting.

The superiority of the scientific approach derives from its systematic character, the application of consistent stringent standards of proof before generalizations are accepted, and its broad, detailed evidential foundation. It is important to note at the outset that although the scientific analysis of memory far surpasses the quality and extent of common-sense analysis, generalization to new cases always requires an inductive leap of the imagination. However, the logic of the generalization process can be strengthened by following several simple procedures: First, it is critical to specify the conditions of the case of which we wish to generalize. What event is the eyewitness reporting? Who is the eyewitness? Under what conditions did the eyewitness observe the event? What has happened to the eyewitness in the time intervening between the event and the interrogation? And, finally, what are the conditions under which the eyewitness is being questioned? Second, care must be taken in matching the variables that characterize the particular case with variables studied in scientific research on memory. There are numerous threats to the generalization at this stage: (a) Inadvertent confusions may arise because scientific usage differs from ordinary language. For instance, the scientific usage of the word "recency" is somewhat different from the everyday usage. (b) Experimental treatments may not be exact analogues of the natural conditions. For instance, laboratory manipulation of stress may not correspond to the stress experienced by the victim of a mugging in quality or magnitude. (c) There may be individual differences between college students whose behavior is studied in most laboratory experiments and the actual eyewitness, differences that make generalization hazardous.

For the most part our attitude toward generalizing from laboratory settings to natural situations is optimistic. First, where efforts have been made to compare subject populations, to replicate systematically laboratory experiments in the field, or to examine the generality of laboratory research, the results have confirmed the generalization. Second, when the accuracy of testimony must be evaluated, the accumulated wisdom of laboratory researchers is the largest, most reliable basis for generalization.

## Substages in the Memory Process

Theoretical analyses of memory processes are almost unanimous in accepting a three-stage breakdown of any memory performance (Klatzky, 1975; Loftus and Loftus, 1976). First, there is the *storage* or *acquisition* stage, in which information is encoded, laid down, or enters into the subject's memory system. If we think of a tape recorder as a type of mechanical memory system, the initial recording of a voice on the tape would correspond to this substage of the memory process. Second, there is the *retention* stage, the period of time that passes between acquisition and the eventual utilization of the stored mnemonic information. In our tape recorder example, this substage might correspond to a period of time during which our tape recording is stored but not played. Third, there is the *retrieval* or utilization stage, in which stored information is recalled, or activated by the subject. Of course, this stage would correspond to our playing the tape recording and listening to the voice "retrieved" from the tape. This tripartite analysis is so central to the concept of memory that it is virtually definitive. If a complex behavior is easily segmented into these three subprocesses, it will probably be described as a memory process. Conversely, a thorough theoretical analysis of the memory process must account for events during each of the three stages.

The central problem in research on human memory is to account for the subject's failure to retrieve or utilize information. Events at any one (or more) of the stages can cause retrieval failure. Information, especially in rich natural environments, may simply not be perceived or encoded. Information may be initially encoded but then be degraded or forgotten during the retention stage. And information may be available in memory but not accessible under interrogation or questioning at the time of retrieval. Of course, to isolate the events responsible for memory failure or even to localize a source of failure in one of the stages requires considerable ingenuity. Often, given a single experiment, it is impossible to conclude that a failure to recall is due to events occurring during only one stage of the memory process.

So far we have talked about failures of the memory system as though we are concerned exclusively with the failure to retrieve information, failures of omission. However, we must also consider failures of memory that involve errors of commission, where the subject distorts the original to-be-remembered events or falsely intrudes incorrect information into recall or recognition reports. The first class of errors will be referred to as errors of omission, incomplete recall or missing recall. The second class of errors will be referred to as errors of commission, intrusions, or false alarm errors.

A well-executed experiment by Marshall and his students (1969) illustrates these distinctions. Subjects in the experiment, drawn from three socioeducational groups, watched a 42-second film. In the film a young man rocks a baby carriage and then flees when a woman approaches him. The experimenters obtained a free narrative report of the incident from the subjects and then analyzed these protocols in several ways. First, they counted the number of correct items reported out of a possible 115 items. This statistic provides an estimate of incompleteness or errors of omission in the recall protocols. Second, they counted the number of incorrectly recalled facts and the number of non-facts ("recall" of material that did not appear in the film at all). These statistics provide an estimate of the number of errors of commission in the protocols. The experimenters also performed a third analysis of the number of identifiable inferences in each protocol. By inferences the authors meant statements about film characters' motives and statements about events that were not directly depicted in the film. The authors note that the distinction between inferences and errors of commission in recall is fuzzy.

## The Acquisition Stage

Before an event can be recalled it must first be perceived in such a way that it is stored or encoded in memory. Before an event can be stored for later recall, the event must be within a witness's perceptual range—the event must be loud enough, close enough, sufficiently well illuminated, and otherwise available to the senses. Beyond perceptual limits imposed by the physical characteristics of the situation or of the event, it is also clear that the witness must attend to events before they are perceived. We cannot see what happens behind our backs, nor can we encode all of the sensory stimulation available at a given moment. In everyday life we find that we frequently miss events that others around us notice.

Why do some events or aspects of events enter into storage while others do not?  For purpose of the present analysis, the determinants of storage can be divided into two categories: characteristics of the stimuli and characteristics of the witness.

*Perceptual Biases and Nature of the Stimuli.*  Even when stimuli are perceived, it often happens that perceptions are distorted or misinterpreted; and when perceptions are distorted, then, of course, the stored memory of the event will contain distorted or biased information.  Bias or distortion *can* originate in faulty sensory organs—for example, an eyewitness with impaired vision is unlikely to see a stimulus accurately and therefore unlikely to produce an accurate and complete report of the stimulus.  But even with normal sensory powers there is ample evidence that perceptions and perceptual judgments can be biased and distorted.

Gardner (1933) noted that observers tend to overestimate vertical distances (e.g., heights of buildings), the size of large objects in the context of smaller objects, the size of small angles, and the duration of events in which much happens, but underestimate the size of filled spaces (e.g., fully furnished versus unfurnished rooms), and the size of small objects surrounded by large objects.  Grether and Baker (1972) point out that judgments of size, distance, speed, and acceleration are especially difficult when the targets of perception are unfamiliar and sizes and distances are unknown.  They further observe that estimates of distance are characteristically biased under certain conditions.  For example, distance and speed are usually underestimated when targets are viewed across water or snow or in the sky—particularly when there are no familiar reference objects in the field of vision.

One classic method of testing eyewitness perception and judgments is to "stage" a criminal event in front of unsuspecting subjects (see Münsterberg, 1915, for one of the first such experiments).  Over forty years ago Gardner (1933) summarized the findings in such studies: Estimates of a man's height varied from 4 feet to 6 feet 6 inches, one quarter of the subjects omitted 50% of the details in their descriptions, height was overestimated by an average of eight inches, ages were missed by eight years, and hair color was missed in 83% of the witness descriptions.

Similarly, Buckhout (1974b) reported that witnesses overestimated the duration of a staged crime by a factor of two and a half to one, overestimated the weight of the "assailant" by 14% and underestimated his age by two years. While the height estimate was close, Buckhout suggests that this may have been due to the fact that the mock assailant was of average height and that eyewitnesses tend to cite facts about the "average" man when they are uncertain.

Myers (1913), in one of the earliest experiments on incidental learning, demonstrated the amazing degree to which perceptually available but insignificant information is not remembered. Sizes and marking of common objects such as currency and watch dials and the background colors, border markings, and nonattended letters in laboratory perception materials were poorly remembered.

One class of stimuli—people (and particularly human faces)—has received substantial attention from researchers.    One specialized body of person-recognition research has focused on eyewitness identification and lineups.

The results of a staged, televised purse-snatching episode on a New York City news program (Buckhout, 1975) are striking.  In December 1974 viewers of a nightly television news program were treated to a twelve-second film of a purse-snatching and were then presented a six-man lineup.  Viewers were told that the assailant in the film might or might not be one of the men in the lineup and were asked to identify the purse-snatcher and telephone in their identifications. Although the "mugger" was one of the men in the lineup, he was correctly identified by only 15.3% of the 2,145 viewers who responded.  This level of accuracy is quite low in light of the fact that simply by guessing the viewers would have selected the "mugger" 14.3% of the time.  In another "staged" assault study, Buckhout (1974b) found that seven weeks after the episode only 40% of the 141 witnesses correctly identified the assailant from a lineup, and 25% of the subjects (including the "victim" of the assault) incorrectly identified an innocent bystander who was included in the lineup.

Brown, Deffenbacher, and Sturgill (1977) have studied lineup recognition of "suspects" under a variety of identification procedures: (1) viewed in an initial lineup and also in mugshots, (2) viewed only in the initial lineup, (3) viewed only in mugshots, and (4) viewed for the first time in a final lineup.  When subjects were presented the final lineup composed of individuals from each of the above four groups and were asked to identify individuals they had seen in the original lineup (members of groups 1 and 2), the subjects "indicted" 65% of group 1 members, 51% of group 2 members, 20% of group 3 members, and 8% of the fourth group. Thus, although subjects did much better than chance in distinguishing "criminals" (groups 1 and 2) from "non-criminals," there was a clear tendency to incorrectly "indict" persons who had been seen only in mugshots.

Some recent experiments by Bower and Karlin (1974) have focused on the significance of the initial comprehension or mental elaboration processes for later recognition. These researchers showed that encoding task (faces were judged for likableness, honesty, or sex) had a dramatic effect on recognition. The "depth" to which a face was processed during its initial exposure was a powerful determinant of later recognition memory. Subjects were shown yearbook photographs and asked to make a single initial judgment about each face: (a) "How likable is this person?" (b) "How honest is this person?" The authors hypothesized that some judgments (likability and honesty) would require the subject to process the faces "deeply." On the other hand, the sex type judgment was expected to demand only superficial or "shallow" initial processing. The results of a later recognition test of memory, in which subjects were asked to pick out the photographs they had judged from a larger set confirmed their hypotheses. Deep encoding, honesty and liking judgments, led to more accurate recognition than shallow encoding, deciding the face's sex.

A second area of person recognition, which has received substantial research attention, is cross-racial identification—the ability to recognize faces from other racial groups. Malpass and Kravitz (1969), for example, found that photographs of previously seen white faces were better recognized than previously seen black faces—regardless of the observer's race; but that white subjects were significantly poorer at recognition of black faces than were black subjects. A considerable amount of research on cross-racial identification has supported the Malpass and Kravitz results. Cross-race identification is poorer than own-race identification, and white subjects are especially poor at recognizing faces of nonwhites. The depth-of-processing notion advanced by the Bower and Karlin experiment summarized above may help us explain these cross-race identification findings. It seems quite plausible that the faces of members of another race are less interesting or important to most of us. Thus for motivational reasons we may "process" these facts "shallowly" and have difficulty recognizing them subsequently.

A nonexperimental field study by Kuehn (1974) analyzed assailant descriptions given to the Seattle police by 100 murder, robbery, assault and rape victims (two homicide victims lived long enough to provide assailant descriptions). Kuehn surveyed the descriptions for completeness in nine categories: sex, age, height, build, race, weight, complexion, hair color, and eye color (these categories are ordered here in terms of the frequency with which each category appeared in descriptions—sex was specified in 93% of the descriptions and eye color in 23%). Descriptions were more complete (complete descriptions mentioned eight or nine characteristics) when the crime took place during the day or night rather than at twilight, when the crime was robbery rather than rape or assault, and when the victim was not injured in the perpetration of the crime. Males gave more complete descriptions than females. Black victims gave less complete descriptions of their assailants than did white victims—regardless of the assailant's race.

While Kuehn's findings are suggestive, they must be viewed somewhat cautiously, for the descriptions can only be assessed for completeness and not for accuracy. It is also possible that some of the effects can be attributed to the victim's emotional or physical condition immediately following their victimization. Finally, racial effects might be due to interracial hostility toward police and merely reflect a reduced tendency for blacks to cooperate with police.

*Temporal Factors.* Three variables have dominated research on human memory in the laboratory: frequency of exposure of the to-be-remembered material, duration of exposure, and serial position (location of a single item within the larger set of to-be-remembered materials). Any modern textbook on human memory will devote considerable space to the effects of these variables (cf. Klatzky, 1975; Loftus and Loftus, 1976). We will mention this vast literature only briefly here because the general conclusions to be drawn from it are almost wholly in agreement with common sense.

First, the more often an event takes place or the longer it endures, the more complete and accurate our memory for that event will be.

For example, if during a bank robbery a robber enters the bank several times, he will be quite likely to be correctly identified by bank personnel on a later occasion. Similarly, the longer he was in view, the more accurate later identification. Second, when a complex series of events occurs, memory will be superior for events that occur early and later in the series. In our bank robbery example, we would expect memory to be sharpest for events at the beginning and end of the robbery.

## Perceptual Biases and Characteristics of the Witness

In the preceding section of this chapter we discussed errors and failures of memory that arise from characteristics of the to-be-remembered stimulus events or the conditions prevailing when they are perceived and encoded. Similarly, enduring characteristics of the witness can affect acuity. The following section reviews attributes and conditions of the witness that influence eyewitness memory.

*Social Expectations and Stereotypes.* Tedeschi and Lindskold (1976) have defined the term *stereotype* as a cluster of traits that is attributed indiscriminately to all members of a group or to a given situation or event. A social stereotype, according to this definition, is a belief representing the consensus of the majority of a group of judges or observers.

The effects of social expectations and stereotypes on memory for an event were noted by early investigators of eyewitness reliability. For example, Whipple (1918) commented that "observation is peculiarly influenced by expectation, so that errors amounting to distinct illusions or hallucinations may arise from this source . . . we tend to see and hear what we expect to see and hear." An illustration was given by Anastasi (1964), who cited the case of a hunter who, mistaken for a deer, was shot and killed by his companions after they eagerly scanned the landscape and fired upon a moving object—their friend.

The implication of these errors for eyewitness testimony is evident: Where social expectations and stereotypes bias or distort perception, perceptual material that enters into stored memory will also be biased or distorted in a manner consistent with the eyewitness's social expectations and stereotypes.

Evidence consistent with this proposition derives from a number of studies. In an investigation by Allport and Postman (1945), subjects were briefly shown a slide of a detailed subway scene. The central feature of the slide was the figure of a black man, empty-handed, engaged in conversation with a white man who was holding a razor. The story was transmitted through a chain of subjects, each person telling the story as he heard it to the next in turn. The typical terminal report has the black man holding the razor. Allport and Postman described this finding as a clear case of assimilation to stereotyped expectancy: black men wield razors, and white men do not. Citing other examples from their study, Allport and Postman conclude that:

> Things are perceived and remembered the way they usually are. Thus a drugstore, in one stimulus picture, is situated in the middle of a block; but, in the telling, it moves up to the corner of the two streets and becomes the familiar "corner drugstore." A Red Cross ambulance is said to carry medical supplies rather than explosives, because it "ought" to be carrying medical supplies. The kilometers on the signpost are changed into miles, since Americans are accustomed to having distances indicated in miles.

The study substantially supports the proposition that expectancy errors are common when "novel," rather than well-known, stimuli violate conventional beliefs.

A convincing demonstration of expectancy errors derived from the novelty or atypicality of the stimulus was provided in another study by Bruner and Postman (1949). In this experiment, subjects were briefly presented with an array of playing cards; certain cards had their suits and colors reversed (for example, two *red* aces of spades were included with three familiar black aces of spades). In response to the critical question, "How many aces of spades were there?" subjects reported three, indicating that distortion resulted from "high probability linkages already learned" (Bruner, 1958).

Finally, evidence supports the assertion that expectancy errors result from objects involved in unfamiliar contextual relationships. Bruner, Postman, and Rodrigues (1951) asked subjects to match colors between a stimulus patch and a variable color mixer. They found that orange-colored tomatoes were judged considerably "redder" than orange-colored lemons; normally red objects were judged redder than "red" objects that are normally not red in color. These findings replicated Duncker's (1939) demonstration that a leaf cut from green felt was judged greener than a donkey cut from the same material, indicating that perception is biased by contextual relationships.

*Personal Prejudices.* Just as generalized social expectations and stereotypes may influence eyewitness accounts, so may individual prejudices affect the entry of material into stored memory. A personal stereotype, distinguished from a social stereotype, represents the idiosyncratic cluster of traits that an *individual* holds for a given individual, group, or situation. Personal prejudices were also mentioned as a source of bias and distortion in perception by Whipple (1918). He commented that "we notice the things in which we are interested and tend actually not to perceive the things in which we are not interested, because to be interested in a thing means that we attend to it readily, naturally, and with satisfaction." Thus, personal prejudices are a subtle source of error in perception and memory, causing us to "encourage the desired and congenial, and repress the distasteful things" (McCarty, 1960). To illustrate, Buckhout (1974a) gives the example of a witness to an auto accident who makes inferences based on his personal stereotypes about "women drivers."

In addition to accentuating the desired and repressing the distasteful, there is evidence that people most readily perceive and remember events that are related to their own interests (London, 1975). Postman, Bruner, and McGinnies (1948), in a verbal learning experiment, showed that a clergyman grasps the word "sacred" faster than the word "football," while an athlete responds more quickly to "football."

Perhaps one of the most convincing demonstrations of the proposition that personal prejudices influence memory for events was provided by Hastorf and Cantril (1954). The context for this study was an Ivy League football game between Dartmouth and Princeton; this match achieved notoriety for the rough and dirty play exhibited by both teams. Dartmouth and Princeton students, later questioned about the game, differed considerably in their recollections of which team was guilty of dirty play and of who had instigated the dirty play. Accounting for their findings, Hastorf and Cantril concluded:

> There was a strong tendency for the students to see their own fellow students as victims of illegal aggression rather than as

perpetrators of illegal aggression. . . . People are not passive receptacles for the deposit of information. The manner in which they view and interpret information depends upon how deeply they are committed to a particular belief or cause of action.

*Attributional Biases: A Social Psychological Context.*  It is evident from the preceding sections that expectations and biases have a subsequent effect not only on the perception and memory for events, but also on the inferences a witness draws after viewing an event. Another line of evidence that has relevance for witness characteristics and eyewitness testimony comes from attribution theory in social psychology.  A witness's memory of an event may consist not only of the facts that he perceived in a concrete sense, but also of the "facts" which he infers from the perceived event.

Attribution theory attempts to describe these processes through which an individual comes to "know" his world.  A central tenet of attribution theory is the proposition that an individual perceives behavior as being caused (Hastorf, Schneider, and Polefka, 1970), and that determining the locus of causality is one major means whereby a perceiver understands an event, assigns credit, blame, or responsibility, and infers information about the situation to allow prediction of future events.

To date rather little research has dealt with the effects of attributions of intent or causation on memory.  An illustration of the possibilities of such research is provided in three experiments by Zadny and Gerard (1974).  These researchers demonstrated that inferences about an actor's purpose (chosen major field of study), intentions toward another person (to steal from him, to assist him, to wait for him), or sexual identity (male or female) affect what is remembered about a person.  For example, in the second study they report, subjects observed two actors having a conversation in a friend's apartment. When the subjects were told the actors were thieves, they remembered from the conversation and objects in the room a different pattern of events from what they remembered when told the actors were looking for hidden drugs to thwart a police search.

The Zadny and Gerard studies merely demonstrate that attributions produce inferences and expectations that affect memory. We suspect that attribution processes are fundamental and pervasive in social perception and that these phenomena are important sources of bias in eyewitness testimony.

*Motivational and Emotional States.*  A further source of error in an eyewitness account of an event derives from the motivational or emotional state of the witness at the time the event took place. Sutherland and Cressey (1966) point out that a problem in courtroom testimony arises from honest mistakes which witnesses make stemming from a tendency to remember what they "want" to remember.    Marshall (1969) has offered a nice example of how reward may operate as a motivation to see particular things:

> A witness who knows that it would be advantageous if he were to remember that the light was red, or that the fire engine was sounding its siren, or the suspect had declared his intention to avenge himself on the victim, may ultimately believe that this was what he saw or heard.  Thus a woman sitting with her rear over the window ledge cleaning her third story window while elevated trains were passing testified that she heard the defendant on the street threaten to kill the victim just before the shot was fired.  She volunteered her testimony to the district attorney and was a neighborhood heroine.  She came to this observation when she read that the defendant and the defendant's former paramour had been talking together on the corner just before the defendant fired the shots.  What would have been more natural, then, than that she had threatened to kill him? . . . If a witness's actual recollection is vague or nonexistent then any dissonance or contradiction can be removed or any void filled by slight but welcome advantage for himself, especially some psychological ego advantage.

Intentionally or inadvertantly, the net effect of a motivational state is to alter the storage of information from which an eyewitness account is drawn.  With respect to emotional states and their effect on perception and memory, the variable that has received the most attention has been *stress.*   The conclusion that Whipple (1915) reached in the early part of this century that ". . . excitement improves observation and memory of witnesses up to a given point (variable for different persons) and impairs it beyond that point" is still prevalent among current investigators of eyewitness testimony.

This principle conforms to the Yerkes-Dodson Law, which asserts that strong motivational states, such as stress or emotional arousal, facilitate *learning* up to a point, after which they inhibit learning (see Figure 7.1). According to this principle, the location of the point at which performance begins to decline is determined by the difficulty of the task. Hilgard, Atkinson, and Atkinson (1975) summarize the law:

> A mild level of emotional arousal tends to produce alertness and interest in the task at hand. When emotions become intense, however, whether they are pleasant or unpleasant, they usually result in some decrement in performance. The curve represents the relation between the level of emotional arousal and the effectiveness of performance. At very low levels of arousal (for example, when one is just waking up), the nervous system may not be functioning fully and sensory messages may not get through. Performance is optimal at moderate levels of arousal. At high levels of arousal performance begins to decline.
>
> The optimum level of arousal and the shape of the curve differ for different tasks. A simple, well-learned habit would be much less susceptible to disruption by emotional arousal than a more

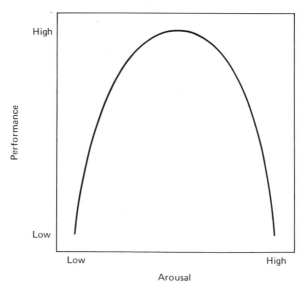

Figure 7.1. The Yerkes-Dodson Law relating emotional arousal to performance.

complex response that depends upon the integration of several thought processes. In a moment of intense fear you would probably still be able to spell your name, but your ability to play a good game of chess would be seriously impaired.

Johnson and Scott (1976) have conducted the most important study of arousal and memory for our interest in eyewitness testimony. The two intrepid investigators enacted a chamber-of-horrors scenario in an abandoned dormitory for the benefit of male and female subjects. In the low arousal condition an unsuspecting subject, waiting to participate in an experiment, overheard a conversation about an equipment failure and observed a bogus subject depart muttering about broken machines. In the high arousal condition the waiting subject listened to a violent quarrel and watched the bogus subject exit clutching a letter opener in his bloody hands. Half of the subjects in the experiment were tested immediately after the staged commotion; the remaining subjects were tested a week later. Test conditions were arranged to mimic police interrogation procedures and included a free narrative report, a controlled narrative (the subject responded to general probe questions such as, "Describe the waiting room"), and a mugshot identification test. The pattern of results was complex, but was obtained in two slightly different replications of the design. First, delayed recall and recognition were less accurate than performance on immediate tests. Second, recall and recognition of male witnesses were more accurate under high arousal conditions than under low arousal. Third, female witnesses' performance on tests measuring memory for the setting and the actions of the actors was higher under arousing than nonarousing conditions. However, female witnesses' performance on tests measuring memory for facts about the bogus subject was lower under high arousal conditions. The authors suggest that this effect may have occurred because the witness's eyes were riveted on the suspect's blood-stained, dagger-clutching hands.

The Johnson and Scott results suggest that their two experimental conditions tap arousal on the left-hand portion of the Yerkes-Dodson curve. (Of course, no two-arousal–condition experiment could disconfirm the Yerkes-Dodson Law.) The subjects' self-rated arousal is consistent with this conclusion, as ratings were for the most part from the lower halves of arousal scales.

It is likely that laboratory manipulations of arousal have not approached the right-hand portion of the Yerkes-Dodson curve. Several reviewers have been willing to extrapolate along these lines (e.g. Levine and Tapp, 1973), and it seems difficult to believe that performance would not deteriorate at extremely high levels of arousal. That leaves us with the questions, "How high?" and "What levels of arousal are produced in crime or emergency situations?" As Marquis, Marshall, and Oskamp (1972) conclude with respect to stress and testimony: "Further experimental inquiry along these lines might be of great use in evaluating and improving the process of courtroom examination."

*Individual Differences.* In this section we will very briefly mention a number of personal and social factors that may vary from individual to individual and which could alter or distort an eye-witness account.

Marshall (1969) studied the effects of social class and education on memory for his 42-second film by comparing the performance of law students, police trainees, and low income settlement house residents. A first analysis for completeness showed that the high-verbal law students correctly recalled an average of 14.0 facts, the police trainees recalled 10.3, and the settlement house subjects recalled 5.3. All of these scores are amazingly low given the experimenter's tabulation of 115 possible to-be-remembered items. It is also important to note that the law students' protocols included more inferences about events not included in the films, as well as more incorrect facts than the other two groups.

Age is another powerful determinant of memory accuracy. Numerous early researchers commented on the low reliability and high suggestibility of very young witnessess. Memory appears to be maximally acute between the ages of 15 and 25, and then performance on various recall and recognition tasks drops. Only two laboratory tasks do not show decreased performance between the ages of forty and sixty, digit memory span (a task where the subject is required to memorize a list of digits in the order in which they are presented) and "recognition" of the missing item in a short series of words or digits. A brief list of the cases that show the greatest age-related deficits would include "paced tasks, tasks which demand a constant switching of attention, tasks which require a change of set, and tasks which require free recall rather than recognition" (Schaie and Gribbin, 1975). It seems safe to generalize from these results and conclude that eyewitness reliability will decrease with age after the age of fifty.

A second biological difference, sex, does not appear to be reliably related to differences in learning or memory performance. Maccoby and Jacklin (1974) in a thorough review of the literature, did not find stable sex differences in any common laboratory memory tasks or in social memory tasks.

## The Retention Stage

As we have seen, when a complex event is experienced, some of the features of that experience are extracted. Early in the process, the witness must decide what aspects of the visual stimulus should be attended to. A number of factors, such as the salience or exposure time of the stimulus or the prior expectations of the witness, will almost certainly determine what aspects get into the memory system in the first place.

Because so many individual and situational factors affect the initial encoding of a new experience, we assume that a witness's memorial representation is not an accurate rendering of the event. To compound the problem, once the material has been encoded, further changes take place. The time interval between an experience and a witness's subsequent recollection or retrieval of that experience— called the "retention interval"—plays an important role in determining the accuracy and completeness of testimony. In this section we discuss the retention interval and how events that occur in that interval affect an eyewitness account.

*The Retention Interval.* It is a well-established fact that people are less accurate and complete in their eyewitness accounts after a long retention interval than after a short one. Ebbinghaus's (1885) research on remembering nonsense syllables is probably the most often cited study dealing with the loss of retention with elapsed time. In this experiment, Ebbinghaus himself learned lists of nonsense syllables, put them away for a certain interval of time, and then relearned them. He recorded the saving in time or the saving in number of readings necessary for relearning. A typical "forgetting curve" plotting performance against the retention interval is negatively accelerated downward: We forget very rapidly immediately after an event, but then forgetting becomes more and more gradual.

Ebbinghaus's forgetting curve has been confirmed again and again in subsequent research, using different types of subjects and different to-be-remembered materials. To give some examples that are closer to the real-life eyewitness situation, we might consider the work of Dallenbach (1913), who showed the influence of retention interval with picture material. In Dallenbach's study, male students were asked to look at a picture; then, after some interval of time, they answered a set of sixty questions about the picture. After answering each question, the students indicated whether they would be prepared to take an oath as to its accuracy, or whether they were only moderately certain about their answer. Dallenbach found that the length of the retention interval affected both the average number of wrong answers and the average number of wrong answers that subjects were willing to swear to. The average number of wrong answers increased from nine in immediate reports to thirteen after a forty-five–day delay, while the number of wrong answers "sworn to" increased from three to seven.

More recently, Shephard (1967) tested thirty-four clerical workers for recognition of pictures after intervals of two hours, three days, one week, or about four months. Shephard found that retention of the picture material dropped from 100% correct recognition after a two-hour delay to only 57% correct after four months. (Keep in mind that simply by guessing one will be correct half the time by chance in this experiment.)

The recent work on the retention interval would have been no surprise to Whipple, who, in 1909, observed that "lengthening of the time-interval between experience and report exerts, as one might expect, a generally unfavorable influence," and eight years later stated that "whenever any interval of time elapses between the actual carrying out of observation and the recording of it . . . , the accuracy and completeness of the record tends to be reduced by errors of memory" (1918).

*Subsequent Information.* Without doubt, then, a witness is less accurate in recalling information retrieved after a long interval than after a short one. It is natural to ask what happens to the memory during the retention interval that produces the loss in accuracy. What events of significance intervene between the initial encoding and the final retrieval that can influence an eyewitness account?

There is evidence that events or information occurring subsequent to the original event (subsequent to encoding) may alter the memorial representation of that event. One way this is accomplished is by simply entering new information into the existing memory structure, thereby enriching, or otherwise altering, that structure.

An early case study by Bird (1927) provides an example of this phenomenon. Bird gave a series of introductory psychology lectures and noticed that the college newspaper misreported the content of the lectures in an article published before an examination. Bird showed that the intervening newspaper report was (falsely) recognized as accurate by many students and led to errors on the subsequent test.

Loftus and Palmer (1974) showed subjects a film of a traffic accident, and then interrogated the subjects about the speed of the vehicles in one of two ways. Some subjects were asked, "About how fast were the cars going when they *smashed into* each other?" while others were asked, "About how fast were the cars going when they *hit* each other?" The former question elicited a much higher estimate of speed, even though both groups of subjects saw exactly the same accident. One week later the subjects returned and, without viewing the film again, answered a new series of questions about the accident. The critical question was, "Did you see any broken glass?" There was no broken glass in the accident, but since high-speed accidents suggest broken glass, it was expected that subjects who had been asked the "smashed" questions might more often say "yes" to this critical question. This is what was observed: those subjects who had initially heard the verb "smashed" were more likely to say "yes" to the question, "Did you see any broken glass?" than the subjects who had heard the verb "hit."

Why does this happen? It appears that the subject, upon viewing the accident, first forms some representation of the accident he or she has witnessed. The investigator who asks how fast the cars were going when they "smashed" into each other supplies a piece of new information: namely, that the cars did indeed smash into each other. When this new piece of information is integrated into the earlier memory, the subject forms a "memory" of a severe accident. Since broken glass is typically associated with a severe accident, the subject is more likely to think that broken glass existed.

To reiterate, information acquired during a complex experience is apparently encoded into some overall memory representation. Subsequent information about that event—for example, facts introduced via suggestive questions—is also integrated and can alter the initial representation.

*Interpolated Retrievals.* During the 1920s and 1930s in Cambridge, England, Sir Frederick Bartlett (1957) performed his now classic studies of how people recall meaningful material. In one series of experiments, Bartlett used the method of repeated reproduction: a subject studied a story or a drawing and was later asked repeatedly to reproduce the information. Bartlett observed that memory for even the simplest material was extremely inaccurate, and that the versions of a story became shorter, more concrete, and more modern in phraseology. In addition, he noted that a final reproduction often reflected objects and events that had been erroneously introduced into an earlier reproduction.

In sum, under conditions where multiple reproductions are required, some accurate content persists. However, the work of Bartlett and others warns us that false items introduced into an early reproduction will also appear throughout later reproductions.

Suppose the final retrieval involves the identification of a person seen earlier committing a crime. Can an interpolated test—for example, using photographs—affect this final identification? The work of Brown et al. (1977) suggests that the answer is "yes." In two of the experiments they reported, showing subjects a mugshot of an "innocent" suspect produced reliable increases in the tendency (incorrectly) to identify the suspect as a criminal. In one experiment 8% of suspects who had never been seen before were "identified" as criminals. If a suspect's mugshot had been seen earlier, his chances of being falsely identified rose to 20%—even though he had committed no crime. In a second experiment, where subjects viewed the criminal under conditions in which they did not think they would have to remember him, the corresponding percentages of false identifications were 18 and 29. This clear evidence of mugshot-induced biases has considerable bearing on questions of criminal identification and admissibility of evidence.

## The Retrieval Stage

The conditions prevailing during the stage of the memory process when information is retrieved from memory are also critically important in determining accuracy and completeness of the report.  A large share of current laboratory research and theorizing focuses on the problems of identifying effective retrieval cues, distinguishing between recall and recognition test conditions, and determining the sources of cue-dependent forgetting.  A number of experiments have explored the effects of variations in retrieval conditions in simulated eyewitness situations.

*Question Atmosphere.*  Marquis and his colleagues (1972; also reported in Marquis, et al., 1971) trained speech and drama students to produce a  supportive or challenging social atmosphere during their interrogations of subjects who viewed a film of an accident in a parking lot.  Under the supportive conditions, the interviewer expressed approval of the subject's responses with smiles, nods, and comments throughout the interrogation.  Under challenging conditions the interviewer maintained a stony, staring silence broken by occasional negative comments on the subject's responses.  Although this variation had powerful effects on the subject's mood and view of his performance, there were no effects on accuracy or completeness of report.  The experiment was unusually well designed and the manipulation of atmosphere powerful, so that the "no effect" conclusion is persuasive.

*Form of Question.*  The form in which a question is put to a witness exerts a strong influence on the quality of the answer.  Four forms of questioning are important in legal settings: (1) narrative, free report, or open questions (e.g., "Write a detailed account of all that has happened today"); (2) controlled narrative, interrogatory, moderate- or high-guidance, or short-answer questions (e.g., "Give a description of what person X was wearing"); (3) multiple choice or leading questions (e.g., "Was the woman wearing high heels?"); (4) recognition or lineup questions, where the witness is shown a test set of photographs, people, or objects and instructed to indicate the previously viewed item.

*Narrative form:*  Marquis et al. (1972) observed that narrative reports included relatively few errors of commission compared to other forms of report.  But narrative reports were also less complete in both experiments (i.e., more errors of omission than other forms). Marshall (1969) compared oral narrative with written narrative recall and observed that the written protocols were slightly more complete than the oral.

*Controlled narrative:*  Relatively little research has included short-answer form interrogations.  Marquis et al. (1972) reported dramatic increases in completeness of report with slight, but reliable, increases in errors of comission as questions became more specific and directive.

*Multiple choice or "leading" form:*  One of the earliest laboratory research programs on eyewitness testimony, reported in Muscio (1915), focused on variations in the syntactic form of leading questions.  Muscio's research was innovative (he was probably the first to employ "moving pictures" in a memory experiment) and ambitious (he included eight sentence forms in his design), but numerous methodological weaknesses make it difficult to summarize his results. First, Muscio did not counterbalance question content and form, so that, for example, questions about one character's clothing were presented in only one form.  Second, Muscio applied an elaborate series of statistical criteria to select questions for analysis; for the most part these screening procedures left only items of intermediate difficulty in the analysis.  Third, Muscio did not use current statistical tests to evaluate the reliability of his results, and many of his results are based on small samples of materials and subjects.  A few of Muscio's strongest conclusions seem to merit summary here. Questions stated in an "objective" form ("Was there a dog?") led to higher false alarm response rates ("Yes," when no dog was present) than questions in a "subjective" form ("Did you see the dog?"). Questions in a negative form ("Was there no dog . . . ?") led to relatively high false alarm rates.  Finally, Muscio found that questions phrased with the definite article ("Did you see *the* dog?") elicited higher false alarm rates than questions with the indefinite article ("Did you see *a* dog?").

*Recognition memory:*  Recognition memory plays a prominent role in the criminal justice system in the form of police lineup and mugshot identification procedures.  Almost all of the relevant psychological research has focused on conditions that produce high false alarm or false identification rates.

Exposure to a mugshot photograph of a suspect has strong biasing effects on subsequent lineup identification.   Brown et al. (1977) demonstrated that presenting mugshot photographs biased subjects to select those "suspects" out of a lineup even when the mugshots did not depict individuals from the original to-be-remembered "crime scene."  Doob and Kirschenbaum (1973) demonstrated that an even more subtle bias could account for the results of a real police lineup identification.  They argued that an eyewitness would depend on his or her own verbal description of an assailant in making a subsequent lineup identification.  In their case a woman described an attacker as "physically attractive" and then identified the most attractive suspect in a subsequent lineup as the attacker.  Of course, Doob and Kirschenbaum are not suggesting that the reliance on earlier verbal descriptions will invariably lead to errors in recognition. However, biases introduced in this manner will occasionally lead to errors of an extremely insidious and unnoticeable character.

Several characteristics of the lineup setting itself affect recognition accuracy.  First, the police officers conducting the test may subtly, or not so subtly, bias witnesses to identify a particular suspect. These "expectancy effects" have been acknowledged and studied in psychological research and educational settings (Rosenthal, 1966; Rosenthal and Jacobson, 1968), but no experimental research has been conducted in the lineup identification situation.  The actual manner in which the expectancy is communicated to the "receiver" is still somewhat obscure and doubtless varies from laboratory to classroom to police station.  However, it is easy to imagine that a police officer could "tell" a witness which lineup member is the major suspect with subtle body or vocal cues or less subtle verbal remarks or displays.

Second, the structure of the lineup—for instance, number of suspects presented, distinctiveness of a particular suspect in the lineup—affects recognition.  Small response-alternative sets increase the chance that a subject will respond to any of the items in the set in laboratory memory research.  It is hard to doubt that this result would generalize to the lineup situation, implying that the likelihood of a particular false identification increases as the lineup becomes smaller.  Buckhout (1974a) argues from his research and from dramatic real-world cases that a distinctive member of a lineup is likely to be falsely identified as a criminal.

*Hypnotic Suggestion and Recall.*   Hypnotic hypermnesia is occasionally used to facilitate retrieval in criminal investigations. Dorcus (1960) reported eight cases, including both successes and failures. Hypnosis was not successful in improving memory in four cases involving misplaced possessions. However, in two of these cases it was not clear that there was anything to be remembered: a watch may have slipped off its owner's wrist unnoticed, and a dentist's tools may have been stolen rather than misplaced. In the second series, four criminal investigations, there was ample evidence that the to-be-recalled observations had been made, and that the subjects were highly motivated to recall the information. Under these circumstances, hypnosis was successfully used in three cases. The recall performances were hardly spectacular: subjects correctly remembered the contents of an identification card, a vehicle registration number, and the color of a truck. Reiser (1974) reports another case in which hypnosis was used successfully to construct a composite sketch of a murderer's face. In this case, the witness had been confused and drugged during the initial observation, but hypnotic suggestion produced a dramatic improvement in the accuracy of the witness's descriptions.

There is also evidence that hypnosis facilitates recall in more traditional laboratory tasks (Dhanens and Lundy, 1975). One conclusion from a review of this research is that hypnotic suggestions are most likely to facilitate recall if the to-be-remembered information is rich, sensible material such as sentences or pictures, rather than nonsense syllables or abstract visual forms. In any case, there is substantial evidence that hypnotic suggestions can facilitate recall in an eyewitness situation. However, it is not clear whether the trance state itself is an essential component of the effect. It might well be that simple instructions to relax, concentrate, and re-create the to-be-recalled event would yield recall superior to that obtained in ordinary police interrogation procedures.

## Expert Testimony on Eyewitness Reliability

We have emphasized the unreliability of eyewitness testimony. Our conclusion is that when a witness attempts to give truthful testimony about directly experienced natural events, there are a vast number of threats to the accuracy and completeness of the report. One implication of our conclusion is that only in unusual circumstances would an eyewitness report, by itself, provide compelling grounds for a verdict or finding. This suggestion was clearly stated in a recent report to the British House of Commons by Lord Patrick Devlin:

> We do however wish to insure that in ordinary cases prosecutions are not brought on eyewitness evidence only and that, if brought, they will fail. We think that they ought to fail, since in our opinion it is only in exceptional cases that identification evidence is by itself sufficiently reliable to exclude a reasonable doubt about guilt. [Devlin, 1976]

We believe that the appearance of research psychologists as expert witnesses in legal trials should be encouraged. Their testimony can be of value both to establish the "exceptional" circumstances that accompany reliable testimony and to summarize the sources of unreliability in an eyewitness's report.

We think that the task of a psychological expert, called to the witness stand to testify on eyewitness reliability, is to summarize the relevant scientific facts. This testimony would include a few remarks on the scientific method, a description of the relevant experimental paradigms, and a list of the specific empirical results obtained with these methods. The jury or judge would then decide the extent to which these facts apply to the particular circumstances of the legal case and draw the appropriate conclusions about that case.

## LIE DETECTION

When the source of evidence is able to misrepresent or lie about factual information, the evaluation of testimony becomes extremely complex. The topic of lying and its detection is central to commonsense, philosophical, and legal analyses of language and social relations. Strangely, perhaps, there is only a small literature of scientific research on the topic. For present purposes we will be concerned with only the most simple kinds of lies: the liar knows that his or her statement is a lie, and lies deliberately. We will discuss three aspects of the lie detection problem: the use of polygraphic techniques measuring physiological responses, the use of truth drugs to detect lying, and the use of verbal, face, and body-language cues to detect lying.

## The Polygraph

The use of physiological cues to detect lying has a long history in legal decision-making institutions (Lee, 1953). The ancient Chinese required a person suspected of lying to chew a mouthful of rice flour. If the powder remained dry, the accused was judged a liar. Arabian Bedouins required suspected liars to lick a hot iron. If the iron burned the subject's tongue, the person was assumed to be lying. In Britain the test was to swallow a "trial slice" of bread and cheese. Failure to swallow was interpreted as a sign of deception. In modern practice these crude measurements of decreased saliva flow during periods of emotional arousal have been replaced by the polygraph, or "lie detector." The principle underlying the use of the modern polygraph is basically the same as the rationale for the ancient saliva tests. The rationale is that the liar's effort to deceive is accompanied by emotional arousal, which manifests itself in uncontrollable physiological signs—most obviously in changes in salivation, heart rate, breathing, and skin temperature; an observer using the proper measurement techniques can detect these changes, regardless of the liar's efforts to control them, and interpret them to distinguish the liar's true statements from falsehoods.

The modern polygraph, really a general recording device used for lie detection among other applications, allows the interrogator to record several physiological signs simultaneously while questions are put to the suspected liar. The technique differs from its hoary forerunners in two ways: the expert has available a much more detailed record of the physiological responses, and the rules for interpreting the physiological signs are much more complex than the ancient "dry mouth, therefore lying" rule.

The polygraph was developed by police officers (Smith, 1967) for use in police work, but today it is widely used in government and industry to screen employees and identify thieves. In 1972, the American Polygraph Association recognized eight schools, each teaching its variant of the basic lie detection technique. There are estimated to be more than 2,000 certified polygraph experts in the lie detection industry today. The basic course of study lasts from four to seven weeks and involves study of the standard Keeler polygraph, invented by a Berkeley policeman of that name.

The Keeler machine records blood pressure and pulse rate, respiration rate and depth, and skin conductance (related to amount of sweat on the fingers). (See Figure 7.2 for example polygraph records.) The trained examiner conducts an oral interrogation session, questioning the subject, and then interprets the polygraph tracks to draw conclusions about the veracity of the suspect's answers. Clearly the examiner's skill is the locus of any successful "lie detection" that does occur.

A typical examination might run something as follows (Reid and Inbau, 1966): The subject of the examination is introduced to the interrogator and induced to relax as much as possible, given the rather strained situation. The examiner attaches the blood pressure cuff, chest (breath) expansion tube, and finger electrodes to the subject and summarizes the interrogation procedure. Usually the questions that will be asked during the actual tests are previewed. This makes it possible to "clear" certain critical questions; for example, to ascertain the details of any thefts or dishonesties not related to the current interrogation so that they may be specifically exempted in the questions put to the subject. Finally, the actual interrogation occurs in the form of a series of carefully worded questions, each answered yes or no. Usually critical questions are separated by neutral questions, and all questions are separated by long pauses to allow emotional reactivity to return to normal.

Two special questioning techniques are employed to make the examination sensitive to lying. In the "peak of tension" test, the interrogator might try to determine the nature of a crime by suggesting a series of possibilities that gradually "narrow in" on the most likely candidate (Smith, 1967). In the "guilty knowledge" test (Lykken, 1960), the interrogator uses detailed knowledge of a crime to construct questions that can be answered only by someone present at the scene. For example, the examiner might ask questions about such details of an armed robbery as the name of the victim's business, the nature of the weapons employed, the amount of money taken, the getaway car, and so forth. In each question a multiple-choice response format would be employed. Lykken (1974) gives the follow-

CARDIAC AND SKIN responses are the most pronounced ones on this record made, like the others on these two pages, by Joesph F. Kubis of Fordham University. In this test the subject was lying as to number 26. The skin response peaks each time the number is called; the blood-pressure change (*top*) is fairly clear the first time. The cardiac change at 22 is probably from an arm movement. (a) Cardiac, blood pressure, trace; (b) Respiratory, breathing, trace; (c) Skin resistance trace.

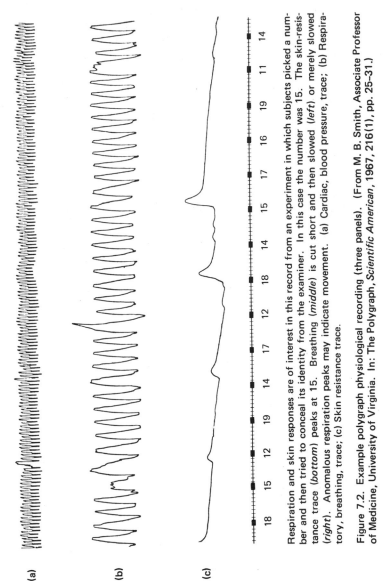

Respiration and skin responses are of interest in this record from an experiment in which subjects picked a number and then tried to conceal its identity from the examiner. In this case the number was 15. The skin-resistance trace (*bottom*) peaks at 15. Breathing (*middle*) is cut short and then slowed (*left*) or merely slowed (*right*). Anomalous respiration peaks may indicate movement. (a) Cardiac, blood pressure, trace; (b) Respiratory, breathing, trace; (c) Skin resistance trace.

Figure 7.2.   Example polygraph physiological recording (three panels).   (From M. B. Smith, Associate Professor of Medicine, University of Virginia. In: The Polygraph, *Scientific American*, 1967, 216(1), pp. 25–31.)

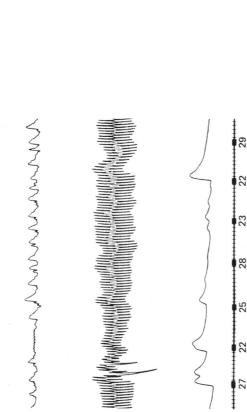

(a)

(b)

(c)

Countermeasure is illustrated by a record from Kubis' series. The subject lied about number 27. He simulated lying about number 22 by tensing his toes. The respiratory trace (*top*) shows that he held his breath as he undertook the first countermeasure. He was able to produce sizable reactions in the cardiac (*middle*) and skin-resistance (*bottom*) traces. (a) Respiratory, breathing, trace; (b) Cardiac, blood pressure trace; (c) Skin resistance trace.

Figure 7.2. (*Continued*)

ing example of such a series of questions:

Item 1. The man we're looking for held up a loan office in Manhattan. If you're the guilty party, you will recognize the name of that loan company. I'm going to name a few loan companies that have offices in the vicinity; you just sit there quietly and repeat the names after me as you hear them. Was it the Ideal Loan Company? . . . Was it the Continental Loan Company? . . . Was it the Guarantee Loan Company? . . . Was it the Friendly Loan Company? . . . Was it the Fidelity Loan Company?

Item 2. Before showing his gun, the robber pretended that he wanted to take out a loan for a certain purpose. If you're the guilty man, you will know whether that purpose was to buy a car, to pay doctor bills, to pay for a vacation trip, to buy a color TV, or to get a present for his wife. I'm going to name each of these five possibilities in order, and I want you to sit quietly and just repeat what I say. Was it—a car? . . . [etc.]

Item 3. If you did rob this loan company, you will recognize the woman you talked to, the one who gave you the money. I have some photographs here of women tellers in five different loan offices, just as they look to a customer. I will show these pictures to you one at a time. Just sit there quietly and look at each photograph.

Consistent emotional reactivity associated with the "correct" answers, regardless of the subject's verbal responses, would be strong evidence of his or her involvement in the crime. In Lykken's example the likelihood that an innocent suspect would show maximum reactivity to the true answer in each of the three five-answer items is $(\frac{1}{5})^3$ or .008. It would usually be possible to construct an even longer series of items, making this "false alarm probability" even tinier.

Lykken has argued that the guilty knowledge test is the only valid application of polygraph methods to detect deception. Unfortunately, these subtle techniques such as the guilty knowledge test seems to be rarely used in modern polygraph interrogations.

After the examination proper has occurred, the polygraph data can be used in several ways. First, the record can be examined and interpreted by the expert. This process is quite complicated and varies considerably across polygraph training schools. As is the case in many of the expert judgment tasks we review in this volume, the technique involves considerable intuition, and expert examiners are typically unable verbally to identify the exact cues and configurations in the polygraph traces that determine their conclusions. Most experts seem to base their decisions on one or possibly two of the polygraph tracks. Second, it is common to confront the suspect with a recording and then accuse him of lying without going through the interpretation process at all. Apparently, this is a fairly successful method of eliciting confessions (Lykken, 1974; Smith, 1967), but it is irrelevant to the scientific merits of polygraph lie detection.

The primary question is, of course, is the polygraphic technique a valid method of lie detection? Does it reliably identify liars and does it reliably *not* classify honest subjects as liars? It is very important to distinguish these two aspects of the polygraph technique's performance. A 90% "hit rate," identifying lies, would have quite different implications if we know that the "false alarm rate," classifying truthful answers as lies, was 80% as compared to a case where the false alarm rate was 20%. Most efforts to study the performance of the polygraph technique have yielded supportive results. For example, Horvath and Reid (1971) gave ten experienced examiners each forty polygraph records and copies of interrogation transcripts. Twenty of the forty records were taken from cases where the subject had committed the crime charged; the remainder were from innocent suspects. The examiners were quite accurate. The overall average accuracy in identifying truly guilty suspects was 85%; the false alarm rate, erroneously classifying innocent suspects as guilty, was 10%. Moreover, examiners with more than six months of experience were slightly more accurate than novice examiners. These positive results have also been corroborated with simulated live interrogations in the laboratory (Kubis, 1962). Barland and Raskin (1973) provide a thorough review of the relevant evaluation research.

There are still several problems with current polygraph methods in industrial and legal settings. First, the evaluation research cited above is biased to show the technique to its best advantage. The clear cases, controlled settings, and well-trained examiners operating in the research surely represent the cream of the polygraph business. Typical practice in the backrooms of police stations and courthouses is almost certainly messier and less valid. Second, in this research it is impossible to separate the examiner's utilization of the polygraph from his reliance on other sources of information (the suspect's overt responses, gross body and facial reactions, and so forth) in arriving at his decision. This issue is of practical concern insofar as there is variation across examiners in their skill at using these other sources of information. It is of critical importance if we wish to assess the reliability of polygraph evidence in a particular case or to characterize the expertise of an examiner. Third, in all of the evaluation research the investigators found appreciable false alarm rates. Polygraph results are clearly neither perfectly valid nor perfectly reliable. Fourth, although polygraph techniques are often refered to as "scientific lie detection," this label is undeserved in several respects. There is no well-formed scientific theory underlying the techniques, there is really very little experimental research on the topic, and most current applications do not employ the most advanced physiological measurement techniques available.

Finally, there are numerous counter-measures that a suspect can deliberately use to attempt to "deceive" the polygraph and its operator, several of which are demonstrably effective (Barland and Raskin, 1973). Mental distraction seems to damp the sensitivity of the polygraph. Dissociation from the questioning achieved by performing a monotonous mental task such as counting holes in ceiling tiles or mental arithmetic calculations seems to be effective under some conditions. A variant on the dissociation method is to "rationalize" answers to the examiner's questions. "Did you take fifty dollars from James Bartlett's wallet?". . . Not really, it was fifty-two dollars and it was in a money clip. . . . 'No'. A second tactic is to generate responsiveness to questions other than critical questions during the session. These techniques are quite effective and are difficult for the examiner to detect. The methods range from thinking erotic, embarrassing, or painful thoughts; flexing or tensing muscles in the toes, legs, arms, neck, or tongue; pressing against a thumbtack concealed in the shoe or mouth; to ingesting depressant drugs.

Direct evidence from polygraph records is not automatically admissible in any American court. However, polygraph examinations are used in police and private investigation work throughout the country. In addition attorneys occasionally attempt to have expert conclusions based on polygraph data admitted as testimonial evidence. Actually the future of the field is quite promising. The techniques already seem to have considerable validity, and additional competent research and higher standards of training and practice may bring them back into the courtroom.

## Truth Drugs

The belief that certain chemicals or drugs will strip away the deliberate controls on a liar's behavior and force him to speak the truth has cropped up at many points in history. The priestesses of the Delphic oracle in ancient Greece ingested drugs before uttering their prophecies. In Aztec Mexico peyote cactus was used to solve crimes, find lost or stolen items, and identify wrongdoers. Recently in wartime certain narcotic alkaloid drugs have been used to assist in the interrogation of prisoners. Some modern psychotherapeutic methods involve the use of drugs such as sodium pentathol to release a patient's inhibitions in discussing emotional subjects.

The use of truth drugs includes applications in criminal investigation to overcome deliberate lying by witnesses and suspects. As with polygraph evidence, evidence secured by such methods is inadmissible in American courts (Falknor and Steffen, 1954). However, truth drug techniques are used in pretrial investigations in much the same manner as in polygraph investigations.

There is very little to be said in defense of such techniques as a method of obtaining empirically factual evidence. All the research on the use of these drugs has shown that subjects can both conceal facts and fabricate falsehoods while drugged. A representative experiment by Dessions and his colleagues at the Yale Law School (Dessions, Freedman, Donnelly, and Redlich, 1953) had subjects reveal embarrassing episodes in their lives and then manufacture false stories to conceal those events. In a second phase of the experiment an unfamiliar researcher administered sodium amytal and then cross-examined the subjects with the aim of uncovering the hidden episodes. Subjects were able to suppress the embarrassing episodes, stick to their cover stories, and substitute completely bogus facts for the truth. Freedman (1960) summarizes this research and defends the use of "truth drugs" in therapy but not in the legal investigation process.

## Behavioral Detection of Lying

All of us are accustomed to detecting deception without the use of the esoteric electronic and chemical methods just reviewed. We are only too familiar with the problem of evaluating the truthfulness of a politician, salesman, or "friend's" statements. Most of us believe that we are fairly skillful at seeing through lies to the truth. Popular culture is rich with rules for lie detection. The liar is unable to meet our direct gaze, his voice quavers, his fingers are active and he tends to touch his mouth or cheeks, and so on. The logic of this conventional wisdom is basically the same as the rationale behind the polygraph methods. Certain channels of communication—voice quality, posture, facial expression—are not as easily controlled as speech content. Therefore these channels "leak" the truth to an acute observer. Recent research suggests that the phenomenon is a bit more complex. Mehrabian (1971) found that deceptive verbal behavior was accompanied by nonverbal signs of negative affect. However, there was no simple pattern in the particular signs of negative affect across types of lies. Ekman and Friessen (1974) found that college students were more accurate judges of deception when they used body cues rather than facial expression. The Ekman and Friessen result is also more suggestive than definitive. They studied only one type of lie: subjects were asked to conceal the true nature of a disgusting film clip from other subjects in the experiment.

Kraut (1976) has conducted a series of experiments using a more common type of lie. The liars were applicants for a dormitory counselor job, and, for the purposes of the research, they were instructed to give false answers to some questions during their job interviews. The videotapes of these interviews were shown to other subject-observers, who were given the task of identifying lies by the interviewees. Kraut also performed a thorough analysis of the videotapes to determine what nonverbal information actually distinguished between lies and truthful responses. Kraut found that observers were moderately accurate, identifying lying at a better than chance rate (64% accuracy) in four of the five interviews (they performed at chance level, 50% accuracy, in the fifth). Interviewees seemed to differ in their ability to lie effectively. Lies were preceded by pauses, and were shorter, and were less fluent than truthful responses. Observers' accuracy seemed to derive from the differences in response length, but inaccuracy was introduced by the tendency (incorrect) to use answer vagueness and amount of smiling to identify lies.

Krauss, Geller, and Olson, 1976 have conducted several experiments along similar lines. They also concluded that vocal, non-content verbal cues, such as speech pitch or timbre and hesitations, were the best indicants of lying. They found that subjects were most accurate when they relied on these cues. Surprisingly, subjects did not appear to be aware of either the relative utility of the vocal cues or their reliance on them. Krauss concluded that the nonverbal "leakage" hypothesis was false, in that effective liars were able skillfully to manipulate the messages sent in their paralinguistic, face, and body languages.

The implications of this research on behavioral lie detection seem to contradict the common belief that we can detect lies and that this ability depends on nonverbal information, especially that available from the liar's face and body. Behavioral lie detection is not impressively accurate. The use of visual communication channels seems to increase the skillful liar's advantage. And, surprisingly, lie detection is most accurate when the observer listens to, but does not look at, the liar.

Although the Kraut and Krauss research shows that subjective judgments of lying based on a speaker's voice are not accurate, there is hope that a mechanical detector will fare better. An industry is growing up around the use of a Psychological Stress Evaluator to analyze physiological tremor of the vocal muscles. Several reports have evaluated the efficacy of these devices, and there is no scientific evidence to support the claim that they are accurate beyond chance levels (Podlesny and Raskin, 1977).

## FREE PRESS–FAIR TRIAL

A special problem arises for the trial judge when a case is striking enough to receive wide publicity in the news media. The Susan Saxe trial in Massachusetts illustrates the difficulties of trying fairly a case that has been saturated with media attention. Saxe, a political radical from a well-to-do family in the Boston area, was accused of participating in a bank robbery in which a policeman was killed. The local newspapers seized the case as a focus of political sentiment aroused during the Vietnam War. Most newspaper coverage of her activities and the case before it went to trial was unfavorable, to say the least, to the defense. A survey conducted a few weeks before her trial found that approximately three-fourths of the adult population in the county where she was to be tried believed she was guilty as charged. In this case the trial judge granted the defense lawyers extra peremptory challenges of jurors during the voir dire proceedings to impanel a jury, to counteract some of the initial pretrial prejudice. In even more sensational trials, such as the Charles Manson, Angela Davis, and Patricia Hearst trials, it is even harder to imagine an unbiased jury.

Several psychologists have directed their research to the free press–fair trial problem. Two questions are addressed in this research. First, how does extraevidential information such as biased press coverage affect judgments, and how pervasive are those effects? Second, what procedures can be employed to reduce or eliminate such biases once they have been introduced?

Most of this research has used a mock jury method in which experimental subjects are shown a prejudicial newspaper article, listen to a tape recording of a mock trial or case synopsis, and then fill out questionnaires indicating their personal verdict judgments (Simon, 1966; Kline and Jess, 1966). Of course, the subjects , case material, and questionnaries used in this research do not approach the natural exposure and jury conditions. One experiment, conducted by Padawer–Singer and Barton in New York (1975), is much more realistic than the others. The experiment was conducted with real jurors in a courthouse using a detailed tape-recorded murder case, and jurors were instructed to deliberate to a verdict. One weakness in the design was that exposure to the prejudicial newspaper clippings occurred during the experimental session a few minutes before the mock trial tapes were played to the jurors. We might wonder just what the experimental subjects thought they were to do with this information provided by the experimenters before the case was presented. Padawer-Singer and Barton found that the prejudicial clippings did indeed bias their jurors to convict the defendant. A neutral set of clippings produced acquittal-prone jurors. Further, in a second study, they found that an extensive voir dire examination was an antidote to the prejudicial newspaper treatment. Juries that were screened with a thorough voir dire examination were acquittal-prone, as were the nonbiased juries in their first experiment.

The Padawer-Singer and Barton study is both sobering and encouraging. Their procedure demonstrates that it is easy to bias the result of a jury trial with "pretrial publicity." At the same time they suggest that some of our current institutions to protect against prejudice are effective. It remains to be seen how a lengthy barrage of sensational media reporting affects judgments, and whether these effects are as easily detected and eradicated.

## SUMMARY

The chapter on evidence was really concerned with the trial witness as a conveyer of testimony. We opened the chapter with a review of John Henry Wigmore's principles for the impeachment of a witness's credibility. Next we covered the psychology of eyewitness perception and memory, concluding that eyewitness testimony was a fragile route to the truth. Third, we reviewed the use of mechanical lie detection devices and concluded that the polygraph was of limited utility for two reasons. Polygraph methods have a nonnegligible rate of "false alarm" errors, where truth-tellers are incorrectly classified as liars. And, certain countermeasures allow the determined liar to damp the polygraph machine's sensitivity. We also argued that unassisted humans are relatively poor lie detectors, performing at only slightly better than chance levels. Finally, we reviewed research on the effects of sensational pretrial publicity on jury decision making.

# 8

# The Court as a Social System and as Part of a Social System

Previous chapters have examined the social psychology of the various components of litigation, alluding where appropriate to their inter-relations with each other, but without really developing the notion that the various actors who come together in and around courts are inseparable from their membership in a social system. Apart from their social system, the individual components become stripped of their meaning and without function. To conceptualize courtroom and conference-room actors as isolated elements overlooks the struc-ture of their relationships to each other. Indeed, it would be more informative to ignore the entities composing the system and to look instead at the relationships among them (Weick, 1969; Katz and Kahn, 1966). In the decision-making and dispute-resolving system that is the court, no decision comes from any one element acting alone; all outputs result from a structured system of social relationships.

## THE ADVERSARY SYSTEM

The meaningfulness of this notion is illustrated by the answer to a commonly heard complaint about the role of lawyers in litigation. The criticism is that lawyers are interested not in truth, but in winning—and in the pursuit of victory they are highly selective (biased) about what they look for and in the cases they present. The answer to this description, whose accuracy is undeniable, is that it is not the advo-cate's role to be fair and balanced, and to do so would be harmful to the search for truth. If an individual lawyer tried to find the middle ground where truth lies, and to present that as the case, then truth would be foreclosed. The lawyer is unlikely to have found it, and the judge or jury, whose role it is to find that middle ground, would be precluded from finding it. Truth, in this social system, emerges from facts and arguments sought and presented by biased adversaries to disinterested decision makers. The respective biases of advocates, linked in an adversary confrontation, offer the best prospect of unveiling truth. It is the system that produces truth, not its constituent elements. And if either advocate failed to perform his or her (biased) role, the system would fail to produce truth.

This venerated Anglo-Saxon-American system is deliberatley dialectical. Competing views of truth are set against each other; and, it is thought, out of this adversarial tension truth has the greatest chance of emerging before factfinders, who are deliberately kept as distant as possible from the facts and parties and interests at issue. Justice comes not from the wisdom and good will of dedicated and sincere people; it comes from a system intended to work with or without wisdom, good will, and sincerity. Truth comes from a *system* that balances competing views of truth, not from well-intentioned seekers of truth. This is typical of our system of "laws, not men"— structures are to be trusted, not people. Hopelessly flawed and biased humans are organized into a structure that, through its dialectic, converts systematically biased inputs into correct and fair outputs. Modern philosophers of science, incidentally, suggest that this is how science finds truth as well, how competing theories, tested in competitive replications by biased scientists, allow truth to make itself felt (Campbell, 1977). Our legal system, too, beginning with the Constitution, puts its faith in structures—in checks and balances, in adversarial dispute-resolving courts. All this, of course, is the concept. Does it succeed?

Thibaut, Walker, and their associates conducted a series of experiments to compare a number of decision-making procedures designed to resolve disputes (Thibaut and Walker, 1975). Their focus was on *procedural justice*—the ability of mechanisms for resolving disputes to do so in a manner that produces fair decisions. It is to be distinguished from distributive justice, which is concerned with principles by which anything of value may be justly allocated among persons or groups. Procedural justice (1) may often lead to distributive justice, (2) arises when allocation is in dispute, and (3) may be applied even when disputes do not involve problems of allocation, as in criminal justice decisions. Considering the centrality of procedural justice to the legal system and to society, the inattention paid by both legal theorists and social science researchers to the topic has been termed "startling" (Hazard, 1963).

The adversary system of dispute resolution, which is the idealized procedure used in American courts, is one such set of procedures for arriving at a decision. The adversary system is characterized by separated presentations of facts and arguments by advocates aligned with and chosen by the respective disputants to represent them. The adversaries present their cases in direct opposition to each other before decision makers who have not participated in the search for facts, do not guide the adversaries in their presentations, and have no personal interest in the outcome of the dispute. This is one system for trying to achieve a just decision; others exist. The major competitor of the adversary system is the inquisitorial system. While the adversary system leaves maximum control of information search and presentation in the hands of the disputants, inquisitorial decision making leans in the other direction. Under the inquisitorial system (in use, for example, in Europe, the Soviet Union, and China), an attorney assigned by the court obtains information from the disputants and presents both sides to the court for its decision. Thibaut and Walker also experimented with intermediate variations of these procedures—such as a double-inquisitorial method in which each party was assigned its own inquisitor who, while not aligned with that party, presented only its case to the court; and the use of assigned adversaries who were aligned with the disputants, but who were chosen by the decision maker. We can see that the inquisitors or double inquisitors are the ideal of the unbiased attorneys who are trying to find out the truth and to present the truth as they see it to the court.

Thibaut and Walker's research, consisting of controlled experimental simulations of the processes under study, was concerned with the ability of these alternative dispute-resolving procedures to produce justice. In their experiments, this meant the differential ability of the procedures to cancel out initial bias of the decision maker, to cancel out internal biases resulting from the sequencing of presentations (see Chapter 5 on order effects in persuasion), and to compensate for sampling error in the discovered facts. The impact of initial decision-maker bias was most successfully neutralized by adversarial presentation of facts. Skewed distributions of discovered facts about a dispute were conveyed by the inquisitors to the decision makers as the same biased distribution. Under the adversary procedure, disadvantaged parties were benefitted by increased information search by their advocates to compensate for the skewed distribution of discovered facts. Unlike court-centered (inquisitorial) attorneys who were content to end the information search once they had achieved stable, confident (though not necessarily accurate) beliefs about the case, client-centered (adversarial) attorneys searched for more facts when they initially failed to come up with a favorable distribution. In contrast to the assumptions of legal theorists (e.g., Freedman, 1970), incidentally, this balancing process did not result from heightened zeal on the part of both advocates. Those whose information search produced a favorable distribution of facts ceased investigating at about the same point as inquisitorial attorneys.

However well-meaning and confident a person might be that he or she is investigating fairly and doing justice to the parties involved, these findings indicate that justice cannot be produced as well by certain procedures as it can be by others. The judgment of an inquisitor that he or she is doing a fair and accurate job is not nearly so reliable as a set of procedures that have built-in bias-neutralizing features, and work with or without the good intentions of the advocates.

Equally important were Thibaut and Walker's findings concerning the subjective judgments of litigants and of uninvolved observers about the ability of the alternative procedures to dispense justice. Figure 8.1 shows litigants' reactions on measures of perceived fairness of procedure, amount of opportunity for presentation of evidence, satisfaction with procedure, and satisfaction with verdict. On all of these measures, we can see that the more the presentations were separated, aligned with each disputant, and client- rather than court-centered (all maximized by the adversarial procedure), the more the procedure was perceived as fair and satisfying. Most interesting, perhaps, is the finding that parties found guilty were least dissatisfied with the verdict when it resulted from an adversarial process. For uninvolved observers, the separation of presentations appears to be the critical feature of procedural justice, since few differences in judgments were made among the adversarial, assigned adversarial, and

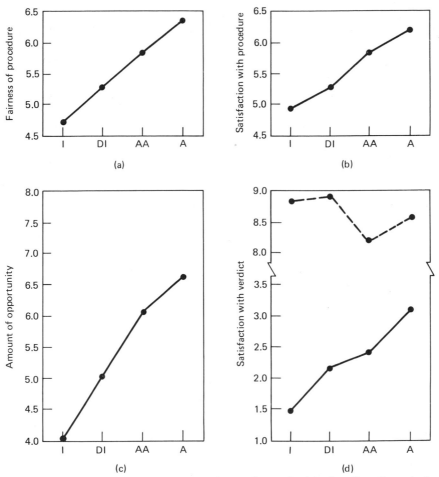

Figure 8.1. Litigants' reactions to various forms of procedural justice. For all panels, I = inquisitorial (the court's officer develops the case to be presented to the decision maker, eliciting information from disputants); DI = dual inquisitorial (two of the court's officers, one for each disputant, develop the case); AA = assigned adversary (each disputant has its own advocate; the advocates have been assigned, not selected by the parties themselves); A = choice adversary (each disputant chooses its own advocate to develop its case and present it before the decision maker). In panel (d), the solid line represents satisfaction ratings for parties that lost; the broken line is for parties that won. We can see that as control of case presentation is placed increasingly in the hands of the disputants themselves, they judge the procedure be more fair, more satisfying, allowing more opportunity to have their position heard, and (even though losing the case) judge the verdict more satisfactory—though obviously parties who won were more satisfied than those who lost. (From Thibaut and Walker, 1975.)

dual inquisitorial procedures, while the inquisitorial was rated much lower.

If trust in justice is placed in individuals, fairness will vary with the individual responsible for dispensing it, and then justice will be achieved less frequently than with the right set of procedures. Research participants, like the designers of our legal system, saw justice flowing more surely from particular systems of procedures than from the efforts of particular persons composing the system.


## ROLES

The patterns of behavior of actors in a social system are thought to be defined and maintained by *roles*—a statement which means essentially that people in social locations behave according to expectations. These expectations are provided by *role senders*, other persons in the role occupant's social environment who hold expectations about how the role occupant should behave (Gross, Mason, and McEachern, 1958). A good deal of convergence exists in the expectations of role senders, enough so that everyone is court would be upset, for example, if the judge began to act as an advocate for one side of a dispute or came down from the bench to ask some spectators what they thought the decision ought to be, or if one of the attorneys began to argue in favor of the other party's case. Yet there also exists considerable incompatibility of expectations, which is called *role conflict*. Such conflicts produce inconsistencies in role enactment as well as personal stress for the role occupant.

Several different kinds of role conflict have been identified. Intra-sender conflict exists when a given role sender has incompatible expectations of the role occupant (as when a client wishes the lawyer simultaneously to take command to solve the client's problem and to defer to the client's decisions on the case). Intra-role conflict exists when different senders have competing expectations for the behavior of a single role (as when a judge is expected by the lawyers to stay out of the case and let them proceed—or not proceed—as they determine, expected by the chief administrative judge to move cases more rapidly through the system, and expected by colleagues to do a careful, conscientious job so that no reversible errors are committed). Inter-role conflict exists when the different roles a person occupies in life impose competing demands on the person's behavior (as when a person is at once an attorney, spouse and parent, town meeting member, scoutleader, and citizen). Some inter-role conflicts are resolved and obviated by law or ethical canon, as when a judge is a member of the same law firm as an attorney whose case is in the judge's court, or when the judge is a friend of one of the parties to the dispute. Research on role conflict indicates with apparent consistency that the greater the amount or intensity of role conflict, the less effectively the role occupant and the organizational system function—with such problems as inconsistency in behavior, anxiety, and low job satisfaction (Kahn, Wolfe, Quinn, Snoek, and Rosenthal, 1964; Wispé and Thayer, 1957). Presumably, resolution of role conflicts, where desirable, would enable the role occupant and the organization to function more effectively.

The courtroom environment provides physical cues as to the roles that various persons are to play (Hazard, 1962). The judge's bench is centered at the head of the courtroom, and elevated above the other persons in court. The attorneys' tables are of equal size and arranged symmetrically before the bench. Some concern has been expressed about the cues given a judge or jury as to the defendant's role (dangerous criminal or innocent citizen), depending upon whether the defendant is kept separate from the proceedings in a defendant's dock or seated at the counsel table, and whether the defendant enters the courtroom through the public entrance (after being free on bail) or is escorted in from the lockup by police, perhaps even wearing prisoner's clothing (after being denied bail or having been unable to raise the necessary amount). Research has indicated that persons who do not go free on bail are more likely to be found guilty than those who do (Single, 1972).

## DISCRETION AND EXCHANGE

The notion of the court as a social system is not limited to relationships among clients, adversaries, judges, and juries, which are formally structured by law. Informal relations exist as well; they are rendered both possible and important by the fact that role occupants have considerable discretion in the decisions they make and actions they perform within their roles, and account for the discrepancy between the law as it is prescribed and the human behavior that is its operationalization.

Consider a given criminal complaint from arrest through disposition, and observe the latitude actors have within the broad constraints of their roles. A citizen observes what is believed to be a crime and can choose to report it or not. The police can choose to respond or not, investigate or not, arrest or not, ask the prosecutor to prosecute or not. The prosecutor can prosecute, alter the charges, or drop the charges. This decision is likely to be made in negotiation with the defense. A judge can dismiss the case at a preliminary hearing or not. About "one half of those arrested are dismissed by the police, a prosecutor, or a magistrate at an early stage of the case" (President's Commission on Law Enforcement and Administration of Justice, 1967). The jury can convict or not. If it acquits it can do so regardless of what the evidence shows, and the defendant must be freed. If it convicts, the judge can set aside the conviction, choose between a range of penalties, or suspend the penalty imposed. The convicted criminal can appeal to higher courts. Or a governor can issue a pardon. If all of that results in imprisonment, a parole board can exercise its discretion in releasing the person.

Role occupants may exercise discretion without exceeding legitimate limits, although some may venture to the borders of those limits. Consider the following description of practices in a Detroit landlord–tenant court:

> If a tenant was unrepresented, the judge ordinarily did not question the landlord regarding his claims, nor did the judge explain defenses to the tenant. The most common explanation given a tenant was that the law permitted him only ten days to move and thus the judge's hands were tied. In addition, judges often asked tenants for receipts for rent paid and corroboration of landlord-breach claims. In contrast, the court supplied complaint and notice forms to the landlords and clerks at the court helped them to fill out the forms if necessary. In addition, the in-court observers noticed during the beginning of the study that the court would not dismiss a nonappearing landlord's case until completion of the docket call, which took approximately forty-five minutes ([while] the tenant sat and waited), but extended no similar cour-

tesy to tardy tenants.    However, once the surprised observers
questioned the court personnel about the practice, it was changed;
thereafter, tenants had thirty minutes after the call within which
to appear. [Mosier and Soble, 1973, p. 63]

Still other role occupants may exceed their role's legitimate limits
in ways that undermine the bias-correcting features of the adversary
system.    In *U.S. v. Rosenberg*, for example, recently obtained FBI
documents indicate that the trial judge engaged in *ex parte* (one-
sided) conferences with the prosecution to discuss the handling of
the case and the penalty the judge would impose, before the trial was
over. (*The Kaufman Papers*, 1977)

Even within the legitimate bounds of the role, each of the system's
actors has a range of choices that may be made.    They are linked
dynamically in a system through which disputes and defendants flow,
where decisions in one part affect decisions in another part, and
where these adjustments can be made with remarkable ease through
the exercise of discretion.    Each component of the system depends
upon preceding and succeeding components to supply it with and re-
lieve it of the matter on which it operates.    Each component tries to
ensure that its own needs, institutional and individual, are met,
which must be done by maintaining exchange relationships with the
rest of the system—exchanging information, support for policies of
other components, competing and cooperating for material and political advantage.    These are the commodities exchanged (Cole, 1975).
Because this is an intelligent system, it meets its individual and sys-
temic needs not only by responding to altered flows of information,
resources, and cases; but its components are alert to cues up and
down stream, trying to anticipate changes in other components of
the system, and trying to get other components to behave in ways
that will serve its own interests.    This often means mutually reinforcing exchange relations and punishing other components if their behavior threatens to harm it (cf. Gergen, 1969; see also Nagel, 1969).
The result is an alert, dynamic social system with a notable ability to
adjust itself to internal (other components) and external (other systems) changes, thereby maintaining remarkable equilibrium, and being remarkably resistant to change.    The most efficient way for the
system to maintain its equilibrium is to expend minimal energy ad-

justing to changes, thereby systemically agreeing not to change, so that routinization becomes the rule.

These abstract points become clear with illustrations. Suppose a prison becomes overcrowded. Its officials transmit informal messages to adjacent subsystems to ease the pressure. Judges respond by suspending more sentences, shortening sentences, placing more people on probation, or even finding fewer defendants guilty. A judge is not eager to make such adjustments, but his or her own subsystem will be in trouble if the prisons cannot hold the prisoners, or if they promote riots or draw critical public attention to the criminal justice system. Because the judge's decisions affect a prosecutor's conviction rate, and reflect on the police officer's arrest record, these system actors will either anticipate or rapidly respond to the judge's altered behavior. Prosecutors may become more selective in the cases they elect to prosecute or press harder for negotiated guilty pleas. The police may relax their arrest frequency or concentrate on more serious offenses. Parole officials may increase the rate of return of inmates to society.

A certain amount of bureaucratic accounting takes place, and these adjustments become favors to be returned at a later time, perhaps when the judge or prosecutor or police have to alter their behavior as a result of some change in material, political, legal, or organizational demands on their subsystem (e.g., the legislature cuts back on funding; someone is running for a sensitive office; a Supreme Court opinion forces a change in practice; the component becomes under- or overstaffed). Reciprocity in such exchanges promotes trust and cooperation among system components (cf. Skolnick, 1967).

System components are able to exert stabilizing pressures on other components of the system. If the police are under pressure to improve their clearance rate for reported crimes, they may begin making more arrests. The prosecutor, not wanting a collection of weak cases with which to go to court or the bargaining table, may send the cases back to the police for further investigation or refuse to prosecute. Police functioning would suffer from too many rejected cases, so police practice is restored to its previous state to accomodate the prosecutor's pressure. A different solution might meet the needs of the police, and the prosecutor, defendant, and defense attorney all at once. The prosecutor could offer a much reduced sentence in return for the defendant's plea of guilty to a longer list of crimes—the more he will confess to, the shorter the sentence will be. This improves the police clearance rate, obtains more convictions for the prosecutor, and supplies the defendant with a lighter penalty. Note that this requires the cooperation of the defense counsel to "sell" the deal to the defendant, and the judge to accept the prosecutor's recommendation of a lower penalty for a longer list of guilty pleas. All of this requires an impressive degree of inter-component trust and cooperation.

In Chapter 5 we discussed plea bargaining between prosecution and defense attorneys, who provide one of the best examples of cooperative relations. The prosecutor and the defense attorney usually have well established, friendly, cooperative relations that help each achieve their goals. What the defense attorney has to offer the client is influence with the prosecutor. In order to maintain that influence, the attorney's cases must be compromised to the prosecutor. In order to obtain negotiated pleas, the prosecutor has to trade acceptable deals to the defense attorney, who will help the prosecutor sell the deal to the defendant. In Chapter 2 we reviewed in some detail the findings of Ebbesen and Konečni (1975) that judges' bail decisions closely track the recommendations of the prosecutor. This probably holds also for sentencing. The judge's cooperation is essential to the bail and plea-bargaining process. And if the judge wishes to keep those 87–93% of plea-bargaining cases out of his court, he must help the defense. Yet the judge has limits, and judges have individual decision-making styles. The prosecution must be able to anticipate what the judge will do in order to bargain effectively. Can you imagine how quickly the cooperation would stop and the system would break down if the judge refused to go along with sentences asked for by prosecutors? Or if, after reaching an agreement, the prosecutor reneged and asked for a heavy sentence? These uncooperative behaviors might happen only a few times before the defense stopped cooperating with the prosecution and the prosecutor and court found themselves with an enormous docket of cases they actually had to try. The behavior of actors in the social system endures because it is instrumental to meeting their needs and achieves their goals. They are locked into their patterns of behavior by a mutually rewarding system of exchange relationships. These cooperative exchange relations among components of the system represent another major way the truth-generating benefits of adversary procedural justice are circumvented. The larger system, in terms of range of activities and time frame, can have still other effects.

The existence of many actors in the system raises the potential for increased *diffusion of responsibility* (Latané and Darley, 1970), wherein, despite wide discretion to act, no action is taken. Each decision-making component may decline to take the responsibility for a decision because it knows that other components are equally capable of taking action. Consider this scenario: The jury convicts a defendant about whose guilt it has some doubts, thinking that if they are wrong, the judge will correct that decision. Although having some doubts, the judge decides that the jury must not have had any, or it would not have made the decision it did; and (anyway) if the verdict is wrong, the governor can always pardon the defendant later. The governor decides that if the defendant had not been guilty, the jury would not have convicted, or the judge would have set aside the conviction. By the time the executioners take over, they can rest in the comfort of knowing that the law and penalty were the legislature's, the jury found the defendant guilty, and the judge and governor accepted that decision. Surely if this were not the proper decision, one of these many system components would have said so.

Defense counsel behavior, which may in an isolated case appear irrational to a client, is quite rational from a systems perspective. Too zealous a defense in a single case (a failure to cooperate) would be costly to future clients of the defense attorney. It would be an instance of losing by winning; a short-term victory would be parlayed into long-term multiple defeat by impairing the ability of the defense attorney to deal effectively with the prosecutor.

This perspective of short-term versus long-term, or narrow versus wide-range rationality, operates in civil litigation as well. The outcomes of lawyer and client may not correspond. Thus, while a client desires to go to court and fight it out, the lawyer would prefer to settle, not only because the code of ethics calls for settlements when possible, but because the lawyer usually can save time and make more money by settling a number of cases in the time required to prepare one for trial. The lawyer's long-term considerations also have to do with maintaining cooperative relations with other lawyers and the effect behavior in this case may have on future cases. Zealous representation today may interfere with cooperation on settlements tomorrow.

The trouble with such a social system is that it precludes the justice offered by the adversarial procedures studied by Thibaut and Walker, which is the way our legal system is supposed to resolve disputes. The level of cooperation created in such a bargain-ridden discretionary system creates a routinization that may deprive clients of justice. While they are viewed as temporary visitors or occasional annoyances in a system run by professionals with long-term interests, it is the clients whom the system is intended to serve. Plea bargaining exists extensively because it provides mutually reinforcing outcomes for all of the major actors in the system; it meets their needs. It keeps court dockets manageable, gets convictions for prosecutors, business for defense lawyers, and individual justice for some defendants. But it may interfere with the production of justice. Is this social system the adversary process? Is it conflict-generating? Is it justice-producing? Or is it cooperation, routinization, collusion? The National Advisory Commission on Criminal Justice Standards and Goals (1973) has called for the abolition of plea bargaining. And many observers of the process have put their judgments of the system into the titles of their studies of it:

> "Pleading Guilty for Considerations: A Study of Bargain Justice" (Newman, 1956)
> *Justice Denied* (Downie, 1971)
> "Did You Have a Lawyer When You Went to Court? No, I Had a Public Defender." (Casper, 1971)
> "In Search of the Adversary System: The Cooperative Practices of Private Criminal Defense Attorneys" (Battle, 1971)
> "The Practice of Law as Confidence Game" (Blumberg, 1967)

## CLIENTS IN THE SYSTEM

The most important participants in the court and its surround are clients. They are the disputants whose conflicts are brought for resolution, the defendants who are processed by the system, the consumers of legal services, the public in whose interest the system purportedly exists. Paradoxically, these most important elements in the system are the least noticed by those who study the system and by the system's components, who worry most about each other. And yet it is logical that they are ignored, for in spite of their importance, they have the least palpable influence on the system we have been discussing. This is so because they flow through it, spending a relatively brief time in it, establishing relations only with their own attorney (often barely), and being little organized among themselves. Books on courts and the legal system have chapters on police, judges, the legal profession, and correction officials, but none on clients. It is not without some embarrassment that this volume as well is deficient on the role of clients and the public in litigation. There simply is little research on clients and their relationship to the social system that exists to serve them.

The research that does exist generally is limited to surveys of clients' beliefs and opinions about the law and lawyers (e.g., Missouri Bar–Prentice Hall Survey, 1963) or about their legal needs (e.g., Special Committee to Survey Legal Needs, 1976). Yet their real or potential influence goes beyond that of the opinions of bystanders or an accounting of the needs of passive beneficiaries or victims of services. Clients in the aggregate affect the system; dynamics of the larger society influence when and how many clients will enter the system of litigation and what impact they will have on it and it on them. The number of clients seeking the services of attorneys (in noncriminal matters) is influenced by citizens' knowledge of what problems are legal problems, how much attorneys cost, how to find a lawyer, and so on, which information is all transmitted through informal social networks (Ladinsky, 1976). These factors are the first filter that determines whether clients enter the arena of litigation or not. These factors, along with skills in dealing with lawyers, have come to be called *client competence* (e.g., Brickman and Lempert, 1976). There are plans on the drawing board for using client feedback to attorneys to help shape the attorneys' services to the client (e.g., Baron and Hoffrichter, 1976). And clients set the extremes of tolerable performance by attorneys in the same way that patients do for physicians: by filing professional malpractice suits against them.

Perhaps the leading study of lawyer–client relations is Rosenthal's *Lawyer and Client: Who's in Charge?* (1974). A lawyer may be the employee of the client, serving the client's needs in a collaborative relationship with the client, or be an agent-mediator, manipulator-coercer of the client, imposing on the client definitions of the problem and decisions about solutions. Clients may adopt role relationships with their attorneys wherein the clients can be essentially passive, allowing major decisions in the case, the gathering and organizing of evidence, and so on, to be made by the lawyers; or the clients can be active in these matters. Client activity–passivity was significantly correlated with dollar recoveries by the plaintiff clients, such that more active clients won larger damages. On the other hand, client judgments do not appear to be sufficient to assess attorney performance. About half the clients were satisfied with their recoveries, and two-thirds were satisfied with the performance of their lawyers. Yet 77% of them won amounts equal to less than that expected by a panel of experts in that area of litigation. This is similar to a finding in health care that most patients were delighted with their surgeons' performance in removing their appendixes, while the pathologists' reports showed that most of them did not need removal at all. Client satisfaction can influence, but is not by itself a reliable measure of, quality.

## THE COURT AS A SUBSYSTEM OF SOCIETY

The delineation of any set of interconnected actors into a "system" is always somewhat arbitrary. Those actors are necessarily connected with actors outside of the system under study, and so systems spill into other systems. Although we endeavored to begin this chapter with attention only to the court and its immediate surround, we have occasionally alluded to other interconnections, as with police, prison and parole officials, appellate courts, and legislatures. It should be clear by now that actions and anticipated actions of police, higher courts, legislatures, news media, business practices in a community, and so on, will have some impact on one or more components of the court system, and the entire system will adapt in order to reestablish equilibrium in the changed environment. These adaptations may take the form of altered screening of cases, more or fewer settlements, changes in decisions made on the cases, and so on. In this final section we wish to view the major actors in our system as fully embedded in the larger society, as persons whose behavior is importantly determined by the information, resources, personnel, and so on, that are imposed, provided, or withheld by that larger social system. This will be but a brief sketch in order to provide perspective, and so that we may appreciate the fact that behavior occurs in a context—in this case a context that exists far from the actors and yet is all about them.

A visit to the local courthouse offers an immediate and striking hint of what that context is. Defendants, their families, and the witnesses waiting to testify in criminal cases represent predominantly the lower socioeconomic strata of society. Across the corridor in the civil division, the clientele tend to be wealthier business people, large organizations, and government agencies doing battle with each other and with people of moderate means. The disputes that arise and the people who are competing for their respective interests do not arrive in court at random. They are delivered there presorted by the structure of the larger society and the interests and conflicts it generates.

The lawyers themselves are filtered by the structure of society into their positions. Higher socioeconomic status persons are conveyed to the more prestigious law schools and thence to the higher-priced and higher-powered firms which serve wealthier clients (Ladinsky, 1963, 1976).

Wealthier litigants are able to select and afford what are presumptively more competent lawyers and are in a better position to control them and receive more conscientious representation. Partly because the lawyers in the civil division are better, and better financed, and thus given more time and support resources, the civil law is better developed and more finely polished than is the criminal law. Because of their position in the larger society and the nature of their concerns, the wealthier and larger organizational interests tend to make repeated appearances in court compared to the average citizen, who may litigate once or twice in a lifetime. The wealthier clients also are better able to press their case on to higher and higher courts. Galanter (1974) has discussed the possible advantages that accrue to the "repeat players" over the "one-shotters." These advantages include advance intelligence about the system and commensurate ability to anticipate legal needs (they have the security deposits and form contracts), established relations with specialists, continuity, a long-term ability to play the odds rather than put all their efforts into a single case, and the ability to use litigation to re-structure the rules so that future cases can be won more easily and inexpensively. The result of this asymmetry of power is that repeat players are the clients who can exert a serious impact on the rules of law that determine the outcome of disputes.

By contrast, the less wealthy often do not even know when they have a cause of legal action, or, knowing that, do not know how to find a lawyer or are not able to afford one if they do find one. The process of defining problems as legal problems and finding a lawyer to represent the client is a process that occurs at some distance from the formal system of litigation, through an informal social network of friends, relatives, and neighbors, who first channel people to lawyers (Ladinsky, 1976). There is some evidence that improved access to and availability of legal services has transferred power to the less powerful, giving them some of the advantages otherwise retained by the repeat players. Brakel (1974), for example, found that once they obtained access to lawyers, and through the lawyers access to the courts, persons previously without such access won a substantially higher percentage of their cases than is typical in civil trials.

The judicial branch itself is but one component of a formal, constitutionally defined legal system. If actions of the judicial branch exceeded tolerable limits, such that public pressure or social disruption resulted, the executive and/or legislative branches would act to compensate for or constrain the judiciary. These adjustments could take the form of presidential pardons, police rendering summary judgment and punishment without trial, or legislatures writing new laws or constitutional amendments to return behavior of the courts to prior, more socially or politically agreeable practices.

When we examine the social system that is the court with an alertness to its equilibrium-maintaining tendencies, both within itself and as part of a larger system, we begin to see the major problem of the courts as being less a matter of maintaining order and more a matter of overcoming resistance to change.

## SUMMARY

While most of this book analyzes components of the court, this chapter adopts a view of these components functioning together as a system. The adversary system is dialectical—justice is produced by the joint operation of its components, not by any one of the individual components themselves. A major illustration of the "system" nature of litigation is given by research on procedural justice. Another principle for conceptualizing the court system is given by role theory, including role occupants, role senders, and the several forms of role conflict, as well as by the physical arrangement of actors in the trial. Actors within the system have discretion in the execution of their roles, yet the exercise of discretion is influenced by such social psychological phenomena as exchange and diffusion of responsibility. This leads to energy-saving but troubling routinization. Clients are a major but neglected element of the system. Also, the court system is a subsystem of society, adapting to and being shaped by other parts of the legal structure and by society. This is illustrated by: the automatic and inadvertent selection by social class of people into civil and criminal courts, "one-shot" and "repeat players" and their relative advantages in altering the system and the law, and court as one branch of a tripartite legal system.

# REFERENCES

*ABA Standards Relating to the Defense Function*, Standard 7.2.

Abraham, H. J. *The judicial process*. New York: Oxford University Press, 1975 (third ed.).

Adorno, T., Frenkel-Brunswick, E., Levinson, D., and Sanford, N. *The authoritarian personality*. New York: Harper, 1950.

Alker, H. A. Is personality situationally specific or intrapsychically consistent? *Journal of Personality*, 1972, **40**, 1–16.

Allport, G. W., and Postman, L. J. The basic psychology of rumor. *Transactions of the New York Academy of Sciences*, Series II, 1945, **8**, 61–81.

Alschuler, A. W. The prosecutor's role in plea bargaining. *University of Chicago Law Review*, 1968, **36**, 61.

Alschuler, A. W. Defense attorney's role in plea bargaining. *Yale Law Journal*, 1975, **84**, 1179–1314.

American Law Institute. *Model penal code, proposed official draft*. Philadelphia: American Law Institute, 1962.

American Psychiatric Association. Durham plus five years (symposium). *American Journal of Psychiatry*, 1959, **116**, 287–348.

Anastasi, A. *Fields of applied psychology*. New York: McGraw-Hill, 1964.

Anderson, N. H. Information integration theory: A brief survey. In D. H. Krantz, R. C. Atkinson, R. D. Luce, and P. Suppes (eds.), *Contemporary developments in mathematical psychology* (vol. 2). San Francisco: Freeman, 1974.

Anderson, N. H. Social perception and cognition. Technical Report #62, University of California, San Diego, 1976.

Apfelbaum, E. On conflicts and bargaining. In L. Berkowitz (ed.), *Advances in experimental social psychology* (vol. 7). New York: Academic Press, 1974.

*Apodaca, Cooper, and Madden v. Oregon*. 32 L Ed. 2d 184 (1972).

Ares, C. E., Rankin, A., and Sturz, H. The Manhattan bail project: An interim report on the use of pre-trial parole. *New York University Law Review*, 1963, **38**, 71–92.

Arens, R. *Insanity defense*. New York: Philosophical Library, 1974.

Arens, R., Granfield, D. D., and Susman, J. Jurors, jury charges, and insanity. *Catholic University of America Law Review*, 1965, **14**, 1–23.

Aronson, E., Willerman, B., and Floyd, J. The effect of a pratfall on increasing interpersonal attractiveness. *Psychonomic Science*, 1966, **4**, 227–228.

Asch, S. E. Effects of group pressure upon the modification and distortion of judgments. In G. E. Swanson, T. M. Newcomb, and E. L. Hartley (eds.),

*Readings in social psychology* (rev. ed.).  New York: Holt, Rinehart & Winston, 1952 .

Bales, R. F. and Borgatta, E. F.  Size of group as a factor in the interaction profile.  In A. P. Hare, E. F. Borgatta, and R. F. Bales (eds.), *Small groups.*  New York: Knopf, 1955.

*Ballew v. Georgia* 46 LW4217 (1978).

Bandura, A.  *Principles of behavior modification.*  New York: Holt, Rinehart & Winston, 1969.

Barland, G. H., and Raskin, D. C.  Detection of deception.  In W. F. Prokasy and D. C. Raskin (eds.), *Electrodermal activity in psychological research.*  New York: Academic Press, 1973.

Baron, C. H., and Hofrichter, R.  Quality control moves to center stage.  *New Directions in Legal Services*, 1976, **1**, 21–22ff.

Bartlett, F. C.  *Remembering: A study in experimental and social psychology.*  Cambridge: Cambridge University Press, 1957 (originally published in 1932).

Bass, B. M., and Klubeck, S.  Effects of seating arrangements in leaderless group discussions. *Journal of Abnormal and Social Psychology*, 1952, **47**, 724–727.

Battle, J. B.  In search of the adversary system: The cooperative practices of private criminal defense attorneys.  *University of Texas Law Review*, 1971, **50**, 66.

Bavelas, A., Hastorf, A. H., Gross, A. E., and Kite, W. R.  Experiments on the alteration of group structure.  *Journal of Experimental Social Psychology*, 1965, **1**, 55–70.

Bazelon, D.  Psychiatrists and the adversary process.  *Scientific American*, 1974, **230**(6), 18–23.

Bem, D.  Inducing belief in false confessions.  *Journal of Personality and Social Psychology*, 1966, **3**, 707.

Bem, D.  Self perception: An alternative interpretation of cognitive dissonance phenomena. *Psychological Review*, 1967, **74**, 183.

Bem, D. J.  *Beliefs, attitudes, and human affairs.*  Belmont, Calif.: Brooks/Cole, 1970.

Bermant, G.  "The notion of conspiracy is not tasty to Americans," *Psychology Today*, 1975, **8**, 60–67.

Bermant, G., and Coppock, R.  Outcomes of six- and twelve-member jury trials: An analysis of 128 civil cases in the State of Washington.  *Washington Law Review*, 1973, **48**, 593–596.

Berscheid, E., and Walster, E.  Physical attractiveness.  In L. Berkowitz (ed.), *Advances in experimental social psychology* (vol. 7).  New York: Academic Press, 1974.

Bird, C.  The influence of press upon the accuracy of report.  *Journal of Abnormal and Social Psychology*, 1927, **22**, 123–129.

Blumberg, A. S.  The practice of law as confidence game.  *Law and Society Review*, 1967, **1**, 15–39.

Boehm, V.  Mr. Prejudice, Miss Sympathy and the authoritarian personality: An application of psychological measuring techniques to the problem of jury bias. *Wisconsin Law Review*, 1968, 734–750.

Bower, G. H., and Karlin, M. B. Depth of processing pictures of faces and recognition memory. *Journal of Experimental Psychology*, 1974, **103**, 751–757.

Bowers, K. S. Situationism in psychology: An analysis and a critique. *Psychological Review*, 1973, **80**, 307–336.

Brakel, S. J. *Judicare: Public funds, private lawyers, and poor people.* Chicago: American Bar Foundation, 1974.

Brehm, J. W. *A theory of psychological reactance.* New York: Academic Press, 1966.

Brickman, L., and Lempert, R. (eds.). *The role of research in the delivery of legal services.* Washington, D.C.: Resource Center for Consumers of Legal Services, 1976.

*Brigham Young University Law Review.* Symposium: The use of videotape in the courtroom. 1975.

Broeder, D. W. The University of Chicago jury project. *Nebraska Law Review*, 1958, **38**, 744–761.

Brown, B. R. The effects of need to maintain face on interpersonal bargaining. *Journal of Experimental Social Psychology*, 1968, **4**, 107–122.

Brown, B. R. Saving face. *Psychology Today*, 1971, **4**, 55–59ff.

Brown, E., Deffenbacher, K., and Sturgill, W. Memory for faces and the circumstances of encounter. *Journal of Applied Psychology*, 1977, **62**, 311–318.

Brumbaugh, L. J., *Legal Reasoning and Briefing*, Indianapolis: Bobbs-Merrill Co., 1917.

Bruner, J. S. Social psychology and perception. In E. E. Maccoby, T. M. Newcomb, and E. D. Hartley (eds.), *Readings in social psychology.* New York: Holt, Rinehart & Winston, 1958.

Bruner, J. S., and Postman, J. L. On the perception of incongruity: A paradigm. *Journal of Personality*, 1949, **18**, 206–223.

Bruner, J. S., Postman, L. J., and Rodrigues, J. Expectation and the perception of color. *American Journal of Psychology*, 1951, **64**, 216–227.

Buckhout, R. *A jury without peers.* New York: Center for Responsive Psychology, 1973.

Buckhout, R. Eyewitness testimony. *Scientific American*, 1974a, **321**(6), 23–31.

Buckhout, R. Eyewitness recall of facts about a person. *Bulletin of the Psychonomic Society*, 1974b, **4**, 191–192.

Buckhout, R. Note. *Social Action and the Law Newsletter*, 1975, 2(3), 7.

Burger, W. Chief Justice Burger proposes first steps towards certification of trial advocacy specialists. *American Bar Association Journal*, 1974, **60**, 171.

Byrne, D. Attitudes and attraction. In L. Berkowitz (ed.), *Advances in Experimental Social Psychology* (vol. 4). New York: Academic Press, 1969.

Byrne, D., and Clore, G. L.   A reinforcement model of evaluative responses. *Personality: An International Journal*, 1970, **1**, 103–128.

Campbell, D. T.   Reforms as experiments. *American Psychologist*, 1969, **24**, 409–429.

Campbell, D. T.   *William James lectures.*   Cambridge, Mass.: Harvard University Press, 1977.

Campbell, D. T., and Stanley, J. C.   *Experimental and quasi-experimental designs for research.*   Chicago: Rand McNally, 1963.

Carlin, J. E.   *Lawyers on their own.*   New Brunswick, N.J.: Rutgers University Press, 1962.

Carlin, J. E.   *Lawyers' ethics.*   New York: Russell Sage Foundation, 1966.

Carlson, A. B., and Werts, C. E.   Relationships among law school predictors, law school performance, and bar examination results. *Law School Admission Research.*   Princeton, N.J.: Educational Testing Service, 1976.

Carlson, R. J.   Measuring the quality of legal services: An idea whose time has not come. *Law and Society Review*, 1976, **11**, 287–318.

Casper, J. D.   Did you have a lawyer when you went to court? No, I had a public defender. *Yale Review of Law and Social Action*, 1971, **1**, 4–9.

Chertkoff, J. M., and Conley, M.   Opening offer and frequency of concession as bargaining strategies. *Journal of Personality and Social Psychology*, 1967, **1**, 181–185.

Clyne, P.   *Guilty but insane.*   London: Thomas Nelson and Sons, 1973.

Cole, G. F.   *Decision to prosecute.*   Law and Society Review, 1970, **4**, 331–343.

Cole, G. F.   *The American system of criminal justice.*   Belmont, Calif.: Wadsworth, 1975.

*Colgrove v. Battin*, 413 U.S. 149 (1973).

*Commonwealth of Massachusetts v. Kenneth Edelin*, 1975, 1–30.

Crano, W. D., and Brewer, M. B.   *Principles of research in social psychology.*   New York: McGraw-Hill, 1973.

Crombag, H. F.   Cooperation and competition in means-interdependent triads. *Journal of Personality and Social Psychology*, 1966, **4**, 692–695.

Crosson, R. F.   An investigation into certain personality variables among capital trial jurors. *Dissertation Abstracts*, 1967, **27**, 3668B–3669B.

Cullinan, E., and Clark, H. W.   *Preparation for trial of civil actions*, 3d ed.   Philadelphia: Committee on Continuing Legal Education of the American Law Institute, 1956.

Dallenbach, K. M.   The relation of memory error to time-interval. *Psychological Review*, 1913, **20**, 323–337.

D'Andrade, R. G.   Memory and the assessment of behavior. In H. M. Blalock (ed.), *Measurement in the social sciences.*   Chicago: Aldine, 1974.

Danet, B.   Language and the construction of reality in the courtroom. I: Semantic issues in the trial of Kenneth Edelin. Mimeo, Boston University, 1975.

Davis, J. H.   *Group performance.*   New York: Addison-Wesley, 1969.

Davis, J. H.   Group decision and social interaction: A theory of social decision schemes. *Psychological Review*, 1973, **80**, 97–125.

Davis, J. H., Bray, R. M., and Holt, R. W.  The empirical study of social decision processes in juries.   In J. Tapp and F. Levine (eds.), *Law, justice and the individual in society: Psychological and legal issues*.   New York: Holt, Rinehart & Winston, 1977.

Davis, J. H., Kerr, N. L. Atkin, R. S., Holt, R., and Meek, D.  The decision processes of 6- and 12-person mock juries assigned unanimous and ²/₃ majority rules. *Journal of Personality and Social Psychology*, 1975, **32**, 1–14.

Dawes, R. M. *Fundamentals of attitude measurement*.  New York: Wiley, 1972.

Dawes, R. M., and Corrigan, B.  Linear models in decision making. *Psychological Bulletin*, 1974, **81**, 95.

Dean, J. M. *Illegitimacy of plea bargaining*.  Federal Probation, 1974, **38**, 18–23.

Denenberg, H. S.   *A shopper's guide to lawyers*.   Harrisburg: Pennsylvania Insurance Department, 1974.

Derbyshire, R. *Medical licensure and discipline in the United States*.  Baltimore: The Johns Hopkins Press, 1969.

Dershowitz, A.   Imprisonment by judicial hunch. *American Bar Association Journal*, 1971, **57**, 560–564.

DeSloovere, F.  The functions of judge and jury in the interpretation of statutes. *Harvard Law Review*, 1933, **46**, 1086–1110.

Dessions, G. H., Freedman, L. Z., Donnelly, R. G., and Redlich, F. C.   Drug-induced revelation and criminal investigation. *Yale Law Journal*, 1953, **62**, 315–347.

Deutsch, M.  A theory of cooperation and competition. *Human Relations*, 1949, **2**, 129–152.

Deutsch, M., and Krauss, R. M.  The effect of threat on interpersonal bargaining. *Journal of Abnormal and Social Psychology*, 1960, **61**, 181–189.

Deutscher, I. *What we say/what we do*.  Glenview, Ill.: Scott, Foresman, 1973.

Devlin, Rt. Hon. Lord Patrick.  Report to the Secretary of State for the House Department of the Departmental Committee on Evidence of Identification in Criminal Cases, House of Commons, April 26, 1976.  Chairman: Rt. Hon. Lord Devlin, London: Her Majesty's Stationery Office.

Dhanens, T. P., and Lundy, R. M.  Hypnotic and waking suggestions and recall. *International Journal of Clinical and Experimental Hypnosis*, 1975, **23**, 68–79.

Diamond, S. S.  A jury experiment reanalyzed. *University of Michigan Journal of Law Reform*, 1974, **7**, 520–532.

Diamond, S. S. and Zeisel, H.  A courtroom experiment on juror selection and decision making.   Paper presented at the annual meeting of the American Psychological Association, New Orleans, 1974.

Dion, K.   Physical attractiveness and evaluations of children's transgressions. *Journal of Personality and Social Psychology*, 1972, **24**, 207–213.

Donnell, J. D.   Corporate counsel and his "client": Use of role analysis to illumine strains in the lawyer–client relationship. *Indiana Law Journal*, 1970, **45**, 514.

Doob, A. N., and Kirshenbaum, H. M. Bias in police lineups—Partial remembering. *Journal of Police Science and Administration*, 1973, **1**, 287–293.

Dorcus, R. M. Recall under hypnosis of amnestic events. *International Journal of Clinical and Experimental Hypnosis*, 1960, **8**, 57–61.

*Dow v. Carnegie-Illinois Steel Corporation*, 224 F. 2nd 414 (3rd Cir. 1954).

Downie, L. *Justice denied.* New York: Praeger, 1971.

Duncker, K. The influence of past experience on perceptual properties. *American Journal of Psychology*, 1939, **52**, 255–265.

Dunn, R. E., and Goldman, M. Competition and noncompetition and feelings toward group and nongroup members. *Journal of Social Psychology*, 1966, **68**, 299–311.

Ebbesen, E. B., and Konečni, V. J. Decision-making and information integration in the courts: The setting of bail. *Journal of Personality and Social Psychology*, 1975, **32**, 805–821.

Ebbesen, E. B., and Konečni, V. J. Fairness in sentencing: Severity of crime and judicial decision making. Paper presented at the annual meeting of the American Psychological Association, 1976.

Ebbinghaus, H. E. *Memory: A contribution to experimental psychology.* New York: Dover, 1964 (originally published in 1885).

Efran, M. G. The effect of physical appearance on the judgment of guilt, interpersonal attraction, and severity of recommended punishment in a simulated jury task. *Journal of Research in Personality*, 1974, **8**, 45–54.

Ekman, P., and Friessen, W. V. Nonverbal leakage and clues to deception. *Psychiatry*, 1969, **32**, 88--106.

Emerson, C. D. Personality tests for prospective jurors. *Kentucky Law Journal*, 1968 (note) **56** (summer), 832–854.

*Estelle v. Williams*, 96 Supreme Court 1691 (1976).

Etzioni, A. Creating an imbalance. *Trial*, 1974, **10**, 28ff.

Fairley, W. B., and Mosteller, F. (eds.). *Statistics and public policy.* Reading, Mass.: Addison-Wesley, 1977.

Falknor, J. F., and Steffan, D. T. Evidence of character: From the "crucible of the community" to the "couch of the psychiatrist." *University of Pennsylvania Law Review*, 1954, **102**, 980–994.

Fine, B. J. Conclusion-drawing, communicator credibility and anxiety as factors in opinion change. *Journal of Abnormal and Social Psychology*, 1957, **54**, 369–374.

Finkelstein, M. O. The application of statistical decision theory to the jury discrimination cases. *Harvard Law Review*, 1966 (December), **80**, 338–376.

Finkelstein, M. O., and Fairley, W. B. A Bayesian approach to identification evidence. *Harvard Law Review*, 1970, **83**, 489–517.

Forston, R. F. Judges' instructions: A quantitative analysis of jurors' listening comprehension. *Today's Speech*, 1970, **18**, 34–38.

Franklin, M. A., Chanin, R. H., and Mark, I. Accidents, money, and the law: A study of the economics of personal injury litigation. *Columbia Law Review*, 1961, **61**, 1–39.

Freedman, L. Z. "Truth" drugs. *Scientific American*, 1960, **202**(3), 145–154.

Freedman, M.   Professional responsibilities of the civil practitioner.   In D. Weckstein (ed.), *Education in the professional responsibilities of the lawyer*. Charlottesville, Va.: The University Press of Virginia, 1970.

Friedman, H.   Trial by jury: Criteria for convictions, jury size and type I and type II errors. *The American Statistician*, 1972, **26**, 21–23.

Friedman, L. M. *Law and society*. Englewood Cliffs, N.J.: Prentice-Hall, 1977.

Friedman, L. M., and Macaulay, S.   *Law and the behavioral sciences*.   Indianapolis: Bobbs-Merrill, 1977 (second ed.).

Galanter, M.   Why the "haves" come out ahead: Speculations on the limits of legal change. *Law and Society Review*, 1974, **9**, 95–160.

Gallo, P. S.   Effects of increased incentives upon the use of threat in bargaining. *Journal of Personality and Social Psychology*, 1966, **4**, 14–20.

Gallo, P. S.   Prisoners of our own dilemma?   Paper presented at the meeting of the Western Psychological Association, San Diego, March, 1968.

Gallo, P., and Sheposh, J.   Effects of incentive magnitude on cooperation in the Prisoners' Dilemma Game: A reply to Gumpert, Deutsch, and Epstein. *Journal of Personality and Social Psychology*, 1971, **19**, 42–46.

Gallo, P., Funk, S. G., and Levine, J. R.   Reward size, method of presentation, and number of alternatives in a Prisoners' Dilemma Game. *Journal of Personality and Social Psychology*, 1969, **13**, 239–244.

Gardner, D. S.   The perception and memory of witnesses. *Cornell Law Quarterly*, 1933, **18**, 391–409.

Gardner, M. R.   The myth of the impartial psychiatric expert—Some comments concerning criminal responsibility and the decline of the age of therapy. *Law and Psychology Review*, 1976, **2**, 99–122.

Gaudet, F. J.   Individual differences in the sentencing tendencies of judges. *Archives of Psychology*, 1938, **32**(230), all.

Gelfand, A. E., and Solomon, H.   A study of Poisson's models for jury verdicts in criminal and civil trials. *Journal of the American Statistical Association*, 1973, **68**, 271–278.

Gelfand, A. E., and Solomon, H.   Modeling jury verdicts in the American legal system. *Journal of the American Statistical Association*, 1974, **69**, 32–37.

Gergen, K. J. *The psychology of behavior exchange*. Reading, Mass.: Addison-Wesley, 1969.

Gibson, J. J. *The senses considered as perceptual systems*. Boston: Houghton Mifflin, 1966.

Gordon, R.   A study in forensic psychology: Petit jury verdicts as a function of the number of jury members. Unpublished doctoral dissertation, University of Oklahoma, 1968.

Gough, H. G.   Clinical versus statistical prediction in psychology. In L. Postman (ed.), *Psychology in the making*. New York: Knopf, 1962.

Gouldner, A. W.  The norm of reciprocity: A preliminary statement. *American Sociological Review*, 1960, **25**, 161–178.

Grether, W. F., and Baker, C. A.  Visual presentation of information.  In H. P. Van Cott and R. G. Kinkade (eds.), *Human engineering guide to equipment design*. Washington, D.C.: U.S. Government Printing Office, 1972.

Griffitt, W., and Jackson, T.  Simulated jury decisions: The influence of jury-defendant attitude similarity–dissimilarity. *Social Behavior and Personality*, 1973, **1**, 1–7.

Gross, N., Mason, W., and McEachern, A. W.  *Explorations in role analysis: Studies of the school superintendency role*. New York: Wiley, 1958.

Grossack, M. M.  Some effects of cooperation and competition upon small group behavior. *Journal of Abnormal and Social Psychology*, 1954, **49**, 341–348.

Gulliver, P. H.  Negotiations as a mode of dispute settlement: Towards a general model. *Law and Society Review*, 1973, **1**, 667–691.

Hagan, J.  Extra-legal attributes and criminal sentencing: An assessment of a sociological viewpoint. *Law and Society Review*, 1974, **8**, 357–383.

Handler, J.  *The lawyer and his community: The practicing bar in a middle-sized city*. Madison: University of Wisconsin Press, 1967.

Hartshorne, H., and May, M. A. *Studies in deceit*. New York: MacMillan, 1928.

Hastorf, A. H., and Cantril, H.  They saw a game: A case study. *Journal of Abnormal and Social Psychology*, 1954, **49**, 129–134.

Hastorf, A. H., Schneider, D. J., and Polefka, J. *Person perception*. Reading, Mass.: Addison-Wesley, 1970.

Hawkins, C. H.  Interaction rates of jurors aligned in factions. *American Sociological Review*, 1962, **27**, 689–691.

Hazard, G.  *Research in civil procedure*. New Haven: Walter E. Meyer Research Institute of Law, 1963.

Hazard, J.  Furniture arrangement as a symbol of judicial roles. *Etc.*, 1962, **19**, 181.

Heider, F.  *The psychology of interpersonal relations*. New York: Wiley, 1958.

Henney, J. G.  The jurors look at our judges. *Oklahoma Bar Association Journal*, 1947, **18**, 1508–1513.

Heumann, M.  A note on plea bargaining and case pressure. *Law and Society Review*, 1975, **9**, 515–528.

Hilgard, E. R., Atkinson, R. C., and Atkinson, R. L. *Introduction to psychology*. New York: Harcourt, Brace, Jovanovich, 1975.

Holbrook, J. C.  *A survey of metropolitan trial courts in Los Angeles*. Los Angeles: University of Southern California Press, 1956.

Homans, G. C.  *Social behavior: Its elementary forms*. New York: Harcourt, Brace, and World, 1961.

Horvath, F. S., and Reid, J. E.  The reliability of polygraph examiner diagnosis of truth and deception. *Journal of Criminal Law*, 1971, **62**, 276–281.

Hovland, C. I., Janis, I. L., and Kelley, H. H. *Communication and persuasion*. New Haven: Yale University Press, 1953.

Hovland, C. I., and Mandell, W.  An experimental comparison of conclusion-drawing by the communicator and by the audience. *Journal of Abnormal and Social Psychology*, 1952, **47**, 581–588.

Hovland, C. I., and Weiss, W. The influence of source credibility on communication effectiveness. *Public Opinion Quarterly*, 1951, **15**, 635–650.

Hunter, R. M. Law in the jury room. *Ohio State Law Journal*, 1935, **2**, 1–19.

Ikle, F. G. *How nations negotiate.* Millwood, N.Y.: Kraus Reprints, 1976 (1964).

"Inept lawyers are the bane of the law," *New York Times*, December 4, 1977 (Week in Review, p. 11).

Institute of Judicial Administration. *A comparison of six- and twelve-member juries in New Jersey superior and county courts.* New York: IJA, 1972.

Izzett, R. R., and Leginski, W. Group discussion and the influence of defendant characteristics in a simulated jury setting. *Journal of Social Psychology*, 1974, **93**, 271–279.

Jacob, H. *Justice in America.* Boston: Little, Brown, 1972 (second ed.).

Jacobs, A., and Sachs, L. B. (eds.). *The psychology of private events: Perspective on covert response systems.* New York: Academic Press, 1971.

*Jenkins v. United States*, 113 U.S. Court of Appeals, District of Columbia 300 (1962).

Johnson, C., and Scott, B. Eyewitness testimony and suspect identification as a function of arousal, sex of witness, and scheduling of interrogation. Paper presented at American Psychological Association Meeting, September, 1976.

Johnson, D. M. *The psychology of thought and judgement.* New York: Harper, 1955.

*Johnson v. Louisiana*, 32 L Ed. 2d 152 (1972).

Jones, C., and Aronson, E. Attribution of fault to a rape victim as a function of respectability of the victim. *Journal of Personality and Social Psychology*, 1973, **26**, 415–419.

Jones, E. E., and Davis, K. E. From acts to dispositions: The attribution process in person perception. In L. Berkowitz (ed.), *Advances in experimental social psychology* (vol. 2). New York: Academic Press, 1965.

Jones, E. E., and Harris, V. A. The attribution of attitudes. *Journal of Experimental Social Psychology*, 1967, **3**, 1–24.

Jones, E. E., and Nisbett, R. E. *The actor and the observer: Divergent perceptions of the causes of behavior.* Morristown, N.J.: General Learning Press, 1971.

Jurow, G. L. New data on the effect of a "death-qualified" jury on the guilt determination process. *Harvard Law Review*, 1971, **84**, 567–611.

Kahn, R. L., Wolfe, D. M., Quinn, R. P., Snoek, J. D., and Rosenthal, R. A. *Organizational stress: Studies in role conflict and ambiguity.* New York: Wiley, 1964.

Kairys, D. Juror selection: The law, a mathematical method of analysis, and a case study. *American Criminal Law Review*, 1972, **10**, 771.

Kairys, D., Schulman, J., and Harring, S. (eds.). *The jury system: New methods for reducing prejudice.* Philadelphia: National Lawyers Guild, 1975.

Kalven, H., Jr. The jury, the law, and the personal injury damage award. *Ohio State Law Journal*, 1958, **19**, 158–178.

Kalven, H., Jr., and Zeisel, H. *The American jury*. Boston: Little, Brown, 1966.

Kalven, H., and Zeisel, H. The American jury: Notes for an English controversy. *Chicago Bar Record*, 1967 *(May–June)*, 195–201.

Kaplan, J. *Criminal justice: Introductory cases and materials*. Mineola, N.Y.: The Foundation Press, 1973.

Kaplan, M. F., and Kemmerick, G. D. Juror judgment as information integration: Combining evidential and nonevidential information. *Journal of Personality and Social Psychology*, 1974, **30**, 493–499.

Katz, D., and Kahn, R. L. *The social psychology of organizations*. New York: Wiley, 1966.

Kaufman, I. A response to objections to the second circuit's proposed district court admission rules. *American Bar Association Journal*, 1975a, **61**, 1514.

Kaufman, I. Watergating on Main Street. *Saturday Review*, 1975b (Nov. 1), **3**, 16ff.

*The Kaufman Papers*, distributed by the National Committee to Re-open the Rosenberg Case, New York, 1977.

Keeton, R. E. *Trial, tactics and methods*. Boston: Little, Brown, 1973 (second ed.).

Kelley, H. H. Experimental studies of threats in interpersonal negotiations. *Journal of Conflict Resolution*, 1965, **9**, 79–105.

Kelley, H. H. A classroom study of the dilemmas in interpersonal negotiations. In K. Archibald (ed.), *Strategic interaction and conflict*. Berkeley: University of California, Institute of International Studies, 1966.

Kelley, H. H. Attribution theory in social psychology. In D. Levine (ed.), *Nebraska Symposium on Motivation* (vol. 15). Lincoln, Nebraska: University of Nebraska Press, 1967.

Kelley, H. H. *Attribution in social interaction*. Morristown, N.J.: General Learning Press, 1971.

Kelley, H. H. The processes of causal attribution. *American Psychologist*, 1973, **28**, 107–128.

Kelley, H. H., and Thibaut, J. W. Group problem solving. In G. Linzey and E. Aronson (eds.), *The handbook of social psychology* (vol. 4). Reading, Mass.: Addison-Wesley, 1969 (second ed.).

Kelman, H. C. Processes of opinion change. *Public Opinion Quarterly*, 1961. **25**, 57–78.

Kessler, J. B. An empirical study of six- and twelve-member jury decision-making processes. *University of Michigan Journal of Law Reform*, 1973, **6**, 712–734.

Kidney, J. Lawyers—Can they police themselves? *U.S. News and World Report*, 1977 (June 6), **82**, 33–35.

Kiesler, C. A., Collins, B. E., and Miller, N. *Attitude change*. New York: Wiley, 1969.

Klatzky, R. L. *Human memory*. San Francisco: Freeman, 1975.

Kline, F. G., and Jess, P. H. Prejudicial publicity: Its effects on law school mock juries. *Journalism Quarterly*, 1966, **43**, 113–116.

Komorita, S. S., and Brenner, A. R.  Bargaining and concession making under bilateral monopoly. *Journal of Personality and Social Psychology*, 1968, **9**, 15–20.

Krasner, L., and Ullmann, L. P. *Behavior influence and personality*. New York: Holt, Rinehart & Winston, 1973.

Krauss, R. M., Geller, V., and Olson, C.  Modalities and cues in the detection of deception.  Paper presented at the annual convention of the American Psychological Association, 1976.

Kraut, R. E.   Verbal and nonverbal cues in the perception of lying.  Paper presented at the annual meeting of the American Psychological Association, 1976.

Kubis, J. F.  Studies in lie detection.  Technical Report 62-205, Fordham University, 1962.

Kuehn, L. L.  Looking down a gun barrel: Person perception and violent crime. *Perceptual and Motor Skills*, 1974, **39**, 1159–1164.

Ladinsky, J.  Careers of lawyers, law practice and legal institutions. *American Sociological Review*, 1963, **28**, 47–54.

Ladinsky, J.  A traffic in legal services: Lawyer-seeking behavior and the channelling of clients. *Law and Society Review*, 1976, **11**, 207–223.

Lana, R. E.  Persuasion and the law: A constitutional issue. *American Psychologist*, 1972, **27**, 901.

Landy, D., and Aronson, E.  The influence of the character of the criminal and his victim on the decisions of simulated jurors. *Journal of Experimental Social Psychology*, 1969, **5**, 141–152.

Latané, B., and Darley, J. M. *The unresponsive bystander: Why doesn't he help?* New York: Appleton-Century-Crofts, 1970.

Lee, C. D. *The instrumental detection of deception*.  Springfield, Ill.: Charles C Thomas, 1953.

Lempert, R. O.  Uncovering "nondiscernible" differences: Empirical research and the jury-size cases. *Michigan Law Review*, 1975, **73**, 643–708.

Lerner, M. J.  The desire for justice and reactions to victims.  In J. Macaulay and L. Berkowitz (eds.), *Altruism and helping behavior*.  New York: Academic Press, 1970.

Lerner, M. J., Miller, D. J., and Holmes, J. G.  Deserving and the emergence of forms of justice.  In L. Berkowitz (ed.), *Advances in experimental social psychology* (vol. 9).  New York: Academic Press, 1976.

Levine, F. J., and Tapp, J.  The psychology of criminal identification: The gap from Wade to Kirby. *University of Pennsylvania Law Review*, 1973, **121**, 1079–1131.

Lieberman, J. K. *Court in session*. New York: Sterling, 1966.

Lieberman, J. K. *The tyranny of the experts: How professionals are closing the open society*. New York: Walker, 1970.

Lind, E. A., and O'Barr, W. M.  The social significance of speech in the courtroom.  In H. Giles and R. St. Clair (eds.), *Language and social psychology*. Oxford, England: Blackwell, 1978.

Livermore, J., Malmquist, C., and Meehl, P.  On the justification for civil commitment. *University of Pennsylvania Law Review*, 1968, **117**, 75.

Loftus, E. F., and Palmer, J. P.  Reconstruction of automobile destruction: An example of the interaction between language and memory. *Journal of Verbal Learning and Verbal Behavior*, 1974, **13**, 585–589.

Loftus, G. R., and Loftus, E. F.  *Human memory: The processing of information*. Hillsdale, N.J.: Erlbaum, 1976.

London, P.  *Beginning psychology*. Homewood, Ill.: Dorsey Press, 1975.

Love, R. E.  *Nonreactive, nonverbal measures of attitudes*, Doctoral dissertation at the Ohio State University, 1972.

Lown, C.  Legal approaches to juror stereotyping by physical characteristics. *Law and Human Behavior*, 1977, **1**, 87–100.

Lund, F. H.  The psychology of belief: IV. The law of primacy and persuasion. *Journal of Abnormal and Social Psychology*, 1925, **20**, 183–191.

Luvera, P. N.  Avoiding legal malpractice. *Case and Comment*, 1975, **80**, 3–8.

Lykken, D. T.  The validity of the guilty knowledge technique: The effects of faking. *Journal of Applied Psychology*, 1960, **44**, 258–262.

Lykken, D. T.  Psychology and the lie detector industry. *American Psychologist*, 1974, **29**, 725–739.

Maccoby, E. E., and Jacklin, C. N.  *The psychology of sex differences*. Stanford, Calif.: Stanford University Press, 1974.

Malpass, R. S., and Kravitz, J.  Recognition for faces of own and other race. *Journal of Personality and Social Psychology*, 1969, **13**, 330–334.

Marshall, J.  *Law and psychology in conflict*. New York: Doubleday-Anchor, 1969 (originally published in 1966).

Marquis, K. H., Marshall, J., and Oskamp, S.  Testimony validity as a function of question form, atmosphere, and item difficulty. *Journal of Applied Social Psychology*, 1972, **2**, 167–186.

Maru, O.  *Research on the legal profession*. Chicago: American Bar Foundation, 1972.

McCarty, D. G.  *Psychology and the law*. Englewood Cliffs, N.J.: Prentice-Hall, 1960.

McGrath, J. E., and Altman, I.  *Small group research: A synthesis and critique of the field*. New York: Holt, Rinehart & Winston, 1966.

McGuire, W. J.  Inducing resistance to persuasion: Some contemporary approaches. In L. Berkowitz (ed.), *Advances in experimental social psychology* (vol. 1). New York: Academic Press, 1964.

McGuire, W. J.  The nature of attitudes and attitude change. In G. Lindzey and E. Aronson (eds.), *The handbook of social psychology* (vol. 3). Reading, Mass: Addison-Wesley, 1969 (second ed.).

McIntyre, D. M., and Lippman, D.  Prosecutors and early disposition of felony cases. *American Bar Association Journal*, 1970, **56**, 1156.

Meehl, P. E.  *Clinical versus statistical prediction: A theoretical analysis and review of the literature*. Minneapolis: University of Minnesota Press, 1954.

Meehl, P. E.  Law and the fireside inductions: Some reflections of a clinical psychologist. *Journal of Social Issues*, 1971, **27**, 65–100.

Mehrabian, A. Nonverbal betrayal of feeling. *Journal of Experimental Research in Personality*, 1971, **5**, 64–73.

Miller, F. W. *Prosecution: The decision to charge a suspect with a crime*. Boston: Little, Brown, 1969.

Miller, N., and Campbell, D. Recency and primacy in persuasion as a function of the timing of speeches and measurements. *Journal of Abnormal and Social Psychology*, 1959, **59**, 1–9.

Mills, E. S. A statistical study of occupations of jurors in a (Maryland) United States district court. *Maryland Law Review*, 1962, (summer), **22**, 205–214.

Mills, L. R. Six-member and twelve-member juries: An empirical study of trial results. *University of Michigan Journal of Law Reform*, 1973, **6**, 671–711.

Mischel, W. *Personality and assessment*. New York: Wiley, 1968.

Mischel, W. Continuity and change in personality. *American Psychologist*, 1969, **24**, 1012–1018.

Mischel, W. *Introduction to personality*. New York: Holt, Rinehart & Winston, 1971.

Mischel, W. Toward a cognitive social learning reconceptualization of personality. *Psychological Review*, 1973, **80**, 252–283.

Missouri Bar–Prentice-Hall Survey. *A motivational study of public attitudes and law office management*. 1963. Cited in American Bar Association, *ABA Compilation of Reference Materials on Pre-paid Legal Services*. Chicago: ABA, 1973.

Mitchell, H. E., and Byrne, D. The defendant's dilemma: Effects of jurors' attitudes and authoritarianism. *Journal of Personality and Social Psychology*, 1973, **25**, 123–129.

Monahan, J. Abolish the insanity defense?–Not yet. *Rutgers Law Review*, 1973, **26**, 719–740.

Morrill, A. E. *Trial diplomacy*. Chicago: Court Practice Institute, 1971.

Mosier, M. M., and Soble, R. A. Modern legislation, metropolitan court, miniscule results: A study of Detroit's landlord–tenant court. *University of Michigan Journal of Law Reform*, 1973, **7**, 6.

Mossman, K. Jury selection: An expert's view. *Psychology Today*, 1973, **6**(12), 78–79.

Münsterberg, H. *On the witness stand: Essays on psychology and crime*. New York: Doubleday, 1915.

Muscio, B. The influence of the form of a question. *British Journal of Psychology*, 1915, **8**, 351–389.

Myers, D. G., and Kaplan, M. F. Group-induced polarization in simulated juries. *Personality and Social Psychology Bulletin*, 1976, **2**, 63–66.

Myers, D. G., and Lamm, H. The group polarization phenomenon. *Psychological Bulletin*, 1976, **83**, 602–627.

Myers, G. C. A study of incidental memory. *Archives of Personality*, 1913, **26**, 1–108.

Nader, R. Consumerism and legal services: The merging of movements. *Law and Society Review*, 1976, **11**, 247–256.

Nader, R., and Green, M. (eds.). *Verdicts on lawyers.* New York: Thomas Y. Crowell, 1976.

Nagel, S. S. Judicial backgrounds and criminal cases. *Journal of Criminal Law, Criminology, and Police Science*, 1962, **53**, 333–339.

Nagel, S. S. *The Legal Process from a Behavioral Perspective.* Homewood, Ill.: Dorsey Press, 1969.

National Advisory Commission on Criminal Justice Standards and Goals. *Report on Courts.* Washington, D.C.: U.S. Government Printing Office, 1973.

Naythons, E. E. Civil settlement conference. *The Forum*, 1973, **9**, 75–81.

Neisser, U. *Cognition and reality.* San Francisco: Freeman, 1976.

Nemeth, C., and Sosis, R. H. A simulated jury study: Characteristics of the defendant and the jurors. *Journal of Social Psychology*, 1973, **90**, 221–229.

Newman, D. J. Pleading guilty for considerations: A study of bargain justice. *The Journal of Criminal Law, Criminology, and Police Science*, 1956, **46**, 780–790.

Nisbett, R. E., and Wilson, T. D. Telling more than we can know: Verbal reports on mental processes. *Psychological Review*, 1977, **84**, 231–259.

O'Donnell, P., Churgin, M. J., and Curtis, D. E. *Toward a just and effective sentencing system.* New York: Praeger, 1977.

Osgood, C. E., and Tannenbaum, P. H. The principle of congruity in the prediction of attitude change. *Psychological Review*, 1955, **62**, 42–55.

Oskamp, S. *Attitudes and opinions.* Englewood Cliffs, N.J.: Prentice-Hall, 1977.

Ostrom, T. M., Werner, C., and Saks, M. An integration theory analysis of jurors' presumptions of guilt or innocence. *Journal of Personality and Social Psychology*, 1978, **36**, 436–450.

Packer, H. *The limits of the criminal sanction.* Stanford, Calif.: Stanford University Press, 1968.

Padawer-Singer, A., and Barton, A. The impact of pretrial publicity. In R. J. Simon (ed.), *The Jury System in America.* Beverly Hills, Calif.: Sage Publications, 1975.

Padawer-Singer, A. M., Singer, A. N., and Singer, R. L. J. Voir dire by two lawyers: An essential safeguard. *Judicature*, 1974, **57**, 386–391.

Partridge, A., and Eldridge, C. *The Second Circuit Sentencing Study: A Report to the Judges of the Second Circuit*, Washington, D.C.: Federal Judicial Center, 1974.

*People v. Craig*, No. 41750, Superior Court, Alameda County, Calif., 1968.

Platt, J. R. Strong inference. *Science*, 1964, **146**, 347–353.

Podlesny, J. A., and Raskin, D. C. Physiological measures and the detection of deception. *Psychological Bulletin*, 1977, **84**, 782–799.

Pollack, M. Pre-trial procedures more effectively handled. *Federal Rules Decision*, 1975, **65**, 475–484.

Postman, L. J., Bruner, J. S., and McGinnies, E. Personal values as selective factors in perception. *Journal of Abnormal and Social Psychology*, 1948, **43**, 142–154.

Prassel, F. R. *Introduction to American criminal justice.* New York: Harper & Row, 1975.

President's Commission on Law Enforcement and Administration of Justice. *The challenge of crime in a free society.* Washington, D.C.: U.S. Government Printing Office, 1967.

Prettyman, E. B. Jury instruction—First or last? *American Bar Association Journal,* 1960, **46**, 1066.

Project '76: What you think about the profession. *Juris Doctor,* 1976, **6**, 28–29.

Proshansky, H., Ittelson, W., and Rivlin, L. (eds.). *Environmental psychology.* New York: Holt, Rinehart & Winston, 1970.

Rapoport, A., and Chammah, A. *Prisoners' Dilemma.* Ann Arbor: University of Michigan Press, 1965.

Raven, B. H., and Eachus, H. T. Cooperation and competition in means-interdependent triads. *Journal of Abnormal and Social Psychology,* 1963, **67**, 307–316.

Reid, J. E. and Inbau, F. E. *Truth and deception: The Polygraph ("lie detector") technique.* Baltimore, Md.: Williams and Wilkins, 1966.

Reiser, M. Hypnosis as an aid in a homicide investigation. *American Journal of Clinical Hypnosis,* 1974, **17**, 84–87.

Reynolds, D. E., and Sanders, M. S. The effects of defendant attractiveness, age, and injury severity on sentence given by simulated jurors. Paper presented at the Western Psychological Association meeting, 1973.

Richey, M. H., and Fichter, J. J. Sex differences in moralism and punitiveness. *Psychonomic Science,* 1969, **16**, 185–186.

Rokeach, M., and Vidmar, N. Testimony concerning possible jury bias in a Black Panther murder trial. *Journal of Applied Social Psychology,* 1973, **3**, 19–29.

Rosenthal, D. E. *Lawyer and client: Who's in charge?* New York: Russell Sage Foundation, 1974.

Rosenthal, D. E. Evaluating the competence of lawyers. *Law and Society Review,* 1976, **11**, 257–286.

Rosenthal, R. *Experimenter effects in behavioral research.* New York: Appleton-Century-Crofts, 1966.

Rosenthal, R., and Jacobson, L. *Pygmalion in the classroom: Teacher expectations and the pupil's intellectual development.* New York: Holt, Rinehart & Winston, 1968.

Rosett, A., and Cressey, D. R. *Justice by consent: Plea bargains in the American courthouse.* Philadelphia: Lippincott, 1976.

Rosnow, R., and Goldstein, J. Familiarity, salience, and the order of presentation of communications. *Journal of Social Psychology,* 1967, **173**, 97.

Rosnow, R. L., and Robinson, E. J. (eds.). *Experiments in persuasion.* New York: Academic Press, 1967.

Ross, H. L. *Settled out of court.* Chicago: Aldine, 1970.

Ross, L. The intuitive psychologist and his shortcomings: Distortions in the attribution process. In L. Berkowitz (ed.), *Advances in experimental social psychology* (vol. 10). New York: Academic Press, 1977.

Saks, M. J. Ignorance of science is no excuse. *Trial*, 1974, **10**, 18ff.

Saks, M. J. The limits of scientific jury selection: Ethical and empirical. *Jurimetrics Journal*, 1976, **17**, 3-22.

Saks, M. J. *Jury verdicts.* Lexington, Mass.: D. C. Heath, 1977.

Saks, M. J., and Benedict, A. R. Evaluation and quality assurance of legal services: Concepts and research. In L. Brickman & R. Lempert (eds.), *The role of research in the delivery of legal services.* Washington, D.C.: Resource Center for Consumers of Legal Services, 1976.

Saks, M. J., and Ostrom, T. M. Jury size and consensus requirements: The laws of probability vs. the laws of the land. *Journal of Contemporary Law*, 1975, **1**, 163-173.

Saks, M. J., Werner, C. M., and Ostrom, T. M. The presumption of innocence and the American juror. *Journal of Contemporary Law*, 1975, **2**, 46-54.

Sales, B. D., Elwork, A., and Alfini, J. J. Improving comprehensive for jury instructions. In B. D. Sales (ed.), *Perspectives in law and psychology.* Vol. I: *The criminal justice system.* New York: Plenum, 1977.

Schacter, S. Deviation, rejection, and communication. *Journal of Abnormal and Social Psychology*, 1951, **46**, 190-207.

Schaie, K. W., and Gribbin, K. Adult development and aging. *Annual Review of Psychology*, 1975, **26**, 65-96.

Schelling, T. C. *The strategy of conflict.* Cambridge, Mass.: Harvard University Press, 1960.

Schulman, J., Shaver, P., Colman, R., Emrich, B., and Christie, R. Recipe for a jury. *Psychology Today*, 1973, **6**(12), 37.

Schum, D. A. The weighing of testimony in judicial proceedings from sources having reduced credibility. *Human Factors*, 1975, **17**, 172-182.

Schum, D. A. The behavioral richness of cascaded inference models: Examples in jurisprudence. In N. J. Castellan, D. B. Pisoni, and G. R. Potts (eds.), *Cognitive Theory* (vol. 2). Hillsdale, N.J.: Erlbaum, 1977.

Sealy, A. P., and Cornish, W. R. Jurors and their verdicts. *Modern Law Review*, 1973a, **36**, 496-508.

Sealy, A. P., and Cornish, W. R. Juries and the rules of evidence. *Criminal Law Review*, 1973b, April, 208-223.

Sellin, T. The Negro criminal: A statistical note. *Annals of the American Academy of Political and Social Science*, 1928, **140**, 52-64.

Shapley, D. Jury selection: Social scientists gamble in an already loaded game. *Science*, 1974 (20 Sept.), **185**, 1033ff.

Shaver, K. G. *An introduction to attribution processes.* Cambridge, Mass.: Winthrop Publishers, 1975.

Shephard, R. N. Recognition memory for words, sentences, and pictures. *Journal of Verbal Learning and Verbal Behavior*, 1967, **6**, 156-163.

Sherif, M., Harvey, O. J., White, E. J., Hood, W. E., and Sherif, C. W. *Intergroup conflict and cooperation: The Robber's Cave experiment.* Norman, Okla.: University of Oklahoma Book Exchange, 1961.

Shure, G., Meeker, R., and Hansford, E. The effectiveness of pacifist strategies in bargaining games. *Journal of Conflict Resolution*, 1965, **9**, 106-117.

Sigall, H., and Landy, D.  Effects of the defendant's character and suffering on juridic judgment: A replication and clarification. *Journal of Social Psychology*, 1972, **88**, 149–150.

Sigall, H., and Ostrove, N.  Beautiful but dangerous: Effects of offender attractiveness and nature of the crime on juridic judgment. *Journal of Personality and Social Psychology*, 1975, **31**, 410–414.

Simon, R. J.  Murder, juries, and the press. *Transaction*, 1966, **3**, 40–42.

Simon, R. J.  *The jury and the defense of insanity*. Boston: Little, Brown, 1967.

Single, E. W.  The consequences of pre-trial detention. Paper presented at the annual meeting of the American Sociological Association, New Orleans, 1972.

Skolnick, J.  *Justice without trial*. New York: Wiley, 1966.

Slater, P. E.  Contrasting correlates of group size. *Sociometry*, 1958, **21**, 129–139.

Slovic, P., and Lichtenstein, S.  Comparison of Bayesian and regression approaches to the study of information processing in judgment. *Organizational Behavior and Human Performance*, 1971, **6**, 649–744.

Smead, A.  Cooperation and competition.  In L. S. Wrightsman, *Social psychology in the Seventies*.  Belmont, Calif.: Brooks/Cole, 1972.

Smith, A. B., and Blumberg, A. S. The problem of objectivity in judicial decision-making. *Social Forces*, 1967, **46**, 96–105.

Smith, B. M.  The polygraph. *Scientific American*, 1967, **216**(1), 25–30.

Smith, R. H.  Disbarments and disciplinary actions: The record for five years. *American Bar Association Journal*, 1961, **47**, 363–365.

Smoke, W. H., and Zajonc, R. B.  On the reliability of group judgments and decisions.  In J. J. Criswell, H. Solomon, and P. Suppes (eds.), *Mathematical methods in small group processes*.  Stanford, Calif.: Stanford University Press, 1962.

Solomon, L.  The influence of some types of power relationships and game strategies upon the development of interpersonal trust. *Journal of Abnormal and Social Psychology*, 1960, **61**, 223–230.

Sommer, R.  Leadership and group geography. *Sociometry*, 1961, **24**, 99–110.

Special Committee to Survey Legal Needs. *Alternatives: Legal Services and the Public*, Special Issue, January, 1976. Chicago: American Bar Association, 1976.

Staats, A. W.  *Social behaviorism*. Homewood, Ill.: Dorsey, 1975.

Steiner, I. E.  *Group process and productivity*. New York: Academic Press, 1972.

Steinzor, B.  The spatial factor in face-to-face discussion groups. *Journal of Abnormal and Social Psychology*, 1950, **45**, 552–555.

Stephan, F. F., and Mishler, E. G.  The distribution of participation in small groups: An experimental approximation. *American Sociological Review*, 1952, **17**, 598–608.

Stevens, C. M.  *Strategy and collective bargaining negotiation*.  New York: McGraw-Hill, 1963.

Stone, A. A.  *Mental health and law: A system in transition*.  Rockville, Maryland: National Institute of Mental Health, 1975.

Strodtbeck, F. L., and Hook, L. H.  The social dimensions of a twelve-man jury table. *Sociometry*, 1961, **24**, 397–415.

Strodtbeck, F. L., James, R. M., and Hawkins, D.  Social status in jury deliberations. *American Sociological Review*, 1957, **22**, 713–719.

Sue, S., Smith, R. E., and Caldwell, C.  Effects of inadmissible evidence on the decisions of simulated jurors: A moral dilemma. *Journal of Applied Social Psychology*, 1973, **3**, 345–353.

Sutherland, E. H., and Cressey, D. R.  *Principles of criminology*.  New York: Lippincott, 1966.

Tapp, J. L.  Psychology and the law: An overture.  *Annual Review of Psychology*, 1976, **27**, 359–404.

Tedeschi, J. T., and Lindskold, S.  *Social psychology*.  New York: Wiley, 1976.

Terhune, K. W.  Motives, situation, and interpersonal conflict within the Prisoner's Dilemma.  *Journal of Personality and Social Psychology*, Monograph Supplement, 1968, **8**, 1–24.

Terhune, K. W.  The effects of personality in cooperation and conflict.  In P. Swingle (ed.), *The structure of conflict*.  New York: Academic Press, 1970.

The Legal Services Corporation Act of 1974.  *United States Code*, 1974, **42**, 2996.

Thibaut, J. W., and Kelley, H. H.  *The social psychology of groups*.  New York: Wiley, 1959.

Thibaut, J. W., and Riecken, H.  Some determinants and consequences of the perception of social causality. *Journal of Personality*, 1955, **24**, 113–133.

Thibaut, J., and Walker, L.  *Procedural justice: A psychological analysis*.  Hillsdale, N.J.: Erlbaum, 1975.

Thomas, E. J., and Fink, C. J.  Effects of group size.  *Psychological Bulletin*, 1963, **60**, 371–384.

Thomas, E. S.  Plea bargaining: Clash between theory and practice.  *Loyola Law Review*, 1973–1974, **20**, 303–312.

Thorne, B.  Professional education in law.  In E. C. Hughes, B. Thorne, A. M. DeBaggis, A. Gurin, and D. Williams, *Education for the professions of medicine, law, theology, and social welfare*.  New York: McGraw-Hill, 1973.

Tribe, L. H.  Trial by mathematics: Precision and ritual in the legal process. *Harvard Law Review*, 1971, **84**, 1329–1393.

*U.S. v. Brawner*, 471 F 2d 969 (D.C. Circuit Ct., 1972).

Uejio, C. K., and Wrightsman, L. S.  Ethnic group differences in the relationship of trusting attitudes to cooperative behavior. *Psychological Reports*, 1967, **20**, 563–571.

Ulmer, S. S.  Supreme Court behavior in racial exclusion cases: 1935–1960. *American Political Science Review*, 1962, **56**, 325–330.

Ulmer, S. S.  *Courts as small and not so small groups*.  Morristown, N.J.: General Learning Press, 1971.

Valenti, A. C., and Downing, L. L.  Differential effects of jury size on verdicts following deliberation as a function of the apparent guilt of the defendant. *Journal of Personality and Social Psychology*, 1975, **32**, 655–663.

Vanderzell, J. H.  The jury as a community cross section.  *Western Political Science Quarterly*, March, 1966, **19**, 136–149.

Vernon, P. E.  *Personality assessment: A critical survey*.  New York: Wiley, 1964.

Vidmar, N., and Crinklaw, L.  Retribution and utility as motives in sanctioning behavior.  Paper presented at the Midwestern Psychological Association Convention, Chicago, May, 1973.

Walbert, D. F.  The effect of jury size on the probability of conviction: An evaluation of *Williams v. Florida*.  *Case Western Reserve Law Review*, 1971, **22**, 529–554.

Walster, E.  Assignment of responsibility for an accident.  *Journal of Personality and Social Psychology*, 1966, **3**, 73–80.

Warkov, S., and Zelan, J.  *Lawyers in the making*.  New York: Aldine-Atherton, 1965.

Weick, K. E.  *The social psychology of organizing*.  Reading, Mass.: Addison-Wesley, 1969.

Weiss, W., and Steenbock, S.  The influence on communication effectiveness of explicit urging action and policy consequences.  *Journal of Experimental Social Psychology*, 1965, **1**, 396–406.

Weld, H. P., and Danzig, E. R.  A study of the way in which a verdict is reached by a jury.  *American Journal of Psychology*, 1940, (October) **53**, 518–536.

Whipple, G. M.  Psychology of testimony.  *Psychological Bulletin*, 1915, **12**, 221–224.

Whipple, G. M.  The observer as reporter: A survey of the psychology of testimony, *Psychological Bulletin*, 1909, **6**, 153–170.

Whipple, G. M.  The obtaining of information: Psychology of observation and report.  *Psychological Bulletin*, 1918, **15**, 217–248.

Wicker, A. W.  Attitudes versus actions: The relationship of verbal and overt behavioral responses to attitude objects.  *Journal of Social Issues*, 1969, **25**, 41–78.

Wigmore, J. H.  *A student's textbook of the law of evidence*.  Brooklyn: The Foundation Press, 1935.

Williams, G. R., England, J. L., Farmer, L. C., and Blumenthal, M.  Effectiveness in legal negotiations.  In G. Bermant, C. Nemeth, and N. Vidmar (eds.), *Psychology and the Law*, Lexington, MA.: D. C. Heath, 1976.

*Williams v. Florida*, 399 U.S. 78 (1970).

Wispé, L. G., and Thayer, P. W.  Role ambiguity and anxiety in an occupational group.  *Journal of Social Psychology*, 1957, **46**, 41–48.

*Witherspoon v. Illinois*, 88 U.S. 1770 (1968).

Wrightsman, L. S., Davis, D. W., Lucker, W. G., Bruininks, R., Evans, J., Wilde, R., Paulson, D., and Clark, G.  Effects of other person's race and strategy upon cooperative behavior in a Prisoner's Dilemma game.  Paper presented at the meeting of the Midwestern Psychological Association, Chicago, 1967.

Wrightsman, L. S., O'Connor, J., and Baker, N. J. (eds.), *Cooperation and competition: Readings on mixed-motive games*.  Monterey, Calif.: Brooks/Cole, 1972.

*Yale Law Journal.*    Notes and Comments: On instructing deadlocked juries, 1968, **78**, 100–142.

Zadny, J., and Gerard, H. B.    Attributed intentions and information selectivity. *Journal of Experimental Social Psychology*, 1974, **10**, 34–52.

Zeisel, H.    What determines the amount of argument per juror?    *American Sociological Review*, 1963, **28**, 279.

Zeisel, H.    *Some Data on Juror Attitudes Towards Capital Punishment.*    Chicago: University of Chicago, Center for the Study of Criminal Justice, 1968.

Zeisel, H.    ". . . and then there were none." The diminution of the federal jury. *The University of Chicago Law Review*, 1971, **38**, 710–724.

Zeisel, H.    Reflections on experimental techniques in the law. *Journal of Legal Studies*, 1973, **2**, 107–124.

Zeisel, H., and Diamond, S. S.    Convincing empirical evidence on the six-member jury. *University of Chicago Law Review*, 1974, **41**, 281–295.

Zerman, M. B.    *Call the final witness.*    New York: Harper & Row, 1977.

Zimbardo, P., and Ebbesen, E.    *Influencing attitudes and changing behavior.* Reading, Mass.: Addison-Wesley, 1969.

# Index

ALSO BY QAIS AKBAR OMAR

*Shakespeare in Kabul* (with Stephen Landrigan)

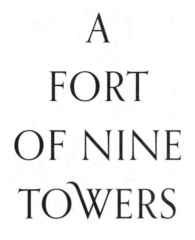

# A
# FORT
# OF NINE
# TOWERS

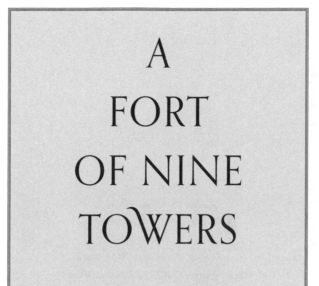

# A
# FORT
# OF NINE
# TOWERS

*An Afghan Family Story*

## QAIS AKBAR OMAR

*Farrar, Straus and Giroux*
*New York*

❖

Farrar, Straus and Giroux
18 West 18th Street, New York 10011

Printed in the United States of America
First edition, 2013

Library of Congress Cataloging-in-Publication Data
Omar, Qais Akbar.
    A fort of nine towers : an Afghan family story / Qais Akbar Omar. — 1st ed.
    p.   cm.
    ISBN 978-0-374-15764-7 (hardcover : alk. paper)
    1. Omar, Qais Akbar.   2. Afghanistan—Social conditions—20th century.
3. Afghanistan—Biography.   I. Title.

CT1878.O63 A3 2013
958.104092—dc23
[B]

                                                        2012034566


Designed by Abby Kagan

www.fsgbooks.com
www.twitter.com/fsgbooks • www.facebook.com/fsgbooks


1   3   5   7   9   10   8   6   4   2

If sorrow settles in your heart, then where is the home of joy?
The sorrows and joys of life are all mixed together.
No one can separate them, except the One who created them.

Real men do not die of death; death finds its death in man.
Real men do not die of death; death finds its name in man.
When a man's name is respected, then death has no name.

*My grandfather said*

# Contents

# MAPS

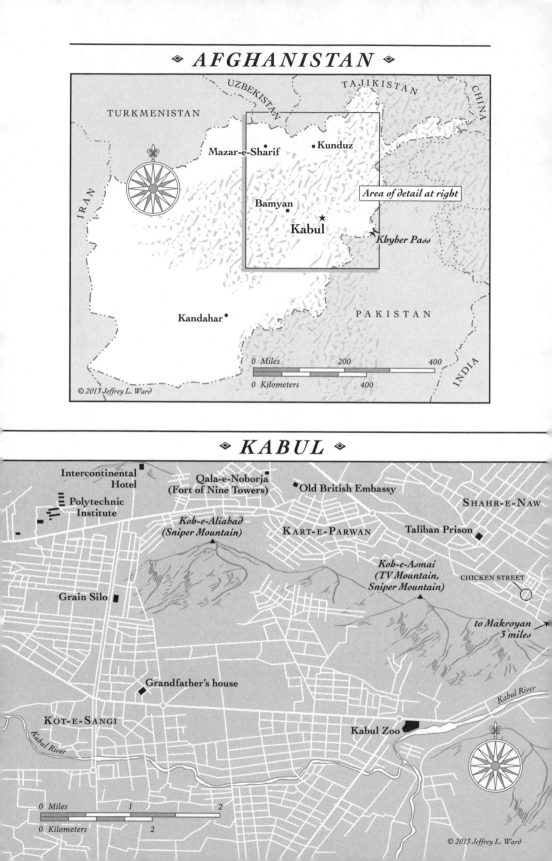

# ❖ AFGHANISTAN ❖

TURKMENISTAN

UZBEKISTAN

TAJIKISTAN

CHINA

IRAN

Mazar-e-Sharif

• Kunduz

Area of detail at right

Bamyan

Kabul ★

✕ Khyber Pass

Kandahar •

PAKISTAN

INDIA

0 Miles 200 400

0 Kilometers 400

© 2013 Jeffrey L. Ward

# ❖ KABUL ❖

Intercontinental
Hotel

Qala-e-Noborja
(Fort of Nine Towers)

Old British Embassy

SHAHR-E-NAW

Polytechnic
Institute

Koh-e-Aliabad
(Sniper Mountain)

KART-E-PARWAN

Taliban Prison

Koh-e-Asmai
(TV Mountain,
Sniper Mountain)

CHICKEN STREET

Grain Silo

to Makroyan
3 miles

Grandfather's house

Kabul River

KOT-E-SANGI

Kabul River

Kabul Zoo

0 Miles 1 2

0 Kilometers 2

© 2013 Jeffrey L. Ward

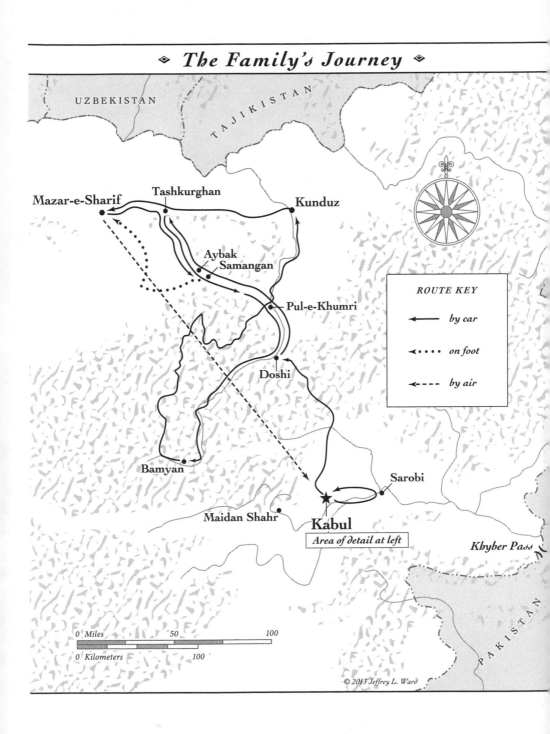

# ❖ The Family's Journey ❖

UZBEKISTAN

TAJIKISTAN

Mazar-e-Sharif

Tashkurghan

Kunduz

Aybak
Samangan

Pul-e-Khumri

Doshi

Bamyan

Sarobi

Maidan Shahr

Kabul

*Area of detail at left*

Khyber Pass

ROUTE KEY

⟵ *by car*

◄···· *on foot*

◄---- *by air*

PAKISTAN

0 Miles  50  100

0 Kilometers  100

© 2013 Jeffrey L. Ward

# A
# FORT
# OF NINE
# TOWERS

*Prologue*

The calls always come early in the morning. Sometimes I am still praying when I hear my mother's phone ring upstairs. I lean forward and touch my head to the carpet and make an extra effort to focus on the ancient verses streaming through my mind.

*Alla-hu-Akbar. Subhanna rabbiyal A'ala . . .*

Even before my mother answers it, I know who is calling.

It is my aunt, in Canada. She has just come home from a wedding party where she met a family with a daughter, a beautiful girl, very intelligent, and funny. A very good family. They are from Kabul, or Kandahar, or Mazar-e-Sharif, and our grandfather knew their uncle, or her father went to Habibia High School with the cousin of our neighbor who used to manage the Ariana Hotel before it was destroyed, or . . .

*Qul Huwa Allāhu 'Ahadun, Allāhu Aṣ-Ṣamadu, Lam Yalid Wa Lam Yūlad, Walam Yakun Lahu Kufūan 'Ahadun.*

My aunt has been in Canada for thirty years. I think she knows all the other Afghans there. She helped many of them when they first arrived, even though she herself was a young widow with a small daughter in a strange land whose language she struggled to master. Afghans never forget a kindness, though. Now, everywhere she goes, she is welcomed by those she helped and respected for the kindness in her heart. Almost every week, except during Ramazan, she is invited to a wedding.

Weddings are where my aunt tracks the young women whom she has known since they were babies. She has watched them become young women, and seen them taking full advantage of opportunities they would never have had in Kabul had their families stayed there over the past three decades. Through it all, she has kept a list of future husbands for them in her mind—nephews, neighbors, sons of former students from her days as a teacher—always waiting for the day when she can be of help.

*Innā a'ṭaynāka al-kawthar, Fa-ṣalli li-Rabbika wanḥar, Innā shaani-aka huwal abtar.*

I am twenty-nine years old. I have a university degree. I run my own carpet business and sometimes work with the foreigners. I have both arms and legs, which is an issue in mine-ridden Afghanistan. I come from a good family and am not yet married. I am a Pashtun with Hazara eyes thanks to a great-great-grandmother whose name no one remembers because she was a woman, and who was from some Central Asian tribe with Mongolian roots. I am the embodiment of this world-spanning mixture of peoples we call Afghan.

I give my aunt a reason to go to weddings on the nights she is tired, or when the snow is deep. I give her something to talk about, and someone to boast about. I sell carpets. She sells me. Her great hope is that I can live someplace where I can prosper and be safe.

How do I tell her, then, that though it sounds mad, I love Afghanistan? That I love being an Afghan? That I want to help rebuild what so many others destroyed? I know it will take a long time. I understand that. I am a carpet weaver. I know how, slowly, one knot follows another until a pattern appears.

Oh, God, can you not weave my destiny to keep me close to these people who mean more to me than any others in the world?

*Ameen.*


When I finish my prayers, I sit near the tall windows that look down over Kabul University and to the mountains beyond. The dust is so thick even at this early hour that I can hardly make out the outlines of the jagged peaks against the dawn.

Kabul has become a very dusty place. How many million people live here now? No one knows. When I was young, there were only eighty thousand of us. A big town with big houses that had big gardens. Now we live on the side of a mountain, like goats, on land sold to us by a squatter.

The sun rises from behind the mountains and burns through the dust with a greasy glare. I lean back on a cushion that was made by nomads who travel each year across miles of arid land in search of a patch of grass for their flocks. My people were nomads until my grandfather settled in Kabul. We have no livestock now, unless you count the cat on the roof.

My youngest sister brings me a thermos of green tea and the news that our aunt has called from Canada. I do not let on that I had already guessed that. I do not want to spoil her excitement at telling me. She has a devilish glint in her eye. I know she wants to make a joke about the girl my aunt was describing. By now, of course, my mother has given all the details to my four sisters who still live at home. My older sister, who is married, will hear everything before long. Marriage discussions in Afghanistan are a family matter, and a major source of entertainment. My youngest sister is trying to decide whether I am in the mood for jokes, or whether I will just send her away.

In the end, she walks off giggling to herself. If I ever leave this place, I will miss her more than I can bear to think about.

Sometimes I wonder whether it was difficult for Grandfather to leave the open lands of his nomad days for the confining walls of the city. I think of my teacher, Maulana Jalaluddin Mohammad Balkhi, known to the world as Rumi. He had to flee our country when the greatest teacher of our warlords, Genghis Khan, swept across our land, destroying everything.

It is time to go upstairs for breakfast. My father has already ridden off on his bicycle to teach his high school physics classes. My mother is preparing to go to her office where they coordinate relief for natural disasters. My two youngest sisters are leaving for school, adjusting their white headscarves over their black uniforms as they go out the door and head down the hill.

One of my other sisters has laid out some yogurt and fruit for me in the kitchen. She is studying agriculture at Kabul University and will soon go for her classes. My only brother, who is eight years younger than I am, is doing exercises in the room above me, sending down tiny clouds of dust as he skips a rope.

These are the things that happen every day. These are the rhythms of my family in the morning. These simple things will stay with me always; that is the one thing of which I am sure.


Uncertainty hangs thick like the dust in the air. I cannot see where the path of life will lead me. It is not my nature to sit and wait for something to happen. For the moment, though, unable to look forward, I have settled for gazing backward, to chronicle what I have witnessed in these few strange and turbulent years I have known.

Perhaps someday I will understand all these things better. Perhaps others will, as well. Perhaps this book will help.

*Insh'allah.*

PART ONE

❖

# THE
# HOLY
# WARRIORS

# 1

❖

## *In the Time Before*

In the time before the fighting, before the rockets, before the war-lords and their false promises, before the sudden disappearance of so many people we knew to graves or foreign lands, before the Taliban and their madness, before the smell of death hung daily in the air and the ground was soaked in blood, we lived well.

We have no photos. It was too dangerous to keep them during the time of the Taliban, so we destroyed them. But the images of our lives before all hope fled Afghanistan remain sharp and clear.

My mother is wearing her short skirt, sitting in her office in a bank, tending to a long line of customers. She is respected for her knowledge of banking, and her ability to solve people's problems.

My father looks like a movie star in his bell-bottom trousers, speeding through the Kabul streets on his motorcycle. Sometimes he ties me to his back with a tight belt. His long hair catches the wind as we ride off. When he turns the corners sharply, the metal guards he wears on his knees shoot sparks into the air as they scrape the pave-ment. The next day I tell my classmates about that, and make them envious.

One of my uncles goes on business trips to other countries. The other uncles and aunts study at universities in Kabul. All of them wear the latest styles. Grandfather, his thick white hair neatly combed, is elegantly dressed in finely tailored suits from Italy that emphasize his affluence. When he enters a room, he dominates it.

Grandfather is an impressive man, tall, with broad shoulders. Unlike many other Afghans, he keeps his well-tanned face freshly shaved. It is his wide, black eyes that you notice most. So deep. So commanding. So gentle.

The images come in a rush. Sometimes they play out in little scenes.

My father is calling me to get ready for school. I open my eyes and look at the clock above my bed. It is too early, but what can I say to him? He is my father. I am his son. Pashtun sons must obey their fathers.

But I am not ready to wake up. I rub my eyes. My father keeps calling, "Get up! Put on your gloves. I'm waiting for you in the ring." He wants me to exercise with him before breakfast. He has started training me to become a famous boxer like himself, and fight as he has in international competitions.

I hate waking up early, but I love exercising with my father. He always lets me beat him, even though I am seven years old.

I love school, too. I have perfect attendance. I am smart and popular. Sometimes the boys complain to the headmaster about me when I punch them in their faces. The headmaster covers for me, because he is Grandfather's best friend. But he never smiles at me.

My sister and I are in the same school. She is a year and a half older than I, and even smarter and more popular, but she never punches any girls, even though she is the daughter of a well-known boxer.

The heart of our world is my grandfather's house.

Grandfather had built it in the late 1960s, when he was the senior accounting officer in the Bank-e-Millie, the National Bank of Afghanistan. The country was prosperous, and he could see that Kabul would outgrow its twisted thousand-year-old streets along the Kabul River.

He bought about five acres on the far side of the small, steep mountain with the two peaks that for centuries had protected Kabul on its south and west sides. The land beyond them was then all farms with mud-brick villages, but not for long.

Grandfather had studied the land, talked to the farmers who knew it, and carefully chose the piece that had the best well. We had always had water even in the driest months, even when our neighbors had shortages. He enclosed most of his land with a sturdy cement wall, but set part of it aside for a school for all the kids whose families he knew would transform the farmlands into a neighborhood.

My father and six of his seven brothers, along with their wives and kids, all lived comfortably within Grandfather's wall. I had more than twenty-five cousins to play with, most of them around my age. Every family had two large rooms of its own. The rooms were clustered in a single-story building on one side of the garden. Grandfather's rooms were on the other side. Between us were sixty McIntosh apple trees. Grandfather's cousin had brought them from America as little branches that he had grafted onto Afghan apple tree roots. They were very rare in Afghanistan, and Grandfather was proud of having them.

At one end of the property was a block-long building with two floors of apartments above the shops on the street level. Grandfather rented out the apartments to people who were not relatives. All the windows in the apartments faced the street. No Afghan allows strangers to look into his family's garden.

My father set up a gym in one of the shops. Every day after school, dozens of young men would come there to train as boxers. My cousin Wakeel and I would watch them from the sidewalk pounding the punching bag, or doing push-ups, or skipping rope, while my father sparred with one or sometimes two at a time inside the ring he had built.

Wakeel was seven years older than I was. He was the older

brother I never had. I was the younger brother he always wanted. He let me use him as a punching bag when I imitated the boxers. Every time I hit him, he laughed.

Grandfather, by then retired from the bank, used one of the larger shops as a warehouse for his carpets. It had a thick door with a strong lock and was filled with the sweet, lanolin-rich smell of wool. He had thousands of carpets in there. My boy cousins and I liked to jump from one high pile of folded carpets to another.

All of my uncles had their own businesses, except Wakeel's father. He was a major in the National Army of Afghanistan. He always said, "Business is too risky. Most of these businessmen have heart attacks, or die at an early age." He was my grandfather's oldest son, and thus had a special place in the family. He and his wife enjoyed a relaxed life on his army salary with Wakeel, my favorite cousin, and their two daughters.

One day he went to his office and never came back. We still do not know whether he is alive or dead. It was in the time when I first heard the word "Communists," but I did not know what it meant then. For more than twenty-five years, his wife has been waiting for him to come home. Even now, she runs to the door whenever someone knocks.

My father was the third son. Like all my uncles, he had only one wife. It was not our family's custom to have more than one.

Our neighbors respected my father like a holy man. They came to see him and talked with him about their businesses and their problems. They called him *Lala*, "older brother," even though some of them were older than he was. They told him, "Your thoughts are older than your age." He was a man willing to try everything. He had no use for the word "no."

He was also the only one of his father's sons who was involved in carpets. His five younger brothers saw carpets as something from the past. They were looking to the future, making money in new ways.

One was importing goods from Russia. Two others were still in university but looking into importing medicine to sell to pharmacies all over Afghanistan.

Often, we all ate dinner together, more than fifty of us sitting on cushions around one cloth spread on the well-trimmed lawn that Grandfather had sown at one corner of our courtyard. Colorful little lightbulbs hung above us. After dinner, my grandfather and his sons sat in a circle talking about their businesses, or to which universities in Europe or America they should send my boy cousins and me.

The women made a separate circle to talk about their own things. It was the responsibility of the older women to find good husbands for the younger ones, such as my father's two unmarried sisters, who lived with us. His two older sisters were already married, and had moved away to the homes of their husbands' families in other parts of Kabul. Discussions on suitors could go on for months and involve the whole family until a choice was made.

My cousins and I sat in another circle, boys and girls together, telling one another scary tales, and staring at Kabul's clear night sky with the moon and stars scattered across it. When we got tired of stories, we shaped animals from the stars and laughed.

Sometimes after we had finished eating, my father or one of my uncles would take the kids around the mountain to buy us ice cream at Shahr-e-Naw Park, or to one of the Kabul movie theaters for an Indian or American film.

Kabul was like a huge garden then. Trees lined the wide streets and touched each other overhead in tall, leafy arches. The city was full of well-tended parks, in which tall pink hollyhocks competed for attention with bright orange marigolds and hundreds of shades of roses. Every house had a garden with pomegranate, almond, or apricot trees. Even the mountain with the two peaks was covered in low-growing weeds and grasses that came to life with the spring rains. In both spring and fall, the sky filled with the brightly colored water birds that rested in the wetlands around the city as they flew between the Russian steppes and India. Ancient underground channels brought water from the mountains, and kept our gardens green.

Every Friday, the Muslim holy day when schools and businesses closed, we carried a large lunch to one of the gardens of our neighbors, or to picnic spots nearby at Qargha Lake or in the Paghman Valley, or sometimes even as far as the Salang Pass, high in the mountains of the Hindu Kush an hour's drive north of Kabul. This was a day for extended families to spend together, visiting and joking and gossiping.

My cousins and I climbed hills, while the elders reclined against huge pillows in the shade of willow trees or under the broad leafy branches of a *panj chinar* tree. My unmarried aunts were kept busy boiling water for the others who drank one cup of tea after another. In these long afternoons they took turns spinning some small event into a big story that made everybody laugh. They all tried to outdo one another, of course. They are Afghans. Of them all, my mother was the best.

My uncles were *tabla* drummers, and my father played the wooden flute, though he had never had lessons. We stayed until late into the evenings, singing, dancing, and cooking over an open fire.

Sometimes on these outings, the cousins held a school lessons competition. Whoever got the highest score could demand that the other cousins buy whatever he or she liked, no matter the cost. We, too, were very competitive. Our parents were the judges, and cheered loudly every time one of us got a correct answer. Sometimes the competition ended in a tie. We hated that.

Occasionally, some of the cousins fought and did not talk to each other for a day or two. But we could not maintain that for very long. Our games were more important, and never ended, whether we were playing hide-and-seek in the garden, or shooting marbles, or racing our bicycles in the park near our house, or especially when we were flying kites from the roof.

Every afternoon in the spring and autumn, when the weather

brought a gentle breeze, hundreds of kites would fill the sky above Kabul and stay there until dark. Kite flying was more than a game; it was a matter of the greatest personal pride to cut the string of your rival's kite. The trick was to draw your kite string against your opponent's with speed and force, and slice through his string.

Wakeel was the kite master, the kite-flying teacher to us all. The kids on the street had given him the title of "Wakeel, the Cruel Cutter," because he had cut so many of their kites.

One afternoon, Wakeel looked at me as we were heading to the roof with our kites and said, "Let's have a fight!" As usual, his long, dark hair fell over his forehead, brushing his thick eyebrows. And below them were his deep-set, dark eyes that sparkled, always.

I said okay, though I knew he would cut me right away. But from the earliest age we are taught never to run away from a fight, even if we think we cannot win.

The roof of Grandfather's apartment block was ideal for kite flying. Rising high above the trees that grew along the street, it was like a stage. People below—adults as well as kids—would see the kites going into the air, and stop everything that they were doing to watch the outcome. A good fight would be talked about for days after.

After we had had our kites in the air for half an hour, taunting and feinting, Wakeel called from the far end of the roof in amazement, "You have learned a lot! It used to take me only five minutes to cut you. Now it has been more than half an hour, and you are still in the sky."

Suddenly, he used a trick that he had not yet shown me. He let his kite loop around mine as if he were trying to choke it. I felt the string in my hand go slack, and there was my kite, flat on its back, wafting back and forth like a leaf in autumn, drifting off across the sky away from me.

Wakeel laughed and made a big show of letting his kite fly higher so everybody in the street could see he had yet again been the victor. I ran downstairs to get another kite.

Berar, a Hazara teenager who worked with our gardener, loved kite fighting. All the time I had been battling Wakeel, he had been carefully following every dive, envious.

Berar was a few years older than Wakeel, tall, handsome, and hardworking. His family lived in Bamyan, where the big statues of Buddha were carved into the mountains. Berar was not his real name. Berar in Hazaragi dialect means "brother." We did not know what his real name was, and he did not mind us calling him Berar.

As the suspense had built between Wakeel and me, Berar could not stop watching us. The old gardener spoke to him impatiently several times: "The weeds are in the ground, not in the sky. Look down." The gardener was always harsh to Berar.

"Give the boy a break," Grandfather told the gardener. They were working together on Grandfather's beloved rosebushes. I had just sent a second kite into the air. Grandfather nodded at Berar. "Go on," he said.

Berar ran up to the rooftop, where I was struggling to gain altitude while avoiding Wakeel's torpedoing attacks. Berar took the string from me and told me to hold the reel.

I had never seen Berar fly a kite before. I kept shouting at him, "Kashko! Kashko! Pull it in!" But Berar did not need my instructions; he knew exactly what to do. Wakeel shouted at me that I could have a hundred helpers and he would still cut me. Though he was tall and skinny, he was very strong and he was furiously pulling in his kite to circle it around mine.

Berar was getting our kite very high very fast, until in no time at all it was higher than Wakeel's. Then he made it dive so quickly that it dropped like a stone through the air. Suddenly, there was Wakeel's kite, drifting back and forth from left to right, floating off to Kandahar, separated from the now limp string in Wakeel's hand.

I climbed on Berar's shoulders, screaming for joy. I had the string of my kite in my hands. My kite was so high in the sky, it looked like a tiny bird. The neighbor kids on the street were shouting, too. They had not seen Berar doing it, only me on Berar's strong shoulders, cheering and shouting: "Wakeel, the Cruel Cutter, has been cut!" I kissed Berar many times. He was my hero. He gave me the title of "Cutter of the Cruel Cutter," even though it was he who had made it happen.

Wakeel sulked, and did not talk to me for two days.

———

We had another cousin who was a few months younger than I. He never really got along with any of the others. Wakeel used to call him a jerk. All the other cousins, everyone, started to call him "Jerk" as well.

If he bought new clothes, he would walk in front of us to show them off and say something stupid. "We went to a shop in Shahr-e-Naw that opened a few weeks ago. They bring everything they sell from London and Paris. The owner told my parents that I have a good taste for clothes. I don't think you guys can afford a suit like this." When I asked how much he paid, he would triple the price.

Wakeel would ask, "Hey, Jerk, do your clothes do any magic for such a price?"

Jerk could never see a joke coming, and would ask something witless like, "What kind of magic?"

"Can they make you look less ugly?" Wakeel replied, his voice cracking into shrieking guffaws.

We'd all laugh, and Jerk would run toward his house and complain to his parents. We would run to the roof, or outside the courtyard, or hide in the garage inside my father's car to escape punishment.

Once when Jerk had on his good clothes and was showing off, Wakeel filled his mouth with water, and I punched him in his stomach. That forced Wakeel to spit it all on Jerk. Poor Jerk looked at us in disbelief and asked with outrage in his voice why we had done that.

Wakeel told him, "We are practicing to be tough. We punch each other unexpectedly, so we will be prepared if we get into a fight with someone. You should be tough, too." Then we punched him in his stomach, but avoided his face so we would not leave any bruises, because we knew that would get us spanked by his parents.

Jerk had one unexpected strength: he was always a reader. For his age, he had more information than he needed. He had a good mind for memorizing, too. That turned us even more against him.

Wakeel teased Jerk all the time when we were at home playing with our cousins. Outside, though, Wakeel would not let anybody bother him. Wakeel was like an older brother to all of us. When Jerk got into fights with the neighbor boys, which happened a lot, Wakeel defended him. When we were playing football in the park, Wakeel always made sure that Jerk and I were on his team, so he could protect us.

Our neighbors were like us, quiet and educated people. When there was a wedding or engagement party in one of their houses, everyone in the neighborhood was invited, along with their kids and servants.

Every week my grandfather talked for ten minutes in the mosque after Friday prayers about how to keep our neighborhood clean, or how to solve water and electricity problems, or how to take care of the public park and create more facilities where the kids could play together. He had never been elected to any position, but people listened to him.

When a family was having financial problems, one of its older men would quietly speak to Grandfather and ask for the community's help. Then, after Friday prayers, Grandfather would explain to the other men in the mosque that some money was needed without ever saying by whom. It was important to protect the dignity of the family in need.

One Friday after the others had left the mosque, I saw my grandfather giving the money he had collected to a neighbor whose wife had been sick for many months. The man kissed Grandfather's hands, and said, "You always live up to our expectations. May God grant you long life, health, and strength." When Grandfather noticed that I was watching him, he scowled at me, and I quickly turned away. This was something I was not meant to see.

Grandfather's house was his great pride, and the McIntosh apple trees were his great joy. He was in his late sixties when I was born, and soon after became a widower. By then he had retired from the bank, and busied himself in the courtyard, planting roses, geraniums, and hollyhocks or watering his McIntosh apple trees, always singing in a whispery voice under his teeth, or quietly reciting the ninety-nine names of God.

And for hours he would sit reading, surrounded by his books. His favorite, in two beautiful leather-bound volumes, was *Afghanistan in the Path of History* by Mir Ghulam Mohammad Ghobar. The title was embossed on the cover in gold. Sometimes he read to me from it.

He also had the *Complete Psychological Works of Sigmund Freud*, which had beautiful covers as well; but he did not read those to me. When I asked about them, he said he would give them to me when I was old enough.

In winter, he studied the poets Rumi, Shams Tabrizi, Hafiz, Sa'adi, and Omar-e-Khayyam. Sometimes he invited his friends to discuss the political affairs of Afghanistan and the world. But before long, the talk would turn to poetry. He always wanted me and my boy cousins to listen to what was being said, and to ask questions.

My sisters and girl cousins were never part of those discussions. Their lives moved on a different path from those of the boys, but they were always allowed to read Grandfather's books. Indeed, Grandfather always encouraged them to do so. "Education," he would say, stressing the word, "is the key to the future." They read lots of poetry, as well as novels by Dostoyevsky, Tolstoy, Thomas Mann, and some Afghan and Iranian novelists whose names no one knows in the rest of the world. All these books were in Dari.

Some of the older girls, including Wakeel's sisters, read Grandfather's books by Sigmund Freud long before I did. We could hear them whispering about something called "the Oedipus complex," and then laughing. As soon as any of the younger cousins got too close to them, though, they stopped talking and looked at us in a way to make us understand that we were not welcome.

One day during one of Grandfather's discussions, Wakeel raised his hand and asked what politics was all about.

One of Grandfather's friends answered, "In fact, politics is really just a bunch of lies, and politicians are very gifted liars who use their skill to control power and money and land."

"They must be devious people, then," Wakeel said.

"That's true."

"Which country has the most devious politicians?" Wakeel asked.

"Let me tell you a story, my son," Grandfather's friend said, clearing his throat. "Someone asked Shaitan, the devil, 'Since there is such a large number of countries in the world, how do you manage to keep so many of them in turmoil all the time, like Afghanistan, and Pakistan, and Palestine? You must be very busy.'"

"Shaitan laughed and said, 'That is no problem. Not for me.' He leaned back on his cushion and raised the mouthpiece of his *chillum* to his scaly lips. He drew in a sour-smelling smoke that made the water in the pipe turn black with oily bubbles, then let the smoke drain out of the corners of his mouth. 'There is one country on the earth that does a better job than me in creating problems everywhere.'"

"Really?" Wakeel asked. "Which country is more devious than Shaitan?"

"'It is called England,' Shaitan said."

My grandfather and his friends all laughed, and then they talked about poetry again.

It would be years before I understood the bad feelings that many Afghans have for England, which three times invaded Afghanistan and three times was driven out. For nearly three centuries, the English used Afghanistan like a playing field to challenge the Russians in a very ugly game. Neither side won, and neither side cared how many Afghans they killed or how much suffering they inflicted on Afghan people.

Those days were long in the past, like the battles between the ancient kings who had fought to rule our country. Life was smooth, and easy, and full of joy, except maybe for Jerk when we played tricks on him. Time moved graciously with the pace of the seasons, and nudged us gently through the stages of life. But then one night the air was filled with the unexpected cries of *"Allah-hu-Akbar,"* and nothing has ever been the same since.

# 2

❖

## Allah-hu-Akbar

Chill winds from the high mountains around Kabul had begun to blow down on the city. Autumn was coming. It had been especially cold the past two nights. Now my parents and my aunts and uncles were using this Friday afternoon to set up the wood-burning tin stoves called *bokhari* in every room. When flakes of last winter's soot fell out of the pipes, some of the uncles said bad words. The cousins laughed and raced to tell one another what they had heard.

Just as night fell, the electricity suddenly went out. I looked outside. It was not just our house. The whole city was completely dark. I had never seen that before. Kabul always had electricity.

My mother said, "Oh, it's as dark as a grave."

I thought for a moment. How did my mother know how dark a grave is?

"Have you ever been in a grave?" I asked her.

"Stop being silly," she chided as she went to find candles.

My older sister had been doing her homework. "There is no electricity in a grave, idiot," she said. "Of course it is dark." She went to help my mother.

I looked out the window again into the darkness. No one was in the street. Could a grave be as big as a whole city?

I could hear voices in the distance. It was like the murmurings of a thousand people from the far side of Kabul. At first, I thought that it must be *muezzins* calling people to prayer. But the prayer time had been twenty minutes ago, and the voices were not familiar like the *muezzins'*. Nor were they coming over a loudspeaker, nor from the direction of the nearby mosques. The voices kept getting louder. Now I could hear them shouting *"Allah-hu-Akbar, Allah-hu-Akbar."* God is great.

I ran to find my mother to ask her why they were saying that. She was searching through all the drawers for candles; my older sister was looking for matches.

"I don't know," she said.

"You're even more than four times older than I am," I told her insistently, "but still you don't know more than me." She finally located a candle and lit it. She held it in her right hand and cupped her left palm around it. The soft light made her look very beautiful.

She kissed me on my cheek, which made me smile, and said, "Go and ask your father. Then you will know more than I know." The wax dripped on her thin, delicate fingers. She flinched and put the candle on the table. The wind blew in through the windows, making the curtains dance and the candle flutter; the voices outside grew louder.


I found my father in the courtyard, up on a ledge of the thick mud-brick wall that separated us from the street. He was leaning over, hoping someone would pass who could tell him what was going on.

The sound grew, like a wind rising. Now we could hear people in many places yelling. They were not organized. Everybody seemed to be saying their own *"Allah-hu-Akbar,"* some louder and some softer.

Suddenly, the man across the street who owned the shop at the corner started calling *"Allah-hu-Akbar"* inside his courtyard. Then I heard his two brothers join him. A couple of more courtyards down the street began having their own voices.

My father jumped down from the ledge. He landed on one of the low wooden platforms where we sometimes spread carpets and ate dinner. He, too, started shouting, *"Allah-hu-Akbar!"*

I was very surprised. I wanted to shout, too. But I did not hear any kids' voices. It was all men, and I was a little bit frightened. I hugged my father's leg.

I put my head against his leg and heard a different voice coming from inside it. Then I pulled my head away and heard his usual voice. I did this several times, then called my older sister and told her to do the same. She grabbed his other leg and put her ear to it. We were fascinated by our new discovery. My father paid no attention to us. He was shouting louder now, and that made it more exciting for us. We were putting our ears to his legs and pulling away, giggling.

I heard some more familiar voices joining in, and even some women. I pulled my head away from my father's leg. All my uncles and my aunts were standing behind my father and shouting, *"Allah-hu-Akbar."*

"Why are they all saying that?" I asked no one in particular.

"It is doomsday," my sister said. "The sun will rise from the west during the night, and the moon and stars will disappear. The mountains will become smooth, and the whole earth will become flat." I was now eight years old and almost as tall as she, but she was frightening me. She was very good at scaring us younger kids whenever she told stories.

"From the east to the west, and from the north to the south, there'll be no mountains at all. You'll be able to see an egg from one corner of the world to the other. All the dead bodies from the beginning of time, which goes back centuries, will come back alive, and God will put the sinners in hell and the honest in paradise." I wanted her to stop, but she kept on, making grotesque faces to emphasize her words.

"Hell is full of fire and wild and dangerous animals. The sinners will die, and be reborn, and die and be reborn, and will always suffer. And that is where you are going, because yesterday you stole my pencil, and lied to Father that the pencil was yours, and then you blamed me for using your pencil. You will go straight to hell, because you committed three big sins. And you will have to stay there for a very long time." I was starting to cry.

"But I didn't mean it, and I gave it back to you. I was just joking and teasing you," I wailed.

"It doesn't matter; you made me suffer. If I don't forgive you, you will go to hell," she said, and she was very firm.

"What do you want me to do for you to forgive me?" I begged.

"You have to kiss my hands and my feet, then buy me a package of candy in school tomorrow. Then I will think about forgiving you," she said.

"But you said it was doomsday. There is no tomorrow!" I said.

"Oh, yes! I forgot. But you must kiss my hands and my feet. Hurry, or you won't have enough time!" she warned.

I hesitated for a minute and did not know what to do.

"Hurry up, if the sun rises now, then your apology won't be acceptable," she said. "Start by kissing the sole of my foot."

I looked at the starry sky and was doubtful that the sun would rise at 8:00 p.m. But when I looked at my sister, she was grimly serious. She was holding up her right foot.

I bent down to kiss her sole. That distracted my father. He looked at me kneeling on the ground getting my clothes dirty and asked, "Hey, hey, what are you doing?"

My sister shrieked and ran away. If I had been sure that this was just one of her stupid jokes, I would have run after her. But I wanted to be certain about doomsday first.

I asked my father, "Is it true that it is doomsday?"

He laughed as he ran his hand through my long hair, which was thick, wavy, and brown in those days and made me look like a foreigner.

"Why is everyone shouting?" I asked him impatiently.

"Because they want the Mujahedin to come to Kabul and make the Russians leave Afghanistan," he replied, grinning with joy at the idea, and then started yelling again.

Sometimes we had seen Russian soldiers when I was very small. The Russians had blue eyes, red hair, and white skin. They threw candy to us when they rumbled by in their huge tanks. We always yelled "*Spaseva*," though we did not know what it meant, and they smiled.

For other Afghans, the Russians brought bombs, not candy. Whole villages and large neighborhoods in cities were wiped out by the

Russians dropping one bomb after another from their planes, which seemed to fly only a few meters above the houses. They did this if they thought there was even one person living there who was opposing them. Everyone was slaughtered, the guilty and the innocent. But how can a man be guilty when all he wants is to protect his family and his land from invaders?

Afghans had only their old hunting guns and their determination to defend themselves against the Russians. Every village in Afghanistan, however, has a council of elders called a *shura*. Once the elders have decided that the village will do something, every family in the village must do it. The *shuras* decided that all the men should form fighting groups and join with others all over Afghanistan. They did, and they called themselves Mujahedin, the Holy Warriors.

My grandfather, father, uncles, and Grandfather's guests had often talked about the Mujahedin long before they came to Kabul. In fact, people had been talking about them from the time they were formed in Pakistan and Iran. When anyone spoke of them, they often referred to them proudly as "our Mujahedin brothers, who will come and liberate this country from these religionless and Communist Russians."

As kids, we heard the Mujahedin spoken of with such respect that we could not wait to see them.

For ten years, they had fought relentlessly against the Russians. The Americans had sent more powerful weapons, and that had helped. Finally, the Russian soldiers were driven out of Afghanistan. Their defeat was so devastating that it helped end Communism in Russia and Eastern Europe. But the new Russian government still tried to control Afghanistan. They put Afghans in charge who had been educated in Russia, and sent them lots of money, as well as food and fuel. But even with all the Russians' help, everyone knew that the Afghan government could not last for long.

My grandfather and his sons talked about it whenever we ate together. One of my uncles imported things from Russia. Like all Afghans, they wanted the Russians to stop interfering with our country, but they did not know what this would mean for their business.

Now the Mujahedin were coming to Kabul to drive away even these Afghans who were running the government for the Russians.

After twelve years of turmoil, Afghanistan would become a place of peace again.

I could not hold back any longer. I started saying *"Allah-hu-Akbar, Allah-hu-Akbar,"* first in a shy voice, then louder and louder.

In the first weeks of the year 1371 by the Afghan calendar (April 1992), the Mujahedin finally took control of Kabul and the rest of the country. A few months before, the Russian government had decided to stop sending money and supplies to the Afghans they had put in charge of our government. Without the Russians' support, the prices for food and everything else, such as flour, cooking oil, rice, beans, chickpeas, sugar, soap, and clothes, quickly started going up and up.

Until the Russians had left Afghanistan three years before, everybody who worked for the government received coupons for these items, which they could buy at the end of each month for a very low price from the government stores. When there were several people in one family working for the government, they often had so much that they could sell what they did not need in the black market, and at a price higher than they paid, but still much cheaper than the market price. Also, the quality of the Russian goods was much better than most of the other things in the market. But once the Russians had left, the coupons stopped.

Food became hard to find in the markets. Even the large food supply in our house began to shrink. We no longer had five things at each meal but only beans with bread, or boiled potato and bread, or rice and slices of tomato and onion. When we asked our mother where all the vegetables were that she usually served along with chicken or lamb, she would make a joke: "The seeds for the vegetables have not been planted yet, the lamb is still a baby, and the chicken is still an egg."

There were times when my two younger sisters would not eat breakfast, because they wanted to have jam and butter to put on their *naan*. But when my mother put two extra spoonfuls of sugar in their milk, they drank it happily with a piece of *naan*. Somehow our mother managed to keep us fed.

One day, even though there was very little food, we had a big party after my mother had given birth to my little brother.

My father was overjoyed to have a second son. To celebrate, he went out to buy a big cake. A couple of hours later he came back with a cake no bigger than a brick. As soon as we saw it, we all laughed, thinking that he was making a joke. He laughed with us as he handed the cake to my mother. Then he told us that he had gone to about twenty shops and could not find even one other cake.

My parents and sisters, with some of my aunts and cousins, stuck a few small candles on the small cake, lit them, and after a few moments everybody blew them out. Then my father cut the cake into very, very small pieces. As he handed everyone a piece, he joked, "At least it is enough to fill the cracks between your teeth." We all laughed.

I was so hungry, though, that I swallowed my piece half-chewed. I asked for another. My father looked at me and said, "Sorry, son, nothing left. Wait for next year, when you will have another brother, *Insh'allah*, then you can have your second piece." Everybody laughed. I never did have any more brothers, but in the years that followed God granted me two more sisters.

As the shortages became more severe, the government became more desperate, and the anger of ordinary Afghans increased. The government tried many things to calm the situation, but they did not know what to do. They tried to work out a deal with the Mujahedin, but it was too late. The president, Dr. Najibullah, fled to the United Nations compound in Kabul to seek asylum. The time of the Communists had ended, and the time of the Mujahedin had begun.

When I heard that the Mujahedin were coming, I had expected to see heroes in uniforms and shiny boots. But they were dressed like villagers with big turbans, the traditional baggy pants called *shalwar*, and the long, tunic-like shirts called *kamiz*. Their waistcoats were filled with grenades and bullets. They all had beards, mustaches, and smelly shoes that wrapped up stinky feet; not one was without a gun.

On TV, the female announcers now covered their heads with scarves. Women singers were no longer seen. Instead, we saw men with big turbans and long beards sitting on the floor, reciting the

Holy Koran. The male TV announcers started wearing *shalwar kamiz* instead of a pressed suit and tie. The TV programs were now filled with interviews with the men we would come to know as commanders. They were talking about their factions, and what they wanted to do for Afghanistan.

They all sounded like professors of the Holy Koran in the way they talked about Islam, and its importance for Muslims and Afghans. They all connected themselves to the Prophet Mohammad, peace be upon him, and claimed to be descendants of Arabs to make themselves sound like they were linked closely to the Prophet Mohammad, peace be upon him, even though we all know that Afghans are descendants of Zoroastrians, Jews, Greeks, Mongols, Aryans, and many other people, as well as of the Arabs who entered our history much later.

Two months before the arrival of the Mujahedin, we had been taught in school that we are related to monkeys. The teacher told us that little by little some of the monkeys changed and became more like humans. Some of them did not want to be human and civilized, because there are many problems in civilizations. We had a series of pictures in our textbooks showing how monkeys became human.

Our teacher said, "Humans are a kind of animal, and animals were created by nature."

"Who created nature?" I asked.

"Nature was self-created," our teacher said.

He took us to the Kabul Zoo to see the monkeys and to compare their faces with ours. None of the monkeys looked like anyone I knew, until I saw a cage with some new monkeys that had just arrived from India. One of them looked exactly like our teacher.

Excitedly, I raced to tell him, "There is a monkey that looks exactly like you."

My teacher was with my classmates and two other teachers. All of them laughed. He came close to me and squeezed my left ear very hard and whispered, "Students don't talk to their teacher like this."

"Maybe he was one of your ancestors," I persisted.

By then, my classmates were confirming my observation. Our teacher shouted at the other students that it was time to leave, though we were supposed to have spent the rest of the day in the zoo.

After the Mujahedin came to Kabul, our same teacher now taught us from a new textbook called *The Creation of Adam*. It did not say anything about monkeys.

We learned that we all came from Adam and Eve. Our teacher started saying things like, "The history of humans started from Adam and Eve, and the earth existed long before them. Do not let Shaitan be your guide; he misled Eve and Adam and drove them out of paradise."

I was confused. "What happened to the monkeys?" I asked our teacher, "And nature?"

The teacher sat on the edge of the desk, and for a minute he did not say anything. "The monkeys and nature are Communist perceptions." His voice was very calm, and he looked straight into my eyes as if there were no one else in the class. "The Islamic perception is: God is the creator of nature and all creatures." Now he was looking at everyone. "Adam is the father of all humans," he said.

I was still confused. I came home and asked Grandfather what all these things meant.

He told me, "Time will show you the truth. You are too young now. Wait and be patient, you will find answers to your questions."

I did not know why grown-ups always said that I was too young now. I wanted to grow up, be tall, and have a mustache and some wrinkles on my forehead, and snore when I slept and know everything.


Once the Mujahedin were in control, everything was cheap, and food became plentiful for a few months after they had opened the government food stores. For the first time in years, people could travel anywhere in Afghanistan without worrying about being caught in a crossfire if some group of fighters suddenly started attacking government cars or Russian military vehicles from their hiding places.

Grandfather was very optimistic. It was springtime, and it felt like the whole world was making a new beginning. Several times, he invited some of the Mujahedin to our house, served them good food, and treated them like his best friends. My father shared Grandfather's feelings at the beginning. But after a while, he began to have doubts. He did not like how they were running the country.

Within weeks, fighting between some of the Mujahedin factions broke out in certain areas of Kabul, small incidents at first. People said, "There must be some misunderstandings. In a family, there are always squabbles. They will solve it."

But those small fights became big fights. Chaos started spreading all over Afghanistan. Afghans who had a little money or relatives in other countries quickly left. Others who stayed were beaten up, or had their property stolen. We heard about women who were raped by the soldiers of the same commanders who had talked about Islam and its importance to Muslims and Afghans only a few months before.

My father wanted to leave Afghanistan for Turkey or Russia, where he had many friends from his days as a boxer, but my grandfather would not give him permission to go. "The borders are still open," my father said. "We should go while we can. We will come back when things quiet down."

"Afghanistan is in good hands now. We are with our own now, and we can decide what we want. Give them time," Grandfather urged. Besides, he needed my father's help. My father was the son on whom my grandfather most depended.


Slowly, one Mujahedin faction took over a part of Kabul City, and another faction took another part. They started by seizing control of a neighborhood where many people of their tribe lived, then tried to take other areas around them. Soon, each faction had its own territory. As spring turned into summer, we started hearing about "checkpoints" and the "front lines." The factions started firing rockets at each other. Now innocent people were being killed, especially in our neighborhood, which by sad chance was about as far as the rockets from each side could fly before they fell.

First it was a dozen people who were killed. Then it was a hundred. Then a thousand. It was like when a forest catches fire, both the dry and the wet burn.

One faction overran Pul-e-Charkhi prison and freed not just the political prisoners, but even those who had committed inhumane deeds against common ordinary people.


One day while two factions were firing rockets at each other over our heads, there was loud knocking on our courtyard door. I had just come out of Grandfather's room, where he was starting his prayers, and I ran to the door.

When I opened it, I saw some guys with guns, grenades, and bullets tucked into special belts and in their waistcoat pockets. The hooks of the grenades were hanging out.

One of them walked through the door without being invited and pushed me against the wall. He had an ugly scar on his face. Two others followed.

"Where is the owner of this house?" he asked loudly.

"He is inside praying," I told him.

"Where?" he asked gruffly. I pointed to Grandfather's room. He kicked open the door. Grandfather was on his prayer rug, with his head touching the ground.

"Give me the key to your carpet warehouse!" the man with the scar shouted at Grandfather, but Grandfather ignored him, and kept on praying. The man shouted again and pointed his gun at Grandfather's head. I started to cry.

My grandfather ignored him until he had finished his prayers. He quietly rose to his feet and folded his prayer rug as if he were the only person in the room. Finally, he looked at the gunman, who had been shouting the whole time.

"If you think I will be scared by your loud voice, you are stupid." Grandfather spoke calmly, like he was talking to one of his clients at the bank.

The shouting had attracted the attention of my father and my uncles. I could hear them running toward Grandfather's room. They were shouting, too, asking what was happening. The thieves took positions in the corners of the room. As my father and his brothers came rushing in, the thieves put their guns to the backs of their necks. Everyone froze where he stood.

My cousins had come running down the long corridor that led to my grandfather's room, their mothers behind them. When they saw the thieves and the guns, there was a moment of horrified silence.

Then Grandfather spoke softly. "Go ahead, kill me, and then you will get the key. Whatever I have earned in life came from the calluses of my hands. I will not give it to a bunch of cowardly thieves."

The one in charge, with the scar, grinned at my grandfather and said, "You stupid old man, I won't even waste a bullet on you." Then he shouted at my uncles, cousins, and their mothers to move back. Everyone did. The thieves braced the butts of their Kalashnikovs against their stomachs, pointed the barrels toward us, and walked backward out the courtyard gate.

When they had gone, my father locked the door after them. My father and my uncles went to Grandfather's room. Their wives were whispering to one another in the courtyard.

My cousins came to me to ask me what had happened. I stood with them all around me and told what I had seen. They paid close attention to everything I said, even the ones who did not get along with me. Now that I had become so important, I told them, "You have to wait until I finish my explanations, then I will answer your questions."

A moment later, we heard three gunshots in the street. My father and two of my uncles ran from Grandfather's room toward the court- yard door. My mother and my uncles' wives cried to them not to go out. But they did not listen.

Grandfather came out of his room and ran after them. Nobody dared to tell him what to do. As he hurried toward the courtyard gate, he nodded at me to follow him. Grandfather always wanted me to see life as it is and not hide from it. I followed him, and my cousins followed me. Outside our courtyard gate, we found my father and my two uncles handcuffed in front of Grandfather's warehouse. Several more robbers were in the street. Two of them were again pointing guns at the backs of their necks. One of the locks to the warehouse had been shot open. One of the thieves was positioned as a lookout at one end of our short street; another one was at the far end. One more was standing in the middle of the road in front of our warehouse.

Two others were still trying to break the second lock. Sweat was dropping from their chins, though it was cold and a light cover of snow had whitened the ground. One of them wanted to blow the lock open with a grenade, but his friend did not let him.

"No!" he said. "They'll hear it. We'll have to share the carpets with the commander." Suddenly, I understood that these guys were ordinary thieves who had joined one of the factions. They were not true Mujahedin who defend their country and faith against the invaders and heretics.

The one who had suggested using the grenade stepped back and shot three bullets at the lock. On the third shot, it shattered and the door opened. The one who was standing in the middle of the road called the two others at the ends of the road to join them. They all went inside.

The warehouse was dark. The carpets were piled one on top of another, all the way to the ceiling. Over the past sixteen years, since my grandfather had retired from the bank, he and my father had gathered more than six thousand carpets. One of the thieves drew the curtains, and sunlight rushed in.

The warehouse was a treasury. Every carpet spoke through its colors and its designs. Many were very old. Each one had been selected carefully by Grandfather and my father, but we could do nothing to stop the thieves from taking them away from us.

Working quickly, three of them loaded as many carpets as they could into their old Russian jeep. Three others stood guard outside with their fingers on the triggers, ready to shoot anyone who bothered them. I saw the carpet that I had helped wash in the courtyard with the washers we hired once a month. They cleaned the old carpets that my father brought back from the villages. That was my favorite carpet, but I could not tell these thieves to not take that one because I liked it.

It took them two days to steal all the carpets. The war had now come to us, as it had to so many.


We were not the only ones who were robbed. Our part of Kabul was almost empty. Most of our neighbors had fled, some in such a hurry they took nothing with them. Soon their houses were stripped bare.

The women were no longer at their windows with their elbows on the ledges, chatting. Now, instead, unfed cats leapt from the ledges and hissed at each other.

Every time the wind blew, the doors of the empty houses started banging, windows slammed, curtains blew in and out. When there were no sounds of rockets exploding or guns being fired, the neighborhood was filled with the howling of the hungry dogs who had been abandoned.

Only a madman would try to go out in the street. Snipers had taken up positions on the small mountain behind us and might take a shot, just for fun. The twin peaks had lost their old names of Koh-e-Asmai and Koh-e-Aliabad and had become known as Sniper Mountain.

As spring brought warm days back to Kabul, it became too dangerous to move around in our courtyard. Some snipers even used Grandfather's high roof where we flew kites to shoot at those on the mountain; the snipers on the mountain shot back. Sometimes they fired rockets. A few landed in our courtyard. The rest fell in the streets around us, on our neighbors' houses, in our park, where they destroyed the trees, and on our small neighborhood school, which had been our joy until it was blasted into dust.

The grass in the courtyard began to die as the weather grew warmer, because no one dared to go outside to water it. In the end, it became too dangerous even to stay in our rooms. We had to move to a large room in the basement under the apartments, where we hoped we would be safer.

It had never been wired for electricity, and both day and night we lit oil lamps and candles. We slept on the cement floor.

We ate together, more than fifty of us sitting on the floor around one tablecloth. Each day's meal was like a little party, but a sad one. Nobody talked, nobody laughed. In fact, we were waiting for a rocket to land on us and kill us all.

All the uncles had radios with tiny earphones. They spent all day listening to news from the Dari-language broadcasts on the BBC World Service and other stations. I wanted to listen to Indian songs. Worry will not change my destiny, I thought; worry brings more worries.

One Sunday night around nine o'clock, the uncles all started telling everyone to be quiet. The BBC announced that the next day there would be a ceasefire in our Kot-e-Sangi neighborhood. It would last for ten hours starting from eight in the morning. This meant we could leave our house. Everyone began to talk at once. What should we do? Where should we go? Who would help us?

As I was falling asleep that night, I could hear rockets whining in flight; when they landed, they made the ground rock like a cradle.

Around three or four in the morning, I woke up needing to use the bathroom. We did not have one in the basement. I walked to the courtyard to pee under a tree as I had done on other nights since we had been forced from our rooms. It was very quiet, but I heard the sound of shoveling. I rubbed my eyes and looked around. In different parts of the garden, all of my uncles were digging narrow, deep holes. They dug in the dark. No one dared light a lantern. It would have been a target for the snipers.

I went to one of my uncles and asked him why he was digging a hole at this time of the night. He did not answer me. I went to another uncle and asked him the same question. He did not answer either.

I went back to the basement to ask my father. He was not there next to my mother. My mother, sisters, and little brother were all sound asleep. I quietly rushed to the corner of the courtyard where our part of the house stood. There was my father digging a hole beneath the mulberry tree we liked to climb.

"Dad, what are you doing?" I asked.

He stopped and looked at me. "Go and sleep," he said. He sounded harsh.

"Why is everybody digging holes?" I asked determinedly.

"I said, go and sleep," he almost shouted at me, but very softly as if he did not want anyone to hear. His voice made me frightened. I did not ask any more questions. But I was angry.

Instead of going back down to the safety of the basement, I went to our own rooms, and I slept in my own bed. It was so good to sleep in my own bed after so many weeks on the hard cement floor of the basement. I did not care if a rocket fell on me. A few minutes later, I was sound asleep, and had no idea of the strange new life that would start for my family and me in the morning.

# 3

❖

## The Other Side of the Mountain

I woke up just before dawn. My father and mother were running all around our rooms, putting clothes into suitcases. My little brother was asleep on a pile of blankets in a corner.

My three sisters came in from our corner of the basement. They were rubbing their eyes and stretching their arms and yawning. Their hair was tangled. My father sat them next to me on the edge of my bed. He crouched in front of us and spoke very seriously.

"We have to leave here today. It is the only chance we may have," he said.

In about half an hour, we were ready to go. It was the first time I had seen our rooms so messy. I told my mother that if she wanted to tidy a bit, I would help her. She nodded and began picking up things that had been scattered in the hurry to pack. My father spoke sharply to her: "What are you doing? Who are you tidying for? Thieves and looters? We are leaving, for God's sake. Get into the car, everybody!"

Were we leaving all our things for thieves and looters? What was going to happen to my kites and my marbles? I started filling my pockets with my best marbles.

"Qais! The car! Now!" my father said. From the way he spoke, I knew not to argue. Several marbles slipped out of my hands and went rolling around on the floor. I left them and ran out the door.

We walked quickly across the courtyard to the garage. I looked under the tree where my father had been digging a hole last night. But there was no hole anymore. The green cucumber vine was there, just as it had been before. I wanted to ask him what happened to that hole, but I thought he might shout at me again like last night.

We got into the car while he opened the garage door to the street. As he started the engine, one of my uncles burst into the garage from the courtyard.

"Where are you going?" asked my uncle, who was a year younger than my father.

"I told you last night," my father replied, "to my friend's house in Kart-e-Parwan."

"Where are the rest of us going to go?" my uncle asked plaintively.

"You have had weeks to think about that," my father replied. There was an ache in his voice.

"Take our kids and wives with you; they want to live, too, like your own," my uncle pleaded.

"This is a small car, not a bus or truck," my father said. "It can only take four people at a time, and we are six already, plus a baby."

"Leave that part to me. I know how to do it. I'm a good packer," my uncle said.

Hardly a minute later, all six of my uncles with all of their kids and wives arrived in the garage and tried to fit themselves into our car. Two of my uncles' wives sat on the front seat, and seven of my cousins sat in the backseat. There was no space left for us. My father slammed the door near the driver's seat. "I'm not going anywhere," he said angrily.

My uncles started to argue with my father. He walked into the courtyard and kept walking slowly around the trees. I had never seen him behaving like this, or talking to his brothers like this before. It reminded me of Indian movies in which the bad brothers did not get along.

Everybody got out of the car and stared at one another. There was a deep silence.

My father came back after a few minutes and told my mother and my three sisters to take the baby and sit in the backseat. Then he ordered four of my cousins to squeeze in there, too. He asked me and three of my other cousins, including Wakeel, to sit in the trunk. Two of my uncles' wives sat in the front seat with my father. The rest would have to stay at the house and wait for him to come get them later.

He backed the car out onto the street. The bottom scraped the road from the weight of so many passengers. My father drove slowly for the four blocks through our neighborhood until we got out to the main road.

What we saw, I will never forget. Thousands of people like us were taking advantage of the ceasefire to flee from our part of the city. Thousands and thousands of people, all walking in near silence. When they spoke, they whispered as if they had been forbidden to talk normally. They were strung along each side of the roadway, moving along like lines of ants. All of them had two or three bags in their hands.

Ours was the only car on the road. When they saw our car, they all rushed toward us, asking us to give them a lift, even though they could see that our car was already fully packed. The crowd that gathered around us was so huge that my father could not move the car forward, not even one inch. Some were trying to pull my cousins and me out of the trunk so they could take our place. My father shouted back to us, "Hold on to each other, and lock your fingers together tightly."

We did what we were told, and my father rolled up his window, pressed the horn, turned on the lights, and drove slowly, then faster until one by one the people let go of us.

For the first time in the two months since the fighting had started, all of us were seeing the destruction it had caused. Things we had heard about, but had not wanted to believe, we were now seeing for ourselves.

The block-long, eight-story yellow grain silo that the Russians had built was full of holes where rockets had hit it. Small mountains of wheat lay at the base of the silo where it had flowed out through the holes.

There were big craters in the road where rockets had fallen. This had been the best road in Kabul. There were still many half-exploded rockets standing in the middle of the road, like nails that had been banged halfway through a piece of wood.

Hundreds of dead bodies were scattered all over the pavement, on the sidewalks, and in the park in the middle of the road. Some looked like they had been there for a long time. Blood was matted all over their clothes. Most were on the main road. Maybe they had been hit by a rocket when they were trying to cross the road. But many of them had been shot with bullets to the head, chest, or back. This was the work of the snipers. I could not believe my eyes; I thought I was seeing an American horror movie, especially when I saw parts of bodies, like arms or legs or even heads, lying by themselves.

My father had no choice but to drive over the ones in our path. Some of the dead bodies were on their backs as if they were sleeping. When our car drove over them, the speed of the car turned their faces toward the road, and the car rose up off the pavement.

To avoid hitting a man who was running toward us, my father drove the wrong way around the roundabout in front of the Polytechnic, then gunned the car up the hill toward the Intercontinental Hotel.


Beyond the top of the hill, everything looked different. The unimaginable scene through which we had just driven suddenly vanished. In its place, we saw real life.

People were buying bread from bakeries for their breakfast. Little kids were holding their parents' hands as they were walking to their school. The dogs were not howling. The roads were not empty. People's windows were not slamming, and their doors were not banging. There was no war. None.

I saw smiles on the faces of people who showed no signs of worry. But they could not stop staring at us; they had never seen a car packed like ours before. The lines of refugees had only just begun to reach that area, and they had no idea how many thousands more were coming. The small mountain that rose between our house and this neighborhood had protected these people from the fighting. Not even the snipers had come around to their side of the mountain, though they could have. But they were fighting over our neighborhood, which lay between two factions. The people we saw acted as if they did not even know that vicious combat was going on less than two miles away, though they would have to have heard the rockets and the shooting.

We came down the hill from the Intercontinental Hotel into the Kart-e-Parwan neighborhood. There were only a few cars on the road, but many people walking. Most of them were Indians going barefoot to their temples, carrying brass bowls filled with milk. Their men were dressed in white or orange. The women wore bright-colored saris. The kids walked behind. The boys' heads were shaved except for one braid. Some of the men had stripes painted on their foreheads.

My cousin Wakeel was sitting next to me in the trunk. He laughed at the kids with no hair, but said he wished he could have one of their bowls of milk.

At the bottom of the hill, we turned sharply to the left a couple of times and drove through a pretty, small park I had never seen. All the flowers were carefully tended.

We passed a large white building that stood behind a high wall. There were guards in strange uniforms with guns out in front of its fancy gate. They stood like statues. Big dogs from Russia were next to them. A sign said "British Embassy" in Dari under big letters in some other language.

We followed a dirt road that ran for two hundred meters beside the wall. That was the bumpiest road in Kabul. It took us down into a deep ravine and then up again as loose rocks slid underneath the wheels of the car. The top of the trunk bounced down on our heads with every bump. The dust stirred up by the car rolled in on us and made us choke. All of our eyebrows and eyelashes got covered with it. We looked like the clowns that used to perform on the stage of our school for Teacher's Day.

My father stopped the car in front of a tall, rusted metal gate in a high mud wall. He blew the horn a few times. Finally, with a scraping sound, an elderly *chowkidar*, the gatekeeper, drew open a small door next to the gate, saw that it was my father, then opened the gates wide. My father drove inside. The *chowkidar* rubbed his eyes to see whether he was dreaming. He closed the metal gates behind us and rushed toward us to help us get out of the trunk. He whispered to himself, "I have never seen so many people in a Volga before."

"I bet you haven't," I said back to him with a grin.

He got red and tried to hide his embarrassment. "I didn't mean to be rude; I'm just shocked." He had not expected to be heard.

We climbed out of the car. Some of my aunts had to be pulled. But the kids were all jumping out and looking around at where we had stopped, hardly four miles from the war zone we had just left.

In front of us rose a massive wall more than two stories high. It had one small opening in its dun-colored expanse, and that was filled with a thick, unpainted wooden door studded with the flattened heads of thick spikes. At the far end of the wall was a tower with eight sides that loomed above the high walls and the tops of some very big trees. We had seen another tower like it just outside the gate, but it was damaged, and half of it was missing.

A few moments later, the thick wooden door opened with the clank of a thick chain that must have been attached to it. A man whom I recognized as my father's business partner came through it, with two house servants close behind. I had seen the man many times in his carpet shop. He had always been impeccably dressed in a silk necktie and tailored jacket, with bright eyes that poured a good feeling into his customers. But this morning, he was wearing only his pajamas and holding a cup of tea in his hand. His eyes were sleepy. He greeted my father, gave *salaams* to the other adults, and welcomed all of us.

His name was Haji Noor Sher. Whenever my father took Wakeel, my older sister, and me to the shop, Haji Noor Sher gave us candy and put some small money in crumpled bills in our pockets. He always had foreign customers in his shop looking at carpets, but he would put his business affairs aside when we came in and give all his attention to us. He never used our real names; instead, he called us "nephew" and "niece," and he told us to call him "uncle."

If he was surprised to see us all at that early hour that morning, he did not show it. We had had no way to get a message to him to tell him that we were coming. But he and my father were close friends, and close friends help each other in times such as those.

My father took him to one side, and they talked quietly for a moment. Haji Noor Sher spoke to one of the house servants, who always stood behind him like bodyguards. The servant ran back into the house to get us some tea and something to eat. Haji Noor Sher acted as if he were accustomed to having visitors every day at this time, and to keeping those words for his servants ready in his mouth.

"Hey, everybody, welcome to my house. Do you like it?"

We really had not seen anything yet except big walls and the towers, but we nodded because we were relieved to be away from the fighting.

"This place is called the Qala-e-Noborja. Did you know that?" He held himself like a famous actor whom everybody knows, but none of my aunts and uncles had ever seen him before. "The reason we call it the 'Fort of Nine Towers' is because when it was built more than a hundred years ago, it had nine towers. It's antique, like me." He had a big smile that was contagious, so we all smiled at him.

I interrupted him: "Uncle Noor Sher, but I only see one tower." I pointed to the one full tower, ignoring the stub of the other one outside the gate.

He looked at my father, winked, and said, "Oh, he is smart." I liked hearing him say that, especially in front of all my cousins. "The other towers," he said with a twinkle in his eye, "are invisible. Just because we cannot see something does not mean that it is not there."

Even though the Qala-e-Noborja had only one tower still standing, it made me feel safe, especially since it had been there for more than a hundred years. Maybe the rockets could not hurt us here.

He handed his teacup to the other house servant and led us away from the door and down a steep, rose-lined path between the old fort and the one-story house to a terrace on the slope below the house. He and my father walked in front, and my cousins and I followed behind them, my mother and my aunts after us. The terrace was covered by a canopy of grapes. The bees were humming around them.

The sky was completely clear, and the sun was floating in a

lapis-blue space shining down at everything through the leaves. The wind gave no rest to the leaves and rustled them. I wondered whether there was still war on the other side of the mountain, or whether everything there had changed, too.

When I turned and looked behind me, I saw the old fort's one last tower rising above me. It looked even higher from where we were standing below it on the terrace. I was curious what was inside those high walls, but was too busy seeing all the new things in this large garden that surrounded them to wonder about that for long. On the terraces—there were four of them cut into the steep slope—rosebushes and vegetable gardens were laid out in neatly tended rows.

On one of the terraces a fountain shot water into the air. Near the fountain were two massive trees. Two of my cousins tried to hold hands with me around one of the trunks. We could just barely reach one another's fingertips.

Down another level, in a flat area at the lowest point in the garden, was a stream. As he led us to it, Haji Noor Sher told us that its cold water came from the Hindu Kush mountains sixty miles away. It was flowing into a pool cut into the rock. More than ten types of colorful fish were swimming in the pool.

Some parrots, canaries, and eagles were in cages near the pool, and cooing pigeons had a place of their own.

In a cage built against the high wall that separated the garden from a street, a big dog with bloodshot eyes was pacing quietly. Some bones lay in a corner. He was the kind of dog the Kuchis, nomads, keep in front of their cattle to protect them from wolves. From other cages next to it, two Russian wolfhounds glared at us.

When we got close to the cages, the dogs began barking at us, and jumping against the sides, trying to break out and tear us apart. They were fighting dogs. We ran away.

There was yet another cage, a very large one, at the base of the tower. At first we saw nothing in it and thought the cage was empty. Then something shifted in the shadows of a small doorway that led into the bottom of the tower. Slowly, the shadow moved toward us. It was very big. My older sister and some of my girl cousins took a step back.

Nobody said anything as a leopard walked gracefully out into the sunshine and looked at us. It was yellow with brown spots. We had seen leopards in the Kabul Zoo. We had been told they were very dangerous. No one dared to speak as the blood ran out of our faces. What kind of place is this that has a leopard in the garden? I wondered.

The leopard had no interest in our fear. He lay down in a sunny place and started licking himself. We all tiptoed away. This garden seemed to me like paradise, but even more interesting than the way my older sister had described it.

The house servants appeared, carrying a huge breakfast on big shiny trays; many types of fruit juices, apples, grapes, milk, tea, butter, cheese, yogurt, hard-boiled eggs, and fresh breads. They unrolled several bright red and green *sofrah*, eating cloths, on the terrace near the fountain, and began to set the trays of food on the ground. Haji Noor Sher invited us to start eating, then went back up to his rooms inside the courtyard of the old fort.

We did not know what to eat first. We had not had a proper meal for weeks. Everybody forgot all their manners as we piled our plates high. My father said, "Slowly, slowly, the food is not running away." Wakeel laughed, but the others were too busy eating.

Above the clink of the knives and forks, we could hear the birds singing as they flew from one tree to another. We had not heard birds in Kot-e-Sangi in months. Twelve baby deer that were grazing placidly in the garden around us occasionally looked up at us.

As we finished eating, Haji Noor Sher came out of the old fort and down the garden steps alongside the terrace where we were seated. Now he was wearing a white *shalwar kamiz*, a silk *chapan* coat, a *karacol* lamb's wool hat, and leather slippers. His two house servants stood behind him. They were much taller than he was.

Haji Noor Sher was so short and so portly he was almost round. My cousin Wakeel whispered to me that he could be a large marble like the ones we played with. My father overheard him and glared at him. Wakeel lowered his eyes sheepishly, but the rest of us were giggling very softly. Even though he was small, Haji Noor Sher had a big presence. I had never seen the king, except on television, but Haji Noor Sher looked like a king to me.

"Do you like my garden?" he asked us. We all told him how beautiful it was. A big smile took over his face.

"Come with me, I will show you my courtyard." Now we would see what was inside the high mud-brick walls of this Fort of Nine Towers that had only one tower. He turned and led the way up the steep path. We all rushed to find our shoes that we had taken off when we sat to eat. I wore one of my own shoes, and one of Wakeel's. He shouted at me. I had to run back and give him his.

Haji Noor Sher pushed open the heavy wood door that led from the garden into the courtyard. Finally, we could see the thick chain attached to the inside of it that made a clanking sound each time the door moved. After the first door was another, but it was at right angles so that anyone trying to invade the fort could be stopped in the passage and not just rush straight in.

Beyond it was a large courtyard half as long as a football field, and half as wide. It was surrounded by two levels of rooms with tall, wood-frame windows. On one side of the courtyard, a room with windows on three sides projected into the garden. On the other, the rooms on the upper level were set back, leaving a broad upper terrace in front of them. A perfect place for flying kites, I thought.

The courtyard was full of fruit trees and roses and many flowers I had never seen before and whose names I did not know. Grapevines covered an arbor in the far corner. A tall acacia tree dominated the end near us, and a very old, spreading *arghawan* tree reigned at the other. In between were peach and pomegranate trees, as well as two enormous thickets of lilacs. Haji Noor Sher made a special point of showing them to us. The lilacs had been a gift to his father from the king. He said that for years after acquiring the fort from the royal family, his father had always sent the first lilacs of the season to the king, large scented armloads of them.

Carefully trimmed rosebushes enclosed beds of brightly colored geraniums and lilies. Haji Noor Sher was proudest of a black rose that he had, and cautioned us against telling anybody about it. He said it was very rare and someone might come and steal it. Morning glory and honeysuckle vines climbed the wall at the far end of the courtyard, where a small door led into a *hammam*, a steam bath.

In front of the *hammam* was a large enclosure with a few deer in it that looked like they were the parents of the little deer outside in the garden. Two peacocks stood watching us with their tails spread. Haji Noor Sher made a funny noise, and they came running to him. He patted them; we all wanted to do that, too. But when we tried, they ran away and screeched, "Fanark!" We soon learned that "fanark" is the most common word in the peacock language. It is always said very loudly.

As we walked across the courtyard, I found a small peacock feather. I picked it up and kissed it, because we had been told they are holy. These many years later, I still use that feather as a bookmark for my Holy Koran.

My father walked next to Haji Noor Sher. He was much taller than Haji Noor Sher. I walked next to my father. The rest of the family walked behind us, and the servants behind them.

Haji Noor Sher showed us five rooms that faced the courtyard and said we could use them all. He was living in the old fort by himself in some rooms above the passageway into the courtyard. He had moved his family to India as soon as the fighting had started so they would be safe. Now he flew back and forth between Delhi and Kabul every couple of months. He had shops in both places. In Kabul, he bought old carpets with my father's help, and in Delhi he sold them.

The floors of our rooms were covered with several layers of carpets. Low mattresses had been placed all around the walls, with long, narrow carpets covering them. In the corner of each room was a pile of quilts and pillows. The carpets made the rooms look like the garden had come in from outside.

Haji Noor Sher told the servants to bring us more tea as we came out of the rooms. We all sat in the shade of the grape arbor and relaxed in a way that we had not done for months.

I entirely forgot about war and those dead bodies on the road. I even forgot about my grandfather and my uncles and unmarried aunts who were still at our house, until we heard the first rocket.

There is a noise a rocket makes when it is fired. You can hear it from miles away. It is not loud, but it stops all conversations instantly. First, there is the *fumf* of the launch, then the silence as everyone waits, and then the explosion as a house is destroyed or a school collapses. Then slowly the conversation resumes, sometimes with a half-spoken prayer.

For some reason, the ceasefire had ended hours earlier than had been announced. My father jumped up and looked panicked. He had been enjoying the magnificent peace in this place for a few moments before heading back to get the others. But if the fighting had started again, he could not go home now.

We were hardly four miles away from our house, but it was too far to go if the snipers had started shooting again. We could not hear the fighting, because the small mountain with two peaks separated us from it. In our mind's eye, however, we could see everything that was happening.

Over the next few days, we settled into our new rooms and worried about Grandfather and the others. We could hear the rockets, but the fighting seemed very far away. The cousins filled the days playing hide-and-seek in the vast garden, or splashing cold water on one another from the pool. The adults said we would not be here long. The fighting would end soon, and we could go home.

On the fourth day, we heard again from the BBC World Service that on the following day there would be a one-day ceasefire between the two main factions that were fighting in our Kot-e-Sangi neighborhood.

Early the next morning, my father woke me up. Then he went to my sisters to rouse them. In five minutes we all were awake, waiting to hear what my father would tell us.

My father kissed my mother first, then he came to me. I was still sitting on my bed, stretching my arms. He crouched on his heels in front of me and said, "I'm going now to bring your grandfather and the others here. If something happens to me, and I cannot come back, you have to forget that you once had a father. You will be your own father, and a good son to your mother, and a kind brother to your sisters and your brother. I leave you all the responsibility of a father. But you have to learn how to take care of your sisters and mother. Understood?"

I did not know what to say. I was now ten years old. I said, "Yes."

He went to my older sister. He sat on his heels in front of her bed and said, "You are my oldest child. You're the most beautiful and intelligent child that I have, but you have to learn how to be helpful to others, and not to feel lonely if I'm not around. You have to educate your little sisters and help your mother. Don't wait for anyone to tell you what to do. If something happens to me, you are responsible for your sisters, to keep them busy, and make them learn one new thing every day. Help with your little brother and keep your mother happy, understood?"

Tears came from my older sister's eyes as she gazed straight at my father. My father hugged her for a minute. Then slowly and gently he rubbed her back and told her to be brave. I did not feel sorry for her. Wakeel and I used to call her "fountain eyes," because she cried so easily, when she was not making stupid jokes.

He went to my two little sisters, who slept together in one bed in those days, because they were scared of the rocket sounds. "Did you have good dreams last night?" my father asked them.

The older one said "Yes." The younger one said "No." Then she changed her mind. "Yes, I had a good dream last night." They both wanted to talk at the same time. Both wanted to talk louder to be heard.

"Stop, stop, stop! One by one! Who had a good dream last night, raise your hand," my father said.

Both of them quickly raised their hands.

He pointed to the littler one. "You tell me your dream."

She thought for a second, then said, "I didn't dream last night. I will try to have a nice dream tonight, and I'll tell you tomorrow morning."

My father smiled and tousled her hair. "You naughty little girl." Then he asked the older one to tell him her dreams.

She cleared her throat, but she was silent for almost a minute. My father was waiting to hear from her. She cleared her throat a second time, but was still silent.

"Come on! Tell me your dream," my father said.

"Why are you in a hurry? Are you going somewhere?" she asked.

"I just don't want to wait till evening, listening to your throat clearings," my father said.

She cleared her throat a third time and said, "Well, it will take seven hours to tell you my dreams, because I slept for seven hours last night. Now, sit properly. You may get tired sitting on your heels."

My father asked both of them to come closer to him, then he hugged them both and kissed their heads, foreheads, and cheeks and said, "I'm going out to buy some milk for breakfast. When I come back, I will listen to your dream stories. Okay?"

They both nodded their heads and smiled at my father. The younger one pulled her blanket off and got up from the bed. The older one, suddenly cold, shouted at her. The younger one shouted back to wake up and brush her teeth. Then they started arguing with each other, as always.

My mother was standing the whole time at the corner of the room with folded arms, leaning against the wall, resting her head on her right shoulder, watching my father. My father got up and walked toward her. He stood in front of her and said, "I have to go. It will get late."

Her face looked very sad. "Be careful." She started to say something else, but her voice caught. We all looked at her. "We are waiting for you," she said softly.

I could read in my mother's face that she had a lot in her heart. She wanted to say something, but her mouth, lips, and throat refused to obey.

My father kissed her forehead and hugged her. He winked at me with a big smile over her shoulder, and I smiled back.

He stood at the threshold of the door, holding the doorknob; he took a long look at all of us and said, "I will be back soon." He looked at my older sister and me and said, "You two, don't forget what I told you." Then he went out. My mother followed him.

Everybody started to fold their sheets. My littlest sister ran outside, but my father had already gone. She came back to tell my mother, "Father doesn't need to buy milk. His friend's servants prepare us a good breakfast every day, and it has milk, too."

"Yes, you are right; I forgot to tell him that." My mother tried to sound surprised. "But don't worry, he'll drink the milk before he goes to sleep."

"I want to drink milk, too," she said.

"Yes, of course. How can he drink it without you?" my mother said.

Later I found out that my cousin Wakeel had gone with my father. I felt very alone. Why had he gone to Grandfather's house and not taken me with him? Maybe he would bring our kites and marbles when he came back.

# 4

❖

## *To Be a Family Again*

My father was supposed to come back that same day, but he did not. We had no idea what had happened to him. My littlest sister kept asking my mother, "Why is it taking Father so long to buy milk?"

"Maybe it is not easy to find milk in this part of town," my mother replied again and again. She tried very hard to be busy, and kept doing things that did not need to be done.

Since the civil war had started, I had seen my mother crying many, many times, though she always tried to hide her tears from us. Now, every night since my father had left, she cried in the dead of night. Mostly she went outside in the courtyard, and cried very softly. Sometimes she just sat on the bottom step of the stairs outside our rooms, and the tears started coming. One of those nights, my littlest sister saw her, and the next day she imitated her by sprinkling water under her eyes and pretending to be the little mother.

On the third day, my father returned with my uncles, their wives, their kids, and my unmarried aunts. Like us, they all had crammed into the Volga with the kids in the trunk, about twelve of them. They looked really dirty, so we made jokes about them. They laughed. Then we sent them one by one to bathe.

The only ones who had stayed behind at our home were Grandfather and Wakeel, my two best friends and the two people for whom I cared most. Grandfather was refusing to leave his house to the thieves and the warlords, but what could he do to protect it?

My father told us that four rockets had landed in Grandfather's courtyard on the day after he had arrived there. A day later, two more rockets had destroyed some of my grandfather's McIntosh apple trees and most of his flowers. Grandfather's heart was broken. He had been so optimistic about the Mujahedin.

"A broken hand can work, but a broken heart cannot," was what Grandfather had told me one day when I did not want to be with my parents, because my father had shouted at me after I had received bad scores in arithmetic at school.

At night I would think about Grandfather on the other side of the mountain, without his carpets, his beloved trees now only stumps and splinters.

A week later, early on a Friday morning when it was still dark, I heard a loud knocking on the front gate. It went on for almost ten minutes, but nobody opened the door.

The *chowkidar* was an old man, and when he slept it was as if he were dead. Someone had to sprinkle water on his face to wake him up.

The knocking continued, followed by low arguments that became louder. I slowly recognized the voices.

I woke up my father. He hurriedly put on his clothes and ran outside. I followed him. A moment later, we saw Grandfather and Wakeel and the *chowkidar* arguing. By now they were shouting. The gatekeeper would not let them in. He kept saying, "If you need some food, come back in two hours, but now everybody is asleep, go, go . . ."

The gatekeeper thought my grandfather and my cousin were desperate beggars looking for a place to stay, or a meal. He was half-deaf. They did not know that they had to shout into his ears.

Haji Noor Sher was not home either. He had gone to visit his family in India, and to check on his shop in Delhi. His *chowkidar* never let any strangers come in when he was away. He was an honest and strict man.

My father rushed and hugged his father and Wakeel, and the gate-keeper stopped talking. My father shouted very loudly in the door-keeper's left ear, which worked a little: "This is my father and my nephew." He apologized and shuffled away with his stick.

My father brought us all into the room where the rest of the family was sleeping in rows of little mattresses on the floor. He turned on the lights and shouted at everybody to wake up and say hello to Grandfather. My grandfather and Wakeel were covered in dust. Their clothes were very dirty, as if they had not changed them for months. We surrounded them and were all waiting for them to say something.

I read a great sorrow on my grandfather's face; I had never seen him so sad, or so dirty before. He had always worn expensive suits with silk ties, his shoes polished to a blinding shine. But that day, his feet and head and even his eyelashes were covered with dust. He did not talk to anyone. He asked my mother for a blanket. When she brought it, he lay on the floor and covered himself from head to toe without washing or saying a word. In five minutes, he started snoring.

We all left the room quietly, tiptoeing outside to let him sleep. We took Wakeel with us into the next room. We asked him to tell us how he had gotten there. He did not want to talk. He was tired and hungry and thirsty, but when we insisted and he had been given a glass of water, he took a deep breath and started.

"We left home around one o'clock in the morning. We stayed in the shadows of the buildings in case there were snipers on the mountain. After we started walking out on the main road, we were stopped in two places," he said, and took a sip from his glass. "At the first place, there were some guys whose faces were all covered. They spoke with a Hazaragi accent. They all had guns and all kinds of other weapons hanging on their chests, backs, even their legs.

Wakeel's voice was deep. Like Grandfather's, it was always calm. He always spoke very clearly in a way that made even grown-ups pay attention to what he said. And he always chose his words very carefully. His face was like a fast-changing sky and revealed his thoughts even before he expressed them in words. His eyes would grow large one moment and tight the next. His mouth changed shape with his emotions.

"They put us in a dark room with no windows. They stood outside talking. We could not hear what they were saying very well, but I think they were worried that we belonged to another faction, and were spying on them. After about half an hour, they came back in. They whispered to one another for a minute or so, then let us go without asking us anything.

"That was near the silo. Then we started walking toward the Polytechnic, but the Panjshiris had a checkpoint there, only we could not see it in the dark."

We had been hearing about checkpoints on the BBC, but this was the first time that they had entered our lives directly.

"Some guy shouted at us, '*Stop! Stop!*' Grandfather said to keep moving, but the guy fired at the sky and cried again, '*Stop! Stop! Stop!*'

"He wore military clothes and searched us from head to toe. He and his friend put their guns to the back of my head and Grandfather's head, and commanded us to walk forward. They led us to a small room. Another guy was there sitting on a bed with dirty sheets.

"He asked Grandfather a few questions, like why we were coming this direction, and who we work for. But Grandfather didn't answer him. He told the commander, 'You guys call yourselves holy warriors, but you are just killers and thieves.'

"The commander smiled at Grandfather and said, 'Behave yourself!'

"Grandfather didn't say anything. He just stared at the commander, and the commander stared back for a few moments, then ordered one of the other guys to search our bags. But all we had was Grandfather's books, so they let us pass."

I looked into the large cotton bag near my foot and saw the two volumes of *Afghanistan in the Path of History* by Mir Ghulam Mohammad Ghobar. Grandfather had to leave his house, but he would not leave his books.

When Wakeel finished speaking, he asked for a blanket and went to the room where Grandfather was sleeping. A minute later, he was asleep, too.

---

The months passed. We stayed in Haji Noor Sher's house, eating the good food cooked by his servants, enjoying fresh fruits from the garden, and playing with the dogs. By then, all the dogs had become friendly. The leopard was not friendly. So we left him alone.

Every night we listened to the BBC World Service and other broadcasts, but there was no good news. Our country was being destroyed more every hour, by factions whose leaders slaughtered thousands during the day, then talked like holy men on their broadcasts during the night. They always introduced themselves as the holy warriors and said that they were fighting against evil. Day killers; night liars.

I started to hate the broadcasts. None of them gave us any good news; they were all the same. They made my grandfather, uncles, and father unhappy, which made us feel sorry for them. I decided to break all the radios. Then I thought that it would make them even sadder. The BBC was the only thing they had to look forward to all day.

Now, for the first time, there was serious talk among my father and my uncles of leaving Afghanistan. My grandfather did not say anything this time. Sometimes late at night when they thought I was asleep, I would hear my father telling my mother what the men had been discussing.

My father again wanted to go to Russia, as he had proposed the year before when we were still at home. He had been in touch with his friends there from his boxing days. They had offered to help us get settled once we arrived. But now the borders were tightly closed, so we would need a lot of money to pay smugglers to get all of us across.

My father's only income in those days came from the carpets that he had gathered from the villages before the fighting had started, and which Haji Noor Sher still sold in his shop in India.

He had not been paid in several months for his job teaching physics at Habibia High School. Though the fighting had closed the school, which had been hit by rockets, he was still supposed to be receiving his government salary.

Some Kuchi nomads had been trapped in the building during one of the times when a ceasefire had suddenly ended. They had been passing through Kabul on their way from their summer grazing lands in the mountains near Bamyan to their winter base in the lowlands near Jalalabad, but had to hide their sheep, donkeys, camels, cows, and horses in the basement of the school. Some of the local factions discovered them and took the sheep to feed their soldiers. For months after the Kuchis left, the whole school smelled like a barn.

Every morning when I woke, I was still confused for a moment until I looked around and saw my family sleeping on the floor nearby and remembered where we were. But in other ways, our lives had settled into routines.

My uncles still went to their jobs in the city when there seemed to be a break in the fighting. Sometimes it would suddenly end, and things would be quiet for weeks. Then, without anybody knowing why, it would start up again as fiercely as before.

My mother stopped going to the bank. She did not feel safe traveling across the city. Also, she was much busier than before going to the bazaars to buy food, which was sometimes hard to find—mostly rice and whatever vegetables the farmers could bring to the market, and not the meat that Afghans love. At Grandfather's house, she had had a lot of help from my uncles' wives, my father's unmarried sisters, and even my older sister and my girl cousins. At Noborja, my grandfather's family was still living together, but we had been shattered into small parts as we tried to survive.

Though his family was in Delhi and he had shops in both Kabul and Delhi, Haji Noor Sher preferred to be in Kabul. In Delhi, he had rented an apartment for his family in the Lajpat Nagar area, but hated living in it, he told us. He had grown up in a large house with a big garden, and the apartment felt like a prison cell to him. Even worse, he did not know many people in India and felt very lonely there.

During his stays in Kabul, his wife often called from Delhi and begged him to come there. He would put off going as long as he could, and then left only when the fighting heated up. As soon as he heard that there was a ceasefire in Kabul, though, he was back with us in the fort.

Each time he returned, his friends would start showing up at Noborja that same day. Somehow they knew he was back. Though we could sometimes hear the sounds of rockets, bombs, and rifles being fired on the other side of the mountain, they laughed and enjoyed one another's company, my father among them. Hearing the sound of their laughter made us hopeful.

Often Haji Noor Sher asked his cook to prepare special food, such as a big *qabli pelau*, with its mountains of rice mixed with shredded carrots, raisins, and nuts heaped over big pieces of meat. Or there were lamb kebabs, or lamb soup. He asked my mother to cook her famous corn bread for dessert. Every day felt like a holiday when he was at Noborja.

In the mornings, as soon as I had woken up and splashed some water on my face, I ran to his rooms, where some mullahs he had known for years were reciting verses from the Holy Koran with melodic voices. I sat in a corner and listened, or took a Koran and followed the lines the mullahs were reciting by heart.

After breakfast the mullahs left, and musicians would come and start singing sweet *ghazals* softly accompanied by a *tambour, sitar, tabla,* and harmonium. The music went on until lunch, when there was a one-hour break for naps. Then some other friends of his, who were the best storytellers I have ever heard, came and told stories about almost anything.

Haji Noor Sher always sat in his chair like a king on his throne while his guests sat on the *toshak* cushions on the floor around the room. His eyes were closed. He fingered his *tasbeh* prayer beads, moving his head gently as if in a trance. If in the middle of a story one of the servants knocked on the door, he opened his eyes and said, "Stop."

The storyteller immediately halted.

He said, "Come in."

The servant would come in with a fresh pot of tea in his hands. Haji Noor Sher looked at the glasses on the floor, which was the sign for the servant to fill them up. The servant stepped lightly from one cup to the next, then left the steaming pot on the floor in the middle of the room and softly walked out.

Haji Noor Sher turned to the storyteller and said, "Continue."

At night, he turned on his generator so that all of the kids could watch an Indian movie with him in his room. He often fell asleep in the middle of the film, half sitting and half lying on his bed. When the movie ended, we pulled his blanket over him, turned off his light, tiptoed out of his room, turned off the generator, and went to our rooms to sleep.

One day, when Wakeel and I were on the roof with our kites, we noticed that below us in the courtyard the house servants and all the other servants, who kept the gardens and looked after the animals, were doing unusual things.

They were shampooing the deer and tying pretty ribbons to their antlers. Later, they strung multicolored lights along the tops of the courtyard walls and hung paper lanterns from the graceful, bending canes of the lilac bushes. Then they hung a very large square of brightly covered cloth from the upper terrace. It draped over the windows of the rooms on the courtyard level until other servants set poles under its lower edge and raised it up to make an awning. Under the awning they built a low platform.

The servants did not stop for lunch but kept on working, washing the large, square paving stones in the courtyard floor. Haji Noor Sher said they had been part of the Buddhist *stupa* that had stood here for centuries before the Qala-e-Noborja had been built by Abdur Rahman, the king, for his *wazir*, his most important minister.

As the evening approached, the courtyard became even busier. Haji Noor Sher was ordering the servants to do this and that. Hurricane lanterns were set up along both sides of the paths around the courtyard and next to the flowerpots overflowing with blooms. Some of the flowers were bright red and tall, some wound like vines up the walls, and some were orange and gold.

Wakeel and I had long stopped flying our kites for the day, and were watching all the activity, wondering what was going on.

My father had come into the courtyard and was standing next to Haji Noor Sher, discussing something with him. When Haji Noor Sher went upstairs to his room, I ran down from the rooftop to ask my father what was happening. He told me that Haji Noor Sher was having some foreign guests for dinner, people who were working for the United Nations. I ran up and told Wakeel.

Haji Noor Sher loved having guests, especially when he could show off his garden, and his wealth, and how many servants he had.

My father went inside our rooms to take a shower. My mother started ironing his best *shalwar kamiz*. Wakeel and I went down to the courtyard to help the servants.


Two servants carrying shiny silver trays with tea and glasses entered the courtyard. They asked us to carry them upstairs, to Haji Noor Sher's rooms. I took the tray that had two pots of tea on it. I could smell the strong scent of cardamom coming from their spouts. Wakeel took the tray of glasses and walked ahead of me, climbing the stairs to Haji Noor Sher's apartment.

When we reached the top, Wakeel carefully pushed the door open with his foot and went in without knocking. Haji Noor Sher had just finished having his shower. He was standing in the middle of the room, drying his head with a small blue towel, but otherwise completely naked.

When he saw us, he gasped and hurriedly looked for something with which to cover himself. I was horrified. It is very shameful to be naked in front of someone else, and even more shameful to look at someone naked. I quickly placed the tray in front of the door on the floor and ran back down the stairs. Wakeel ran after me, laughing, and nearly knocking me over as he raced down. I started to laugh, too.

Haji Noor Sher shouted at us. We did not hear what exactly he said, but we knew that he was very angry that we had not knocked on the door before we came in. But how could we? Our hands were full.

Wakeel and I ran out of the door, across the courtyard, and back up to the roof terrace. There we collapsed into embarrassed laughter. Wakeel asked, "Did you see them?"

"What?" I asked, still giggling.

"Did you see that he had five testicles?" Wakeel asked.

"Five?" I asked in disbelief. "How could he have five?"

"I counted them very carefully," Wakeel said seriously, then fell into a heap as he exploded laughing. And each time that the laughter started to ease, we would look at each other and Wakeel would say "Five," and it started even fiercer than before. When Wakeel laughed, his eyes glowed and his brilliantly white teeth shone.

Several minutes later, we saw Haji Noor Sher, now very nicely dressed, coming out of his door into the courtyard. We peeped from behind a low wall in a corner.

Haji Noor Sher was standing in the middle of the courtyard, in a white *shalwar kamiz* and a black waistcoat, ordering his servants to lay carpets on the paths around the courtyard, and to bring the peacocks from the garden. He wore a small, round red hat with a tassel.

A group of musicians walked in through the low door and greeted him as if he were a prince. He directed them to sit on a platform in the middle of the courtyard that had been covered with an old Bukhara rug made soft and shiny from years of use.

The musicians were dressed very elegantly with beaded black waistcoats. Each wore a brightly colored turban. One started tuning the twenty-two twangy strings of a *rabab*. Another was blowing the Kabul dust out of his flute-like *ney*. The oldest one sat with a *tambour* rising from his lap, running his fingers up and down its long neck, playing silent music that only he could hear in his mind. And the fourth had a shining pair of brass *tabla* drums that he kept tapping on the sides with a small hammer to tune them, and put a snap into their sound. After a few minutes, they finished their preparations, and the courtyard was filled with their soft, sweet music.

When my unmarried aunts and my cousins heard the music, they joined us on the rooftop, watching everything from there. By now, it had become dark, and nobody could see us.

For a few minutes, Haji Noor Sher left the courtyard, then returned with four foreign men. Haji Noor Sher looked too short to be standing next to those people, who were extraordinarily tall and strong, with long, yellow hair, blue eyes, and unusually white skin.

Haji Noor Sher talked to them in a strange language, showing them the carpets on the paths and talking about them. The guests asked questions in the same strange tongue.

I asked one of my aunts what language they were speaking. She said, "English." I liked the sound of it. It sounded very much like Dari, but even though I paid close attention, I did not understand a word of it.

From time to time, Haji Noor Sher would have one of the servants pick up a rug so one of the guests could inspect it more closely. He would turn it over and show them the knotting on the back side, then rub his hand across the pile as if it were his favorite cat.

Suddenly, I understood what was going on. I had seen him do this many times in his shop. He was trying to sell carpets to these foreigners. As the fighting in Kabul had become worse, Haji Noor Sher's customers had stopped coming from other countries. He still sent a few carpets to people who phoned him from Berlin or London, and he had taken many carpets to India. But he had not sold any carpets in Kabul for a long time.

My father shared in the profits with Haji Noor Sher, and he spoke about these things with my mother at night. Now the only foreigners in Kabul were the aid workers. If these foreigners bought some carpets, perhaps we would have enough money to pay smugglers to get us out of Afghanistan.

My father came out of our house and shook hands with the visitors. My father talked to them in their language. I was amazed. I did not know that he could speak English.

The servants brought tall glasses of pomegranate juice on trays filled with plates of nuts and dried fruit, as the musicians continued playing soft music. We watched as if it were all a movie. Haji Noor Sher had the servants bring several very old carpets from inside and lay the carpets out on the carefully cut grass. These were the most expensive pieces, the carpets my father had found when he had gone to the villages and knocked on doors. One of the visitors got down on his knees as he was admiring the old carpets. The discussion about prices would happen after they ate. Haji Noor Sher, like any good rug dealer, wanted the customer's excitement about a carpet to build until he could not stand the thought of leaving it behind.

Haji Noor Sher led the guests to the awning under which the servants had arranged large cushions and several layers of carpets on the platform so they could sit comfortably while they ate. Some were at ease seated, like Afghans, with one leg folded on top of the other. But one of the guests kept shifting his position, trying to get comfortable. A servant brought a pitcher of water and a bowl. He stepped carefully among the guests as they settled on their cushions and poured warm water over their hands into the bowl so they could wash. Another servant followed him with small towels.

Then the food started to come. The servants, who were now dressed in even nicer clothes, carried big rice platters heaped with *qabli pelau* covered with raisins and grated carrots and set them on the cloth that had been spread in front of Haji Noor Sher, my father, and the guests.

An Uzbek man who usually helped Haji Noor Sher in the shop had been cooking kebabs out in the garden outside the courtyard. The smoke had started curling up to us on the rooftop, making us all feel hungry. A few minutes later, the Uzbek came running into the courtyard with long swords of grilled meats, and set them down in front of the guests, where they sat under the awning. Then other servants brought dishes filled with roasted aubergines and spinach. There were bowls of salads and yogurt and large baskets piled with freshly baked *naan*. It was still warm, and we could smell it. Someone else brought all kinds of drinks.

There were only four guests, plus Haji Noor Sher and my father, but there was enough food for everyone living at the Qala-e-Noborja.

We were happy about that, because we knew that later when the guests had left, the leftovers would be offered to us.

When the guests had all eaten too much, and Haji Noor Sher had insisted that they eat more, they patted their stomachs, while Haji Noor Sher pretended to be offended that they had eaten so little. The servants brought them *chillums*, water pipes, and carefully lit the apple-flavored tobacco using pieces of glowing charcoal.

One of the foreigners sucked a lot of air through the embroidered tube and made the *chillum*'s water bubble. But he did not manage to get any smoke. When he breathed out, expecting to see a blue cloud as when my father had done it, there was nothing. Wakeel laughed; the foreigner heard him and looked up at us. Haji Noor Sher looked up, too, and then the other foreigners looked at us as well.

Wakeel whispered to us, "There is the man with five testicles." His disheveled hair framed his dark, shining eyes.

I burst out laughing. Wakeel laughed out loud, too. My other cousins who were hiding with us in a doorway on the roof terrace laughed without knowing why. The foreigners laughed out loud. The musicians stopped playing, and they laughed, too. Haji Noor Sher looked at us with sparks in his eyes for a second. But when he saw all his guests laughing, the frown on his face was put away, and it became a big smile with a loud laugh.

"Five," Wakeel repeated, nodding his head convincingly.

And then, somewhere to the north of us, the first rocket exploded. Perhaps it had hit Khair Khana, a Panjshiri neighborhood about five miles away. Perhaps it had been sent by Gulbuddin Hekmatyar. Perhaps by Sayyaf. It did not matter. The guests quickly got up from their cushions. They thanked Haji Noor Sher, and said good night to my father. They took lingering looks at the carpets on the grass and carefully stepped around them, as their security man hustled them to their cars without taking any carpets with them.

My father and Haji Noor Sher smiled as they saw them off. If they were feeling disappointed at having sold nothing, they were too polite to show it.

That was the last party that Haji Noor Sher ever gave in that court-yard. A few weeks later, a rocket landed in the street in front of his shop. He had seen what had happened to my grandfather and his carpets. He was one of the last carpet dealers still in Kabul. Now he knew it was time to go. The next day, he closed his shop and shipped all of his best carpets to Delhi, where he would go to join his family in the apartment he hated.

Early the next Friday, while we were still eating our breakfast, we were told that some men had come to take the leopard to a new home. All the kids wanted to go watch, but Haji Noor Sher had already or-dered his house servants to chain the courtyard gate so we would not get hurt if the leopard somehow escaped. Haji Noor Sher watched it all happen from the safety of his bedroom, which overlooked the gar-den from the window on one side, and the courtyard from the other.

Later he told us how the men had put a small cage on wheels in front of the leopard's home at the bottom of the one tower that was still standing. Being a cat, the leopard had to see what this new cage on wheels was all about. He sniffed it for a minute, walked into it, sat down, and started licking himself as the door was dropped closed and he was rolled slowly down the hill and out a rarely used gate that led through the high wall to a small street that ran beside it.

Haji Noor Sher then called out to Wakeel, my other cousins, and me from his window that faced the courtyard: "Now you can go to the garden." We ran out through the right-angled passageway in the high walls as if we, too, were being released from a cage. We jostled one an-other against the heavy wooden door with its clanking chain and down the hill to the leopard's cage. It now had one of the large dogs in it. It had been his cage before the leopard came, we had been told. Maybe he was happy to be home. We looked at the dog and at each other, and were not sure why we had run so fast to see what was no longer there.

Over the next few days, Haji Noor Sher gave away all his birds to different friends, except for the pigeons, which you could not give to anyone because they would only come back to their roost that rose at the far end of the courtyard. He made his funny noises at his peacocks one last time as they were being taken away.

As for the deer, as things worsened for us in the weeks ahead, they became food for us, and we threw their bones to the dogs in the cages.

Then the day came for Haji Noor Sher himself to leave. My father, my grandfather, and my uncles all lined up outside the courtyard gate to see him off, and to thank him for having saved us by giving us a place to stay. They all shook his hand and hugged him. All the cousins stood around, watching silently.

He asked my father to take care of the Qala-e-Noborja as he took a long look at the last remaining tower. Then he got into his car. As his driver pulled off, he waved at us kids.

His two house servants watched him being driven out the gate to the airport, and had no idea what to do next.

# 5

❖

## The Long Road Home

Every morning before sunrise, I was awakened by the sound of water splashing in the bathroom next to the room where I slept. It was Grandfather taking ablutions before he prayed.

When the splashing stopped and I knew he had finished, I went to the bathroom and took ablutions myself. Then I went to Grandfather's room and put my prayer rug next to his while he was still praying. Before I started my prayers, I looked up at him. A smile appeared on his face and soon transferred to mine; but he continued his prayers without looking at me, and I started mine feeling his smile all around me.

After Grandfather finished his prayers, he sat cross-legged on the prayer rug. He kept his eyes closed, his *tasbeh* prayer beads in his hands, softly reciting verses from the Holy Koran. I still remember the sweet sound of his mumbling. Whenever I think of it, it brings my grandfather back to me.

After I finished my prayers, I sat cross-legged on my prayer rug, exactly like he did, kept my eyes closed with a *tasbeh* in my hands, audibly reciting the verses of the Holy Koran that I knew by heart.

Sometimes I looked at Grandfather and wondered what he thought about when he was meditating. Twice he had gone to Mecca, and as with all pilgrims to that holy city everyone called him "Haji," except for his children, who called him *Agha*, Dad. We called him *Baba*, Grandfather.

After breakfast, Grandfather usually went to the large garden outside the courtyard with a book in his hand. Haji Noor Sher had a large collection of books and he was happy to have Grandfather read them. He sat under the grapevine, but he could not read like in the old days, with full concentration. After a short while, he put the book aside and started walking back and forth under the trees, making a path in the grass of one of the long terraces below the tower. He seemed to me the way the leopard had been in the cage, restless. The sight of him made me sad.

Sometimes I went to walk with him. When he saw me approaching, he would smile, but I could see that this was a forced smile. I walked with him back and forth under the trees, without uttering a word. All we could hear was the sound of the dry leaves under our feet.

Every now and again, I looked up at him and saw a deep sorrow on his face. His face was like a mirror, accurately reflecting everything he was thinking.

Sometimes he talked to me of his business, and how hard he had tried to accomplish so many things in life. Sometimes he talked with regret of things he had not achieved. Sometimes he talked of soul, or heart, or essence, or spirit. But most of the time he talked of his carpets that had been stolen, his house that lay in ruins, his apple trees and his rosebushes that had been destroyed, and his lost peace of mind.

Grandfather hated idleness. For three months now, he had been at the Qala-e-Noborja doing nothing. Finally, he could sit there no longer. His house had been his life, and he had to go see it. He asked my youngest uncle to join him.

"With all respect, no, I don't want to go. You shouldn't go either. The house is there, no one can take it. The looters have probably plundered everything else. They might even have taken the windows and beams and cut the trees for firewood. But the land will always stay there," my uncle said.

"I brought you up for such a day to tell me 'No'? Huh? Huh?" my grandfather asked, as he stared at my uncle.

"You know I have never said 'No' to you in my entire life, Agha. Please, at least once in your life, listen to me. Let's not go today," my uncle politely said.

"If you don't want to go, just say you are a coward," Grandfather retorted.

My uncle grinned to hide his embarrassment. "I'm not a coward, but I am afraid of being killed by a coward. Those who kill thousands of innocents to make themselves rich are cowards. If we go there, they will smell money on us, even though you have lost everything. We have a little money left, we can survive for a while. Who knows what is going to happen next? They have been fighting for months; it cannot last much longer. Let's not risk the things that we buried there!"

I did not know what he meant. What things were buried there? But I knew I should not ask.

Grandfather turned away from my uncle. He looked at me, and for a moment, he did not say anything. Then, very coldly, he said to me, "Prepare yourself. We will leave in ten minutes."

I looked at my father. From his eyes, I could see that he was not happy. Grandfather looked at my father. I looked at Grandfather. My father looked at me.

"Do what your grandfather says," my father said quietly. My mother's face went pale. But it was not her place to challenge Grandfather.

I knew from my father's tone of voice that he was not pleased with Grandfather's idea. But he was too respectful to say "No."

"Are you a coward like your uncle?" Grandfather asked me.

I looked at my uncle, who was only a couple of years older than Wakeel. His face was full of hurt at having been called a coward by his father.

"I will do what my father and you say," I replied softly. But I did not want to go.

Grandfather smiled, but sadly. "You are a good boy."

———

We left home in midmorning. We got a bus that took us halfway. The bus had to stop before it reached the front line between the Panjshiris and the Hazaras. The front line moved from time to time as one side gained a temporary advantage over the other. No one ever knew for sure where it was.

We got off the bus and started walking. The road was empty. This was the same road that had been crowded with lines of refugees on the morning we had fled our home. It was the widest road in Kabul, so wide it had a park with big trees running down the middle. Before the fighting, young men met young women there to sit under the trees. Sometimes we saw them kissing and laughed at them. Wakeel called them pigeons.

Now the pavement was all broken. Everywhere there were holes where rockets had exploded, and craters made by bombs dropped from planes by some of the factions. Some of them were so deep that they had filled with groundwater from far below. All around us were pieces of twisted metal. It was so quiet, we could hear the sound of the bees humming.

As we were walking, my grandfather asked me whether I had ever been in love with someone. I was too shy to say "Yes," so I said "No." I desperately wanted to say, "I am in love with my classmate, Yaldda." But I was only ten years old, and boys that age are not supposed to have girlfriends.

My grandfather looked into my eyes. His voice was uncharacteristically gentle. "The person who doesn't have love in life has emptiness. I'm sure you are in love, but I know you don't want to tell me."

I had never kept anything from Grandfather. He had always advised me on everything important. Whenever I told him my secrets, I felt very light and happy.

"I love a girl in my old school," I confided to him. "She is my age, her name is Yaldda, and she is very beautiful!"

My grandfather laughed very loudly. "A woman can keep you warm like wine, or turn cold like ice. Be patient, little man. A person without patience is like a candle without wax. Sometimes love makes you very impatient. Keep control of your feelings."

We said nothing more for a while as I thought about what he told me. And I thought about Yaldda. I had never seen her again after the fighting started. I wondered where she was, and whether she was safe. Had her family left in time, or had they waited too long? Sometimes I wrote poems about Yaldda in my diary, where I kept all the important things that Grandfather told me.

Our steps were surprisingly loud as we walked down the middle of the road with not a single creature in sight, except for some sparrows occasionally flying past, making their *chuk-chuk* noises. The sky was completely blue. Had it not been for the destruction around us, it could have felt like we were going on a picnic.

"Were you impatient, too, to marry Grandmother?" I asked.

"I was in love with her. I was very lucky to have a wife like her, but I didn't know until many years later that marriage has three stages," he said, and sighed as he gazed up at the mountain with two peaks. Its bare rock rose up steeply behind the large yellow grain silo that the Russians had built.

"The first stage is that you talk, and your wife listens. The second stage is, she talks and you listen. And the third stage is, both of you talk, and your neighbors listen," he said with a grin growing wide at the corners of his mouth until it became a big and loud laugh. "The first stage is the best," he said. Grandfather had not told a joke in months. I laughed to hear the happiness in his voice.

But there was more to Grandfather's story than that. His great-grandfather, Khaja Noor Mohammad, had come from a village near Herat in western Afghanistan and had settled in the Maidan Valley about thirty miles from Kabul, where he built a large mud-brick fort with high walls, as was common all over Afghanistan. Though it was large enough to hold his extended family, it was much smaller than the Qala-e-Noborja.

From their base in Maidan, several generations of his descendants have followed the seasons with their herds. They raised sheep and camels for their wool, which they sold to carpet weavers and cloth makers.

Grandfather's father was the third youngest among his six brothers, yet he was to die before his older brothers. Grandfather was only four years old when he lost his father. His younger brother was born two months after their father's death.

Two years later, Grandfather's mother was married, but not, as was the custom, to one of Grandfather's uncles, but instead to one of his cousins, who was closer to her age. Though he was now his stepfather, Grandfather still called his cousin *Lala*, older brother, as he always had.

Grandfather's father had not left much for him and his brother, except for some livestock, a bit of land, and part of the old fort. Grandfather wanted to do more in life than raise sheep and goats. His own grandfather, Mullah Abdul Ghafor, had been a very holy man. And his oldest uncle for several years had been the district governor in Kandahar, where he had become a rich and respected man.


Grandfather wanted to earn respect like his grandfather and wealth like his uncle. He taught himself how to read and write, and told us that he always had a book in his hands. He was determined to educate himself. When he was twelve, he decided to go to Kabul. But when he first arrived, he had nowhere to live. He slept in mosques and shrines for several days until he finally got a job as a clerk in a branch of the Ministry of Transportation called Inhisarat, which transported wood and government goods to other countries.

The job became his school, though he had never gone to one. He studied other people around him very carefully and learned what they did. He learned how to dress well and never forgot the practical things of life his mother had taught him. Soon he had his first promotion and moved to an office where he became an accountant.

He got a job as a clerk in the National Bank of Afghanistan, where he continued to teach himself new things. He studied the law, and how the courts worked. He learned how to look after other people's money and talk to the king.

Despite his success, he told us, he had never felt more lonely, though he had been alone for many years. He kept looking for someone to give color to his life of carefully written columns of numbers.

One spring day, as he was coming out of a restaurant after lunch, he saw a caravan of Kuchis crossing through Kabul. The Kuchis are the Pashtuns who live as nomads. In fact, the word "Kuchi" in Pashto means "nomads." They were coming from their winter quarters near Jalalabad and heading toward their summer pastures in the high mountains at the center of Afghanistan in Bamyan. He saw a beautiful girl among them walking next to a camel.

He recognized her, because he had seen her many times years before when he was young, when the nomads had come to Maidan and stayed there for several weeks in early spring. He told us that he fell in love with her instantly. They had one brief moment of eye contact that afternoon, and that glance became the first link in the chain that connected their lives for the next fifty years.

He went back to the bank and explained to his boss that he would have to be absent for a few weeks, then he followed the Kuchis as they made their way along their usual route to Maidan, where they stopped for a month to let their herds graze. Finally, after a couple of weeks of indecision and fear, he went to the uncle of the girl, who was the lord of that caravan. He expressed his love for the man's niece. The uncle threatened to kill Grandfather, because Kuchis marry only Kuchis to bring more Kuchis.

My grandfather was frightened and almost went back to Kabul. But after a few days of thinking about his situation, he asked his mother to go and broker the deal.

His mother, a very courageous woman, explained to the uncle that our family came from a background similar to his. We, too, had been herders for generations. She told him how we were descended from the Arabs who had come to Afghanistan more than a thousand years before, and who were related to the family of the Prophet Mohammad, peace be upon him. She recited the names of the twenty-nine generations between the Prophet's family and her son, Khaja Ghulam Jallani.

The girl's uncle listened, but said nothing. Grandfather's mother was happy with his silence, because that meant "Yes." There were no threats this time. Grandfather now understood that he was engaged to his beloved, though he would not be able to see her again until their marriage.

The nomads left Maidan soon after to move on to their summer pastures in Bamyan. But in early autumn when they came back, Grandfather had made all the preparations for the wedding ceremony and was waiting for them.

He had the grandest marriage ceremony in the valley of Maidan. It went on for days. When the nomads left to go back to their winter quarters in Jalalabad, their daughter stayed behind with Grandfather and his mother.

Grandfather returned to his job at the bank and started building his house on the land he had bought in Kabul. Though we always called the place Kot-e-Sangi, after the nearby neighborhood, it was actually in Dehnaw Dehbori. He was busy for ten years constructing it and planting his courtyard. Meanwhile, his wife was giving him children. In the end, there were sixteen, though two sets of twins died before they reached six months.

Grandfather had one promotion after another at the bank until he became the head of its Accounts Reconciliation Department. It was his responsibility to review the papers of every deal the bank made. Everybody respected him highly, and after a few years they started calling him "President," even though that was not his title, because he stepped in and ran the bank when the president of the bank and his assistant went to other countries.

With his knowledge of banking and transportation, Grandfather was asked to come work as the head accountant for the Afghanistan Customs Bureau in the Ministry of Commerce. A few years after he went there, though, he uncovered a serious fraud by one of his colleagues. Grandfather went to the minister of commerce to report what was happening, but the minister defended the man who was stealing the funds. Grandfather walked away from the ministry that day and never worked in a government office ever again.

Several high-ranking officials came to him in the weeks that followed, apologized to him, and asked him to come back to his job. But he did not go back. He had lost his faith in the government.

To earn money, he started dealing in carpets he bought from weavers he had met when he was traveling as a boy with his father, who had sold them wool.

Over the years, he bought and sold thousands. Every spring and summer, Grandfather would travel to the villages. Often, he took my father with him, just as his own father had taken him as they followed their herds. It was Grandfather's way of reliving his old nomadic life.

As they went from house to house buying new carpets, Grandfather trained my father to recognize beautifully woven old carpets and *kilims*—flat woven rugs without a knotted pile—that had been made with natural dyes. He also taught my father how to bargain until the last moment to get the best price. They would sit and drink tea for hours and tell jokes and learn the names of all the sons of their hosts.

By the time I was born, Grandfather was not traveling as much. He sent my father to look for carpets while he stayed in Kabul and carefully picked the best times to buy and to sell, quietly amassing a fortune and an inventory of valuable rugs without anyone knowing how he was doing it. And then, of course, he had seen them all stolen from him by those who falsely used the word "Mujahedin."

A pack of stray dogs came in our direction, then stopped and ran away. We turned into the street that led to our house, and a few minutes later we could see the yellow apartments at the end of our courtyard that rose above the surrounding one-story houses. At least that part of the building was still there. Grandfather stopped for a moment when he saw it.

"Life is a gamble," he said as if he were speaking mostly to himself. "You may lose, or you may win. If you search for its meaning, you may never find it, and lose. But maybe you will find it, and win."

He looked at the sad evidence of war all around us. Nearly all the houses on our street had been reduced to jagged, broken walls.

As we got closer to our house he started humming something in the whispery voice he used when trimming his roses. Grandfather was happy to be back in our own neighborhood, even with so much destruction around us. Then a strange voice behind us shouted, *"Stop! Stop! Stop!"*

We turned around and saw two men pointing Kalashnikovs at us. Their faces were covered with the bandannas. I could only see their eyes, which looked like cracks in a grain of wheat. They came toward us and one of them asked my grandfather, "What are you doing here?"

"Visiting my house!" Grandfather said.

"Where is your house?" he asked.

Grandfather pointed with his right hand.

"You must be a rich old man to have such a big house!" one of the guys said. He was tall and thin. His voice was harsh. "Let's talk for a minute," he said, and then pointed his gun toward our neighbor's house.

The gunmen were Hazaras; they were in their late twenties and part of one of the factions who were trying to control that area of Kabul. They wore black *shalwar kamiz*. Each had grenades in his belt, and a knife strapped tightly to his right leg.

"I will come talk to you later, after I see my house," Grandfather said.

"Do what I said," the tall one shouted. He shoved his gun at Grandfather's chest. I heard evil in his voice.

We had no choice but to go with them to our neighbor's house. He had been a successful importer, and had built one of the most beautiful houses in our street. When one of our captors opened the door of the courtyard, I smelled blood like a butcher's shop. There was also a stink of something that had been rotting for days.

The first gate opened onto a twenty-foot corridor that led to a door into the courtyard. I remembered having been there two years earlier with my father for an engagement party. That night the grass in the courtyard had been neatly trimmed, making a green carpet. Roses were in bloom all around. A few McIntosh apple trees in the center, a gift from Grandfather, had big apples hanging from their slender branches. There were some pear, apricot, and pine trees, too. Every path around the courtyard was lined with flowerpots. The rooms around the courtyard had beautiful lamps in them that sent a glow over their fine furniture. The owner often went to London and other places, and brought back fancy things that no one else had.

Musicians had played from a low platform covered with deep red Afghan carpets. Men and women sat together around the courtyard, chatting. Some were on chairs around small tables, others on cushions spread on the grass. They all had a drink in their hands as they talked and laughed. The man's son had just come home from Harvard to meet the bride his parents had selected for him.

My father and I stayed until one in the morning. When we left, some of the guests were still listening to the soft music and talking to one another about their lives, their businesses, their families, their futures.

In those days, grown-ups were always talking about these things. The Afghan Communists were still in control even though the Russian soldiers had left, but they were being challenged fiercely by the Mujahedin in many places. I listened to them out of curiosity, but never understood why they sounded so worried. The only thing that they knew for sure was that no one could know for sure what would happen.

Now here I was standing in that place again, and finally understanding exactly what they had been talking about. These beautiful rooms had no glass in their windows, and it looked as if it had been centuries since anybody had been living in them. There was no sign of any tree in the courtyard. They had all been cut down for firewood.

In the center of the courtyard where the platform for the musicians had been, there was now a ditch filled with the heads of men and women. Dozens of them. I looked at them with their eyes open, staring at me with their shabby hair matted with blood. I started to vomit, but controlled myself.

I did not know who they were. I did not know how they had ended their days on this earth in this place. But I have never been able to forget them, though I have tried many times.

The two men pushed Grandfather and me along a pathway that ran between rosebushes that needed to be pruned. Thorns grabbed my sleeve as I brushed past. I remembered the time I had cut a rose from one of these bushes. The owner told me, "A flower looks happiest on its bush. That is where it belongs." Since then, I have never cut a flower, because he was right. But I could not imagine how anyone had cut the heads off these men and women. They belonged on their bodies, I thought.

The stench in the heat was unbearable. I did not want to be there for even a minute. I felt tears coming from my eyes, and a tightening in my throat was cutting off the air flow. Even though I closed my eyes, the pile of heads, legs, and hands with no fingers was still there in my brain, sending pictures to my eyes.

I looked at those two guys with their faces behind their bandannas. Those who carry a gun are the most cowardly of all, I thought, because they cannot protect themselves without it.

I did not have a gun for killing them. I had no shovel to cover those lost souls with earth. And I had no ability to ask for any of those things.

The two guys pushed us into a room at the end of the courtyard. It was damp and smelled of blood. He locked the door after us. The walls were covered with writing in chalk and charcoal. Someone had written, "Once you come to this room, you will not leave alive. This was my brother's fate, and it will be mine."

On one side of a wall was written, "Don't be afraid of death. You were born one day, and you will die one day."

Another person had written, "No matter how much you have prepared yourself, there is no guarantee for the future." I closed my eyes so I would not have to read any more of them.

An eerie feeling inside me was getting stronger and stronger. I wanted to scream, "If you kill me, I will be one of these heads, but it is unkind to show me these hundreds of innocents whom I did not know." I was too afraid to scream, though. My voice hid inside my chest. I did not dare to say a word.

I kept my eyes tightly closed, trying to force what I had seen from my mind. Silence filled the room until Grandfather spoke in a strange voice.

"You have to find a way to survive. And the secret of survival is to open your eyes. Closed eyes can never see the path." I slowly opened my eyes to see Grandfather down on one knee in front of me so that his face was level with mine. He looked very shaken. "If they kill me and keep you, you have to promise me to find your way home."

"Why will they keep me and kill you, and why are you saying all these things? I'm not going anywhere without you," I said defiantly.

"I'm old, and they don't need me. But they will need you for work, or for their sexual pleasure," my grandfather said.

He could see the confusion in my eyes. "I don't have to tell you what that is, but when the time comes you'll know it. They may use you for a while, but you must find an opportunity to escape. I'm sure you can do that. Don't show them that you are smart. Always act stupid."

"No, no, don't tell me that you can't come with me. Please stop," I said. I never liked crying but was afraid I might start, and I did not want Grandfather to see that, because maybe he would call me "fountain eyes," the way my older sister did to get back at me for saying the same thing about her.

"Just listen to me. We may not have another chance to talk again. If these people here make you very unhappy with your life, you may think that killing yourself is the best way to overcome all your sorrows. But believe me, it is not," Grandfather sternly said. It was the first time he had ever spoken to me like that.

"You have to be a brave boy, and if they do kill you, accept the death with open arms, and never beg for your life, because in the end death gets us all one way or another."

"Before they kill me, I want to see my family once more, I want to say goodbyes to them, and I want to tell them I love them," I said. My voice choked as I spoke.

I started remembering my father's jokes, my mother's smile, and my sisters' innocent looks. I remembered sitting around one tablecloth with my parents and sisters, eating breakfast and laughing.

He stared into my eyes for a moment, then said, "The past is like water that flows in a river, you can't bring it back with a shovel. Let the past be in the past, and move on; you won't lose anything. Remember all that I told you. Okay?"

"Yes, I shall remember," I said. I was looking into his eyes, and they were getting watery. When he finished, he turned his face away and blew his nose with his pocket handkerchief. He looked at the walls and started reading what had been written on them. He said, "We need to leave our words, too." He picked up a piece of charcoal on the floor and gave it to me. "Write, 'Death only breaks the cage, but it does not hurt the bird.'"

It was a great relief to hear such a wise saying from him instead of these other despairing statements. I wanted to hug him, but his face was lost in his handkerchief.

The tall, thin guy unlocked the door and came in. He pointed his right hand at my grandfather. "Bring me four hundred thousand afghani, and I will let you go. But the boy will stay with us till you come back with the money," he said.

"I'll find you four hundred thousand afghani, but you will get none of it if you hurt my grandson!" Grandfather said.

"As long as you stand by your word, we won't hurt the boy," he said. Then he went out to talk to his friend, leaving the door open.

"How will you find the money?" I asked my grandfather.

"Don't worry about money. It is not the issue. We have to get out of this situation," Grandfather said.

"I think it is very good to be rich in such circumstances," I mumbled.

"We were rich, and that is why we are here. Being rich from now on will be like cooking a sheep for dinner and inviting wild and hungry wolves with sharp teeth to join you. When the dinner is not enough for them, then they'll invite themselves to eat you," Grandfather said with a worried tone. "For now, we just have to keep them talking."

The tall guy came back and pointed at my grandfather. "Are you Sunni or Shi'a?"

"Sunni and Shi'a are the two wings of one body, and thorns to enemies' eyes. They are both believers in God and Mohammad, peace be upon him," Grandfather said, his voice oddly relaxed. The separation of Sunni and Shi'a started with a dispute among those closest to the Prophet Mohammad, peace be upon him, over who would lead Islam in the years after his death. Both Sunni and Shi'a share the same Islamic beliefs and articles of faith.

The guy suddenly acted ashamed of his question and walked out, as if not sure what to say next.

The other guy, who had said nothing until now, came in and grabbed Grandfather's collar and pulled at him. "I'm gonna make a deal with you. How much do you have to give us now?" Then he slapped my grandfather on the face. I stood up to defend Grandfather, but the guy pushed me in the chest and knocked me backward. He rolled up his sleeves to make his hands ready for more slapping.

My grandfather recited in Arabic one of the Hadiths of the Prophet Mohammad, peace be upon him: "The Messenger of God, Mohammad, said, 'He is not one of us who does not treat our young with compassion or acknowledge the dignity of elders.'"

He stared at my grandfather fiercely for a moment, hesitated, then left the room without saying anything more. His tall, thin friend came and locked the room, leaving Grandfather and me alone again.

I looked at Grandfather. His face was red, and I saw the print of four fingers on his left cheek. If my father had been there, he would have punched those two guys brutally and changed the geography of their faces.

Grandfather smiled at me. "That was an adventure." Then he began pacing from one corner of the room to another.

I thought about my death. What if my family receives my body without my head? Will they put my body in the grave without it? What will be in the grave? Only earth under me and big stones on top of me. I would be covered with a white sheet. I thought about how lonely a grave must feel. That was even more frightening than looking at the heads and legs that I had seen in that ditch. At least the heads were together. They did not eat and chat with one another, but they were not alone.

Suddenly I wished for oblivion, to be at rest. I would drink a glass of poison if that would take away the sight of those heads and send me to sleep forever.

I heard footsteps in the courtyard. I saw a third Hazara man through the broken window of our room. He was not wearing a bandanna, or even carrying a gun except for the pistol in his belt. He was a couple of years older than the other two, but probably not more than his early thirties. He was very muscular. His little finger was halfway up his nostril.

The tall guy unlocked the door and shouted to us, "Come out and talk to our commander."

We went out. The commander was standing at the edge of the ditch, staring at the severed heads. He did not seem to mind the bad smell. He did not pay any attention to us for almost five minutes. The commander continued cleaning his nostrils, then rubbed his finger against his vest, which had little pockets and compartments for holding bullets and grenades. All his grenades had fuses hanging out. I thought for a moment of pulling one of those fuses and pushing him into the ditch.

He cleared his throat with a fake cough, still staring into the ditch, and asked my grandfather, "Do you know why I have kept all these heads here?"

"No," Grandfather said.

"Do you want to know?" the commander asked.

"Do you want to tell me?" Grandfather replied.

"Do you want to know, young man?" the commander asked me.

"No. Because it is obvious. You are a killer," I said sadly.

The commander turned toward us for the first time. He looked at me with dead eyes.

Grandfather squeezed my shoulder and hurriedly said, "He is a kid. He doesn't know what he is saying."

"Kids are honest, and they know exactly what they are saying. I like people who talk frankly. I also like to collect human skulls. Sometimes I plant flowers in them; they look beautiful that way. Do you want to have your skull become a nice pot for a rosebush?"

Grandfather said nothing.

"Your skull will turn to earth after a while anyway. Why not use it for something?" the commander asked with a smile. His little finger was still going in and out of his nose, searching for something. "A man should be happy to be turned into blossoms."

Grandfather was watching the commander, who in turn was enjoying the sight of those heads. The other two guys watched us from the side of the garden.

"And do you know what rotten human flesh is good for?" the commander asked.

"Tell me," Grandfather said.

"It makes good fertilizer. Didn't you know that?"

"No. I didn't know that," my grandfather said, almost as if he were interested. But I could tell he was afraid.

"Yeah, me neither. I just found out a few months ago when I put some in one of my skull pots. That rose blossomed like crazy; it's still in bloom. Maybe you would like to see it?" he said, smiling, and looked straight at my grandfather for the first time. He cleared his throat again. "In fact, why don't you choose which kind of rose you would like to have growing in your own skull?"

"As you wish," Grandfather said very softly. "But may I ask your permission to visit my house across the street one last time?"

The commander laughed, much too loudly. I looked at him and wondered what he found so funny. "That is not your house," the commander said.

"Actually, it is," Grandfather replied, as if he were making a point to a customer. "I built it. I lived there, and it was my hope to return to it when you all go back from where you came."

The commander narrowed his eyes and looked at Grandfather with disgust. "I told you I like people who tell the truth. I know the owner of that house, and he is not you. He is my teacher. And my trainer. I went there every day to train in his gym." He drew his pistol. "You are a dishonest man, like all these people with money."

"Are you speaking of Abdul Basir?" Grandfather asked quietly.

"Of course! Abdul Basir is a man of honor, a man of respect."

"Yes, I know that," said Grandfather.

"That is his house, not yours!" The commander was shouting now.

"Abdul Basir is my son," Grandfather said.

The commander narrowed his eyes again. "Don't try to fool with me."

"He is my father," I said emphatically. "If he were here and saw you talking to Grandfather like this, he would have broken your nose by now."

The commander looked at me. "This boy doesn't look like Abdul Basir. He looks like a Hazara, like us," the commander said to Grandfather.

"From his mother's side," Grandfather replied. Was that true, I wondered? I had never heard that before.

"Tell me about your son. Where is he a teacher?" the commander shouted.

"At the Habibia High School. He is a boxing trainer, too. He had one gym there and one gym in our house, at the corner. He used to train two hundred people in Habibia High School every day, and fifty people in this gym at home. He has been in many international boxing matches, and won most of them," Grandfather said. "What else do you want me to tell you about him? What he eats for breakfast, or what color he likes to wear, or what kind of motorbike he rides?" Grandfather was on the edge of sounding disdainful.

"Tell me about his motorbike," the commander said edgily.

"English. Four cylinders. Fifteen hundred cc. It was noisy and big. Two years ago, a tourist from Denmark came to Kabul and bought it from him. Then he used the money to buy a Russian Volga."

The commander's face changed. A small amount of life seemed to have crept into his eyes, but only just a little. "You are right," he said in a low voice. His whole body relaxed. Then he took my grandfather's right hand and kissed it and touched his eyes to it several times. This is how we were taught to kiss the Holy Koran and a holy man's hand as a sign of respect and honor.

I was not sure whether to be relieved, or more frightened. Everything that had been happening was so strange. Now, just by his having said my father's name, it was becoming even stranger.

The commander led us out of the courtyard. He seemed very embarrassed. His two friends followed. When we got outside, he asked my grandfather whether his men had treated us badly. His behavior had totally changed. He was not a bully anymore. He was acting like a servant to a king.

"Ask them yourself," Grandfather said.

"Did you treat them badly?" he asked his men with a harsh voice. They were standing behind him, staring at their feet. He asked them once again, but very quietly this time. They still did not answer. He slapped one of them so hard on the face that mucus exploded out of his nose and all over the commander's left hand.

The guy started wiping his nose, and the commander beat him on his back with his heavy fists. And as he was beating him he was saying, "Snot-filled bastard, do you know who you are dealing with? This holy man is the father of my teacher. His son was very kind to me. He has won more boxing matches than you have hair on your head!" The commander pummeled the man mercilessly, until he was on his knees wailing. The commander must have been a strong boxer.

Grandfather asked him to stop the beating.

The commander kicked his underling, then ordered the other to bring us tea. He asked my grandfather what type of tea he drank.

"Let me visit my house now; we will have tea another time," my grandfather replied.

"I'm sorry; you can't go to your house today." His voice was much calmer when he talked to Grandfather. "Your house was the front line last week, and our guys put mines all around the courtyard." Grandfather's face fell. "They are fighting in Bamyan now but they'll be back in a few days. By next week your yard will be fully cleaned, I promise!" the commander said.

Grandfather had just survived a near encounter with death, yet he was even more devastated to know that though our house was right in front of us, we could not go in. We walked into the street. We stood there and stared at our house and said nothing.


That street had once been full of joy. I watched as two stray dogs went into the house where only a few minutes ago we had been held captive. One of them came back with a forearm in his mouth. Our neighborhood had become a fast food restaurant for dogs.

The commander insisted that we have lunch with him, but Grandfather wanted to go.

"You seem to be a good man," Grandfather said. "Did you really kill all those people whose heads were in that ditch?" His voice was very calm, like he was talking to one of his sons.

"No, Uncle. I'm not a good man anymore. I am a killer. I used to be a good man, but that seems like a very long time ago."

"What happened?" Grandfather asked.

"I used to be a student in Habibia High School. I always got the highest scores in the class. I was preparing for the university. You can ask my teacher, your son, Malem Abdul Basir. I was also one of the best boxers in the school gym. But this war has destroyed everything good in my life. It has taken everything from me." He sighed and looked at the mountain.

"It is not just you," Grandfather said. "It is everybody in Afghanistan."

"No. It is not true. For centuries we Hazaras have been treated like slaves in this country. Pashtuns and other tribes always thought of us as outsiders, and treated us like dogs. A few months ago, one of my cousins was captured. He had an air hose put in his ass, the kind you use for tires. They pumped him full of air until he exploded. Do you know who did that? Gulbuddin Hekmatyar. And who is he? A Pashtun, who hates Hazaras. Then one of my brothers had a nail hammered into his head by one of Masoud's commanders. They laughed while he screamed. Do you know who Masoud is? A Panjshiri who hates Hazaras. Everybody in this country looks down on us. What have we done to this country to be treated so badly? Name me one Hazara who is working in a high position in this government. I assure you there is none." His face was getting red with anger.

"But what you are doing is not good either. You cannot clean blood with blood," Grandfather said.

"I want revenge." He said those words very slowly. His voice was getting higher and louder. "I want revenge! My whole family has been killed by Gulbuddin, Masoud, and Sayyaf. Their commanders raped my mother and my sisters before they killed them. Do you want to know how I know that? They made me watch them! One of my sisters was only seven years old. I am the only one who survived, and I know that sooner or later I will be killed, too. But before I die, I'll kill as many of their people as I can. I will rob them, rape them, and murder them," he said, getting even louder.

"This is not a very smart way to solve the problem," Grandfather said.

"I think this is a very smart way. Other tribes should count Hazaras as Afghans, as one of them. If they think they can do all these bad things to us, now they should learn that we can do bad things, too. We tolerated too much for too long, for centuries. Now the bowl of our patience is overflowing."

Grandfather did not say anything and the commander was silent, too. The commander was looking at the mountain. Grandfather was looking at his house. The commander broke the silence. "I am sorry that you cannot visit your house today."

"Thank you," Grandfather said.

As we walked around the corner, I automatically looked for my good friend Muhammad Ali, as I always did at that place. He had lived in a nice house across the street from ours, but it looked empty now. He and Wakeel were the same age and were friends in school together. He was one of several Hazara neighbors we had. He taught me how to ride a bicycle, and he was very good with kites. I wondered where Muhammad Ali was now. Many of his relatives had gone to Germany. Was he there safely with them? Or had the Hazara-hating warlords done terrible things to him and his family?

"I can drive you halfway back from where you came," the commander offered.

Grandfather nodded. The commander walked ahead of us, and we followed him to a Russian jeep that was parked along the road. The commander climbed in, and we did, too. We sat in the car and the commander drove us along the road past the yellow silo where we had walked an hour and a lifetime before. He stopped near the bus stop, where no bus had stopped since the fighting had begun. He stepped outside. "I cannot go farther than this. This is the front line between Hazaras and Panjshiris. They will kill me if I go past here," he said.

We climbed out of the jeep. The commander did, too. He came around to our side of the vehicle. He kissed me on my cheeks and urged me to give my father his warm regards. He told us his name. His breath smelled so bad that again I nearly threw up. Once more, he kissed Grandfather's hand. He stood watching us for a long time as we walked away.


When I got home, my mother was cooking dinner. As soon as she saw me, she ran and kissed me on my cheeks. Her hands smelled of onions, and that scent meant everything that is good in the world.

She kept asking me how our house was, but I could not talk. I thought of the pile of skulls, and the dogs. My grandfather went into his room without saying anything. My uncles and aunts quickly started gathering there to hear about what he had seen. My cousins stood outside the door, watching me but saying nothing, waiting for me to say something.

My mother insisted that I tell her what we had seen, but instead I started to cry, sobbing uncontrollably, and I could not stop. My mother cried, too, but without knowing what had happened to me. My sisters cried softly also, except my older sister, who had a wicked gleam in her eyes.

My mother was one minute shaking my shoulders and the next hugging me. "What's wrong?" she asked me forcefully. I sobbed even louder to try to release the grief in my soul.

I do not remember when I stopped, but I do remember falling asleep with my mother holding my head on her chest and rubbing my back, while my older sister was smiling at me. I knew why she was smiling at me. She was planning to tease me with "fountain eyes" for the rest of my life.

The next day when I woke up, I felt so ashamed that I had cried in front of everybody that I did not want to see anyone. I tried not to look them in the eye, but everyone was nice, even my older sister. By now they all must have heard about what had happened to us.

I went to Grandfather's room, where he was reading a book. He smiled at me and continued reading. I just sat there in front of his stretched-out feet and took a book for myself. I looked at it for a long time, but I could not concentrate.

After a while, Grandfather took an apple from a dish next to him and made a few little jokes as he peeled it with his knife. He offered some of the pieces to me and talked about a few things that were of no importance. But he never mentioned what had happened to us. When we had eaten a couple of apples he said, "Okay, Gorbachev, it's time for you to go out and play while I do some writing."

"Gorbachev" was one of his nicknames for me, though I never knew why.

As I left his room, my older sister ran to me and gave me a big hug, holding me in her arms for several minutes. Then she looked at me with her eyes full of tears and kissed me several times. Taking my arms in her hands, she said, "You know I love you very much." I nodded, unable to say a word.

I went up on the roof, where Wakeel was already flying a kite, and Jerk was holding his reel. When Wakeel saw me, he took the reel from Jerk and gave it to me and told me to do a good job, because he was in a fight.

Surrounded by those who I knew loved me, I felt the pain from the day before begin to ease, at least for a time.

# 6

❖

## Under the Earth

Now everything was different. Now we knew we would not be going back to our home. Now we understood that the fighting would not end soon. Now my father and my uncles were more open in their discussions about fleeing the country. Grandfather listened to them, but said nothing.

We had been at the Qala-e-Noborja for half a year, longer than any of us had expected. After Haji Noor Sher left, some other people who were either Haji Noor Sher's distant family or close friends moved into the fort. That made us more aware than ever that we were not living in our own home. We had lots of room at Noborja, but no Afghan wants to live in someone else's house.

A school near the Qala-e-Noborja opened sometime in the late summer but closed two weeks later, when the principal heard a report on the BBC that a faction was threatening to attack our neighborhood that afternoon. We were sent home.

The principal told us to listen to the radio. "As soon as the radio announces that the schools are open again," he said, "you must come." Some of my classmates were very happy, because they did not like school. I found their attitude very strange. I had had so much fun in our old school. What do these new classmates like, then? I asked myself.

I thought that the school would be closed for no more than a few days. But we did not go back to school for two years.

Our parents started teaching us at home. It was not fun; there was no one to compete with. I could not compete with my older sister. She knew all my lessons much better than I did, because she was two classes ahead of me.

My father often taught us. He was very strict. Sometimes in school we had joked with one another when our teachers were writing things on the blackboard. I could not do that at home. I started to lose interest in all subjects, except for astronomy, which was not then taught in our schools. I read the textbook all the way through a couple of times. At night I went out in the courtyard and stared at the sky for hours, drowned in strange thoughts. But my father emphasized math, and the more pressure he put on me to learn, the more I lost interest.

Wakeel and my older cousins, who were in upper grades, often just read novels, or magazines, or books on subjects that interested them. I felt envious of them. Nobody pressured them to study boring school subjects. Wakeel read poetry for hours and could recite line after line of Hafiz by heart. Hafiz was his favorite.

As children we had our own world. We went to the garden every day after breakfast, played with the animals that were still there, or swung from the branches of the trees. We found new friends among the kids in the neighborhood.

After lunch we flew kites. The roof of the fort was even higher than the one at home. With enough string, we could almost float our kites over the top of the twin-peaked mountain that separated us from our house. Wakeel was cutting all the other kites nearby, but nobody in our neighborhood knew it was he. For some reason, they thought it was I. Soon my name was famous, and all the kids called me "Qais the Kite Cutter."

Wakeel just smiled at me when he heard them. That made me feel a little bit small. But, still, I never told anybody that it was Wakeel who had cut them. Wakeel was my closest friend, but we were very competitive when it came to kites.

Then, strange things started to happen with my kites. I would put them up very high and look for somebody to cut. Usually, once one kid had a kite up, others would quickly rise to challenge him. But before another kite even had a chance to appear in the sky, my kite was suddenly floating free, as if somebody had cut it. Wakeel came running over to see what had happened.

"Did you cut your own kite?" he asked. He was laughing, of course.

I did not know what to say to him and just shrugged.

About two days later, the same thing happened. I told myself that the wind must have been very strong up high where the kite was, and maybe it had ripped the kite from its string. That had never happened before. But I was looking for an explanation.

I had been using the string for two years. Wakeel and I had prepared it very carefully. It had taken weeks. First we had collected old light bulbs and ground up their glass into a fine powder. Then we mixed the powdered glass into the paste we made from boiling rice down to a soggy mess. We rubbed the paste and glass into the string to make it like a razor when it went into the sky. My string had cut every kite it fought, except Wakeel's. Now it was cutting itself.

What was worse, after my kites were cut, they floated into the grounds of the old British Embassy, which had been abandoned when the Russians came, and whose walls were topped with barbed wire. There was no way to get over those walls and bring back the kites that had fallen inside them.

The next week it happened again. And then five more times. It was very mysterious. Now the kids in the neighborhood were all laughing and calling me "Qais Who Cuts His Own Kites."

At the Qala-e-Noborja, we did not often eat together as we had at Grandfather's house. There was no room large enough to hold us all. Sometimes, though, we squeezed ourselves into a couple of adjoining rooms, especially when my mother made a special meal and invited my grandfather, my uncles, and their families to join us.

The grown-ups sat at the upper end of the tablecloth, and my cousins and I sat at the bottom. Sometimes we would throw bones at one another, or rub hot peppers on bread and leave it for someone to eat without knowing. Mostly the grown-ups were silent; they were always unhappy. Whenever any of them talked, it was about how to leave Afghanistan.

Every day my father and uncles went out to look for smugglers to get us across the border to one of the nearby Central Asian countries. Most of the smugglers in those days were taking Afghans to Iran and Turkey. Those borders were easier to cross, but the smugglers demanded a lot of money because the trip was long and dangerous. We simply could not afford to go with them.

One night my father came home very happy. He made a few jokes as he took off his jacket. A few minutes later we were all sitting around the tablecloth. When my cousins and I started throwing bones at one another, my father joined us, throwing bones from the upper end. We all looked at him, wondering what was going on. He made a few more jokes that made everybody laugh. It was the first time in months that I was seeing everybody laughing.

After dinner we had tea, and my father announced that he had found a smuggler to take us all out of Afghanistan to Russia and, eventually, Germany. He was very expensive, and we did not have enough money to give him. But the smuggler was willing to wait. He knew my father had been a famous boxer and wanted to help him.

Later, there was quiet talk among the grown-ups about "the garden." My mother frowned and flatly stated, "No. You are not allowed to go there." And then they went back to speaking quietly again.

A month passed. My father tried to call Haji Noor Sher in India several times to ask him for a loan of some money to pay the smugglers, but the Afghan phone system had been completely destroyed.

Then we heard from the BBC World Service that the opposing factions who were battling for control of Kabul had agreed to a ceasefire for a week.

That night my father announced that he was going to our house the next day. Grandfather tried to stop him, but my father was the most stubborn of his sons. Once he said he would do something, no one could stop him from doing it. The next morning, he told me to get ready to go with him.

"No way. You have no idea what I saw there the last time, and I don't want to see it ever again," I said as stubbornly as I could. A look of pain crossed Grandfather's face as I said that. He studied his hands.

"You will come with me," my father said firmly. "I expect you to obey me."

In the end, I went. I would soon be eleven years old and felt nearly like a man. A Pashtun son obeys his father, no matter what the son's age. His voice softened a little, and he explained that he thought he would attract less attention if he had me with him than if he were on his own.


We took a bus from Kart-e-Parwan as far as the Polytechnic, where the Panjshiri control stopped. We got out and walked along the wide, empty avenue that led to our side of town. Even though there was a ceasefire, the Panjshiri soldiers were searching people who were coming toward them from the far side of the front line. I was wearing my jeans and a white shirt with a blue sweater on top. My father had a white *shalwar kamiz*. He was carrying a cloth sack with a shovel in it. He did not explain why.

I walked next to my father, both of us looking around and not saying anything. The leaves on the trees in the park that runs up the middle of the road had gone yellow, like the big yellow silo we were passing that the Russians had built. A wind moved a cloud of dust from one place to another place. There was no one else besides us, except for fat dogs running up and down.

We turned into the narrow streets that led to our house. We had been walking for a half hour by then. Silence hung over the neighborhood, except when a dog howled. As always at that time of year in Kabul, the sky was clear and beginning to have the glow that comes with autumn.

Finally, the high yellow wall of our house was in view. All the windows were broken. The walls had many holes from bullets that had not been there when I had come with Grandfather two months before. Some of the curtains were still in the windows, but they were dirty, and some had been shredded by gunfire. The heavy wooden door that led inside was splintered. It looked like it had been used as a target. My father pushed it gently, as if he were trying not to make it hurt any more than it already did. It swung smoothly on its strong hinges.

As we stepped into our courtyard, we heard a gunshot at the end of the street. We looked around. Two guys were coming from one end of our street, and four more from the other. One of them pointed a gun at us as he walked.

"Again!" I thought. I wanted to run into our garden, but I froze instead. My father tried to pretend he knew them. They said nothing when my father told them about the ceasefire. One of them walked up to us and handcuffed us without telling us why.

"Gentlemen, do you think that we have committed a crime?" my father asked politely. They did not answer. Instead, they kicked him in his back.

The handcuff rings were too big for my thin wrists. They slid down over my hands. I moved my hands in and out of them several times, but I never let the guys with the guns see that. In fact, I was holding the chains in my hand so they would not fall off.

They marched us all the way back to the silo. My father and I were in front. Our captors were spread out behind. Like the guys who had threatened Grandfather and me before, they were Hazaras, but not the same ones. I was looking around to see whether I could find my father's student. The Hazaras continued to control that side of Kabul. But he was not there.

These guys were wearing Western-style clothes. They had boots that were laced tightly up over their ankles. One with big shoulders wore a red headband showing that he was willing to be a martyr. Their hair was nicely combed. They were clean. If there had been no war, they would have been running shops or doing metalwork, for which Hazaras are famous. These guys did not look like bad people. They seemed like those who had been trained to do bad things.

When we arrived at the courtyard of the high, yellow Russian grain silo, they made us crouch on our knees in front of a hole in the ground with steep stairs going down almost like a ladder. The guy with the red bandanna unlocked my father's handcuffs. I slipped mine off and handed them to him. He looked at me holding out the handcuffs to him and laughed. Then he kicked my father down the muddy stairs into the hole, and then me. I rolled down the stairs and dropped onto my father's chest. My father was breathing heavily. He had a few cuts on his face, but they were not deep wounds. His clothes were streaked with dirt.

From where we had fallen, we saw that we were at the mouth of a tunnel. We heard footsteps coming toward us from somewhere inside. In a moment a man stood in front of us with a lamp in his hand. I was trying to stop the bleeding on my father's head with a piece of the toilet paper that my mother had taught us always to carry when we left the house.

"Get up! Follow me," the man said.

I helped my father to stand, then we followed. It was very dark. My father had to walk hunched over because the ceiling was so low. We could barely see our steps. We walked for several minutes. With each step, the air got heavier and damper.

When we got to the end of the tunnel, we saw in the dim light a few men and women sitting along its wall. The man told my father and me to sit next to them. Then he knotted our hands and feet to the others with rope, like slaves. When any one of us moved, the rest of us were forced to move, too. The guy with the lamp who had brought us there sat on a chair in front of us, pointing a gun at us, his finger on the trigger.

A few minutes later a couple of other ragged-looking Hazaras with guns and grenades attached to military belts came to inspect us. They were different from the well-dressed guys who had captured us. They counted us. We were eighteen. There were five women among us. One of them was pregnant, and about twenty-five years old. The rest of the women were middle-aged.

The guards talked among themselves, put a lantern on the ground in front of us, then left.

None of the captives said anything. Some were staring at their feet, some at the tunnel wall. We were all deep in our thoughts about how to get out. The faces of the women were filled with resentment, the men's with anger. It was a moment of heavy silence. Then all of a sudden the pregnant woman began screaming. She had her hands on her stomach and was shouting for help, wailing, "My dear mother, come and help me!" And she kept repeating the name Ahmad.

I asked my father, "What is happening to her?"

"A labor contraction," he said. I had no idea what a labor contraction was.

We were all staring at her, as she was howling in agony, grunting, and occasionally yelling high, piercing shrieks that were made louder by the echoing walls of the tunnel.

One of the women sawed through another woman's bindings with a piece of stone, and she in turn untied the other women. The four of them quickly made a circle around the pregnant woman. Then they asked the men to help them. Two of the women started untying our hands and feet. One of the women said to the men, "We need some hot water. She is going to give birth to her child now."

My father was freed first since he was on the end of the line, then he untied me. He patted my head and said, "I'm going to ask one of those guards to let that woman go to the hospital. Stay here and don't move until I come back." Then, bent over like a cripple, he disappeared down the long, narrow tunnel.

Ten long minutes later my father returned, followed by the commander, who had his gun at the back of his head. My father's hands were tied up with a rope behind his back again. The guy pushed my father hard on his chest against the wall and said, "You don't move from there, or I'll shoot you in your head, understood?"

My father nodded.

He pressed the button of his walkie-talkie and said, "Hey guys, come here, we have a movie without a ticket."

Minutes later, five other guys rushed up the tunnel toward us like wild dogs. They grabbed from behind the four women who were trying to help and dragged them away from the pregnant woman.

By now her cotton *shalwar* trousers were off. She was screaming for help. One of the women said, "For God's sake, she needs to be in a hospital now. She needs a doctor."

"I'm a doctor. Don't you see my Kalashnikov?" One of the men laughed as he held up his battered weapon that had probably passed through a dozen arms dealers before it reached him. "I use this to do my operations." He was about twenty-five years old, and as thin as a stick. His gun was hanging from his right shoulder, and its weight made his shoulder droop. The rest of them laughed loudly.

They were all standing around her and one of them invited me to watch. My father looked at me fiercely and whispered, "Don't go."

"No thanks, I'm fine here," I said.

"It is an order! I said 'Come,' otherwise I'll shoot you," he shouted.

I looked at my father again, and he nodded at me to go. I stood next to those guys and closed my eyes.

The guy next to me slapped me hard on my head and said, "Open your eyes and watch."

When I did, I saw that the woman had a kindly, beautiful face that was twisted by her pain. Her nostrils flared, and her voice shook as she screamed for help. She lay down on her back. Blood was coming from between her legs.

She kept taking deep breaths. Every time she breathed in, her whole body shook, and her face got redder. I knew that I should do something to help her, but I did not know what.

She kept screaming for almost an hour until finally the baby came out, and she went numb. One of the women jumped from where the guards had dragged her, grabbed the baby, and held him upside down. The baby screamed, and the woman told the new mother, "It is a boy."

The guys with guns cheered and said, "It's a boy! It's a boy!" as if he were their nephew. Then one of them said, "Let's go, the movie is finished." They all left.

The other women made a circle again around the new mother and did what they could to help her. The men, sitting shoulder to shoulder, were deeply embarrassed.

The young mother woke up after half an hour. When she opened her eyes she started saying "Ahmad! Ahmad!" again.

We did not know who Ahmad was. We all looked at one another to find whether there was an Ahmad among us. But there was no Ahmad there. A woman who had torn her scarf in two, and wrapped the baby in half of it and tied the other half around the young mother's head so she would not feel ashamed at being uncovered, asked her gently, "Who is Ahmad?"

"Ahmad is my husband. Who are you? Why am I here? Why is it so dark here?" She sounded confused, as if she did not remember what had happened to her. She asked all those questions in one breath.

The men and women all looked at one another and did not know what to say.

She repeated, "Why am I here? Where is my husband? Who tied up my head with this cloth? Oh, I'm feeling dizzy. What is wrong? Why is everyone staring at me?"

"Calm down, calm down, sister! You just gave birth to this child. He is a boy. We are here because we are in the captivity of those warlords, and we don't know what is going to happen to us next. Don't you remember anything?"

The new mother touched her stomach, then looked up at the woman next to her, not really understanding what she had just heard. She grabbed her child from the woman and started kissing his bloody face. Then she looked around her once again and asked, "Did I give birth in the presence of all of you in here?" She was looking at everybody's eyes, one by one, to hear an answer. Then she fainted. The woman next to her caught the baby just before he hit the ground. He cried from the shock.

The men and women looked wearily at one another. There was no water to give her.

The woman who had torn her scarf left us and disappeared up the dark space of the tunnel. She came back in ten minutes with a bucket. She sprinkled some water on the young mother's face and gently tapped at her cheeks. Slowly, the mother regained consciousness and drank some water from the woman's hand.

We all drank from that bucket, too. We had not eaten lunch, and a minute later our stomachs began making noises.

We did not know what time it was. The guards had collected our watches along with our money and the women's earrings, necklaces, rings, and bracelets before they had imprisoned us in the tunnel. But after what must have been several hours, one of the guards came with eighteen *naan* flatbreads and gave everybody one. They vanished in minutes. Those who finished first looked at the others who were still eating. Some of them had not had any breakfast either.

One of the women asked the time, and the man who had brought the bread said it was 6:00 p.m. We had been in that tunnel since midday, but it felt as if it had been much longer.

Some of the men were yawning and ready to sleep, but there was not a mattress or a blanket. My father asked one of those ragged-looking men for something to sleep on.

"You would be the luckiest man to have it," the warlord said.

He disappeared along the tunnel and came back in half an hour with five mattresses and five blankets for the eighteen of us. The tunnel was filled with the stale smell of sweat.

The young mother was shivering from the cold, damp air. She needed a warm place and good food. Her baby needed to be kept warm in a soft bed. The other women gave her one of the mattresses and two blankets. But she still was shivering under the blanket, and crying and saying things that we could not hear clearly.

We now learned that she had lost her husband that morning, when a rocket struck their house.

"The last time I saw my husband was this morning when he was half-alive and half-dead," she told us after a long silence. She spoke softly, as if she were talking to herself. It was the first time I heard her talking like a normal person. "He said, 'I cannot make it, let me die here by myself.'" Her lips trembled, and tears streaked down her cheeks. She sighed deeply, full of pain, and continued.

"We had eaten our breakfast together. He said we would go to Pakistan, where his parents live, to get visas for England.

"We'd met each other and become engaged when we were studying in the Faculty of Social Law at Kabul University. Then his parents fled Afghanistan when we were in our fourth semester. They had to go; his father was involved in political affairs. My husband was their only child, and they did not want him to come back to Afghanistan. But we were in love, and he suffered from being away from me. Two years ago he returned to marry me."

She was speaking in a whisper. Slowly, by telling us her story, she was making us a part of her family, as if she were our sister, to ease the shame of everything that had happened to her in front of us. "This morning when we were eating breakfast in the dining room, he looked at me and said that he was so lucky to have a wife like me, and he kissed me. I went to the kitchen to get butter and jam from the fridge, then I heard a huge noise. Then I was under the ceiling beams, with the earth and straw from the roof all on top of me. When I wanted to stand up, I could not move. But I was at the corner of the kitchen, and there was less rubble than in the middle. I finally pushed a beam off me. When I stood up, my mouth and nostrils were filled with dust and the smell of gunpowder and smoke. I started calling my Ahmad for help. He did not answer me. The beams from the ceiling were blocking the door. I was stuck in the kitchen with the smashed jam jar still in my hand. I climbed out from the kitchen window to the courtyard.

"The dining room ceiling had totally collapsed. I struggled to move the thick beams, but they were too heavy for me. I looked around the courtyard and found a shovel to dig the earth from the roof that had buried my husband.

"As I was working, the contractions came several times, but I still continued. And then I saw my husband's leg. I recognized his jeans. It was the only part of him that I could see. I nearly fainted, but I said to myself, 'Be brave.'

"After an hour of hard work, I dug my husband out from under the rubble. He smiled at me and said, 'You made it through, I'm very proud of you, just remember that I love you so much that I can't put it in words. I don't think I will live, but tell my parents that I love them so much. Tell them they are the greatest parents in the world.' Then he touched my stomach and said, 'Tell our child I wanted to see him, but God didn't want us to meet in this world. Tell him I am waiting for both of you.'

"Then he put his head on my lap and asked me to pat his hair. I patted his hair and I was crying. He looked at me and said, 'I hate seeing tears in your eyes. Don't cry for me, it was my destiny, and I'm going to a better place.' Then he said, 'Smile, smile, smile!'

"His breathing became very heavy. Then, after a great shake, it stopped. He still had a smile at the corners of his mouth but his eyes were wide open, horror-struck. I closed his eyes and left him there." At last she started to weep. Then she started shaking because of the cold, and the loss of so much blood.

One of the women went to her and held her tightly to try to keep her warm. No one said anything. We were feeling the woman's agony at being here with strangers at a time when she should have been with her family.

I started to shiver.

My father took a blanket for me. I used half of the blanket as a mattress and half of it to cover my body. I fell asleep right away, thinking about Ahmad and the son he would never see.

I woke up a few hours later. My father and some other men were doing push-ups to warm themselves up. Some of them were shivering and their noses were red. When they breathed, little clouds came out of their mouths. My father patted me on my head and told me to sleep; I slept again.

Three or four hours later, somebody was kicking me on my back. At first I thought I was dreaming, but it was real, and it was painful. When I woke up, I saw a big guy standing in front of me and shouting, "Wake up, wake up . . ."

My father was begging him not to hurt me. "He's a little kid," he said.

A minute later, still half-asleep, I found myself with the others at the place where the tunnel ended in a wall of dirt. Everyone had shovels.

We were separated into three groups. Most of the men were set to digging, making the tunnel longer. We were never told where the tunnel led or why it was being dug. We knew we should not ask. The women put the loosened earth into buckets. And four men and I carried the buckets of earth to the entrance of the tunnel and dumped them outside. I wanted to stay outside even though the sun hurt my eyes, but one of the guards was always standing there to make sure we did not escape. Once when one of the men was slow going back into the tunnel, the guard beat him with a heavy stick.

The young mother was holding her baby. When the baby cried, she began breast-feeding him. A few hours later, she was released, because she could not do any work.

We worked for a couple of hours. Then we had a loaf of coarse, dark bread—the Russian kind they made at the yellow silo bakery for poor people—and a glass of water for our breakfast. Breakfast, lunch, and dinner were all the same, a loaf of Russian bread and a glass of water.

That second night, we started talking to one another and trying to get to know one another better. We made some jokes, too, even though everybody's lips were sealed against laughing. Everybody started talking about their lives, kids, wives, husbands. But no one talked about politics, or why we were being held captive, because we were all afraid of one another.

The commander and four of his thugs came with their guns hanging from their shoulders. One of them had a bag on his back that was so heavy that he could hardly carry it. He put the bag in front of us and opened it. The bag was full of handcuffs. The commander started handcuffing the hands and feet of all the men. Then, with a long chain and heavy padlocks, he connected each of them with the man next to him. My father was right in the middle. No one could move. Even a small shift in position could hurt the others.

He handcuffed three of the women together, separately from the men. Only one woman and I were not handcuffed. The other four captors watched passively as he fastened the handcuffs and tugged on them to make sure that the locks held tight.

Then he looked at the woman who was not handcuffed and said, "It is better you don't struggle and yell or curse. It is better you take off your clothes now for me. Soon, one by one, we will be finished. You cannot imagine how fast we release. We are away from our homes and our wives. We are at war, and war without sex is like poison."

She was confused at what she was hearing. "Are you fighting for peace in this country, or to do shameful things?" she asked sharply, as if she were a teacher speaking to a naughty student.

"You're going to be a problem, I can see that," the commander told her.

The commander started tearing the woman's clothes with his knife.

My father moved to stand up and say something, but the handcuffs held him down. Then one of the thugs hit him on the head with the butt of his Kalashnikov. I tried to run to him, but the commander grabbed the back of my collar.

I yelled, "Let me see my father," but instead of letting me go, he slapped me on my head so forcefully that for a moment I saw strange lights, though the tunnel was very dark.

Blood was running from the top of my father's head to his jaw and was dripping from his chin. He was slumped over and unconscious. The men handcuffed to him on either side tried to ease him into a sitting position.

In a few moments, the woman was naked, cursing and spitting at the commander. He climbed on her. I closed my eyes. I was deeply ashamed to be seeing these things. She screamed piteously. When he had finished, he wiped the spit off his face with his sleeve, then stood up.

"Don't use all your energy on me, there are more coming," he said with a laugh. As he spoke, three more thugs came up the tunnel to where we were being held. They were laughing, too.

The other women wept in low voices. They knew that tomorrow night the same thing would happen to one of them. They should have been in their homes with their families. All that seemed so far away. The men closed their eyes, but they could still hear the sound of the woman's cries.

She continued cursing for six of them, her voice growing coarser and coarser. By the seventh man, she went quiet.

They continued long into the night. After the last one had finished, a boy who was about eighteen came with a bucket of water and left it in front of the woman. She was unconscious.

Later, five men whom I had not seen before came with sleepy eyes and guns hanging from their shoulders. One of them splashed the bucket of water on the woman. She took a deep breath and sat up, and then she looked around to find something to cover her body. All she saw were her torn, wet clothes. She covered herself as best she could, then put her head on her knees and wept.

One of the other guys bent down to unlock the men's handcuffs and unlocked the padlocks. The other four were pointing their guns at the men and women, their fingers on their triggers. Once the locks were open, the captives started rubbing their wrists and ankles. I ran to my father, who had regained consciousness by then but was badly hurt.

Suddenly, one of the captives jumped at the guard who was collecting the handcuffs and chain and knocked him onto the ground. The captive was on top, punching his opponent's face with his right hand, trying to get his gun with his left hand. The other four captors pressed their backs against the tunnel wall, pointed their guns at us, and said, "If any of you move, we will kill you all."

One of them took a grenade out of his military waistcoat pocket and said, "This will be enough for all of you. *Do not move!!*"

The captive kept struggling, but the guard under him managed to push his gun into the captive's chest. Suddenly, we heard a loud gunshot. The captive's face went pale; his eyes were wide open with horror, and his brow glistened with sweat. He raised himself up and looked at all of us, then dropped onto the guy under him.

The guard on the ground struggled to get up. The other thugs had to help him. When they turned the victim on his back, there was a tiny hole right at his chest where his heart was. The exit wound was bigger than the entrance. The exit wound is always bigger than the entrance; this is something children in Kabul had come to know.

I looked at my father. He made a motion with his eyes that told me, "Do not say anything." Throughout the time we had been in the tunnel we had hardly talked at all, and never about what was happening to us. I was young, but old enough to understand that it was dangerous to speak.

They half carried, half dragged the body out. One of them stood in front of us, pointing his gun at us. Nobody spoke. Everybody was staring at the bloodstains on the ground.

Now there were sixteen of us.

Days passed. The routine was the same every day. The commander and his men used the women during the night in the presence of all of us, and forced the men to work as slaves in the day. The commander was always there, but the others changed every night. We never saw the same ones twice. Our food was a piece of bread with a glass of water three times a day, though twice we were given rice and lamb. Those who did not work hard were whipped like donkeys.

I lost track of the days. I was very hungry, and feeling weak. I had hardly enough water to drink in all this time, and could barely walk.

By the end of about two weeks, only seven men and two women were left besides us. The rest of the men had been killed by the commander, two I remember for refusing to work, one because he was too weak and sick. One of the women was let go because she cried so loudly and in such pain all day and all night the commander got fed up with her. Another woman was dragged outside after they had used her. We never saw her again.

One day as we were starting to fill the buckets with earth, a tall Hazara guy came to the tunnel to inspect the commander's work. I turned my back, tried to make myself appear very busy in the dim light, and did not look at him.

The commander was trying to be very nice to that tall man, but the tall man did not care and paid no attention to what the commander was saying. The tall man walked the length of the tunnel to see how far we had gone. He looked at his commander and said coldly, "You have done very little."

Instantly, I knew his voice.

"Hey, Berar!" I shouted.

He looked at me and said, "Who are you?"

"This is Qais," I said.

He pointed a torch toward my face.

"Qais *jan*, what are you doing here?" There was surprise in his voice as he spoke to me, using the title "*jan*," a sign of affection and respect.

"I didn't come here by myself. My father and I were brought here. To work like slaves. Berar *jan*, I'm very, very thirsty, but I am not allowed to drink water at work time," I said. "Please, can I have something to drink?"

"Whose order is that?" he asked me, as he knelt in front of me.

"This man's," I said wearily as I pointed at the commander.

"How do you expect people to work for you if you do not give them enough water? You don't buy water, do you?" he said.

"No, sir," the commander said, staring at his feet like a bad child.

"What is 'No, sir'? Get the hell out of my sight! Bring some water, for God's sake," he shouted, and the commander hurried off.

Berar asked me for how long I had been working there. I said for maybe two weeks. Then he asked me what I had been eating. I told him. I also told him about the commander and his men having sex with the women in front of us, and about killing the men.

Berar put his hand on my mouth, closed his eyes, and said, "Stop, stop, it is enough." He was silent for a moment and then he shouted, "Stop working, please!" He stood up, and the men stopped shoveling, wondering what was happening.

"I do not know why this man has been so cruel to all of you. And I do not know what to say to you now. There is a war. You know that. The people who are trying to kill us Hazaras all have guns that the Americans gave them. Maybe you know that, too. All we have is shovels. We need a tunnel to protect ourselves.

"I told him to use new people every day. I told him to get people from the street, and to give them good food, and make them work for one day, and at the end of the day let them go home. How can I apologize to you for all that he has done to you?" he asked. His face looked stricken.

"Please go to your homes, go to your families who are waiting for you," he said softly. We dropped our shovels and buckets and headed silently toward the mouth of the tunnel.

For a second time, we had been rescued by somebody we had known in our old life, from the time before being Hazara and Pashtun meant we were supposed to think of ourselves as enemies. Kabul was a small town then, and people like my grandfather and my father knew everybody, or so it seemed when we walked through the shopping district and many people greeted them by name: Pashtuns, Tajiks, Uzbeks, Turkmen, Jews, Hazaras, Sikhs, and Hindus—everybody.

We came out into the daylight and the air. The men were happy to stand straight again after so many days, but the two women were ashamed of how they looked and kept trying to cover themselves.

"Wait," Berar announced. "There is one thing that must happen before you leave." We froze in fear. Our minds were set on leaving. And now there was something else we had to do.

Berar told us to walk with him to the silo. He also called his commander to join us, along with two other Hazara men we had not yet seen.

The commander, who had been so ruthless, carried a bottle of Coca-Cola in his hand. After a sip he belched.

Inside the yellow silo, we climbed a staircase all the way to the roof. It was about eight stories, but it felt much higher as we climbed one flight of steps after another. We could hardly make the climb, we were all so exhausted. Our fear increased with every step. We did not know what would happen next. I knew that Berar was my friend, but I did not know what he was doing. Even I was afraid.

When we stepped out of the stairwell onto the roof, it was very windy; it could have easily knocked any of us down, because we were so feeble. Everybody held on to somebody else. I held my father's hand. The roof had a railing around the edge, but it did not look sturdy. The weather was very clear, and we could see for a great distance.

Berar was standing in the middle of the roof. He called us to come. We all surrounded him. His commander was standing near to him. Still sipping his Coca-Cola, and still burping. Suddenly, Berar turned around and kicked the commander in the stomach. Berar was very fast, like in the kung-fu movies. The commander fell to the ground and coiled like a snake.

He cried out, "Why?" He was rubbing his stomach. Berar did not answer. Then he nodded at the other two men. One man picked the commander up on his shoulders, and in one fast move carried him over to the edge of the roof and tossed him off.

We were too shocked to know what was going on. We all listened to one long scream, and then a thud. There was fear in everybody's faces. They thought he would toss all of us, one by one. But I did not believe Berar would do that, though he looked a lot taller and broader and stronger than the last time I had seen him.

Berar picked up the half-drunk bottle of Coca-Cola and flung it over the edge of the roof. "Now we are all happy!" he said.

But no one was. Not even Berar, who studied the ground far below, searching for words.

"This man was supposed to have been put to death in Pul-e-Charkhi prison, but he was freed when the Mujahedin overran it," Berar told us. "In a war, every man is needed, so he was sent here. But wicked people like him bring shame to us Hazaras and to the Mujahedin. Some who were released from the prison are now seeking their private revenge in the name of Mujahed. Some of them joined the factions that came from Pakistan. They have taken weapons from all these countries who are using Afghanistan as their playing field. They are everywhere. They are sick, and their only cure is death."

He had turned his face back to us now. "Please, go to your homes. I ask your forgiveness for all the bad things that have happened to you here."

He came close to me, sat on his heels before me, and patted my hair. "Give my best wishes to your grandfather," he said quietly, then he kissed me on my cheek and left. His men followed.

An old man who had been held with his sons walked first toward the staircase, and his sons followed him. Then the two women, then my father and me, and the others after us. In front of the silo gate, we all said very formal and cold goodbyes to one another. We knew we would feel shame if we ever saw one another again. We all went quickly in our different directions.

My father and I headed for Qala-e-Noborja. My father was very weak. He could hardly walk. As we left the silo, he said, "The life of cruel people is short." He said nothing else all the way home.

When my father opened the courtyard door, we heard the women crying. My father asked me what was wrong. He asked me in a way as if he thought I would know, as if I had been at home and not with him for the past two weeks. I just said, "I don't know."

"Do you think someone died?" he asked with an exhausted voice.

"I don't know," I said again.

"But why are they crying? Something must be wrong!" my father said.

"I hope not," I said. Because all I was thinking about was eating something and washing all the mud from me that had turned us the color of dust. My sweater, my jeans had lost all their color. I wanted to sleep for a day, not listen to women's weeping.

We walked into the courtyard. I could hear my mother's crying all the way from the room at the far end where we lived. There were other unfamiliar voices with her, voices raised in sorrow.

Through the thicket of lilac bushes at the center of the courtyard and the fruit trees, I could see my uncles and cousins preparing lunch in one corner of the broad courtyard, with flames licking the big pots, and huge amounts of smoke rising around them.

The courtyard was full of men. Even from across the courtyard I recognized most of them. They were our relatives. I could see other men I knew in one of the ground-floor rooms. A nice voice was reciting from the Holy Koran. All the men were facing away from us, listening to it.

We went to those pots, and my father asked his brother through the curtain of thick smoke, "What is wrong? Who died?" I was standing next to my father and looking into those pots to see what was being cooked. One was full of meatballs. I grabbed one. It was very hot, and I could not hold it in my hand. It dropped on the ground and rolled on the earth. No one noticed. They were all busy.

My uncle touched my father's face. "Am I not dreaming? Are you here?"

"I'm very tired and hungry. Can you give me something to eat?" I said.

My uncle did not answer me. He walked away very slowly, backward, looking at us as he went as if he had not heard me. It was weird seeing my uncle acting like that. He looked frightened. He was still not sure that we were alive and not ghosts. My father followed him.

My cousins circled around me, but none of them talked to me. I thought they wanted to tease me, and I did not have the energy to play now. Wakeel was taller than all of them, with pale skin that looked even whiter than usual. He touched my shoulder, fast, as if I were hot as fire, and said, "Is that you, or your ghost?"

"What?" I narrowed my eyes.

"We thought you and your dad had died. Your mother has been crying for you for two weeks."

This was not making sense to me.

"We thought that you both had been killed. Grandfather invited all of our relatives to hold a funeral. All these people are here for you and your father, because you are dead."

"Please stop saying stupid things. I'm very hungry; I just want something to eat."

"We are not joking, Qais. This is all for you." Jerk was standing next to him, nodding vigorously. "Look, there are your coffins. We were about to do the burial rituals after lunch," he said. The coffins were made of wood, and they were covered with black cloth. One was about six feet long and the other one was four feet.

"What is in it? It is definitely not me in there," I said.

"Things like your reel and a few kites, and some of your best marbles that you used to keep and never played with, and your school clothes and some of your notebooks and your diary. We put them there. Grandfather asked us to do it," Wakeel said.

"You put in my reel, and my kites, and my marbles and my diary? What the hell are you thinking?" I said. I ran toward the coffins and opened the small one, and I saw all my stuff there. Wakeel wanted to take them out. I shouted at him, "Do not touch anything! Those things are mine!"

"I'm not getting them for myself. I'm taking them out for you," he said.

"No. Leave them there," I said.

Wakeel looked at me strangely. "Do you want us to bury them, then?"

"No, just leave them alone!"

One of my other cousins said, "Maybe he wants to get buried with them." All the rest started laughing.

I opened the long coffin. Inside was my father's favorite carpet, which he used to put on his bed. Now it was nicely spread inside the coffin. His physics books were piled in one corner, and his boxing gloves were next to them. There was also his suit, shoes, socks, and his favorite mug, which had a crack in it.

"If my father sees all these things in this box, he will beat you all like his punching bag," I said. My cousins were always a little bit afraid of my father, and this quieted them.

"We did not do this," Wakeel said. He was sounding very panicked. "Our uncles have put all your father's things here. We were busy doing yours."

One of the other cousins looked offended and said, "We were just trying to give you a good funeral."

I did not usually talk to him, so I did not answer him.

Jerk came up to me, looking very sad. "I'm very sorry for what I did to your kite string." I could not understand what he was talking about, and I did not care. "Those times when they said you were cutting your own kite, I did that. I used a razor to cut halfway through your string, so that it would break when you put the kite in the air."

I suddenly understood, and felt anger rising. That miserable little Jerk. My hunger and exhaustion faded as I felt my fury growing. I pulled my arm back to swing at him, but I was so weak I knocked myself off balance and started falling backward. Jerk reached out to hug me. He was crying now. But I was already too far off balance when he embraced me to keep from falling, and I pulled him down on top of me. I did not have the strength to push him away. I would beat him up later.

"Where were you for these two weeks, anyway?" Wakeel asked earnestly.

"Why are you so dirty?" a girl cousin asked.

"Please don't tell us that you returned from your grave," another said.

Even though Wakeel was my best friend, I did not want to go through telling all that had happened to us. Instead, I looked for my father.

My sisters came out of our rooms, drawn by all the noise. My older sister looked at me strangely, as if she were not sure whether I was actually me. Then, looking frightened, she quickly took my two little sisters' hands and led them back inside.

Then I saw my mother kissing my father and hugging him and crying and muttering something that I could not hear. She seemed to me like a kind of crazy woman I had seen in Indian movies. She and my father were surrounded by all our women relatives.

I heard her ask somebody where I was.

"I'm here, I'm okay." I waved at her from where I was standing. I had thought about her many times when we were in the tunnel, wanting to tell her the things we were enduring. Sometimes I wondered whether I would be like Ahmad, who did not live to see his son in this world, and I would never see her again. Now she was running toward me, shouting.

"Get away from those coffins!" She hugged me and kissed me more than a hundred times. My face was almost wet from her lips and tears. Or maybe they were my tears.

My mother drew my father and me inside and led us to a corner of our room and sat us there. My mother was fluttering around us like a butterfly. She kept drying her eyes and her runny nose with her sleeves. She gave my father three pillows instead of one. She did not know whether to laugh or cry. I had never seen her like that before. She was not herself anymore.

Relatives whom I usually saw only at wedding parties followed us in and crowded along the walls. My youngest aunt whispered into my father's ear, "Ask your wife to sit next to you. She has been crying for two weeks. She'll go crazy if you don't help her control her feelings. She is in a state of shock. Do something."

Numbly, he asked my mother to sit next to him, though usually men and women do not sit together when there are visitors present. She sat next to my father for a few seconds, then jumped up again. "I have to prepare lunch for you two."

"No, no, we're not hungry; I want you to sit next to me," my father exclaimed.

"I think Qais is hungry. You both look very thin," my mother said.

"No, no, he is all right. We had a huge breakfast this morning and we're still fully stuffed. Just come and sit next to me," my father said.

I smiled at her and pretended I was not starving.

My father wanted me to make room for my mother, but she said, "No, no!" and squeezed herself between both of us. She started patting my hair and staring at my father without a word, as if she had not seen him for years.

Kids were peeping through the windows and giggling. No one knew what to say. Maybe no one wanted to say anything, because it was the sweetest moment any of us had had in the time since the fighting had started.

My mother broke the silence. She jumped up from between us and almost frightened me. She kneeled in front of my father with her back toward the others. She cried very loudly, "Is this really you or am I dreaming? Please tell me it is true!"

My father leaned forward on his knees to embrace her. "Yes, this is me. I am here for you. I will never go anywhere. I'm fine, I am fine. It is okay now, it is okay."

I could hear the heavy breaths of my mother and my father as they clung to each other. My father was rubbing her back. My mother was shaking silently. Tears came from her eyes, though they were closed; my father's, too.

The men and women in the room were now laughing in low voices, but at the same time wiping their own eyes. Finally, my mother stood and asked me and my father to come with her to another room nearby that was empty. She seemed suddenly to be aware that everyone was watching the three of us, and she wanted to be alone with us. She turned to the others and said, "We will be back soon." She ordered my uncles to prepare lunch for everyone. Now she seemed to be herself again.

In the empty room she kissed me and my father over and over again. She never minded the dirt on our faces, or maybe she could not see it, or maybe she did not know what to do except to kiss us. She never asked me or my father what had happened to us during the past two weeks. Maybe she did not want to know. She was only happy to have us back.

A few minutes later, we rejoined the others. Everyone was laughing and enjoying one another's company; the funeral had turned into something like a wedding party. We spent the whole day singing and dancing, with my uncles playing flutes and drums, even though there were two coffins in the courtyard ready to be buried. Instead, we used them as benches for the guests. I was worried, though, that if the thin wood on the lid broke, my kites and reel would get smashed. Each time I looked at Jerk, I wanted to smash his face. "I'm not going to let him get away with what he did," I told myself. "He made me look very stupid."

My sisters told me about the new novels they had read and the new movies they had watched. My little brother looked at me and smiled. My cousins told me about their past two weeks' adventures and who won the bets on kite fighting with the neighbors. They showed me their money to make me feel jealous. They had no idea what had happened to me, and until now I have never told them, or anybody.

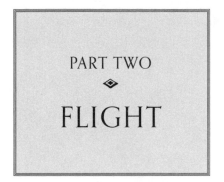

PART TWO

◆

FLIGHT

# 7

❖

## The North

By now we had been living in the Qala-e-Noborja for well over a year while the war in Kabul writhed around us. All this time, the front lines shifted like angry snakes. Today the Panjshiris would control one sector; tomorrow it was in the hands of the Hazaras; and the next day it would be held by Sayyaf, and a couple of days later, Gulbuddin, or Dostum. Rockets streaked over our heads, not caring where they landed.

Almost every evening, there was more talk among my uncles and my father about leaving Kabul. The smuggler who was going to take us to Russia had heard that a funeral had been planned for my father. We had never given him any money. So he took somebody else. He did not know that we had come back from the dead. We never saw him again.

One morning at breakfast while my father was eating some yogurt, he very calmly told my sisters and me, "I have decided that we shall go to Mazar and stay with your mother's sister for a while." Mazar is up north, on the other side of the Hindu Kush mountains. We had gone there many times before the fighting had started. Once we had flown there in an airplane.

I asked whether Wakeel was coming with us. My father said "No." Then I asked if Grandfather was coming. He said "No." I was stunned that we were going away and leaving them. I went to the other room and told Wakeel. He thought I was joking. He came with me to our room and saw my mother packing. He asked my father whether he was coming with us.

"Not this time, Wakeel," he said kindly. "We are not going on a picnic. We are heading to Mazar to spend some time with Qais's aunt. My hope is that while we are there, I can find a way to take everybody out of Afghanistan. Then I will come back and get you guys."

"Shall I come, too?" Wakeel asked, as if he had not heard what my father had just told him. My father always bought him whatever he bought for us and took him wherever he took us, and he could not understand why he was being left behind.

"No, there is just not enough space in the car for all of us," my father said.

"There is plenty of space in the car," Wakeel said insistently. "There were fifteen of us and the baby when we came from our house to this place. Don't you remember?" He looked at me and my sister for confirmation. We were afraid to say anything, because my father was in one of those moods where we could not tell whether he was angry. We nodded, but tried to avoid looking at our father's eyes.

"That was a short distance," my father said. "Now we are going to the other side of Afghanistan, easily ten hours of driving." His voice was getting a little bit hard.

"That is okay," I said, "we can squeeze in the backseat."

"No more discussion," my father said with a loud voice that startled us all. "I said 'No,' and it stays that way. No more discussions."

After Wakeel's father had disappeared, all my uncles had done their best to help him. But he was closest to my father, who had always included him in everything my immediate family had done, as if Wakeel were his own son. I did not understand how he could even think of leaving Wakeel behind.

This was the first time I was going to be really separated from Wakeel. With all the uncertainty that had contorted our lives since the day his father had disappeared, the one thing that each of us could count on was the other.

One day about a year before, I had searched for him everywhere, but I could not find him. I climbed the ladder to the roof of the Qala-e-Noborja to look in the hiding place that we always used when we played hide-and-seek. He was sitting there, alone, staring into space. When I tapped him on the shoulder, he acted startled and looked at me. I asked him what he was thinking about. He said it was nothing. He sounded sad. I asked him whether something was wrong. He said "No."

Wakeel was always cheerful and happy. Is he hiding something from me? I asked myself.

I sat down next to him and said nothing. I started staring at where he had been looking. For a few minutes we remained silent. He glanced at me several times, and I kept staring into space. He waved his hand in front of my eyes, and I pretended that I did not notice. He tapped on my shoulder and asked me what I was looking at. I told him I was imitating him. He smiled.

He said, "You are lucky that you're Qais, and not Wakeel."

"Why?" I asked. "I wish I were Wakeel, who is very good at flying kites, and having lots of friends, and being very popular at school, and climbing trees, and being the oldest child of his mother and the older brother to his sisters so he can order them around to polish his shoes and bring his tea and water. Who in the world doesn't want to be Wakeel?

"Look at me," I went on. "My friends are the little kids. I am no good at flying kites. I'm not as popular as you are in school, and not all of my cousins, aunts, and uncles love me like they do you. I can't order my older sister to do anything for me. She always bosses me around. Who in the world wants to be Qais?"

"I do," Wakeel said.

"Why?" I asked, very surprised.

"Because you have a dad, and I don't," he said, his voice shaking. "Every day when you wake up, your father kisses you on the cheek. Every day you exercise with your father, he lets you beat him, he plays with you, he teases you, he sits on your bedside when you are sick, he wakes up in the middle of the night to check on you when you're having nightmares or you mumble in your dreams, he warns you when you do something bad, he points out your mistakes, he tries to fix them with you, he wants you to climb higher on the ladder of your life, he is with you all the time. You can let yourself fall back, and you know there is your father, who will hold you." The words were coming out in a rush. "Who will hold me when I fall back? When I tumble and break into bits and pieces, there is no one to collect me. I have to collect myself and get back with my life. I want my dad. I want him to hold me when I fall back." He burst into tears and rushed out of the hiding place, tripping as he climbed down.

I did not know what to do. Should I run after him and give him a hug? No, I was younger than he; I cannot do that, I told myself. His dad should give him that kind of a hug.

An hour later, Wakeel had his cheerful glow on his face again and was making jokes that made everyone laugh. But suddenly I understood that for all these years his jokes had been chasing a shadow from his soul.

"Only a dad can fill the space of a dad, not your uncles nor your grandfather, only your own dad," he told me. Then he recited a couplet from his favorite poem by Hafiz: "To make one heart happy can be greater than making a thousand sacred journeys."

Once, when we were sitting in the lowest part of the garden of the Qala-e-Noborja near the pool, Wakeel told me that he was worried what would happen if his father came home; he would not know where to look for us. He would go to Grandfather's house and not find us there.

"I think he is still alive," Wakeel said. "If he had died, he would have sent a sign."

"What kind of sign?"

"I don't know. I will know it when I see it."


An hour later, we were ready to go. We did not have much to take. Our few clothes quickly went into our two suitcases and then into the trunk of the car. My mother gathered up whatever food we had in the house and put it in large sacks. Grandfather and my uncles and aunts and cousins all stood around the car to say goodbye to us as we drove away from Noborja.

Wakeel ran after our car. The car was faster than he was and left a track of dust in the air. I popped my head out of the front seat and waved at him, trying to smile. My sisters were looking back at everyone from the rear window and were waving as well. When we disappeared around the corner near the British Embassy, Wakeel stood in the middle of the street, despair all over his face, shoulders drooped, breathing hard and lost in the dust.

I felt very sad. I was very angry at my father for leaving Wakeel behind, and did not talk to him as we drove out of Kabul and up the steep hill at Khair Khana that leads north. I put on a frowning face, and my sisters did the same. My father made some jokes. And though they were new and funny, I did not laugh and my sisters did not either.

"Look, we could have taken Wakeel, but what would his mother do?" He was looking straight ahead, but we knew he was talking to us. "She has no one else. I will come back for him and the rest of them in two weeks." Then he turned on the car radio to the BBC World Service.

My sisters and I wanted to hear Afghan or Indian songs, but my father only wanted to listen to the news, especially for any information about Mazar. We did not tell him to change the station, since we were determined to maintain our anger with him.

As we left Kabul behind and started driving north across the Shamali Plain, I looked out through my window and saw the remains of Russian military trucks everywhere. Some lay sideways or upside down. Most of them were broken into bits. Almost every field had one, and people farmed around them. A burnt-out tank lay in a river; water was rushing through it and little kids with wet clothes were sitting on it, watching the passing cars. Years of rain had rusted the hulks; the sun and dust had bleached their paint. Some of the kids were pulling on their steering wheels, taking long journeys across their fantasies. A Russian jeep hung halfway down a steep valley wall, as if it were held by some kind of superpower.

I started counting them. I quickly reached one hundred. After a while, counting became boring, and I stopped.

We climbed up the side of the Hindu Kush mountains next to a fast-moving river that twisted back and forth around tiny villages perched high on its banks. Near the top, we reached the Salang Tunnel, which cut through the high peaks. Many of the lights in the tunnel were broken. Some were very yellow and gave a little light. The tunnel was filled with exhaust from other cars and big trucks. We raised the windows. My father drove very slowly to get around the holes in the road.

The hours rolled by faster than our car could go on the badly damaged road. As we drove down the north side of the mountains, we started following another river, this one much wider. On either side, fields were green with growing things even though it was early autumn. But beyond the fields, where the sides of the valley rose up, everything was bare rock. I looked at all these things very carefully, because I knew we were soon going to a different country and I might never see them again.

By midafternoon, we were driving through a beautiful valley on a narrow gravel road, toward a high gorge between two steep mountains. As we passed through the gorge, my sisters and I popped our heads out of the windows to see the birds flying from one hole in the cliffs above to the next. We could hear a fast-moving river as it crashed over the rocks at the bottom of the gorge and echoed between the high walls above.

We passed through the gorge and out onto the flatlands that stretch north to Russia. Suddenly, my father pulled the car over to the side of the road and stepped out. He stood in front of the car and took a deep breath. He looked at the blue sky and gazed at the mountains. A smile appeared on his face, as if something unknown were revealing itself only to him.

"Is something wrong with the engine?" my mother asked, as she stretched her head out the window.

Without turning around my father shouted, "This is Tashkurghan!" Ahead of us we could see many walled gardens and a small town a mile beyond. Crowning a hill between us and the town was a very large mosque with a high dome. My father started walking across a field toward where all the water in the broad river we had been following was rushing through the narrow gorge.

I leaped out of the car and followed him. He kept walking with big strides, looking up the wall of the gorge at the mountains, until he reached the riverbank. He splashed some clear water on his face and did not care that it dripped on his clothes.

"I have been dreaming about this place for months," he said. "I used to camp here with my friends for weeks at a time."

"When was that?" I asked. By now we were friends again, even though I had not forgotten my anger. I had realized that if I stayed openly angry because Wakeel and Grandfather were not with us, everyone would be very miserable. So, I was friendly to him. But I did not tell him my secret thoughts, which were still wrapped in bitterness.

"Oh, it was a long time ago. Before I married your mother," he sighed. "Well, not very long. It just seems like a long time ago. It seems like ages. All of those friends are living in Europe now, and I'm still here."

He reached over and ran his wet hand through my hair. "Come on, let's camp here for a few days." He walked toward the car, and I followed quickly after him.

It sounded great to me. Sometimes we had camped for a night next to Qargha Lake near our home or in a neighbor's garden, but never in a wide-open place like this.

By now, everybody was out of the car. My father took a large sheet of blue plastic out of the trunk. In each corner was printed "UN" in big letters. "We will use this as a tent," he said. He led the way down across some stony places to a flat field near the river, which flowed away from the road once it had escaped the gorge.

My sisters started helping my father and me to set up the plastic over some straight tree branches we found along the road. My mother was quiet, and my father looked at her several times to see whether she liked the idea. She just seemed happy to see us happy again.

A village man on a mule approached, sitting on a load of carrots piled in handwoven bags on the mule's back. As he came closer he asked, "What are you doing here?"

"We're camping," my father said.

"Be careful, this place has wolves. They come out at night," he warned us.

"I'm not afraid of wolves. But thank you for telling us," my father said, and the man rode on. Then my father drove the car down the gentle slope from the road into the field and parked it near our tent.

It was the middle days of autumn, sometimes windy, warm during the day and cool at night.

Each day, we swam in the river after breakfast and fished there in the afternoon. At night we made a fire in front of our tent and listened to my father's jokes and my mother's folktales, which sometimes frightened us. Some nights we just gazed at the sky, sparkling with millions of stars.

After all the bad things I had seen in Kabul, especially in the past couple of months, I felt like these were the best days of my life. I wanted to stay there forever, away from Kabul, away from the war. But then I would think about Grandfather and Wakeel, and wonder what they were doing while we were enjoying ourselves surrounded by such beautiful nature.

After a week, my father was ready to move on to Mazar, to my aunt's house. But we urged him to stay next to that river for one more week.

We continued our swimming and fishing. Sometimes we climbed in the mountains.

One morning after breakfast, the sky was very cloudy, and we stayed in our tent to study our schoolbooks, which we had brought. A gentle wind was blowing through our tent, occasionally turning the pages of my book. The wind was coming from the north. It grew stronger, and the sky got darker. Low clouds were bearing down on us.

My father gathered us in the corner of our tent. I wanted to go out and feel the wind blow against me, but he did not let me. "Stay here," he commanded in his I-am-the-father voice. The wind grew stronger by the minute. Then rain started falling, driven hard by the wind, and then harder and harder, and louder and louder. It was almost screaming, with lightning occasionally shrieking across the sky. We almost never had storms like this in Kabul. It was very exciting for me.

My father clutched my little sisters to his chest, as if the wind might take them away. My mother held on to my little brother so tightly that nothing in the world could separate them. My brother was crying most of the time because his teeth were starting to come in. We called him "the crying machine." We all had nicknames. Mine was "Dizzy," because sometimes for several minutes I would stare at nothing while I was thinking about something. When someone called me, I did not notice. I do not know what that had to do with being dizzy, but that is what they called me.

Now the rain beat our tent in waves. It was so loud that we could not hear one another speak. Lightning cracked again, each time getting much closer. The thunder was so close that it hurt our ears. This was no longer any fun. We were in the middle of nowhere under a makeshift tent.

The rain stopped as quickly as it had started, but the sky grew even darker, almost like a black night, though it was only midmorning.

Suddenly the ground started shaking like a small earthquake. We heard huge crashing noises above us in the gorge that were louder than the wind. When we looked out from underneath our piece of blue plastic, we saw a massive stone bouncing down the side of the mountain behind us at a furious speed. My father yelled at us to get out of the tent. We all rushed out, not knowing where we were headed, and scattered in three directions.

I had escaped death twice in Kabul in the past year. Now it looked like I would be killed in this place that had seemed like paradise. I thought of Prophet Noah and the storm and the rain for forty days, and how he survived and saved others' lives. But he had no problem with stones roaring off a mountain and shaking the earth.

The stone rolled right through our tent. It smashed the center pole, snapping it like straw, and kept going down to the river. Our food and clothes were crushed into the ground. Not knowing what else to do, we went and sat in the car, still very frightened.

We were stunned. The stone could have rolled so many other places. My older sister said, "Maybe the stone did not like our tent." For the first time ever, I thought she was right.

Half an hour later, the sky was perfectly clear. The sun was a bright orange ball. The wind was fragrant. The birds started singing again. It seemed that nature thought nothing had ever happened, but we had lost our tent and everything we had in it.

We spent the rest of the day in our car. Before dark, my father and I walked around the area to see whether it was safe to spend another night there. He was carrying a heavy stick in his hand, and I was carrying a thin one. We had not seen any wolves or any other wild animals. But the evidence of the storm was all around us. We found a branch of a tree to use as a new center pole. It was not straight.

Night came. Through the many holes the rock had made in our tent, we could see clouds passing quickly in front of a half-moon. We ate smashed bread with squashed mulberries for dinner. The crying machine was quiet now, and his mouth was half-open as he slept next to my mother on the one pillow that only he had.

My father listened to the BBC World Service on the car radio. They were saying something about a fight in Mazar between two factions. When I asked my father what they meant, he told me things about a man named Dostum. I had seen Dostum on television, sitting on a tank with his trousers rolled up to his knees. But I had not paid much attention to who he was.

For seven more days we stayed there, a bit shaken, but not sure what to do next. In the mornings the sun was not so bright as when we first came. We could feel the seasons changing, as the days grew shorter and the nights longer and cooler.

After a week we heard from BBC World Service that Mazar was safe again. The fighting between factions there had ended, at least for now.

My father told my mother at breakfast that after lunch we would leave for Mazar. All this time we had been in Tashkurghan, we had been only one hour away from Mazar, had the road not been broken by the fighting. It had rained hard again during the night. We were all a little cold and damp. That made it easier to leave this place that we had come to love. Also, our supply of food was low. Breakfast did not take long to eat. All we had was some apples we had found on trees that had planted themselves near our camp. My father had caught some wild ducks by the river early that morning using long, sharpened sticks, but he had not had time to cook them yet. He had learned to hunt as a young man, when Kabul still had wetlands. He never let me go with him, though, because he said he needed total concentration, and the slightest noise would frighten the birds and we would go off hungry.

After breakfast I helped my father clean our car. My mother and my sisters were collecting our clothes in the tent. My father started to check the engine. There was no need for me to be with him; I let him do it by himself.

The rain had stopped now, and I went to see the river, which was about half a mile from our tent. I said goodbyes to all of the trees, stones, and birds that I had come to love. I felt as if the mountains were saying goodbye to me as well. We had all become good friends, except for the big stone that had rolled onto our tent. I did not go to him, though he was still nearby in the river.

But something was not right with the river. The water was gray and breaking in waves over the stones. Dust floated on its surface. The fish seemed unable to swim, as if they had been struck blind. Some of them were dead and were being carried away on the rising water.

I could not understand why the river was acting this way. I stood on the bank and let the water run over my toes. Very quickly it rose to my ankles, and then to my knees. I was beginning to feel a little afraid of the gray water. I wondered whether it was angry at us for leaving.

I picked up a fish that stared at me and wiggled only weakly. As I was holding it and saying my thanks to the river for all it had given us, the water suddenly climbed up to my thighs. It was very strong and nearly took me away with it. I scrambled up the bank and looked up the gorge between the two mountains. The water was climbing its walls and speeding in my direction.

Nothing could hold back that water. It was much bigger than the river. I could see that it ran wherever it wanted and washed away everything that stood in its way.

Would it reach our tent and our car? Would it take away my family, and I would never see them again? This river would never let such a thing happen to me. He knows me, I told myself.

I quickly climbed to the top of the riverbank and raced toward our tent, shouting at my father, "Get them out of the tent. A flood is coming!"

My heart was beating like that of a frightened deer, but I never stopped running or shouting. My father was in front of the tent, lighting a fire to cook the ducks that he had caught. He stood up, confused. The rain had stopped an hour ago. How could a flood be possible? he appeared to be asking himself.

I fell down several times. My clothes were muddy, but I kept running, gasping for breath and shouting at him to start the car. At last he saw the wall of water where the peaceful river had been. By the time I reached the car, everybody else was already in it.

The water was fifty feet behind me, rushing fast as if it were trying to knock me down. It made a terrifying roar as it pushed large stones and tree branches in front of it. The water was no longer gray, but almost black.

I was the last person to get into the car. As soon as I put my first foot inside, my father hit the accelerator. The tires spun in the muddy ground for a second. Then the car jerked forward and sped up the sloping field to the road as if it, too, were afraid of the oncoming flood.

Everybody except my father looked out the back window and saw the flood wash our tent away like a nasty person destroying a kid's sand palace like the ones we had built in the large sand pile at Grandfather's house. The flood took all of our clothes and what remained of our food with it.

Before we could reach the road, the flood overtook us. First, it

covered the tires, then rose halfway to the windows. The engine began to sputter, and the car slowed down. My sisters and brother were
crying.

My father was in a panic and mumbling prayers under his breath.
My mother was saying, "Calm down . . . calm down . . . we will be all
right," but we did not know whom she was talking to. No one was
listening to her anyway.

Now the water was inside the car, almost up to our ankles. My
sisters were holding their feet up as the water came level with the seats.
The engine kept sputtering, but the car finally lurched onto the road.
When we reached a high spot, we opened the doors, and the dusty
water rushed out even faster than it had come in.

We got out and looked back at the field. It was all underwater now.

We had escaped from death once again, only to discover that we
had nowhere to go.

The announcer on the BBC World Service was saying, "A mis-
understanding between two commanders has resulted in a resump-
tion of hostilities in Mazar-e-Sharif this morning. The fighting resumed
shortly after one in the morning, with both sides reporting casualties.
Two children and an old man who were on their way home after
shopping were killed this morning." The announcer mentioned their
names, and asked their families to come to the hospital in Mazar to
collect their bodies.

Now we could not go to Mazar. But we no longer had a tent, or food.
My father drove half a mile toward the town, then parked the car
by the side of the road, where it widened. Everyone was stunned. My
father's face was white, as if there was no blood in it. My mother was
rocking the crying machine in her arms. The rest of us were silent, too
numb to say anything.

The sun began to disappear behind the mountains, and the moon
started to rise. The night air became cooler, and we were all hungry.
My parents had some money, but there was no shop where we could
buy anything.

My father left the car to say his evening prayers on the roadside.

We locked the door behind him. Whenever another vehicle approached us, I was afraid they might stop and kill us to steal our car. I was even afraid of the people who were riding donkeys when they ambled past. They looked frightening to me, even though they were normal people. They had not seen many cars, and they kept staring as they swayed by. I am sure that when they got home they talked about us.

When my father had finished praying, he winked at me from where he was sitting on some gravel. I said to my mother that I wanted to take a leak. She nodded, and I got out of the car. I peed, then I went to my father.

He put his hand on my right shoulder as we were walking away from our car toward several walled gardens at the edge of the town.

"Tonight you have to steal something. Can you do that for your father?" he asked me with his eyes wide open, looking for me to answer him. I stopped walking, but he kept going. I became a little afraid and ran to catch up with him.

"But you told me that stealing is a big sin, when I stole your money from your jacket pocket a few months ago. I told you I had made a mistake, and you said that kind of mistake can happen only once. If I repeat it, it becomes an unforgivable sin. Do you remember that, Father?" I asked, as he walked past one walled garden after another.

"Yes, I do remember. But sometimes you have to do something that is wrong to make things right," he went on in a steady voice. "If you steal some pomegranates, you will save your sisters and brother from hunger. You and I can sleep with empty stomachs for a night, but I'm worried for your mom. She doesn't have enough milk to feed your brother. She has to eat something," he said.

Then he stopped and pointed with his right hand to a large garden nearby and said, "You have to go over there very carefully. Nobody should see you. Be aware of your four sides, and fill this bag with pomegranates." He always carried a large plastic bag in his pocket for when he went to the bazaar, and now he gave it to me. "When you come back with pomegranates, tell your mother that you bought them from somebody who was selling them," he said.

I said "All right" and started walking toward the garden bravely.

But then I thought about it some more, and I felt very sad that my father picked me among all his children to be a thief.

I remembered Grandfather telling me, "Avoid three evils: lying, stealing, and gossiping." Even though Grandfather was not here, his words were there with me, and they were stronger than my father's. I walked back toward our car, but stopped when I saw my father walking slowly toward me.

"What is wrong? Why are you back with nothing?" he asked.

"Everyone will call me a thief!" I said.

"Who is everyone? You're doing this for your father! You know that. For me. I wouldn't call you a thief," he said.

"Why don't you ask one of my sisters? Is it because I have skills in stealing, because I stole your money one time in my life? Everyone called me a thief for weeks after." I felt like I was about to cry.

He sat down on the big round stone where we were standing. All around us were small white stones brought by floods years ago. He asked me to sit next to him.

"I respect your feelings, but you have to try to understand the situation. We cannot buy food for dinner, and we did not eat lunch. We do not have any place to go, and no one will receive us in their houses in this village. It is war, and everyone is afraid of others. The whole village is afraid of us, as we are afraid of them.

"It will take me at least a week to make the villagers my friends so they'll trust me. You go and steal pomegranates from that garden now, and somehow I'll make the owner my friend, and afterward we'll tell him everything about tonight. I'm sure he'll forgive us both. The reason I'm not doing this is because you're smart, and little. If they catch you, they won't kill you. But if they catch me, they'll think of me as someone dangerous. Do you get my point?" he asked.

I thought about all he said. I agreed that he was right about everything.

"All right!" I said. I walked toward the garden. I talked to Grandfather in my heart and told him that I was sorry to be doing the thing that he told me strictly to avoid. I also told him that I was doing this for my father, and he was the one who should be blamed, not me.

———————

When I was next to the wall, I sneaked into the garden very carefully, like I had seen heroes do in movies. Maybe somebody would make a film about my stealing. That made it seem a little funny.

When the wind blew, it moved the leaves of the trees and made them sound like someone's steps. I watched my four sides as I was told. I saw nothing but trees with big pomegranates hanging from thin branches, nearly breaking them. I picked five huge pomegranates that made my bag full and heavy.

It is not enough, I thought. But there was no more space in the bag for even a small one. If I take this to my father, he will fuss about that. "Why did you not pick small ones?" he would ask. But then I thought that I am not paying money for these; nobody should ever complain over something that cost nothing.

First, I tossed the bag over the wall. I was just starting to climb the wall to jump out when I heard dogs barking, very close. I thought the dogs were outside the garden and that they had seen my bag and were fighting over it.

I waited to hear better where the sound was coming from. Suddenly, I saw two big dogs running very fast toward me. They were inside the garden. From the light of the moon shining through the trees, I could see their muscles straining as they ran.

I froze in place. My mind was not signaling me what to do next. I thought for a moment and asked myself, "Should I stand here and let the dogs tear me into pieces for my stealing, for the sin I just committed?" I thought that Grandfather was punishing me. But Grandfather always told me, "Never be afraid of anything; let others be afraid of you." I knew I had to escape even though they were bigger than any other dogs I had ever seen, even bigger than the ones in the garden of Haji Noor Sher in Kabul. Water was running from their mouths as they barked. Their eyes were so red, they looked like they were filled with blood. I tried to be courageous.

They had now reached me and were close enough that I could have petted them, but they were not those kinds of dogs. I felt a wave of fear. The instant they saw that, they snapped at me. Their teeth were long and sharp. But I got my courage back and continued staring in their eyes, stiff like a sculpture. They stepped back. Each of them seemed twice as big as me.

Someone called to them from the other end of the garden, an old man's voice. One of the dogs turned halfway toward the voice, then he came back and barked at me a few more times before running off. The other one bared his sharp teeth, but held back. The old man was still calling and whistling.

Someone started throwing stones into the far side of the garden, making the trees rustle. The dog stopped barking at me and looked at the trees instead. The stones were big. It was definitely not a kid throwing them. The dog ran to find out what was dropping from the sky.

I heard my father's voice whispering urgently from behind the garden wall for me to climb out.

I pulled myself up on the wall and was halfway over when the dog lunged and bit my leg. I could almost feel which of his teeth were tearing into my flesh. My father saw my face and guessed what had happened.

"Don't shout! Be brave!" my father said hoarsely.

He thrust his hand up to me and pulled me toward him. The rough mud-brick wall scraped my stomach. The dog let go and started barking again.

I jumped down from the wall and landed on the leg that had been bitten. I started to shriek in pain. My father put his hand over my mouth.

My leg was bleeding. I could not see how badly I was hurt. My father tore his prayer bandanna that he always carried on his shoulder and tied it tightly around the wound. The dog on the other side of the wall was going crazy.

I wanted to look at the injury, but my father did not let me see it.

"It is nothing; it is just a small scratch. You'll be fine," my father said.

I did not believe him. There was fear in his voice. I never heard my father speak with a shaky voice like that. I kept walking like a cripple with all my weight on my right leg. The skin on my stomach felt like it had been scraped off.

I made it back to the car and climbed into the front seat. My mother was in the backseat, tapping my little brother's back and singing a lullaby to make him sleep.

She did not notice my leg, but she could see the fatigue on my face. She stopped singing and gave my little brother to my older sister, who had snuggled next to her. "Are you all right? You look like hell!"

I said nothing. She looked at my father, who was standing outside. He said nothing. "I'm fine," I told her. "We were just attacked by some dogs, and one of them bit my left leg, and it hurts a little."

"What dogs? We didn't hear any dogs," she said.

"Because your windows were all rolled up," I answered, trying not to let the pain be heard in my voice.

"Let me see it," she said quietly. I turned around to show her. She looked at my wound, shook her head, and started to clean it with a handkerchief. It was still bleeding and dripped into my mother's lap.

She rolled down the window all the way to the bottom and shouted at my father, "Why have you let such a thing happen? Did you just let the dog chew his leg while you watched?"

My father was quiet. My little brother woke up and my mother shouted at my older sister to take the crying machine out of the car.

She asked my father for a bottle of water from the trunk, washed my wound, and put some alcohol on it, which stung. Then she sat next to me in the driver's seat while my father was out walking up and down the road, holding my little brother and breathing the fresh cool air.

"You didn't buy those pomegranates, did you? I know there is no shop anywhere nearby." She was looking into my eyes very intently. "So tell me what happened, and don't make me ask you twice, and don't disappoint me with your lies," she said sternly.

Her eyes were fixed on my mouth until I finished.

"I'm afraid to let you out of my sight till we get home. Don't do anything like this again," she said, then she hugged me.

"Okay!" I said. I wanted to cry. I remembered being in our courtyard, helping Grandfather weeding, eating on one long tablecloth, making jokes with my cousins and aunts and watching TV together.

Those things seemed so far away. I sighed several times to ease the pain.

"What is the matter, Qais?" my mother asked. She was holding my head against her chest and rubbing my back. I could not force words out. There was a faint ringing in my ears, and I wanted a place to hide.

"Is it still hurting?" she said.

"Yes, Mother," I said.

"Or is there something else that you haven't told me yet?" she said.

"No, there is nothing. It just hurts and it is itching, and I'm very tired," I said.

"Okay, then sleep as long as you want." She tapped me on the back as if I were a baby. I fell asleep in her arms. But I knew that I was a thief, and that my sin was unforgivable.

# 8

❖

## The Garden of Hamza's Father

I woke up and was alone in the car. My parents, sisters, and brother were seated out on the ground having breakfast. They had cheese, butter, milk, yogurt, homemade jam, hot *naan*, and fresh tea. I rubbed my eyes to make sure I was not dreaming, but it was real. Everybody's mouth was full. My stomach was floating from hunger. I opened the door to join them. When I put my left foot on the ground, the pain was so sharp I felt as if a hot knife were ripping through me. My father came and helped me. I did not ask where all the food came from. I was just happy to be seeing butter, jam, and milk after two weeks.

"A villager invited us to his house," my mother said.

"A villager? Who is he?" I asked.

"Oh, I think you know him," she said.

"I know him? How?" I said.

"Because last night you heard his voice calling his dogs," she said.

I froze with fear and shame. "The man in the garden where I stole pomegranates?" I asked. My sisters looked at me sharply. They all said in one voice, "You stole pomegranates? You are a thief?" Then they started softly hissing, "Thief, thief, thief."

"Not again!" I said.

"Shut up, girls! He did it for me. I told him to do it. If anyone says the word 'thief,' she will be spanked!" my father said.

"His son knocked on my window this morning," my mother said, "while we were asleep in the car. He already had set this cloth here with all these things. He said that his father thought that we were modern nomads with our car."

We all laughed at "modern nomads."

"Do they know that I stole pomegranates from their garden last night?" I said.

"Yes, his son saw you," she said.

"They will call me a thief," I said. I felt shame rising in me.

"I don't think a host calls his guest a thief," she said.

"He may call you Mr. Thief," my old sister said, and my other sisters hid their faces as they laughed, too. I sighed as I sat down to eat.

After we had finished, a boy my age crossed the road and said hello to us. Then he started collecting the dishes, stacking one plate on top of another. When he stood up, he invited us to go with him.

"My family is waiting for you," he said very warmly.

The boy led us to the garden of the pomegranate trees and opened the gate. The garden was very large. It had two small one-story houses, one built along the northern wall, the second along the southern wall. There was a long tent in the middle made from some simple black cloth that was stretched over some poles and staked to the ground to make a place of shade. An old man appeared from one of the buildings and came toward us. He shook hands with my father. He greeted my mother and gave *salaam*s to us. Then he asked me what was wrong with my leg.

"Your dog was hungry last night, so I let him have a chew on my leg," I said, trying to make a joke to cover my shame.

He laughed and replied, "You should have knocked on my door. I would have given you more than five pomegranates."

My father said to the old man, "It was my fault; I was afraid that no one would welcome us in this village, especially in the night. Since the fighting started, everyone is afraid of everyone else."

"That is true, but now I know you, and we're not strangers anymore. We are a family," the old man said.

The dogs started barking. I jumped, but I could not see them.

The old man continued, "You are welcome to stay in my house for as long as you want. Those rooms over there are for guests." He pointed to those along the south wall of the garden. "You have water, electricity, TV, and radio. I will send you some blankets. There are mattresses and pillows in the rooms already. If you want to eat with us, you're most welcome."

"You are very generous," my mother said. "But we cannot be bothering your family with unexpected guests." She smiled, and the old man smiled, too.

"Yes, you are right! You are unexpected guests, but unexpected guests are gifts from God. Our door is always open to them; they bring the charity of God with them," the old man said. "I'll send you some dishes, and you can cook your own food. Please use any of the herbs, vegetables, and fruits of this garden."

"You are very kind," my father said.

"This garden is not mine, it is God's," the old man replied. "He gave it to me for use by those who need it for as long as they want. In fact, He is the owner of everything, and whatever He gives us, it is with us for only a few days."

His family came to greet us. He had four daughters and three sons. Among them was a woman who was much younger than he, almost the same age as his oldest daughter, and very pretty.

"Is she your wife?" my mother asked.

"Yes, she is my second wife. We married five years ago," the old man said. His wife was very shy. She invited us to her house at the far end of the garden, and we followed her as my father began discussing politics with the old man and his sons. A few minutes later, he joined us and whispered to my mother that our host was a great man.

Later, after we had had our first hot baths since leaving Kabul, we ate a magnificent lunch with them in an area shaded by almond trees. It seemed as if we had known one another for years. The old man told us to call him uncle and call his wife aunty. We talked about our lives. My father told them how he and Grandfather had lost their six thousand carpets, and now he had nothing except his family and a car.

"God gave them to you, and He took them back," the old man said.

"I'm a boxer. I can beat any man. Afghanistan has sent me to Russia and all those Central Asian places for matches. But how do I fight against madness like this?" my father said with a heavy sigh; I could tell he was thinking about his boxing victories in Tajikistan, Uzbekistan, and Turkmenistan.

"The good times and bad times are both the same, like spring and autumn of life. Neither of them last forever." The old man had a gentle smile on his face, but when he talked he was a very serious man. "The problem for our country is where we are located and the neighbors we have. Our stupid politicians let them interfere in our affairs."

After lunch he showed us the guest rooms. When we passed the tent in the middle of the garden, the two big dogs jumped out of it and frightened us. My little sisters hid behind my mother. Strong chains were fastened to thick collars around their necks, but they were jumping with so much force, I was afraid they would break free.

"These dogs are good for security, especially during the night. They will tear anyone apart who tries to get in this property," the old man said.

"Do they have names?" my father asked.

"Yes, the white one is Shir [Lion], and the gray one is Palang [Tiger]. Shir doesn't harm anyone unless someone attacks him or tries to hurt him. He is a fighting dog and has never lost a game. But Palang is very cruel; he likes to wound people."

"Palang bit my leg," I said.

"Don't worry, my son; he'll be your best friend soon," the old man said, then he called one of his sons to bring him the leftovers from lunch. He gave them to me to feed them to the dogs. I threw the leftovers to them. First they tried to leap at me, but soon they were busy eating.

The guest rooms were nicely painted. A beautiful red carpet with big motifs lay in the middle of the largest room, and mattresses stretched along all the walls; they were covered with long, narrow carpets. A small TV with a video player was in the corner.

"Perhaps you'll let my eldest son take your kids out and show them around," the old man suggested. We heard a big engine start with a roar behind us. His son, who was about Wakeel's age, was seated on a large tractor and invited us to get on it with him.

"How is my airplane? It makes a lot of noise, doesn't it?" he said as we climbed up to the platform behind the seat, and he put his foot on the gas.

"Yes, and it has bigger tires than other airplanes," I said.

"Do you like this place?" He shouted into my ear over the big noise of the engine.

"I don't know yet. You have to show me around, then I can tell," I said as we drove out of the garden onto the main road.

The sky was churning with dark and white clouds. The sun was lost among them and seemed ready to drop like a stone. The wind ruffled the surface of the wheat fields.

On both sides of the road as far as I could see, the fields were yellow and ready for harvest. The farmers were working with their scythes, holding a bunch of wheat stalks in one hand and cutting them with a smooth sweep of the other. Others were collecting pomegranates and almonds in sacks that drooped behind them on their backs. Their hands moved deftly through the branches.

I asked the old man's son whether he had ever traveled out of his village.

"No, and I don't want to. I love my village. I can find all that I need here. People respect my father, and me because I'm his oldest son," he said.

He pulled over and told his sister to take my sisters to the riverside, where she could introduce them to the other village girls. This was a branch of the same river along which we had camped, but there was no sign of the flood that had nearly carried us all away only a day earlier.

"All the girls from the village go there every day in the afternoon to fetch water for dinner. The village boys meet at the mosque," the old man's son said.

"Can we go to the river, too?" I asked. "I want to go swimming."

He laughed. "Don't ever try to go to the riverside at this time of day. If you are seen, someone will shoot you. Sometimes the girls take baths there."

"Are the girls carrying guns?" I asked.

"No, no. One of their fathers or brothers will shoot you."

"You have snipers here, like in Kabul?"

"No, but we have hunters, and they are everywhere. If one of them sees any boy or man going to the riverside at this time of the day, he will shoot."

"What about strangers? They don't know this rule," I said.

"You're not a stranger anymore. My father already announced in the mosque this morning that he wanted to host you guys for as long as you want to stay."

"You mean, all the villagers know about what I did last night?" I asked with a renewed sense of shame rolling over me.

"That is why all the villagers agreed to let us help you. They said that you guys had nothing to eat and nowhere to go," the old man's son said.

"They will call me a thief," I said despondently.

"No! They are not so stupid and rude to call their guest a thief." My mother had said the same thing. I was very relieved to hear this.

He showed me his hunting place nearby. He had some wooden ducks in a pool of water he had dug where the land began its rise to become a mountain. A narrow stream of water flowed down from the mountain's springs into the pool. Each time the wind rippled the surface, the wooden ducks bobbed as if they were real.

"When the birds are crossing over our village, they see my wooden ducks and think it is safe to land. When they land here to play or drink water, I catch them. I will teach you how to shoot," he promised.

"Have you ever seen Kabul?" I asked.

"No, I don't want to. It is a horrible place. Every trouble starts from there, and it spreads all over Afghanistan. I wish Kabul did not exist. I belong here. Everything that makes me happy is here."

He started reciting an old poem:

"'There is no room left in my heart for anything but the beautiful faces of my village girls. You have to know, how you will see her face with the light of the sun and the moon reflecting in her eyes. Wait and hope with all your vain fancies and dreams to see her face on a cloudy dark night.'"

He stopped and smiled at me. "I'm talking about my girlfriend. I'll show her to you, but you must promise not to fall in love with her, because she is mine. Okay?"

"Yeah, all right!" I said.

"If her beauty enslaves the heart of any man, I'll tear out that heart," he said with a suddenly serious, almost harsh voice, despite his poetic words. "Be careful, okay?" he said. I nodded my head, but I was a little afraid of him now.

We got off the tractor and walked for ten minutes without talking. He took me to the end of the village, where a very large courtyard with a garden stretched as far as I could see along the base of the low mountains that rise up behind Tashkurghan.

"That is her house," he said. His voice was soft now, and I relaxed. "We really love each other, but nobody knows, except for my mother. Please don't say anything about it to anybody."

"I can keep a secret," I said.

"Now, I'll make you my reason to get into the house to see her," he said. He sounded excited.

"How?" I said.

"I'll knock on the door. She or her brother will open it, and I'll introduce you as my guest. I'll say that you would like to see the garden. If she opens the door, she will know everything, but her parents won't. Your job is to tell them that you are my cousin, and you came from Kabul to visit us, and you would like to see the garden. The rest of the talking is up to me. Do you understand everything?"

"Yes," I said. This was an adventure, and I was enjoying it.

He knocked on the door, and a young girl opened it. She was a real beauty.

She instantly lowered her eyes and hurriedly said "*Salaam.*"

"I dreamed about you last night, and now I'm here to kiss you," the old man's son teasingly said.

"Get out of sight! My parents are at home, and my brothers are watering the flowers in the courtyard," she said in a panicky voice.

"Today I'll ask your parents for your hand. I'll ask them to make you my bride and sharer of my life," the old man's son said sweetly, with a smile as gentle as his father's.

"Don't make a fool of yourself. My brothers will beat you to death if they hear this. Go away before someone sees you," she whispered, and looked behind her.

One of her brothers suddenly appeared behind her like a mushroom after the rain.

"Who is it?" he asked.

"Oh, it is me," the son said. "This is my guest, Qais. I mean, my cousin. He came from Kabul with his family. I was showing him around, and he asked me if it was possible to see this garden. I told him it is my father's friend's garden. So, if you don't mind, I want to show him inside."

The brother welcomed us in.

"Sarah, show them around, and make them some pomegranate juice," he said to his sister. "You guys feel at home. I have some work to finish. We'll talk later."

Sarah took us to the garden. I could see almost every kind of fruit tree there is, with ripe fruit hanging from the branches. When we got to the end of the garden, Sarah turned to me and said, "If you don't mind, we want to talk in private for a few minutes. You just walk around, and eat whatever you like. Meet us here in ten minutes. Is that all right with you?"

"Sure, it's not a problem," I said. She gave me a grateful smile.

I walked all around for almost half an hour, until I got tired of being alone. I snuck behind a tree to see what kind of private talks they were having that were lasting so long.

But not a word was being spoken. They were just sitting face-to-face. The old man's son was looking right into the girl's eyes, and she was beaming at him. When he broke the silence, he spoke in a strange, poetic way.

"Do not forsake me," he beseeched her. Maybe he was making a joke. But the girl did not laugh.

"How could I forsake you?" she replied tenderly. "For you are all my life."

"You are mine, for I love you and must die if you forsake me," he said.

"I feel the same for you," she replied.

Do all the men in this village talk like that to their girlfriends? I wondered. Maybe they had seen too many Afghan movies where both lovers die before they get to see each other a second time. I eased out of my hiding place and ate another pomegranate.

An hour later we were ready to leave the garden.

"You can come anytime you want," Sarah said to me. "Next time, introduce me to your sisters. I want to meet them. Hamza will drive you here." It was the first time our eyes met. I felt warm inside, but nobody else saw it. I felt guilty, because I had promised not to fall in love, but what could I do? It was not up to me. It was up to my heart, and the heart cannot be controlled when it comes to love. I knew this from the Indian movies.

"Who is Hamza?" I asked her.

"I am Hamza," the old man's son said.

"Oh, I am sorry. I never asked your name. It is good to know your name," I said.

Sarah looked at both of us as she was standing at the threshold of the garden gate and holding the doorknob. "I thought you two were cousins," she said sharply, and waited for a reply.

"Yes, that is right. He is my cousin, but he didn't know my name. I think he never asked," the old man's son said.

"Hamza, what is going on? Is he your cousin, or someone you don't know? My brother will talk about it in the mosque tonight. If they find out that you lied to them, it will be dangerous for both of us," she said with great worry.

"Oh, relax, relax. It is not a problem. He is my cousin, I mean my guest. He will explain everything to you the next time he and I come. Sometimes cousins forget their cousin's name," Hamza teasingly said.

"Tell me one thing. Is he your cousin or guest?" she asked.

"The truth is, we didn't know each other until this morning. He is my guest."

She looked at him angrily. Someone called her from inside; it was an old woman's voice, probably her mother.

"Do you trust me?" Hamza asked.

"Yes, I trust you," she said with forgiveness edged with concern. The calling became louder, and she shouted back that she was coming.

"This is not a problem for us. You just have to relax. Everybody in the mosque knows him and his family. They are our guests, and they'll be with us for a few weeks at least. And I call him cousin. We are a family now," Hamza said.

"I trust you," she said with a beautiful smile, and closed the door after us as we left.

We spent three weeks in the garden of Hamza's father while we waited to hear that the road to Mazar was safe. The dogs did indeed become my friends. I took them for walks to the mountains and wished that Wakeel were there to go with us. I showed Palang the sign of the wounds that he had given me. He did not know what I was talking about, and he licked them.

Hamza taught me how to hunt. Every other day we went to his beloved's garden. She always had pomegranate juice waiting for me, and while I drank it, they had their private talks. The first day it was for a short while, but after a week it seemed like hours. One day I sneaked behind a tree again. They were not having those stupid movie dialogues that day. It was more interesting than that. I felt guilty, and never watched them again. I walked all around until Hamza called me to go home.

My family was happy, too. My mother sang old Indian songs when she cooked. Everything came from the garden and tasted better than anything we had eaten since we had fled Grandfather's house. In the mornings, my job was to take two straw baskets into the garden and fill them with tomatoes, cucumbers, squash, eggplant, peppers, pomegranates, apples, walnuts, and almonds, and then give them to my mother. Some days I could hardly carry the baskets by the time they were filled, we had so much to choose from.

My older sister became very busy, helping my mother with all the cooking. They spent many hours together talking about things. Other times, she asked my father to climb the mountains and see the view. My father was always happy to take her and our next sister on long walks in the fresh air. He loved the exercise and their company.

When my mother took her nap in the afternoon while my little brother was sleeping, my older sister took my younger sisters to the river to get drinking water with Hamza's sisters. They learned from the village girls how to carry a clay water pot on their heads without holding it with their hands, or at other times how to embroider hats. My older sister told them stories about life in Kabul, and what it was like to go to school. None of Hamza's sisters had ever been to school, though they knew how to read.

Since I had never seen my older sister act so pleasantly before, I decided to be nice to her. But when it came to me, she had not changed. She always found some way of making fun of me. She and I were supposed to eat from one plate. Afghans believe that sharing a plate improves the appetite. She would say things like, "He finishes everything on the plate before I take three bites. And he makes noises while he eats, like a cow." I stopped being nice to her.

Late one afternoon after hunting ducks, Hamza and I climbed up to the highest mountain to look down on the whole village. The sun was setting in the west. There were no clouds, just the gold of the sun and the deep blue of the sky.

"Have you ever talked to nature?" Hamza said.

"Sometimes," I said.

"Do you hear when it talks back to you?"

"What do you mean?" I asked.

"Nobody knows what I mean. Anytime I tell anyone what I can see and hear, they think I'm crazy. But you have to know that everything talks to you if you are very honest with them," Hamza said.

"You mean like mountains, and trees, and rivers, and the wind, and things like that?" I asked.

He nodded. "And to learn how to be honest, you have to start thinking about who the architect of the skies and earth is." Hamza was quiet for a moment. "When you build a building, you have to put pillars and walls to hold up the roof. But the sky has no pillars or walls. Only God can make architecture like that."

"Does God talk to you?" I asked, very surprised.

"No, He talks to us through his creatures," Hamza said.

"How?" I asked.

"The moon floats in a dark blue space, and shames billions of stars by its light. She has things to tell you; in fact she is talking to you," Hamza said, then we looked at the moon, which was just rising behind us. He had a funny way of speaking poetically, even when he was not with Sarah. At first I had found this strange. But after a couple of weeks I was beginning to enjoy it. The moon was perfectly round, and as the last of the daylight faded, it spread its softening glow across the land so we could see the whole village below.

"How did you learn all these things?" I asked.

"Open your eyes and ears, and you can learn anything you want," he said in his sweet voice. "The rose has given its power away to its thorns for its protection. But the nightingales never give their voices to crows. The moth flies around a candle until it burns its wings. But a deer runs away from hunters as far as it can."

"You are a poet," I said.

"No, I have eyes that are open, and I use them well," he said.

The wind started blowing. A few small clouds edged over the horizon, and the moon took control of the sky. We carefully climbed down.

I opened the garden gate. The dogs jumped playfully at me as I was thinking about what Hamza had told me. What he said has stayed with me from then until now. He made me think about things I had never thought much about before, like how God had created the stars, moon, sun, sky, the universe, and all of nature, and for what reason, why we are here, what is our mission in life, and how one can take pleasure from all these things we have been given.

That night, our families ate dinner together. Afterward, when my father and Hamza's went to listen to the BBC World Service, we heard that the fighting in Mazar was coming toward Tashkurghan.

My father made his decision right away. He said to the old man,

"It sounds as if we must leave Tashkurghan tomorrow morning." Hamza's father nodded.

My father had been going to mosque early in the morning with the other village men to say their morning prayers together. After prayers the next day, he shared what he had heard the previous night from the BBC. Then, in the way that Afghan people always do when they must leave the company of those who have welcomed them, he asked their permission to go.

When he came back from the mosque, we were having breakfast. He sat down and took a cup of tea from my mother, then told us, "We cannot now go to Mazar. I don't think it is safe to go back to Kabul. So we will head for Bamyan. We have heard no reports of fighting there, and I believe that we will be safe there. I have received the mullah's and the village men's permission to leave here today. They say that they will leave their homes, too. The war will reach this place in two days, maybe sooner. As soon as we finish eating, we will pack," my father said.

My older sister looked at him and said, "But, Father, Bamyan is in the middle of Afghanistan. We are supposed to be going to another country where there is no war."

My father looked at her and said very kindly, "We will. But not today."


After breakfast we went to the old man's house on the other side of the garden to say goodbye and to thank them. The old man was again listening to the BBC; his sons were playing chess; his wife and daughters were embroidering a tablecloth together. Each daughter had a corner in her hand.

Hamza's father rose and embraced my father. "This is your home, and its doors are always open to you." Then his sons hugged my father and me, and his wife and daughters hugged my mother and sisters.

"Are you staying or leaving?" my father asked.

"I think we are leaving as well," Hamza's father said. "We will go to Pakistan, to my brother's home; he has been living there for ten years. I received his letter yesterday. He is very worried. He wants to send Hamza to America to live with his son."

"What about your garden? Will you leave it just like this?" my father said.

"Yes, I cannot do anything about it. We all know that these holy warriors don't fight to drive out foreign troops from our country. They fight to loot us. This factional fighting is just an excuse to steal from us, and even to steal our wives and daughters."

"Alas, alas," said my father, nodding his head.

His wife wrapped two fried chickens in newspaper and put some fresh beans in a pot, along with two pumpkins, some potatoes, and a few cabbages in bags. My mother did not want to take them, but the woman kept insisting. Finally, my mother accepted the food and thanked them for their hospitality and all their help.

Just as we started to drive off, Hamza's father ran toward our car with a big bag on his shoulders. He stood in front of our car, panting. He winked at me to come out. He gave me the big bag and asked me to lift it. I tried but I could not. It was very heavy.

"Can you eat them all?" he asked me.

"What is it?" I said.

"Pomegranates!" Hamza's father said.

He was smiling, but I felt very small. "No, I can't eat them all," I said with a renewed sense of shame that not even the kindness of the old man could dismiss.

"I'm sure you can, and I know you'll share them with others. Remember me and my dogs when you eat these pomegranates. That is all I want," Hamza's father said. I felt a little bit better when he bent over and kissed me on my forehead.

He helped me put the bag into the trunk and waved us off toward Bamyan.

The town's mullah was standing on the roadside and signaled for us to stop. My father halted in front of him and rolled down his window. After greeting the mullah, he introduced him to us.

The mullah wore a white *shalwar kamiz* and a long green-and-blue-striped *chapan* coat on top of it. He had a black turban, and the rims of his eyes were darkened with kohl, as men do who are religious. His mustache was shaved, but his beard was long, almost to his belly. When he talked, his beard waved, though he was a calm talker.

He gave my father a *tasbeh*, a string of prayer beads, and said, "I can't give you more than this. I should have invited you to my house so we could eat together, but I didn't know that the war would come here and separate us."

"Your *tasbeh* will always remind me of you and God," my father told him. "If God is willing, one day we will see each other again, and we'll talk about these days."

"I'm waiting for that day, if not in this world, maybe in the next one," the mullah said.

"Are you staying or leaving?" my father asked.

"I'm staying here. You know I can escape from my country, but I can't escape from my death. I'm breathing the last days of my life anyway. I'm seventy-five years old. If death comes tomorrow to me, I'm happy to welcome it. There is no difference between today and tomorrow," the mullah said.

"You are a brave man," my father said.

"I wouldn't call it bravery. Death is part of life, and whoever takes it earlier, he or she will be at the head of the caravan for the next world. Either today or tomorrow we will join that caravan, so why not sooner rather than later?" the mullah said.

"Let me tell you something," he added, "a story of Mullah Nasruddin:

"Mullah Nasruddin was awakened in the middle of the night by the cries of two men quarreling in front of his house. Nasruddin waited, but they continued to argue. He was unable to sleep. He wrapped his quilt tightly around his shoulders and rushed outside to separate the men, who had come to blows. But when he tried to reason with them, one of them snatched the quilt off Mullah Nasruddin's shoulders, and then both men ran away. Mullah Nasruddin, very weary and perplexed, went inside.

" 'What was the quarrel about?' his wife asked him.

" 'It must be about our quilt,' replied the mullah. 'The quilt is gone, the dispute is over.'

"You see what I mean? Our country has become a Mullah Nasruddin story. This war is all about what we have in this country, not about you or me. Once they get what they want, then they won't care about anything else," the mullah said. "Almighty God protect you and your family from all dangers."

They hugged, and my father got back in the car and began driving quickly toward Bamyan before the mullah could tell another story, or anyone else showed up.

# 9

✦

## *Inside the Head of Buddha*

The Kuchi nomads follow their goats, sheep, and camels through the mountains in search of new pastures. They never settle anywhere for long. Though my grandmother was born a Kuchi and my grandfather had come from herders who spent long seasons in the mountains with their flocks, my family and I did not think of ourselves as nomads. Yet we were enjoying our new life on hillsides, in the gardens of strangers, a few days here and a few days there, never in the same place for long. I knew we were looking for a quiet place to hide from the rockets while we found a way to leave Afghanistan. But despite rockslides, floods, and biting dogs, we had found a way of pushing the everyday threat of war from our minds as we thought about where we were going next, or where we had just been.

Bamyan is at the very center of Afghanistan, high in the mountains. We had to go back across the Hindu Kush to get there, but this time we took an unpaved road through a mountain pass to avoid any fighting along the main road. It took fifteen hours of slow, rough driving over deeply rutted roads to reach the Bamyan Valley. It had been an endless day; our bodies were longing for rest. It was well after dark when we were finally on a better road approaching the town.

The car jerked to a halt, waking those of us who were falling asleep. A blue plastic rope was stretched across the road between two wooden poles. It was called the Bamyan Door. It did not look like a door to me.

A man rushed from a mud house next to one of the wooden poles. He had a Kalashnikov hanging from his shoulder. He asked my father where we were going. My father explained that we were heading to Bamyan City. The man said we were not allowed to go in this late at night, and we must park somewhere along the river and come back tomorrow.

My father did not try to argue; the man had a gun. He drove back in the direction from which we had come for a few hundred yards, and parked the car on a level spot next to the river. My mother gave us some of the food that Hamza's family had shared with us.

It was a beautiful night, but much cooler than in Tashkurghan. In the crisp air, the sky was like a dark piece of silk studded with tiny diamonds. The silence was dense, with only the quiet sound of the river and the twittering of some night birds to challenge it. We squeezed ourselves into the car's seats to stay close together and keep warm as we slept. Though it was crowded, I felt as if I were on a soft bed after the hours of bumpy roads.

We set out a picnic breakfast along the river the next morning and took our time over it. After all, we were nomads now; we moved when we wanted to. When we finished eating and had packed everything back into our car, we headed once more to Bamyan City. The guy who had stopped us the night before at the "door" was sitting in front of the mud house with his friends. They all had Kalashnikovs hanging from their shoulders.

They stopped us again and my father explained that we were refugees from Kabul, looking for a safe place to live for a while. They silently searched our luggage piece by piece, though there was not much, then to our relief lowered the blue plastic rope and let us drive through.

My father slowly drove toward the main Bamyan bazaar. The town was small and filled with the smell of wood fires and horse manure mixed with saffron, pepper, cardamon, and dust.

He pulled into a car *serai*, an enclosed parking area. We walked up and down Bamyan's one main street for a while. It was full of donkeys, goats, and people dressed very poorly. Then we went to a *chai khana*, a teahouse, for lunch. We climbed a bamboo ladder to the second floor, though a few of the rungs were missing. My father went first, with my mother and my baby brother behind him. My little sisters had a hard time climbing up. I had to help them, since I had been appointed to look after them. Another bamboo ladder led up to the third and fourth floors. There were no proper stairs.

The *chai khana* was a large room filled with kebab smoke. A tiny TV was in the corner of the room; I could hardly see it through the smoke. The men were sitting on platforms two feet high, their shoes left behind on the floor. The plates in front of them, whether filled with food or only scraps, were alive with flies. Some of the men were eating, some were drinking tea while watching an Indian movie, and some were snoring while hundreds of flies had parties on their hands and feet and around their mouths.

My mother was the only woman there, and my sisters the only girls. The men who had been chewing kebab stopped chewing. Their mouths hung half-open as they stared. The ones who had been drinking tea and watching TV put their glasses on the floor and turned where they sat to get a better view of us. My mother pulled her headscarf forward an inch and pretended she was there alone with my father and her children.

All the men's faces were furrowed like plowed earth. Deep wrinkles cut into the corners of their Asiatic eyes and along their foreheads. They watched us for the most part in silence, and when they did speak they whispered.

All of them were Hazaras. I remembered Grandfather having told me that most of the Hazaras lived in central Afghanistan. He said that when he was still traveling with his father and uncles, driving their flocks to Bamyan to find high mountain pastures that stayed lush all summer from the last of the melting snow, they had been treated very warmly by the Hazara people there. Though they were not Kuchi nomads like my grandmother's family, who traveled in regular routes around the country, my grandfather's people also were herders, who left their home with their flocks each summer to search for pastures. Often, they had spent summers in the green Bamyan Valley, which was only a week's walk from their village in Maidan.

They traded some of their sheep, goats, or cows with the Hazaras in return for grazing rights and a place to set up their tents for a couple of months. I hoped the Hazaras would treat us well, too, even though we did not have any animals to trade with them, and we were not real nomads anymore but modern nomads in a beat-up old car.

Berar used to tell me good stories about Bamyan, where he was born. When he worked for our family, he used to leave all his money with Grandfather. After several months he would ask for it, and then send it all home to his parents. Grandfather always made jokes with him, telling him to spend some money on women while he was a young man.

Berar used to say, "If you build a house, a lot of people can use it, but a woman can be used only by a husband. A house is more efficient than a wife."

I looked through the smoke in that *chai khana* to see whether he was among those men, but he was not. I was disappointed. Since that morning on the roof of the silo, I had never seen or heard of him again.

We ordered kebab, which is about the only lunch you can get, not just in Bamyan but in restaurants all over Afghanistan. On the wall was a photograph of the two enormous Buddha statues that had been carved into the cliffs at Bamyan almost two thousand years before. They looked very strange to me. They did not have faces.

After we had finished eating, my father suggested that we go see the Buddhas and their caves cut out of the cliffs behind them. They were just a short walk from the *chai khana*. We climbed down the bamboo ladder, with me passing first my hesitant younger sister to my father and then a very happy crying machine who kept smiling and pointing at all the donkeys. There were no cars on the road, so my sisters and I could run ahead of my parents, shrieking as we went, feeling free and lighthearted in a way we had not been for a couple of years.

As we approached the smaller Buddha, though, we all became

very quiet. He towered over us, and I found myself holding my breath. I had seen a photo of him in my schoolbook, but there he looked as flat as the page. Here, I felt that Buddha could walk right out of the mountain. How could a statue be so tall? I asked myself.

I had never seen a statue before, not even a small one. In Islam, statues are *haram*, forbidden, and have been since the time of the second law of the Prophet Musa, or Moses. Only God can make a living creature and breathe life into it, we are taught, and men should not make statues and try to be like God. Nothing had prepared me for the sense of awe that filled me.

Grandfather once told me that he had climbed to the top of the statues with his stepfather. The statues had been carved from the soft stone of the cliffs, their backs merging with the hill. He had told me about all the caves in the cliffs behind the Buddhas, and of all the paintings on their walls. He said that Bamyan had once been a place filled with holy men.

"Buddha lived six hundred years before Prophet Issa [Jesus]. And Prophet Mohammad, peace be upon him, came six hundred and thirty years after Prophet Issa. If you learn about Christianity and Buddhism, you will value Islam even more than you already do."

My father found the opening to the stairs that led to the top of the smaller Buddha. I had never seen stairs like those before. They were cut from the stone right inside the cliff. Each step was at a different height and angle, just as Grandfather had said.

Slowly, we all made our way up. The only light came from occasional holes cut in the rock; we had to feel our way along in some places. My father was carrying my little brother, who was enjoying the adventure as much as the rest of us. By the time we got to the level of Buddha's shoulders, we had all run out of breath, and our faces were red, even my father's. Through a large opening in the rock wall, we had a spectacular view across the valley with its rows of crops and fruit trees everywhere. We edged one another to get a better look, and to smell the sweetly scented air that rose off the fields below.

We climbed a few more steps, and just behind the head of Buddha found ourselves in a cave as big as our living room in Kabul. The walls of the cave were twenty or more feet high; the floor was littered with loose rock. The air was still and cool, and the only sound was the wind blowing through the small openings on the stairs, like the finger holes on a flute.

The cave was connected to other smaller caves beyond it. Just as Grandfather had said, the walls of all the caves were covered with paintings. Even in the dim light, the colors were bright in rich shades of red, white, green, black, blue, and purple. Some showed bare-chested men and nearly naked women in strange poses. Others were of birds and animals of many kinds, like lions, tigers, cats, eagles, and pigeons, and men hunting them with spears or bows and arrows. They were all interlaced with patterns and symbols, some looking like the tracks of the creatures being hunted. Others were more difficult to understand.

I asked my father what those paintings meant. He was looking at the hunting scene and replied, "Do you see the man hunting the lion with his arrows?" I nodded. "The others are proud of him. So, they painted a picture of him on the walls to remember his courage. That is how people passed history along to the people who came after them. This was the way of telling stories before the alphabets were invented."

I pointed to a large wheel with many spokes that looked like a spider. "What does that mean?"

"I don't know. It meant something to somebody. The archaeologists and historians might know." Then he looked at my mother and said, "You know, this cave is a perfect size for us. We can stay here for as long as we are in Bamyan."

My mother looked at my father the way she did when he was telling jokes. But my father said, "I am serious. It is our home now." My mother smiled at him. All the rest of us smiled, too. My father always told good jokes.

"It is impossible," she said flatly when she realized he had actually meant what he had said.

My father did not hear her. "You know, even the king used to buy a ticket to visit this place. Tourists from all around the world used to come here." But tourists had stopped coming years ago, and the local people had no reason to climb up to the caves.

My mother had a lot of looks. We could tell by her look what she was thinking, and her eyes were disbelieving. But when she saw how excited we were by the idea, she looked at my father again. "Do you know how high this place is?"

"Yes, and I have never lived in a place like this before." He walked over to one of the holes in the wall. "Look, you can see the whole world from here," my father said excitedly. "I think this is the mouth of Buddha, and we can look right through it." Buddha actually had no mouth; his whole face was missing. But that did not hinder my father's imagination. The opening was long and low, and it did, in fact, have a great view.

"You're just like a little kid," my mother said.

"So, you tell me what to do," my father responded a bit plaintively. "I don't have money to pay for a hotel, and I have no idea how long we'll have to stay here."

"But what if somebody falls?" my mother said. "What about these babies?" She held up my little brother and gestured with her arm toward my youngest sister. "Do they have wings to fly if they fall out those holes?"

In Kabul, I was always afraid of being killed by a rocket, but if I fall down from Buddha's head, I thought, at least I will die happy.

My father knelt on the ground and asked everybody to come closer. We all stood in a line in front of him, except my mother, who stood behind us holding my little brother, who was gurgling at the paintings on the wall.

"Do you want to live here?" my father asked us, and we all shouted "Yes," almost in one voice.

"But I have rules. If you accept them, we will live here," he said. "Rule number one: Everybody has to be careful climbing up and down the stairs. Rule number two: Everyone is responsible for the one younger than him or her. Rule number three: Those are all the rules." He smiled at us, and we smiled back, then he looked at my mother, and we all looked at her. We could not tell whether she was happy with the idea or not. But we stayed, perhaps because there was no place else to go.

For an hour, my older sister and I kept running up and down the stairs, bringing things up to our mother that our father took out of the car. There were so many stairs, and they were so hard to climb. But I was moving as fast as I could because my father had promised a bigger ice cream to whoever made more trips. She was moving very slowly, and I knew I would win. By the time we had taken everything up, I was soaked with sweat. But I had made almost twice as many trips as she. I told her proudly that I had won. She smiled and said, "You're a complete idiot! There is no ice cream in Bamyan. These people don't know what ice cream is. This is not Kabul, stupid!"

I looked at my father. He had a silly smile on his face. I was furious at him for tricking me.

"I owe you a huge ice cream," he said. "A huge one. You show me the shop around here, and I'll buy it for you." Now he was making fun of me. My sisters laughed at me. I ran to the next cave, ashamed of having been so stupid. But my curiosity soon led me back to my family when I heard my father banging two big nails he found in the car into a spot on the walls of the cave where there were no paintings. Then he strung up a cradle for my little brother across a corner of the cave. Later, he hung a *kilim* at the entrance of the cave to make a door.

My father went to the bazaar to buy some cooking pots, plates, spoons, forks, and other necessities. My mother sent me to get her some water in buckets. I went to a spring not very far from the Buddha. My older sister collected a few bricks and flat stones at its feet. We took the bricks and water to my mother, who built a hearth for cooking in one of the smaller caves next to the large one. That small cave became our kitchen.

My father brought back some lamb along with some tomatoes, onions, carrots, potatoes, radishes, and parsley. My mother built a fire, which she was not used to doing. The smoke made her cry. She was wiping her eyes and nose. Soon her face was covered with black smudges from the smoke. My father teased her, but then helped arrange the wood in the fire and put stones around it so my mother could set a pot on them. She cooked the meat with all the vegetables and made a simple stew that was as good as anything we had ever eaten. We ate it in the large cave, where the men with the bows and arrows watched us.

Soon it was dark, and we had no light. My father had forgotten to buy candles. He always forgot one or two things whenever he went shopping; that is how my father is. If he did not forget something, how could we know he was actually our father?

Through the opening that my father was calling "Buddha's mouth," a ray of moonlight was weaving itself into patterns of white lace on the floor. It was our lightbulb for that night, a huge one, and very far away, but all we needed for our new home.

I was the first one to fall asleep that night, even though my mattress was not long enough, and my quilt could barely cover me from head to toe. It was cool in the cave. A gentle breeze kept blowing through it all night long. I woke up after a while and had to pee. My father told me to use the ledge of the next cave down. It felt very strange peeing from such a high place. I was already finished before I heard it hit the ground. It was amazingly loud.

The next morning I was up earlier than the others. I looked out through an opening in one of the cave walls. The sun was still halfway behind the bare and sharp rocks of the mountains. But already daylight was flooding in, making patches of bright light amid the darkness. Below me, the valley was full of fields and trees. The leaves on some of the trees were still green; others had already turned yellow in the midautumn chill. A gentle breeze was moving the branches, and some of the yellow leaves were falling down into the white-tipped, fast-running water of the river. Dogs were playing along the banks. Piles of wheat that had been harvested on each plot of land made neat piles at regular intervals. Cows were eating straw as women milked them. There was no sign of war. A warm feeling just from being there swept through me.

I decided to see what was in the other caves while my family slept. When I pushed aside the *kilim* door, a burst of cold wind whirled through the opening into the cave. I shivered in my thin cotton *shalwar kamiz*, but I knew that in these caves, and outside in the valley, adventures were waiting to happen. It was time to start.

———

As the days passed, the memory of war began to fade, like the image of a bad dream. I wanted the rest of our family to be with us. Especially I wanted Wakeel, so we could explore all the other caves and the secrets of the mountains, like a place called the City of Screams, where another war had happened long ago. A man named Genghis Khan had killed many people there. It was hard to believe that anything like that had ever happened in Bamyan; it was so peaceful now.

Grandfather had told me that for centuries people from all parts of the world had come to Bamyan to understand the wisdom of Buddha. I wanted to know more about Buddha, but I could not find anybody who could tell me much. Everybody was Muslim. But I noticed that the local people still felt something special for the Buddha statues. They believed that he was taking care of them.

I discovered that several other families were living in the caves. Most were Hazaras who had fled from Kabul; some came from a neighborhood close to ours. My sisters and I soon had many friends from among their children.

Early one morning as I was climbing down from behind Buddha's head to play with some of the other kids, I saw a group of unusual-looking men in one cave walking in a circle around a fire, completely silent. They were dressed in white and reminded me of Gandhi from the movie we had seen; they wore the same kind of clothing.

One of them looked Hazara; the rest were Asians, but not Afghans. They kept making circles around the fire. I wanted to join them, but then I was afraid that they might push me into the fire. It was not such a big fire, but enough to burn my feet and clothes.

I waited near the door for them to stop. I wanted to ask them what they were doing. But after they had finished, the short ones bowed to the Hazara-looking man, who bowed back to them, and went out without saying anything. They walked right past me without looking at me, as if I were not there. Only he stayed in the cave.

I went in and bowed to him the way I had seen the others do. He bowed back to me as he stood next to the fire. I asked him why they had been circling around the fire.

He said, "Fire has two faces, like woman." He had a strange accent, unlike anything I had heard before, and when he spoke, he left out some of the words. "If you worship it, it gives you its blessings, and if you insult it, it burns you as it burns itself." Since then, I have always thought of fire as a woman with two faces. But I did not really understand what he meant, or who these men were. Were they Muslim? I had never seen such a thing in a mosque. I never saw them again, except for the one who looked like a Hazara, though I later learned he was not. In my explorations I discovered that he lived in a cave nearby. Sometimes I would go to visit him. He did not say very much, but his silence made me feel calm.

I told my mother about him. She said that maybe he was a monk from another country visiting Bamyan.

My little brother was beginning to walk. He wanted to do it all the time. In the caves this was a problem. We all had to watch him so he did not fall out. He never went far from my mother. When my mother had to feed our youngest sister, he became jealous. She had to give him a small lump of sugar to distract him. He loved sugar and would eat as much as anybody gave him. Sometimes when I wanted to take him out of the caves to go walking with me, I put a little sugar in my palm. He ran to me. I gave him some, and he followed me all the way to the river, or to wherever I wanted to go. He held on to my middle finger. For a time when we first arrived in Bamyan, he was my special friend, though a quiet one, but I had to trick him to be with me.

Autumn showed its face by turning everything completely yellow. The days shrank, but we enjoyed the clear weather and went for long walks through the town. Nearly every day we passed the larger Buddha statue, but we never went into his caves. They were filled with other fleeing families like ours, and we did not want to intrude on their privacy. The larger Buddha was very impressive, but he was not our Buddha, so we did not have such strong feelings for him.

Winter came unexpectedly early that year. Soon the bumpy roads disappeared under thick snow. Every morning my father had to shovel aside the snow at the bottom of the steps so I could go get our bread fresh from the baker's clay ovens.

After a few days the entry to the cave was reduced to a narrow lane between two walls of snow. Our cheeks got red as we slid down the slope that led down from the bottom of the stairs to the road. In front of Buddha, our breaths became small clouds, and we laughed at the sight of them. We had never seen this much snow in Kabul.

When my father came back from shoveling or shopping, he had to shake the snow from his large felt coat. Under it, he was wearing a jacket with its fur turned inside out. Felt and fur coats were what everyone wore in Bamyan. I could not find anyone who did not have one. It was not like Kabul, where it snowed only for a day or two, and then warmed up. Here it snowed for weeks without any end. When it did not snow, it was sunny, freezing, and windy.

My mother was always making tea to keep us warm. On days when it was snowing too hard to go out, my father built a fire in a part of the cave that had no paintings, and we all sat around wrapped in our quilts while my mother told stories about all the Afghan kings and heroes. Amazingly, it seems that they had all spent time in our cave, or at least that is how my mother told it.

One day the snow was too deep for me to go to the bakery. My father went and brought back some extra flatbreads, so we would not have to go out again later. Since there were so many, I asked my mother whether I could bring one to my friend the monk. I never saw him eat, and sometimes I worried about him, since he was an old man and had no family to take care of him. She gave me a piece that had been on a hot stone by the fire and was still warm.

I went down the stairs to his cave and found him sitting near his own fire, though it was too small to make much heat. He wore only his light cotton clothes, with his shoulders wrapped in a white woolen *patu*, the long blanket that for most Afghan men is their only coat in winter. Yet he did not shiver. He was very happy to receive the bread, and offered me some tea that he had made from leaves that he had gathered from the valley.

We sat together for a long time. When he poured the tea into a very small bowl and passed it to me, his hands moved very precisely, very gracefully. It was only tea in the bowl, but the way he offered it made it seem like something far more valuable. I drank it very slowly, to make it last, and looked at his face as I did. He spoke with his eyes more than with his mouth. I felt very happy to be with him, though I do not think I could have explained why if I had been asked.

I asked him to tell me about Buddha. For a long time, he said nothing. He just looked at the bowl of tea he was holding. Slowly, he shifted his gaze to me and spoke very softly.

"The earth will never be without flowers and trees," he said. "For as one dies another comes to take its place, and it has been like this since the creation. Like a rosebud, the world and its affairs are closed up tight, waiting for a warm spring breeze. We must always be like the warm spring breeze, and open the buds of every kind of flower."

The cave felt very warm, despite that small fire.

In the cave where we were living, though, everyone complained about being cold, especially at night. One day my father found someone selling mattresses that were filled with wool and he bought five of them. These were much better than the thin ones we had brought from Kabul. My mother stitched the new mattresses together, then sewed several of our quilts together, as well.

That night we all slept together. My mother and father lay in the middle with my little brother between them. I was next to my father, and my sisters next to my mother. We all clung to each other to stay warm.

Two and a half months had passed since we had come to Bamyan. We worried all the time about everybody, and worried even more because we had no way of getting news. We heard reports of fighting in Mazar and Kabul, so we knew it would not be safe to go there. We settled into our caves, where we had developed our routines. Every day included time with schoolbooks, with my mother teaching us reading and writing, and our father teaching us arithmetic.

My father became very friendly with many of the men in the town. He went with them to their mosque on Fridays, though they were Shi'a and we are Sunni. But a mosque is a mosque and anybody can pray there. People with good hearts can always rise above narrowness.

When they heard that he was a teacher, they asked him whether he would teach their sons physics and chemistry when school opened again in the spring. My father told them that he was happy to help them.

We heard rumors about a terrible battle that had been fought somewhere north of Bamyan near a place called Doshi. We had driven through Doshi on our way to Bamyan. We did not want to believe it. It had been such a peaceful place.

"Mazari's troops attacked Masoud's troops and were defeated badly. Masoud's troops are coming to Bamyan." We heard this from men, women, kids, everyone. The people in Bamyan were afraid of Masoud. He was a Tajik from the Panjshir Valley. His soldiers had treated many Hazaras very cruelly. Mazari was a Hazara commander who had gained the reputation of a cruel warlord. His forces had clashed with Masoud's in other places, such as our old neighborhood in Kabul, but so far there had been no fighting in Bamyan.

Though we are Pashtuns, we had been treated very well in Bamyan by everyone there. Whenever another one of the refugee families in the caves cooked something special, they sent some to share with us. We did the same for them. The shopkeepers in the main bazaar were all Hazaras. When I went to one of their shops to get something we needed, I told them that my father would pay them later that day or the next day. They did not mind.

It felt like our old neighborhood in Kabul, where everyone respected my father. Even now, when the divisive brutality of war was threatening to overtake us again, none of our neighbors ever failed in their hospitality even for a moment.

But there was a feeling in the air, a look of worry that settled into people's eyes. There was only one topic of conversation anytime anyone met. My father and the other men would gather in shops, and in the caves, and in the mosque, sometimes listening to a radio with its poor reception because of the mountains, sometimes speculating what might or might not happen. If a newcomer came to Bamyan, everyone wanted to know what he knew, and then whatever he had said would be talked about for days after.

People said that Kunduz was peaceful. It was back across the Hindu Kush mountains, almost on Afghanistan's northern border with

Tajikistan. My mother was born there, and we had lots of relatives there. Some of the other refugees had already decided to go there. My parents talked about whether we should try that ourselves.

With all our moves, I began to wonder whether Wakeel and Grandfather would ever find us. The day we had left Haji Noor Sher's house, Wakeel had said that he would go to Mazar by himself and join us there. Had he gone? Was he there looking for me? Had something happened to him? There was no way of knowing. I had no information about him or Grandfather, only a great worry.

I became very sad and went to talk to my friend the monk. He had always answered my questions so wisely. I wanted to ask him why men always want to kill each other.

"Everyone has a purpose," he replied. "Everyone has to be good at something to feel fully connected to this cruel world."

I did not understand. "But they kill thousands of innocents," I said.

"Warriors are born with certain skills. But still, the warrior has a mind, too, and knows the difference between bad and good. Those who kill the innocent are confused. They are men with damaged souls," he said.

"Do you feel connected to this cruel world?" I asked.

"There is a time for being connected to this world," he replied, speaking slowly and choosing his words very carefully, "and a time for not being connected." We sat quietly for a few moments. We both knew that if Masoud's forces reached Bamyan, they might kill him.

"Will you stay here if the warriors come, or will you go somewhere to save your life?" I asked.

"I will do what is best," he said.

"You mean you have a place to hide?" I queried.

"Of course I do," he said.

"Far from here?" I asked. "Is it in Afghanistan?"

"I can't tell you that," he said.

"You will never leave this Buddha, will you?" I said knowingly.

"As a candlewick drowns in its own wax, and a moth flies around it till it dies, I want to drown in Buddha's knowledge and die at his feet. To tell you a hard truth, even the king when he is away from his home is like a beggar."

"It is the last time I'm seeing you," I told him. "We're leaving here for Kunduz tomorrow." I asked his permission to go and stood up. He also stood and laid his right hand on my head.

"Go well, tomorrow and always. Never hesitate to do good things. I'm sure you will be successful in your life," he said. He shook hands with me as a gentle smile spread across his full, wrinkled face.

That night, we made a fire to light our cave as we organized our few belongings. The fire crackled in front of us, and from time to time a spark jumped out, as if trying to escape. I wished we could escape from Afghanistan like the spark from the fire, but there was no way out. All the paths were blocked; all the doors were slammed against us.

Early the next day we packed the car and prepared to leave Bamyan. It was snowing, and all the mountains were covered. It was very beautiful to see, but very cold. The Buddhas did not mind cold or heat. They had been standing there days and nights for centuries.

I bowed in front of our Buddha as I had seen those monks do and said my goodbyes. I felt sorry for leaving the Buddha there alone, especially after we had been made to feel so welcome living somewhere inside of him. But he did not mind, or maybe he did. But I could not see it. A few minutes later we were in the car heading toward Kunduz, all shivering from the cold.

I had always expected I would see our Buddha again. But the storm of ignorance that has been raging in Afghanistan for so many decades smashed him to bits before I could return. I once lived inside his head. Now he lives in mine.

# 10

❖

## *Borderlands*

A fter about six hours of driving over the Hindu Kush once more, we made our first stop in a place that was in the middle of nowhere and surrounded on four sides by mountains.

We could not see a track, or a road, or an animal footprint, or anybody to give us directions. We had not used any of the regular roads, since we did not know where the front line and its fighting was. We had followed several old dirt tracks that seemed to lead in the right direction and which we hoped were too small for the factions to use with their trucks full of guns. But now we were lost, and had no earthly idea where to go next.

Also, in these few hours, we had gone from winter to summer. Bamyan is very high in the mountains, and we were now nearly a mile below it. The weather had changed completely. The sun glowed orange, the sky was perfectly clear. We had left the snow behind and could see heat rising from flat stones.

A couple of hours before, we had packed away our fur and felt coats, and now we were in a desert, sweating. The water we had brought from Bamyan was long gone; we had expected to be in Kunduz by now and had not used it as sparingly as we should have. Our throats were dry, and we kept hoping that our route would go past a brook or a stream. But there were none.

My father parked the car under the shade of a mountain rock. Dragonflies hummed all around. He let the car engine cool for a while, then with a small pipe he took some water out of the radiator. It did not look very good, but it was the only thing we had to drink. Everyone wanted the first drink. There was not enough for all of us to have as much as we wanted. He gave us one sip only, not more, and in the end, there was nothing left for him.

We were desperate to find someone who might know the road to Kunduz, but there was no one, only the dragonflies, and we could not speak their language to ask them.

Finally, after an hour, when we were happy just to be out of the car, we saw a man on a mule making his way slowly down the side of the mountain. My father and I ran to him to ask him where, in fact, we were. If we knew that much, perhaps we could find our way.

"This place is called Nahreen," he said from atop his mule. "And this mountain in front of us is called Mongol's Mountain. If you continue driving to the north for four hours, you'll get to a town called Shekamish, which belongs to Takhar Province, then after another four hours you will reach Khan Abad, which belongs to Kunduz Province, and then another two hours will get you to Kunduz City."

The man told us that the roads were not good, but that came as no surprise after what we had driven over. He also warned us not to stop for anyone, "not even for little children, because they are all robbers and killers."

We thanked the man and got everybody back into the car.

Now we had another ten hours of driving ahead of us. We had wanted to get to Kunduz before dark, because of the robbers. My father started driving as if he were in a race. He hit every bump of that very bumpy road with too much speed, and the car jumped off the ground, squashing us against the ceiling. In the wild ride, we forgot our thirst and hunger. As we flew along, my father kept one eye on the road, and the other on the gas gauge. We had not seen a gas pump in hours, not even a village. About an hour after leaving the old man, we saw a little boy with a few gallons of petrol standing along the road. There was no pump station in sight, just the boy. We were afraid to stop, thinking he might himself be a robber. But we had no choice.

My father told us to stay in the car with the doors and windows locked, and be ready to go in an instant if anybody else came along. Even my father did not get out of the car, he just rolled down the window and spoke to the boy. The boy charged my father twice as much as we usually paid, and he was very slow about putting the petrol in the tank. Every set of eyes in that car swept the landscape around us as he did so, looking for the first sign of trouble. But no one came to bother us, and my father gladly gave him the money.

That was the only stop we made. In several other places small kids waved at us to give them a ride to the next town. We sped past as the old man had told us to do. As we did, my sisters and I saw men come out from behind big rocks nearby with their Kalashnikovs hanging from their shoulders. That was how it worked in those places. If you stopped to help a little kid who looked poor and desperate with torn clothes, guys with guns would jump out from hiding places and rob you, and maybe rape the women, too.

It took us two hours longer than the old man had predicted for us to get to Kunduz. We arrived long after dark, exhausted, hungry, and very, very thirsty.

We went straight to the home of my mother's brothers. They were extremely surprised to see us at one in the morning, but woke everyone and welcomed us to their compound. Their wives and daughters quickly set about making a meal for us, and bringing us jugs of water and pots of tea. The men and the boys showed us their houses, which were each surrounded by good-size courtyards that had doors connecting one to the other. Quickly, they arranged spaces for us to sleep, and some of the older boys carried our belongings from the car.

There were so many cousins I had never met before. They looked a lot different from my cousins on my father's side in Kabul, whom I knew well. They had bigger eyes with darker eyebrows and crinkly hair. They were a little shorter, and had narrow shoulders.

As late as it was, my aunts quickly prepared rice with chunks of meat and carrots, and a big plate of salad and roasted aubergine with some apple juice. We ate while my cousins, uncles, and aunts watched us. There were so many of them. They did not all fit in one room. Some of them were peeping in through the window at the back.

They were very talkative, all speaking at the same time, like sparrows. There were no rules like those my grandfather had established for us in our house. He used to say, "When someone talks, you listen until he finishes, then you talk. If someone older than you talks, you don't talk." But no one knew about that in Kunduz. I could not hear who was saying what. I ate and wished Grandfather were there to teach them the rules.

Some of them talked to me in Pashto. I found this very strange. My sisters and cousins and I in Kabul always spoke Dari at home, even though we are Pashtuns and can speak Pashto fluently. Sometimes when we had guests who could not speak Dari, we spoke Pashto among ourselves to put the guests at ease. But here everyone spoke Pashto. Maybe they thought I could not speak Dari, as I was a guest.

A few days later I found out that they could not speak Dari properly. When they used Dari, it was as if they were translating Pashto expressions into Dari. It sounded funny, and they had a strange accent. My sisters and I found that very entertaining. A few times we caught them laughing at our accent. But it did not take us very long to become good friends. We had discovered twenty new cousins our own ages.

We spent three weeks with them, enjoying living in a house again, though I missed our cave sometimes. We could go out walking in the street. My father finally bought me the ice cream that he had promised me in Bamyan. My cousins went to school, and we helped them do their homework and read their books. Maybe we could live here now, I thought. We will find a way to tell Grandfather and Wakeel where we are. Maybe they were in Mazar-e-Sharif now, waiting for us.

I saw how happy my mother was. With the restrictions on travel imposed by the Russians, and then dangers from the factions, she had not been home to Kunduz for many years. She spent hours every day greeting old friends and distant relatives whom she had not seen in a long time. Her brothers' wives did not allow her to do any housework. They gave her some of their very best clothes and treated her like a queen, bringing her tea and fruit. My father had known several of my mother's brothers when they had been in Kabul studying or working for the government. He went to see their businesses and talked with them all night, with lots of laughing about old times.

But war never stopped chasing us. Now it came to Kunduz. Small groups started fighting to control each neighborhood, exactly as had happened in Kabul. Both day and night, we heard gunfire, especially Kalashnikovs, as well as rockets and bombs. Kunduz is a very small city; gunfire at one end is easily heard at the other. We knew about war, and we guessed that these fights between factions would soon get out of control as they had in Kabul. Then it would be hard for us to leave. We had never planned to be in Kunduz anyway; our real destination was Mazar. So we decided to leave while we could. Some of our cousins did, too, after they heard our stories of how the war had trapped us in our basement in Kabul while many horrible things happened around us.

The grown-ups knew the names of all the commanders and the factions, but to me they were all the same, and I shut them out. They were the guys who were keeping me separated from Grandfather and Wakeel. That was all I needed to know about them.

Now they were about to separate me from my new cousins as well.

One morning we all got up early to say goodbye to two of my Kunduz uncles and their wives and kids, who were leaving to go over the mountain passes to northern Pakistan. It was a difficult journey, with no certainty of what they would find when they reached Pakistan. They would drive as far as they could, but they knew that they would have to leave the road at some point and go over the mountain pass on foot. They took very little with them, mostly food. We gave them some of our warm clothes from Bamyan. They would need them, along with very good shoes.

Some of my uncles decided to stay in Kunduz, hoping for the best. Some others were planning to head to Wakhan, the little finger of Afghanistan that points east, toward China, where it is very cold in all four seasons. They had summer houses there. War rarely reached Wakhan even when there was fighting in all the rest of Afghanistan.

"Let's go there," I said. "We can all go together."

My uncle was sitting on a *toshak* cushion, drinking tea. He put down his cup, leaned forward, and gave me a gentle hug. I knew that meant "no," but I wriggled free from him, though I was very fond of him, because I did not want to hear "no." But we could not go to Wakhan, my mother said, because we were not used to such cold weather.

My father had been looking for smugglers from the day we had arrived in Kunduz. Perhaps, if he had had more time, he would have been able to find one. But with the fighting coming to Kunduz, the border crossing to Tajikistan was being closed more tightly than ever, and even the smugglers would have had problems getting us out. The largest bribes that the smugglers paid to the border guards would not be enough with the war raging so near.

In the end, instead of trying to go north across the mile-wide, swift-flowing Amu Darya River, which separates Afghanistan from Tajikistan, we fled west to Mazar, where my mother had a sister, and which we had been trying to reach since we had left home six months before. We had heard on the BBC that things there had settled down for the time being. We had to travel on a small road that was usually full of bandits. But even they had fled.

My father drove very fast. I held on to the padded armrest on the door. My mother held on to the little ones but did not say anything, because she, too, wanted us to finally get to Mazar.

The fighting did not get fierce in Kunduz right away, but in the end Kunduz was destroyed as thoroughly as Kabul. We lost six of our relatives before it ended.

In Mazar, my mother's sister was very relieved to see us. My mother had sent her a letter from Kabul a week before we left, explaining that we would be coming to Mazar. Then we had been stuck in Tash-kurghan and had gone to Bamyan and Kunduz. She had no idea what had happened to us. No one did. She told us that she had written a couple of letters to Kabul, but that she had no idea whether they ever got there. No one had answered her.

Like my mother, she is a very calm person. Once she got over the excitement of seeing us, she quickly found room for us. We had visited her many times in the past and enjoyed her large house near the edge of the city, where the streets end and the open fields stretch a mile southward to a line of blue mountains that rise with no warning.

There was no sign of Wakeel. Why had he not come? I was very worried about him and Grandfather. We had had no news from any-one in Kabul in all these months of travel. I asked my aunt, hoping she had had a letter, or maybe even a phone call. But nothing.

Every day we went to the shrine of Hazrat Ali and prayed for peace in our country and to keep Mazar safe. Hazrat Ali was the cousin and son-in-law of the Prophet Mohammad, peace be upon him. Some people believe that Ali is buried in Mazar. In fact, the very name of the city—Mazar-e-Sharif—means "the very important grave." Other people say that Zoroaster, the great Aryan prophet, is buried there, too. For all these reasons, people go there to pray.

Hazrat Ali is my ancestor, so when I came to the shrine I had a special feeling of visiting an important relative, and being in a place where other relatives had done important things.

My grandfather's grandfather, Mullah Abdul Ghafor, had come to Mazar during the holy month of Ramazan for several years, and had copied the entire Holy Koran in great swirls of calligraphic script as he sat in silence for forty days in a special building next to the shrine called the Chila Khana. His Koran is now in the National Archives in Kabul. It is one of the largest ever copied. When he was getting old, he said goodbye to his sons and walked to Mecca. As he left, he told them to celebrate his death rituals when they saw an unusual white bird at the top of the minaret of the mosque near his home.

Many years later my grandfather—Mullah Abdul Ghafor's grandson—went to Mecca. According to people he met there, Mullah Abdul Ghafor was well remembered as a man of great humility, who for many years had been the cleaner of the area around the Holy Ka'bah, the House of God. The people in Mecca spoke highly of him, though years had passed since his death. In his honor, they treated my grandfather with great respect.

My grandfather told them about the white bird that had come one day to the top of the minaret, and mentioned the year and the season.

The people in Mecca said that that was when Mullah Abdul Ghafor had died.

I thought about my grandfather's grandfather and the white bird, wondering how such miraculous things could happen in this same world where we had had to flee our home to survive.

The shrine became my life. As long as I was there, my parents knew that I was safe. Some days I would study its blue and yellow tiles for hours, looking for patterns. Each one did not mean much by itself. Together, they had a big meaning and looked very beautiful. During these weeks in Mazar, though, I began to feel that my life was only a set of loose tiles and nothing more, and a deep feeling of loneliness settled over me.

I had been sure that when I reached Mazar, Wakeel would be there.

When I tried to talk with my father, he did not want to talk with me. He left the house early in the morning and came back late at night, always in a bad mood. He stopped trying to teach us school lessons.

My mother was busy either doing housework for my aunt, who went to work every day, or visiting cousins and friends. She had relatives in more than one hundred houses in Mazar, and they all wanted to see her.

There was no school. It was winter, and school would not be open until the second day of spring. Even if there had been school, we would have had to spend weeks to get our records transferred from Kabul. Our schools there, though, were closed because of the fighting, and there was no one who could send us anything.

My older sister spent most of her time with two girl cousins who were a few years older than she and a couple of other girls from the neighborhood. They spent hours together, whispering. Whenever I came close to them, they stopped talking and looked at me strangely, and asked with their eyes, "Why are you here?" If I stayed even for a minute, they would start to say things like "Hey, what do you want here? This is for girls only. Go about your own business." I tried my best not to be near her when she did not want me around, which was pretty much all the time. One day, though, I saw her in the neighbors' house when she and the other girls were putting on makeup.

They had lots of cosmetics in front of them. One was shaping her eyebrows with a pencil, another was darkening the area under her eyes, another was putting something on her eyelashes. Each one had a different color of lipstick. I was very excited, because I knew I could get my sister in trouble. But when she came home to eat, her face was scrubbed clean.

At the shrine, I asked the mullahs many questions. They always invited me to say prayers to the throne of God Almighty and told me that prayers are the key to every earthly problem. They also said that destiny shapes human life; whatsoever is written in man's destiny, that is what comes. Our complaints cannot change anything. We must embrace life happily with all its sorrows and joys.

At first, I enjoyed listening to them, but after a while, they just said the same things over and over with different words, and I got tired of it. Nothing they said could stop the war.

I never got tired, though, of being at the shrine of Hazrat Ali. I loved everything about it: the tiles that caught the sunlight and looked like gems, the towers all around it, the white pigeons outside, and especially the place where Hazrat Ali is said to be buried, under a monument full of precious stones and surrounded by a gold railing with the Holy Koran carved on it in great vines of sweeping letters.

Every day after breakfast I went there to see the pilgrims who had come from all over the country, despite the dangers of traveling in wartime. They spoke in many languages and with many accents. I liked to imitate the sounds that they made and let them roll around inside my mouth until I could turn them into words.

Later, I joined the young boys who came each afternoon to the shrine's garden to play a game called *gursai*. I remembered Grandfather's telling me how he had played in there when he was little. It was probably the same game. A boy takes his left foot in his right hand and hops about on his right leg, and using his right shoulder tries to knock down his opponent, who is advancing in the same way from the opposite direction.

I made so many new friends while playing *gursai* that I decided

I was never going to leave Mazar, even if the war came there. I had never had so many friends outside my own family before. I just wanted Wakeel and Grandfather to come soon, and I prayed for that every day. I knew that Wakeel could beat all the other boys at *gursai*.

In many ways, our life had become like a game of *gursai*, as we went hopping from one place to the next, hoping nobody would knock us down.

# 11

❖

## *My Teacher*

One day when it had snowed overnight and I was not able to go to the shrine, I stayed home. All day long, I could hear thuds coming from next door. The following day it snowed again, and the thuds continued. In fact, I had been hearing this sound from the first day we had arrived in Mazar, but I had not been home enough to pay attention to it. Finally, I asked my aunt about it.

"Those people are carpet weavers," she said. "They moved in a few months ago. They are good people, except for this noise they make."

I had learned how to make a simple carpet knot in school two years before and had made a small carpet, which I'd given to the principal of my school. He put it in a green frame in the hallway. Whenever I passed it, I felt very proud to see my name under it, even though it was not very well made. I had long wanted to learn how to weave a complicated pattern in a carpet, but I had never had anyone to teach me.

"Do they make big carpets?" I asked my aunt. "They make so much noise." When I had made my little carpet, I had not made thuds like the ones I was hearing here.

"Go and see for yourself, if you like," my aunt said.

I borrowed my aunt's sandals to walk the short distance from our gate to theirs. The snow stung my feet and went halfway up my legs inside my cotton *shalwar* pants. I began to run and was happy to see their door was open. Nobody invited me, but I ran inside anyway. In the courtyard, the snow had been shoveled away, and a warm sun was drying up the puddles left behind.

The house had big rooms. Each one held a large, flat loom that stretched out only a few inches above the floor, like a Chinese table. In the first room, about seven people were making a big carpet on a very wide loom, men and women together. They sat on the part they had already woven and leaned forward to tie the next row of knots.

They stopped when I came in, some in the middle of tying a knot. I told them I lived in my aunt's house next door. None of them said anything. I was too curious about what they were doing to feel uncomfortable.

At first, they were shy, and no one spoke to me. But when I sat next to them and tied a few knots, they relaxed when they saw that I could tie a knot correctly. They spoke softly in Turkmeni, and I did not know what they were saying. The kids were working with their parents. Everything was very different from my aunt's house, where my cousins and I spent most of our time playing games, and my older sister tried to boss me around, when she was not watching one of the Russian television channels that we did not have in Kabul. Here the kids looked at me quickly when they were speaking. Even though I did not know their language, I knew they were talking about me. Slowly, they tried speaking Dari with me, and we found a way to understand one another.

The women wore lots of jewelry. Their bracelets and bangles made music when they were pounding the weft threads tightly into place with a heavy metal comb. Their earrings hung low each time they bent forward to tie their knots. They wore rubies, pearls, and emeralds, and their clothes had these same bright colors.

I spent time tying some knots at each loom—nobody told me to stop— and I ate lunch with them, too. It would have been impolite to leave at lunchtime. They all sat around one tablecloth; it looked like they were having a party, like the dinners we had eaten in Grandfather's courtyard. At least sixty members of the Turkmen family were crowded into that house.

After lunch I went to the far end of the courtyard where I could hear a single person's combing. I opened the door and I saw a woman seated at a loom that, unlike all the others in the house, rose up in front of her. It was much smaller than the others. Though her loom had space for two people, she was alone. The other weavers in that house used ten to fifteen colors of wool. She used more than fifty. Her wool was a better quality, and her knots were much smaller than the others. She was making small geometric patterns; the others made big traditional patterns that were easy to weave.

She was a woman of unusual beauty, probably in her early twenties, with very dark and expressive eyes. When a Pashtun man sees such a beautiful woman, he becomes a poet. It is what we have been doing for thousands of years. I was far from being a man, but I quickly made a poem in my heart about her. She was paradise, and music, and charm. And she was making a magic carpet.

I said "Salaam," and she smiled in reply. I said "Salaam" again. And again she did not answer.

I took the extra hook and sat next to her. I made my first knot. She looked at me. She opened my knot and redid it. There was nothing wrong with my knot. Why did she open it, I asked myself. I made a few more knots. She continued to look at me with a silent smile. When I looked at her, she lowered her eyes, then opened my knots once again and redid them. I was a little bit annoyed, but I said nothing. After all, I was a guest. I continued making more knots, and when I finished, she opened them all and redid them.

"What is wrong with my knots? Why are they not acceptable to you?" I asked.

She smiled at me and continued tying her own knots. She was very fast. She could make sixty knots in a minute.

"It is very rude not to answer someone's question," I said in a joking kind of voice to be polite, but I meant what I said.

This time she ignored me and did not even look at me.

"What, do you think I am stupid?" I asked her. The joking voice had gone.

She smiled at me again and began combing. She slipped the teeth of the comb through the threads of the warp, and pounded the knots she had just tied with surprising force for such a delicate hand until they were snug against the row below.

"Say something, please!" I said.

But she never talked to me, and she never accepted my knots. I felt very insulted.

I got up from her loom and went to an old woman whom everyone called Mother, and I told her what had happened. She laughed at me, and I began to dislike her, too. Maybe they are all insulters, I thought.

"No, my son, she doesn't hate you, and she doesn't aim to insult you either." She spoke Dari, but with a strong Turkmeni accent, and I had to listen very carefully to understand what she was saying.

Mother sighed. "She is the sweetest of all among my children."

"But she never talked to me. She didn't even say 'Salaam,'" I said.

"Because she can't hear you," Mother said. "She is deaf. And she is mute. She is pure love, and her thoughts are even more beautiful than she is. She has never had any bad feeling for anyone. She is the happiest creature, I think."

"Is she your child?" I said.

"Yes, my youngest child," she said.

"I didn't see her at lunch," I said.

"She eats when she is hungry, not at regular times like the others. She has her own strange habits. Sometimes she sleeps for twenty-four hours, and sometimes she is awake for twenty-four hours. She never uses the same wool as we do, and she has never woven the same patterns we weave," she said.

"What kind of wool does she use?" I asked.

"Only the wool from the back of the sheep, which is finer and softer than any other. She spins her wool much finer, and she colors it with her own dyes. She makes all the dyes from plants. When we dye wool with such dyes, we often have to use some chemicals to get the right color. Not her. She uses only vegetable dyes," she said.

"Where did she learn all these things?" I asked. Mother shook her head and shrugged.

"It is her special talent. She was born with it," she replied.

"It would be very interesting to watch her make dyes from plants. My grandfather says that the best carpets have vegetable dyes," I told her.

"She doesn't let anyone watch her when she dyes. Not even me. She is very private. We want her happy, so we do not interfere," Mother said.

"Her designs are prettier than yours, and much finer," I said.

"We draw our designs on paper and have two of the boys put them on graphs. Then we work according to the graphs. But sometimes she doesn't sleep for a couple of nights, and all that time she is making a new design in her mind, as if she were drawing it on paper," Mother said.

"What are you asking my mother?" A handsome man who looked about twenty-five came out to the courtyard and knelt before his mother. In his hands was some wet wool. He was the first person I had met in that house who spoke Dari easily.

"We are speaking of your youngest sister," she replied.

"Oh, she is a real mystery," he said. "She is an unanswered question, an unsolved puzzle." He handed the wet wool to his mother and asked her something in Turkmeni. They spoke for a few minutes, then he walked to some pots nearby with fires below them and threw the wool into the pots.

He stoked the fires below the pots until they were blazing and made the dye in the pot boil. Then he took a batch of light-colored wool and dipped it in what looked like black water. It came out dark blue. Then he rinsed some gray wool in reddish water until it was a deep red, like mulberry.

The old woman took her water pipe from the shelf of the cupboard behind her. She packed it with tobacco and lit it. She sucked the smoke, and the water pipe made a bubbling noise.

"Does she read and write, your daughter?" I asked.

"How can she read or write, since she can't hear or talk? You tell me," Mother said.

"Well, because she is special and unusual," I said.

"She is special in many ways, but she doesn't read or write. She writes numbers only. To be frank with you, none of us can read and write; we are all illiterate, but we are the best carpet weavers."

I was always surprised when adults said they were illiterate. Grandfather had taught himself how to read and write both Dari and Pashto, and even Arabic. I wondered why other people could not do that.

"When she finishes her carpet, she writes the price in sand with a stick. First we thought they were very high, but later we discovered that she chose correct prices," Mother said. "When she made her first small carpet, we sold it to one of our dealers. He kept it in his shop for a year, happy to have such an unusual piece. Soon it became famous, and people who saw it in the shop started calling it Suleiman's magic carpet. That dealer became my daughter's special customer. But he does not sell her carpets to anyone. He thinks her carpets are holy," she said.

"No," I said. "I don't believe it."

"It sounds strange, doesn't it? First we didn't believe it either, but his wife told us that he spends at least one hour of every morning in a room where he keeps them. He does not allow anyone else to go into that room," she said, puffing some smoke out of the pipe.

"Can I buy one of your daughter's carpets?" I asked.

"Don't ask me. Go and talk to her yourself. We have never interfered in her business. You should also talk to her customer. He says they are beyond value. That is why he never sells them," she said.

"So that means he has never used them either," I said with amazement.

"Exactly. He says they are not for use. They are made to be worshipped," she said, and breathed out another plume of smoke.

"Do you think he is right?" I said.

"No, not for a minute. It is all delusions," she said. "He says she is another sun in the earth, and his eyes sting when he looks at her. My daughter is only my daughter, not the sun. But I have seen that his eyes hurt when he looks at her. Tears start dropping after two minutes only."

"I wonder if I could work with her to learn a few things?" I said excitedly.

"Take an ablution, then you can work with her. Tie small knots, and don't make mistakes. And don't waste wool. These are her rules, and she will let you work with her for as long as you want. But be careful, she can read your mind, too," she said as she began sucking her water pipe once more.

"I never saw anyone take ablution to make a carpet." I laughed. "I'm not praying or going to the mosque. I just want to tie a few knots with her."

"That is her rule. If you want to work with her, respect her rules," Mother said.

I went to their bathroom. I did the ablutions for my head and my hands, splashing the water above my wrists, almost to my elbows. I skipped those for my feet, since it was so cold. I went to the daughter's loom and sat down next to her. When I picked up the hook, she grabbed it from me and she told me with hand gestures that my ablutions were not completed.

I went back to Mother and angrily asked whether her daughter was spying on me while I was taking my ablutions.

"I told you that she can read your mind," she said, grinning. "She knows more than you think. Be honest and truthful with her."

This time I took a complete ablution. I went back, sat down as before, and this time she let me work with her.

The minute I sat next to her, I felt something unusual, something inexpressible. Although I did not know as much about carpets then as I do now, the carpet on her loom was unlike any other I had ever seen. She had started with the basic geometric patterns that Turkmen people have woven for centuries. Inside each one was a small floral pattern like those that Iranian weavers have perfected. The scrolling vines and flowers just seemed to grow out of the geometrics and wind around them as if they were a trellis. Because she was using more than fifty colors, the flowers almost looked three-dimensional, like a wood carving.

After I tied a few knots I looked at her face, which was so beautiful. She had such transparent eyes that it seemed possible to look straight through them. Sometimes I found myself staring at her. This made her uneasy, and she narrowed her eyes, twisted her head away. It was her way of asking me not to stare at her.

Whenever I tried to tie knots fast like she did, she pressed on my forehead with her index finger, smiled, and shook her head. She was telling me not to try to compete with her. I tried hard to be as fast, but it was impossible. She motioned for me to fill in the areas of a solid color, and showed me which shade to use.


I stopped going to the Hazrat Ali shrine except to pray on Fridays, and I forgot about my *gursai* friends. I had found someone who was quickly becoming as important to me as Grandfather and Wakeel.

Every night I told my family about the carpet weavers next door. My father was not interested. He was listening to the BBC, as always. But my aunt told me many things about them. She explained that a lot of the Turkmen people had come to Afghanistan when the Russians were making problems for them in their own country. And many others had been here from long before.

"They are the ones who brought carpet making to Afghanistan from Central Asia somewhere. That was centuries ago."

"The best carpets made in Afghanistan are made by these people," my mother added, "especially by the women."

I wondered who was cooking for the kids, if they were all making carpets.

"They marry in their early teens, and become mothers of large families before they are thirty," my aunt went on. "They spend most of their lives on their looms, from early childhood until they become grandmothers. They are always competing to see who is the best carpet maker. People tell me that they can tie as many as ten thousand knots a day," my aunt said boastfully, as if she were one of them, "because they have small fingers."

Every night, I had a dream about the young woman. I could hear her speaking very clearly to me then. Sometimes she teased me, and I teased her back. That never actually happened when I was sitting next to her. We were serious about our work. Though she was more than ten years older than I, it would have been unusual for an eleven-year-old boy like myself to be allowed to spend time alone with a young woman like her, at least among Pashtuns. But Turkmen, like the Hazaras, are more practical than strict. These people knew my aunt well. She was highly respected throughout her neighborhood and was always doing kind things, such as bringing medicines to the neighbors when they were sick, though she had no medical training. They expected me to be as decent and polite as she was.

Whenever I needed to ask my teacher something, I just looked at her and she knew I had a question. The first time I asked one, I spoke very loudly. She smiled and let me know that I did not need to shout. She drew her finger across her lips, then pointed at her eyes and then my mouth, indicating that she could read my lips.

She conveyed information to me mostly with her hands, though she could make perhaps a dozen different sounds. In the first days before I understood her gestures, she sometimes got red with frustration when she was trying to tell me something, such as "Go and do your ablutions." When I thought I had understood what she was saying, I would repeat it slowly to her. She would watch my lips. If she shook her head from side to side, I would have to try again.

I discovered that she did not like to be asked several questions at once. So when I did ask her a question, I waited until she was ready to answer it, even if that meant a few hours later, or a few days. Anyway, we could not talk much while we were working, because our hands were busy tying knots. But if she stopped to eat lunch, or when we had finished for the day and she was sending me home after the *muezzin* called the *azan*, then she would respond.

By the second week, I had to repeat what she said less and less often, maybe only once in five times. In the third week, it was almost as if we were talking normally. When I was with her, hours melted away, and then she was telling me that I had to go home so she could say her prayers. It was only when I looked out the window that I realized it was almost dark. Day after day went by this way. My parents were happy I had found a hobby where I could learn new things and enjoy my time, but they never said much about it. They were relieved that I was not wandering in the streets, making friends with boys whose families they did not know.

Strangely, my older sister had nothing to say about it either. But our cousins, who were the same ages as some of the kids in my teacher's family and knew them, often teased me. They whispered into my ears things like "I know you are in love with her," as well as some other vulgar things that made me feel very shy. There were too many of them for me to challenge, so as soon as they started saying those things, I walked out of the room to their loud laughter. I turned red and could not dare to face them for hours.

One thing I wanted to know was how my teacher invented her designs. She explained that she studied many other carpets before she made a design of her own. When I asked whether she took the patterns from other carpets, she firmly shook her head "No."

She then tried to tell me what she had in her mind when she was creating a design. But she could see that I did not understand what she meant. She took the hook she used for pulling the carpet threads through the strings of the loom and started drawing odd shapes in the dust of the courtyard. They looked almost like Chinese letters. I really did not know what they were.

"Are those some kind of patterns?" I asked, pointing first at what she had drawn, and then at a design on a carpet. She shook her head emphatically.

Suddenly I said, "Signs?" I do not know why, or where that word came from. But she smiled and nodded vigorously. She went on to convey to me that if I wanted to design carpets, I must never just copy. I should be creative, and there would be no limit to the designs I could invent.

I never really knew what she meant by "signs," nor could I ever truly understand the connection between the shapes she drew in the dirt and the patterns she wove on the loom.

She taught me how to graph a design on paper. I explained to her I could weave a traditional large, octagonal, dark blue *fil poi* (elephant foot) motif from memory, having included one on my carpet that had hung in my old school, but she insisted that I use a graph until I had woven a pattern many times, especially when weaving a complicated design of my own. I never saw her use a graph herself, but it was a good lesson, and one that in time would help my family and me survive.

As I got better at tying knots, I began trying to compete with the other weavers my age, and the ones younger than I, in a friendly way. Maybe I was just trying to show off. I was faster than a few of them, and desperate for some kind of attention. My father did not even see me anymore. I wanted somebody to notice that I could do something well.

Whenever she saw that I was trying really hard, she looked at me and smiled. Sometimes my fingers got tired, but her smile was more precious to me than my hands. My hunger for it turned me into one of the fastest weavers in her house.

As I watched my teacher's carpet take shape, I sometimes had dreams of Suleiman's magic carpet at night. Suleiman, they said, was given so much power by Allah that not only was he very wise, he also could rule over the beasts, the evil spirits known as *jinns*, and other creatures that we cannot see. And he could order his carpet to lift from the earth and carry him anywhere he wanted to go. I wanted to go high in the sky and fly to beautiful places. But mostly I wanted to go up to the best kites, cut them, and bring them to our courtyard, so Wakeel and I could fly them.

On Fridays, she did not work and her family always had guests. Once I went, but she was very busy with other girls, laughing often. I felt jealous that they were with her and I could not be, and I ran out. The next Friday, she saw me and introduced me to them. I felt pleased that she had allowed me to meet them. But once I had done that, I felt shy to be with the women and excused myself and ran back to my aunt's house. Anyway, my aunt always made a big lunch on Fridays.

On the other days, though, I was happy to eat with my teacher's family. They ate at exactly 12:30 p.m., while in my aunt's house there was no fixed time, which I never liked.

Everybody had a job. The boys prepared the eating cloth in the middle of the floor of a large room that had no loom. They spread the bread around the cloth along with plates, spoons, napkins. The girls brought the bowls of food from the kitchen.

We sat around one large cloth. Mother and the other adults all sat at one end. The boys sat along the sides, three or four eating from one bowl or a large plate. The girls sat from the middle to the bottom, doing the same. Everyone seemed to talk at once. I did not understand a word, only that they were really loud and talked very fast. When Mother spoke, though, they all listened.

When we finished eating, the boys and girls collected everything together and took them to the kitchen, where Mother washed the dishes as she hummed or sang Turkmeni songs softly. Then she came back to her place, loaded her water pipe, and smoked for a time before we all went back to work.

A couple of times, they invited me to stay with them for dinner. I ran to my aunt's house, told my mother that I would eat next door, and ran back. They cooked over the fire in the courtyard. Even in the cold winter while there were mountains of snow all over the court-yard, the girls gathered around the fire, cooking, chatting, and enjoy-ing one another's company, dressed in their colorful clothes. The boys had a circle of their own around another large pot, mostly showing the power of their arms to one another. The grown-ups drank tea around the large woodstoves inside, laughing and shouting for more tea. And the younger ones ran one pot after another to them.

When it was time to eat, they all gathered around one cloth, as at lunch. Everybody took a piece from a large homemade *naan* while waiting for the food to arrive. First came small bowls of soup, made of seasoned vegetables along with chickpeas, beans, corn, and smashed wheat. Then there were large round plates of delicious *qabli pelau*. My mother is a good cook, but I will never forget that *qabli pelau*. Then bowls of meat cooked with potatoes. Then an enormous salad. Then a large bowl of yogurt. And finally jugs of water with glasses. As soon as the grown-ups took their first bites, the others followed their lead.

For the first few minutes nobody talked. All you could hear was the sound of spoons against the plates, and noisy sounds of chewing, as if they had not eaten for years. As the plates became half-empty, joking and laughing rose above the noise of eating.

Once, when my teacher ate with the rest of the family, I watched as she "talked" as much as the other girls with her limited sounds, signs, hand gestures. They were quick in understanding her. She even must have told jokes, because from time to time they all laughed at something she had conveyed to them. I enjoyed watching her laugh, which made her more and more beautiful to me.

The grown-ups leaned back on their huge pillows and asked for more tea and sweets, while the girls collected the plates. The boys folded the tablecloth. Then one of them brought a pitcher of water and a large bowl for everyone to wash their hands, followed by another boy carrying small towels.

After the girls washed the dishes in the courtyard near the fire, they collected some charcoal in a pot and covered it with ash. They brought the pot inside, set a small table over it, and covered it all with a large quilt. Then they tucked themselves around the table and pulled the quilt all the way up to their necks, leaning back on the pillows behind them. Warm, they gossiped and giggled as they ate sweets, especially the sesame-filled meringue known as *conjit* that is famous in Mazar.

The grown-ups soon left for their beds. The boys sat around the woodstove and were warned strictly to not make more fire, so they would have enough wood left to last the rest of the winter. As soon as the grown-ups started snoring in their rooms, the boys sneaked in more wood. They drank tea and played cards, winning small amounts of money from one another, sometimes shouting at one not to cheat, and the girls hushed them.

A TV was on for as long as there was electricity, but nobody watched it. As soon as the electricity went off, the girls brought lanterns and lit them.

This continued until midnight, when they finally went to bed so they wouldn't fall asleep on the loom, tying one knot after another and, as they said, "making a wall with knots of thin wool." From the sounds we heard through the wall of my aunt's house, they seemed to have feasts like this every night.

After a few months in Mazar, my father heard on the BBC that the leaders of the various factions were holding an assembly for peace. They said they would go to Mecca and take an oath together that they would not fight with one another anymore. My father said it was time for us to go to Kabul, to go home. We were all very happy, especially me. I wanted to tell Grandfather and Wakeel and my other cousins about all we had done and seen.

Early the next morning I told my carpet teacher about our leaving. I delayed telling her until the last minute because I thought that my father might change his mind. When I went to see her, the car was already waiting outside for me. She looked at me for a few seconds. Quite unexpectedly, her eyes filled with tears.

We could communicate now as if we could speak with our voices. She told me to use my mind skillfully, and I would be a brilliant carpet weaver and have a successful carpet business one day.

I kissed her hands in the custom of showing respect for a teacher, and she blessed the top of my head with a kiss. Then I said goodbye to her family, and she escorted me to the courtyard gate, where we said our goodbyes. I started missing her even as we were waving to each other.

I remembered one of Grandfather's sayings, "Love makes the old feel young, and it makes the young feel like a child. If you separate the lover from his beloved, they both feel destroyed."

I felt a little bit destroyed, but the destructions were inside me, and only I could feel them, nobody else. This was a time for rebuilding.

The fighting was over, and we would help Grandfather rebuild our house. We did not need to go to another country. We would fly kites again from the roof. We would all sit around one cloth for dinner. And Wakeel and I would never have to be separated again. It was a time for joy.

But at that moment, as I settled into the front seat and we headed toward Kabul, I felt a deep sense of emptiness that increased as mile after mile separated me from my teacher.

# 12

❖

## *Caravan*

Once again we were on the road, but for the last time. The sky was clear; the sun was bright. Winter had ended and quietly turned to spring while we had been distracted by our life in Mazar. Everything was turning green. The peach, almond, and apricot trees had clouds of pink blossoms filled with humming bees. The sparrows' *chuk-chuk* calls were everywhere.

We said little as the car moved away from Mazar. We were all lost in our own thoughts.

I was already thinking of when I might come back and see my carpet teacher again. Perhaps she would teach me how to dye the wool the way she did. Then I thought of my school, my classmates, my cousins, and all the things that I would tell them about, what I had seen and been through. And I wondered what they had been doing.

My father was probably thinking how he would start his life again with all his carpets gone and his gym in ruins. I had heard my mother tell her sister in Mazar that she missed going to her job. Maybe she was thinking about the bank, and whether she would find her job waiting for her when we got back. She had never quit. But like most people in Kabul, she had just stopped going when it became too dangerous to move around the city. That was nearly a year ago now.

No one talked, not even my littlest sister, whom we called "the chatterbox." And the crying machine was silent, too. The truth is, it had been a long time since he had been a crying machine, but somehow the name stuck to him even though he had a nice row of teeth now. That morning he was looking out the window and smiling at everything he saw.

Mazar was soon behind us. The road had bumps now. Holes were everywhere from the rockets, but the earth was damp from the spring rains, and in some places we could see grass where there was only desert the rest of the year.

Two hours later, we passed through Tashkurghan. The road goes around the village, on the side of the hill. We all looked down as we passed to see if we could spot the garden where I had stolen the pomegranates. We wondered what had happened to that kind family in the months since we had seen them, but we were too much in a hurry to return to our own home to stop and visit theirs.

For another hour or more we moved across the low, sandy hills of Samangan Province toward the Hindu Kush. Suddenly my father was shouting, "Hold on! Everybody hold on!"

My mother grabbed the little ones. "What's wrong?"

"The brakes are not working. Something's broken."

He kept pumping the brake pedal, but the car kept moving at high speed.

"Relax, relax," my mother said. "Let the car slow down on its own."

A few minutes later the road leveled out, and the car began to slow down. My father eased it over to the side of the road, where it stopped. He let out a sigh of relief and jumped out and checked under the hood.

"The brake fluid box is empty," my father said. "We can't go anywhere without brakes, but they won't work unless we find some brake fluid."

My mother looked around at the empty land and asked in her usual practical way, "Where will you find brake fluid?"

"We should wait for a car to pass by, and I'll borrow some. Just enough to take us to the next town," my father said.

We waited on the roadside for two hours, but no car passed, only a group of Kuchi nomads who stirred up a huge cloud of dust as they drove their cattle across the unpaved road and moved on up the hillside to pasture their herds. Every time we saw nomads, they re-minded me of Grandfather. I have always thought that being a nomad is the best way to live, constantly moving from place to place, away from city troubles.

My father took his teacup from the dashboard and told us that he would be back in a few minutes, and then headed toward the Kuchis. We watched him as he went farther and farther off until he stood in front of a herd boy who was sitting on a big rock, blowing his flute. We watched as the herd boy got up from the rock, milked one of his sheep, and filled my father's cup. My father came back with a cup of milk in his hand and a funny smile on his face.

"What are you going to do with a cup of milk? It is not enough for all of us," my mother said.

"But it is enough for our car to quench its thirst. This time, our car will drink milk," my father said.

He poured the cup of milk into the brake fluid box, then he started the car. He drove a short distance and braked.

"Our problem is solved," he shouted excitedly from his window. He put the car in reverse and backed up very fast to where we were standing, then hit the brakes. The car threw up a plume of dust.

We all climbed back in the car and headed for the town of Saman-gan up ahead, where we would get lunch. We went to a local restau-rant in the heart of town with beautiful views on all sides. We ate kebabs and drank tea, then headed back to the car to continue our journey toward Kabul. I was still thinking about my carpet teacher, and the unexpected combinations of many bright colors that she used in her carpets, instead of only the deep reds and dark blues that most other Turkmen carpet weavers used.

My father tried to start the car, but it sounded broken. He checked the engine but could find no problem. He did not know very much about cars, anyway. Maybe the car did not like the taste of milk, I thought.

I asked the owner of the restaurant whether there was a mechanic shop around. He told me that there was one a quarter mile to the south.

My mother and my sisters went back inside the restaurant while my father and I pushed the car all the way to the mechanic shop. It was a small, shabby place with old tires and used spare parts all around.

There were more than fifty cars and trucks in a long line waiting to be fixed.

A guy whose face was completely blackened with oil shouted at us. "Hey, hey, hey, stop, stop! Where the hell are you putting that car?"

"Our car is broken," my father said.

"Are you blind? Can't you see these other cars and trucks?" the mechanic said.

"No, I'm not blind, I can see them, but what is that supposed to mean?" my father asked.

"It means your car will be fixed after I finish fixing these cars," the mechanic said.

"You must be joking," my father said.

"I don't make jokes with my work, and I don't have time for talking. Either park your car at the end of the line over there, and come back in two months, or get your car out of my sight," the mechanic said. My father shifted from one foot to the other, as he did when he was about to enter a boxing ring. He looked directly at the mechanic and spoke softly and urgently.

"I'm with my wife and kids. We have been on the road for almost eight months. You have no idea what we have been through. Now we're finally able to go home to Kabul. Please fix my car. It worked perfectly well until an hour ago. We don't have any house here, and we don't have relatives to stay with. I don't have enough money to pay for a hotel for two months," my father said.

"Look, I don't know you. My job is to fix people's cars. It doesn't matter whose car I'm fixing. But I have to fix these cars first, then it is your turn. Some of them have been here for months. If I spend all day today fixing your Russian Volga, tomorrow my other customers will kick my ass," the mechanic said.

"So I have to wait for two months for my car to be fixed?" my father said.

"Exactly," the mechanic said.

"It is not possible," my father said. His voice was tight in a way I had rarely heard it.

"Look, I understand your problem, but you should understand my problem, too. Most of these cars belong to warlords. If I don't fix their cars by exact dates, they'll put their guns up my ass and shoot. I have a wife and kids, too, and they need me."

"Is there any other mechanic around?" my father said.

"There were five in this town, but the bastards ran away because of this fucking civil war," the mechanic said.

"If you're the only mechanic in this town, you must be making a lot of money then," my father said, trying to tell a joke and make the mechanic his friend.

"Oh, fuck the kind of money that comes with threats from war-lords," the mechanic said.

"Oh, this is very sad," my father sighed.

"Yeah, it is really fucking sad," the mechanic said. "Excuse my language, young man." He pointed to me. I did not answer, and just smiled at him. I found it very entertaining the way he talked. I had not heard many people in Kabul talking that way.

"Can you just take a look at my car, and see if it is anything that I can fix?" my father asked.

"Yeah, let's see," the mechanic said, relenting a little.

The mechanic opened the hood, climbed up on top of the grille, and squatted over the engine block. He spent ten minutes probing the engine, checking dipsticks, pulling on belts.

"It needs a few days' work," he said as he climbed down. "So, in this case it has to wait its turn, and that's going to be two months, at least."

"What is the problem?" my father asked, very surprised.

"You used bad gasoline that was full of sand. Now the sand is all through the engine. I will have to open even the smallest parts to clean them," the mechanic said.

My father sighed deeply, and with the mechanic's help we pushed the car to the end of the line. As my father and I walked unhappily back to the restaurant, his face was once again drowned in worries; a cloud of sorrows surrounded him.

We rented a room above the restaurant and spent the night there. My father could not sleep at all. Every ten minutes I heard him sighing until I fell asleep. I woke up early in the morning and saw big brown bags under his eyes. He looked very tired as he gazed at the mountains through the window.

As we were eating breakfast my father said, "I have enough money to feed us for a week, and after that God knows what is next."

"Let God take care of things. He can see us. He will help us, as always," my mother said.

"Maybe you're right, I should not worry so much," my father said with a heavy sigh. But he remained deeply anxious.

After breakfast my father went to the mechanic's shop to see whether he could find a solution. My mother and my sisters stayed in the second-floor room. But I wanted to get away from the smoke that filled the room from the restaurant below, where they cooked kebab from early in the morning until late at night. The restaurant always had customers.

I took one of my younger sisters and walked up the slope behind the restaurant. We sat on a large rock surrounded by mountain grass near the road. We had a sweeping view of the rounded hills that stretched for several miles until they became mountains in the distance. Everything was green in those early days of spring. I counted more than twenty shades of green and wondered how to capture them in a carpet.

I could hear the songs of a donkey driver from the bazaar and the flute of a herd boy from the hillsides. The whole land seemed ready to burst into song. I saw the girls from the town going down to a stream to fill their pitchers with water. They wore their best clothes. Young men stole glances at the girls as they walked past with their pitchers on their heads.

When the villagers passed us, they saw that we were strangers. They made *salaam*s to me, and some of them shook our hands. They all invited us to their houses. They all seemed very hospitable and sincere. No one seemed to be in a hurry, and their deep peace created an air of timelessness. They had a world of their own, calm, serene, and indifferent to what was going on anywhere else.

The next day I went again to the same spot. I found the herd boy there with his sheep and goats pasturing around him. He looked about my age. He was sitting on the big, round rock where we had been sitting the day before, blowing his flute. I said "*Salaam*," and sat next to him. He said "*Salaam alaikum*," somewhat formally, and hurriedly hid his flute under his shirt.

"I heard the sound of your flute yesterday. I tried to find you. You play very beautifully, like the masters on the radio," I said.

"You liked it?" he shyly asked. He lowered his eyes.

"Oh, yes. I love the sound of a flute, especially when I am hearing someone who plays as well as you," I said.

He spoke to me in Pashto, and I replied in Dari, but we could understand each other.

He took his flute out from under his shirt and started playing again. His hands were shaking a little. He played a few traditional Afghan songs.

"I only know these four or five songs. If you know better songs, play them for me. I want to hear them from you," he said.

"No thanks, I can't play," I said. "My father plays well, but I never learned."

"It is very easy to play," he said. "Sing me any song, then I can play it for you," he said.

I sang an Indian song. We laughed, and then he played it. We did that several times until we got tired of it.

As we sat there, he started making letters in the sand with his shepherd stick. After a few moments, I could read "Omar Khan."

"Who is Omar Khan?" I asked.

"It is my name," he said. "Can you read and write?"

"Of course I can," I said, surprised by his question.

"I know how to write my name only," Omar Khan said. "Can you teach me how to read and write?"

"Yeah, it is not a big deal. I'll teach you how to read and write, and you teach me how to play the flute," I said.

"Done!" he said as we shook hands.

I wrote five Dari letters in the sand. I pronounced them and he repeated them after me. Then he wrote them again, several times. By then it was midday, and I had to go to the restaurant to eat lunch with my family. As I said goodbye, he asked me to come back after my lunch. I did, and he was there waiting for me, with his sheep and goats quietly grazing around him. I taught him five more Dari letters. By the end of the day he had learned them all.

The next day we met again, and I asked him about his life. He told me that he was a Kuchi boy. I told him that my grandmother was a Kuchi long ago, and that my grandfather had been a shepherd when he was young, had lived with my grandmother's Kuchi family for a year after he married her, and had traveled with them all over Afghanistan.

A broad smile appeared on his face. He looked at me for a few seconds without saying anything, and then he said, "We are cousins!"

He jumped up from his stone, grabbed my wrist, and pulled me after him. "Let me introduce you to your other cousins over there," he said, pointing toward several long black tents hung with colorful bands down by the river. The tents were surrounded by children, goats, sheep, and camels, along with some donkeys and horses. The children and the baby goats were running in and out between the legs of the camels as if they were pillars carved from stone.

As soon as I walked into the Kuchi camp, I was overwhelmed by the strong smell of animals, which were all over the place. Girls my age and older, dressed in bright red, blue, and green, rushed inside their black and gray tents as soon as they saw me. I knew I was not supposed to look at them, but I could not help looking at the long woven bands strung across the tents.

Then I saw the men, all staring at me. They were tall and muscular, with dark eyes, thick eyebrows, and long hair. They were dressed in khaki-colored *shalwar kamiz*. All wore turbans or hats. Some had long daggers hanging from their waists that looked like swords. There were several men near a tent cutting large chunks from a cow they had just slaughtered. Their clothes were bloody. They stopped when they saw me. Boys my age came out of their tents as Omar Khan and I walked farther into the camp.

About a hundred pairs of eyes were staring at me. I began to feel a little nervous and somewhat shy. Old women slowly emerged from their tents and added their curious eyes to my discomfort. Apart from them, I did not see any other women anywhere, as they all remained inside their tents. I was only eleven, but because we had not had very much to eat for many months, I was very thin, which made me look taller. The women could see that I was a stranger, and they must have thought I was a man.

All around me, I was surrounded by Kuchis. Nobody spoke. The only sounds were kids crying inside some of the tents, and some sheep that were baaing and cows that were mooing. The baby goats kept jumping and running after one another, paying no attention to the people as they played with the chickens and the cats.

I looked at Omar Khan. Unlike the others, he had a big smile on his face and was completely at ease. He introduced me to his father, Amir Khan. His father looked at me sternly for a long moment, then gave me a big, welcoming hug. As he wrapped his arms around me, I could see over his shoulder that all the faces in the camp were growing big smiles. Now I did not feel like a stranger anymore. I felt like I was at home. Their smiles had the warmth of my grandfather's smile. The men all looked like they were my uncles.

After hugging Amir Khan, I had to do the same with all the other men and boys my age and older. Then I kissed the old women's hands as a sign of respect. They kissed me on the head in return, and rubbed their right hands on my head in blessing.

I was filled with excitement and wished I had known these people all my life. I had very unexpectedly entered the world of my grandmother, whom I had never known but had always wondered about. I wanted to tell Grandfather everything that was happening.

Omar Khan's father asked me to introduce him to my father, and I took him to the restaurant. My father talked to him in Pashto in the Kuchi manner, which is very loud, like you are shouting at each other instead of speaking. The boy's father was very happy to hear my father talk as he did. He asked my father about his ancestors and figured out that my father's great-grandfathers and the man's great-grandfathers truly were distant cousins. So that meant we were all part of the same family.

My father and the man hugged each other warmly. Then the man kissed me and my sisters and told us to call him uncle, and he called my mother "sister." Straightaway, he invited us to his tent. He would not let us stay in that restaurant for one more minute. He helped us collect our stuff. An hour later we were in a Kuchi tent, drinking green tea, with more than a hundred men, women, and kids watching us.

Their tents were dark inside. They were made from black goat hair that had been pounded into long, wide strips of felt and stretched across a wooden framework that could be taken down easily, folded, and carried on the backs of camels. A single tent could shelter a very big family. During the day it furnished shade; at night its sides could be lowered to give protection from the cold and wind. From a distance, an encampment of Kuchi tents stretched long, black, and low across the dry land.

Their life was measured in their herds of camels, sheep, and goats, and in the passage of the seasons and the years as they moved their herds from one grazing place to the next, from one end of Afghanistan to the other.

Omar Khan introduced my older sister and me to more than forty kids. They wore ragged, dirty clothes. They looked like they had not washed for months. He told the other kids that we were their cousins. I wondered how many more cousins I had whom I did not know. Finding so many cousins from my mother's family in Kunduz had been a big surprise. Now here were all these Kuchi cousins from my father's family who looked at us with wide eyes, but said nothing.

Omar Khan's father, Amir Khan, set up a new tent and put all our belongings inside. Like on many of the other tents, colorful, long woven bands were hung on the outside of ours. Then he invited my father and me to another big tent, where we found all the Kuchi men. My father said "Salaam" and embraced them all. I imitated him. They tied a turban on my father's head and gave him handmade slippers. Amir Khan put an embroidered hat on my head and called me Qais Khan. And a few hours later we ate with the Kuchi men while my mother and sisters ate with the Kuchi women in another tent.

We ate Kuchi bread-cake, spiced rice, kebab, and thick Kuchi-style yogurt. I could see that my new uncles and cousins were very fond of meat. Amir Khan said a Pashto proverb as his mouth was full of kebab: "Even burnt meat is better than vegetables." And the rest laughed. After dinner we drank green tea and ate dried melon until midnight. In every sentence they used a proverb. Some of them started their sentences with a verse or two from a famous poet.

At midnight we went to our tent, which we found full of Kuchi women surrounding my mother and sisters. My mother was telling them about our travels since we had fled Kabul.

A few minutes later, they all left us to sleep. My mother blew out the lantern that they had given to us, which is called a "hurricane," though we have never had a hurricane storm in Afghanistan. Some foreigners had brought us that word along with the lanterns. My mother and father slept in one corner with my little brother. My sisters slept in another corner, and I slept in a corner of my own. Before long, though, my whole body began itching, like I was having some kind of reaction to a drug. My father whispered to my mother that something was biting him. My sisters and I shouted that something was biting us, too.

I lit the hurricane lamp and looked at my legs. An army of tiny grayish insects were all over me, jumping and hopping like they were playing *gursai*. I hurriedly shook them off. My mother told me to take off my clothes outside of the tent and shake them there. I went outside, tearing off my clothes. A minute later I was naked and shaking my clothes as hard as I could.

I heard someone giggling. I looked all around me, but I did not see anyone. All the tents were dark and quiet, and the sky was very starry with no moon. I heard the giggling again as I continued shaking my clothes. This time it was more than one person's voice. I looked to my right, and I saw nobody. Then I looked to my left, and saw a group of kids hiding behind a tent and laughing. I narrowed my eyes to see whether they were really there and took a step toward them; I saw more than twenty kids, including Omar Khan, staring at my naked body. I ran quickly inside our tent without stopping to put on my clothes before I entered.

"What the hell are you doing?" my father shouted.

I saw that my mother and my sisters were staring at me. I was deeply embarrassed and quickly ran outside as I heard my sisters laughing. Then the Kuchi kids started giggling and looking at me again.

I walked toward them, still naked, and stood before them with my clothes slung over my shoulder. I was angry now, and I did not care who looked at me, although it is very shameful to be naked in front of another person.

"What the hell are you laughing at?" I demanded.

They became quiet for a second, then ran off laughing very loudly. I put on my clothes. The itching had stopped for the moment, and I went back to our tent, wondering how to face my father, mother, and sisters. I thought about the day that Wakeel and I had seen Haji Noor Sher after his bath and made fun of him. Maybe I was being punished for laughing then.

"What is wrong with you?" my father said.

"When I was shaking out my clothes, a lot of kids were looking at me. I panicked, and without thinking I ran inside," I said.

"All right, go to your bed and sleep. Be careful next time," my father said.

My sisters were still giggling. I looked back at them fiercely, daring them to tease me in the morning, and they started to laugh openly. My father shouted at them to shut up, and this made them laugh even louder.

I lay on my bed, angry and bitten, but before long I was asleep. I was glad that Grandfather was not there to see me. He would have made jokes about that night for the rest of my life.

I woke up later than usual. There was no one else in our tent. I found Omar Khan outside giving orders to the other kids. When the kids saw me, they grinned. I greeted them and asked Omar Khan about my family. First, he laughed a little about the night before. Then he told me that my family was in the stream, bathing.

I asked him about the insects that had been biting me.

"Those are fleas from the sheep and goats and camels," he said. "You will soon get used to them."

Get used to them? I thought. How does someone get used to fleas?

I went to the stream nearby. My father was in the water in his underwear. He was splashing around as if he were in a warm bathtub. He told me to jump in. I took off all my clothes except my underpants and jumped in. It was freezing, and I yelped. My father laughed as I ran out of the water, where the wind made me even colder. I started shivering. My feet were muddy and there was no towel to dry myself.

I looked for my father to ask him for his towel, but he was no longer in the stream. Suddenly, he was behind me, pushing me into the water. It felt even colder than before. My father was standing above me and laughing as I shivered.

"You are a Kuchi now," he said. "So you have to learn how to live like a Kuchi." I slammed my open palm across the top of the water and drove a wave of freezing river water into his face. He laughed and dove for me, while I wriggled out of his way. When I landed a fist against his left shoulder, his eyes lit up.

"Okay, now we are going to be boxers!" he exclaimed as he started fending off every punch I aimed at him. Sometimes I stumbled backward when one of his blocks hit me squarely. He was laughing. I was laughing. He was my father again, but this time he was not letting me beat him. After I began tiring, he grabbed me to pull me out of the water, and it turned into a big hug like I had not had from him in months.

An hour later we were back in our tent having our breakfast. We had tea, milk, butter, yogurt, and bread. After breakfast Omar Khan took me to an empty tent. There, to my amazement, was a blackboard and a piece of chalk. When I asked him where he had found these things, he just laughed. He left me there and ran outside and whistled three times. A moment later he came back in with more than twenty other boys. Each had a notebook and a pencil. Once again Omar Khan introduced me to his cousins—my cousins, too—and told them that from today I would be their teacher. Omar Khan ordered everyone to sit in a line on the dusty ground. Then he asked me to write the Dari letters on the blackboard.

Everything happened so fast that I had no chance to think about it. I did what he asked. The boys became very quiet and started copying what I had written on the blackboard.

"Teacher, what do these signs mean?" asked a boy who was older than I.

I felt a strange shyness, because he called me "Teacher." My father was a teacher. No one had ever called me a teacher before. I cleared my throat with a fake cough, then I said, "These are Dari letters. All together, they make the alphabet. If you learn them, you can read and write."

I pronounced each letter. They repeated them after me. Then I checked everyone's notebook for mistakes. I remembered my teacher had done the same to me and my classmates. But that was in a real class where we sat on chairs and wore clean clothes.

Their handwriting was straggling, but not large. Most of them wrote very tiny to save space in their notebooks for the next lessons, since they were not given money often to buy books and pens.

A few hours later our class ended. I thought that if Grandfather were here, he would have been very proud of me. I ran to our tent to tell my mother that I was now a teacher. My mother was sitting outside of the tent, milking a cow. I was shocked. I had never seen my mother milking a cow before. She had been born into a wealthy family who had servants to do this kind of work. I asked when she had learned to do that. She smiled and said, "About twenty minutes ago!"

She looked sideways at me with her cheek against the side of the cow and asked me, "Am I doing this right?"

"No, you are squirting the milk onto the ground, not in the pot," I said.

She looked down and started laughing. The cow kicked the pot, and the milk spilled onto the ground, where the thirsty earth drank it quickly. The cow walked away as if she did not like to hear us laughing. Maybe she thought she had been insulted.

A Kuchi woman who was very beautiful was sitting next to my mother, rocking a large clay pot. It had a small opening at the top and I could not see inside it. Something in the pot was sloshing loudly. I asked the woman what she was doing.

"It is whey, for lunch, and it is good for putting you to sleep," she said. "The rest we will eat tonight," she added, nodding at the pot.

As I was talking to my mother, I heard a crowd of girls pronouncing "Alef, bey, pey, tey, sey, jem, hey, khey, dal, zal, rey, zey . . ." These were the first letters of the Dari alphabet. The sound was coming from inside our tent. I entered and saw my older sister in front of a blackboard with ten Dari letters already written on it. She pronounced the letters, and the Kuchi girls repeated them after her. My sister had become a teacher, too.

From then on, all the Kuchi kids called my sister and me "Teacher," even though most of them were older than we were.

A week later, my class and my sister's class held a reading and writing competition. It was just simple words using the letters everybody knew. My class won, and two days after, we had another. This time, my class lost. Every day, the Kuchi kids were getting better and better. They were very fast learners and drew the letters in the dirt whenever they had a free second during the day. They had their own competitions, one on one, and soon they were writing words we had not yet taught them, though full of spelling errors.

My father thought it was very funny to have so many new teachers in the family. Every night he asked us what we had done, but he never tried to tell us how to do it. Meanwhile, his beard grew. He always wore a turban now. My mother started wearing Kuchi clothes and jewelry. Sometimes I could not pick her out of a group of women, milking the sheep and the goats as well as the cows, and shearing the sheep's wool. My father learned how to wash wool in the river and slaughter animals and cut them into pieces for cooking or for sale to the villagers.

My older sister and I taught the kids, our cousins, for three hours early every morning. Afterward, I went with Omar Khan and other boys to take the flocks to the pastures for grazing on the hillsides. My older sister went to the stream with the other girls to fill their pitchers. She also learned how to make Kuchi embroideries. She already knew how to hold a pot of water on her head without holding it with her hands. She had learned that in Tashkurghan. The Kuchi girls were very surprised to see her doing it like they did.

When my father went with the men, and my mother was with the women, and my older sister had gone off to get water with the Kuchi girls, it was my job to take care of my younger sisters and my brother. One of my sisters was happy with her own company. She would be next to me for hours, but I would hardly know she was there. She did not say much, did not complain about anything, and never cried to have something.

The next sister, though, cried for hours when she did not get what she wanted. She was afraid of no one, neither my mother nor my father. She would just cry stubbornly until somebody solved her problem. Then she became friendly and did not leave that person's side.

My brother would be very quiet until he wanted to eat something sweet. Then he would live up to his nickname. Both of my parents loved him, because he had such soft cheeks. He never went far from my mother.

On the first Friday that we were with the Kuchis, Omar Khan said we should go to the river and catch some fish.

"Do you have fishhooks?" I asked.

"We don't need fishhooks," he said.

"Do you use a net?" I asked.

"No," he said.

"Then how do you catch the fish?" I asked.

"With a generator," he said.

I did not know what he was talking about.

"It is a Kuchi trick. I will show it to you, but you have to help me carry this generator to the river," he said.

The generator was heavy. It was a struggle to get it to the river. Meanwhile, the other Kuchi boys were pasturing the herds on the hillside.

We put the generator on a flat rock about twenty meters from the river. Omar Khan connected one end of a wire to the generator and put the other end on a tree branch near the river. A few minutes later, all the uncles came. They carried many big stones to the middle of the river. Two hours later the river was dammed.

Everyone got out of the water. One of the uncles turned on the generator. Another one dropped the end of the wire into the river. The generator made some sputtering noises and stopped. I did not know what was going on until I looked at the river and saw that it was filled with fish floating on the surface. They had all been electrocuted. While some of the kids pulled the wire out of the water, Omar Khan and several of his uncles jumped into the pool and started throwing the fish to the riverside. The rest of us began collecting them. Half an hour later, we had four large bags of fish on the back of a horse and carried them to the tents for a Friday fish party.

The next Friday we did not have gasoline for the generator, but Omar Khan asked me to go to catch fish with him anyway.

"How will you catch any fish today?" I asked.

"Today I will show you another Kuchi trick," he said.

We all hid behind a big boulder that was way back from the river. One of the uncles took a grenade from his pocket. He pulled out the fuse and threw the grenade into the river.

Seconds later, the water splashed all over the riverbank with bits of sand, gravel, and fishes flying into the air. Even where we were hiding, little pieces of fish found us and stuck to my face and in my hair, which was long then. I smelled like fish for hours after. The river turned gray as hundreds came to the surface. We waited there for a few minutes to let the silt in the water settle down. Then Omar Khan and his uncles jumped in to throw the fish onto the riverbank. This time it was five big bags we put on the back of the horse. A few hours later we had another fish feast.

On the third Friday, there was yet another trick.

The grenade had completely destroyed our dam from the week before, so it took us about three hours to block the stream. Then the uncles came leading a horse that was carrying a large bag of caustic soda, and another bag full of empty bottles. The uncles and Omar Khan filled the glass bottles with the caustic soda, and then we crouched behind that same big rock and threw those bottles into the river. When the caustic soda in each bottle touched the water, it exploded like a bomb, though not as forcefully as the grenade. Again, we went back to the tents with five bags of fish.

Everybody had to clean his or her own fish and cook them. The Kuchis used only powdered laundry detergent to wash their hands, and it smelled worse than the fish. I saw Omar Khan rubbing his hands with lemon and orange to kill the fish smell. This was another Kuchi trick, of course.

———

We spent more than a month camped with the Kuchis in Samangan. The spring rains had ended, and the pastures on the hillsides were starting to brown. There was not enough grass left for the herds. On the Friday night of the fourth week, Amir Khan said that by Monday they would move to Mazar, and then farther west to Andkhoi, where they could find fresh grasses for their flocks.

Our car had not been fixed yet, and we still had to wait another month. But my father did not have enough money to feed us and rent a room for a month. My father decided that we should go with the Kuchis as far as Mazar. There my mother, my sisters, and I would stay with my aunt, while my father would return to Samangan to get the car fixed. He would rejoin us as soon as it was repaired, then we would go to Kabul together.

On the Sunday night of our fifth week, the Kuchis collected their stuff. Early the next morning we started our move back toward Mazar. Though we wanted to be heading home to Kabul, we were excited to be traveling with the caravan.

The caravan moved slowly, with huge, shaggy camels lumbering down the rocky slopes followed by sheep, goats, and fierce-eyed watchdogs. The men, tall, lean, and severe looking, walked proudly back and forth among their herds and cattle. They carried rifles on their shoulders. Sometimes, the silence suddenly was broken by harsh words from the leading camel driver, who spoke in a jargon known only to those of his profession and to his camels.

At both the head and the rear of the caravan, the women walked openly, contemptuous of veils, as they swung along blithely near their camels. They were as beautiful and ethereal as old romantic paintings. Some of them were black-eyed and tan-skinned with raven hair. Others were fair and blue-eyed with golden or red hair. The sun and wind had given them red cheeks and lips that contrasted sharply with their dresses of somber black.

The littlest kids, two or three years old, were strapped between the two humps of the Bactrian camels. As the camels joggled along, the kids slept in a sitting posture. Every now and then a child would whimper, but would soon be lulled to sleep by the padding camel feet and the tinkles of bells that hung on the camels' long necks. Older kids would walk alongside the one-humped camels, but when they got tired, they climbed up on the striding camels' backs like monkeys. There they settled themselves in front of the hump for a nap.

Occasionally, a newly born camel walked up from the rear and nuzzled its mother, its woolly body in strange contrast to its long, unsteady, thin legs.

The Kuchis carried all of their possessions with them. They lived very simply, but not poorly, and had many richly colored carpets of their own working, with big traditional geometric patterns; from what I had learned from my teacher in Mazar, I could see they had used many vegetable dyes, and they were as soft as velvet. These carpets were bundled together with the tents and cooking utensils and slung on either side of the camels.

From a distance the camels looked like they were bobbing up and down like large rag dolls.

The nomadic life was accustoming us to hardship, making us strong and teaching us courage. We walked for six hours, until we stopped for lunch. Then we walked again until dusk approached. It was very trying, but I could now understand why Grandfather was so much in love with the way the Kuchis lived; as he had said, "It is carefree, and secure, and finds the best in every season in a way that can never be monotonous, like Kabul life."

I walked in front of the herds with my father and the other Kuchi men. They spoke Pashto very loudly, as if they were all deaf. I asked my father why they were speaking so loud. He said, "This is how Kuchi people talk."

Then I spent some time with my boy cousins who were lost in the dust among the sheep and goats. They each carried a stick in their hands. Then I went to see my sisters. Their colorful skirts and embroidered jackets were covered with a thick layer of dust, which turned them the dull colors of the men's clothes. When the Kuchi girls saw me, they stopped talking and glared at me to let me know that I was not welcome there. I was their cousin, but Kuchis have strict rules about men being with women and boys being with girls, which I was still learning. After I left them, they started talking to one another again.

My mother was always in the back, coughing and sneezing from the chalk-like, powdery dust. She could not walk as fast as the others. She did not have proper shoes, only sandals. The dry air and the dust made her heels crack. Sometimes she rode on one of the one-hump camels. Everybody stared at her as if she were doing something wrong, since usually only little kids and old people did that. Her white skin was becoming tanned by the sun, but the dust made her look as if she had put her head into a bran flour bag.

When the sun dropped behind the mountains, we stopped wherever we were: one day on the skirt of a mountain, one day in a desert, and one day in a green valley near a village. In less than an hour, a few Kuchi men could set up a few tents, while the women began to prepare dinner. Some breast-fed their babies as they cooked. A few hours later darkness covered us, except for where the starry sky with a half-moon dropped light toward us.

We had three huge fires every night, one for the men, one for the women, and another for the kids. Every now and then the fire cracked and a spark broke free. Youngsters were busy boiling water for tea, while the men reclined against huge pillows to drink it. They were as fond of drinking tea as my aunts and uncles, draining several cups, one after another, in minutes.

These were sociable people who enjoyed every meal like it was a feast. The Kuchi women often cooked *shorba* for lunch, a meat soup filled with carrots, potatoes, turnips, spices, and lots of dry or fresh hot pepper. When townspeople came to the encampment to buy animals, skins, or fleeces, the cook just added another few cups of water to the pot, boiled it, and there was enough to serve the guests. To eat it, we tore our *naan* into small pieces and put the pieces in a large bowl. Whichever woman was in charge of cooking that day would then pour the *shorba* over the bread chunks. Five to ten people would then eat from that one bowl. If I did not eat in a hurry, I might eat only one or two bites before the bowl was empty. Then I had to fill myself with bread and yogurt, whey, or *quroot*, dried yogurt that is hard and sour and always carried by the Kuchis.

At night, the Kuchi women would sometimes make kebab, or rice with lamb. They did not clean the rice before cooking it. Each time I took a bite, sand crunched in my teeth or I would find myself chewing a stone. Several times my father joked, "The sand and pebbles are cooked very well, but why is there so much rice mixed in?" The men laughed and boasted, "Kuchis' stomachs can digest even iron."

I was grateful for the food that the Kuchis were giving us, but I did not like eating so much meat. I often cut an onion into small chunks, mixed it with yogurt, and ate it with bread, while the others stretched out their hands to eat their soaked *naan* from one large bowl.

After dinner two men played drums, the deep-sounding *dol*, and other men formed a circle and danced the *attan*. Slowly at first, they raised one foot and spun around, then faster and faster as the *dol* drove them into a spinning fury. One by one, some of the men dropped out when the beats came too quickly and they got too tired. On the last pounding beat, everybody cheered the couple of men still dancing.

The whole night was spent enjoying one another's company, singing and dancing. Sometimes they hooked up a string of bulbs to the generator and made the desert night come alive with electric light. The women continued cooking until very late.

Finally, we drifted into the tents and slept. The flocks dozed outside, and the fierce-eyed watchdogs stayed vigilant.

Three weeks later, late on a Monday afternoon, we got to Mazar. We left the open country, and our line of camels swayed into the town along the main road. When we reached the shrine of Hazrat Ali, the caravan stopped briefly so the men could go pray. After the prayers, my father told Amir Khan that we could not continue walking with them any longer, and that we had to leave them there.

Amir Khan became very unhappy upon hearing this, but he forced a smile. He and the others had known we would leave them in Mazar, but none of us had wanted to think about it or talk about it.

"We will always carry this great memory of being with you and your kind family," my father said as he was hugging Amir Khan goodbye. "And we will be always thankful for your hospitality and sincerity."

"We also will remember you and your family as one of our good memories," Amir Khan said. "Don't forget to visit us in Jalalabad in the wintertime. Please bring your father."

Jalalabad stays warm all year. That is where the Kuchis had their permanent homes.

Then my father hugged the other Kuchi men one by one and said his goodbyes. I imitated him again, like the first time we had met them. This time, though, we knew all their names. We knew who were the best dancers, who told the best stories, who were the best kebab cooks, and who were poets.

My mother and sisters kissed the Kuchi women. My father and I waved farewell to them from a proper distance.

Then I went to my boy cousins. I hugged Omar Khan first, then the others. Omar Khan held out a handmade envelope to me and asked me not to open it until the next day. I promised I would. Then all the other boys handed me their own envelopes and said their shy good-byes. They tried to disappear from sight quickly. They were not good at goodbyes at all. My hands were full of their envelopes.

I noticed that my older sister was surrounded by a group of Kuchi girls handing her Kuchi jewelry and kissing her farewell. They hugged her very tenderly, then one by one they disappeared inside the dust of the herd.

We stood on the roadside in front of the shrine and its blue-tiled towers, and watched them as they went farther and farther away until they disappeared from our sight. The farther they went, the closer I felt to them.

My father said wistfully, "They will just go on walking and walk-ing over the same routes that our ancestors have followed for centu-ries. I wish Dad were here."

We did not say anything. I put the handmade envelopes into my pockets as we got into a taxi. But the taxi did not feel right, somehow. I wanted to run after my cousins. I wanted to shout at them to take me with them.

A few minutes later, we were in my aunt's house. She was very happy to see us again, but very surprised. We had had no way of letting her know what had happened to us, or that we would be coming back to her house. Happy as she was, she did not let us go into her rooms, because we were so dusty and dirty and full of fleas. She brought us tea in the courtyard. After we drank a cup, she sent us one by one to the bathroom for a shower, while she found us clean clothes and sent what we had been wearing to be washed in very hot water with strong soap. Then she let us in.

After I had bathed, I ran next door to surprise my carpet teacher. I knocked on the door several times, but nobody opened it. Then I pushed the door and entered the courtyard. All the rooms were empty. No one was there. Frightened, I ran back to our house to ask my aunt about what had happened to them. She told me that they had left for Tajikistan a few weeks before. Tajikistan! I was stunned with disappointment. How would I find my teacher in Tajikistan?

My aunt went to her bedroom and came back with a small package. "She left this for you," she said.

Even before I unwrapped the plain white cotton, I knew what it was. I looked at it very carefully. It was my teacher's rug hook. I could see her beauty in that hook, and it reminded me of her smile and her eyes filling with tears when she said goodbye.

I kissed the hook. It smelled of her perfume. I cried without knowing why I was crying. My aunt kissed me on my forehead, hugged my head, and said, "She loved you, too, but it was her decision to go to Tajikistan. She convinced her family to leave Afghanistan, and her family always listens to her. They believe that she is always right about her decisions."

"She is not an ordinary person," I murmured, then asked my aunt many questions about why my teacher would have wanted her family to move. But neither my aunt nor anyone in her family knew the answers.

I wrapped the hook in a pure silk handkerchief that I had bought from the Mazar bazaar when we had been there a few months before, and I put it in my suitcase with other special things that I had found in all the different places we had gone.

That night I went to sleep very early, and I saw my carpet teacher in my dreams. I also saw Omar Khan and my monk friend in Bam-yan, and Hamza and my other friends in Tashkurghan. Wakeel was there, too. We were all together.

I woke up early in the morning, and everyone else was still asleep. I started reading the letters that I had been given by my Kuchi cousins. I began with Omar Khan's letter. He was the one who was dearest to me, and the one I most understood. I had learned a lot from his love of life.

*Dear my best friend and kind cousin,*

*I will always remember you in the cage of my heart, for you gave me the sight to see my path. Until I met you, I always thought I was living in darkness, and from the moment I met you, I found my light.*

*You lit a candle in me. Its light can show me my path, and this light will always remind me of you.*

*Sincerely, Omar Khan*

I read this letter several times. Omar Khan, I could see, was a poet as well as a herd boy. What he meant by "light" was being able to read and write.

I opened the second letter and it was from Aaron Khan. Aaron Khan was dark and skinny, with bulging eyes like a crab. He spoke in a hurried voice, half swallowing his words, and glancing furtively about as though he was planning to run off and hide. When he was excited his very eyeballs seemed to tremble.

*Knowledge is the candle of life, and you gave me a candle that I can use for the rest of my life. I don't know how to say my appreciations for the precious gift that you gave me, but I believe someday I will meet you and give you a gift that is worth giving. If not in this world, in the next world, as we all believe this world is a bridge to the next.*

*Best regards, Aaron Khan*

The third letter was from Solomon Khan. He was quiet and had his father's combination of sad eyes and winning smile, even though his teeth were very ugly; they protruded from his mouth and grew in a double row in his upper jaw. This kept him busy, as his fingers were constantly in his mouth, trying to loosen and yank out the teeth in the back row. He meekly permitted those who wished to put their fingers in his mouth to feel his teeth. I could find little in common with him that we could talk about. He was always sitting off by himself in some dark corner of a tent, or spending his evenings at the hillside.

Still, it was pleasant to sit close beside him there on a big rock and say nothing for a whole hour, watching the crows wheel around the domes of the tents when they stood out in relief against the red glow of the sunset. The birds soared and plunged, then suddenly spread a black net across the fading sky and disappeared, leaving a vast emptiness behind them. When we watched something like this, we had no desire to speak, for our hearts were full from the joy of seeing it.

*Dear my cousin,*

*Knowledge is that precious wealth that nothing can compare to it. You gave me that wealth and I gave you nothing but silences. I know that you understood the secret behind the silences. That was all I could give you for the time being. I hope we meet another time and exchange more.*

*Best wishes, Solomon Khan*

One by one, I read them all. The letters had many writing mistakes, many misspelled words, large and straggling, but I could read and understand them. With practice our cousins would get better, my older sister and I agreed. That is how we had learned Dari. What moved me was how creative their writing was, and how full of images. And when I finished reading them, I read them all again, over and over.

The next day, I went to the Hazrat Ali shrine and met my friends with whom I had played *gursai*. They all were amazed by my story of living with the Kuchis. While I was in the shrine, I prayed to ask God to keep my carpet teacher safe wherever she was. My father spent a week with us in Mazar, and then he decided to go to Samangan to get our car, which should have been fixed by now. He would come back to Mazar and drive us all to Kabul. For the most part, the ceasefire seemed to be holding, according to the reports my father heard on the BBC. There had been no serious fighting during the weeks we had been with the Kuchis. My parents felt it was safe to go home. After nearly a year of wandering, they wanted to be settled again.

There was no more talk, at least for now, of going to another country. I was disappointed; I had thought that perhaps I could look for my teacher. But I was also desperately missing Wakeel. He had not come to Mazar as he had promised he would. But I understood how hard it was to travel.

We waited for my father for three days, but he did not come. On the fourth day, my aunt introduced us to her neighbor who was a helicopter pilot.

He told us that he had a flight to Kabul the next day. If we wanted to go, he would take us. That sounded like a good idea to me, but we wanted to wait for my father, so we could all go together.

My mother, my aunt, and her husband talked about it late into the night, while I listened from my bed.

My aunt said, "If you wait for him to come back to go to Kabul together, maybe on the way the car will break down again. It may take days to fix. Then the poor man has to drag you all with him to somewhere, and you know he has no money left. But if the car does break, he will find a way to fix it, or just leave it behind, and make his own way to Kabul."

Finally, around midnight my mother agreed, though reluctantly. Before she could change her mind, my aunt immediately went to her neighbor who had offered to fly us. She took me with her, while my mother started gathering what few belongings we had, and knocked on the neighbor's door, waking him up. My aunt apologized and told him that tomorrow he should pick us up before going to the airport. He smiled sleepily, nodded, and closed the door.

The next morning, my mother, sisters, brother, and I climbed into the helicopter without my father. The cockpit was full of pomegranates in big bags. We ate them as we looked down through little windows to the Hindu Kush mountains that we had already crossed three times, so slowly, in fear and in hope. In only fifty minutes we were at the Kabul airport. We took a taxi, and a half hour later we were at Noborja. Nobody knew we were coming. We had not known ourselves.

As we walked through the outer gate into the garden and then past the heavy wooden door with the clanking chain into the courtyard, a couple of my cousins saw us and then their mothers, and then my uncles. They started shouting and running toward us. We got only as far as the tall acacia tree before we were totally surrounded by them.

Then I saw Wakeel. He came out of one of the rooms on the upper floor to see what was happening. For a moment or two, he stood very still, watching us as we were being hugged and kissed by many of our relatives, while still others were running out of their rooms as they got the news. Then he bolted toward the stairs and sped down them like a kite dropping for a kill, and raced across the courtyard to us.

I was so happy to see Wakeel again. In the months since I had seen him, he had lost some weight and looked skinny and a little taller, but his face glowed with happiness. I could sense that he was feeling waves of relief, like a dry land after the rain. But he could not find words for his emotions.

He hugged my sisters and my mother, but when he reached me, he tagged me on the shoulder and said, "Hey, where the hell were you?" Everybody was watching both of us.

"That is all you can say?" I asked disappointedly as emotions were racing inside me.

He could not hold his tears anymore, and I was not ashamed to let mine go. He hugged me as I shook silently with sobs and squeezed me tighter in his arms. Finally he got back enough breath to say, "I was so worried that something had happened to you guys. You said you would be gone for one month. But it was almost a year." He wiped his eyes.

I could not answer him. My throat was still blocked. I wanted to see my grandfather. He was inside the house and had not come out. Wakeel took me to the upstairs room where he was seated with two of his friends. When I saw him through the door, I ran to him and kissed him on the face over and over, and hugged him for several minutes without saying anything. I did not want to look in his face, because my eyes were full of tears, and I did not want him to see them. My heart was pounding, and I was trying very hard not to cry out loud. Grandfather did not say anything, but simply held me in his large arms.

After a while, Grandfather said, "Hey, Gorbachev, how did you get here?"

I pulled myself away from him enough to look him in the face. I kissed his hands formally and managed to say, "We all came in a helicopter. The others are downstairs." I felt like I was choking when I spoke, and I could not say more.

Grandfather's eyes were now as full of tears as mine. "Give me another hug," he said, maybe because he did not want me to see this.

Trying to make a joke, he said, "You didn't say hello to my friends. Did you forget all your good manners?" I unwrapped my arms from around his neck and said *"Salaam"* to them, but it came out with a squeak. One of them was drying his tears with the end of his turban.

At that moment, my mother and the others walked in. For the first time ever I was glad everyone was there with us. Usually, I wanted to be the one talking to Grandfather for hours without any interruption. But that day I could not. My mother kissed Grandfather's hands as he kissed her head. Then my grandfather asked about my father.

She sat near him and told him everything, as my aunts brought us tea and my mother gave everybody presents, which were only round Mazar flatbread and candies that we had taken to the shrine to be blessed. After an hour, as the grown-ups kept talking, I walked out of the room and found Wakeel in the corridor all by himself, weeping. That made me start again. Then we were both laughing. This was one day when nobody was feeling any shame about crying. We would have broken the noses of anybody who had said anything.

Before the day ended, everything was like it always had been. We both had a lot of stories to tell each other. He had five good kites for me. One had my name on it. He had made that for me himself. He told me that he had flown that one and cut lots of other kites with it. He said that the neighborhood kids were afraid of that kite.

That is how he made me famous in Kart-e-Parwan. Every kid in the town thought that I was the one flying that kite and cutting them all. But it was Wakeel. It had been very mysterious for the kids in our neighborhood that they never saw me outside, but saw my kite every afternoon high in the sky as it proudly roared around, cutting other kites that tried to rise a little higher than mine.

The next day when I walked outside to buy some bread for break-fast, all the kids were looking at me from the corners of their eyes and whispering to one another, "There he is, there he is. 'Qais, the Cruel Cutter.'" I pretended that I did not hear them. I walked past them, holding my head up like a tyrant.

I gave Wakeel some rocks that I had collected from the Buddha in Bamyan. I had to explain everything about Buddha, and why I thought those rocks were precious. He thought I was joking when I gave them to him, but after I told him about the Buddha, and living in a cave behind his head, and meeting the monk, he did not want to take those stones. He thought they were part of my adventure memories and I should keep them. I told him that he was the *padshah*, the king, of all my memories and that he should have them.

Five days later, my father arrived home with our car, which was now running well. Once again we were all together. We all tried to lead a good life. The war seemed to have ended in Kabul. But we were not living in our own house, which lay in ruins on the other side of the mountain. We were still refugees in Haji Noor Sher's Fort of Nine Towers, which had only one tower left.


While we were away, Grandfather had the idea to scatter his sons, so that if the war started again, we would not all be stuck in one place and could look to one another for help in another part of the city. My uncles had been wanting to leave for some time, but they were waiting for my father to come back before they did. Now, one by one, they left the old fort.

One took his wife and children and moved in with his father-in-law in the Taimaskan blocks in the northwest corner of Kabul. Another uncle shared a house with his brother-in-law in Parwan-e-Seh, not very far from Kart-e-Parwan. Another went to live in Khair Khana with a friend.

A week after we returned, Grandfather himself moved to Makroyan to live with his eldest daughter, who was now a widow. The ceasefire had been going on for more than a month by then, and people were beginning to be hopeful that it would be permanent.

Makroyan was a neighborhood of five- and six-story apartment blocks built by the Russians back when they had come as friends. It was now controlled by one of the factions whose soldiers were raping many young girls there, along with looting people's houses and sometimes killing people. My father's sister had lived there for many years but had become afraid of being there alone.

Her husband had been executed during the short-lived Communist presidency of Hafiz'allah Amin, whom no one remembers now. But he had held power long enough to kill many of the best-educated Afghans. One day, my aunt heard her husband's name announced on the radio as being among those who had been purged. No reason was ever given.

Though she subsequently had many suitors, she never remarried and lived with her daughter and her brother, my youngest uncle. He was only a little older than Wakeel, so we thought of him more as our cousin. Grandfather wanted to be with his eldest daughter as long as things remained bad in Makroyan.

Wherever Grandfather lived, that is where Wakeel's mother wanted to be. Grandfather told her to remain at the Qala-e-Noborja with the rest of us, even though he especially loved her cooking. But she insisted on going to Makroyan with him. And so did my unmarried aunts. They wanted to be with their oldest sister, who was like a second mother to them.

———

Now, for the first time in Kabul, we were living without Grandfather and without Wakeel. Since the fighting had started, nothing had made sense. I could never have imagined that we would ever have left my grandfather's house. And now after so many months away, living without Wakeel or Grandfather made the least sense of all.

The big mud fort felt very empty. At night when the wind hit the large trees and lilac bushes in the courtyard, it made a lonely and even sometimes frightening sound. The dogs outside howled in the rutted road. The Qala-e-Noborja no longer felt like the magical place it had been the day we first arrived.

I thought about my friends in Tashkurghan, and about the Kuchis, and the monk in Bamyan, and my teacher in Mazar, and the kids at the shrine. And most of all, I thought about Wakeel. I had waited so long to be with him again, and now he was on the other side of the city.

Because he was older, he was allowed to come from Makroyan to the Qala-e-Noborja on Fridays by himself. Over the next couple of months the ceasefire held, and he came almost every Friday around midmorning. For an hour, he would sit with my parents and talk with them. Then he and I would fly kites for the rest of the day. He always had to be home before dark, though, which meant he missed the best kite winds at dusk.

Sometimes he spent the night with us, but most of the time he returned home since he was the youngest boy among all the family now in Makroyan, and it was his job to run to the bazaar anytime his mother or one of the aunts needed vegetables or herbs, or had *naan* dough ready to be taken to the bakery.

I wanted to tell all my adventures to Grandfather. But he was not there. Makroyan was on the other side of Kabul. It was only a couple of miles away, but it felt like the far side of the world.

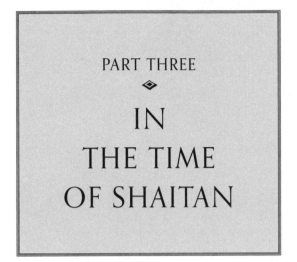

PART THREE

IN
THE TIME
OF SHAITAN

# 13

❖

## The Gold

Now we began the time of pretending. The signs of war were all around us, but we pretended that we did not see them. All but one of my uncles and their families had moved to different parts of the city, but we pretended that we would not be apart for long. We missed sitting around one tablecloth, but we pretended that eating by ourselves was the same as eating all together.

Once or twice everyone came back to the Qala-e-Noborja on a Friday. The grown-ups sat and talked inside, while my cousins and I played in the garden as before, or flew kites. We pretended that we were still living in one courtyard like in the old days. But the grown-ups did not make jokes as they always had. And they never talked about rebuilding Grandfather's house.

When they all left at dusk, we pretended that we would see each other again the next day. Instead, we met after a month or two, because as the weeks passed and the ceasefires came and went, it was still not safe to move around the city.

The war started again in full force five months after we had arrived back in Kabul, even though the leaders of all the factions had gone to Mecca and had sworn that they would never fight again. We pretended that their broken oaths were normal, though every Afghan knows that to break an oath is a serious offense, especially one made in Mecca in the House of God.

The war between the oath breakers locked us all in one room for days and weeks. Sometimes we could not even go to the kitchen across the courtyard, afraid that a sniper might hit us, or a rocket might land as we ran to get some rice, which was often the only food we had left as the days passed and our meat and vegetables were all eaten. We slept night after night with empty stomachs, but we pretended we were practicing for Ramazan.

Once, after several days of eating nothing, I had no choice but to go to the kitchen to get flour so my mother could at least cook us some bread on the woodstove we used for heating the room where we spent our days and nights. My father took me aside and apologized with tears in his eyes for asking me to go, but he explained that if he were killed, there was no one to look out for the rest of the family. I understood. But it took me hours to gather the courage to run the twenty steps there. I ran in zigzags to the kitchen, pretending I was playing hide-and-seek with the snipers on the mountain. They often shot anything they saw that moved. It was their game. But they did not see me. I won the game that day.

Rockets fell by the hundreds. First they made a whistling noise in the air, and then a huge blast that shook the earth when they landed. Bits of rocket and anything they hit rained all around. We pretended that it was fun. We made a whistling noise along with the rockets when we heard them; sometimes we ran out of breath before they landed, and sometimes we did not. When they struck, we made an explosion noise with our mouths and shook our bodies, and pretended we were the earth. Some nights it was hard to sleep because so many rockets were exploding over the city. We pretended it was fireworks on holidays like Great Eid, which honors Ibrahim's willingness to sacrifice his son Ishmael, or Naw Ruz, our new year on the first day of spring.

Sitting every day in one room nearly drove me and the others crazy, but we pretended it would end soon. For days and weeks we did not see the sky, so we pretended that our ceiling was our sky. We read the same books over and over, until we could almost recite them. Sometimes when the stress became too much, I went to another room where I had hung my punching bag from the ceiling. I punched that bag for hours until sweat was running all over me. I pretended that I was getting myself prepared for a match.

A lot of people did go crazy. They walked out of their houses and were hunted down by snipers, who shot them just for the joy of shooting.

As one strange event followed another, we understood—even if we did not say it—that we were living in the time of Shaitan, the devil. Pretending that we were leading normal lives was the only thing that allowed us to survive.

I did not know how to start this new life. Every day I woke up and breathed in and out, and waited for the times to change. I learned that waiting is a skill that must be mastered.

I told myself that my past was finished, and that I had to do something new now. But every day in the cage of my heart, I felt the weight of the memories of the time before.

Many times, I thought about the mother of my carpet teacher, who had told me many old stories that always included a wise lesson. I thought about the bright sky, and snow around us as she spoke in her quiet, mysterious voice. Her face was always close to mine, her wide eyes gazing into mine. Sometimes it felt like she was pouring strength into my heart. She sang rather than spoke. The longer the story went on, the more musical she became. It was an inexpressible joy to listen to her.

I had never known my grandmother. She had died before I was a year old. Sometimes when I was with my teacher's mother, I wished she could be married to my grandfather. When I was with her, it was like she was holding me when I was falling backward.

Grandfather came back to visit and spent several days with us. I would sit next to him while he was reading. It was not important to me that he did not say anything. I was just happy to be there, and, though I was now getting too old for it, I liked to put my head on his lap, to look up and watch him eat an apple and listen to the crunch as he bit it. Sometimes, he would read aloud a poem by Rumi or Hafiz and he would ask me what it meant. I would try very hard to say something wise, to please him. He would smile and tell me, "You learned a lot on your travels."

I told him about our time with the Kuchis. He loved to hear how they ate and made jokes in front of the bonfire until late at night. He asked so many questions about the way they made music, danced, slaughtered their animals, bargained with the people in the towns where they passed and extended their hospitality. As I told him, I relived it all for myself.

He told me that his wife, my grandmother, would always have a strange feeling when she saw a Kuchi caravan passing through Kabul. A part of her wanted to run out of the house when she saw a line of camels plodding through the streets and follow along with everybody else.

One day when my grandfather was reading his favorite book, *Afghanistan in the Path of History* by Mir Ghulam Mohammad Ghobar, my father came in. He had a tray with tea, but only two cups. When he saw me, he told me to go out, but my grandfather put his arm around my shoulder.

My father said, "At least go get a cup for yourself."

When I came back, my father was talking about some man in Hayratan, a town that was on the border with the Soviet Union, which we always just called Russia, about an hour's drive from Mazar-e-Sharif. I listened, though I did not understand what he was talking about at first. Slowly, however, I understood that all those days in Mazar when he had left the house so early and had come home so tired, he had been going back and forth to Hayratan, trying to arrange to have our family smuggled across the border.

Suddenly, I felt stupid for having been so unhappy with my father in those days. I had not known what he was trying to do.

He had been doing the same thing when we were in Kunduz. He had gone north to the border many times but had never been successful. Being smuggled is expensive. We had had enough money when the fighting had first started. But as time passed, we had had to use most of it just to live on. Now there was very little left.

I looked at my father as he was telling these things to his father, and I felt a kind of respect for him in a way that I never had before. I had blamed him for not having enough money to get us out of the country, for not taking us someplace where nobody could tell us what to do or how to be. Many times I had wanted to ask him why all his friends were living in America or Europe, but we were still in Afghanistan. I had never dared to say that. But I had been resentful. Now I felt ashamed.

I understood as I never had before what a tough man my father was. I thought of how he had carried us from one place to another to save our lives, like a cat carrying its kittens in its mouth.

My father now had to start his life again. Once, he and Grandfather had been important carpet sellers. Now he had no carpets to sell, and no money to buy new ones. He borrowed some money from a friend and bought one carpet from a shop in Chicken Street, a small one. Then he sold it to another dealer for a tiny bit of profit. That was the start of his new business.

Every day, he carried a carpet on his shoulder all over Kabul to sell it for a few afghanis more than he paid for it. Slowly, slowly one carpet became two, and two became four, and four became eight, until one day after five months he had eighty carpets and owned them all. As he sold them, he built up a small cash reserve to pay smugglers. To get to Russia, though, he would need to sell hundreds of carpets.

He never stopped worrying.

Perhaps on that night, now more than two years before, I knew what my father and my uncles were doing when I discovered them silently digging holes in the garden. Or perhaps I just pieced together the bits of talk I had overheard whenever there was any mention of smugglers. Someone would mutter something about "the gold" that would pay for them. And "the garden."

My mother and my uncles' wives all had had boxes and boxes of gold jewelry. My father was very much in love with my mother. When they got married, he spent everything he had to buy her gold. Every year at Eid, he would buy her so many new gold bangles that they stretched from her wrists to her elbows.

Whenever my father bought gold for my mother, his brothers had to do the same for their wives, too. Everyone wanted to show off. One uncle's wife wore gold anklets; another had a thick belt, all gold; my mother had a crown of gold. I had seen her wear it only once, at a wedding, and then just for a couple of hours, because too many people were staring at her and wanted to touch it.

At night, when we had gone back to our rooms after a big party, my mother would comment on all the other women's gold. She enjoyed pointing out that her bangles and necklaces were always thicker and heavier than theirs. Probably my uncle's wives were saying similar things about their gold, too. Afghans are competitive about everything.

One afternoon when I was alone with my father, and he was talking about trying to get smuggled to Turkey, I asked him whether he thought all the gold that he and his brothers had buried in Grandfather's garden had been found by thieves. He looked at me with his head tilted slightly to one side, trying to decide how much I really knew.

"It is a big garden," was all he said. I could tell he believed there must still be some gold there.

Now I understood that this was why we had gone before and been captured and sent down into the tunnel. I also understood why he was now insisting on going back, even though we all knew the house had been destroyed.


My mother tried hard to stop him. They argued about it for weeks, but my father is stubborn, possibly the most stubborn man that I know. The ceasefires were irregular and ended unpredictably. But on the days when the guns had gone quiet, my father became profoundly impatient. I could see his thoughts of our old courtyard on his face.

One Friday as we were finishing breakfast, my father asked me to get ready to accompany him. He spoke in a distant tone. I looked at my mother. She was staring at her plate.

I had not forgotten what had happened the last time we had gone there. I knew it would be dangerous. But I was willing to take any chance that could end the pretending and the waiting. Maybe there was still some gold in the garden. Maybe we would find it. Maybe we could pay smugglers and actually escape this time.

We went to the crossroads at the Polytechnic. The flashing yellow traffic light was still over the main crossroad. It had not been shot out yet. We took that as a good sign.

The neighborhood was not at all as I remembered, even from our previous visit. Roofs had fallen in; wild house cats were sneering from broken windows. Ration cans and Russian helmets were scattered everywhere.

When we got to our house, my father pushed open the splintered remains of the thick wooden door. Inside, we walked across the garden to our rooms, staying on the stone path, just to be safe. Once when we had been in Mazar and we were speaking about our house, I had asked my father why somebody would put mines in our garden. He said that maybe they had, but maybe they had not.

"Maybe the man who told my father about those mines was only trying to keep you out of there," my father said. "Did you ever actually see the garden that day?"

"No," I replied.

There were several large holes in a few places that probably had been made by exploding rockets. But most of the garden looked as if it had not been disturbed. I tried to remember where the cucumber plants had been. But after two years, I could not be sure.

All of a sudden I remembered the folk tale of how Mullah Nasruddin had dug a hole on top of the mountain and had hidden his money there. He came back two years later and started digging along the bottom of the mountain, looking for it. After a while, when he could not find anything there, he started to weep. Somebody who was passing by asked, "Why are you crying, Mullah?"

"Two years ago I dug a hole here and hid my money, and now it is not here anymore," Mullah Nasruddin said.

"Are you sure you hid it there?" the man asked.

"Yes, I am very sure, because two years ago the cloud was right here in the sky, and it gave me shade while I was digging. And now you see the cloud is here today, too, but not my money," Mullah Nasruddin said.

The room where I used to sleep was roofless. Dust covered everything. I went inside to look for my bed. The room was empty. It was like no one had ever lived there.

Suddenly, from outside I heard a heavy thud. I looked out and saw five guys in our courtyard, jumping up on the roof of Grandfather's room across the garden from our rooms. They had bundles of thick rope in their hands. They were surprised to see me. One of them wore dusty and torn clothes. He had narrow blue eyes, a brown bushy beard, broad shoulders, and short legs. My father was in another room. He came out and stood next to me. The man came closer and asked my father, "Who are you?"

"I am the owner of this house," my father said sharply.

"But it is ours now," the guy said with a bitter smile. "It is the wheel of life. One day you have everything, and one day I have everything. You enjoyed being in these rooms, and now we are taking the beams to make rooms of our own." He placed an empty clay pot he was holding on the ground. Maybe he had been planning to steal it.

Two of the men had climbed up a bamboo ladder to the roof while we were talking. They tied their ropes into the end of one of the roof beams that lay across the tops of the house's brick walls. One of the others tied the other end of the ropes to a truck that was parked on the road outside. We heard the truck start, and its wheels spin. Black smoke rose over the walls as one of the roof beams was pulled free from its spot and went crashing over the wall into the street.

My father could no longer hold himself back. He was furious. "You bastards! What the hell are you doing?" he shouted at the guys on the roof, who were tying more ropes to other beams.

"Hey, big man, mind your own business," the short guy said.

"Fuck you! It is my fucking business. This is my house," my father shouted. It was the first time I heard words like those from my father.

The short guy climbed down the bamboo ladder. He came over to my father, walking like a lion preparing for a fight. His head hardly reached my father's chest, but he looked very brave, very sure of himself. He tugged hard on my father's beard. With his other hand he tried to grab my father's hair. But my father stopped him with one push and a punch in the nose. The guy's nose broke, and blood spattered all over his clothes.

The two on the roof, who had by then climbed down the bamboo ladder, saw his face was covered with blood. One of them jumped at my father from the back and tried to choke him with a rope.

My father reached over his head and twisted the guy's neck. It made a cracking sound like when you break a dry stick. The guy shrieked. He let go of my father and collapsed onto the ground.

Another guy lunged from the front with a knife. But my father punched him full in the face before the blade could get near. The guy dropped his knife. It fell on the ground. He held his face within his two hands as crimson dripped through the cracks of his fingers.

Two others were holding shovels and looked ready to attack my father. But they looked at their friends and hesitated. One was very pale.

My father ran toward them. They dropped their shovels and sped toward the courtyard wall, climbed it like monkeys, and jumped outside into the street.

My father climbed the wall. "You fucking cowards! Run, you sons of bitches," he shouted.

Two of those in the courtyard were lying on the ground, holding their noses. By now blood was all over their clothes. The other one was still clutching his neck as he walked toward the courtyard gate, groaning.

My father kicked the two guys on the ground. "Leave my house, or I will break every bone you have," my father shouted.

He stood there, breathing heavily, looking around. He asked me whether I was okay.

"You were great!" I said admiringly.

"Oh, come on, I've done sixteen years of boxing. This kind of fighting is like sipping tea," he said with a satisfied smile.

He picked up the intruders' shovels and hid them under some leaves.

"We might need these when we come back," he said.


We went all over our courtyard and checked each room. There was nothing that we could take home with us. Everything had been stolen. There were holes in the walls and floor of each room. The thieves probably thought we had buried something beneath them.

My father and I walked all around. He saw that the earth had not been disturbed where the cucumbers had grown. I thought he would start digging, but he turned and said, "We better go home now before they come back with some more guys." I had been thinking the same. "I will come here tomorrow with my brothers."

My father stepped outside the courtyard with me behind him. Two feet in front of us a strange spray of sparks rose up from the sidewalk accompanied a popping sound. I instantly knew it was bullets. My father ran to the other side of the street and yelled at me, "Move it!" As we ran, a line of bullets followed us, hitting the pavement inches from our feet. We crouched along a shabby wall opposite our courtyard. The shooting stopped.

By now, we had learned that ceasefires did not mean too much. The snipers on the mountain were Panjshiris. But the flat land around our old neighborhood was controlled by the Hazaras. A ceasefire meant that they were supposed to stop launching the rockets at each other that had come from the Americans to be used by the Mujahedin against the Russians. But the Russians were defeated and long gone. However, that did not stop the snipers from shooting people for fun. Sometimes, even in the middle of a ceasefire, there would be a small fight with rockets fired between two factions, and then everything would go quiet again quickly.

My heart was racing, and my clothes clung to my back with cold sweat. I had no time to think about how I had allowed myself, once again, to be drawn into the very heart of the madness of this war. My eyes were fixed on the next building that would provide some cover. We ran to it, then around a corner wall. Under an overhanging roof, we found four middle-aged men sheltering there who had also come to visit their houses. They were trembling like leaves.

We sat there for a few minutes and had no idea where to go. A guy with a rifle crept slowly toward us. He was a sniper, too, trying to shoot the sniper on the mountain.

He pointed his rifle upward and took aim. High on the mountain, we saw a flash of light, and a second later a bullet hit the leg of our sniper. His clothes erupted in bursts of bright red, and his face showed a terrible pain as he cried out.

We all ran from that hiding place to the opposite building, and again a line of bullets rained down next to our feet. I could feel chips of the pavement hitting my legs, but no bullets hit us. We sat there pressed tight against the wall and stared at our sniper. There was nothing we could do to help him. He stood up and ran toward us to take shelter. When he got to the middle of the road, dragging his leg, three bullets hit him in his back. His body hurtled forward, jerking with each hit. His face showed an agony beyond describing.

He turned around, faced the mountain, and fired three times, with spurts of blood jerking out of the back of his hand. Crimson bursts spattered across his broad chest as more bullets hit him.

A friend of his appeared from another corner of the road, but the sniper on the mountain was very quick and hit the sniper's friend, too. The force of the bullets knocked him backward. He died right away.

Our sniper had collapsed into a sitting position. He was still in the middle of the road. He gazed at his feet, saw his torn flesh, blinked with a glazed and mystified look. Then he raised his rifle toward the mountain.

"You bastard! You must die, too," he shouted, and it echoed. We looked where he was pointing. We saw a flash of light like before. Maybe the sniper on the mountain had already squeezed the trigger. The blast thudded into the throat of our sniper. He grunted loudly. His eyes rolled into his head. He never had a chance to pull his trigger. His head slumped onto his arm.

My father stood up, and a bullet hit the wall next to his head. He quickly scrunched down.

"Probably we should just wait here a while," my father proposed. "Maybe they will get bored and forget about us." The other men agreed. We sat quietly without saying anything and let an hour pass.

We were beginning to think about moving again when a large dog ambled toward us. He went to lift his leg against the wall on the other side of the street. As he did, a sniper sprayed him with bullets. The dog was flung into the air, howling. The sniper had let us know he had not forgotten us.

We sat there until night fell.

"We have to creep all the way out of this area," my father finally said.

The other four nodded their heads as a sign of agreement, and then slowly we inched ourselves along the wall all the way to the end of that street and the next one until we got to a roundabout. There we saw trucks with black smoke boiling up from under them, and people running up and down the road.

Hesitantly, we stood up and walked normally. Here on the main road, with so many people, the snipers would probably not shoot at us. This was how war in Kabul was fought. Nothing made sense.

We said goodbye, and we all went our separate ways. Nobody mentioned our sniper who had been killed. But we all knew he had saved us.


My father and I sat on that roundabout and waited for a taxi. I stared at the park across the road where I used to race bicycles with my cousins and play hide-and-seek with my classmates after school. Now the park was dry and dirty. Bullet casings were everywhere. Our neighborhood is cursed, I thought, as a taxi slowed to a halt in front of us.

We climbed into the backseat and headed toward Kart-e-Parwan. It took almost an hour to get there. Neither of us said anything all the way home. And I did not mind.

# 14

❖

## *Wakeel*

My father opened the door of our room. My mother had just finished her evening prayers. She folded the prayer rug and put it on a shelf. She turned around to go out and prepare dinner. Then she saw us standing on the threshold of the door. She looked like she had cried a lot in the hours since she had expected us to reach home.

My father hugged her. "It's okay, it is okay. We're fine. You see, nothing happened to us. We are the cats with seven lives," my father whispered as he rubbed her back. My mother opened her arms for me, and the three of us stood clinging to one another as if the world and whatever it might bring would never be allowed to separate us.

I needed to bathe, but I wanted to find Wakeel first. My mother said that he had waited for us, but when we did not show up and it was getting dark, he went back to Makroyan to be with our grandfather.

Ever since his father had disappeared, Wakeel always felt very lonely if Grandfather or I was not nearby. He always had friends. Everyone enjoyed being with him. But he needed to know that either Grandfather or I was somewhere close.

"He said he wanted to get a real bath in a tub," my mother explained. There were no bathtubs at Noborja. We washed by pouring small amounts of water over us from the buckets I carried from the ancient water channel known as the *karuz* at the bottom of the garden. Sometimes we heated it first in one of Haji Noor Sher's large Russian samovars. "He said he will come back tomorrow."

I wanted to go to Makroyan, too, for a real bath in a tub, and even more to talk to Wakeel, to tell him what I had seen. I felt like I was carrying a terrible weight in my soul. I knew he could help take it from me. He would listen very carefully to everything I told him and ask questions that only good listeners ask.

But I was too exhausted to go anywhere. I would wait and see him the next day. I knew his habits, though, and as I lay half dozing on my bed I could picture in my mind everything he was doing.

After his bath, he put on the blue *shalwar kamiz* that he recently had had made. He had outgrown all his clothes in recent months and was getting taller. He stood before the hall mirror after and combed his hair carefully. He carried his other freshly washed clothes to the balcony and hung them on the line. From there he could see some young guys he knew sitting around a fire they had made in the small park between the buildings. They each had a glass of tea in their hands and were talking and laughing.

Wakeel hollered at his friends, and they invited him to come down for tea. He hesitated for a second, trying to decide whether to join them. He turned on the switch to see whether there was electricity to watch TV, but there was not.

He said his evening prayers, and then stood before the hall mirror again and looked at himself. He liked his hairstyle very much. He had found a new barber in Makroyan who could cut hair very stylishly. He was almost twenty now and had begun to think about such things.

He went down the stairs and met his friends where they were sitting around their bonfire. He shook hands with all of them and made a few jokes as he always did. They asked him to sit, but he kept standing.

"Did you come from a city of standing people?" one of his friends asked him.

"No, from the city of people who just took a bath and don't want their clothes to get smoky," Wakeel joked back.

Everybody laughed.

"Do you want tea?" another friend asked.

"No, thanks!" Wakeel said, smiling. He was already thinking that he should go back into the apartment. The autumn breezes felt cooler down here than they had on the balcony, and he had recovered from the flu only a few days earlier.

He gazed at the clear sky where the half-moon had started to shine, and daylight was fading to dusk. The sparrows' *chuk-chuk* calls were the only sound. They were flying from one branch to the next, from one tree to another, to find their nests and prepare for the night. Wakeel looked around him and took a deep, happy breath.

He was the first to hear the whine of the rocket.

"Get down! Everybody! Down on the ground! Cover your heads. Cover up!" His shout was lost in the explosion of a rocket that landed a few feet behind him. A moment later, another one hit nearby, and then a third.

Then it was so quiet, it was as if the whole world had stopped. The air was laced with the smell of burning cordite, and a cloud of dust rose swiftly to hang above the place where the rockets had landed.

Afterward his friends told us how Wakeel had been the only one standing when the rockets hit. In warning his friends, he did not cover himself in the few seconds that he had. Now he wavered and could not stand anymore. His slender body dropped to the ground. His eyes were wide open, still staring at the sky, at the half-moon. His friends rushed toward him.

Wakeel lay on his side. Springs of crimson spread over his freshly ironed blue clothes. Rocket shrapnel had made dozens of holes in his back. Labored sounds escaped his heaving chest. His mouth quivered. One of his friends sat on the ground and cradled Wakeel's head on his lap and begged him to talk, even as he cried out for help.

Wakeel whispered something and went silent. He had seen so much death. He understood what was happening. Perhaps he had a last wish that he needed to tell someone. Every breath was a fight for him now.

My youngest uncle, who was barely older than Wakeel, appeared from somewhere and rushed toward him, his nephew, his best friend. My uncle sank to the ground and knelt over Wakeel's bloodied body. Wakeel was still gazing at the half-moon. My uncle lifted him onto his shoulder and ran to the road. For the longest time, he could not find a taxi, and even when he did, he knew Wakeel had already said his goodbyes to this world.

Still, he took him to a hospital. He had lost Wakeel's father, his own brother, fifteen years before. He could not accept that he was losing his last connection with his beloved oldest brother.

"He is dead," the doctor said.

It was around eight o'clock. We already had had our dinner. I was ready to sleep, hoping that image of the sniper's body would not stay lodged in my mind and keep me awake. My father was watching the news on television, which reported that rockets had landed in Makroyan, despite the ceasefire. They were Gulbuddin's rockets. Ceasefires meant nothing to him.

I heard a loud knocking on the large gate that opened to the street. My father sent me to see who was there. I had nearly been asleep. Resentfully, I went out of the courtyard and across the open space where Haji Noor Sher had always parked his large Chevrolet with the canvas roof that was a twin to the one owned by the king.

I opened the gate and found my uncle with his face and clothes drenched with blood. We looked at each other, but he said nothing. It was several moments before I realized that the blood-soaked body on his shoulder was Wakeel, and then only as my uncle was already walking past me. He carried Wakeel's lifeless body to the courtyard.

I wanted to follow him, but my legs were shaking. There was no strength in them to carry me. I held tight to the handle on the gate, then tried to walk again, but I felt that my stomach was falling down. Somehow I managed to close the gate. My uncle disappeared through the archway that led into the courtyard. No! I could not let him take Wakeel from me. No! Suddenly, I was running after them. No!

My uncle laid Wakeel on the ground in front of our windows beneath the tall acacia tree.

My father came out and saw his beloved nephew wrapped in blood. He was shaking his head from side to side, not willing to believe what he was seeing.

He took a deep breath and screamed at heaven, "Oh God, why are you doing this to us?" His voice echoed throughout the courtyard.

Immediately, all of our neighbors in the courtyard were at their windows. A minute later they had surrounded the body, staring at Wakeel, whom they all loved so much.

My only uncle who was still living in the old fort came running out of his rooms holding a book. When he saw Wakeel on the grass, he dropped the book and started slamming the palms of his hands against his head, moaning, and calling out the name of God. His wife tried to make him stop, but he could not.

Wakeel was remarkably long. I had never thought of him that way. His toes were strangely widespread, and his hands were quietly crossed on his chest. I looked at him and looked at him and looked at him. Why was he lying like that? What was I seeing? Nothing was real. A light breeze stirred the carpet of yellow leaves from the acacia tree that had woven itself on the grass. A few of them brushed across Wakeel's immobile face.

A loud cry burst from me, and I wept. I wept for Wakeel. I wept for me. I wept for everything that had happened since the Holy Warriors had destroyed our country and our lives. I do not know how long I cried, but after a while I found myself folded in my mother's arms. She was crying, too.

A few hours later, Wakeel's mother arrived from her brother's house. She had been at her nephew's engagement party. She knelt beside Wakeel and kept muttering things in a deep, hoarse voice. Her eyes were larger than I had ever seen them.

She spent the entire night on the ground next to her son, crying and laughing, like a crazy woman, and sometimes muttering things that we could not hear. I lay in my bed, letting the tears roll silently down my face.

More than at any time in my life, I wanted to be with my grandfather. But it was too dangerous to cross Kabul at night.


Early in the morning, Grandfather and my uncles arrived to take Wakeel for burial. I wanted to help carry him, but though I was thirteen years old, I was too short. I walked next to my father as he and my uncles carried Wakeel out of the courtyard on their shoulders. They carried him on a bamboo litter, still wearing his bloody clothes. His body had not been washed, since he was a martyr.

His mother ran after us, trying to stop us from taking her only son away, but her feet would not let her. She stumbled and collapsed on the ground. She stood again briefly, but then fell down again and rolled onto her back. The other women came and tried to help her. Her hair streamed over the ground, her unseeing eyes gazing into some other world, her teeth clenched. She cried out loud. Slowly they helped her get up.

The other women knew they should try to hold her back, but they let her go, though there is no place for a woman at a Muslim burial. She stood yet again to run after us, but again she fell down, and for a time she went unconscious.


We finished the rituals and put the body in the grave. We had not been able to go to our family cemetery since it was near Grandfather's house on the other side of the Koh-e-Aliabad, and we had no way of knowing whether the snipers on the mountain would respect us as we carried Wakeel's body. So we left him with strangers in a small, old cemetery called Nawabad that was protected from the snipers by the spur of a low, steep hill.

A butterfly appeared over the loose earth of the grave and fluttered around for a few moments before settling on it. The undersides of its wings were powdery white. When it opened them, the tops were such a dark red that it looked like an open wound.

It was lifted by a breeze and borne away. I watched it go. It grew smaller and smaller. I knew it was Wakeel's soul leaving his body, and us, and I knew he was trying to tell me that he was all right. He had always believed in signs. I wanted to be flying away with him, too. I wept again, but a strange, warm feeling filled me that brought a sense of peace of a kind that I had never known before and never have since. The butterfly disappeared from sight as it drifted across the top of the steep cemetery hill.

All around me, Grandfather, my father and my uncles, and all my other male relatives stood frozen in grief. Jerk stood next to his father, looking down and not trying to hide his tears. Though he had been the target of Wakeel's relentless jests, he loved Wakeel, as we all did. Jerk had no one to protect him anymore, or to tease him, or to help him fly kites, or to make him run faster when we played football, or to help him with his homework.

Shortly after we finished the prayers, Wakeel's mother arrived with the other women. She was crying as if she herself were dying. She lowered herself to the ground and knelt next to the grave, arranging and rearranging the stones on the loose earth. We all started weeping with her, but there was nothing we could do for her. I was very grateful that Wakeel had shown me his soul in that butterfly, and that Grandfather was there with me, too.

Though we had finished what we had come to do, we knew we could not leave until Wakeel's mother was ready to come with us. After half an hour or so, she rose and quietly started walking away. The other women, who had been waiting at a distance, quickly surrounded her and let her lean on them as they picked their way down the cemetery's rocky slope.

We walked slowly all the way home. I walked next to Grandfather, but he was so upset that he hardly noticed me. I tried to talk to him, so he would not feel so sad. He did not seem to listen. Then he spoke.

"I have always thought that people's sorrows come from three reasons," Grandfather said. "They always want everything immediately, without effort. They want more than they need. And they are not happy with what they have. But now I realize that the greatest sorrow of the world is to lose a gift from God."

I did not understand.

"Wakeel was the gift of God to us, but we hardly noticed its worth. So, God took it back," Grandfather said.

I told him about the butterfly. He crouched down on one knee, then opened his arms and embraced me. "You always find something that makes me feel better."

His face was level with mine, and for the first time I could see that even his eyes were red and wet. "Do you know what happens to people when they die?" Grandfather asked with a sad smile.

"Yes, of course I do. That is the first lesson the mullah taught me and the other boys on our first day at the mosque," I replied.

"Right. When we die, we believe we go to heaven, or we rest forever, or we turn into angels, or we go to paradise. That's probably all true. But let me tell you something: I believe that when we die at least a small part of our soul enters the one whom we loved the most, and makes that person wiser."

Grandfather had said things like this to me many times. I always understood the words, but sometimes it took me weeks to know what real meaning lay behind them, and what lesson lay in them for me.

Grandfather spent a week with us, then he said he must go to be with Wakeel's mother. I understood. I loved Wakeel's mother and could not imagine how lost she was feeling. She was like a second mother to us. That is why we called her Abbo, which in Pashto means "mother." When we were little, she often looked after us when my mother was at the bank and my father at his school and for some reason they could not come home to prepare our lunch. Abbo fed us, washed us, put us in bed for our naps, woke us up, and took us to the other side of the courtyard to play with her children and our other cousins.

Abbo was always a good storyteller. She knows many stories, funny and sad ones, but now she tells her son's story more than any other. Every time she tells it, her eyes get red, tears roll out of them, and her voice shakes, but she continues until she finishes. Even though it is painful to hear, no one can leave in the middle, because she always tells it as if she had just heard all the details a short while before. She always says the same words, as though reciting something from a holy book. Once I left the room when she started telling a distant relative what had happened. But though I did not want to hear it, I found I could not stay outside and leave her alone with Wakeel. I went back in and sat next to her.

She had asked hard questions of all of Wakeel's friends and others who had been there that evening. She knows every detail as if she had seen them with her own eyes. I cannot imagine how painful that has been for her. It is even painful to listen to her, but we listen to her because we love her.

When Grandfather left to go back to Makroyan, I felt more alone than I ever had before. I had so many things to ask him.

Some days I sat under the acacia tree in the courtyard where Wakeel's body had lain. I was waiting for the butterfly. But it never came back.

# 15

❖

## *Inferno*

A rocket landed in the room upstairs where my father stored his carpets. It was late on a Friday afternoon in the middle of the summer, when everything was dry and the weather was windy and dusty.

When it hit, my father was drinking tea with the next-door neighbors and trying to buy their carpets, along with an old silver vessel from the twelfth-century Ghaznawi dynasty. It had two hundred pounds of rice in it. The neighbor was moving to Pakistan, and from there to Canada to stay with relatives who had made arrangements through the United Nations.

My father wanted to buy their carpets, because they were at least a hundred years old and still in good condition. He could sell them for twice what he paid. He also wanted to buy the old silver vessel, because he knew that the guys who took those old pieces to Pakistan paid good money. He was trying to buy their rice as well since it came from Kunduz, and was a bit cheaper than the market price for imported rice.

I was just coming back into the courtyard, carrying water in buckets from the tap at the mosque below the garden. In those days, all the neighborhood water pumps installed around Kabul by the municipal government had dried because of a drought, and most of the pipes had been destroyed. Now we had to go long distances to find a working well. The mosque had one in its garden. I had just made my fourth trip. I was tired and was trying to catch my breath.

The noise of the rocket exploding was so loud that in actual fact I heard nothing. I could only feel a heavy and deep wave that shook the entire fort. Smoke mixed with dust started pouring out first one, and then another of the three large windows that faced the courtyard. I was stunned and confused. What should I do with such smoke? How could I turn it off? I was afraid to get close to that room. But I did not want all of my father's carpets to burn while I watched and did nothing. But I could not think of anything. I was very dizzy, and completely deaf.

I saw the mouth of my neighbor's son was opening and closing, but I could not hear a word he was saying. He began touching my entire body, starting from my legs and going up and up. He was looking to see whether I was injured. He nodded at me that I was all right, and we turned and looked upstairs.

My father had rushed back from the neighbors' house when he had heard the explosion. He met me just inside the gate of the courtyard, where I still held my buckets full of water.

I read horror and fear on his face. He asked me something. I could not hear him, but I instinctively knew he was asking whether my mother and the rest of the family were okay.

My mother and sisters had been watching a Bollywood movie downstairs, directly under the room that was hit. When the rocket exploded, it shook the whole fort, and the dust puffed out of the ceiling and cracks in the old mud walls.

Now my mother came running out into the courtyard with my sisters. She was almost dragging my little brother, even though he could walk now. In her arms, she had my newest little sister, who was only a few months old. From head to toe they were all covered with dust. They looked lost and confused and were probably deaf like me.

My father could see that they were not injured, and so he looked up at the storeroom, where all his hard work and our hope of ever fleeing Afghanistan were turning into smoke.

He grabbed my two heavy buckets full of water as if there were nothing in them and rushed up the outside stairs to the terrace in front of the burning room. I followed him. He jumped inside the room through the one window clear of smoke, holding one bucket. Then he gestured to me for the other.

Now he was inside. Lost in the thick, black smoke, he threw the water from the first bucket, unsure of where it was going. Where it hit, the smoke turned to fire, as if he had poured gasoline on it. He threw the second bucket, but he was suddenly surrounded by fire; he was in the heart of it. I could see he was shouting for help.

I shouted at him to run out through the fire before it got stronger and even more uncontrollable. I heard myself in my head louder than I actually sounded, and it was painful. Perhaps he heard me, or perhaps it was just his instincts. He leaped through the fire and jumped out the window. His shoes and trousers were in flames. The fire quickly rose to his chest and back.

Someone screamed at him to roll on the ground, probably my mother. The fire on his back appeared to go out when he rolled on it. But when he rolled onto his chest, the flames on his back flared up again. He kept rolling back and forth. My mother brought a bucket of water from our bathroom inside the house and poured it on him. Smoke mixed with steam rose over my father as he kept rolling back and forth on the earthen, now muddy terrace.

He stood up, surrounded by steam with smoke rising up all around him. We could hardly see his face. His clothes were badly singed, but somehow he was unharmed.

He grabbed another bucket of water that my sister brought from the house and rushed toward the windows. By now the fire was pouring out all three of the big windows. There was no doubt now that my father's carpets were fueling that fire.

My mother raced after him, yelling, and held his shoulder to stop him from going into the blaze again with his small bucket of water. It was like spitting on such a fire.

My father shouted back at her as she tried to drag him away by one arm, but he shook her off and stood there as every second the fire grew bigger. I watched it all like a silent movie, as I could still hear nothing. The roof beams by then were burning, and one of them collapsed onto his carpets. Slowly, his head fell down on his chest in despair. He put the bucket full of water by his feet.

One hour later, when the fire had already consumed the thick beams of the ceiling and what was left of the carpets, the firefighters arrived. None of their equipment fit through that one very small door into the courtyard and the angled passageway within. The fort with its high walls was like a large open box, and the firefighters had no ladders long enough to climb over and get inside it.

Our neighbors brought their narrow bamboo ladders, and eventually three firefighters climbed up the walls from the garden side and started pouring water into the heart of the fire. The blaze sent shadows of the dark and bitter-smelling smoke of burning wool over the whole neighborhood. The sky choked on it.

More neighbors arrived. But when they heard the muffled, defiant roar of the fire, they knew there was nothing they could do.

There was now thick, white smoke in place of the orange flames, and the black smoke lessened. The firefighters were finally able to go into the room and check for hot spots. The fire still smoldered in crevices in the walls.

After a couple of hours, it appeared to have died down. But the firefighters did not let us go in. The mud bricks in the walls had a lot of straw in them, with wooden posts and beams buried within. It could all flare up and start burning again at any time.

The courtyard was still full of our neighborhood people. Slowly, one by one they left, as night came, shaking their heads sadly, and talking about how big the fire had become in such a short time.

My father and I walked inside the burned-out room. The ceiling had fallen in, and everything was hot and steaming. He started looking for his carpets under the tons of mud that had been the earthen roof. He was breathing very hard.

He tried to dig the hot earth with his hands. It singed his fingers, and he shouted at me to bring him a shovel instead of staring at him like a nutcase. I was now beginning to hear again, but with a loud ringing in my ears.

I brought him a shovel. He shoveled for half an hour without stop. He was soaked in sweat. His burned clothes clung to his back, and I could see every muscle straining. With each minute, his shoveling got faster and faster. Finally, he reached the floor and found nothing except a layer of ashes where his carpets had been.

"Oh God, why have you done this to me? Do I deserve this?" he cried out. It scared me. Such heavy grief from the depth of his soul.

A strong wind started to blow. Some of the half-burned wood caught fire again. My father cried for water. I brought him two buckets from the storage tank in our bathroom, and he poured them where the fire had blazed up. A minute later another crevice in the wall caught fire. We threw water there as well. Then another place flared up, and another, until seven o'clock the next morning. My father and I did not sleep that night, or eat either.

He did not want my mother and sisters sleeping in the rooms beneath the one that had burned, and so he made a shelter in the corner of the courtyard for them. All night, they kept waking up, hungry and cold, dreaming that there was another fire they had to put out.

The next night, my sisters were still afraid to move back into those rooms downstairs, though by then they were safe. Everything smelled of smoke, though, and was covered with dust.

We all slept in the shelter my father had made the previous night. We made a fire in front of it for light. It reminded me of those nights with the Kuchis when we ate and laughed and told stories with the sounds of the animals nearby in the darkness.

But we were not with the Kuchis anymore. Fire had a different meaning to us now. I was lying between my father and mother, and the sound of their breathing assured me of their sleep, though with my mother you could never tell. Sometimes she would wake in the middle of the night and stare into space with tears on her cheeks.

That night I had seen her crying again. I reached out and touched her on the shoulder and asked whether she was all right. She quickly turned her back without replying. She never sobbed or wailed or sniffed like an ordinary person. She cried when nobody could see or hear her, letting the tears empty out of her in a stream of silent sorrow.

The next day we moved back into the downstairs rooms, even though they still smelled smoky. My father was deeply depressed. He did not help us carry our things back in. He sat under the acacia tree where Wakeel's body had lain, his head on his knees, sitting like that for hours. It was as if he were dead himself. My mother asked him to have lunch with us, but he did not eat or drink anything. His lips were dry, and brown bags had formed under his eyes.

Finally, around one o'clock in the morning he came in and lay next to my mother. He was cold and shivering. My mother covered him with her blanket and hugged him until he stopped shaking. The next day, he did not talk to anyone. He just sat next to the window, staring outside at one spot, not knowing what he was looking at. When my sisters and I talked, we whispered. When we walked, we tiptoed. And when we ate, we tried not to make any sound with our spoons and forks.

After a week, he began to ask for a few things, like a glass of water, or a cup of tea. My mother began to cook everything salty or oily, knowing that my father did not like this. He started fussing about the salt and oil. My mother shouted back at him not to complain. He left the room and went out. My mother smiled at us and said, "He'll come back happy like before." We did not know what she was talking about.

Three hours later my father came back with bags of fruit and a few kilos of beef. He had a sad smile on his face, like his own father's. That night my mother cooked us good food, and my father began to make jokes. The noise of forks and spoons started again. We did not have to whisper or tiptoe anymore.


The factions had started fighting yet again, and again trapped us in one room like mice in a hole.

The rockets were raining all over Kabul City nonstop. Gulbuddin was firing his American rockets at the Panjshiris who lived in the area around our Fort of Nine Towers. Dostum, the Uzbek commander, was also sending his rockets against the Panjshiris, both to our area and to Makroyan. The Hazaras were sending rockets against the Panjshiris, who were also sending rockets to the Hazaras. Sayyaf fired rockets from the high mountains west of Kabul aimed at the Panjshiris and the Hazaras. Sometimes three thousand rockets fell on Kabul in one day. When the rockets stopped for a few minutes, it was unnaturally silent. But, in fact, there was never truly silence. The house was always talking to itself, the clicking of the clock in the next room, the periodic judder and whir of the refrigerator when we had electricity. From the bathroom the drip, drip, drip of water from the nozzle into a big pot full of water. Every now and then out on the road, there was the whoosh of a passing car or the rumble of a truck.

We listened for the sound of the releasing of the rocket, then its landing that shook the ground like an earthquake. In two months, twenty-nine rockets landed in that fort and its garden. The last of the nine towers still stood at the corner of the old fort, but it no longer made me feel safe. For more than a hundred years, the towers had protected the people inside. Not anymore. Not in this time of Shaitan.

One reason why Grandfather and the rest of the family had all moved to the solidly built blocks of Makroyan was that they thought it would be safer there. But they were as trapped in Makroyan as we were at the Qala-e-Noborja in Kart-e-Parwan. For weeks we had no idea what was happening to them. Were they still alive, dead, wounded? We had no phones; no one was in the street to carry a message. My father stopped listening to the BBC and the other news channels, because they made us even more anxious, telling us about the casualties and announcing the names of the injured in hospitals and the lack of blood for transfusions, or medicine, or doctors.

For whole days and weeks we sat at the corner of the room, murmuring our prayers and waiting for a rocket to kill us all together. One night when the noise of the exploding rockets was too loud to let me sleep, I climbed up on the roof of the old fort and sat near the one remaining tower. I watched one rocket after another fall on the flatland neighborhoods in front of me. Each time when a rocket whistled overhead, I was momentarily surprised that it had not killed me. But a part of me no longer cared. I simply presumed that one of them would soon land next to me, and that I would not live to see the morning.

Sometimes my father, mother, sisters, and I wrote letters to my grand-father, aunts, uncles, and cousins. When there was ceasefire for a day or two, we sent those letters that we had written days or weeks ago with anybody in the neighborhood we could find who had to go to Makroyan for some reason. In the same day we might receive a bunch of letters from all of them, if one of my uncles could make the trip. Then the war would set in again, and we would not hear from each other for weeks.

Those were the worst days of my life. Yet there was something sweet about them. Whenever I wrote letters, I was very careful to use the right words in the right places. I expected the same careful atten-tion to detail from those who answered my letters. In those days when most people were worried about staying alive, I was focused on how to write a beautiful letter and express my feelings accurately about everything, and in precise chronological order. I was only just finding my way into my teenage years, but with life so fragile, the schooling I might have had, or the sports I might have played, or the work I might have done meant nothing.

After two months of constant war all over Kabul, once again we had a ceasefire for a few weeks. Grandfather came to our house and spent those days with us. I was so happy to sit next to him, and to put my head on his lap and listen to his breathing when he was reading or eating or talking to others.

The night before he returned to Makroyan, he talked with my father and mother late into the night, long after the rest of us went to sleep. After he left, I went to sit under the acacia tree feeling a deep loneliness. A short while later, my father came and sat down next to me.

"We made a decision last night while you were asleep." My father paused, and then continued with a deep sigh. "Now while we are having this ceasefire, you and I are going to Pakistan. We'll rent a house there, and then come back for the others. We'll stay there until Kabul gets peaceful again."

"Isn't it going to be hard to live in a strange country?" I asked.

"We will all die if we stay here. At least we will survive in Pakistan. I'm sure you'll get used to it soon. You'll find good friends, and you will go to school again, I promise you," my father said. He had a kindly half smile. That made me feel like this was really going to happen.

I asked when we would go.

"Tomorrow," he said. He put his arm around me and let me fall against his strong chest.

# 16

◈

## The Dog

The next day around five o'clock in the morning, we said good-bye to my mother, brother, and sisters. By six o'clock, I was on the seat next to my father in an old minibus full of people. Some of the people were sitting on the floor on bags of clothes.

I had a glass of black tea in my hands and was slowly sipping it to wake me up. I enjoyed looking at the mountains and thinking about nature after the months trapped inside the fort. Now Kabul was behind us, and we were heading toward the Khyber Pass. I had heard about the Khyber Pass from my history teacher in school, as I had about the Buddhas in Bamyan, but I had never seen it. I was excited that soon I would be passing through it.

The minibus was quiet, except for the sound of the engine, and the occasional coughing or sneezing of some of the passengers. Some were having a nap. Some were looking out the windows as we twisted our way down the sides of mountains where Kabul was nestled. Sometimes the driver had to slow down because of large holes in the road. Mostly, though, he drove fast despite the steepness of the mountains.

Just as we were approaching the small town of Sarobi and almost out of the mountains, the driver hit the brakes, and my tea spilled all over my clothes. I felt the warmth of it spreading across my lap.

The other passengers shouted at the driver to be careful. The driver turned around in his seat and put his index finger on his lips and hushed us for silence. The bus doors opened, and a man followed by two bodyguards stepped inside our bus.

They eyed us coldly. There was nothing even close to a welcoming smile and no Afghan hospitality in their eyes. We were all quiet as they scanned us, one by one.

The old man who was sitting in the seat in front of us turned around and whispered to my father that the man's name was Commander Zardad.

Commander Zardad had badly pitted cheeks and the thickest black eyebrows I had ever seen over big, dark, sunken eyes, so black that they demanded full attention. He weighed only about one hundred fifty pounds, all of it bunched tightly into a black leather jacket and *shalwar kamiz*. He selected several men and women from our minibus, including my father, and led them off the bus, then told the driver to continue his journey to Pakistan. The panicked driver started the engine. I jumped off before he could drive away.

Zardad looked me in the eye and said, "You are not invited."

"You have my father, and I want to stay with him," I said.

"Then you must come," he said, and slapped me on my shoulder gently like an old friend.

We walked for ten minutes up the side of the steep mountain to get to his camp. He had more than two hundred men, all armed and resting under the shade of their tents. Some of them were drinking tea, some of them were asleep, and some of them were just staring at us.

We were led into a large tent that was open on one side and told to sit down. None of us did. We stood there frozen. Inside the tent, several corpses were laid out on the ground. They were naked and looked like they had been badly bitten all over.

One was a girl who looked to be in her early twenties. She was petite with yellow hair that streamed all around her head. She had a pretty face and a slender body with long legs. Her shoulders were narrow, hardly more than a dozen inches across. Her breasts were small, but they looked almost like they had been shredded.

There were bite marks up and down her arms and legs, especially around her thighs.

A dead man next to her looked like a statue that had been cut from white stone, as if all his blood had been drained. Like the girl, he seemed more like an American or a European than an Afghan. He was very muscular. But he, too, had been bitten all over. His throat had been slashed, and so had his wrists and thighs and ankles. I could see no bruises on his hands; he had not been able to land any punches on his attackers. There was a cold, desperate horror frozen on his face. His mouth and eyes were wide open.

Some other bodies that lay near them were covered with white sheets that had bloodstains all over them.

"You see these people?" Zardad said. "They avoided giving me their money, and in the end they lost their lives as well as their money. If you guys love your lives, give me your money, and you are free to go."

My father took out all his money from his pockets and gave it to Commander Zardad.

"Where is your house?" Zardad asked.

"In Kabul," my father replied without emotion.

"Why are you going to Pakistan?"

"To see if we can live there," my father said.

"You don't have a wife and more kids?" Zardad asked.

"Yes," my father said.

"Why are they not with you?"

"I couldn't take them with me to Pakistan now. I have no house for them there. After I find a place, I will go back for them," my father explained matter-of-factly.

"You must be a rich man. Let's make a deal. I let your son go home and bring more money, then you're free to go. Does it sound good?" Zardad asked, his big eyebrows raised up.

"We don't have much money. Just enough for us to live on for a while. If I give it all to you, how will I feed my kids?" my father asked.

"Don't answer me with a question," Zardad shot back.

My father lowered his head and said nothing.

Zardad shouted out, "Dog!" I looked around, expecting to see one of his men come with the kind of dog that was used for fighting.

I looked at the corpses with their bite marks and became very frightened. Why did Zardad want a dog?

A man entered the tent. He had big teeth, like long, yellow fangs. He laughed when he saw us.

Zardad rasped an order. "Tie him."

Two of his men grabbed my father from behind while another one pulled off his *kamiz* shirt, then his *shalwar* trousers. They tied his hands and feet with chains to a large frame made from thick wooden beams. They pulled his wrists upward to the top corners of the frame. His feet were spread apart and chained to the bottom. He looked like one of the carpets I had seen him stretch so many times.

When my father could not move anymore and all eyes were fixed on him, Zardad ordered the man he called Dog to start. Dog opened his mouth wide and sank his teeth into one of my father's biceps.

My father cried out in pain and shouted that he did not have any money. This time Zardad ordered the man to hang by his teeth from my father's other arm. He closed his jaws on my father again and raised his feet from the ground as he had been told. My father was screaming now, and turning redder and redder.

I watched in disbelief. I had seen so many things since the fighting had begun, and so much cruelty, but I had never imagined anything as unspeakably strange as this.

The fanged man continued biting my father all over: his arms, shoulders, thighs, chest, underarms, neck, and buttocks. My father continued shouting while Zardad sat casually on a chair, twenty feet away, watching him and sipping his tea. He showed no emotion despite my father's piercing yells.

I could hardly even breathe. I understood that I was watching my father die, and my mind raced as I thought, "How can I take the responsibility for my family? I'm only thirteen years old."

And then the shouting grew quieter, as my father began to lose strength. His eyes closed. His body hung limply in the chains. His wounds were bleeding badly.

Zardad finally ordered two other men to release him. They undid the chains, and my father collapsed on the ground. They grabbed him by his wrists and dragged him thirty feet across the gravel, scraping the skin off his back as they went. He lay there, not moving, just moaning.

Then the two guys came and grabbed me. They pulled off my clothes except for my undershorts and a thin chain around my neck with a picture of Mecca hanging from it. They fastened the chains that they had used on my father around my wrists and ankles. Strangely, as they pulled the chains tight, cutting into my skin, I felt a sense of relief. I had cheated death so many times since the war had started. Today it would all end.

The man with the fangs slowly walked toward me. His mouth was outlined with my father's blood, but his skin was deathly pale, as if he had no blood of his own in his veins. When he walked, he seemed like he hardly had enough energy to propel himself.

When he bit me the first time, it was like a saw or a sharp piece of metal was sinking into my arms. The pain was so powerful that the light started instantly going from my eyes, and everything around me got darker and darker. I shouted louder than I ever have.

"Don't touch him," my father shouted hoarsely. He tried to stand. Two men ran over and held him back. Dried blood covered his whole body, except for his face. "Come and do it to me!"

"No, your son has fresher blood and tender skin," the man whispered so softly that I hardly heard him. "You've got old blood. This is more fun with your son." Then he bit me on my left leg. This time it was worse than before. Then on my shoulder, and on my back. I could do nothing but howl.

One of Zardad's soldiers stepped forward. "Please stop for a while, sir. Give them a break." The soldier spoke in Pashto.

"I'm not taking orders from you. You're taking orders from me," Zardad snapped back. Until now he had spoken only in Dari. He did not even look at the soldier. He was still staring at me.

"Yes, sir, I know it, but I just want to have a couple of hours of sleep and these bastards keep screaming and waking me up," the soldier said.

"Hey, I'm having a good time. Don't fuck with me," Zardad said.

My father forced himself up from the ground. "What kind of a Pashtun are you?" he spat hoarsely at Zardad, speaking in Pashto.

"Are you Pashtun?" Zardad asked in amazement.

"Of course I am," my father said, his voice hardly louder than a whisper.

"Why the fuck didn't you tell me?" Zardad said. He got up from the chair where he had been watching and walked toward my father, studying him more closely. He stood over my father for a moment, then ordered his men to untie me and give us our clothes back. "I don't torture my Pashtuns," Zardad said airily as he walked back to his chair.

My father and I put on our clothes as best we could. Every time I moved, the places where the fanged man had bitten me ached like something was still tearing my skin. I was so stiff with fear, I hardly knew what I was doing. Blood ran out of the wounds and soaked my clothes. All the while, the man with the fangs was looking at me fiercely, angry that he had lost his prey and could do nothing about it.

"What about the others?" my father asked. He could not stand up straight. "Release them, too."

"You're free to go," Zardad said, like he was giving an order.

"You're not torturing these people for their money, are you? You're torturing them because you enjoy doing it," my father said.

"If you say one more word, I will forget you're a Pashtun. Understood? Go, and don't ever look back," Zardad shouted.

My father did not say anything. We left there and walked in small, painful steps along the steep path back down to the road. Ten minutes later we were in a highway taxi coming along the main road from Jalalabad to Kabul, headed toward our home.

"What is all this?" my mother asked, looking at the blood on our clothes. Her eyes were wide, her mouth open, and her face pale.

"We were bitten by a dog," my father said as he was hugging her. Then he fainted, and his body slumped onto hers.

My mother cried to me to help her with my father. We half carried and half dragged him to his bed. I told my mother what had happened to us but kept it short, because I wanted to lie down as well.

She ran outside and came back with our neighbor who was a nightshift doctor.

A few minutes later, the doctor injected him with something that made him totally numb. The doctor started to wash the wounds, first with alcohol to disinfect them, and then with a few things he mixed all together. He rubbed the wounds gently, then covered them with rolls of bandages.

When the doctor had finished my father's wounds, I showed him mine. My shoulders and arms had begun to itch and then ache. The puncture wounds of the bites were still bleeding a little, especially those on my right arm, which were the deepest. He did for me the same things that he had done for my father. He was amazed how I had endured the pain so far. But pain was our way of life now.

I woke up early the next morning and was still in bad shape. There was a blotchy redness and intense heat around each bite wound. Each one throbbed. I noticed a nasty drainage from the bites on my left leg. All the wounds were swollen to nearly twice the size they had been the night before. When I moved, I felt like something was tearing my skin.

It took us two weeks to recover. My mother would not let my father even speak of going to Pakistan again. She said that what had happened to us was a bad sign. She said that if we lived in Pakistan, it would be worse than Kabul.

"You are superstitious," my father said.

"Yes," my mother said bluntly. She was pacing the bedroom like the leopard that had been in the garden. My father watched her for a few minutes, and then told her he would like some tea.

She stopped, looked at him, and raised her finger like she was pointing to me or my sisters. "I am not going to Pakistan," she said very firmly. "I'm going to stay in Kabul. And if I die, so be it. But I'm going to die on my own piece of earth, not in some strange country."

My father knew argument would not change her mind. She walked silently from the room to get him his tea.

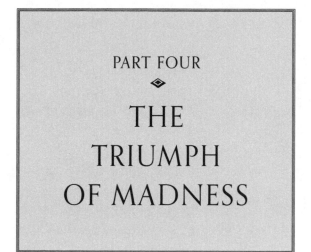

PART FOUR

THE
TRIUMPH
OF MADNESS

# 17

❖

## A New Kind of Justice

We entered a time of waiting. The fighting would end, we said, if we waited. Our lives would come back to us, if we waited. Or we would find a way out, if we waited. If our gold was still in Grandfather's garden, then it would wait there for now, just as we would wait at Noborja.

The fighting in Kabul eased, and a school near Noborja reopened. After so much thirst to go back to school, I was now disappointed by it. The school was shabby, not like the well-maintained building that the educated families in our old neighborhood had supported. There, all the teachers had known my name and my family. I was treated well and was excited by every new thing I was taught.

In this new school, many of the students came from rural areas north of Kabul, like Shamali, Parwan, and Panjshir. They spoke Dari with accents from those places that sounded strange to me. Some of their families had come to Kabul with the Mujahedin. Some of them liked to fight more than to study. In Dari we say, "If you sit with good people, you will become a good person. If you sit with bad people, you will become a bad person." The students were not really bad people, but I picked up a lot of bad habits from them.

I went every day, though, mostly because there was nothing else to do. I had missed more than two full years of school, but so had most of my classmates. We were all behind, even though some of them, like me, had been educated at home by their parents. Living in a war had also taught us many things.

Somehow I had ended up in the eighth grade. Perhaps that was because I was thirteen and looked like I should be there. I went for four hours every afternoon. The kids in the first six grades came in the morning, including my younger sisters. My older sister went to a girls' high school not far away. For as long as the ceasefires held, we could go every day.

Most of the teachers were as discouraged about life in Afghanistan as the students. The teachers tried hard to convince us that what they were teaching was important for us to learn. Maybe it was.

Sometimes in our classes we talked about the various factions, and which one was good and which one was bad. In the end, we agreed that none of them were good. Rockets still fell on Kabul sometimes, though we were never sure which faction sent them. Meanwhile, we were hearing about a new faction called the Taliban that was taking control of the cities in the south and was slowly moving into the east. Many people said they would make a circle around Kabul and drive all the other factions away. We did not know much about them. We were sick of commanders and factions.

We were more worried by our principal, who had eyes that were red like fireballs. Every day he slapped students who had been fighting until they started to cry in front of all the other students. He was a stupid man who told us to fix a faucet that was dripping precious water by jamming a stick up inside it. We did that, and we got very wet when the water squirted all over us. Then he slapped us for getting ourselves wet.

Nobody slapped him, though, when somebody discovered a dead cat in the cistern. It had been there for at least a week, and we had been drinking the water.

The one class that I did enjoy was taught by our Dari language and literature teacher. She was pretty and always cheerful. She helped me understand for the first time that there is more to a story than its plot. She told us that images created by words can have hidden meanings. I started rereading all the books that we had at home, like a detective, looking for hidden meanings that other people who were not as smart as I was could not see.

The textbooks that the school gave us had very little literature in them. Some poetry, some short stories with hard and fancy words, and some history about famous poets and writers. So, our teacher assigned us other books to read, mostly novels. A lot of the boys hated reading, and they sulked. But there were a few of us who found that every book that our teacher asked us to read was better than the one before.

Our teacher recommended novels she thought would help us understand things that are not taught in school textbooks. Mostly they were novels by Iranian authors such as Amir Ashiri, Parwiz Qazi Sayed, Aroniqi Karmani, and Jawad Fazil. She also suggested a few Western authors as well, such as Maxim Gorky, Fyodor Dostoyevsky, Leo Tolstoy, Anton Chekhov, Jack London, and Thomas Mann. *Crime and Punishment* was too much about hardship, misery, and pain. I read the first few pages, but then put the book back in its place in my cabinet and told myself that I would read it when I was no longer living in Afghanistan.

She spoke to us softly in a low voice, but in a way that everyone could hear her. When she came into the classroom, everybody stopped talking immediately, and nobody teased anyone during her lesson as we did during other classes.

One day she told us that she had received her degree in Russia, and she would have liked to have been a professor at Kabul University. But she had three sons, the oldest four years younger than we were, and she had to be home most of the time. I do not think she taught for money, because her husband had a good business in an electronics shop he owned. I think she taught because she loved literature. I was only beginning to understand what literature was, and I was excited to learn from somebody who loved it as much as she did.


As the months sifted into years, I began to notice hair on my body where it had never grown before. At first I was frightened that all the tension of the war was turning me into a monkey. I remembered the pictures in my schoolbook from all those years ago. Could it be possible that war turned humans back into monkeys?

Then, new kinds of dreams, especially about women, left me excited and self-conscious. Whenever I looked at a picture of a pretty girl in a magazine, I felt something strange.

It was not like in the old days, when a young Afghan guy could take a girl on a date. Since the Mujahedin had come, a young man had to get married to have a girlfriend. I did not want to get married at that early age.

Instead, I spent hours and hours in the gym lifting weights and training as a boxer. My arms were getting thick, and my chest began to look like a man's. Sometimes when I stood before a mirror without my shirt, I saw a body full of muscles, like those statues in the books about Plato and Socrates.

One day I pretended I was the statue of Apollo. I was posing like that with my left arm raised for a couple of minutes without knowing that my father was at the door watching me. He made fun of me for several weeks afterward. He would look at me, then hold up his left arm. I did not like him making fun of me, but at least I got to hear him laugh.

My father told jokes when we ate, but he was not happy, except when he put on his boxing gloves and was showing me how to fake a right jab, or come back with a left hook. He would not allow anyone to mention carpets, or smugglers, or Grandfather's house.

A day came when I felt like I had been living at Noborja longer than in our own home. But it had been only four years.

On a Thursday night in September 1996, we heard lots of cars running up and down the roads. There was no shooting, and no rockets. But all the roads all over Kabul were unusually busy all night.

The next morning, like other Fridays, I planned to eat my breakfast late with my family, and then, if no factions were firing at us from the mountain, go watch our neighbors playing football for an hour in the road in front of the fort. Afterward, I would come home and listen to the radio drama before we ate a big lunch with my grandfather or any of my uncles who had been able to come. While they sat and drank tea for the rest of the afternoon, I would go to the garden and sit in the shade of the grapevines to listen to sparrows make *chuk-chuk* calls and read one of my Iranian novels.

But on that Friday as I approached the gate, I could not hear any football noises from outside. Only silence.

Our front gate of corrugated steel had been shot full of holes like a colander when a rocket had landed in front of it five years before. The rocket also killed a little boy who had been feeding his donkey from a pile of trash nearby. We never had money to replace the gate and used it the way it was.

I looked through one of the holes outside to see why no one was kicking a football where the dirt road widened between the gate and the wall of the old British Embassy to make a broad playing area. But there were no footballers. Instead, I saw men who were strangers. I had never before seen such people, not even in my dreams, or in movies, or in any novel or history books.

They looked like Afghans, but were dressed strangely in long black and white turbans and very long *kamiz* that hung down over their *shalwar* trousers way below their knees. They were carrying whips.

All of them had outlined their eyes in kohl. Their beards were untrimmed and long. None had proper shoes. Instead, they wore slippers, and their feet were dusty. Most of them had snuff in their mouths. A few of them spat brown saliva into the dust in front of them, and then cleaned their mouths with the ends of their turbans.

None of them spoke. They looked lost, like men who had come from a forest or caves and had never seen buildings before.

I thought at first they might be vampires. I knew that vampires did not exist, except in stories to scare kids. But what else could I be seeing?

I could not see even one of my neighbors around. Not one. A fear rushed through me. Perhaps they had all left the town the night before without telling us. Or maybe these vampires had eaten them and were now staring at each house to see whether anyone was still inside to prey on.

"It is not possible," I reassured myself, while not being sure of anything.

Ever since the conflict between the factions had started, it usually took months for one to overcome another and take control of a neighborhood. Now this new faction seemed to have taken over the whole town with no fighting and no casualties. I had to know what was going on.

I opened the door as quietly as I could and stepped outside. Three of them heard the squeak of the gate and ran toward me. Their faces were fierce. They raised their whips.

One of them came close and asked me whether I knew where Ahmad Shah Masoud was. They were all speaking Pashto with the Kandahari accent, which has more ups and downs than the Pashto we speak in Kabul. Maybe they were part of this new Taliban faction that we had been hearing about.

"I don't know," I said fearfully in Pashto. They softened when they heard me speak their language.

"Do you know Fahim?" the same guy asked me.

"Everybody knows him," I said. Marshal Fahim was a Tajik and one of Masoud's close allies.

Another one of them pushed the two others back and grabbed me by my collar. His hands smelled like shit.

"Are you Fahim's son?" he yelled.

"*No!*" I shouted back.

"Where is his house?" he asked me as he held my collar tightly. I pointed toward the Bagh-e-Bala, a tree-covered slope that rises up steeply half a mile west of Noborja, where there used to be a garden built by the Moguls.

He was still holding me and said, "Show us his house."

I took them to Fahim's street, and from the far end pointed out to them where his house stood. The guy who had held my collar let me go.

I raced home and told my family what had happened. But they thought I was making it all up, except for my mother. I could tell by the way she listened to me that she believed me.

As he always did on Fridays when guests might come, my father had shaved very carefully that morning, and was wearing his best trousers and a neatly pressed, white short-sleeve shirt. He decided to go out to see what I was talking about.

My mother did not want him to leave the house until we heard some more news. But my father, always practical, said, "There's no fighting going on. If there is a new faction in town, I want to make them my friends."

My father came back in half an hour looking angry. There were stains of fingerprints on his face and the mark of a whip on the back of his white shirt.

"What happened to you?" my mother asked, her voice high with worry.

He did not answer. He walked across the room, sat on the floor in the corner, and put his head on his knees and his arms around his legs.

My three little sisters stopped jumping on my parents' *toshak* and throwing pillows at one another. My mother sat in front of my father and raised his head up. "What is wrong?"

"They whipped me," my father said.

"Why?" my mother asked in amazement.

"Because I had shaved my beard. They called me an infidel and a Communist," my father said, incredulously. "They said that the beard is the symbol of Islam."

"Islam is about what is in your heart, not what is on your face," my mother stated.

"I told them that if the beard is a symbol of Islam, then a goat must be a Muslim since it is born with one," my father said, looking slightly dazed as he spoke. "Then they whipped me."

"What kind of people are they?" my mother asked with disgust.

My father put his head back on his knees, and my mother kissed his head. She beckoned for us to leave the room with her and let him alone.

My mother covered her head with a scarf and went to find out for herself what she could about this new faction.

She came back after fifteen minutes. Her eyes were full of fury, and she was limping.

"Some guy with a big black turban and torn clothes and a long beard whipped me on my legs," my mother exclaimed.

"Why?" my father asked, angered and bewildered. He jumped up from where he was sitting, prepared for a fight.

"Because I was not wearing a *burqa*," my mother said. We could all see that she was suffering from the lashes.

"What the hell is going on today? Where did these weird people come from?" my father asked.

All of my sisters had come to see what was going on. "I don't want any of you to step outside of this house today," my mother said to them firmly.

"Who are these people?" my oldest sister asked my father.

"I don't know." He gazed at the ceiling and murmured, "I never had a chance to ask them."

My mother asked my older sister for a bandage and alcohol to disinfect the whip wounds on her legs. One of my little sisters turned on the radio to hear the Friday drama. Instead, we heard a strange kind of singing. We thought it must be a part of the drama, but it continued for hours. From that day, we did not hear the radio drama again for five years.

All the songs were in Pashto with no instruments, no soft background music. We heard the same type of songs from outside, from cars going from one street to the next with loudspeakers at high volume. They were songs, but they were without music.

None of our relatives would be coming for lunch that day, I was sure. And I had no appetite. I went earlier than usual to the garden to sit under the grapevine and to read and to put these new guys out of my mind. As I was settling into my usual place, I saw something shining on the ground next to the garden wall. I left my book on the ground and went to see what was there. A Kalashnikov with several boxes of bullets next to it lay in the tall grass by the wall. Nearby was a plastic bag with thirteen grenades in it.

I did not touch any of them. I was afraid that they might be wired to a mine somewhere. I called our old *chowkidar* to come see them.

The doorkeeper shuffled toward me, leaning on his stick. The end of his dirty turban hung in front of his face. It was covered with stains from the tobacco juice he was always spitting. He looked at the weapons and spat.

"They must belong to Masoud's people," our doorkeeper said. "Masoud escaped from Kabul last night. Zalmai's wife told me."

"But why are these weapons here?" I asked.

"Those who couldn't escape with Masoud had to get rid of their weapons. This new faction is saying that if they find any weapons in anybody's house, they will put them in prison," the doorkeeper said.

He knocked at a grenade with his stick. I jumped back.

"We have to hide them somewhere," he said. He opened his turban and spread it on the ground. With no fear, he gathered the Kalashnikov, the bullets, and the grenades into his turban, then he slung them onto his hunched back. He carried them across the garden to the far side where there was a pit toilet. Carefully, he dropped them one by one down the hole. Then he pressed them with a shovel until they all disappeared under the filth.

I walked all over the garden to see whether there were any more weapons. I found more grenades and some mines that looked like a yellow butterfly, two RPGs, hundreds of bullets, and six guns.

I hid one of those guns under my trousers for myself. It was the kind I had seen many times in James Bond movies. Now that I was fourteen, I understood that I had the responsibilities of a man. A gun felt like a good thing to have. We put the rest in the toilet and pressed them down until they all sank under the mess in the pit.

I continued to walk all around the garden to see whether I had missed any other weapons. While I was pushing aside some bushes, someone from the street threw two bags of grenades over the wall into the garden.

"Who the hell is that? Is our garden your trash ditch?" I shouted. I climbed the wall to see who it was.

He was a tall man with broad shoulders, running like a scared dog, trying to disappear from sight.

I shouted at him several times and cursed him for being a coward, but he did not look back as he disappeared around the corner.

I opened the bags. Each bag had twenty grenades in it. I took them to the toilet and dropped them one by one until they had all sunk out of sight.

For a week, more and more weapons came over our wall. We

collected an armory of guns, grenades, RPGs, bullets, butterfly mines, and things we had never seen before. For a week we kept putting them all in that pit toilet.

By the end of that week, there was no longer enough filth to cover all the weapons. We sent everyone in the fort to use the weapon-toilet to help cover what was in there.

One day, as I was relieving myself, I looked down through the hole to see the barrel of a Kalashnikov pointed up at my bottom. It was too late to stop.

At the beginning, some of our neighbors were afraid to use the weapon-toilet. They thought that they might cause explosions. But my father was a very good convincer.

He said that there was a rumor that if the Taliban—now we knew that was who they were—found anyone with weapons in his house, they would put the suspect in prison and whip him to death.

We all heard, "Once you are in their prison, it is almost impossible to get out, unless you bribe them with a huge amount of money." I do not know how people knew these things. The Taliban had been in Kabul only a week.

We still did not know much about them. Most of what we had heard came from the BBC. They told us how the Taliban had taken control of Jalalabad, the last city in Afghanistan before the Khyber Pass leads into Pakistan. From there, the Taliban were moving toward Kabul. Other Taliban fighters had taken control of the main road to Kabul that comes from Kandahar and the west. And still more Taliban controlled a smaller road through Logar Province to the south. The only road from Kabul that was still open was the one that went to the north.

The Mujahedin government had become weaker and weaker as the years of civil war had gone on. They could not fight back, because they were so busy fighting each other. When they heard that the Taliban had captured Sarobi, a town halfway between Jalalabad and Kabul and close to where Zardad had his camp, they panicked. They knew that thousands of Taliban would be in Kabul by the next day, showing no mercy.

So the Mujahedin factions raced out of Kabul in the middle of the night on the last road that was open. They hauled truckloads of guns and ammunition to their bases in the Panjshir Valley and across the Hindu Kush mountains in the north, so the Taliban would not get them. But that did not matter. The Taliban had been given all the weapons they needed by Pakistan.

When the first group of Taliban had arrived in Kabul, they had expected a fierce fight. Instead, they found that the Mujahedin factions were gone and the streets were empty. They were confused to find themselves in such a silent city, but they did not take long to let us know that they were now our rulers.

Every day we heard new decrees from Mullah Omar, the head of the Taliban, from Radio Sadai Shariat (The Voice of Islamic Law), received from the office of Amer bel Maruf wa Nai As Munkar (Department for the Promotion of Virtue and the Prevention of Vice).

One day: "Every man in Afghanistan should grow a beard."

The next day: "Every woman over twelve should wear a *burqa*."

The next day: "Kite flying is forbidden."

The next day: "No one should be seen to keep pigeons or fighting birds in his house. Pigeons are for shrines and mosques."

The next day: "No one anywhere in Afghanistan should watch TV. If anyone is ever found to be watching movies, he will be punished in public and imprisoned for six months."

The next day: "Every man should go to the mosque five times a day for prayers."

We could say nothing. Everyone knew, however, that sooner or later a new faction would take over and things would change. This was Afghanistan, after all. This was how things worked.

At the end of the broadcast Maulvi Nazami, the head of Radio Sadai Shariat, said, "We say the right things so that we can be loved."

A few weeks after the Taliban arrived, I saw one of them hanging out the back of a van with a loudspeaker in his right hand. He was shouting, "We, the Students of God, are bringing justice to this city and the other cities all over Afghanistan. If anyone has any interest in our justice, come to Kabul Stadium and witness our justice. Today at two o'clock."

I had been on my way to school and told some of my classmates whom I met about the strange announcement I had heard. I said that I wanted to go to the stadium to see what the Taliban meant by justice.

Some of my classmates said that they wanted to go, too. Afghans are always hungry to learn anything new. So instead of going to our classes, we headed across Kabul, hanging out the doors of an over-crowded bus.

The stadium was filled with men and schoolboys as full of curiosity as we were. A pickup truck drove into the middle of the field. That was surprising. Grass is hard to grow in Kabul, and no sensible person would drive a truck, even a lightweight one, onto a playing field. There was a loudspeaker on the back of the truck. Two Taliban wearing black *shalwar kamiz*, long hair, and white turbans stood on the truck. Even from the seats we could see the black rings of kohl around their eyes.

"We call ourselves Taliban, which means the Students of God. We never do wrong," one of the men on the back of the truck said into a microphone. "We never do wrong even by mistake. Everything we do is right, so we can be loved. Everything we say is right, so we can be cherished." As he spoke, he kept rotating so he could address every part of the stadium.

A moment later, two other Taliban brought a man onto the field with chains around his wrists, feet, and neck. The Talib with the microphone said the man was a thief who had stolen a pair of shoes from a shop.

The Talib's voice got higher and louder, which made the loud-speaker screech. "This guy has stolen a pair of shoes from a Kabul shop. He deserves amputation. Our justice for thieves is amputation. If we don't have justice toward thieves, they will take control like Genghis Khan, or English people, who are the biggest thieves of our time. Then it will be impossible to control them."

They stood the thief in the middle of the football field and opened his handcuffs. Two Taliban held his right arm down on a table. A doctor injected the man's right arm with anesthetic, then took a saw and cut off the man's hand while he watched. One of the Taliban took the hand and waved it around to the crowd. The hand was still bleeding, and the pale fingers seemed to our horrified eyes to be moving very slowly. The thief went numb and collapsed. Two other Taliban took him by the arms and dragged him off the football field.

The spectators were shocked. A stunned silence filled the entire stadium. I had been to the stadium many times with my father, but this was the first time I had experienced such total quiet there, though it was packed with thousands of men.

My classmates and I did not want to stay any longer. We stood up to leave. Some other people stood up to leave, too. But Taliban came from all directions, beat us with whips, and ordered us to sit and see the execution.

They brought another man with cuffs on his hands and chains on his feet.

The eerie silence was broken by the Taliban announcer: "This man killed his neighbor four years ago, then he escaped to Iran. When he came back, we arrested him. Now someone from the victim's family will shoot the killer in the head, and you will be witnesses."

Then a Talib handed the victim's relative a gun and asked him to shoot. The relative fired the gun and shot the murderer through the head. The bullet hit his forehead and came through the back of his head. His body shook for a few moments on the ground.

At the end, the announcer said, "We will conduct two more acts of justice on Friday. Now you can go, and you will come back next Friday. No tickets needed."

I ran out of the stadium, determined never to go back there ever again. But in the weeks that followed, a new principal who was a Talib was appointed to our school. He ordered us to go several more times, to see more of the Taliban justice. We saw women whom the Taliban said were prostitutes stoned to death. We saw men who were accused of being homosexuals killed by having a mud brick wall toppled on them. Since the Taliban left Kabul, I have never gone there again.

At the front gate of the stadium, a few Taliban gave every passerby a paper with a big headline in large black type at the top:

### JUSTICE
### REPRESENTS EQUALITY

Imprison the violators. Amputate the thefts, execute the murder, topple wall on homosexuals, and stoning to death the prostitutes!

We imprison the violators to be a lesson to them for futures that no one denies our Islamic virtue.

Amputation is needed for thieves to stop more thefts in the future.
Execution is needed for murderers to stop more murderers.
Stoning to death is needed for prostitutes to stop more adultery and prostitutions.
Adultery and prostitutions carry AIDS with them. Killing prostitutes are every Afghan's duty.

There are three types of punishment for homosexuals.

1. Take these people to top of the highest building and hurl them to death.
2. Dig a pit near a wall somewhere and put these people in it then topple the wall on them. If one does not die, then he is not a sinner and not a homosexual. The wall should be toppled on blamer.
3. Homosexual hair should be shaved and he should be taken around on top of a donkey upside down with a blackened face displaying to society.

Be aware! We bring in action the second punishment.

*We beat the sinners with whips for the minor offences. If they die under the whipping, it means they were the sinner of sinners and he or she died clean.*

Whoever had written the announcement was somebody who did not know correct grammar. When we turned the paper over, we saw a headline about the Taliban's rights for women. Below it was a long list of things that women could and could not do. My friends and I read it. I turned to my friends and said, "Wow, women are in cages." The list was long. Some of the rules were strange.

### WHAT ARE THE TALIBAN RIGHTS FOR WOMEN?

The parents should not keep their daughters inside their house. They should get them married as soon as they are ready. This is the advice from us, and since we are the Students of God, we know better than others.

Poor and widow women should be assisted financially by their blood relatives. Widows should be remarried by her father-in-law's family.

Women should not step outside of their residences. In case of emergency, they can go out but they should not wear fashionable clothes to attract the attention of other men, because she belongs to only one man (Husband) or soon she will be property of a man (Husband). If any woman is seen outside with fashionable, tight, and charming clothes, she will be chased to her house, and her brother, father, or husband will be punished and imprisoned. Woman should only be attractive to her husband inside her house. Women have the responsibility of a teacher for their children and a helper to her husband.

Women's makeup is forbidden unless they do it for their husbands inside the confines of her house, but men can use kohl outside of the house and inside.

Women do not have as much brains as men, therefore they cannot think wisely as man. So, we refuse to allow them to become involve in politics.

Whoever is holding this paper; he or she should give it to other women or read it to them, so they know our rules and observed them.

Sincerely! The Taliban rules.

I took that paper home and showed it to my mother and sisters. They showed it to our neighbors. Soon everybody had read it or had a photocopy of it.

At first, people made fun of the incorrect grammar and bad spelling. But soon, women understood that these things were serious.

When the Mujahedin factions had arrived and had issued their version of Islamic laws, women were forced to cover up, but they could still go anywhere and do anything they wanted, if the fighting allowed. Now that the Taliban were in control, females mostly disappeared from Kabul's streets.

The men faced their own strict set of rules, as well. One of the strictest was having to go to the mosque five times a day rather than praying wherever they found themselves. The mullah there had an attendance sheet. He called out our names to find out who was present and who was not. He would put a cross before the name of an absent man and report him to the Department for the Promotion of Virtue and the Prevention of Vice. The next day a Talib might come and imprison that man for a week or so.

For the first few weeks, every day someone was imprisoned for being absent. But as the months passed, the decree was not enforced so strictly, unless one of the mullahs disliked someone.

In our neighborhood, there was a man we used to call *Malem-e-chaq*, the chubby teacher. He had six sons and was extremely rich. He even had a swimming pool in his garden. The mullah did not like him at all, though I do not know why. *Malem-e-chaq* was a good man. Yet, the mullah kept a strict account of when he came to the mosque, so the poor man had to be there five times a day, except when he went to other countries for his import-export business. But before he left on a trip, he had to tell the mullah where he was going, and how long he would be away. So did his sons, who had shops to run in other parts of Kabul. A few times my father did the same thing when he had to go somewhere.

Before prayers, the mullah talked about Islam and religion for ten or fifteen minutes and asked people in the mosque basic questions about Islam. In these new days, the mullahs in charge were either all Taliban or had become Taliban, or acted like them, except for one old mullah who had seen his entire family—wives, sons, daughters, brothers, and his mother—wiped out by a Russian bombing raid. He was then a farmer. One day he had stayed a bit longer in the fields after the others had gone to the house to eat. A Russian plane roared overhead. Bombs exploded and threw him to the ground. When the dirt that was swept up into the sky by the blasts had settled, there was no sign that there had ever been a house, or that he had ever had a family. The Taliban were told these things about him and left him alone.

One evening before prayers, our mullah asked the first line of people in the mosque, "If you fill two buckets, one with alcohol and another one with water, and take them both to a thirsty donkey, which one will the donkey drink?"

A guy from the first line said, "Of course the water."

"Since the donkey avoids drinking alcohol, then you have to hate it yourselves and not even touch it," our mullah said.

A guy raised his hand from the second line and asked, "If there are a few drops of alcohol in a glass of water, is it still as bad as pure alcohol?"

"If I piss a few drops in your glass of water, will you drink your water?" our mullah said.

"Of course not," the guy answered.

"The alcohol is a million times worse than my piss," our mullah said.


In my family, now only I could go to school to study, and my sisters had to stay at home. The women teachers in my school also were told to stay at home. I missed my literature teacher's lessons, but I never stopped looking for hidden meanings in my books.

The school year ended for the winter a few weeks after the Taliban arrived. When we got the results sheet for our exams, I had the highest grade for Dari literature. I wanted to tell my teacher, but I did not know where to find her. I never saw her again.


When the schools reopened for the new school year on the second day of spring, it was time for me to start high school. I had wanted to go to the school where my father taught, Habibia. It was the best school in Afghanistan. But it was about five miles from the Qala-e-Noborja, and my parents were afraid to have me travel so far with so much uncertainty.

Instead, I went to a school nearby. It was named for a king who was dead. Our king who was alive was in Italy and had not come back to save us. We had stopped waiting for him.

For all my life, except when we were fleeing or the fighting was too heavy, I had seen my father go to his school. I had watched him prepare for his classes the night before. I had seen him thumb through his well-worn books with the eagerness of somebody discovering something new. I had heard his enthusiasm when he spoke about his students. I thought high school must be an important and exciting place. But the Taliban took from me all the joy I had expected to feel.

The boys were told to wear *shalwar kamiz*, a long one according to Taliban standards—tunic below the knees, trousers above the ankle, with a black turban and slippers instead of proper shoes. We were prohibited from wearing shoes in school, because we were told that shoes get stinky easily. The Taliban did not like to wash.

Most of the teachers had taught at that school for years wearing suits and ties, but now they all wore turbans and *shalwar kamiz*, except for the academic dean, who wore a suit and a necktie every day for nearly a year before he, too, found a *shalwar kamiz*. A Talib was appointed as the principal of the school and told the teachers to stress religion in all our subjects. We were taught that the history of humankind began with religion, and we were born with religion, and we had to die with religion. Religion was involved in the sciences, history, philosophy, psychology, arts, everything. If we know our religion, the Taliban principal said, we will know ourselves.

At the beginning, it was interesting to learn about Islam, because in the time of the Communists, we had no religious studies at all. All we were taught was how to respect Communism. They told us that it was our duty to invite others to be Communist to enlarge the wheel of Communism, because only Communism could help mankind.

My formal schooling seemed to have had two subjects only: Communism and Islam. Perhaps it was not surprising, then, that I was happiest at school when I was wrestling with my classmates in the classroom, breaking their noses in boxing competitions or flexing our arm muscles for one another to show our strength. We talked a lot about sex and played card games with cards that had sex pictures on them, which we passed around in school.

My head was always shaved now; I looked like a bald man. I could no longer wear my choice of clothes. I could not watch movies. I could not fly kites. In short, I could no longer be myself.

We heard that some Taliban were now living in what was left of our old house. Our former neighbor told us. He had gone to visit his own house nearby. He was asked by the Taliban in our place who the owner of the house was. He told them that we were not in Afghanistan. The Taliban instructed him to inform them if he heard that we had come back to Kabul. They told him that they would get money from us and split it with him. The next day he came to the Qala-e-Noborja and told us all this.

With the Taliban living there, there was even less reason for anybody to talk about the gold in Grandfather's garden.

We heard rumors that if the Taliban knew that you had a lot of money, they would put you in prison until you gave it all to them. So, in my family everyone became silent about the gold, and we were told never to talk about it to anyone.

On the streets I noticed that people were now wearing dirty clothes. Even people whom I knew had money wore clothes that were dirty, trying to look poor. One of our neighbors was imprisoned. A few months later we heard that his brother had come from Pakistan and given the Taliban a lot of money, and then they both left quickly for Iran.

Sometimes we heard talk about a rich Arab named bin Laden. We were not sure who he was. One of our neighbors said he was living nearby in the big house that had been owned by the man everyone called the Pimp of the King. We went by that place many times, but we never saw him. And we were careful not to look directly. There were always many Taliban at the gate. They used the place for big meetings, and their black Land Cruisers were always going in and out.

Grandfather came from Makroyan twice in a month and stayed with us for a night or two. Now that I was in high school, he talked to me like I was a grown-up man. He talked about things that made me feel shy at first. Sometimes he would ask me questions about these strange feelings I had when I thought about pretty girls. Sometimes he would ask me philosophical questions about Socrates, Plato, and Aristotle. Sometimes we would talk about Judaism, Buddhism, Islam, and Communism.

I think he wanted to see how much I grasped from life, how much I had learned from school, from the books he had given me to read, and from the things he had told me.

Since he knew I was very interested in Socrates and liked to read Plato, he asked me questions exactly the way Socrates asked them of Callicles, Chaerephon, Gorgias, and Polus when they met in Callicles's home. It was very much as if I had found myself with Socrates, whom I revere, and he was present in the body of Grandfather, whom I loved more than anyone in the world. It was a pleasure beyond description, to be with two such people at the same time.

These conversations lasted for hours; we hardly noticed how time passed.

I did not feel that I had to go out or entertain myself when he was with us. But when he was not there, I felt imprisoned sitting at home, with little to distract me but reading or doing push-ups. And any time I did go out, it was uncomfortably quiet. The streets should have been filled with kids playing, and vendors pushing carts, and donkeys. Instead, all I saw were Taliban, everywhere. They always acted so strangely.

People looked nervous all the time, too. They were not afraid of rockets anymore. Now we had peace in Kabul, and we did not see blood and corpses and body parts on the streets anymore. But it was an unhappy peace, a frightened peace. We did not know what was going to happen next.

We waited.

# 18

❖

## The Prison

In the second year of the Taliban, I got fed up with their rules, and I began breaking a few of them: growing my hair out, sometimes not wearing my hat or turban, and dressing in jeans and T-shirt— but only in our neighborhood. I did not go beyond half a kilometer from our house.

One day before going to school, I bathed and did not have enough time to wait until my hair got dry. I slung my unwound turban on my shoulder, took my books, and walked toward school, letting the sun dry my hair as I went. The weather was balmy, and it felt good to be without a turban for once.

All of a sudden, a black Land Cruiser filled with Taliban popped up from nowhere and stopped in front of me. A black pickup truck with more Taliban followed. One of the Talibs stepped out of the car and started beating me on my back with a heavy whip. I did not know what my crime was, and he did not give me a chance to ask him. Everything happened very fast.

After beating me for almost five minutes, he pushed me toward their vehicles. I asked them what this was all about. But none of them answered or even talked to me. They kept whipping me.

I stopped asking questions and punched one of them in his face. He fell on the ground like something heavy that someone had dropped.

All those hours in the gym practicing boxing had taught me some things.

Now there were ten of them, jumping out of the Land Cruiser and the truck, running toward me. They began beating me again with three heavy whips, and kicking me as I lay coiled on the ground. Every time a whip or a foot landed on my head, I saw stars in the daylight. I forgot about being so strong and looking like the statue of Apollo.

Finally, they carried me to their pickup and dropped me into the back. As they handcuffed me to the side rail, I lost consciousness. Sometime later, I found myself in a barber shop, sitting on a chair in front of a mirror. I hardly recognized myself. My face was covered with wounds and marked with dried blood. My hands and feet were still handcuffed, and all of my body ached like I had a severe fever.

The barber shaved my hair, then the Taliban drove me to the Shahr-e-Naw prison in central Kabul, right across from Zajanton hospital, where I had been born. They still had not told me what I had done, and they did not let me contact my family.

In the prison, they put me in a dark room, alone. For the first few days, usually early in the morning, someone came and tied my hands to chains that were hanging from the ceiling and beat me with a whip. Each minute passed like hours. Whenever I demanded to know why I was in prison, he remained silent. When I insisted on an answer, he said that he was told to say nothing.

The beatings left me with a dislocated shoulder and lots of whip welts all over my body, especially my back and chest. For those first few days the pain was intense, and the heat was stifling. There were no doctors to treat my shoulder. Flies swarmed around the cuts on my face, hands, and feet and drove me crazy; after a while I did not have the energy to brush them off.

They slid me a piece of hard bread and a glass of water under the door. A bucket in the corner of the room was for me to use as a toilet. It took all my strength to crawl to it.

From time to time, I could hear jeeps coming and going in the yard outside. Each time, the guards made noise unlocking the padlock on the slatted gate to the street. Every time the gate swung open, I squinted out the tiny window to see the Talib commander lounging in the driver's seat of one of the jeeps, and leering at all the little windows like mine where about twenty other prisoners were being held.

Later, when he came to my cell, he thwacked his whip against his boot tops while he accused me of blasphemy against Islam and beating a Student of God. He was the only to wear boots.

When I asked him what my blasphemy was, he beat me. After that, I decided that silence was my only course. It reminded me of my Kuchi cousins, who had taught me how to use silence to step back from the world around me and let the answers to my problems form in my mind.

The only company I had was the Holy Koran, which they left for me and the other prisoners on a shelf in each cell. At the mosque, the other boys and I had already read it several times in Arabic. We had been taught how to make the sounds of the Arabic words, because we used their alphabet for our language, Dari. But we had never been taught what the words meant, except for sometimes when my grandfather translated some of the verses for me. So, we had no way of understanding what we were reading, even though we held competitions to see who could finish memorizing his verses first.


This copy of the Holy Koran had a translation in Dari under each line. It was like I was reading the Koran for the first time. I could finally understand what these Arabic words that I had recited for years actually meant. I discovered what a treasure trove of tales the Koran is, filled with good advice, a real guidebook to the human experience.

At night in my cell, after I had put down the Holy Koran, I played those tales and their wisdom over and over in my head like movies. And I thought for hours about their meaning and what lessons lay in them for my own life.

For example, Sura 29 begins: "Do people think that when they say: 'We are believers,' they will be left alone and not be tested? We tested those who have gone before them. God surely knows which of them are truthful, and He surely knows which are liars. Or do the evildoers think they will escape Our reach? How poorly they judge."

I read this in less than a minute, but I thought about it for hours, searching for the deeper meanings, in the same way that our Dari language and literature teacher had taught us to look for what we could not see even in books that were not the Holy Koran.

I thought about the Taliban. They said they were believers, but a lot of what they were doing was not in the Holy Koran. The Koran says that "God surely knows which of them are truthful, and He surely knows which are liars." Did the Taliban and the other factions and all the other evildoers think that they would escape God's reach? "How poorly they judge."

But what about me? I began to think about the evil things I had done, like when I had broken our neighbor's window and then denied it, or had rung people's doorbells and run away, or made fun of the weak boys in our neighborhood, or called people names behind their backs, or beaten up guys in school for no reason but to show that I could. These are all *haram* in Islam, forbidden. But I had done them all. Before I could think about what the Taliban were doing, I felt I must first repent for all these things I had done. I promised to myself never to do them again.

I read the whole of the Holy Koran as fast as I could. Then, after a couple of days, I decided to read this Dari translation again, to understand it better, and to savor the stories. Reading also kept my mind from the physical pain I was experiencing.

But the lessons I was drawing from the Holy Koran slowly worked through my mind and made the emotional pain inside me even worse.

I lay on the cement floor, staring at the ceiling with the Holy Koran open next to me. Tears rolled out of my eyes as I recalled one wrong thing after another that I had done. I kept thinking about my parents, sisters, and brother, and how I had been so mischievous toward my parents, and how I had bossed my sisters and made them do things for me, because I was a boy, such as ordering them to polish my shoes or iron my clothes, then criticizing them for not doing it the way I wanted, or complaining when the food they cooked was a little salty or oily. I had used my position for the wrong reason. And I easily could have done those things for myself.

I thought about my mother and how worried she would be, not

knowing where I was. I began to think about how much pain I had caused her. Carrying me for nine months. Feeding me, washing me, clothing me, taking care of me day and night. And what did I give back to her? Always pain and worries. The same with my father. He had worked day and night to make life possible for us, sometimes under the worst conditions, and what did I do for him besides give him anxiety? What was he feeling now? And as the older brother to my sisters, what had I done for them? Slapped them when my parents were not home, knowing they had no one to whom to complain? Called them names? Why?

For hours I would ask myself what made life worth living. Is there only pain that you give to others, or pain they give to you? Why do we misuse our power? I in my way, and the Taliban in their ways. What good does this bring to humanity? I'm no better than the Taliban, I thought. Maybe I deserve this treatment. But what about my parents? How can I send them a message that I am in the right place, being punished for all the wrong things I have done, and they must not worry?

"Maybe I should kill myself," I thought several times, especially when the ache in my shoulder felt like a piece of hot steel being pushed into my bone. But I did not want to give my parents even more pain. They would blame themselves. I could not do it, though there were many times in that stinking cell when I had stopped caring about this world, this life, or my feelings, desires, and wishes.

After a week, the Taliban took me out of that small, dark room and put me in a larger one with other prisoners. We had to pray five times a day and study religious subjects in the prison mosque. After prayers, we had to carry heavy stones from one room to the next, and then carry them back.

During the night, we did not have enough blankets to keep ourselves warm. Sometimes I woke up in the middle of the night, shivering, and did push-ups. I remembered that my father had done the same thing in that tunnel four years before. Some people ran around the room to keep the blood in their veins circulating. We could not exercise for more than about ten minutes at a time, though, because we did not have enough energy.

I did push-ups with the right arm only, which is very painful to do. For a few seconds it made the pain in my left shoulder go away. I learned then how to cheat my brain; a temporary pain in one part of the body makes you forget the permanent pain in another part of your body, at least for a few moments. I felt I was triumphing over the Taliban by overcoming my pain. I could do four push-ups at the most. Sometimes I laughed, though only for a second as sweat clustered over my forehead. Laughter in the depth of pain is an uplifting feeling, though a short-lived one. I suddenly understood what Socrates meant by "Pleasure can also come from pain." Suddenly, something I had never understood made sense. I felt as if my head were illuminated with millions of lightbulbs.

Over the next ten days, I lost twenty pounds. I could hardly move my body or talk.

One day, after I had been in the prison for nearly two weeks, I saw a piece of broken mirror on the ground, about the size of a hand. When I looked in it, I saw a face that was not mine. I laughed at myself, but that exposed my teeth. Even in the times when we had had very little to eat, I had never seen myself so toothy and skinny. I still had a few muscles left on my arms and chest, but only very tight ones.

At the end of two weeks two of the jailers asked me some basic questions about Islam. I answered them all. They took me into a room that was cleaner than the rest and asked me some more simple questions about Islam, like how to take ablutions, whose answers I had known since I was a child. Then they told me to recite the verses from the Holy Koran that are used every time we pray. I kept waiting for something more difficult.

The older jailer, who was in his forties, kept nodding his head as I responded. His sandy-colored beard moved up and down in time to the rhythm of the prayers that I was reciting. For every answer I gave, he smiled and said "Very good, son!" in a calm voice, as he rubbed his left hand on the large belly beneath his gray *shalwar kamiz*.

The other man was skinny and half his age. He looked at me, as we say, "as if I were his family's enemy." His dark brown eyes, tan skin, and black *shalwar kamiz* contrasted sharply with his white turban. He asked harder questions in a loud voice and acted disappointed when I answered them correctly. I wanted to ask him some questions, as well. I was sure he would not know the answers. But I did not.

Finally, they told me I could go home. Some of the prisoners who could not answer the questions stayed for two more weeks.

"Why did you imprison me?" I asked the older jailer as I was leaving the room. But it was the younger one who answered.

"Because you were not wearing a turban, and your hair was too long."

"But it was not more than three inches," I replied.

"You must keep your head shaved at all times, and wear a turban or a hat. We keep the violators at our prison, so they understand how serious their crimes are. It is our job," the jailer said forcefully. "We are here to help you."


When I came out of the prison, the sun's glare blinded me for a few seconds. Slowly, slowly I opened my eyes and everything began to look normal.

I did not have any money to get a taxi to go home. I could hardly walk, because of my lack of energy, but I had no alternative. I knew my family would have been looking all over Kabul for me for the past two weeks I was in the prison. That forced me on. Somehow I managed to walk the two miles from the prison all the way home, stopping several times to rest. I was worried that people might somehow know that I had been a prisoner. Maybe they would ask me how I had hurt my shoulder, which still ached. But there was almost no one in the street to see me.

When I arrived home, I found my mother on a prayer rug facing toward Mecca and praying in a loud voice, "Oh God, keep my son in your peace. Save him from any dangers of the world. Wherever he is, give him the message that his mother is always waiting for him and tell him to come home . . ."

"Your prayer is accepted," I said softly from behind her.

She turned around with an amazed look on her face. Unusual for her in the daytime, tears sparkled on her cheeks. A smile spread across her face, which revealed the wrinkles that now owned the corners of her eyes.

Later that day, my father brought his friend who was a champion wrestler to the room where I was trying to rest. He told me to stand up, and when I did, he grabbed my arm and forced my shoulder back into place. I screamed like somebody had thrown me into boiling water. By the time I finished howling, I realized that the pain in my shoulder was mostly gone.

The ache in my soul, however, was not so easily fixed. It is still there, as fresh as if these things had happened yesterday.

# 19

❖

## A Precious Jewel

I was beginning to feel that I should take care of my family. My despair in prison had forced me to think about my life in a new way. I did not feel like a kid anymore. I was almost seventeen years old. "At seventeen, a Pashtun son should be a shoulder to his father." This is what Grandfather used to tell me. In Afghanistan, even a sixteen-year-old is considered a grown man. But I did not know how to help.

My father had become so discouraged after the fire destroyed all his carpets that he quit the carpet business completely. He had kept his teaching job at Habibia High School during the fighting, though neither he nor any of the other teachers or the students could actually go there for about two years. Once things quieted, he was again riding his bicycle the five miles around the mountain every day to the school to teach his physics classes. Teachers, though, were paid very little. To keep us going, he also began buying and selling flour and cooking oil that came from Pakistan.

He worked very hard. For a while he disappeared from our life. We woke up in the morning and he would not be there. We went to sleep late at night and he would not have returned. When we did see him on Fridays, he seemed to be in agony. After breakfast, he would ask my youngest sister to walk on his back and his legs to ease the pain in them. The rest of his Fridays were spent sleeping; we whispered when we talked and we tiptoed. He was too busy to pay attention to what we were doing. It was not like the old days, when he had made a schedule for me every day to do things in an organized way.

I felt that I was getting to be like a stray dog. I was trying to find a sense of peace for myself, trying to find someone who could guide me in the right direction, to the right path. I went to several mosques to listen for the invisible voice, but the mosques did not feel the same as before. It felt like I was being forced to say prayers the way the Taliban wanted. Talibanism: it was not the Islam that I knew from what I had read in the Koran or from what Grandfather had taught me.

I went to Grandfather to get his advice, but he was too busy thinking about how to get our house back, and he was very afraid, not knowing what to do. I had never seen Grandfather like that. He had always made me feel safe, but now I did not know how to make him feel safe. He told me not to be dependent on anyone else. The time had come when I should make up my own mind and be my own guide, he said. I was not so sure.

I started thinking about my carpet teacher, seeking her advice. I went to quiet places, trying to hear her.

Under the Taliban, the country grew increasingly poor, dismal, and isolated. The Taliban's chief concern above all others was that men must respect the hours of prayers and women must be separated from the rest of society.

I frequently cursed my country for allowing ourselves to be ruled by our neighbors, by the English, by the factions, and now by these Talibs. Most Afghans had nothing but contempt for the Taliban, whom we considered illiterate peasant extremists. They had originated from the poorest and most backward parts of the country, where literacy hardly was known.

While the Taliban ruled, no one smiled. It was as if the Taliban had stolen our smiles. Or maybe the people just forgot how, except when they went to the jewelry shops to buy gold for their daughters' weddings. Afghans were still determined to give their daughters gold when they married, even if they could have no music at the wedding.

A jeweler friend who was a few years older than I had a shop near the Qala-e-Noborja in the Kart-e-Parwan neighborhood. We had met playing volleyball in a nearby park, and I spent a lot of time in his shop; it was one of the few places where I could hear laughter. His customers would spend an hour or more bargaining to get the cheapest price, and they made lots of funny jokes while they did so.

My friend knew how to make his customers feel happy. That way they would spend more money and buy things they did not need.

One day I was sitting next to one of his assistants, who was polishing an old necklace with hot water and sawdust. He dipped the necklace in boiling water for a minute, then he rubbed it hard with a toothbrush and put it in sawdust. Half an hour later, he took it out and polished it with a kind of soft brush until the gold gleamed like it was brand-new. I was getting interested in becoming a jeweler. This, I decided, was how I was going to help my family.

That day nobody came to buy anything. My friend was bored. He kept yawning and gazing at the busy road, frowning at the frowning faces of the people who were walking past the shop. He was deep in his thoughts. The only sound was the whooshing of the Taliban cars, running up and down the road recklessly.

A woman with a dirty *burqa* entered the shop and raised her hand to my friend. She was a beggar and was asking for money. Her hand was dirty like her *burqa*, and her brown skirt was full of tiny little burned holes. I thought she was some kind of drug addict.

My friend was still staring outside with his elbows on top of his desk and hands under his chin. The woman gently pulled on my friend's sleeve as a way of asking him to give her a few small afghanis. My friend looked at the woman, took a few afghanis out of his pocket, and gave them to her. She got the money and stuffed it into her pocket, then she raised her left hand. Her left hand was clean with long nails and they were polished red. She had a beautiful hand.

On her palm was written, "I am available, and my price is 10,000 afs." This was about fifty dollars.

"Can I see your face?" my friend excitedly asked.

She looked outside to make sure there were no Taliban nearby, then she pulled up her *burqa* for a second and covered her face again quickly.

"Let's go to the back room," he said to her.

My friend had a small storage room at the end of his shop.

They were there for almost fifteen minutes. My friend came out with sweat on his forehead and a look of contentment. He told me to go in, that it was my turn. He would pay for me if I did not have money.

I did not know what to say. I had never had sex before. My mind was screaming at me to go and experience these feelings that were filling my dreams. But my heart was whispering to me not to do it.

I remembered the woman whom I had seen stoned to death in the stadium, because her husband complained to the Department for the Promotion of Virtue and the Prevention of Vice that his neighbor had had relations with her. Indeed, the Department for the Promotion of Virtue and the Prevention of Vice had stoned the woman and the neighbor both.

I thought that if the Taliban captured me, they would stone me to death in public. That would be not only a severe death, but very shameful to my family.

"What are you waiting for? Go in! She is waiting for you," my friend said as his assistants snickered quietly. "She's fantastic." I looked at him, and then at his assistants. They were not more than eight or ten years old. Their coolness assured me they had seen my friend with other women before.

"Do you want to go in, or should I dismiss her?" my friend asked with an annoyed tone.

I did not know what to say. Then without knowing what I was doing, I walked toward the back room.


She appeared to be in her midtwenties. She wore a red bra and panties. She stood straight and relaxed, like the letter *alef*, with her back against the wall. Her skin was soft, and faintly glossy.

I did not know what to say or what to do. She smiled at me and asked, "Do you have any experience?"

I did not answer her. In fact, I did not know what to say. I was frozen there. My eyes stared at her, and my mouth was paralyzed. It was the first time in my life that I had seen a beautiful woman nearly naked, waiting for me to have her, and she was right in front of me, asking me a question that I was unable to answer.

"I said, do you have any experience?" she asked again, and her tone was a little more serious.

"No," I said.

"It is okay. I'll help you," she said.

"How?" I asked, as I stood there staring at her perfect legs. I felt like I was in an oven, and sweat began to form on my forehead and on my back. My heart was beating fast and seemed to be in my throat.

She slid down and slowly crept toward me on her knees on the bare concrete floor. Now I could see her breasts. I trembled. She grabbed the bottom of my *shalwar kamiz* and tried to pull me toward her.

I stepped back, suddenly afraid to touch her, or to let her touch me. I felt like I was a deer being attacked by a lioness. At the same time, I was trying to look brave, and not to show my fear. Deep inside me, I wanted to let her do whatever she wanted to me. I ached to learn the feeling of being with a woman, and to feel her body against mine.

"It is okay. You don't have to do anything. I know it is your first time. But trust me, it'll feel great," she said.

I stepped back a few more steps. Now my back was on the cold wall. She was standing again, very close to me. Her breasts were touching my chest. I could feel her warmth, smell her perfume. We both stared into each other's eyes as if we were trying to find something there. Her breath brushed my face. My heart started to beat faster, even faster than before. My legs began to shake. It was as if she were sending electric current into me, and my body was too weak to receive it. I could feel that I was getting redder every second, as all the blood came to my face.

"We don't have to do this if you don't want to. Maybe you should do it with someone your age," she whispered kindly. She understood my shyness.

She stepped back and turned toward her clothes. Now her back was turned to me. She put on her trousers first, then her shirt and skirt. I wanted to hug her from the back and kiss her entire body, and hold her in my arms. But I did not have the courage. I was filled with confusion.

Now she put her *burqa* on her head, and, with the veil still up so I could see her brown, almond-shaped eyes, she turned around and walked toward me. She stood before me, but not as close as before, and said with great sadness, "I'm not doing this for the joy of it. I'm doing this because I have to. Selling myself is the only possible way I have to earn any money." Her eyes began to fill.

"Can we talk for a minute?" I asked her. I did not want her to leave.

"Talk about what? About my blackened life?" she asked as a tear rolled down her cheek, then dripped onto the concrete floor.

I did not know what to say. I did not want her to cry. "Why don't you marry someone who would look after you? You are a pretty woman; you can make a good wife," I said. I did not know why I was saying this. I just wanted to make her feel good.

She sat on a chair in the corner. I was still standing. She motioned to me to get another chair and sit.

"Who is going to marry me?" she asked.

I did not know what to say.

She took a deep breath in and lowered her head. She was looking at her hands as she kept intertwining and releasing her fingers. "I was not born a prostitute, I was not born in a prostitute's family either. I was born in a well-educated family, in a family of well-respected people." She spoke very clearly, using good grammar and a high form of Dari that is not usually heard on the street.

"My father was a general in the Ministry of Interior Affairs; he was a man of honor, a man of respect, a man of pride. He was educated in Russia, and he was very serious about our educations. My mother was a teacher, like me. My brother was studying in the Medical Faculty, and my sister was studying social law at the University of Kabul."

I was listening carefully to what she was saying, but still very conscious that she was a woman whom I might touch.

"I taught chemistry in the same school with my mother, who taught literature. I had graduated from the Pharmacy Faculty. I'm the oldest child of my parents. I was married six years ago, and I have two children." The words were tumbling out.

"My husband had gone to my parents' house to tell them the news of my newly born son. A rocket landed in my parents' house and killed them all. In the end, there was nothing left for a burial. They were all turned into pieces and bits and mixed with the earth.

"I was living in a rental house with my two kids when the Taliban came. They closed the girls' school, and did not let any women work outside of their houses, as you know. I had no money to pay my rent. So, I was kicked out of that house by the landlord. Now I'm living under a tent in Parwan-e-Seh.

"I don't have any relatives from either side of my family in Kabul. They have all fled to foreign countries. I don't have their addresses to ask them for help. After the Taliban closed my school, I started begging for a few months. But I never collected enough money to buy five *naan*. Most of the time, I went hungry. I put my kids to sleep with empty stomachs."

I was becoming absorbed in her story, and forgetting about what had brought us together.

"About a year and a half ago I met another beggar, and she told me to sell myself. She said that there are a lot of customers for a body like mine. She also told me that prostitution is an art, not a black or shameful act. I cursed her and walked away from her. I continued my begging for another month, but I still couldn't collect enough money, and my kids began to get skinny and sick. My daughter is the older one, and she is four years old; my son is three.

"One day while I was begging along the Kabul River in the jewelry shops there, a jeweler showed me a bundle of money. He said if I came to the back room, he would give me all of it. I told him that he was disgusting, and he laughed at me as I walked away.

"I thought about my kids, who were suffering from malaria. I went back to that shop and I went straight to the back room. He came and used me. I didn't know what was happening to me. I was there like a body without a soul, like a doll. I was used by a couple of his friends, too. An hour later, I had the bundle of money, and I took my kids to a doctor.

"That night I cried the whole night without knowing why I was crying. I had not cried that much for my parents, my brother, my sister, or my husband when they died. The next day I didn't go out. Whomever I looked at, I thought they knew the truth about me. I couldn't even look at my own kids. I hated myself, and I wanted to kill myself. But I couldn't do it. 'Who would give my children the love of a mother?' I thought." She wiped her tears with her sleeves and looked at me.

"Why am I telling you all these things? You don't know me, and I don't know you," she said, and started to sob softly with her head down.

"You have to tell them to someone, to feel light, to feel free. You can't carry them all within you. You have to share them with someone," I said. I was surprised at the words that were coming from my mouth. How did I know to say these things? I was using all the proper forms and grammar, as she was, though almost no one ever spoke that way anymore.

"You're just a damn kid. You haven't seen the cruel face of life," she said, standing and covering her face with her *burqa*. She ran out of the shop without taking her money. My friend shouted at her to come back later for it.

I grabbed the bundle of money from the desk and caught up with her, walking slowly next to her. She did not see me because of the *burqa*, but I could hear that she was still crying quietly. The street was nearly empty. It was in the hot days of July. A few dogs were resting in the shade of walls, and little boys were carrying pots of yogurt with herbs toward their houses. She noticed me after a few moments; she stopped in the middle of the street and pulled up her *burqa* to look at me as I was standing in front of her. The hot sun was cooking my back. The little boys stared at her, because they had not seen any woman's face on the street for two years, since the Taliban had come.

"Why do you care for me? Do you know me?" she asked me. Her voice shook. Her beautiful eyes were full of tears waiting to come out.

"No, I don't know you, but I'm a human like you, and we should share the sorrows and the joys together," I said.

"And how will you share my sorrows with me? It is not just me who needs someone to share her pain with. There are thousands of people like me who are even more desperate."

I did not know what to say. She grabbed the money from me, pulled her veil down, and walked away without looking back, the dust blowing after her and settling on her blue *burqa*.

# 20

❖

## The Length of a Hair

My mother gave me some money and a list of what she and my sisters needed: trousers, skirts, shawls, scarves, and other small things.

After the arrival of the Taliban, they hardly went out. They did not like wearing the *burqa*. They could not see through those little holes. In fact, if they left the house, it was only to go to the wedding parties or funerals of close relatives. For those occasions, I hailed them a taxi, or I called a relative with a car who collected them from our gate and dropped them at another gate. While they were in the car, their heads were completely covered with shawls, even their faces, and they could not see which road they were on.

I hated shopping for them, but what could I do? I was the only one available; with my father always working, they had no one else. We left the crying machine with a neighbor. My little brother had, in fact, become a joking machine. Everything he said was funny, and he made everyone laugh. He was the sweetest kid and knew how to keep us entertained.

I took my shopping bag and headed to the main bazaar in mid-afternoon. On my way there, I was stopped by a Talib in front of the high-rising Ministry of Communication. He wore the usual long, white turban and long, black *shalwar kamiz*. But he had a pair of scissors in his hand instead of a gun or a whip.

He asked me to take off my shirt. I thought he was joking. Nobody in my life had ever asked me to take off my shirt in the middle of the road.

"What do you want to do with my shirt?" I asked him in Pashto.

"I have nothing to do with your shirt. I want to see your armpits," he said.

"Why?! Look, look, there is nothing in my armpits. No hashish, no opium. I'm an athlete. I don't use drugs. You see I have muscles," I said as I raised my arms and flexed them.

"I need to see how long the hairs of your armpits are. They shouldn't be longer than one inch," he said insistently, and commanded me to take off my shirt.

"What does the hair of my armpits have to do with you?" I wanted to ask. But I had been to the Taliban prison once and did not want to go back again. I pulled off my *kamiz* in the middle of the road. The passersby on either side of the road watched me from the corners of their eyes, but they kept moving and kept their silence.

The Talib pulled out a hair from my left armpit and measured it. It was a tiny bit longer than one inch. He frowned and told me that I was in big trouble. I pleaded with him to measure a different one. He pulled out another hair from my right armpit and measured it. That one was just less than one inch.

"Some of the hairs are long, and some of them are short. When was the last time you shaved under your arms?" he asked.

"Two, three weeks ago," I answered as I was putting my shirt back on.

"Give me an exact date," he shouted, frowning.

"I don't remember," I said. In fact, I had never shaved my armpits at all.

"I want to see your penis and testicles," he said matter-of-factly as he stared between my legs.

"What? Why?" I asked. Panic was replacing my anger.

"Because I said so," he calmly replied.

"You know they look the same as yours," I said very seriously to mask my fear. I did not want to take off my trousers in the middle of the road for a stupid and illiterate villager who called himself a Talib.

"This is your last chance. If you don't show me your penis and testicles, you'll be in prison in ten minutes, and I'll see them there," he warned.

"Oh God! What the hell is wrong with this man? Please God, help me!" I screamed inside myself.

"Why don't you show me yours first," I challenged, playing for time until I could think more calmly what to do.

"Do you have an interest in my penis? It is quite big, and there is a lot of semen in my testicles," he said with a totally different tone. "My boy loves it, but he is not as white as you." He suddenly smiled a warmly engaging smile, even though he was a Taliban, and they hated any sign of happiness.

Now I understood why he had stopped me. We had heard rumors that the Taliban who had been fighting on the front lines against the Mujahedin would go to the prison during the night so they could relax by raping young boys who had been imprisoned for no crime.

This man wanted to use me every night with his frontline friends until they got bored with me and found someone new, or younger, or with whiter skin. I had seen some of those frontline Taliban, as we called them, a few days before in the park near the Qala-e-Noborja. They had long, dirty hair and untrimmed beards. They were full of lice since they did not wash for months, despite what the Holy Koran told them about cleanliness. The worst ones were from the tribal lands between Pakistan and Afghanistan, or from Chechnya or some of the Arabic countries such as Yemen and Syria. They had no interest in Afghanistan. They just wanted to kill people.

I could not let such a thing happen to me, to my life. I would bring shame to myself and to my family, even if it was done by force.

I did not know what to say, but I knew that I had to get away from this man any way I could. I opened my trousers and, very self-consciously, lowered them to my knees. Passersby stared at me. I glared back at them.

The Talib sat on his knees and pulled out two hairs, one which he called "the hair of your penis forehead" and another one from my testicles. Then he asked me to tie up my trousers. He measured them both with a ruler. I was looking closely at his hands, which were trembling. Both hairs were curly; I could not even guess how long they were. The one from "the forehead of my penis" was nearly two inches, and the one from my testicles was one and a half inches.

"Boy, you are in big trouble. I will have to sentence you to one month in prison," he said, a devilish sneer growing as the corners of his eyes narrowed.

He gripped my right arm tightly and pulled me toward his car, which was parked at the roadside. Another Talib, who was lounging in the driver's seat, stood up and opened the door. They pushed me into the back. Then my captor went off and stopped another young man who was hardly more than a boy.

As I sat in the backseat, the Talib in the driver's seat was holding the steering wheel and listening to one of those Taliban songs without music. The singer was mixing verses of Persian love poems with some random Urdu words. Only the singer himself knew what he was singing about.

We both watched as the Talib examined the armpits of the boy he had stopped. The boy was younger than I, and paler, and very handsome. They loved white-skinned boys.

I was determined to escape.

Not far from me, in front of the Ministry of Communications, I saw a group of builders who had been working nearby, constructing the largest mosque in Kabul. They had finished their work for the day and were heading home. As they came alongside our car, I opened my door, jumped out and shouted very loudly, "Bomb! Bomb! Bomb! Bomb! Bomb! Bomb under the Taliban car!"

There were more than thirty builders. Instantly, they panicked and scattered like a flock of frightened pigeons. People on the sidewalks also started running to get away from that Taliban car. The Talib who had been in the driver's seat was equally frightened. He raced toward the new mosque with some of the builders.

I ran in the opposite direction, toward a bakery. When I entered, the baker asked me what was happening outside. He could see the panicked people through his window. It was real chaos. Nobody knew what was going to happen next. Everywhere, people were yelling "Bomb! Bomb! Bomb!" They were all trying to hide. I saw a few middle-aged men who had stuck their heads under a pushcart with the rest of their bodies hanging out.

"They think there is a bomb," I answered, breathing hard. "But there is no bomb. I shouted, 'Bomb! Bomb!,' so I could jump from that Talib's car. They arrested me for nothing. So, they could use me in the prison," I told him.

The baker looked at me in bewilderment, then terror.

"Get out of here! Get out of my shop!" he shouted at me.

"If I were your son, would you let them take me to prison and use me for days and nights? Are you a stonehearted man?"

"You can see I'm a Hazara. You know that they hate us. If they find you in my shop, they'll kill me," he said. I tried to stay where I was, standing inside the shop. But he was a strong man with big arms and broad shoulders and was a head taller than I, and he pushed me out the door.

Now I was outside on the street again. The people were still running up and down. I did not know where to go or where to run. I felt very desperate and lonely. Suddenly, I felt myself being pulled back inside the shop. It was the baker. He practically picked me up and carried me all the way to a room at the back of his shop. He was gripping my left arm very tightly. I tried to speak, but in my terror I could not think of anything to say.

The back room was huge, almost twice as big as his shop. It was full of very large sacks filled with wheat flour, corn flour, and sugar. The baker brought me to a corner where there was a mountain of flour sacks. They were put one on top of another, all the way to the ceiling. He told me to climb over those sacks and jump in behind them.

I did what I was told. There was hardly enough space between the sacks and the wall to squeeze myself in. My nose filled with flour. I sneezed several times, one after another. The baker shouted at me to shut up. I tried my best to hold my sneezes back, but it was very hard.

My nostrils kept itching, and I had to sneeze. The man shouted again with his thick voice.

I stayed there for four hours until it was completely dark and there was no sign of any Taliban outside. By then, people were hurriedly walking toward their homes, as they always did. The pushcart men were pushing their carts slowly, as they always did.

The baker called for me to come out from my hiding place. A boy who was younger than I brought me a pot of water to wash my face. I was powdered white with flour.

Some moments later, I was standing near the window and peering outside, still afraid that if I stepped out, the Talib would grab my wrist.

"I'm not letting you go out by yourself. That is even more dangerous for me. I'll take you to your house. I have a car. If someone asks you anything, tell them you're my son," the man said.

I looked at him, not knowing how to express how grateful I felt. All I could say in a shaking voice was, "You are a hero."

Half an hour later, I was sitting in the backseat of the baker's car along with his son as he drove toward my house. He dropped me in front of the main gate. I insisted they come inside and eat dinner with my family. He said that he had to go, otherwise his wife would get frightened if he came home late.

I watched as he drove down the dirt road away from Noborja, then stepped through the gate feeling a weakness that was now replacing my fear.

When I went into our house, everybody was angry at me for being so late. I told them what had happened. I do not know whether my father and mother believed me. But my sisters did not believe me, and they were unhappy that I had not brought them the clothes they had asked for. If what I said were true, they taunted, then I would have been imprisoned for a month at least. I was probably at a friend's house, or playing volleyball in the park, or using the parallel bars, because I was addicted to parallel bars in those days, and won every bet I made when I swung on them.

But that night, I shaved my armpits and also between my legs in case any more Taliban wanted to see them.

# 21

❖

## The Secret of the Pigeons

The next day, I never even left our rooms to go into the courtyard. I tried to sleep, but I could not sleep in daylight. I thought
about the baker. I had never asked him his name.

I arranged some pillows in one corner near a window where I
liked to read, and sat down with a copy of the Bible that had been
translated into Dari. My mother's brother had brought it to me from
Pakistan, where he had to go sometimes. He had a job in the Ministry of Interior Affairs drafting official papers, because he had very
clear handwriting. He had held a similar position under some previous governments, and had simply kept his old job. In the third year of
the Taliban, he came to live with us at the Qala-e-Noborja. Though
he worked for the Taliban, he was not one of them, and he hated their
decrees. But he kept that to himself. He needed to use his skills to
support his family, who was in Pakistan.

Every morning a car came to pick him up at the fort and dropped
him off at the end of the day. That gave us some protection from the
Taliban assigned to control our neighborhood.

He brought other books, too, by Maxim Gorky, Aristotle, and one
called *Plato Selections*. It was his way of defying the regime. All such
books had been banned by the Taliban. Philosophers such as Socrates, Plato, and Aristotle were infidels as well as foreigners. So,

their books should not be read in the Taliban's Afghanistan. Furthermore, since they were written before Islam, they were full of non-Islamic thoughts.

That, of course, made me more curious to read them.

At noon prayers on Fridays, the mullahs in the mosque would say that the Holy Koran was the only true book that was sent by God. But I wanted to read other books that other people believed were sent by God. I had heard that these books had helped solve the problems of millions of people for hundreds of generations before me.

I had already read this Dari translation of the Bible once when my uncle first brought it. I found that it was filled with poetic stories about the prophets who came before the Prophet Mohammad, peace be upon him.

Having recently read the Holy Koran in Dari in prison and now understanding it for the first time, I wanted to understand the Bible better, so I could compare it to the Holy Koran. The mullahs, however, said that the Bible had ceased to be the word of God a long time ago, because it had been rewritten and translated many times by different people. The Holy Koran, they said, has never been rewritten, nor will anybody ever rewrite it, nor can anyone rewrite it. Whoever rewrites the book of God is an infidel. He is in battle with God, like Shaitan.


Suddenly, I heard an unfamiliar voice calling my father's name: "Basir, Basir, Basir . . ." I looked through the window to see who was out there. My father was taking a nap, as most of my family did after lunch in the July heat. There were more than twenty Taliban in the middle of the courtyard, looking all around. One of them was tall and thin, dirty as the others with a long beard and a big, black turban. He kept shouting, "Basir, Basir, Abdul Basir!"

I hurriedly woke my father.

"Who let them in?" my father asked as he was rubbing his eyes.

"I don't know," I replied. I heard anxiety in my voice.

"Did they knock on the door?" My father was rising from the *toshak* where he had been lying.

"I didn't hear any knocking. I didn't open the door for them," I answered, my voice now shaking. "Are they looking for me? Did they come to arrest me?"

"I don't know. Let me go and talk to them. You stay here, and don't come out," he replied.

I woke my mother, my sisters, and my mother's brother. When my uncle heard the word "Taliban," he hurriedly went out to talk with them.

We stood back from our windows and looked at the Taliban through the little holes in the curtains. My father was surrounded by them, just inside the passageway into the courtyard. He was talking with the tall, thin one. My uncle showed them his ID card from the Ministry of Interior Affairs. A few of them kissed my uncle's hand as a sign of respect and honor.

They moved toward our rooms at the other end of the courtyard, looking searchingly at the niches high in the wall where my pigeons nested and laid their eggs.

"They're looking at your pigeons," my mother said. "Didn't I tell you a hundred times to take them to a shrine or a mosque somewhere? But you are so stubborn like your father, you never listen to me."

The pigeons had been living in the Qala-e-Noborja long before we moved there, in holes made for them in the mud-brick walls above our rooms.

I had always wanted to keep pigeons, as many Afghans do, even when we were still living in Grandfather's house. My father would not let me, though, saying, "You'll waste all your time on pigeons and not spend it on your lessons. When you have finished nine grades, I'll let you keep some." But I did not have to wait that long.

When we were living in Grandfather's house, one of our next-door neighbors had some pigeons. I used to go to his roof and watch him cutting the extra feathers from their wings and putting rings around their legs. They were of many breeds and colors, and each breed had its own name. I loved it when he held seeds in his hands and they came and sat on his hands, his arms, his shoulders, and his head.

I helped my neighbor keep two large pots filled with water for the pigeons to wash themselves, and two other large pots filled with sand for them to rub the insects out of their feathers.

When we moved to the Qala-e-Noborja, Haji Noor Sher already had many pigeons there. After a while, the pigeons knew me. As soon as I walked into the courtyard, many of them flew to me. Even when I just stood at our windows, they all came.

Most of the time I did not have enough money to buy them seeds. So, I cut hard pieces of stale *naan* into smaller bits for them. I purposely did not eat all my rice, so I could give some to my pigeons. Sometimes even my parents did the same.

The only one who did not like them was my older sister, because it was her job to keep our section of the courtyard swept. She complained that the pigeons left their droppings everywhere, but she liked when they chortled to one another in the early morning. She said the noise helped her sleep better.

"Will they kill my pigeons?" I asked my mother plaintively.

"No, no, I won't let that happen," my mother said, and she pulled me toward her and kissed the top of my head.

"I don't think they'll listen to you. They hate women. Why would they listen to you?"

"But I'll still try," my mother said.

"Are they here because I escaped yesterday and created panic?" I asked my mother.

"I don't know," my mother said.

My older sister was looking at me with one of her evil looks. Everyone said she was pretty; and she was. But she saved certain looks only for me, and this one was not so pretty. "If they arrest you, and send you to prison for a few weeks, then I'll believe that you were not lying yesterday," she said.

"You just shut up!" I hissed at her, and she giggled.

From out in the courtyard, we could hear the tall, thin Talib talking to my father. Most people spoke to my father with respect, because he was a *malem*, a teacher. But the Talib spoke very insultingly.

"You keep pigeons, too?" the tall, thin Talib asked. "Don't you know about Decree Number Nine that was issued by the Department for the Promotion of Virtue and the Prevention of Vice about pigeons and fighting birds? It was released almost two years ago."

My father's face went pale. He did not know what to say. My uncle hurriedly interjected, "Nobody is keeping these pigeons. They're wild pigeons. They came here by themselves."

"Yes, that is right," I heard my father confirm.

"Let me read Decree Number Nine about pigeons and fighting birds for you once again," the Talib said as he took a paper from his pocket.

"'Prevent keeping pigeons and fighting birds! This habit should stop. After ten days this matter should be monitored, and the monitors should go house to house to find the fighting birds. The pigeons and any other fighting birds should be killed by the monitors, and the bird fighters should be punished and imprisoned.'"

The Talib folded his paper. "Now I want to know who the bird fighter in this house is. He needs to be punished and imprisoned."

I was seized with fear. I loved my pigeons. And I knew that if they took me to prison, the Talib who had tried to arrest me the day before would recognize me, and I would have no hope of coming home soon, or of not being shamed.

My mother put a shawl over her head and covered her face. She went to the doorway. She stood behind the curtain that was spread across the door and said in Pashto so the Talib could understand her, "I'm feeding those pigeons."

"Who is that?" the tall, thin Talib said.

"I'm the wife of that man who is standing next to you, and I'm feeding these pigeons. I have one question to ask you: Do you think it is a bad thing, or a sin, to feed a hungry, living being?" my mother asked him.

"No, not at all. In fact, it is a good thing," the tall, thin Talib said. He was suddenly almost polite. It was impossible to know why, except perhaps her Pashto was of a very high form and revealed her as a woman whose sense of dignity demanded respect from others, even Taliban.

"As you say, I am doing a good thing. Then, you don't have to punish and imprison me, do you?" my mother said.

"No, no, not at all. The pigeons will stay here, and there will be no punishment and imprisonment for the keeper," the tall, thin Talib said.

My mother came back into the room with a triumphant smile on her face. We all looked at her with adulation. I kissed her hands. Then I walked outside and greeted all those Taliban as the laws of hospitality demanded, and stood next to my uncle.

The Talib asked my father for an ax and a ladder. My father brought them without asking why.

The Talib ordered one of his men to climb the ladder to one of those holes where my pigeons were nesting. He gave him that ax and asked him to chop a hole near the top of the dried mud wall.

"I think we agreed that we should not hurt the pigeons, right?" my father asked.

"Yes, that is right. But we are here to look for a weapon in this house. I was informed that there is a rifle with a bag of bullets in that pigeonhole," the Talib said.

"We have been living in this house for almost seven years, and I haven't seen any kind of weapon," my father said.

"You don't mind if we dig that hole?"

"No, I don't mind, but if you don't find anything, then you have to fix the mess," my father said confidently.

"Agreed," the tall, thin Talib said.

His man took out a pigeon with her week-old babies and put them carefully in another hole. The other pigeons in that hole started to fight with her; they did not want her there. She did not know where to go. She was worried about her babies and kept struggling and fighting with the other pigeons to protect her little ones. A minute later, the father pigeon flew down and walked near the babies to defend them, but the fighting never stopped.

The Talib kept chopping away. We were all watching him as he made a big mess of the wall. A few minutes later he pulled a rifle from deep inside the pigeonhole. With it was a bag of bullets, just as the tall, thin Talib had predicted. My father's face went ashen.

"You choose a very good place for hiding your weapons. But don't you know that we have better spies?" the tall, thin Talib said.

"It is not my weapon. I have no idea who put it there," my father said. His voice trembled.

"Every criminal says the same thing, but after some beatings they confess. So, now, tell me where the other boxes of weapons are." He paused as he was looking into my father's eyes. "Or I will beat you until you confess."

"I don't know what you are talking about. There are not any weapons in this place."

"Is that right? But you said that there is no rifle in that pigeon's hole, yet there was. We are going to search all these rooms. If we don't find them, then you have to show them to us, or you will die under interrogation," he said viciously. He pressed the button of his walkie-talkie and said, "Send us fifty more Taliban to surround the court-yard and the garden. Don't let anyone out of this place."

Thanks to my uncle's work in the Ministry of Interior Affairs, he had a walkie-talkie, too. He could have asked for help, but if any more weapons were found, he would be implicated as well. He stayed silent. He grabbed my left arm and half dragged, half carried me just inside the doorway to our rooms and ordered me to destroy all those books that he had brought me from Pakistan.

"I'm not going to destroy any of my books. They're not looking for books. They are looking for weapons," I said.

"You idiot, just do what I tell you. If they see the Bible or any of those philosophy books, they will hang us all," my uncle said with a rasp.

"Why?" I asked, confused.

"They will think we all have converted to Christianity or Com-munism or paganism," my uncle said.

"But that is stupid," I told him. "It is nonsense!"

"What is not stupid and nonsense about them?" he replied. He went back outside to find ways to delay the Taliban from coming into the house.

Now I was afraid. I ran toward our rooms. I put all of my books in front of me. I kissed them one by one. I loved Socrates's dialogues. I still did not want to tear them. But I had to.

I took the Old Testament first. I had only ten more pages left before I finished it for the second time. But there was no chance for that now. I tore out the first page, then the second and third. Then I started tearing bunches of pages at a time, as the sound of the coarse voices of the Taliban outside gave me extra strength and speed. A few minutes later, there was a pile of pages in front of me. Then I took the *Plato Selections* and tore out all of its pages. My mother and sisters helped me to tear apart the other books.

A short while later, my uncle came back in. We could hear the Taliban still at work in the courtyard, breaking down the pigeon roost. He said we must burn all the torn pages. My mother started a fire in a back room we never used that had no windows and no way for the Taliban to see any smoke. They probably would not have come into the house anyway, knowing that there were women inside.

I separated the pieces of the Old Testament and *Plato Selections* and burnt them separately in a metal bucket. I am not even sure why I did that.

My uncle told my mother to bring all our photo albums. He said we had to burn all our family pictures, like my parents' wedding pictures and the pictures that they took on their honeymoon to the Central Asian countries.

In most of those pictures, my mother and father wore Western clothes. If the Taliban saw such photos, they would imprison my parents, or maybe even kill them. These things happened often, and were announced from the backs of their pickups as the Taliban drove from one street to the next, shouting over loudspeakers.

My uncle and my mother started tearing up all those pictures. Tears streamed down from my mother's eyes, and this time she made no effort to hide them.

They put all the torn photographs in the fire with the torn books. The flames rose up, and a few minutes later every image of our family had turned to ashes.

There were pictures of my grandfather receiving a medal from his bank, and standing in front of our old house when it was new, and dedicating the school he had built. There was another one of him with the king, Zahir Shah. One showed him with all of his fourteen children. Several showed him dressed as a pilgrim from the time he had walked most of the way from Afghanistan to Mecca. In moments, his whole life as we had known it from those photos became ashes.

Everybody was coughing from the smoke, which had nowhere to go. I took a deep breath, determined to hold the smoke in my lungs even if I could not keep the books. I put the bucket full of ashes into a *bokhari* stove that we were storing in the back room.

"What about videocassettes and the video player?" my older sister asked my uncle.

"Break them all. Hurry up, quick, quick," my uncle said.

We had more than fifty Indian and American films on video. We had watched them all more than twenty times each. My favorite was the one called *Conan the Destroyer*. I had seen it at least fifty times, even though I did not know a word of what they were saying, because it was in English. Still, I loved to watch it again and again.

I grabbed that cassette and looked at the picture of Arnold Schwarzenegger on the cover. He wore underwear with boots and was holding a sword. Every muscle of his body stood out. I wished he could have been here with us now with his sword to beat all those Taliban. But he was not.

I said goodbye to Arnold Schwarzenegger and tore the cover first. I did not know how to break the cassette. I did not want to put it on the floor and break it with my feet as my uncle was doing to other cassettes. Instead, I took a decorative sword that was hanging above the door to the courtyard. It had been given to my father by the Indian government as an award for winning a boxing competition.

I put the cassette on the floor and held the sword over my head. I looked at my arms and chest. They were not as big and full of muscles as Arnold Schwarzenegger's. Though I had spent a lot of time in the gym, we never had enough to eat. But I decided that he would not mind if his cassette got broken by a person like me and with a sword used only for decoration, not with a real sword like the one he had used in the movie.

My uncle broke the video player into small pieces. He dropped the jagged bits down a hole in the floor where the toilet was supposed to go when we got running water. We threw the broken cassettes after it and burned their covers.

In the hour or so that it took for the Taliban to make sure that no pigeon would ever live in our courtyard again, every one of those so-called infidel books, videocassettes, and photographs had disappeared from our house. And that was a good thing.

As soon as the Taliban had finished tearing up the pigeon roost, they started searching through every room around that courtyard. Even though they did not find any more weapons, they wanted to take my father and me for interrogating. My uncle talked on his walkie-talkie to some people in the Ministry of Interior Affairs who told the Taliban in the courtyard not to bring us in after all. That outraged the head Talib. He was determined to find a picture or a book or anything to use as evidence against us, but nothing remained for him to find.

They did find a picture of a cow that my little sister had drawn in her drawing book with unusual colors. One of the Taliban tore it from my sister's drawing book, held it against my father's face, and said, "I can put you in prison for months for this drawing, but I will stay calm, because I am known as being kind."

"I can see you are a kind man with a soft heart. Your eyes tell me that," my father said, even though the Talib had eyes that were hooded like a cobra.

The tall, thin Talib raised his brows, then winked at the other Taliban to follow him, and they headed toward the door. My father asked them to drink tea with us. The tall, thin Talib declined, saying he was fasting. And they left.

The pigeons stayed for a couple of days, trying to make sense of this madness that was affecting them. But in ones and twos, they flew away to some other roost where they could build a nest and have a life of simple expectations.

Every time I looked at the ruins of where they had lived, I felt that far more than pigeons had been taken from me. Before the last of them left, I buried the ashes of my beloved books under a mulberry tree in the garden.

The next day my father used the public pay telephone, which we called the PCO, and which was very expensive, to reach his friend Haji Noor

Sher, who had never returned to Kabul since the night of his last party and remained in India with his family. There were two PCOs in our Kart-e-Parwan neighborhood. My father and I went to the closer one on the Bagh-e-Bala road. It was very busy, though, and we would have had to wait a couple of hours to make a call. We went to the other one in Baharistan, but the line there was even longer. So, we went home and got my father's bicycle and went to a larger PCO in Da Afghanan, a ten-minute ride from the Qala-e-Noborja if the streets are not too crowded with cars. My father pedaled while I sat on the back.

Noor Sher wanted to know about everything that was happening in Kabul. My father asked him about that rifle. At first he did not know what my father was talking about. He had completely forgotten about it. After a while he said, "That was my father's rifle, and when he died, it disappeared. How did it end up with the pigeons?"

"The pigeons must have taken it there," my father said, trying to make a joke.

"It could be true. Things like that happen from time to time," Haji Noor Sher replied, missing the joke, perhaps because of a poor connection. He asked my father to please go to the Taliban and get the rifle back. But my father never did. Even now, we still do not know how that rifle got there.

My father talked for longer than he could afford with the money in his pocket, and when he finished, the PCO owner told him the cost. I searched my pockets and gave my father all the money I had. It was still not enough, only half. My father gave the man his watch, which he had worn for many years and liked very much. It was a good Russian watch and worth more than the money my father owed the man. But the man agreed that if my father brought the rest of the money we owed, he would give back the watch. For two weeks my father was unable to make enough money to pay the man and get his watch back. When he finally did go to pay after three weeks, the PCO had moved from that place and the watch had gone with it. My father never saw it again.

Before long, we bought another video player on the black market. You could find anything you wanted during the Taliban time if you knew where to look in the back streets of the bazaar. Even porn videos, if that was what you wanted. Owning one was a form of rebellion and a source of personal pride. I found another cassette of *Conan the Destroyer*. One by one, I located copies of Socrates and the other books.

But my parents' photographs of their wedding and honeymoon now lived only in our hearts. They had become ashes, and would remain ashes forever.

# 22

❖

## University of Taliban

At the end of the second year of the Taliban, I graduated from high school. On the day when the classes ended, my classmates and I wanted to have a big celebration. But a celebration without music, which was not allowed by the Taliban, is like a funeral. I had already had one of those.

Most of my classmates were boxers like myself. Since there was nothing else to do, six of us decided to go to the gym, put on our gloves, and have some fun sparring. The gym was in an old building not far from the school. It was nothing more than a room with a few weights, a punching bag, and an area the size of a boxing ring marked out on the floor. We had no ropes. We did not even have proper boxing trunks; when we practiced we just wore our underwear. And, of course, there were no showers. But we did not know about those things and were interested only in seeing who could be the best boxer.

We started punching one another. Not one on one, but everybody on everybody, all at the same time. We punched one another from eleven o'clock till five in the afternoon, until we could not lift a hand even to defend ourselves. Our heads were dizzy and our faces were swollen and badly bruised.

When I came home, nobody recognized me at first. They thought somebody had beaten me up. "We celebrated our graduation!" I explained.

"I'm so glad you graduated only once, not twice," my mother said.

I went straight to my bed and slept until the next morning. It was Friday, and my father was home. When I woke up later than usual, around eight o'clock, I tried to open my eyes, but I could not. I felt my way to the bathroom. I stood before the bathroom mirror and forced open my left eye with my finger. When I saw myself, I was really scared.

Every feature was twice as big as normal. I did not know what to do. I thought I must have had some kind of reaction, maybe from the bite of some insect or a large scorpion. I called my mother. She came and stood at the threshold of the bathroom door. I turned around, and she screamed as if she were being attacked by a wild animal. She began crying and murmuring, "What did you do to yourself? What happened to my son? It wasn't like this yesterday."

Everybody heard my mother's shouts, and they all rushed to the bathroom. My father stood at the door next to my mother. I looked at him with my left eye, which I was holding open with my fingers.

He said, "Who is he?"

"He is Qais, your son," my mother wailed.

I tried to speak but it was painful to open my mouth.

"Hey, watermelon head, what happened to you?" he asked. There was no sympathy in his voice. "Shame on you for letting somebody beat you up like this," my father said.

"Nobody beat me up. I boxed with five of my classmates, and I couldn't defend myself against them all. But I made sure I hit them as hard as they hit me," I said, not knowing whether to laugh or be angry.

"Five? Are you crazy? Are you talking about your friends who have had professional training?" The best I could do was to nod my head.

"Oh my God, he is crazy! He is mad! He is brainless! He is fighting his ass with an ox horn. This is complete stupidity. I haven't heard of such a thing in the history of boxing," my father said. He was looking first in one direction, and then another, but never losing sight of me. He was boxing with his words.

"Now I have become a part of boxing history," I said with a smile that stung all across my face.

My father came closer and slapped me. I shouted very loudly. It really hurt. Even opening my mouth to shout was painful.

"You ninny," my father said, and left, and then my mother and sisters left and I was alone again. I began laughing at myself, though it hurt.

I did not go out for a full week. My parents did not bring me a doctor either. They said it was my punishment. I did not mind. It is hard to explain, but that pain was in its own way a relief from the frustration of not being free to challenge the Taliban. My friends and I are Afghans. We had been trained never to allow anyone to do to us what the Taliban were doing. Our genetic code screamed for revenge. Suffering helped us forget that, at least for a while.

Every morning I washed my face with warm water and salt. It stung like hell, but it was the only way to keep my wounds disinfected. A week later when I was starting to feel better, I went to my classmates' homes. Each one looked at me shyly; some of them were in even worse condition than I.

Three weeks after school graduation, we had recovered enough to sit for the CONCOR examination required for admission to the University of Kabul. It is a very competitive exam. Far more students want to study at the university than there are places.

Most of my classmates had studied mathematics, biology, and chemistry in special private courses to get high scores so they could be admitted to the engineering or medical faculty. None of them had studied religious subjects, at least not the way the Taliban taught them.

I did not go to any of those special courses and was nervous going into the test. I still do not know how I had passed twelve years of school. I was extremely bad in mathematics. My classmates always solved the problems on my math exams for me, because they were afraid that I would break their noses if they did not.

We had four hours to answer the CONCOR's 210 questions. I

finished them all in just under two hours. There were almost no mathematics questions, and nothing on physics or biology. They were all about Talibanism.

I gave the answer sheet to the teacher. He looked at it for a moment, then looked at me and asked in disbelief, "How do you know so much about these things? All your answers are correct."

"I took a special course," I told him with a wise-looking smile. I decided it was better not to mention the prison where I had studied.

I was admitted to the Kabul University, Journalism Faculty. This was where I had most wanted to study, though with my high score on the CONCOR, I could have done medicine if I had wanted.

On the first day of classes, I ironed a white *shalwar kamiz* very carefully and wore my new Afghan-made leather sandals. The Taliban did not allow students to wear shoes, but only to make the point that they were in charge. They said shoes stink. But they never said that about themselves, though they did not wash for weeks and always smelled of dried sweat. After a few weeks, when we saw them wearing shoes, we did, too.

I also put kohl on my eyes with a small stick, like a toothpick. I looked at myself in the mirror. Each year at Great Eid, Muslims slaughter a sheep, goat, cow, or camel when we remember the Prophet Ibrahim's willingness to sacrifice his son Ishmael when God asked him to. My family always slaughtered a sheep. And before slaughtering it, we put some salt in its mouth and kohl around its eyes. I thought, "Somebody is going to slaughter me now."

I took my new notebooks and some old journalism books we had been assigned, tied them on the back of my bicycle, and excitedly headed around the twin-peaked mountain toward the university. It was not far from our old house.

I had wanted to go to university since I was in the third grade. My father had promised to buy me a car on my first day there. Now, here I was with a used bicycle that I had bought on the black market. In the three months since I had been admitted, I had dreamed of sitting behind a microphone with a pressed suit and tie and asking difficult questions of presidents, ministers, and high-ranking officials.

Not far from the looming yellow silo where my father and I had been forced to dig the tunnel, one of my tires had a puncture. As a result, I was five minutes late for my first class.

The class was full of students of different ages from all over Afghanistan. There were about three hundred of them. Most were older than I, with long, unkempt beards, long *shalwar kamiz*, big turbans, and dusty sandals. They all smelled like chicken sheds. "These are the classmates with whom I will have to spend four years," I thought.

The professor was standing before the blackboard, dressed like the students and equally dirty as they. His clothes were full of wrinkles, as if he had worn them for days and slept in them, too. I felt shy for having worn clean clothes that were carefully pressed.

I sat in the third row next to a man about thirty years old who had thick eyebrows, sunken eyes, a bony face, and a slender body. I soon learned that he could not speak Dari. He could not read or write either. I had no idea how he had ended up in the Faculty of Journalism.

But a few days later we found out that ten more people like him were in our class. They had come from the front line after two years of fighting the Northern Alliance, factions that had once fought one another and had now joined forces to drive out the Taliban. They had not passed any exams. They were introduced by the Ministry of Higher Education as "special students."

The professor banged his fist on the desk in front of the blackboard, demanding quiet. We all stopped talking and looked at him. He took his snuffbox from his pocket and put some snuff under his tongue. For a full minute he looked at all of us, then he spat the snuff into the corner of the room. It was the color of chicken shit. He wiped his lips with his turban and spat again. He opened a thick book, read a few lines, and began lecturing about the Taliban version of Islam. He was pacing from one corner of the room to another, and we all wrote down what he was saying in our new notebooks.

The special student next to me was looking unblinkingly at the professor. After one hour of lecturing, the professor asked a few questions about what he had said. The special student next to me raised his hand at every question. He answered nearly all of them.

"How do you know so much?" I asked him after the professor had left and we were having a fifteen-minute break before the next subject.

"I was born in a Muslim family and brought up Muslim, then learned a lot more with my fellow Taliban before I joined them," he said.

"I was also born in a Muslim family, but I don't know as much as you do," I said.

"Then you are half Muslim, and half something else," he said.

"What could that other half be?" I asked curiously.

"I don't know. I guess Communist, or Jewish, or Buddhist, or something else that I would hate to be," he said disgustedly as he walked away.

I wanted to make some friends, and it seemed that was not going to happen with this special student who could not read or write but knew all the answers for our Talib professor.

Fifteen minutes later, a real professor came and lectured us on the use of microphones in studios. He sounded like he had had real journalism training. Though he was dressed in the style of a Talib, his clothes were clean and his appearance tidy. While other students were busily writing what he was saying in their notebooks, the special student next to me stared blankly at him.

Suddenly, we heard loud beeps, and everybody looked at the special student next to me. It was his walkie-talkie. He pressed the bottom and talked loudly in Pashto, then he went out without asking the professor's permission. Twenty minutes later he came back and sat next to me, again without asking permission. The professor stopped lecturing.

"Who let you in?" the professor asked the special student.

"Who is supposed to not let me in?" the special student asked.

"I have the right to say who can stay in my class, and who cannot," the professor said.

"In my village, that is not how it works," the special student said.

From his accent we could guess that he was from somewhere in the south, where most people are very poor.

"This is not your village; this is Kabul University. No one in the ten years that I have been teaching here has ever entered my class without my permission," the professor said.

"It shouldn't matter if it is Kabul University or my village. It is the same land under the same sky," the special student said, and the rest of the class laughed.

"Then why are you here and not in your village?" the professor asked. "It is the same land and the same sky there."

"It is up to me to decide where to be. It is none of your business where I should be, or not. If you go to my village, nobody would ask you why you're there. They may even feed you, and treat you like a guest, like a friend of God," the special student said.

"You are my student, not my guest," the professor said.

"In my village, we go to the madrassa to learn the Holy Koran, and the mullah says that the mosque is the home of God and anyone can go there. Now I'm here to learn something. To me there is no difference between the madrassa and the university," the special student said. "We gain knowledge in both places."

His walkie-talkie beeped several more times, and he ran outside and talked into it. When he came back, he sat next to me again. This time the professor ignored him.

After ninety minutes, the next professor came. He was a Talib. He taught us more about the way Taliban thought Islam should be.

Later, I asked one of the real journalism professors why we had been taught journalism in only one class in the whole day.

"I cannot give you an answer to this question. We do what we are told," he said.

I came home. My mother wanted me to do some clothes shopping for her and my sisters. I told her that shopping for her and my sisters had brought me bad luck the last time. "I am not going to do any clothes shopping for anyone anymore," I said. Besides, I was feeling very discouraged by my first day of university.

She put on her *burqa* and asked me to accompany her, since women were not allowed to walk out without a male relative. Two of my sisters quickly joined us. They had just been invited to a wedding party that night and needed some things to wear. Wedding parties in Afghanistan usually are announced only a day or two in advance, and sometimes on the same day.

In the two and a half years since the Taliban had come, it was the first time that my mother and sisters had gone out to the bazaar. I had bought those *burqas* a long time ago in case some emergency forced them to go out, but they had never once worn them, preferring to stay inside the walls of Noborja. The *burqas* were brand-new, and bright blue, the color favored in Kabul.

We walked all the way to the main road to take a taxi. My sisters were complaining that they could not see through the small netted peepholes of their *burqas*. But there was nothing that I could do for them except try to keep them from walking into other people or falling into holes in the pavement. We took a taxi to Mandawee, the main bazaar in Kabul.

There you can find anything. It is always crowded. Before the Taliban came to Kabul, it was full of all kinds of people: men, women, children, poor, rich, young, and old from all over Afghanistan. Now there were mostly men with turbans and long *shalwar kamiz*. They all looked like they were Taliban, but they were only normal people who just dressed like Taliban. It was safer that way. Occasionally, I could see some women with bright blue *burqas*.

My mother and sisters went into a shop that sold women's underwear. I never liked buying those kinds of things for them. One of my sisters tripped going up the steps into the shop when her *burqa* got caught under her foot. My other sister walked into her, and they both fell sideways onto a pile of underclothes. It was hard for them to get up, because they could not see what they were doing.

The shop was dark. There was no electricity, and only a faint light filtered through the overhanging roofs of the bazaar. A few other women were in the shop already. My mother could not see what was for sale. She pulled up the front of her *burqa*. My sisters did the same. Three other women who were already there did the same as well, once they saw my mother do it.

When the other women heard my mother talking Pashto to my sisters, they started speaking to her in Pashto as well. They were from southern Afghanistan, talking in a way that was loud and a little bit coarse.

The shopkeeper respectfully asked my mother and the others to cover their faces. He seemed a very nice and educated man. But women were not allowed to show their faces to an unknown man. If the Taliban saw that, they would beat the women on their ankles with the cables or whips they always carried with them and slap the shopkeeper.

One of the other women, who was older, said, "Don't worry. My son is a Talib. He will protect us." We all thought she was joking. My mother, sisters, and the other women smiled.

Not even five minutes later, a Talib came along the narrow street of the bazaar, looking into all the shops. When he saw my mother and the others with their *burqa* fronts raised, he marched into the dark shop and started whipping the women's ankles with a thick cable. The women yelled and tried to jump out of the way.

The Talib was shouting in Pashto, "Cover your faces, you silly women," as he swung the whip.

My mother and sisters followed his orders. The others did the same, except for the older one who had spoken to my mother.

Instead, she picked up a teacup from the shopkeeper's table and threw it at the Talib. The cup hit the ground and smashed into pieces. She picked another cup and threw it at him. This one hit him in the chest. The Talib was stunned. So was I, as I wondered whether any woman had ever hit a Talib or thrown anything at one before.

Then the old woman picked up a teapot and threw that at the Talib, too. The tea had been made only a few minutes earlier. It was very hot. The pot shattered, and the fresh-boiled tea scalded him. He began shrieking and holding his clothes out from his skin to lessen the pain.

The shopkeeper quickly started collecting all the other cups from the table. He could see that the older woman was looking for something else to throw. He was afraid all his cups would be smashed. In a harsh voice the woman barked at the Talib, "Go home and behave yourself. Have I brought you up for such a day to whip me on the ankles with a cable? You son of a dog!" she yelled, making a bad reference to his father.

"Mother! What are you doing here?" the Talib asked as he was still holding his sopping *kamiz* away from his chest. He gazed at her with wide eyes.

The shopkeeper, who was fearfully holding the tray of cups, slowly put them back on the table.

She picked up another cup and threw it at her son. The cup hit him on his right arm as he turned around to avoid it, then fell on the ground in pieces.

"Don't you see what I'm doing?" the woman said. She picked up an extralarge red bra and showed it to her son. She was a solidly built village woman. "I'm buying this. Could you buy this for me if I sent you?" she said.

"Put it away, Mother," the Talib said. He was shy and covered his eyes with his right hand.

She reached for another cup, but the shopkeeper had picked up the tray again before she could get one. Instead, she grabbed a package of bras and threw it at her son. It was heavy and landed at her son's feet.

"Get out of here," the woman said. "I'll teach you tonight how to behave."

The Talib turned around to walk out. The shopkeeper said, "Excuse me. Excuse me." The Talib turned around to see what the shopkeeper wanted.

"Your mother has broken three cups and a teapot," the shopkeeper said. "Somebody has to pay for them."

"How much?" the Talib said, annoyed.

The shopkeeper told him the price, and the Talib paid without any bargaining. He did not even look at his mother or the other women. All the women's *burqas* were pulled up again as he walked out. He did not tell them to cover their faces.

The old woman apologized for the inconvenience that was caused by her son. The other women told her that she was a brave woman, and she was very happy to hear that.

My mother quickly became very good friends with her. For the rest of that day, my mother followed her around to all the other shops so nobody could beat her or my sisters if they needed to pull up their *burqas* while they were buying things.

After shopping for several hours, we had lunch in a restaurant and invited the old woman to join us as our guest, which she was happy to do. She had many funny stories, and we laughed like we were having a picnic with an old friend.

My mother gave her our home address and asked her to come and visit us sometime. She said she would, but she never did.

# 23

❖

## *Grandfather*

We all came home from our shopping trip very happy. When we got there, we found Grandfather sipping tea in our sitting room. I ran to him and kissed his hands, and he kissed my forehead and congratulated me for starting university. I was so happy having my grandfather next to me, sipping tea and patting my head like in the old days.

He had brought some gifts for me to celebrate my first day. He gave me three expensive notebooks and his collection of the *Complete Psychological Works of Sigmund Freud*. I have no idea how he had saved those books all those years, or where he had been keeping them. Perhaps years ago he had lent them to a friend who lived where the fighting or the Taliban had never reached. I was too happy when I saw them to ask. "Now is the right time for you to have them, Gorbachev," he said.

"*Tashekur, Baba*," I replied, as I gave him a long, heartfelt hug, upsetting his tea onto the carpet. I was thankful not just for the books, but to have him with us. It pushed my disappointment with the university to the back of my mind.

It was only forty minutes by bike to Makroyan, where he lived with my aunt, but I was not allowed to go. My father was afraid to let me go anywhere alone. Whenever I walked out of the courtyard, somebody called after me, either my mother or my father, asking me where I was going. Nobody was worried about my sisters, because it was not possible for them to go anywhere; but after all the things that had happened to me, they were always worried about me.

Grandfather was slowly becoming an old man. It was hard for him to walk all the way from Makroyan the way he once had, and he found the bus tiring. Sometimes he wanted to visit us, but he had no money for a taxi. He was too proud to ask anybody for any. We did not have a phone to call him. Afghanistan did not have much of a phone system anymore. It had all been destroyed in the fighting between the factions. Now, whenever he came to visit us, one of my uncles would accompany him.

One of my sisters brought me a cup, and I poured more tea for Grandfather and some for myself. It felt like the old days, but I could read a deep sadness in Grandfather's eyes, though he tried to hide it.

I knew he did not want to ruin my first day of university. He did not know that I was already bitterly disappointed, and I did not want to spoil his happiness for me by showing it.

I was looking for a right and quiet moment to ask him what was troubling him, but nobody wanted to leave us alone. It had been a month since we had last seen him, and everybody had been missing him.

Night fell and covered everything with its black coat. My grandfather went out to the courtyard and sat on one of the low, wooden platforms scattered around where my father had once washed carpets. He was gazing at the star-filled, moonless sky. He did not notice me at first when I came out and sat next to him. He was lost in his thoughts. I sat there for a long time before I spoke.

"You are hiding something from me," I said finally. "What is it inside that keeps burning you? Why don't you take it out and share it with me?" I asked.

He looked into my eyes for a full minute. I could feel his discomfort through his eyes, which got watery. Then he looked at the stars again.

"I have kept that fire for a month inside me. If I take that fire out, its flames will burn everyone," he said with his head pointed toward the sky. "It will make you sadder than others," he said. He got up and walked back into the house.

We ate dinner together. My father made some of his jokes, and everyone laughed. I kept looking at Grandfather. His mouth made the gesture of a smile, but not his eyes.

After dinner as we were drinking tea, Grandfather said, "I have unpleasant news for everyone." We all looked at him. He was quiet for a moment and then said, "I have been receiving a letter every morning since a month ago. In the letter someone is threatening me and my sons with death if I don't sell my house to him. He is working with the government, and he is a powerful Talib."

We were all very quiet. Nobody knew how to break the silence as we tried to understand what might happen to our home, the place where we expected to return. Finally my father said, "How do you receive these letters?"

"Somebody is sliding them under the door around three in the morning. When I wake up for morning prayers, I find them. Each one is the same, the same writing, the same words. It has come every day for a month," Grandfather calmly said.

"Have you told anyone else yet?" my father asked.

"No, not yet," Grandfather said.

"While you are here tonight, will he slip another letter under the door?" I asked, deeply concerned about my aunt alone in the apartment in Makroyan without Grandfather with her.

"No. Two days ago I wrote him a letter, and left it for him under the door before morning prayers. I asked him to show me his face. Yesterday I met him. He is a dangerous man. He likes our house, what is left of it, and he wants to buy the land and rebuild. He will choose a price for it. He said he would tell me the price tomorrow," Grandfather said.

"We are definitely not going to sell him the house," my father said. "Let him dream about it. I'm sure he can do nothing."

"He can do anything he wants. He is not afraid of anyone. He would destroy whatever comes into his path. He may kill one of us if I say 'No,'" Grandfather said.

I noticed that my uncle's face had gone pale.

"May I go with you and see him tomorrow?" my father asked forcefully.

"No, he doesn't want to see any of you. He said that if I tell any of my sons, he will kill me. But I'm telling you, and you'll all keep your father's secret," he said as he looked into everybody's eyes. We did not know what to say.

"Do you want to sell him the house, then?" my father asked, more quietly.

"I want to talk to him and solve this problem peacefully, but if he gets serious and stubborn, then I don't know. He is one of those Taliban from the border. They capture a village and torture people and club them to death, then afterward ask the young boys to do the same to their parents. They tell the young boys that this will make a man of them.

"I don't want the same thing to happen to my sons, my grandsons, and my granddaughters. I don't want to see my daughters-in-law in widows' clothes. I don't want to ruin my family. Money is the dirt on our hands; it comes and goes. We may have some money again, and we will buy a better house," Grandfather said. He said all this with a calm voice.

No one talked after him and there were several minutes of silence. He asked for a blanket, which he wrapped around himself, then went back out into the courtyard and lay down; he fell asleep on the platform where we had been sitting earlier, even though the night had turned cool.

The rest of us sat inside; no one said anything for a long time. Finally, my uncle spoke.

"I went to the old house about six weeks ago. I had to know if any of my wife's gold was still there. I mean, how long are we going to go on living like this?" His voice was filled with frustration.

Nobody answered him. My uncle had gone to the house without telling any of his brothers or his father. Grandfather did not want anyone to go there.

"The garden was full of sacks of potatoes. It looked like they are using it for storage. They saw me and chased me all the way to Makroyan," he said sorrowfully.

Somehow they figured out that he was part of the family who owned the place. This was how they found Grandfather. The Taliban could have just taken the house, but even they knew they could never claim to own it without the papers.

Early in the morning, Grandfather left our house without telling us where he was going. While we had our breakfast my father said, "If Dad sells the house, the gold is gone with it. But I don't know how to stop him. If I did, we might face bad consequences. I don't want to be blamed for the rest of my life by the others."

"So, are we just going to lose all our gold?" my mother said. "We'll never get to another country." The gold was the only wealth we had left. The belief that we would one day get it back had made it possible for us to think that somehow someday we could leave Afghanistan and have something like a normal life.

"What do you want me to do, then?" my father said. "It is not just your gold; others have theirs, too."

"Can you not just go and get the gold, before Father sells the house?" my mother asked. My mother always called my grandfather "Father."

"You heard what my brother said last night. The whole courtyard is full of potato sacks. Thousands of them. We would have to shift all those first. Then, if they see us taking it from the ground, they'll think we have a lot more somewhere else. Then we'll be in worse trouble. They may kidnap us, and ask us for money we don't have. How will I be able to convince these illiterate Taliban thieves of that?"

My mother did not say anything.

All I could think about was having seen Grandfather's spirit so broken.

A few days later, we heard that Grandfather had sold the house for less than half of what it was worth. A few days after he received the money for it, he was threatened by the buyer and forced to give half of it back. Grandfather did what he was told.

From the time he sold the house, he became a quiet man, a man who spoke only two or three words a day.

He bought a new house. It was on our side of Kabul, only a thirty-minute walk from Noborja, about halfway to his old house. It had two floors and a nice courtyard, but it was tiny compared to what we had had before. Two of my uncles lived downstairs with their families. Grandfather lived on the second floor and stayed in his rooms for months without leaving the house. He never talked to anyone. He read and read and read. That was all.

Sometimes I visited him, but he hardly noticed me. We said "Salaam" to each other, and a few minutes later he said "Salaam" again, and a few minutes later he said "Salaam" again. He never said anything more. He just kept reading for hours, occasionally gazing at the blue sky.

Other times, he talked about whatever book he had open. But the two thick volumes of his favorite book, *Afghanistan in the Path of History* by Mir Ghulam Mohammad Ghobar, were always on his top shelf. They were never opened now, and were covered with dust.

After a while, he even stopped reading, and he became gloomier. Dark circles appeared under his eyes, and he neglected his appearance, going about the whole day in a wrinkled *shalwar kamiz* with an unbuttoned collar without combing his hair. It hurt me to see him so uncaring about all the things he had told me were important.

One day in late winter, Grandfather woke up before dawn to take ablution for morning prayers. He still did not like his new house, especially his bathroom with its floor covered with blue tiles. They were very slippery. He liked white marble from our mountains, as he had had in his bathroom in his old house. He always said that Afghan marble is the best in the world. "The rest of the world will notice it one day, and it'll have great value. It will be exported everywhere," he would tell us.

That day, he took ablution as always with cold water and was shivering from the cold. As he hurried to get to his bedroom to get under his blanket, he slipped. His head hit the edge of the sink. He went unconscious and lay there for several hours.

When he came to, the sun was already flooding into the bathroom through a small window. He had missed his morning prayers. He did not remember what had happened to him and did not know why he was lying on the bathroom floor. He wanted to stand up and go to his room, but he could not. He called for my uncle who lived downstairs with his kids, but his voice was not loud enough to wake anybody up.

My uncle came upstairs around seven o'clock as always to ask his father about his breakfast. Sometimes Grandfather wanted his eggs boiled, and sometimes fried. Some days he wanted milk with sugar, and some days he wanted green tea with honey. But this morning my uncle could not find him in his room reading a book, as Grandfather usually did.

My uncle opened the bathroom door and saw Grandfather lying on the ground with blood pooled under his head. He carried Grandfather to his room and asked him what had happened. But Grandfather could barely talk. His face was blue from cold. My uncle covered him with blankets and lit a blazing fire in his tin *bokhari* heating stove. The room was warm after a few minutes, but Grandfather could not feel anything, neither cold nor heat. He fell asleep.

My uncle quickly came to Noborja to tell us about Grandfather. He and my father and I went to several private clinics to look for a doctor. But it was too early, and the clinics were still closed. It was not like the old days, when we could call an ambulance any time of the day or night.

Nobody wanted to take his sick relatives to public hospitals, either. They were filthy. A person would get sicker there instead of getting cured. Besides, the hospitals did not accept patients unless they had been injured on the front line, or had stepped on a land mine, or had been wounded by a rocket.

We waited for more than an hour in front of a private clinic. Finally, the doctor arrived. He was a close friend of my uncle. We took him to Grandfather's house. By now all my other uncles and their wives and my cousins had arrived there, as well as my mother and my sisters and my little brother. There were too many people for that small house.

The doctor examined Grandfather and said, "Some blood vessels burst inside his brain. He needs to have an operation within twenty-four hours. Nobody can do this operation in Afghanistan. We don't have the surgical tools for it. You'll have to take him to India."

"Is there no alternative?" my father asked.

"No. I'm afraid not," the doctor said.

"That will take three or four days!" my uncle protested. "His passport is expired. We have to renew it first. Then we have to apply for Indian visas. God knows if they'll give them to us."

"The best I can do is to take him to my clinic, but I cannot promise anything. Without an operation, he will lose his ability to speak in twelve hours or sooner. If he talks, his words will be loose, and he won't be able to pronounce them properly. In twenty-four hours, he will start losing his memory. In thirty hours he will not recognize anyone. And after that, he will go into a coma. God knows how long he will stay alive after that," the doctor said with a sigh.

Grandfather was listening to all that the doctor was saying. "Will I be able to walk before I start losing my memory?" Grandfather said.

"No, I'm sorry," the doctor said. "Your brain will not help you control your body. You won't be able to lift your arms, or your feet, and you won't feel anything unless we get you operated on."

"So, I will die like this?" Grandfather said as if he were hearing a joke.

"Not if we get you to the operating table on time," the doctor said.

"Otherwise, yes," Grandfather said.

The doctor nodded his head as he was looking at his hands.

There was a moment of silence, a bitter silence. Nobody knew how to break it. My father ordered my uncle to start working on passport renewal.

Grandfather said, "Let's have a good *qabli* for lunch, and celebrate the last hours of my life, and enjoy eating and talking while I can. You don't go anywhere for lunch, Doctor. You stay with us."

The doctor nodded.

Grandfather tried to sound cheerful. We all had cold smiles on our faces to make Grandfather feel good, but inside we had flames of sorrow burning us, and we did not know how to cool them.

"I know I can't bring a real smile to your lips," Grandfather said, "but maybe my joke will. Mullah Nasruddin said, 'When my wife died, half of the world died for me. When I die, the whole world will die with me.'"

Everybody laughed.

"You see, I can still do it," Grandfather said with a trace of pride.

My aunts started wiping tears and blowing their noses.

"Hey, hey, I don't want to see you crying and wiping your noses for me," Grandfather said cheerfully.

We all smiled with tears in our eyes.

My uncle left the room to start working on Grandfather's passport renewal. My father went to find out about whether an Indian visa would be possible. My aunts started cooking the rice and the meat for the *qabli pelau* and shredding the carrots they would mix with it. The doctor wrote a prescription, which he handed to me, and I ran off to the pharmacy. The room was full of my cousins, and Grandfather told them to sit in a circle around him and joked with them.

I came back with the medicine in a plastic bag. In the short time that I had been gone, Grandfather's face had become noticeably paler. But he tried to sound happy and full of energy.

Several hours later we had lunch around one long tablecloth in Grandfather's room. My father had to feed Grandfather, like a little baby, as he was lying on his *toshak* in the corner near the woodstove. Grandfather made some jokes about old people, and we laughed, quietly.

After lunch, the doctor injected him with some painkillers since his head was hurting, and he fell asleep. We did not let the doctor go. Late in the afternoon my uncle returned with a new passport for Grandfather. Early that evening Grandfather woke up. His saliva started coming out of the corners of his mouth without his noticing it, and he was saying things that did not make sense.

My uncles tried to talk to him, but he could not focus on what they said to him. My aunts wept, but he did not object anymore.

"I should take him to my clinic," the doctor said. "It is happening faster than I thought. He may need oxygen very soon."

My uncle stayed with him in the clinic that night; the next day we busied ourselves trying to get visas. The next night I stayed with him. I sat all night long on a chair in front of his bed, looking at him as he was breathing softly. Occasionally, he opened his eyes, looked at me, and then closed them again.

Early in the morning he opened his eyes. This time he did not close them. He wanted to say something. I lifted the oxygen mask so he could speak. He called my name, and I said "Yes." He called my name again, and again I said "Yes." His voice gave out, but his lips still moved a little. And then they stopped. His eyes remained open, seeing the invisible.

We brought the body to his new house. I did not cry at all. I could not tell whether it was nighttime or daytime. They seemed to me the same. I was not feeling hungry or thirsty. I did not know whether I was walking or sitting. Everything seemed like it had stopped.

Meanwhile the little house was filling up with people from all over Kabul who had somehow heard the news.

My father took charge of organizing cars to take us all to Grandfather's village. Though he had left the village many years ago, Grandfather had always kept in touch with many of our relatives there, and had helped many of them without telling anybody.

That same day, we carried him to his village, about thirty miles from Kabul. Even before we arrived, Grandfather's friends and relatives had heard the news. The high-walled house where he had grown up was full of people.

Once we reached there, the news quickly spread all over the village, and thousands of people came. No one there had ever seen so many people at a funeral before. Our family had lived in that village for several generations. The village people used to call my grandfather "President" from the time he was working at the National

Bank of Afghanistan. My grandfather had brought my grandmother there for the first five years of their marriage to live with his mother, and would visit her once every three months while he was working in Kabul. He had fixed up many of the rooms in the old house and had made its walls higher and stronger, but they offered no protection during a war fought with rockets.

One of my uncles, whose wife is from that area, had wanted to go to the village instead of staying in the Qala-e-Noborja. He decided to go with his wife's brother to see whether it was safe. On the way there, they were robbed by one faction who took all their money. On the way back, they took a different route to avoid the robbers and were beaten badly by another faction, because they had no money left to be stolen. We heard worse stories about those roads from other, distant relatives. So, we never tried to take refuge there. Yet the village was a beautiful place, filled with the apple orchards that Grandfather had planted.

When the time came to take Grandfather from the house to the place for his burial about a mile away, my father and his brothers tried to carry his coffin, but everybody there wanted to help carry it. So, they passed Grandfather's coffin over their heads to the next person in front of them.

When they put the body in the grave, and I saw the earth taking Grandfather away from me forever, I could no longer hold back the feelings I had been carrying inside me. I broke down and cried loudly. I could not stop, though I remembered Grandfather's long-ago admonition: "Brave boys don't cry." But I was not brave anymore. I knew that my bravery had been buried with Grandfather.

Many people rubbed my back and hugged me. But it had no effect on me. I would stop only when I was asleep.

We stayed in his village for three days to be with the people there who wanted to say their condolences. Every day, several hundred people came. Sometimes, we had to keep all his close friends and relatives for lunch. After the three days we went home.

————

Several nights later, I saw Grandfather in my dreams, very happy in a field of roses. I called him, but he did not seem to hear me. I called him several more times, but he never answered. The next morning I stopped crying.

I went through all of Grandfather's papers and books. I gave some of his books to my cousins, but I kept all his papers. He had written the story of his life in those papers. On the first page he wrote, "The richer you get, the more you lose your respect, love, and closeness to poor people around you. Don't forget that once you were one of them, and that your ancestors were among them."

# 24

❖

## *One Knot at a Time*

After going to Kabul University for only three months, I stopped. I did not have enough money to fix my tire punctures every day, or to pay for the bus. We had spent all our savings on Grandfather's funeral, feeding people in his village. This is how it works in Afghanistan. People come to your house offering their condolences and expecting a lunch or dinner.

My father made barely enough money to feed us poorly three times a day. We could not afford milk, butter, or jam for breakfast anymore. We ate bread and tea with a little sugar. Sometimes we boiled the same tea leaves for several days until there was no color or taste left in them. For lunch, we ate beans and cheap Afghan rice. Most of the time, we ate the leftovers from lunch for dinner, and from dinner for lunch. My uncles and aunts were in the same situation.

I stayed at home for a few days after I stopped going to the university. I did not know what to do with my life. Most of the young men were going to Pakistan or Iran for work. When they came back after several months or years, they brought money and gifts and told about eating good food while they were away. But some of them had also been kicked out of those countries with no money in their pockets. Their money was left behind with their employers. Some of the honest employers sent their money, many did not.

Several times I made plans to go to one of those countries. But my father never gave me permission to go. He was still buying and selling flour and oil. Sometimes we did not see him for weeks. We knew that he had been home only from the rumples we saw in his bed in the morning. Sometimes, I think he was so discouraged, he did not want us to see him.

Once when I tried to talk to him about buying carpets again, he just shook his head. "Carpets are a cursed business," he said, and he would not say anything else.

I was looking for advice, for someone who could guide me in the right direction. Grandfather was not there to help me anymore. Every now and then I saw him in my dreams, always wearing white clothes and a big smile, but he never talked to me. He never told me what to do to help my family. But I was still so happy to see him, to feel that he was in some way still with me. Sometimes I saw him with Wakeel. Wakeel always had his kite and reel with him, and looked as if he had just won a kite battle.

One day when I felt completely desperate, I went running for a couple of hours without stopping. As long as I was running, watching carefully where I placed each step on the broken pavements and roadways, my mind stopped thinking about the poverty that we were suffering, or about my father, who was working so hard and was losing weight from lack of food, or the loss of Grandfather and Wakeel.

I ran so hard that sweat was pouring from all over my body in a way that it rarely does in the dry air of Kabul. Finally, breathing deeply, I sat under a tree on the slope of the Bagh-e-Bala, the very formal High Garden built by the Moguls four hundred years ago at the top of a steep hill just west of the Qala-e-Noborja. I was exhausted. But as soon as I leaned back against the tree to rest, the distraction that the running had brought went away. Once again, all I could think about was our problems. From the Bagh-e-Bala, I could look down and see Noborja with its one last tower. I closed my eyes.

My carpet teacher came into my mind. I had not thought about her for a long time, and when I had, it had always seemed as if she were very far away from me. Now I felt that she was close to me, sitting right next to me. I opened my eyes and looked around. There was no one, only the trees and sparrows making their *chuk-chuk* noises.

I closed my eyes again and thought about the last time I had seen her, when she had said goodbye. "Use your mind skillfully, for you could be a brilliant weaver and seller of carpets one day." She said this with her hand gestures.

As I sat there against the tree, her message rang through my mind very loudly, as if she were saying it forcefully into my ears. I opened my eyes again and looked around to see whether anyone else had heard. But there was no one around. I was alone, but I was not alone. A feeling of peace came over me, and I felt very relaxed and fresh, except the muscles of my legs, which began to cramp and hurt when I got up to walk home.

At home, I looked at the carpet that we had in our sitting room. I thought, I can make a carpet, too. I had learned that from my teacher.

A sudden idea sang in my mind: why not draw a design for a carpet? I took a piece of paper and roughly sketched a design that had been circling in my mind for several months. A few hours later, it had begun to really look like a carpet.

That night I stayed awake until my father came at midnight. He asked me why I was not asleep. I asked him for some money to buy graph paper for drawing my carpet design properly. He did not like the idea. He asked me what I would do with the design. I said that I would be able to sell it and make some money.

"Maybe that is my career," I told him.

"Stay away from carpets," he said with a sad voice. "They will only disappoint you."

The next morning when I woke up, I found the money that I needed next to my bed.

I went to one of the stationery shops in the Shahr-e-Naw business district and bought some sheets of graph paper. As soon as I got home, I started working on my design for a carpet about six feet long and four feet wide. Every day I could see mistakes from the day before, and I had to correct them. Also, the longer I worked, the more ideas kept streaming through my imagination, and I wanted to include many of them. It took me four months to finish it.

When I was finally satisfied with it, I took my design to several carpet factories to sell it, but none of them were interested. Some of them did not even look at it. They said that they received their designs from buyers overseas and worked only according to their customers' orders.

As the weeks passed, I became very discouraged. I nearly tore the design into little pieces. But then I thought about how much of my father's money had been spent on the paper and the pencils, though we hardly had enough to eat, never mind the time I had wasted on it.

"I am not going to university anymore. If I go, I will not learn anything new," I told myself. "I am getting like a stray dog. I should not be like a dog. I eat and shit, that is all I do. I must be like a human, and do something. But what?" I asked myself. "I don't know," I answered myself, despairingly.

"You have to make your own carpet with your design," a voice inside me exclaimed.

"What if nobody likes that carpet?" I asked the voice inside me.

"You don't know that yet," the voice replied.

"Yes, I don't know that yet. Nobody knows what will happen tomorrow," I said back. It was several days later when I suddenly realized that the voice I had heard was like that of my teacher when she had spoken to me in my dreams.

I told my father that I was going to make my own carpet. At first he thought I was joking. But I insisted until he understood that I was serious. He gave me some money to buy wood for a loom. I went to a wood market and bought three long beams. I took them to a carpenter who was my father's friend and asked him to make me a carpet loom.

A week later the loom was ready. I did not have money to pay the carpenter, and I did not want to ask my father for more money. I told the carpenter that I had forgotten to bring the money, and he said that it was all right, that I could bring it the next day. I said I would. But that particular tomorrow never came, or at least not the next day. After four weeks he came to our house for his money. I told him that

I spent the money on something else, and that my father did not know that. I promised him that I would give him his money within a month. I begged him to please not tell my father about it. In fact, I had already told my father about it. He was not happy that I had not been truthful to the carpenter.

The loom had been in my house for two weeks before I had wool, a comb, or any of the other materials I needed, or the money to buy them. I still had the hook that my teacher had given me, but that was too precious to use.

I asked my neighbors to lend me some money, but they said they were in the same situation as we were. I asked my friends and they said the same thing.

I went to the street where the wool shops are located and asked the owner of one of them to give me six kilos of different-colored wool. The shopkeeper weighed the wool, put it in plastic bags, and told me the price. I searched all my pockets, but there was no money in any of them. The wool seller thought somebody had robbed me on the bus. I said, "No. I must have left my money at home." I told him that, if he did not mind, I would bring it the next day. He said that was okay.

I told him, "I am the owner of a carpet factory, and this carpet is an experiment. If it works, and my customers like the new design, I will buy tons of wool from you." He said that he would provide all that I needed. I said that I would buy it only from him, because he was a good man. This is what we say in Afghanistan when we are doing business. And, because we are desperate and poor, we believe it.

My mother gave me all her tiny savings to buy the hooks, comb, and the other tools. The next day I started my work. I had never set up a loom before and did not know how to wrap the yarn around the top and bottom of the loom to create the warp on which I would tie knots. No one in my family had ever made a carpet; we had only sold them. I looked at the book that had pictures of Turkmen people making carpets. I read the book several times. But it was still hard for me to understand. I only knew how to make knots. Not even my carpet teacher had taught me how to set the warp on the loom.

After many days of seeing my warp suddenly sag where it should have been tight, I gave up. I had no idea how I would pay the carpenter and wool seller.

I went back to that same tree in Bagh-e-Bala and sat under it. I closed my eyes, but did not see or hear anything. I sat there for several hours, but nothing happened. Darkness came. I became very hungry. But I did not want to leave without an answer to what I should do. I was pleading in my heart for my carpet teacher to tell me what to do.

Finally, I had to leave. I walked home slowly. By the time I got there, everybody was asleep, except my father, who was not home yet. I went to my bed but just lay there. I was staring at the ceiling. Some hours later, I heard my father come in and fall into his bed. I do not remember ever falling asleep. But that night I dreamed of my carpet teacher. She said, "A carpet cannot be woven in one day. It causes pain, and demands patience. If you let the pain poison you, you will never get to the fringes."

I woke up the next morning. I decided that the time had truly come to follow Grandfather's advice to make patience my companion. It took me two more days to find the right way to do the warping, and then to weave my weft yarn back and forth through the warp threads, as my people have been doing for thousands of years, to create a few inches of the flat-woven *kilim* needed to anchor the beginning of a carpet. Uncertainty filled my every move. Finally, I had reached the place where the knots started and my design began.

Once I started tying the knots, my mother and sisters sometimes came upstairs to see how far I had gone. Two of my sisters wanted to learn, too. But I did not have time to teach them. Anyway, who was I to be a teacher? Every day I was teaching myself new things. I worked from early in the morning until my father came home at midnight.

My father really did believe that the carpet business had become cursed for us. He would say that we were carpet sellers, not carpet makers. But I listened only to what the voice inside me told me to do. I did not say "Yes" or "No" to any of my father's comments. I pretended that I was deaf like my teacher, and I kept my silence like she did.

Jerk's father was the worst. He always made fun of me. Maybe he was the one who taught his son how to be a jerk. He would say, "Soon your back will be bent like an old man's. You'll look like a cripple, shuffling around. You'll lose your fingers, and eat with your palms. You'll lose the sight in your eyes, and you'll wear thick glasses. Wool will grow inside your nostrils." I did not mind; I kept working.

It took me three months to finish my first carpet. I took it to a carpet shop on Chicken Street, which got its name from the Jewish shopkeepers who had sold chicken there for decades from the time the street was first laid out. After most of them had moved to Israel, carpet sellers took over nearly all the shops, but everyone still called it Chicken Street. The shopkeeper, whom my family had known for many years, looked at my carpet and laughed. I asked him whether something was funny. He said my design was hilarious. He also said that he did not want to buy it.

I insisted that he keep it in his shop. If by any chance anyone saw it and liked it, he should sell it to him. He agreed, only because Grandfather had been his friend.

"But only for a week," he cautioned. I promised him that I would come back at the end of the next week and take it back.

Three days later, early in the morning, I heard a steady knocking on our gate. I was afraid it might be the carpenter or the wool seller. I still had no money to pay them. The carpenter had come several times and asked me and my father for his money. We kept saying "Next day," "Next day," but he complained that the "Next day" never came. I had told the wool seller that I was too busy with my factory to come to his shop and pay him. He believed me. But that had been weeks before. Now, perhaps he was here demanding payment.

I opened the door. There was the Chicken Street shopkeeper. I thought he had brought my carpet back, and I was ready to argue that he had promised to keep it for a full week. But I did not have a chance. He extended his hand, which was holding American money. He gave it to me and asked me whether it was enough.

---

It was two hundred dollars. I thought he was making fun of me again. I gave him back his money and almost said a bad word to match the hard look in my eyes.

He asked me how much more I wanted. I told him to stop mocking me, but he told me that he had found an Afghan who was selling carpets in Germany and who was very excited about my design. He had asked for one hundred more like it. Could I make them? He extended his hand with the money again, but this time he gave me three hundred. I took it and counted it as if I were concerned that it was all there. But, really, all I wanted to do was to touch it and to feel it moving through my fingers. I felt him watching me, and suddenly I realized I was being very rude. I quickly invited him to come into our house, and I asked my mother to please make us some tea.

Inside, I was thanking God and my carpet teacher. I so much wanted her to be there to hear what the shopkeeper had just said. My eyes filled for a moment, and I told the voice inside me that it seemed what she had said those years ago was really beginning to happen.

When he noticed my wet eyes, the shopkeeper asked me whether anything was wrong. I wiped them with the back of my sleeve and said I would make more carpets if he gave me money to buy more wool and looms. He gave me a thousand dollars. I had never once touched an American dollar. The edge of the paper was so stiff and so sharp, so different from our small and tired afghanis. I looked at it and told him, "I could kill sparrows with this sharp edge." In those days, you could buy a good car for a thousand dollars. You could even buy a visa to Italy for that. Here I was holding it in my hand. But I did not want to go to Italy by myself. I wanted all my family to go with me. So, I spent every penny of it on wool and looms and started making more carpets.

I went to the carpenter and gave him his money. He grabbed the money from my hand without saying a word and looked at me sideways. I asked him whether he could make me a few more looms.

"I will never make a loom for you in my life ever again," he spat with disgust.

"What if I give you the money for them in advance?"

"You don't have money even to buy yourself a *naan*," he said derisively. "How can you give me the money for a few looms in advance?"

I gave him the money for five looms, and told him that I would collect the looms in a week. He looked at me, a little startled, and even though he had my money in his hand, he remained a little unconvinced. I walked out of his shop without listening to what he had to say.

"All right! Don't worry! They will be ready next week! Thank you!" he shouted behind me.

I lifted up my right hand without turning around and made the sign of bye-bye. Money was making me arrogant.

I went to the wool shop and apologized for keeping him waiting for so long for his money. He said not to worry, that all carpet factories were like that, and he was used to it. He did not know that I had lied to him about my factory. But my lie had turned to truth. I bought a couple of hundred kilos of wool.

"I can provide you any kind of wool you need," he said. "I will deliver it to your factory."

My factory. I liked the sound of that. I was beginning to believe it myself. I had not really thought about it yet, but if I was going to be able to make all the carpets that the man in Germany wanted, I would need a factory.

"Okay," I said as I left. "Thank you." My factory, I thought.

That night my father came home very late as always. Everybody was asleep, but I was waiting for him.

"It is midnight. Go to bed," he said. Then he asked me for a glass of water.

When he finished drinking it, I gave him the three hundred dollars. He looked at the money and asked me whether they were forgeries, or some kind of joke.

"No. They are the result of my seven months' hard work," I said very proudly.

He studied them all very carefully, then smiled in a way he had not done for months and said, "Wonderful! Now you are making more money than I do." Then he opened his arms and gave me a big, long hug.

I told him about the shopkeeper, about the thousand dollars, the five looms, the several hundred kilos of wool, and my plans for opening a carpet factory. He looked at me in amazement. But I knew he was pleased.

I taught two of my younger sisters and my brother how to make knots. My brother was still very young, but he had become a very helpful member of our family. He and my sisters and I took turns working on our one loom.

My younger sisters had been spending time with our neighbor's girls in the garden every afternoon. Since they were banned by the Taliban from going to school, all they did was chat or read Iranian novels. When my sisters failed to appear in the garden after lunch for several days, the other girls became worried. At first, my sisters were very secretive about making carpets. They thought they were doing something special, and they did not want anyone to know. But they could not keep secrets from their friends. After about a week, they finally told the other girls about it.

The neighbor's girls came to me and asked me to hire them for no salary. They just wanted to learn how to make carpets. We were Pashtuns. They were Hazaras. Weaving carpets was something that Turkmen did. But we all worked at it together.

Within a few days, most of the other girls in our neighborhood were coming to our house to ask me to teach them how to make carpets. Somehow they had heard about what we were doing. They had all been at home doing nothing and were very bored.

My first reaction was to be worried. If the girls had heard about what I was doing, maybe the Taliban would as well. But I needed weavers, and all the girls were willing to learn.

In a couple of months, my one loom had turned into a carpet factory. My father and I had rebuilt the walls of the storeroom where his carpets had been destroyed by the rocket. We made all the bricks our-selves, filling more than a hundred molds every day with mud that had been mixed with straw, then letting them dry enough to empty the molds and fill them again. We did not have the money to buy cooked bricks, and besides, the whole of the Qala-e-Noborja had been built this way from sun-dried mud bricks. For privacy I blocked the large windows facing the street with bricks, but kept a little space at the top to let some air come through.

I had twenty-five looms and about forty girls, including my sis-ters, making carpets. As soon as I could get new looms made, new girls would start. From early in the morning until four o'clock, all those girls tied knots except for one hour when they stopped to have lunch.

From four o'clock until six o'clock, we had classes. My father taught them basic mathematics, my mother showed them how to do accounting, and my older sister taught Dari grammar and literature. Though she had no interest in making carpets and never learned how, my older sister was a very good teacher, as she had been when we had taught our Kuchi cousins. I was very happy that she was teaching my weavers, though I never told her that. Even though we were now at peace, I never knew when, like with the rest of Afghanistan, the fighting would start again.

Hanging over us every minute was the fear that the Taliban might find out what we were doing. It was against the Taliban laws for the girls to be working outside their homes, or to be getting an education. Had the Taliban known, terrible things would have happened to all of us. In the end, we probably would have been killed, but that would have been easier for us than what they would do to us first. Even though it was dangerous, my parents and older sister stood with me at every step.

My rule was that the girls should be present at the factory by eight o'clock. But they were not allowed to enter through the same door at one time. The spies of the Taliban would have noticed that. Instead, they had to come a few at a time from six o'clock in the morn-ing until eight o'clock.

Two of them came in the main gate of the fort. Three of them came in from another door at the bottom of the garden. Four of them came in from a different door at the far corner of the garden that was hidden from the street. The neighbor's girls climbed over the walls between their house and our courtyard on a ladder. At eight o'clock, all the girls were present at the factory. The ones who came earlier did their homework until starting time.

Once my factory started to be successful, so many girls were coming every morning to work for me that Jerk decided to become friendly. He begged me to accept him as one of my students and teach him how to make carpets. I agreed, though a little bit reluctantly. But I did not have any friends, and in those times when he chose to be intelligent, I enjoyed his company. He had a good sense of humor. He was still a jerk sometimes. But that was not his fault; he was just being himself.

He was a fast learner. He learned everything about making a carpet in two months. All his life he had been very competitive with me, but somehow he never learned how to get ahead. He always remained one step behind. Maybe he had been smart all along, though, letting me take the risk first, then doing it better by imitating and improving on what I did.

Soon he bought his own looms and wool and started his own factory on the other side of the courtyard in the rooms his family used. He taught all his brothers how to make carpets and organized a factory like mine. He began hiring all the boys of our neighborhood, paying them more than I paid the girls, feeding them better food and making lots of jokes with them.

Soon I started hiring boys, too, especially some younger ones whose big sisters would have been looking after them, except they were now working for me. But after a while, some of my boy weavers joined his factory for better food, more wages, and funnier jokes. Then all of them went.

Jerk started making fun of me to my face, pointing out that all my boy weavers had come to work for him.

I soon found some older ones who could work faster, but I wanted back some of the first crew, because I had trained them well. For a while, I did not know what to do. Then I had an idea. With the help of a friend who was deeply committed to education, I rented a building with five rooms near the old fort. We bought some chairs and blackboards. We hired a few Dari and English teachers. At the end of each day, I sent all my boy weavers, many of whom had never once been to school, to a course for two hours to learn to read and write Dari and English.

Soon, all the rest of the boy weavers came back to me. Before long, most of Jerk's own weavers wanted to work for me as well. After a month, there was no room on any of my looms and I had to buy more looms so I could hire them.

Jerk was really annoyed. When he saw me, he spat on the ground with disgust. But he could not afford to be disgusted forever. A few months later, he came to me and begged for his weavers, because he could not manage to run a factory with the few who remained.

I told him to stop being a jerk, and he promised he would. But a jerk is a jerk. Even if he lives on the moon, he will still be a jerk.

I sent his weavers back, though they did not want to work for him. But I had promised. I told the boys to come to the course afterward for free lessons, as if they were still working for me. And they did.

A year after I had started the factory, I graduated the first group of girls. They started making their own carpets in their own homes, hiring their relatives and neighbors. Some of them asked me for looms and wool. I had to lend them some since they could not afford to buy them. A few months later, though, after they had sold the carpets they had made, they returned my looms and paid me for the wool. Some of them made carpets for me in their own houses. I paid them for their work. I started paying regular salaries to all the students in my factory. Sometimes I gave them bonuses for very good work.

Soon my neighborhood turned into a carpet-making area. We were making the best carpets in Kabul. Some of the girls had great ideas about colors and were bringing in new patterns. I gave them complete freedom to make what they wanted.

———

After I had shown that I could make and sell carpets, my father started taking me seriously. He listened to what I had to say. When he saw that we might have some money again, he revived the idea of leaving Afghanistan. I told him that I would make enough money to take everybody out. I told him that we were Kuchis and wanderers by nature, that I would take care of the money, and that he should look for smugglers. He was doubtful at first, but after long discussions in which I wrote out all the numbers on paper of my costs, my production, and my profits, he finally agreed. He was a physics teacher, and he understood numbers.

He started listening to the BBC World Service again to find out what was happening in different parts of Afghanistan, so he could decide which route to take to get us out of the country safely. We made lots of plans. Then we would go over our plans and see what was missing.

The final plan was to go to Iran first, then to Turkey and, eventually, to Italy. Once we were there, we would try to get one of my uncles and his family out. We would work hard and make more money, and then invite another uncle. Slowly, slowly we would get everybody out. None of us had ever been to Italy, and had only a vague idea of where it was. But we were determined to go there.


While my father was looking for smugglers, I went back to university. Though the university taught me only what I had already learned in the Taliban's prison, nevertheless it would provide me with a degree after graduation. That could help me get a job somewhere, and the Taliban's prison could not.

With the money that came from carpets I had sold, I bought a new bicycle. I could even have afforded a motorbike or a car, but I did not want to flash my money around. Most of my classmates were poor, and I wanted to look like I was the same as they.

"When there is danger, conform to the crowd," Grandfather used to tell me. So I conformed. Grandfather was gone, but I carried his good words and advice in my heart.

For the next two years, I studied hard and worked hard. The credits I needed for my degree slowly accumulated, as did the profits from my carpet factory. The strange peace brought by the Taliban made it safe for foreign buyers to return to Kabul, and my sales increased. A woman might be beaten for leaving her home alone, but in other ways the Taliban regime provided a sense of security. Many things worked. The banks. The mail delivery. Offices. Safe transportation all over the country. My father began going out to the villages again to look for older rugs, and to find customers for them among the foreign rug buyers who had started to come back to the Taliban's strange but stable Kabul.

We never lost our desire to leave, though. My mother quietly but insistently reminded us to focus all our energies on getting out. Ironically, the Taliban were making it possible for us to do so.

Then, as so often happens with Afghanistan, events on the other side of the world changed everything for us.

# 25

❖

## *A Change in the Air*

In the summer of 2001, we started hearing from the BBC World Service that Ahmad Shah Masoud was planning to challenge the Taliban. Masoud was a very intelligent man who had attacked the Russians relentlessly for many years and had prevented them from ever capturing the Panjshir Valley, which controlled the main pass across the Hindu Kush mountains.

After the Russians were driven out, Masoud had served as defense minister of Afghanistan at a time when the fighting between many factions to control Kabul caused thousands of deaths and terrible destruction. He was the leader of one of those factions who were driven out of power by the Taliban.

Everyone was terrified that if he tried to retake Kabul, the mindless war would start all over again, and all our gains of the past few years of stability under the Taliban would be lost. The Taliban were cruel and ignorant, but they had brought order to Afghanistan. We lived in constant fear that the brutal fighting among the factions would start up again. Even the Taliban's strangest laws were easier to survive than the chaos of the commanders.

Masoud had been born in the Panjshir Valley, an hour's drive north of Kabul. Neither the Russians nor the Taliban had been able to capture him. Now he was serving as the military leader of the Panjshiris who bitterly opposed the Taliban. If he attacked Kabul, all the roads would be closed, and we would not be able to get out. Everyone would be hiding in their houses. The streets would fill with bodies, and the gutters would fill with innocent blood. Again.

Only a few weeks before, my father had finally found a smuggler who seemed to be the right one for us. He came to our house several times. We all met him and felt we could trust him. He seemed to be an honest man, not one of those smugglers who take your money and leave you in the middle of nowhere. We had met him through my uncle's friend, whom we had known for many years and trusted.

The plan was that after we arrived in Turkey, my uncle would give his friend in Kabul the money he wanted for getting us there. Then he would hook us up with another smuggler who would take us to Italy.

We were all very relieved that soon we would be making a peaceful life in another country, the rest of our relatives following soon after. We never thought for one minute about the dangers and the hardships that we would face. Nothing frightened us except staying in Afghanistan, despite the calm brought by the Taliban.

The smuggler gave my father a date when we would leave. We had about six weeks to prepare. My mother had already started packing. We could not take much, so she was very carefully choosing the things we could carry. My father was sorting out our belongings. He made several piles. Each pile was intended for a different uncle.

My sisters were going through their clothes, deciding what to take and what to leave behind. They all knew that they could get better clothes in any of those countries where we were planning to go, but they were very sentimental and kept some of their favorites from childhood even though they did not fit. The whole house was a mess, with piles of clothes everywhere in all the rooms.

I was going through all my looms upstairs in my factory. Some of my looms had carpets on them that could be finished before the date we were scheduled to leave. Some of them had carpets that were half-made, and others that were only just started. I put the best weavers to work on finishing the ones that were nearly done and placed one of my better students in charge of the rest of my factory. It was her responsibility to finish all the carpets after we left. She would then contact my uncle, who would take them to my buyer on Chicken Street. These carpets were part of the money we would be paying the smugglers once we arrived in Italy.

After we had gone and the carpets were finished, this same girl would distribute all the looms among my other students, so they could start making their own carpets in their houses. These looms were to be their salaries and bonus for this month. They were very happy about that. But I still had to dye the wool and silk for them for at least one month, since they did not know how to do it. I had been showing a few of my students how to dye wool and silk, but dyeing is very unpredictable since the strength of the dye, the quality of the wool, and the heat of the fire under the dye pot can be slightly different from batch to batch. Learning how to get the same shades of each color in every batch takes time, and they were still making the kinds of mistakes that I had made when I had been teaching myself these things.

It was around seven o'clock in the evening. We were about to have an early supper after a long and tiring day. My mother was cooking kebab on a grill in the courtyard. Every meal now was like a celebration, because we would be leaving on October 15, only a month and five days away. It was also our way of not feeling sad about having to leave our own country, where our family had lived for thousands of years, and where I had lived the first nineteen years of my life.

My mother gave everyone a stick of kebab. It was lamb, very juicy and delicious. My father said, "Let's listen to the news." My mother did not want to hear anything from "the devil box." That is what she called the radio, because it always broadcast evil news. She said it would ruin our time together in this life.

My father chuckled and said, "It is all right. We're leaving this country very soon. Let me hear it while we're here." Then he turned on the radio to the BBC World Service. My mother did not want to argue, because she knew that it would not change anything. Instead, she fussed over the food.

Suddenly, we heard news that made us stop eating.

"Ahmad Shah Masoud was wounded in a suicide attack today at his stronghold near the Tajikistan border. The attackers were two Arabs who had posed as journalists. While they were interviewing Masoud, a bomb in a belt worn by one of them exploded.

"That man was killed instantly. The other was captured and shot while trying to escape. Masoud was rushed to the Indian military hospital at Farkhor, Tajikistan."

We were completely stunned. We did not know what to think. Should we eat and continue our celebration? Should we start mourning? What did this mean? We did not have suicide bombers in Afghanistan.

In the morning we heard that Masoud had died during the night in the hospital while they were trying to save him. All around us, our many Panjshiri neighbors wept loudly.

I had not told any of my classmates that I was leaving. I did not want to make them feel bad that I was going and they were staying behind. I was planning to send them gifts and sweet letters from Italy.

We had all become good friends in the past three years, despite my time away from the university. We even had made those Taliban who had come from the front line our friends. We had taught them how to read and write. We also taught them how to use parallel bars in the gymnasium, how to play basketball, and how to dance. Sometimes we even secretly listened to Indian music with them in our breaks between classes. A few of them quit being Taliban. They were not bad people after all. They were just guys like us who wanted to have a chance at life. They wanted to marry Kabuli girls and to continue living in Kabul.

We told them that they would have to share all the housework with their wives. At first they thought we were making fun of them. Then they realized that we were serious. But they did not want to go back to their lives in the village. In the end, they accepted that they should work equally as hard as women in their homes.

The day after Masoud's death, my classmates and I talked about his assassination. Some expressed deep concern at losing yet one more of our Afghan leaders. Others, who remembered all the rockets that he had thrown at Kabul during the civil war, were happy about his death.

Some of our classmates chided the others as if we were already journalists, saying, "Our job is not to take sides. Our job is to tell the truth and get all the facts." We listened to the BBC World Service as a model of how to present news accurately and as soon as it happens. We carried small radios in our pockets and listened to them during our breaks between classes, usually with small earphones.

One of my classmates was listening to the news while we were talking about Masoud. Suddenly, he shouted, "Quiet! Quiet! Something terrible has happened in New York."

He pulled the plug for the earphone out of the radio, and we listened to the news that a plane had hit one of the towers of the World Trade Center in New York. We had seen the World Trade Center in many movies, especially one with a giant monkey who had climbed it like it was a ladder. We could picture its two towers clearly in our minds. Then, as we stood in the late afternoon sun under the trees on the university campus, we heard with disbelief from that tiny radio that a second plane had hit the other tower. Now the horrors that had filled our lives for so many years were happening even in America. We felt as if something had been taken away from us. "What hope can we have for Afghanistan, if this is what is happening in America?" we asked each other.

The death of Masoud was instantly overshadowed. We completely forgot about him. The BBC World Service said something like:

"The timing of the Masoud assassination, coming just two days before these attacks on the United States, is now considered significant by observers who believe that Osama bin Laden ordered the assassination to help his Taliban protectors and ensure that he would have their cooperation in Afghanistan. The assassins are also reported to have indicated support for bin Laden in their questions of Masoud."

Osama bin Laden. Was that not the name of the Arab they said was living near us in the house of the Pimp of the King?

Some of my classmates said that soon America would attack Afghanistan. The Americans would be like the Russians. They would drop bombs everywhere, destroying every village and city.

I was not so sure. I thought America was too far away to attack Afghanistan. It was on another continent. Why would they come to Afghanistan? If they wanted Osama bin Laden, they would send their intelligence services to arrest him. But they would not attack the whole of Afghanistan for just one person.

"Even if they do," I told myself, "we will be gone. We will be in Turkey, or maybe even Italy by then. But an attack is not likely."

We kept listening to the BBC every day after that, almost every hour. They kept saying that America would attack Afghanistan. One month passed. Nothing happened.

The roads were still open. As each day brought us closer to our departure, we became increasingly hopeful that we would really get away this time, and equally worried that something would happen to stop us.

One week to the day before we left, some of my uncles, aunts, and cousins were at our house. It was late on a Sunday evening, and we had had a long dinner together. They had come to say goodbye and collect the things that my father had separated out for them.

It was a cool evening, so we ate in one of the rooms of the Fort of Nine Towers, instead of in the courtyard. It was good to be together like a family, eating around one cloth. We knew it probably would not happen again in Afghanistan. My cousins were asking me whether I would send them nice presents. I promised to send lots of gifts as soon as we arrived.

In the middle of somebody's joke, we heard an extremely loud noise, like a bomb exploding. The whole ground shook. Some of our windows shattered, but no one was hurt. For many years now, we had lined all our windows with a sheet of plastic to keep the breaking glass from falling on us. We all rushed out into the courtyard and climbed the stairs to the terrace and then a bamboo ladder up to the roof to see what had happened.

We saw a large cloud of black smoke that looked like a giant mushroom rising from one peak of the small mountain between the Qala-e-Noborja and my grandfather's old house, which was topped by TV antennas. Everyone now called it TV Mountain instead of the name it had had for centuries, the Koh-e-Asmai.

We had not heard any planes. We thought that maybe one of the Taliban weapons on TV Mountain had caught fire. But then there was another bomb, which exploded in another Taliban area very close to our old fort. Again, the whole ground shook. We all held on to each other. My father and his brothers ran along the top of the roof toward the last remaining tower to get a better view. Then we heard an airplane that was very high, "way out in the sky, very close to heaven," as my older sister said.

It was too high to be hit by any guns on the ground. Soon there were more of these planes. As we watched, they began to bomb the Taliban camps, and Taliban air defenses, and Taliban training sites. Then they focused on places where the Taliban commanders were and where they had their communications equipment, and their military bases.

"These are not blind bombers," my mother said. "They're not like the Russians or the warlords who just drop their bombs anywhere. Look how carefully they are hitting targets."

We still did not know who these bombers were.

We all tuned our pocket radios to the BBC World Service. By now, everyone had climbed up the ladder to the roof. The BBC World Service was saying something like:

"American and British forces have begun an aerial bombing campaign in Afghanistan, targeting Taliban forces and al-Qaeda. Strikes have been reported in the capital, Kabul, where electricity supplies have been severed at the airport, and in the military nerve center of Kandahar, the home of the Taliban's supreme leader, Mullah Omar, and also in the city of Jalalabad, which has many Taliban training camps."

We saw a large bomb explode out near the airport, where the

Taliban had a big camp. We looked at each other in amazement, but said nothing so that we would not miss a word of the BBC news.

We were all suddenly distracted, though, by my mother, who was shaking her hands in the air and shouting at my father.

"No way! No way!" She was shrieking.

"What's wrong?" my older sister asked, sounding uncharacteristically frightened.

"He says he doesn't want to leave! Your stubborn father doesn't want to leave Afghanistan! Everything is all ready to go, and he says we are not going!" she railed.

I could not believe what I was hearing. So many strange things were happening this night. I had just given away my best kite to my cousin, even though I knew he would lose it the first time he tried to fight with it.

"He is behaving like a camel again," my mother said with despair in her voice. "Once he makes up his mind, nobody can change it," she said as she climbed down the ladder to the terrace below. My aunts went with her.

"What is going on, Dad?" I asked.

"Come here, son. Come here, everybody," he said. Unlike my mother, he was calm and in control. We all sat in front of him in a semicircle. The American warplanes continued firing their rockets at their targets. We saw a flash each time a rocket was released from an invisible plane, and a second flash when it hit its target with a big explosion that shook the ground.

"Afghans have fought each other for millennia," my father said as he was looking at each one of us in the eyes. He had become our teacher, and we were his students. "We have a long tradition of raiding and plundering each other. But two things unite us: love for Allah, and hatred for our invaders and enemies. We are not leaving Afghanistan until we find out if these Americans are our real friends, or enemies in the mask of friends."

"So, this is it? We're not leaving after all?!" my older sister asked. She sounded disappointed and irritated.

"Who cares who invades us?" one of my cousins asked. "I'm sure they'll be better than the Taliban or the factions."

"No, my son," my father said as he reached to him and drew him closer. "Our land is our mother. We don't let strangers invade our land. It's our duty to protect her."

"Our duty is to leave this mess you call a country!" my mother shouted insistently from the terrace below. We all turned our heads around to see her. She was standing in the dark, invisible, except when the rockets hit a target and their flash illuminated her for a second. "Our duty is to save our lives." She strode to the bottom of the ladder that led up to where we sat with my father. She looked my father straight in the eye.

"Before the Mujahedin came to power, we thought of them as life-savers. But they turned out to be the life takers of the innocent. The Taliban are the same. These ones will be no different. They all have the same goal, but come with different names. Don't you get it? Don't you see the pattern? Don't you see where it started, and where it's going?" All the anger of all the years since we had been driven out of Grandfather's house raged in her voice.

"You might be correct," my father replied quietly. "But I'm not leaving until I find out who these people are."

We turned our heads around to see what my mother might say in response, but she was gone. She knew my father better than he knew himself. She knew what answer he would have. She had gone even before he opened his mouth.


The day we were supposed to leave came and went. My father said nothing about it. My mother said nothing to him. I sat in my room, deeply disappointed. I wanted to talk to Grandfather more than at any time since he had died. But he was not there for me.

In the evening, I went and sat under the acacia tree in the court-yard. It had become my habit to sit there when I was feeling badly. In a strange way, I felt close to Wakeel there where he had last been with us. Would I, too, have to die to be able to leave this place?

The bombing continued night and day. This war was totally different from the one with the Russians. Russian warplanes had come in low, destroying whole villages at a time. American warplanes flew high above their targets, unleashing only small numbers of bombs at one time.

Calls were growing from the mosques for prayers as the bombs rained down nightly and neatly on the Taliban and other religious fanatics from Pakistan, Chechnya, Punjab, and Saudi Arabia who had joined the Taliban.

Winter was approaching and the weather was turning cold. Daily life went on. We were so used to war. There was so little left to be disrupted in Afghanistan.

With all the bombing, no one left home except to try to find whatever food was available. It was hard to get news about what was really happening in Kabul. But we had started to notice changes. As the weeks passed, the Taliban, with their long *shalwar kamiz*, black and white turbans, and black-rimmed eyes, began to disappear. They did not go all in one night, the way the Mujahedin had done when the Taliban had taken over Kabul. It was more gradual than that.

From the first day the Taliban had arrived, we had learned quickly never to look them in the eyes, and always to put our heads down and stare at the ground when they passed. Now it was just the opposite. There were fewer and fewer Taliban to be seen, maybe only two or three in our neighborhood. When they saw someone approaching, it was they who looked at the ground and walked past in a hurry, heading to one of the compounds they had seized.

Other things amazed us. A Talib had always sat on a chair in the middle of the intersection near the large mosque not far from the Qala-e-Noborja. Whenever the *muezzin* began his call for prayers, the Talib would take off his turban and place it on the chair as a sign that he had gone to take his ablutions. Sometimes he would even leave his whip. Instantly, everything in the streets nearby—in fact, in the whole city— would come to a standstill. Drivers would stop their cars in the road and head for the mosques. Shopkeepers would rush out from behind their artfully arranged piles of pomegranates and grapes without even thinking about locking their doors. They knew that no one would steal anything. Under Taliban justice, a thief would have his hand cut off.

The day came, though, when there were no turban, no whip, and no Talib on the chair in the intersection. No one knew what to make of it, but just to be safe everyone still followed the Taliban rules.

The American bombings continued week after week, some nights more, some nights less. The planes had no lights; we could hear them for only a few seconds before their bombs hit the ground.

Two or three times since the bombing had started, my mother, her brother, and I climbed the ladder to the roof, wrapped ourselves in blankets against the autumn chill, and watched the flashes of light where the bombs exploded. A few seconds later, we would feel their impact roll right through us as the whole city shook. We would pass the time by making bets on which Taliban base the bombers would hit next. Sometimes my uncle won, sometimes my mother won, and sometimes I won.

We had heard that some of the planes dropping the bombs were being flown by women. That astonished us. How could women do such things? we asked. America must be a great country, everyone said, that they could send their women to defeat the Taliban. We had not seen any of their men yet. No soldiers were on the ground, only planes in the sky.

One night, after the mullah had finished the last call to prayers, we went to the roof. The bombing had been going on for more than a month by then. As we sat down near the one last remaining tower, we started hearing music. Real music, not the Taliban's tuneless singing. It was coming from the house of our neighbor *Malem-e-chaq*, who lived across the street below the garden. We looked at one another with puzzled smiles. *Malem-e-chaq* had been brutalized by the Taliban several times because he was rich. Now his sons had placed very large speakers in their windows and music was pouring into the street.

"Have the Taliban finally gone?" my uncle asked, his voice and eyes full of expectation. We could not answer.

We had been hearing stories for the past four days that people in the apartment blocks in Makroyan had been playing music during the night from their darkened windows on the upper floors, but we had not really believed them. Maybe the stories were true after all.

Soon after, we heard more music from another house along the street. Then from another. Then another. Then from our next-door neighbors whose daughters had climbed the ladder to come work in my factory. And then from our own courtyard, where someone had hooked up a cassette player to a car battery, as we had no electricity that night.

Everyone was pulling their speakers out of hiding and placing them in their windows. They were playing music as loudly they could. Any kind of music. Ahmad Zahir. Hangama and Ahmad Wali. Ustad Sarban. Lata Mangehkar. Mohammad Rafi. Jagjit Singh. Ustad Rahim Bakhsh. Ustad Beltoon. Ustad Doray Logari . . . It was overpowering, and it was spreading.

Below us in our courtyard, and in the streets, and in our neighbors' courtyards, people were coming out of their houses, cheering, shouting, and just laughing in a way they had not dared to do for all these years. Now, with each note of music ringing through the darkness, a message came through that we could hardly believe: The Taliban are gone. The Taliban are gone!

All my sisters, my cousins, and our neighbors in the old fort rushed into the courtyard to find out what was going on. They went from one to the next asking questions for which no one had any answers.

I saw my father standing near the acacia tree watching them. From all that he had said since the bombing raids had started, I knew he was waiting to see what would happen next. Had these Americans come to help or to invade? He needed more than music to know that Afghanistan had been returned to us. He looked around for a few minutes, then quietly went back inside.

*Malem-e-chaq*'s sons started playing a recording of the traditional *attan* drumbeat. It cut through all the other music. By the light of a motorcycle that had stopped in the middle of the street behind the garden, we could see two dozen men and boys streaming toward the blasting rhythm. Some wore tight jeans or brightly colored T-shirts they had kept hidden since the Taliban had taken over. Others who had come out wearing *shalwar kamiz* quickly turned around and disappeared into their houses; a few minutes later they were back on the street dressed in Western-style clothes. One young man was in a suit and a necktie. Not even one had on a turban.

A couple of them raised their hands above their heads and gave a clap to signal that the *attan* had begun.

The shapeless mob quickly formed a circle to dance the first steps of the first *attan* I had seen in five years. It hardly lasted ten seconds, though, before all the men started laughing too hard to continue. They stood there shouting and hugging one another, amazed to find themselves dancing, even though that is how Afghans have been expressing their joy for hundreds of generations—until the Taliban. The beat continued booming down the street, and before long, the circle had reformed. Some began to make the measured, graceful steps— ever so slowly at first—while others cheered them on.

Tears had filled my mother's eyes at the sound of the *attan*. She made no effort to hide them, and was smiling too much to care.

As the drumming grew more insistent, she rose up, untied her scarf, and opened the knot of her hair. She leaned back slightly and in the darkness shook her head from side to side. A breeze blew through her hair and lifted it a little. A bomb exploded not far from us, probably at the house of the Pimp of the King, where many Taliban had been living. In the bluish flash of the bomb's light, I caught sight of my mother's face. It was the first time in years that I had seen her with no scarf, just like in the old days. She looked so pretty.

I got up and stood next to her as we watched the men in the street below fling themselves into the accelerating pace of the *attan*, whipping their bare heads around as they spun. A part of me wanted to join them. I was nineteen years old and had never danced; I had always wanted to, even though I worried that I would look like a sheep if I tried. Another part of me, though, was like my father: I could not celebrate until I knew more about these people dropping bombs on my country.

My uncle stood up. He spread his arms wide like an eagle, as if he were going to start his own *attan* right there on the roof of that Fort of Nine Towers. But he only looked up at the sky in wonder.

As another explosion punctuated the pounding rhythm of the *attan*, I put my arm around my mother and thought about all she and my father had done to keep our family safe. I was taller than her now. I had reached the age when it was an Afghan son's duty to take care of his parents. How could I ever do as much for them as they had done for us?

My mother reached around and hugged me as she rested her head on my shoulder. She sighed deeply. I pulled her closer as I thought about all the uncertainty of the coming days.

The men in the street had now been joined by a guy beating a deep-throated *dol* hanging around his neck. In sharp contrast to the others, he was wearing traditional Afghan clothes and a sparkling golden cap. The onlookers went into a frenzy as he strode inside the circle of dancers, beating in time with the drums from the speakers, adding to their urgency.

The *attan* reached the point when the drumming becomes so fast that the dancers generally start to drop out one by one, exhausted. But the faster the drums beat, the more furiously the men threw themselves into it, whirling first in one direction, then the other. On this night, no one was going to quit. In fact, others joined them.

I cheered for those men, though I knew they could not hear me. I shouted at them never to stop.

And they danced. They danced. They danced.

# Epilogue: A Journey Still

My mother was right. The foreigners were more interested in their own politics than in our country. They chased the Taliban away, for a while. But they brought back the same factions who had claimed to be Mujahedin and who had destroyed our country.

Many of the foreigners who came here claiming to help us left very rich. We are waiting to see what they will build, besides their military bases.

For many years we were hoping that they might help us construct water systems so we do not have to carry water in buckets from public pumps, or sewer systems so we can get rid of the stink and diseases of the open ditches we now have. We finally got electricity, but it comes from other countries, even though we could make our own if we had some help rebuilding our hydroelectric dams.

When I see how much money has been wasted by the foreigners, I think of my grandfather. One day, as he was settling himself with a pot of green tea on the long cushion next to the window, he said to me, "Let me tell you a story."

I was becoming a teenager by then, and was finding stories of my own. But I always had time to spend with Grandfather. I sat down beside him and looked into his old yet unwrinkled face.

"Mullah Nasruddin used to live in a village not far from here." I knew that was not true, of course. Mullah Nasruddin lives in folk tales throughout the Muslim world, but Grandfather always claimed he was our neighbor. I smiled at Grandfather as he put an arm around me and drew me close to him.

"Every morning, he rode his donkey out to a place where no one ever goes. Why would they? God had made it to show people the true meaning of a wasteland.

"After a while, his neighbor Ali Khan became very curious as to why the old man went back to that same spot day after day, but was too respectful to ask directly. He sent one of his sons to ask if there was anything he could do to make Mullah Nasruddin's life better.

"Mullah Nasruddin was delighted to see Ali Khan's son, and offered him a piece of hard candy that had bits of lint on it from where it had stuck to the inside of his pocket. The boy politely declined. Then, Mullah Nasruddin asked him, 'Why are you alone? Where are the others?'

"Ali Khan's son asked Mullah Nasruddin, 'Whom are you expecting?'

"'Well,' he said. 'Someday something good might happen here. And if it does, a large crowd will gather, and since I am here first,' he declared with his famous smile, 'I will have a good view of everything! Until then, I am waiting.'"

Grandfather raised a cup of tea to his lips, while I chuckled. Though I was too old for Mullah Nasruddin stories, and too young to understand how much wisdom has been distilled in them, I laughed, because I loved being with my grandfather. Now, however, these many years later, I finally understand it. If something good comes from all the foreign money in Afghanistan, like Mullah Nasruddin I will have a good view of it. Until that time, though, every day I am waiting, and waiting, and waiting.

When the Americans came, they needed interpreters. In six months, I taught myself enough English that I could work for them and earn dollars. They were desperate for anybody who could help them and were not concerned about proper grammar. I started listening to the BBC in English and watching American movies to practice the language even when I was not with the Americans. I was never shy about making mistakes when I spoke or wrote, and was always grateful when somebody pointed out my errors.

My first job was with American soldiers. I learned many interesting words from them. Later, when I was working with the United Nations, I discovered that I could not use these words in the office. A few times I did, and I saw shocked and puzzled faces.

Now that I could speak some English, I revived our family's carpet-selling business with my father. I never tried to restart my factory, at least not in the way that I had it. I had given away my looms and did not want to take them back, since many of my weavers had no other way of earning money. The flood of foreigners into Kabul created a large, new market for all the carpets that people had been making in their homes for years and now wanted to sell. I did not need to make my own carpets to have a business. Since I spoke English, I could sell other people's carpets to the foreigners. This gave me the chance to meet people from many countries.

The Americans are always very friendly. They buy a lot of carpets and pay me the price I ask. They always want to know everything they can about the carpets: where they were made, who made them, what the meaning of the pattern is. They have invited me to their embassy several times to make presentations on Afghan carpets. "Carpet makers are poets," I tell them. "And the carpets are like poems." I try to teach them how to read their verses.

The French come, look at carpets, throw them around in all directions, point out all their flaws, then do not want to pay what they are worth. They bargain for hours for even a small discount. Some of them have become my good friends, though, and bring me dark chocolate from France. Twice I went to France for short visits, and they invited me to their houses. They cooked meals for me that were so good that I had to wonder whether anything else I had eaten all my life could really be called food. I admire how they value their history, their traditions, and their old buildings in a way that Afghans do not.

The Italians are always loud. Before they look at carpets, they ask for a cup of tea. Then we talk for a long time about many things. Finally, we start discussing carpets while they go through the piles. They ask for more tea and start to bargain and make jokes. This can go on for hours. Suddenly, they pay the full price and leave in a hurry, because they are late for something. They are very much like Afghans, always friendly, dressing nicely, eating big meals, one minute laughing and the next minute shouting. When I went to Italy I saw all these things and I told myself, "I am at home."

When I had a chance to visit England, I was treated very well by everyone I met there. The countryside in England is so beautiful that I felt I was in paradise. But many of the English people I knew in Kabul lived up to the old reputation the English have in Afghanistan.

A skinny Englishman with a bony face rented part of the Qala-e-Noborja. He cut down all the large, old trees and the lilac bushes in the courtyard, even the towering acacia tree under which we laid Wakeel's body. He said they were in the wrong places.

I had kept those trees alive during the worst years of drought by carrying water twice every day in buckets strapped to my bicycle from the only place that had water, a pump more than a mile away up and over the hill by the Polytechnic.

This Englishman also decided he wanted more rooms at the Qala-e-Noborja. So, two very poor Afghan families who had lived for more than thirty years in their houses just beyond the courtyard were forced to leave. One of them was the Hazara family whose daughters had climbed over the wall to work in my factory. When they left, they had to sell their cow, whose milk gave them their only income. That meant that their daughters had to leave their schools and go find work.

My grandfather and his friends are somewhere nodding at one another knowingly about all that. Please, God, put some mercy in that Englishman's heart, and lead him to the right path.


Meanwhile, the Afghanistan that we had dreamed about during all those years of bombs, whips, and stonings still has not returned to us.

After we held our first presidential elections in 2004, we were very hopeful. For a couple of years, a lot of Afghans came back from the foreign countries where they had fled and started businesses. Some put up tall, modern buildings in Kabul and other provinces. There was a real feeling that finally Afghanistan was ours again.

But then things changed. Not everything, we soon learned, is the fault of the foreigners.

I went to the Ministry of Commerce to register my carpet business. I knew the special adviser to the minister. With her help, I finished all the necessary paperwork there within an hour. Then I had to take my papers to the Ministry of Finance, to the Ministry of Justice, and to police headquarters for more processing.

In all these places, I had to get stamps from many people, even though no one could tell me what the stamps were for. Every single person from whom I sought a stamp demanded a bribe. They did not ask directly for money, of course. They said, "Please, may I have some candy." I gave them a few afghanis, and they did what needed to be done.

As the day wore on, my money was nearly finished, and I was disgusted. I went out to a street vendor and used what money I had left to buy a bag of hard candy, the kind we put in our mouths when we drink tea. After that, whenever anybody asked me for candy, I gave them a piece from my pocket. They glared at me with one eyebrow up, one down. I acted stupid and smiled at them, as if I did not know what "candy" meant.

One said, "I don't want this. Give me real candy."

"This is real candy, and it is very good," I said, trying to sound innocent as I took out the bag and showed it to him. "Look, it comes all the way from Poland. And the ingredients are all healthy and organic. They used honey instead of sugar, and real milk. It tastes delicious!" Then I ate one, and yum-yummed.

"Idiot! I want money," he said sharply.

"Money? For what?" I asked, trying to sound surprised.

"For processing your papers," he said, somewhere between a shout and a whisper.

"But that is a bribe," I replied with my eyes wide with amazement. "And a bribe is a sin! In Islam it is forbidden! Are you trying to make us both sinners?"

"Are you stupid?" He looked at me in disbelief.

"Nobody has ever called me stupid before!" Then, more kindly, I added, "I'm just trying to explain to you the basic principles of Islam."

Soon he decided not to waste any more time on me, knowing he could get a bribe from the next person. He processed my papers and pressed the bell on the desk. A guard came bustling in and was told, "Get this psychopath out of here!"

"I'm not a psychopath! I'm not a sinner, either. I'm not a bribe taker, or angry all the time. Now, tell me who is a psychopath?" Then I walked out, smiling, without waiting to hear the answer.

More than ten years have passed since that night on the roof when we saw the first American bombs. From time to time, I think about some of the people—good and bad—whom I had known during the worst years, and I wonder what has become of them.

I have never seen Berar again, though I have looked for him in many places. If he is dead, please, God, keep his soul at peace. If he is alive, I pray to God to make us meet again one day.

The garden where Grandfather and I saw the skulls now has three houses covering the place where the fountain was.

Sometimes when I am riding in a taxi, the driver might take a shortcut on a street where a horrific memory comes back to life. I lean forward and ask him please to go another way, as being there reminds me of something from the war that I want to forget. Every driver understands this, and they always turn around and find another route.

I never again saw the young teacher who was forced to sell herself. I hope she earned enough money to go to another country and start a new life. I will always think of her with deep respect, despite the circumstances in which we met.

I have never seen the family in Tashkurghan from whom I stole the five pomegranates. Maybe they are living in America by now. I heard the garden was in ruins until five years ago, when somebody replanted it. I went there once, but the people living there said they had never heard of Hamza or his family. I wonder how Hamza can be happy anywhere else.

Sometimes our Kuchi cousins call my father when they are passing near Kabul with their sheep and camels in late spring, heading from their winter homes in Jalalabad to the central highlands. They are still Kuchis, but they all have cell phones now.

Omar Khan, once a herd boy with a flute, is now in Germany. He became a car mechanic. He is running a garage with another Afghan who was born there. He speaks German fluently. He has not returned to Afghanistan in the years since he left. He is waiting for the German government to give him a German passport, so he can travel to Afghanistan to visit his family.

Aaron Khan is living in Greece. He became a tailor. He got married to a pretty Greek woman. His parents are unhappy with him for marrying a Greek, because a Kuchi should marry another Kuchi and produce more Kuchis. They are not in touch with him, but know about him through Omar Khan.

Solomon Khan remained a Kuchi. He has two beautiful wives. He has three beautiful daughters from his first wife, and two handsome sons from his second wife. He still does not talk very much, but he taught his wives and kids how to read and write.

Many of my classmates, including those with whom I celebrated our graduation by punching one another, are still in touch with me. A few of them went to India for a couple of years for education. A couple of them got visas to European countries by marrying their cousins who were already there. Five of them are in Kabul, running good businesses. Three of them died in suicide bombings, two while they were walking toward their houses with bags of fruit for dinner. We carry their memories in our hearts.

One night at a party in Kabul, I heard that Zardad, the sadist, is in jail in England. He was hiding in London, but a journalist from the BBC found him, and he was arrested for crimes against humanity.

A foreigner, one of the few who truly has helped Afghanistan, told me in a garden full of music being performed by masters that he had been asked to testify against Zardad. It had taken two trials to convict him. The foreigner also said that Dog is dead, executed at Pul-e-Charkhi prison. Before that night, I had once tried to find out about Zardad and Dog using the Internet, but doing so made me feel violently sick. It reminded me too clearly of those days. I do not care whether they are dead or alive. If they are dead, I pray they are in the depths of hell.

For Gulbuddin Hekmatyar, whose rocket killed Wakeel, hell is too good a place, and eternity too short a time. He is still alive, still doing evil.

When the foreigners began to come to Kabul after the Taliban were driven out, Haji Noor Sher returned from India and reopened his carpet business at the heart of the Shahr-e-Naw shopping district. He came back to live in his rooms in the Qala-e-Noborja. No one had used them in all the years he had been away. One day he just appeared in the courtyard and yelled "Malem," the Dari word for "teacher," meaning my father. We had just finished lunch and my father was about to have his nap, but when we heard that familiar voice, we all quickly ran outside and were overjoyed to see him.

For the next couple of years he lived at Noborja, while his family remained in India. Sometimes he went to visit them, but he was happiest in Kabul among his carpets and his friends. He and my father spent hours together gathering and selling carpets again, and just enjoying each other's company after so many years apart.

He began to show signs of health problems, though he never said what they were. He went to India a couple of times to see doctors, and seemed to be sicker when he came back to Kabul. Then a few weeks after he had gone there again, we got a call telling us that he had died. A part of ourselves died with him. His kindness and generosity had made it possible for our whole family to survive the fighting.

Recently, I went to visit that Hazara baker, to thank him for saving me from the Talib rapist.

Three times I went to the baker's shop. Each time I could not bring myself to mention these things. There was no one else in the shop. He was always just sitting behind the counter, looking at the pedestrians and traffic on the road.

Somehow, for no particular reason, I felt weak, though I wanted very much to talk to him and tell him who I was. Instead, each time I got a plastic bag, went through trays of cookies, and filled it. Then I gave him the bag to weigh it. He did not look at me while he was putting it on the scale, even though I kept staring at his face, wanting to say something, but nothing came out. Then I would pay and walk out.

He was a little heavier than all those years ago, but otherwise he looked much the same. His shop was the same, too, except that the back room where he had hidden me was now filled by a large, modern oven. His son had become a tall man, with broad shoulders. He operated the oven with several other workers.

The fourth time I went, I said, "I'm not here to buy anything." I ran out of breath, and my heart was beating very fast. He could tell I was nervous about something.

"Slow down, young man," the baker said. He had a calm voice, very different from that afternoon, years before, but still deep. "What do you want, then?"

"I'm here to thank you," I said, still with no breath left, as if I had run for miles.

"Thank you to you!" he said with a smile. "I'm glad you like our cakes and cookies."

"Yes, they are delicious, but I want to thank you for saving my life several years ago," I said.

Suddenly, the smile disappeared from his round, Asiatic face, and he looked into my eyes with no expression. He narrowed his eyes. "What are you talking about?"

"I was arrested just across the road there by a Talib. To escape from them, I shouted 'Bomb, bomb, bomb, bomb under the Taliban car.' People ran everywhere to—"

He interrupted me: "And you came here, stood behind this window, and you said, 'There is no bomb. I created this chaos, because a Talib arrested me for no good reason.' And I pushed you out, because I was afraid for myself." He stopped for a moment. "Then I saw a look of despair in your eyes . . ." His voice trailed off.

"You pulled me back inside, and hid me behind the flour bags—"

He interrupted me again: "And you kept sneezing . . ."

The baker came out from behind his counter and gave me a long and big hug. Now we were the same height. His chest was soft and fleshy, and he smelled of bread and ovens. We held each other very tightly.

"I have thought about you many, many times. I didn't know what happened to you. You never came back," the baker said.

"I was very scared," I said.

"After that night when I dropped you off in front of your house, several months later I was arrested three times for no reason. But you know they hated us. What wild animals they were! I was a good prey for them. The bastards got all my money. The third time I had nothing left to give them. They beat me like a dusting machine beats a carpet," he said.

He had a broad smile on his face, as if he were telling a funny joke. That is what I love the most about my countrymen. He should have been scarred for life after experiencing so many horrible things, but he was talking about his past as if it were funny.

"Are you still living in that old fort?" he asked.

"We lived there for sixteen years, but not anymore," I said. "After the Taliban were driven out of Kabul, one of the widows of the owner, Haji Noor Sher, came back from India and wanted to rent the old fort to the foreigners to earn big money. She asked us to leave. We did not mind. We wanted to have a home of our own without a lot of other families sharing our courtyard. But we had no home to go to. The Taliban had forced us to sell our own house in Kot-e-Sangi to them, to give it to them, really. We could not afford to buy any property on the flat land. A squatter who had lived for a long time up on the Koh-e-Aliabad—what we used to call Sniper Mountain—across from Kabul University sold my father a small plot at a good price. We have built a house there. I hope you will come and meet my family."

"I shall," he said.

I wrote my address on a piece of paper. He wrote his address and gave it to me. It was lunchtime, but he could not serve me anything because it was Ramazan. He made me promise to visit him in Eid days, when we celebrated the end of our month of fasting with three days of visits to the homes of all our relatives and friends. We talked about other things. He was a great talker and a good storyteller, sophisticated and full of funny jokes.

He was not just a baker, I discovered. He had graduated from the Literature Faculty of Kabul University and had taught at Kabul University for two years. But he did not earn enough money there to support his big family. He stopped teaching and took over his family's baking business. He built up the business and now has three shops. He has three sons and two daughters. All of them are married and have their own kids, but they all live with him in one big courtyard, the way we did with Grandfather.

"Do you still have to be home on time for dinner, otherwise your wife will be worried?" I asked him.

"Oh, of course! She is the boss after all!" he said with a huge smile.

My older sister accomplished her dream: she finished her education and became an architect and an engineer. Then she got married, and has a sweet son, who was given the name I had chosen: Suleiman. It was a name I always liked. Suleiman was an important man in many folktales as well as in the Holy Koran and the Bible. More practically, it is a name that people rarely mispronounce. And when I was little, I often dreamed of Suleiman's magic carpet, on which I could fly to interesting places, and cut the most beautiful kites along the way.

Now my older sister can tease her husband instead of me. Her husband is a good man. He teases her right back. She complains about that. I smile and tell her, "What goes around comes around."

These days, she has become my best friend, even though sometimes she still says that when I eat I make noises like a cow. Maybe I do.

But I do not think I do. These words bring memories of our time in the garden of Hamza's father, and the stealing of the pomegranates.

One night about six months after their wedding, her husband asked her, "Tell me a few things about your brothers and sisters. I don't know much about them." He had been living in other countries for several years before they were married.

She told him about our childhood at Grandfather's house in Kot-e-Sangi, and how everything changed when the civil war started, how we took shelter at the Qala-e-Noborja as refugees, then tried so hard to get away from the madness that was destroying our country. Later he told me that as she started telling him how hard I had tried to help my father support us, her voice began to shake. She burst out sobbing and could not stop, though her husband held her in his arms.

Around midnight, I heard knocking on our door and I opened the window to see who had come at that late hour. I was very surprised to see my older sister and her husband. I went down the long flight of stairs to the door and opened it for them. Before I had a chance to greet them, my sister hugged me and kissed me many times, her face soaked with tears.

"What is wrong?" I asked with alarm.

"Nothing," her husband said. "She got talking about you, and suddenly said she needed to see you."

I led them upstairs. The rest of the family were asleep, except for my mother. She was surprised to see my sister, who by then had calmed down a little. Her husband found a blanket and a *toshak* and went to sleep, but my sister, my mother, and I stayed awake for hours while the muted TV flickered at us, having an unexpected tea party and talking about things of the past. We almost never do that. The wounds from those days are deep and can easily be opened. It is better to leave them in the past.

The crying machine is a big man now, handsomer than I am, taller than I am, stronger than I am. He is full of muscles and can beat me when we arm wrestle. He has not cried since he was a baby. In fact, he is like my father, and can always tell good jokes. But I like to remember his old name. It reminds me of the time when we were with the Kuchis. Now he studies law, and hopes to bring order to our country.

My four younger sisters are all being educated, even though some people in Afghanistan still say that educating girls is a bad thing. They have high ambitions. One of them studies management, another agriculture. Another wants to be a writer and reads any book she can find. The youngest says she will be a nurse. Afghanistan will benefit from having good managers, agriculturists who can plant trees, writers to record the joys and sorrows of our people, and nurses to cure our wounded hearts. The older two have married very good men.

My mother had never really quit her job at the bank. She just stopped going during the civil war when the fighting made it too dangerous. And then she was prevented from working by the Taliban. But after they were driven out, she went one day to see what was going on at the bank, and then the next day she started back at her old job. No one had been hired to fill it, because no one had been there to do any hiring. After a few years, she finally left the bank and took a job with the Afghanistan Disaster Management Authority, where she feels she can be more useful. She works very hard to get government assistance quickly to communities that suffer earthquakes or blizzards or other calamities.

My father is still teaching physics at Habibia High School. He is the only teacher from before the war who was not killed or did not flee the country. All the younger teachers respect him like they do their own fathers. The school has a gym, but no equipment. He is trying to find money to buy what is needed and to start training again. He is still in great shape, and very strong, except for the arthritis that is creeping into his knees.

After so many years of trying, my father did finally manage to leave Afghanistan, though only briefly. He achieved his lifelong ambition to make a pilgrimage to Mecca. Now we are proud to call him "Haji."

My cousin Jerk can still be a jerk sometimes, but despite that he has done very well for himself. He has always been kind to his siblings and parents, and has willingly shouldered his family's burdens, as I tried to do with mine.

After not having seen him for a couple of years, I went to his house one day to deliver my second sister's wedding invitation card. He had put on a little weight, and had a few white hairs on his temples, which made him look distinguished. I pointed those out to him, and said, "You are getting old." Suddenly I felt *I* was being a jerk, since he is the same age as I am.

He ran his right hand over his temple and said, "Well, that's the story of life. As Grandfather said, 'We are raw, we get cooked, and finally burned.' I'm in the process of being cooked."

"Will you stay in this country until you get burned?" I asked, trying to be funny.

"Yes, I will stay in this country and will do my best to fix things," he said, sounding serious. "Things that my father and his generation could not fix. I believe that there is a future for this country, but only if we do something about it now. If we don't do it, then who will?

"Somebody has to have the guts to step in. We know that no country is here to help us. They are here to help themselves. We have to tell the world that Afghanistan has a new owner, and that owner is our generation."

I gave him a big hug for the first time in many years—a lifetime— because I was so moved by what he said. I admire him for his determination.

A few years before Wakeel was killed, we received a letter from Russia. Who knows how it found us. But some friend of my grandfather's brought it to him. It was on a scrap of a Russian newspaper, stating, "I'm still alive. I can't write more. We're living in a dark hole. I'll come home one day." The handwriting belonged to Wakeel's father who had mysteriously disappeared all those years before. But we have never heard any more from him.

If he goes to look for us at Grandfather's house, he will not find us, or even the house. Most of it is completely destroyed. The part where my father and mother had our rooms is only a mound of dirt. Every one of Grandfather's beloved McIntosh apple trees is gone. There is no sign that once we had a good life there. Perhaps someday somebody will build a new house in Grandfather's garden. Perhaps they will find our gold.

There is one person I have never seen again, but I am determined to find her, because she has given my life its purpose. I now have my own carpet company called Kabul Carpets & Kilims. It is still small, but it will grow. Grandfather used to say, "Small streams make an ocean."

A few years ago, when I had a chance to go to Holland, I visited a Dutch woman who had once come to Kabul and has become my good friend. In her house in Haarlem, I saw one of my carpets that I had made in my factory in the worst days of the Taliban.

There is no way to describe the feelings I had when I saw that carpet again. It reminded me of my good memories, my hardships, my eagerness for a future, my factory, and eating lunch with my weavers around one cloth with everyone laughing, even though we knew terrible things would happen if the Taliban caught us. Now all of that history, my history, is being preserved in that faraway country.

None of this could have happened without my teacher.

I think she might be in Tajikistan. Maybe in a city. Maybe in a village. I have not dreamed about her in a long time. There is too much noise in my life now. But soon the time is coming when I shall set out to look for her.

I am sure she will know when I am coming. And, with her help and Allah's, I shall find her.

I have long carried this load of griefs in the cage of my heart.
Now I have given them to you. I hope you are strong enough to
  hold them.

*Qais Akbar Omar*

## Author's Note

*A Fort of Nine Towers* chronicles the past three tumultuous decades in Afghanistan. For part of that time, I was very young. Many things happened to my family and me, and for the first years of the fighting I cannot say exactly when they occurred—only that they did. I have included specific dates when I can be sure of them, and done my best to reconstruct them when I cannot.

Readers from outside Afghanistan may wonder why I have rarely included the names of my family in this account of our lives together. Afghans, however, will understand.

While this book focuses on my family's experience, every Afghan family has stories similar to ours. They all need to be told. They need to be heard. They must not happen again.

## Acknowledgments

This book is dedicated to Afghanistan and its people, to the spirit of Grandfather, who still leads me in good and bad times like a guardian angel, to Wakeel, who visits me every three or four years in my dreams, to my parents, who mean everything in the world to me, to my sisters and brother, who will make their own families soon in Afghanistan or in other countries, to my uncles and aunts and cousins with whom I shared so much and whom I deeply love.

This book would not have been written if Stephen Landrigan had not come to Afghanistan, and I had not met him. He listened quietly when I spoke of the memories that haunted me, and encouraged me to write about them to ease their grip on my soul. His guidance helped me discover a love for writing. Someday I will write a book about all the good things he has done for Afghanistan. It will be a thick book.

A profound thanks to J. Garcia and Linda Nicita of Colorado, who read an early draft before I knew so much about the English language, and who cleaned up all the grammatical errors and misspelled words. Thanks also to Laurence E. Landrigan, whose careful reading and editing of my manuscript provided many helpful insights. Their generosity has been deeply impressed on me, and I welcome the obligation of passing it on.

Khaled Hosseini and Michael Patrick MacDonald not only inspired me by their own writing, they were helpful in opening doors to agents and publishers, and to them I am grateful.

I am especially appreciative of the professionalism and kindness extended by Courtney Hodell, my editor at Farrar, Straus and Giroux, who nurtured this book through many drafts. Also, a big thanks to Jessica Papin, my agent with Dystel & Goderich Literary Management, for her positive energy and hard work that led me to the team at Farrar, Straus and Giroux, where Marion Duvert and Devon Mazzone helped this book find publishers in many other countries and languages and Lottchen Shivers spread the word as its publicist.

And finally, thanks to Janie Harris, who gave me the first review long before *A Fort of Nine Towers* was even published. It was deeply moving to have somebody who lives on the other side of the world so excited by what I had written.

I hope this book will lead others to become curious about the many layers of Afghan culture that so unexpectedly and for so many of the wrong reasons have become the focus of the world's attention.

A NOTE ABOUT THE AUTHOR


Qais Akbar Omar (whose first name rhymes with "rice") manages his family's carpet business in Kabul and writes books. In 2007, he was a visiting scholar at the University of Colorado. He has studied business at Brandeis University and is currently pursuing an MFA in creative writing at Boston University. Omar has lectured on Afghan carpets in Afghanistan, Europe, and the United States. He is the coauthor, with Stephen Landrigan, of *Shakespeare in Kabul*.